Prehistoric Man
in Wales
and the West

Prehistoric Man
in Wales
and the West

essays in honour of Lily F. Chitty

edited by Frances Lynch and Colin Burgess

BARNES & NOBLE, BOOKS ● NEW YORK
(A Division of Harper & Row Publishers, Inc.)

First published in 1972 by
Adams & Dart, 40 Gay Street, Bath, Somerset

Printed in Great Britain

Published in the United States by
Harper & Row Publishers, Inc.
Barnes & Noble Import Division

ISBN 389-04136 X

Contents

Preface

Most *Festschriften* are filled with papers written by eminent senior scholars, contemporaries, or near contemporaries, of the person to whom their essays are addressed. It is perhaps a reflection on the unique place of Lily Chitty in British archaeology that this volume, while it does have distinguished contributors of this order, also includes contributions representing various generations right down to young newcomers to archaeology. Some of the contributors confess to having known Miss Chitty for more years than it would be gentlemanly to record, while others have had their new careers immeasurably helped by her in just the last few years. Her influence on recent generations of archaeologists is all the more remarkable when one considers that she has never held a professional teaching post or, indeed, any full-time archaeological appointment. The fact is that she still has by far the largest private archaeological records in the country, so that any newcomer to archaeological work sooner or later has to turn to her for help. The help is always freely and generously given and, remarkably, it has been so now for over half a century. So unassuming is she, so spontaneously but quietly has she given of her knowledge that, although her work has been widely absorbed into the publications of generations of scholars, she herself has never received a fraction of the credit due to her.

With the prodigious increase in archaeological publication of the last few years, occasioned by the flood of graduates from our new schools of archaeology, there has been a growing awareness of Miss Chitty's crucial place in British archaeology. And it is these newer, younger archaeologists, their writing owing so much to her, whose idea this *Festschrift* was. We feel Miss Chitty will not mind if we record that this project was born in a pub. The pub in question is one in Piccadilly where young archaeologists are wont to gather after Prehistoric Society meetings, to exchange news, discuss developments and new finds and, eventually, dissect British archaeology minutely. The name of Chitty crops up continually; so many had been helped by her that the feeling grew that this help should be acknowledged. A volume of essays seemed the most appropriate way of doing this.

Little could be done during those brief Piccadilly evenings, but a Neolithic Conference held at the University of Newcastle upon Tyne in January 1969 provided two of us with a better chance to discuss more concrete plans. From there this volume has grown. At an early stage we decided that the work should have a coherent theme, as it seemed that most *Festschriften* were too general in their scope. Of all the aspects of Miss Chitty's work, we chose the pre-

Preface   history of Wales and the West as the one with which she has been most closely associated. Even within these limits, it was not possible to approach everyone who might have contributed something relevant, and in addition to those whose efforts are included here there are many more who could not contribute for one reason or another, but who would like to be associated with the project. Finally it is a measure of Miss Chitty's unique position that a number of contributors, when they came to write their piece, found they could not do so without furtively referring to her on various points. Unsuspectingly the information came back freely and copiously as ever. May it continue to do so for many years to come.

C.B.B.

F.M.L.

Lily F. Chitty, 1971

Lily Frances Chitty

W. F. Grimes

On a day vaguely to be defined as falling within the closing years of the reign of King Edward VII a young lady was walking down Castle Street in Shrewsbury in her best new hat when a sudden rainstorm came on. Caught without an umbrella, she walked into Hammonds the fishmongers, asked for one of their fish-baskets, put it over her hat and, thus protected, went on her way triumphant down Pride Hill. To a permissive age, in which fish-baskets may well become standard female head-gear, there is perhaps nothing remarkable in an event so baldly stated; but in 1910 or thereabouts, society was not in the grip of the freedom that some part of it enjoys today, and those who know her will be in no way surprised that the wearer of the hat, at once feminine and unorthodox, was Miss Lily Frances Chitty.

At the time of the above happening Miss Chitty would have been seventeen or eighteen. The daughter of the Reverend James C. M. Chitty and his wife Gwen Ethlin Georgiana (*née* Jones), she was born on 20 March 1893 at Lewdown in Devonshire; but the family had settled in Shropshire in 1902, when the Reverend James Chitty became rector of Yockleton. Her mother's family had long associations with the Marches and it is not surprising that they are of both Welsh and English stock; on the Welsh side they claim ultimate descent from the Kings of Dyfed. A fourteenth-century ancestor, having murdered a Chief Justice of Carmarthen, adjourned to Powysland and there married an heiress. Another ancestor, Sir Gruffydd Vychan, a descendant of the princes of Powys, is said to have been knighted at Agincourt and, less fortunately, beheaded in Powys Castle.

On the English side there was a link with the Salopian family of the Heighways of Pontesford, tanners who became landed gentry in the eighteenth century with large estates in western Shropshire. It was her mother's cousin, Heighway Jones junior, who introduced Miss Chitty to archaeology. She accompanied him on the expeditions of the Shropshire Archaeological Society and in due course inherited some part of his very good library of local archaeology. An interest in archaeology is also detectable in the Catons, an East Anglian family having connections with Shropshire. Two nineteenth-century members of the family were Fellows of the Society of Antiquaries. Miss Chitty's grandfather married Frances Eliza Caton.

The Chittys, on the other hand, had a strong legal tradition. Joseph Chitty the elder, 'friend of George IV', was a legal writer. *Chitty on Contracts* was the work of his son, Joseph Chitty the younger, a step-great-great-uncle; *Chitty's Forms*, of a great-grandfather, Thomas Chitty. Two great-uncles were judges, Sir Joseph W. Chitty, Lord Justice of Appeal, and Sir James

Shaw Willes. An uncle, Sir Thomas Willes Chitty, first baronet, was King's Remembrancer. The Reverend James Chitty, though named after three judges, broke away from this legal tradition to be ordained, in this being followed by his sons, John (now a medical missionary in Africa) and Derwas, whose name echoed one of the early Welsh connections on the mother's side. Here also there is an attachment to antiquity, for Herbert Chitty FSA was a cousin – and the father of Miss Letitia Chitty, another remarkable woman of varied interests, who took a First in engineering at Cambridge in 1922 and was awarded the Telford Gold Medal in 1969.

These family particulars are set out at some length (though omitting much) because in one way or another they have relevance to Miss Chitty's own character and achievement. Her interest in archaeology may be said to be endemic. It is not surprising that Shropshire and Wales should take first place in her affections or that she should bring to her work a high standard of factual accuracy and the flair for detail that, in the words of one member of it, 'always seems to have been a mark of the family'.

It has already been said that Miss Chitty's introduction to archaeology came by way of the Shropshire Archaeological Society; the county and the Society – and, in parallel, Wales and the Cambrian Archaeological Association – have benefited from her loyal support ever since. She was educated at home and early showed an artistic talent which was to stand her in good stead when her more serious archaeological work was to begin. But before that came the First World War and secretarial training which also she was later to find valuable. It is said that she watched the first daylight air-raid on London from the roof of the General Post Office. The writer of this note as a small boy witnessed the same event from a vantage-point farther along Holborn, and can see now with memory's eye the 'Gothick' windows of the Prudential building across the street quivering as the bombs exploded.

Miss Chitty's introduction to the wider world of archaeology came in 1923, when, as she herself has recorded, she met H. J. E. Peake. The immediate occasion was 'local', since it sprang from an undertaking to do the Shropshire cards for the British Association Bronze Implement Catalogue. Miss Chitty acknowledges Peake's continuing kindness and influence. His geographical approach to prehistory appealed to her and she has well described the wide-ranging enthusiasm with which he discussed the things that interested him or that he thought should interest others.

The other great influence was Cyril Fox, whom she met for the first time in Cambridge in 1924. Out of this meeting grew a collaboration which was to have led to a new prehistory of Britain. Miss Chitty's contribution was to have been the distribution maps which were to form an essential, if not the central, element of the work; to the compilation of these maps and their associated records she devoted all her energies into the early 'thirties, but Fox, after an illness, abandoned the project. It was some consolation to her that the original (as distinct from the borrowed) maps in *The Personality of Britain*, thought of as the precursor to the larger work, were from her hand and acknowledged to be so on the title-page of the later enlarged editions. But the major disappointment remained, unspoken but sensed by her friends. Later the hope was entertained that the material would be assembled as an archaeological atlas, but, having been compiled to meet her collaborator's requirements, it did not lend itself to this kind of treatment. Nevertheless, when copied, it formed a valuable nucleus for the archaeological index which C. W. Phillips inaugurated later at the Ordnance Survey.

Study of Miss Chitty's publications suggests that in what might be called her Salopian phase she was in the true tradition of local antiquarianism. She met Harold Peake, as already noted, in 1923. From 1925 her writings are almost entirely concerned with prehistory: with the meticulous recording of discoveries over a wide area – but never neglecting Shropshire (for which for many years she has been Archaeological Correspondent for the Ancient Monuments Department of the now Department of the Environment) – and always with an eye to their relationships in space as well as in time. Fieldwork seems to have been difficult, particularly after 1933, when the death of her mother gave Miss Chitty added domestic responsibilities. The 'sketch (drastically condensed from records enough for a volume)' of the Clun–Clee ridgeway which she contributed to Cyril Fox's *Festschrift* is a pointer both to the range of her material and, by implication, to the contacts with local workers whose activities she has fostered. It is in a spirit of sadness rather than of criticism that those of her colleagues who concern themselves with this kind of archaeology will regret that more such 'sketches', the essential condensation of so much detail, have not yet appeared.

Lily Frances Chitty

The scientific spirit that informs Miss Chitty's attitude to her subject emerges in other ways: in her anxious wish to hear the archaeological opinions of colleagues, her readiness to share her own knowledge and to help others, younger archaeologists in particular. One example of this last must suffice: a kind invitation to Yockleton in the late autumn of 1933 to examine the stone circles in that part of the Marches. Two days of rapid progress from one monument to the next culminated, in the fading light of late afternoon, in a situation which was sufficiently absurd but might also have been very uncomfortable, if not disastrous. A track on the 6-inch map which should have been a time-saving short cut between sites started optimistically but faded out on the ground; and the small car which at one time or another had suffered the indignity of being pushed up most of the steeper hills of Wales found itself with its forward end propped in the air on an erratic boulder deceptively concealed in long grass. Miss Chitty's anxiety for the grunting owner of the vehicle as he laboured with the car-jack was real, as also when the retreat involved his travelling backwards solo and obliquely over sundry banks which had somehow been missed on the journey out. She very properly enjoyed the incident none the less.

This enjoyment is her other great attribute. It is all-embracing, applied to the countryside at large, to the simple business of being *in* the countryside. She is knowledgeable about flowers: they command her delighted attention as much (or almost as much) as the earthworks that bear them. This zest has remained with her down the years, but the zest for information has also never deserted her. Miss Chitty on safari travels with all that she will need to inform herself on the sites to be inspected. From one bag or another she will startle her fellow-travellers with full references to the monument engaging their attention. 'I looked it up before we came: I thought people might like to know.'

OBE, MA (*honoris causa*) of the University of Wales, Honorary Member of the Prehistoric Society, Honorary Member and Vice-President of the Cambrian Archaeological Association 'for services to archaeology'. But perhaps nothing will give Lal Chitty greater pleasure than this volume, unless it be the thought that her editors and many of their contributors are of the younger generation of archaeologists who recognise how much they owe to her.

Archaeological Distribution Maps

Leslie Grinsell

The essential basis of any reliable archaeological distribution map is a really comprehensive if not complete inventory of the sites or finds to be shown on the map. The great work done by Lily Chitty during the past fifty years or so, in compiling and maintaining as complete a card index as possible of British prehistoric material, has enabled her to produce not only many of the maps included in *The Personality of Britain* (Fox, 1932 and later editions to 1943), but also to prepare numerous other distribution maps, and to assist many other workers to develop theirs.

This survey will deal mainly with the archaeological distribution map in Britain; but incidental references will be made to foreign work.

HISTORY

Among the earliest British archaeological maps are those produced by Philip Crocker, surveyor, of Frome, and published in *Ancient Wiltshire* (Hoare, 1812, 1819). These were particularly comprehensive for barrows: those opened by Hoare and Cunnington were shown by solid circles; those left unexplored, by open circles. Another early landmark in the history of archaeological mapping in Britain is J. Y. Akerman's three-colour map of the distribution of Ancient British Coins (Akerman, 1849). Charles Warne's map of Dorset, although good for its date, illustrates the disadvantages of showing sites of several different periods on the same map (Warne, 1866).

On the Continent, Montelius produced a map of the megalithic monuments of Scandinavia in 1874 (Montelius, 1874); since that date a long and notable series of distribution maps has been published from the three Scandinavian countries, of which perhaps the most distinguished are the maps in *Danmarks Oldtid* (Brøndsted, 1938–40). These are remarkable in particular for their mapping of very large numbers of barrows by red or blue spots which, although small, are remarkably effective because they are in colour.

In Britain, major contributions to distributional studies were made over a long period by O. G. S. Crawford, who took an Oxford degree in geography in 1910. From his early 'teens he had shown a remarkable flair for field archaeology, and on 4 May 1911 he read to the Oxford University Anthropological Society a paper on the 'Distribution of Early Bronze Age settlements in Britain', which was afterwards published (Crawford, 1912). In this paper he contrasted the distribution patterns of flat copper axes (mostly in Ireland) and beakers (mostly in England). He created a precedent which was to be followed by other archaeologists: to prepare and publish distribution maps of the objects of their study; but for obvious reasons little was done until after the war of 1914–18. Crawford himself wrote a stimulating chapter on distributions in *Man and his Past* (Crawford, 1921). His appointment as the first Archaeology Officer at the Ordnance Survey in October 1920 was followed by the publication of an Ordnance Survey Professional Paper on the long barrows and stone circles of the Cotswolds and the Welsh Marches (1922), which was later expanded and published as *The Long Barrows of the Cotswolds* (Crawford, 1925). In due course other Ordnance Survey archaeological publications appeared—*The Long Barrows and Megaliths in . . . Kent, Surrey, and Sussex* (1924), the *Map of Neolithic Wessex* (1932), the *Map of the Trent Basin, showing Long Barrows . . .* (Phillips, 1933), and the *Map of South Wales showing the Distribution of Long Barrows and Megaliths* (Grimes, 1936). It is intended that these will eventually be merged in an Ordnance Survey map of Neolithic Britain.

In 1923 a scheme for an international atlas of prehistory was initiated in Paris, and its development has been described in detail elsewhere (Antoniewicz, 1966). The early post-war years also saw the publication of *The Archaeology of the Cambridge Region* (Fox, 1923), with its fine series of distribution maps which formed the basis of a set of revised and extended maps in Fox's presidential address to the Prehistoric Society of East Anglia (Fox, 1933). In August 1932 he gave the substance of his *Personality of Britain* as an Evening Special Lecture before the First International Congress of Prehistoric and Protohistoric Sciences, in London – and a memorable occasion it was. Since the publication of that work, it has become standard practice to include distribution maps in a high percentage of archaeological publications. The following notes on the base-map, the overlay, and their relationship, have resulted from the writer's experience, combined with a study of a selection of maps produced by others and listed in the bibliography.

THE PREPARATION OF DISTRIBUTION MAPS

It is recommended that base-map and overlays be produced separately, at least in the first instance. Almost any well-drawn base-map is likely to be used more than once and many are likely to be used for dozens of different distribution overlays. It is worth while trying to persuade an editor to sanction the inclusion of two-colour distribution maps. Failing this, it is possible to produce a two-tone distribution map in only one colour by producing the base-map with Letraset or other dry-transfer appliances, by using one of their forms of mechanical stippling, and then using fairly heavy black symbols for the overlay (Coles, 1963) (fig. 1). It is worth trying publishers of outline maps, such as W. & A. K. Johnston Ltd, or G. Philip & Son Ltd, who sometimes produce excellent outline maps which can be used either as they are, or as a basis for one which meets the archaeologist's requirements more precisely.

Drawings for both base-maps and distribution overlays should always be made on plastic sheet such as Permatrace, Ethulon, or Ozalid, as they are dimensionally stable under all normal changes of temperature or humidity. This dimensional stability is essential to ensure correct registration of the overlays on the base-map.

THE BASE-MAP

This should always be drawn before preparing the distribution overlays. It should be prepared from an Ordnance Survey map which is National-Gridded, as this will greatly facilitate the plotting of the overlays. It should be drawn between twice and three times the linear dimensions of the map as intended for publication. First of all, the National Grid squares of the area to be covered should be indicated at any rate in pencil, and the area to be covered finalised. Then the coastline (if any) and political or other regional land boundaries should be drawn, preferably

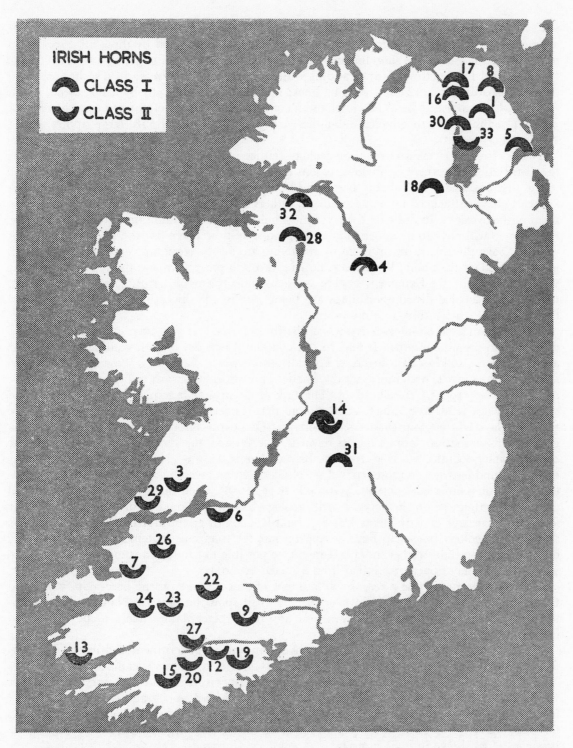

fig. 1 Map of Ireland showing the distribution of Bronze Age horns of classes I and II, by J. M. Coles, *Proc. Prehist. Soc.*, XXIX, 1963, 331. This illustrates the achievement of two tones by the use of only one block.

with a fairly thick line for the coastline and a dot-and-dash line for the land boundaries. The appearance of any map showing a coastline can be vastly improved by thoughtful treatment of the sea or the coast. The shoreline can be indicated by stippling (fig. 5); by a series of two or three parallel lines getting thinner and/or wider apart as they increase in distance from the coast; by shading in horizontal parallel lines; or (perhaps best of all) by a horizontal ripple (fig. 2), which can easily be drawn freehand if controlled by the use of squared (graph) backing paper, or applied by a mechanical self-adhesive such as Letraset LT 118 (large ripples) or LT 126 (smaller ripples).

The addition of rivers and relief or geology (either solid or drift) will assist in interpreting the distribution patterns. For obvious reasons the adding of rivers must be highly selective, and in the first instance it is probably best to add only the most important rivers and any others known to have influenced human settlement. Others can be added as required by the development of the overlays. In drawing the rivers, it should be borne in mind that at a later stage the river names will have to be added; and a decision should be taken on whether they should be written above the rivers, or 'in' them by removing any of the straighter portions long enough to accommodate the name. With rivers flowing through narrow valleys the latter choice may well be preferable: the Exmoor rivers are a case in point (Grinsell, 1970). It is astonishing how many archaeological distribution maps are being published which show no rivers at all and thereby reduce their utility to a minimum.

For a base-map to be informative when distribution overlays are superimposed, land detail of some kind should be shown. It may be hill-contoured without or with shading, or shaded to accord with the solid or drift geology. For normal purposes, base-maps showing hill-contours at two or three levels, preferably suitably shaded, are straightforward to prepare and effective in use (Grimes, 1963; Grinsell, 1970). The task of drawing a base-map showing either solid or drift geology tends to be more laborious and that is probably why most archaeologists go to press on layered (contour-shaded) base-maps. The extra effort involved in producing a geological base-map sometimes has its rewards. For Wessex, the spread of settlement from the chalk downland to the heaths during the Bronze Age is thereby clearly shown, as well as the rarity of round barrows on those parts of the chalk downland which are covered with clay-with-flints and other superficial deposits (Grinsell, 1941; 1958). Such maps also show the rarity of prehistoric settlement on the clays. A drift geology base-map would seem to be most suitable for period overlays of settlements based primarily on an agricultural or pastoral economy; and a solid geology base-map may be appropriate for mapping settlements based primarily on a mining and industrial economy. It might be possible to produce a compromise base-map when the settlement pattern resulted from a mixed economy.

It is desirable to include a reasonable number of place-names on the base-map, because if they are added to the distribution overlays they will spoil the pattern. Names of the major towns should therefore be added, and also any other place-names likely to be mentioned in the accompanying text.

It has for many years been a standard convention among government and most other professional cartographers, on both sides of the Iron Curtain, to use *italic* capitals for the names of seas and estuaries, and *italic* lower case for the names of rivers and streams and other smaller water surfaces including lakes. The *italic* fount has a 'liquid' appearance and can be easily fitted into the often sinuous courses of rivers. By contrast it is convenient to use roman lettering for place-names. Names of tribes and tribal areas of the Iron Age (not quite so static) are, however, often shown in *italic* capitals.

When preparing a series of period distribution maps, the writer has found it essential to test each period overlay with the base-map by drawing the overlays on plastic sheet and superimposing each on the base-map. Assuming that the distribution maps are the result of physical fieldwork as distinct from 'travels in one's study', this process will involve the making of certain

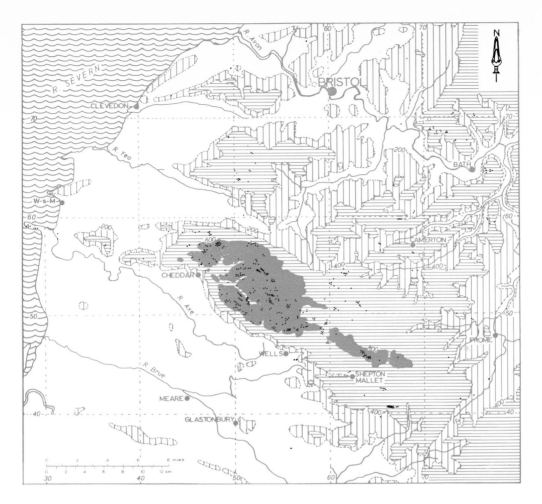

fig. 2 *Bronze Age Round Barrows on and around Mendip*
The *base map* has the sea indicated by a hand-drawn ripple controlled by the use of graph paper behind the plastic sheet. Contour-layered at 200, 400 and 800 feet, and main rivers shown. Space provided in N.E. corner for a north point to be included on the overlay. This map has been designed for any archaeological overlays covering this area, and the style of north point can be varied with the period or subject mapped. The *overlay* illustrates the difficulty of accurately plotting a large number of sites with symbols small enough to be more or less in their relatively correct positions, and yet large enough to provide an effective distribution pattern. Special attention has been given to showing the main nucleated and (mostly) linear barrow groups. In view of the difficulty of distinguishing between round barrows and lead-mining spoil heaps on Mendip, only those sites that are certainly or almost certainly barrows have been included. The need for a dominant overlay and a recessive base map is imperative here.

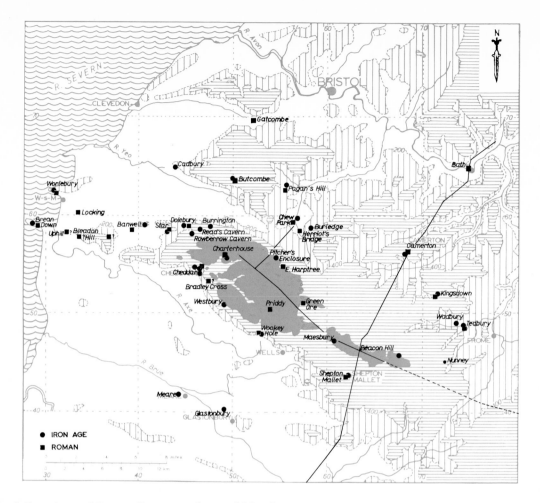

fig. 3 *Iron Age and Roman Sites on and around Mendip*
This is not intended as a distribution map in the strict sense. Only the main sites are shown and all are named, as it was prepared partly as a guide to visitors. An important point about a map which shows more than one period is that continuity or recurrence of occupation can be shown, and the symbol for the later period site must of course partly overlap that for the earlier. An important series of maps of this type is produced by the Italian Ministry of Public Instruction, on a scale of 1:100,000.

minor corrections to the base-map: the lengthening of a river here, or the adding of a small river not previously shown; the amendment of a contour there, or a slight change in the coast-line somewhere else. Where a series of period overlays has been prepared, it will be found that a study of each in relation to the base-map will necessitate a few slight alterations in the latter, which cannot therefore be finalised until each overlay has been tested against it (Grinsell, 1958; 1965; 1970).

Finally, if the national grid square divisions are retained on the published map they should of course be lettered and numbered. It seems best to add north point and scale although these are often omitted in the case of very general maps such as a map of England. There is no reason why the north point should not be made to look attractive providing that it is not so ornate as to take attention away from the overlays. In the case of a series of period distribution maps, the north point can with advantage be omitted from the base-map but added to the overlays and varied in design so as to be appropriate to the period of each overlay (figs. 2, 3). Above all, the use of some of the extremely ugly dry-transfer north points now on the market should be avoided. For the next ten years or so it is desirable to give the scale in both miles and kilometres.

THE DISTRIBUTION OVERLAYS

These should be prepared on plastic sheets superimposed on the base-map. The present writer always starts by inserting the four corners of the base-map to ensure exact registration between overlay and base-map.

The Coastline (if any)

If, during the period represented by the overlay, the coastline was different from that of today, the conjectured coastline of the period can be indicated on the overlay (Cunliffe, 1966).

The Artefacts to be Mapped

The type of artefact which is the subject of the distribution map can be illustrated by a drawing in an otherwise unoccupied part of the map, as it is essential that the reader be left in no doubt as to what is being mapped (Piggott, 1938). In general there should be a separate map for each type of artefact; but sometimes two or three types can be effectively shown as contrasting or similar distribution patterns on the same base-map. Further multiplicity of types of object by the use of several different symbols on the same base-map usually results in confusion.

The Shape and Size of the Symbols

(a) SHAPE   It has recently been written that 'the ideal symbol should be so designed that the reader immediately associates it with whatever feature it indicates without reference to a legend or key' (Hodgkiss, 1970, 109). In the opinion of the present writer representational symbols are a failure if they are long and thin. Symbols as broad as they are long are generally the most effective, and these include circles, squares, equilateral triangles and equal-armed crosses, of which all can be varied in size for different types of site and the first three can be either solid or open. A distinction between precisely and only vaguely known find-spots can be made by the use of large and small symbols or of solid and open symbols. Similarly, in the case of field monuments, a certain example can be shown by a solid, and a doubtful one by an open symbol. The principle of designing symbols in the form of miniature drawings of the objects represented is in the writer's opinion a failure if carried out on a large scale (Grinsell, 1957). It can however be successful with certain types of object such as gold lunulae (Fox, 1932) or bronze horns (Coles, 1963). The use of letters as symbols is not very effective and can border on failure (Allen, 1961). The use of certain shapes of symbol for particular types of antiquity has for many years received general acceptance, e.g. circles (single or concentric, solid or open) for hill-forts, and triangles for Roman villas. It is wise to follow such standard practice unless there are strong reasons for departing from it. The Ordnance Survey period maps provide excellent guidance on this.

(b) SIZE   There is no hard and fast rule concerning the size of symbols on a map. If there are very few plottings the tendency will be to draw the symbols rather large, but the appearance of the map will be spoiled if this is overdone. Sir Cyril Fox, in his critical review, done twenty-five years afterwards, of his own maps in his *Archaeology of the Cambridge Region*, admitted that his own spots tended to be too large (Fox, 1948, 7). A series of Implement Petrology maps done by the present writer has spots that are equally clearly too small (Grinsell, 1962). In general, the greater the contrast in tone between the base-map and the overlay, the smaller the spots can be while yet remaining effective (fig. 2). The maps in *Danmarks Oldtid* illustrate this point (Brøndsted, 1938–40).

Should the Symbols be Numbered or Named in the Overlay?
The addition of numbers tends to detract from the effectiveness of the distribution pattern unless they are smaller than the symbols. If the numbers are put between brackets the effect is even worse. W. F. Grimes once solved the problem by extending the numbers to areas outside the field of the distribution (Grimes, 1963). The addition of names beside the symbols almost invariably spoils the distribution pattern. It is justified only when the map is intended to function as a general-purpose rather than a distribution map.

The Period represented by the Overlay
This should not be too long. A map of the British Isles in the Bronze Age, covering the period between *c.* 1900 and *c.* 550 BC is not as meaningful as a map of Ancient British coins which, by the nature of the material, must cover the period between *c.* 100 BC and AD 50.

The Area represented by the Overlay
Sometimes it happens that although the base-map covers, for example, the whole of England or the British Isles, the data mapped have been assembled for only a part of the area. In such instances the area for which the data are comprehensive should be distinguished from the rest of the area of the base-map by a line of dots or dashes (Grinsell, 1962).

The Mapping of Negative Evidence
Where, for example, several excavations of sites of a particular period in a region have failed to yield a specific type of pottery found elsewhere, the fact can be shown by the use of a special symbol, which should if possible have a 'negative' appearance (Jope, 1963).

The Adequacy of the Supporting Inventory
(a) FIELD MONUMENTS
In general it is easier to compile a reasonably complete inventory of the field monuments of a particular type in a region (providing that adequate fieldwork has been done) than of chance finds. However, aerial photography in the middle Thames Valley, along the coastal plain of Northumberland, and in other lowland parts of England has shown, during the last forty years, that field monuments in lowland areas have been destroyed on a scale which could never have been imagined previously (RCHM, 1960).

(b) SMALL OBJECTS AND CHANCE FINDS
The distribution of these depends largely on that of archaeologists, and particularly so in the case of flint implements; but the supply of flint implements in a region will generally over a

period result in an adequate number of archaeologists searching for them. Where such finds result mainly from archaeological excavation, this is usually related to various circumstances including the distribution of population within the last century or so, the existence and potential of the local archaeological societies, and the amount of earth disturbance which is usually related to modern development in areas of urbanisation. Over a period of a century or two these factors may cancel one another especially over a large area. The fact remains that most of our inventories of chance finds are based on what has been taken out of the ground during the last two hundred years. To what extent can that material be considered representative of what there was originally?

Relationship between Base-Map and Distribution Overlay

It is desirable for the author to have complete control of both base-map and distribution overlay and to be equally interested in both. If the editor's girl friend has drawn the base-map it will almost certainly be printed so that it steals the limelight from the overlays. It is imperative that the overlays should be dominant and the base-map recessive when published. On the other hand the base-map should be printed so that it can be seen in detail when desired.

Blockmaking and Printing and Binding

In his chapter 'How not to write local history', H. P. R. Finberg (1967, 78) has this to say on maps: 'Let the blockmaker reduce it so drastically that most of the names become illegible; and finally let the binder insert it into the book in such a way that it tears every time you open it.' It is enough to add that all the trouble taken in drawing a perfect base-map with overlays can be thrown away by bad editing or bad printing.

Copyright

If a base-map is drawn from an Ordnance Survey map published more than fifty years ago there is no copyright to be cleared. Strictly speaking, any base-map drawn from or founded substantially on a more recent Ordnance Survey map needs copyright clearance. Application should be made to the Ordnance Survey, Romsey Road, Maybush, Southampton, SO9 4DH, on their form OS 23. In cases of doubt it is well to consult the Publication Division, Ordnance Survey, at that address.

ADDENDUM

Since this essay was written, the author has seen a long forgotten but most important paper by Sir John Evans, 'Note on a Proposed International Code of Symbols fo ruse on Archaeological Maps', *Jour. Royal Anthropological Institute*, vol. 5, 1876, 427–36. The question of developing an international code of symbols for archaeological maps was first considered at the Bologna Congress of Prehistoric Archaeology in 1871, and it was reconsidered at the Stockholm Congress of Prehistoric Archaeology in 1874. The report by Sir John Evans published in 1876 embodied the findings of the committee set up at Stockholm for that purpose. It recommended a set of *radical* symbols for the chief types of monument, and sets of *derived* and *complementary* symbols for secondary and complementary information on those types of site. For example, the radical symbol for a cave is an inverted U over a horizontal line ($\underline{\cap}$). The derived symbols of the same shape are open for an artificial cave, and solid for a natural cave; with a curve added for a cave that is sepulchral. Complementary symbols include the addition of an annulet for a cave that has been excavated; a diagonal line for a dilapidated cave; and a diagonal cross for one that has been destroyed. All readers are strongly recommended to consult this paper which is full of useful suggestions.

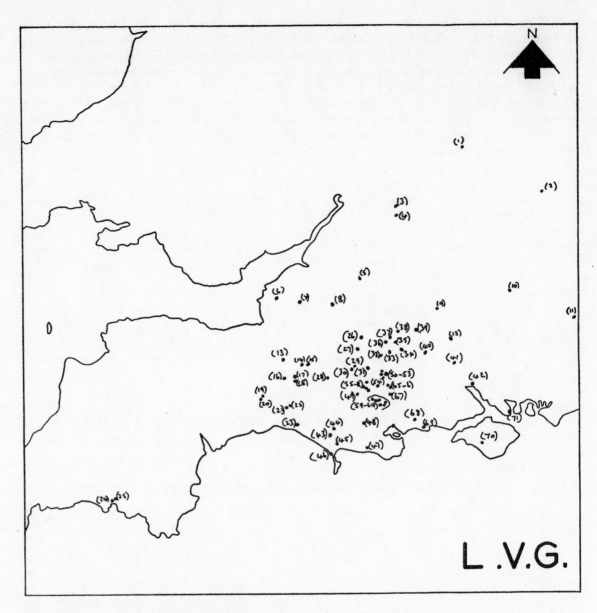

fig. 4 *How not to draw a distribution map*
The Coins of the Durotriges. Based on R. P. Mack, *The Coinage of Ancient Britain*, 2nd edn (1964), 116.
1. No proper distinction between land and sea.
2. No rivers.
3. North point too large and also ugly, and scarcely necessary on a general map of this type.
4. Spots too small, drawn freehand, and lacking in uniformity.
5. Pattern spoiled by addition of site-numbers, made worse by being written freehand and enclosed in brackets.
6. No distinction made between hoards and single finds.
7. Initials of cartographer are too large and badly spaced; in any case they should not have been inserted because the distribution has been copied from the source stated.
8. Area covered by map does not include the whole of the known distribution; in particular it omits the vitally important hoard from Jersey.

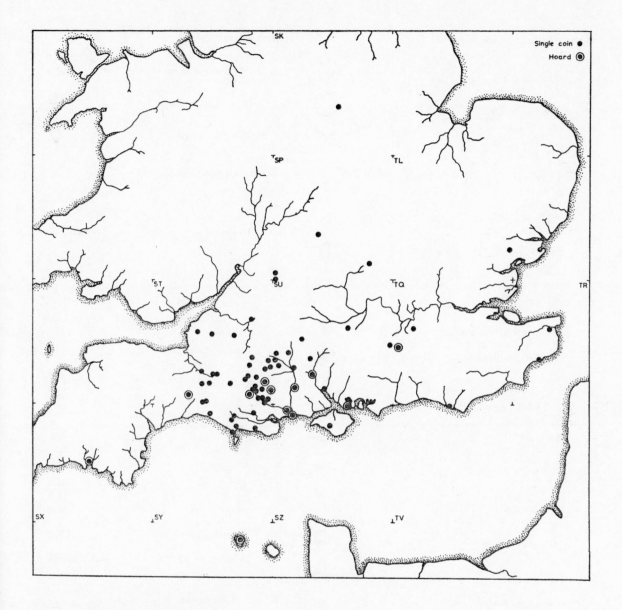

fig. 5 *How to draw a distribution map*
The Coins of the Durotriges. Based on R. P. Mack. *The Coinage of Ancient Britain*, 2nd edn (1964), 116.
1. Coastline emphasised by stippling.
2. Main rivers shown.
3. North point omitted as Grid North implied by the lettered divisions.
4. Spots about the right size and traced by standardgraph stencil and therefore of uniform size. (Dry transfer by Letraset or similar method would have been equally effective.)
5. Numbers within brackets omitted in order not to confuse the distribution pattern. Angles and letter prefixes to national grid squares have been sited so as not to detract from the distribution pattern. Their purpose is to control plotting and to enable the reader to check the spots with any accompanying inventory.
6. A distinction has been made between hoards and single finds.
7. Initials of cartographer omitted as unnecessary.
8. Area of map extended to include the whole known distribution area, including the hoard of crucial importance from Grouville, Jersey.

13

Ceremonial Sites

Stone Circle

Earthen Circle

Stone Row

Stone Setting

Standing Stone

Temple (Iron Age or Roman)

Defensive Sites

Hill-fort, univallate

Hill-fort, multivallate

Cliff-castle
   (sited to promontory)

Rampart

Ditch

Living Sites

Inhabited Cave

Lake Village

Hill-slope Enclosure

Hill-slope Enclosure
   (with outworks)

Other Enclosure

Industrial Sites

Mine or Quarry

Kiln, for pottery

Kiln, for tiles

Communications

Road (Roman)

Trackway

Burial Sites

Long Barrow
   (correctly orientated)

Burial Chamber
   (shape of original
    mound uncertain)

Round Barrow: Bowl

             Bell

             Disc

Single Grave

War Grave

Cemetery

War Cemetery

Miscellaneous

Submerged Forest

Shipwreck (Roman)

fig. 6 *Some Symbols recommended for Field Monuments*
A wide range of additional symbols is given in the keys to the Ordnance Survey period maps, especially those on *Southern Britain in the Iron Age* and *Roman Britain*. There is a need for a commercially produced stencil for archaeological symbols most frequently used. In general principle, the writer considers that the most successful maps of distribution of small artefacts are produced by the use of a straightforward circle or other simple symbol, and the type of object mapped to be shown by a sketch in an otherwise unused corner of the map.

This section includes notes on numerous distribution maps published in the *Proceedings of the Prehistoric Society*, *Archaeologia Cambrensis*, and elsewhere.

Akerman, J. Y., 1849. 'On the Condition of Britain from the descent of Caesar to the coming of Claudius; accompanied by a Map . . . showing the finding of Indigenous Coins', *Archaeologia*, XXXIII, 177–90.

Allen, D. F., 1961. 'The origins of Coinage in Britain: a reappraisal', in S. S. Frere (ed.), *Problems of the Iron Age in Southern Britain*. Univ. London Inst. of Archaeol. Occasional Paper No. 11. London. pp. 97–308.

Allen, D. F., 1967. 'Iron Currency Bars in Britain', *Proc. Prehist. Soc.*, XXXIII, 307–35. The symbols on the maps on pp. 309, 313 are rather large, and some at least have been drawn freehand.

Antoniewicz, W., 1966. *Sur l' Atlas Archéologique du Monde et de la Pologne*. Warsaw. p. 42.

Archaeologia Geographica, 1950 onwards. A periodical devoted to the study of archaeological distributions. It is published in Hamburg and the contributions are normally in German.

Balchin, W. G. V. & Lavis, W. V., 1945. 'The Construction of Distribution Maps', *Geography*, XXX, 86–92.

Brøndsted, J., 1938–40. *Danmarks Oldtid*. Copenhagen.

Bunch, B. & Fell, C. I., 1949. 'A Stone Axe Factory at Pike of Stickle', *Proc. Prehist. Soc.*, XV, 1–20. On the map on p. 12, the spots are rather large and their numbering tends to add to the appearance of confusion.

Campbell Smith, W., 1965. 'The Distribution of Jade Axes in Europe', *Proc. Prehist. Soc.*, XXXI, 25–33. The map on p. 26 has everything about right, except that more rivers than only the Thames might have been shown in Britain.

Case, H. J., 1961. 'Irish Neolithic Pottery: Distribution and Sequence', *Proc. Prehist. Soc.*, XXVII, 174–233. Maps on pp. 215, 216, 218, 219. Their clarity is slightly reduced by the addition of numbers to the symbols.

Chitty, L. F., 1932 and later editions. Maps in Fox, Cyril, *The Personality of Britain*. Cardiff. The classic series.

Chitty, L. F., & Barker, P. A. and C. J., 1963. Map accompanying 'The Clun–Clee Ridgeway: a Prehistoric Trackway across South Shropshire', in Foster, I. Ll. & Alcock, L. (eds.), *Culture and Environment*. London. 171–92. The map has shaded contours, and rivers are adequately shown. Symbols for chance finds are about the same size as those for field monuments.

Clark, J. G. D., 1946. 'Seal Hunting in the Stone Age of North-Western Europe', *Proc. Prehist. Soc.*, XII, 12–48. The distribution pattern on the map on p. 16 is somewhat confused by the addition of site numbers.

Clark, J. G. D., 1965. 'Radiocarbon dating, and the expansion of farming culture', *Proc. Prehist. Soc.*, XXXI, 58–73. The map on p. 65, showing the three main periods of expansion, by means of three well-chosen and clearly distinguishable types of symbol, is most effective. The unobtrusiveness of the small numbers by each site is a big improvement on Clark, 1946.

Clarke, J. I., 1959. 'Statistical Map Reading', *Geography*, XLIV, 96–104.

Coles, J. M., 1963. 'Irish Bronze Age Horns and their relations with Northern Europe', *Proc. Prehist. Soc.*, XXIX, 326–56. By using a mechanically dotted base-map he has achieved the effect of a two-tone distribution map although it has been printed from only one block. The symbols are rather heavy. The map is on p. 331, and is reproduced in this essay as fig. 1.

Cowen, J. D., 1967. 'The Hallstatt Sword of Bronze: on the Continent and in Britain', *Proc. Prehist. Soc.*, XXXIII, 377–454. The maps comprise red overlays with sites numbered to correspond with inventories, on a black outline base-map.

Crawford, O. G. S., 1912. 'Distribution of Early Bronze Age Settlements in Britain', *Geogr. J.*, XL, 184–97, 304–17. The first archaeological distribution map on modern lines?

Crawford, O. G. S., 1921. *Man and his Past*. Oxford. Chapter XIII.

Crawford, O. G. S., 1925. *The Long Barrows of the Cotswolds*. Gloucester.

Crawford, O. G. S., 1953. *Archaeology in the Field*. London. Chapter 3, 'Archaeology and Maps'.

Crawford, O. G. S., 1955. *Said and Done*. London. Chapter 16, 'Period Maps and some others, 1932–38'.

Cunliffe, B., 1966. 'The Somerset Levels in the Roman Period', in Thomas, C. (ed.), *Rural Settlement in Roman Britain*, London. 68–73.

Deffontaines, P., 1924. 'Cartes Préhistoriques', *Revue Anthropologique*, 320–2.

Eogan, G., 1964. 'The Later Bronze Age in Ireland', *Proc. Prehist. Soc.*, XXX, 268–351. On the maps on pp. 284, 312, the author has done his best to produce effective distribution maps as well as maps of Irish place-names for the benefit of those of his English readers who are more or less ignorant of Irish geography; but such dual-purpose maps are successful only when (as on p. 312) the spots are almost evenly spread over the whole area of the map and it is not really necessary to study their pattern in detail.

Finberg, H. P. R., 1967. 'How not to write local history', in Finberg, H. P. R. & Skipp, V. H. T., *Local History: Objective and Pursuit*. Newton Abbot.

Fox, Aileen, 1936. 'The Dual Colonisation of East Glamorgan in the Neolithic and Bronze Ages', *Archaeol. Cambrensis*, XCI, 100–17. Two maps, both in red on black, showing glacial drift and alluvium, contours, and adequate rivers. Probable and conjectural trackways are shown in red.

Fox, Cyril, 1923. *The Archaeology of the Cambridge Region*. Cambridge. Perhaps the earliest comprehensive series of English archaeological distribution maps.

Fox, Cyril, 1927. 'A La Tène I Brooch from Wales: with notes on the Typology and Distribution of these Brooches in Britain', *Archaeol. Cambrensis*, LXXXII, 67–112. The base-map is a colour-contoured 'diagram hand-map' published by the Diagram Co. and G. Philip & Sons Ltd.

Fox, Cyril, 1932 and later editions to 1943. *The Personality of Britain*. Cardiff. Includes many maps from earlier publications, brought up to date.

Fox, Cyril, 1933. 'The Distribution of Man in East Anglia, 2300 BC–AD 50', *Proc. Prehist. Soc. East Anglia*, VII, 149–64.

Fox, Cyril, 1948. 'Reflections on the Archaeology of the Cambridge Region', *Cambridge Hist. J.*, IX(i), 1–21.

Griffiths, W. E., 1951. 'Early Settlement in Caernarvonshire', *Archaeol. Cambrensis*, CI, 38–71. The map on p. 58 is dominated by the thick alternating parallel lines for the sea shading, diverting attention from the distribution pattern which is shown by the minutest dots.

Grimes, W. F., 1936. *Map of South Wales, showing . . . Long Barrows and Megaliths*. Ordnance Survey.

Grimes, W. F., 1963. 'The Stone Circles and Related Monuments of Wales', in Foster, I. Ll. & Alcock, L. (eds.), *Culture and Environment*, London. 93–152. The map on p. 99 has layered contours and well-selected rivers; the sites are numbered from lines extended from the map area, thereby not disturbing the effectiveness of the distribution pattern.

Grinsell, L. V., 1941. 'The Bronze Age Round Barrows of Wessex', *Proc. Prehist. Soc.*, VII, 73–113. The author's first maps comprising a black overlay on a green base which in this instance incorporates drift geology.

Grinsell, L. V., 1953. *The Ancient Burial-Mounds of England*. London. Part I, chapter 6, 'Maps and Distributions'.

Grinsell, L. V., 1957. Maps in *Victoria County History of Wiltshire*, I (i). These comprise black overlays on a blue base that is rather dark. The principle of showing each type of find by a miniature drawing of it was here applied with results that are not too satisfactory.

Grinsell, L. V., 1958. *The Archaeology of Wessex*. London. This work includes six period-maps (Neolithic to Pagan Saxon) in black overlay on a green base that is a shade too powerful. The base-map incorporates drift geology and is divided into national grid squares to facilitate plotting and to eliminate the need for numbering each site. Only the field monuments are mapped, and the more important sites are named for the benefit of non-specialist readers.

Grinsell, L. V., 1962, in Evens *et al.*, 'Fourth Report . . . on the Petrological Identification of Stone Axes', *Proc. Prehist. Soc.*, XXVIII, 209–66. The spots on most of the maps are rather too small; but this was done to prevent them from fusing together in concentration areas, while still preserving accuracy of plotting.

Grinsell, L. V., 1964. 'Settlement in Prehistoric and Roman Times', in Monkhouse, F. J. (ed.), *A Survey of Southampton and its Region*, 189–204. Six maps in black on green (Palaeolithic to Roman). The Bronze Age map shows that the distribution of hoards of bronze implements is coastal and quite different from that of round barrows most of which are in the hinterland of heath and downland.

Grinsell, L. V., 1965. 'Somerset Archaeology 1931–65', *Proc. Somerset Archaeol. Natur. Hist. Soc.*, CIX, 47–77. Ten maps in black overlays on a green base-map carrying rivers and contours and divided into national grid squares to facilitate plotting. Notes are given on the chief sources on which each map is based.

Grinsell, L. V. *et al.*, 1966. *The Preparation of Archaeological Reports*, London. pp. 55–6.

Grinsell, L. V., 1970. *The Archaeology of Exmoor*. Newton Abbot. This work includes eight period-maps (Palaeolithic to Medieval), in black overlays on green. The base-map is contoured and shaded and shows the main rivers, and is divided into national grid squares to ensure accuracy in plotting. Each map is supported by a comprehensive inventory of sites and finds with their national grid references.

Gulley, J. L. M., 1960. 'Some Problems of Archaeological Mapping', *Revue Archéologique*, 141–59. The best general survey so far.

Harris, S., 1928. 'Distribution Maps and early movements into Britain, and their relation to legendary history', *Archaeol. Cambrensis*, LXXXIII, 182–91. A critique of Fox, 1927.

Hoare, R. C., 1812, 1819. *Ancient Wiltshire*. London.

Hodgkiss, A. G., 1970. *Maps for Books and Theses*. Newton Abbot. A book of outstanding importance by a professional cartographer. It is particularly good for its explanations of artificial aids and how they should be used.

Jope, E. M., 1963. 'The Regional Cultures of Medieval Britain', in Foster, I. Ll. & Alcock, L. (eds.), *Culture and Environment*. London. 327–50. The maps on pp. 330, 331, 333 show a special symbol for negative evidence, i.e. where an excavation on a medieval site has failed to yield a particular type of pottery.

Keiller, A. *et al.*, 1941. 'First Report . . . on the Petrological Identification of Stone Axes', *Proc. Prehist. Soc.*, VII, 50–72. The maps on pp. 52, 59, 62 have their distributions confused by addition of site numbers.

Mackay, J. R., 1949. 'Dotting the dot map: an analysis of dot size, number, and visual tone density', *Surveying and Mapping*, IX, 3.

Monkhouse, F. J. & Wilkinson, H. R., 1963. *Maps and Diagrams*. London.

Montelius, O., 1874. *La Suède Préhistorique*. Trans. J. H. Kramer. Stockholm.

Phillips, C. W., 1933. *Map of the Trent Basin, showing Long Barrows . . .* Ordnance Survey.

Piggott, S., 1938. 'The Early Bronze Age in Wessex', *Proc. Prehist. Soc.*, IV, 52–106. The maps on pp. 59, 81 show sketches of the types of object plotted. On p. 104 is an adequate Wessex base-map hill-contoured at 400 feet, with plenty of rivers, and horizontally-shaded sea.

RCHM, 1960. *A Matter of Time: an archaeological survey of the river gravels of England*. London.

Savory, H. N., 1948. 'The Sword-bearers. A Reinterpretation', *Proc. Prehist. Soc.*, XIV, 155–76. The maps (figs. 1–5) show an effective thick-line coast and the main rivers. One senses a tendency to have too many different types of symbol on each map.

Sumner, H., 1913. *The Ancient Earthworks of Cranborne Chase*. London.

Sumner, H., 1917. *The Ancient Earthworks of the New Forest*. London.

Sumner, H., 1923. *A Map of Ancient Sites in the New Forest, Cranborne Chase, and Bournemouth District*. Although not distribution maps in the strict sense here used, these maps are models of what can be achieved by an archaeologist who is also an artist. The reader can only admire the beauty of the lettering, the treatment of the north points, and other incidental details which convey to the reader the spirit of the region.

Wainwright, G. J., 1963. 'A Reinterpretation of the Microlithic Industries of Wales', *Proc. Prehist. Soc.*, XXIX, map (by J. Christiansen) opposite p. 104. The coastline is emphasised by a thick line, and the main rivers are also shown. Submerged forests are indicated by a neat tree-stump symbol.

Warne, Charles, 1866. *Ancient Dorset*. Bournemouth.

Winterbotham, H. St. J. L., 1934. 'Dots and Distributions', *Geography*, XIX, 211–13.

ACKNOWLEDGEMENTS

The writer is grateful to Mr R. W. Feacham (Archaeology Officer, Ordnance Survey) for reading this text and making some suggestions which have been adopted. For improvements on various details he is indebted to Dr John Coles and Mr A. J. Sutcliffe.

The Irish Sea Element in the Welsh Mesolithic Cultures

R. G. Livens

The object of this essay is to draw attention to an element of the Mesolithic cultures of Wales which has not hitherto received the attention which it merits, and which seems to display clear affinities with material found elsewhere on the western seaboards of the British Isles. I feel that it is appropriate to offer this study in affectionate homage to Miss Chitty, who has done so much to emphasise the essential unity of the Irish Sea area in British archaeology, and from whose writings and companionship I have derived so much inspiration.

CHARACTERISTIC FEATURES OF THE IRISH SEA COMPLEX

In his study of the Irish material, Professor H. L. Movius (1940) isolated and described a quantity of worked flints, occurring mainly on coastal sites, whose date seems to span the maximum of the local post-glacial marine transgression. The chronological bracket occupied by these industries may be a wide one, for the industry at Toome Bay, Lough Neagh, is of late Boreal date or earlier (Evans, 1867; Knowles, 1912, 198–206), while at Ballynagard, Rathlin Island, a flint industry may be associated with pottery of Neolithic type (Whelan, 1934); this association appears to be uncertain.

The most striking feature of these Irish industries, by comparison with their counterparts elsewhere in the British Isles, is the relative unimportance of the microlithic element. Recent studies of the British mesolithic material have demonstrated that the cultural and chronological significance of the various microlithic forms has to be radically reassessed: the 'Tardenoisian' element in some British industries has been virtually abolished (Clark, 1955), while at the Cathole, Cwm, Gower, typical microlithic forms have been found associated with a late Palaeolithic industry and a late-Glacial fauna (McBurney, 1959, 268). Though any extensive discussion of these questions is outside the scope of this paper, it appears that in certain areas the development of microlithic forms may be interpreted more as a reaction to particular environmental conditions than as a reflection of any particular cultural affinities or date. Certainly, in the industries which I wish to discuss here, there is no evidence that microlithic forms were either made or used to any noticeable extent.

Mr A. D. Lacaille, in his analysis of the material from South-West Scotland (Lacaille, 1954, 124–60), has shown that certain sites in that area – mostly located on the coast, but showing some penetration inland into the Clyde area – have produced stone industries which, within the

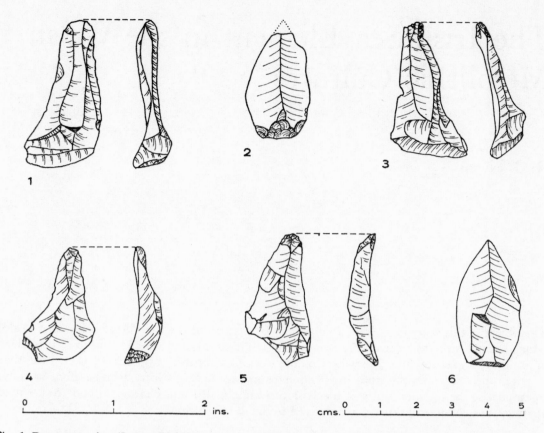

fig. 1 Representative 'Larne Picks' (1,3–5) and 'Bann Flakes' (2,6) from Ireland and Scotland: 1, Cushendun, Co. Antrim; 2, Rough Island, Co. Antrim; 3, Annieston, Lanarkshire; 4, Albyn Distillery, Campbeltown, Argyll; 5, Woodend Loch, Lanarkshire; 6, Risga, Argyll.

limitations imposed by inferior raw materials, may be regarded as cognate with their counterparts on the Antrim coast. This is reflected in the application of the term 'Larnian' to some of the material from the Scottish sites (Mitchell, 1947): they share with the Irish sites the characteristic lack of good microliths, and the similarities are emphasised by the occurrence in Scotland of such implements as the 'Larne Pick' (fig. 1). Where dates can be established, the majority of Scottish sites date from after the maximum of the marine transgression (Lacaille, 1954, 140–9), though occasional sites have produced hints of earlier activity (Livens, 1956).

The 'Larne Pick', as defined by Movius, is not the most satisfactory of implements. Among the material from the Antrim sites, there is a quantity of large, approximately triangular, flake implements, which bear traces of use at the narrow, bulbar end (fig. 1, no. 1). Most of these implements are fashioned on large, plunging flakes, and many of them bear cortex on the wider end; in many instances, this enhances their resemblance to implements of the 'handpick' type and some published examples exceed 5 inches in length. In an industry as devoid of characteristic implement types as Movius's 'Late Larnian' these objects are conspicuous by their relative uniformity of size and shape, although one suspects that many of them may be merely utilised core-trimmings.

The Scottish 'Larne Picks' (fig. 1, nos. 3–5) studied by Mr Lacaille (1954, 189–93) present a different picture from their alleged Irish counterparts, on two grounds: in the first place, their distribution shows some inland penetration, whereas the Irish specimens seem to occur exclusively on coastal sites. Secondly, it is notable that the Scottish specimens are uniformly smaller than the Antrim examples: the one 'Larne Pick' from Albyn Distillery, Campbeltown (fig. 1, no. 4) is a mere 1¼ inches long, and those from Woodend Loch (fig. 1, no. 5) and Annieston (fig. 1, no. 3) are no bigger. It must be emphasised that the difference in size may be due partly to the inferior raw material available in Scotland, but the smaller size of these implements must have rendered them correspondingly less useful as any sort of hand implement. It is notable, too, that at Woodend Loch (by contrast with Campbeltown) the range of identifiable implements was far more varied than that from any Larnian site (Davidson, Phemister & Lacaille, 1949). It cannot be established, however, that the Woodend Loch industry is the work of a single group of people with a uniform material tradition.

More convincing evidence of affinities can perhaps be adduced from the presence in both Scotland and Ireland of characteristic implements of the 'Bann Flake' type (Livens, 1957). These implements are leaf-shaped, prismatic-sectioned flakes, which normally bear retouch of a distinctively coarse pattern only around the base. This retouch either narrows the bulbar end of the flake to form a crude tang, or takes the form of resolved flaking at the bulbar end of the upper surface, to reduce the thickness of the butt-end of the point. The 'Bann Flake' occurs extensively in Ireland, in both Larnian and later contexts (Knowles, 1912, 198–206), and implements of this type have been noted in the Isle of Man (Clark, 1935, 74–5). In Scotland, the inferior raw material available to the flint-worker resulted in a decrease in size, but the Scottish examples are nevertheless plausible missile-points. The function of the Irish 'Bann Flakes' is not certainly known: the tanged points could be used as either spear-heads or knife-blades; one example appears to have a surviving knife-handle of moss (Knowles, 1912, 201). It is difficult to envisage the points which are reduced in thickness at the butt end being used as anything other than arrow- or spear-heads.

The so-called 'Limpet Scoop' is also represented on both sides of the Irish Sea: in Ireland, specimens are known from a single site, Dalkey Island, Co. Dublin (Liversage, 1968, 119, 147). In Scotland, they are numerous on sites of the Obanian complex (Lacaille, 1954, 193–243) and their occurrence in Wales has been noted by Mr T. C. Cantrill (1915, 179–96) and the Rev. J. P. Gordon-Williams (1926, 100–9). On the sites on the island of Oransay, Argyllshire (Bishop, 1914), they are associated with a flint industry distinguished only by its poverty, but they also occurred in quantity on the rich site at Risga, Argyllshire[1] (Lacaille, 1954, 229–43). The Risga industry contains 'Bann Flakes' (fig. 1, no. 6), in addition to a few relatively coarse microliths, some possible 'Larne Picks' and a number of highly distinctive awls. Professor J. G. D. Clark (1957) has shown that the extensive antler-work from Risga relates to that from other Obanian sites. The shell-mound at Risga overlies deposits of the marine transgression, so it cannot be of a particularly early date, but it must be noted that the worked bone from the site contains some remains of elk; so, if the deposit is a cultural and chronological unit, its date cannot be too retarded. The two most recent studies of the deglaciation and littoral history of Scotland (Lacaille, 1954, 30–91; Donner, 1963) suggest that the submergence phase terminated during the third millennium BC. The maximum of the marine transgression may be placed nearer to the commencement of the submergence phase than to its termination. It is accordingly difficult to assume that the Risga site dates from after 3000 BC and it may be as early as 4000 BC.

The purpose of the finger-like pieces of bone or stone, described by the Abbé Breuil (1922, 267–71) as 'flaking tools', but by Mr A. H. Bishop (1914) and others as 'Limpet Scoops', is a mystery. Evidence that these objects have been used as implements is to be found in the traces of either abrasion or battering upon their extremities; traces of both forms of wear may occur upon the same implement. G. D. Liversage (1968, 147) records that the wear upon a stone

---

[1] Much of the unpublished material from this site is lodged in the Hunterian Museum of the University of Glasgow; I am indebted to the University Court for permission to examine and refer to it.

example can be reproduced by rubbing it on a rock, but this explanation accounts neither for the battering upon some specimens nor for the almost polished appearance of the worn surfaces of some of the bone examples. It seems improbable that they can be regarded as flint-working tools, because many of the sites upon which they occur in profusion (notably the Oransay shell-mounds) have extremely poor flint industries. The association of these objects with shell-mounds or littoral sites suggests that they played some part in the preparation of a diet which consisted largely of shell-fish, but neither the sheer quantity of these implements nor the form of the wear upon them can readily be explained in this way. It is possible that the 'pebble rubbers' which occur upon certain sites in southern England (Rankine, 1952, 34–5) may be related to the Irish Sea examples, but the English specimens show no signs of battering nor have they apparently been noted on any coastal site. It must be remarked also that 'Limpet Scoops' of either type are not apparent among the great quantity of material from the many shell-mounds in the Baltic area. The only examples which I know to occur on sites outside the British Isles are two from the megalithic site on the isle of Thinic (Morbihan), now in the Carnac Museum (Jacq, ?1942, 39); their significance and associations are not clear.

It appears, then, that some of the mesolithic material found on both sides of the Irish Sea has certain distinctive features in common: these may be summarised as the poverty or complete absence of the microlithic element and the presence of certain distinctive implement types, of which the most notable are the 'Larne Pick', the 'Bann Flake' and the 'Limpet Scoop'. We have no information about the forms of Mesolithic antler-work from Ireland or Wales, so the cross-bearings which this material might provide are denied to us. The three distinctive types listed above appear to have few direct counterparts on English or Continental sites, and they therefore suggest the presence of a cultural or economic unity of a distinctive character in western Britain. This I propose to categorise as the Irish Sea Complex and to examine its occurrences in Wales.

SITES IN WALES

In his study of the microlithic industries of Wales, Dr G. J. Wainwright (1963) has noted the occurrence of a certain quantity of this material, found on sites which he was considering on other grounds. There is now a considerable, though scattered, amount of material of the Irish Sea Complex from coastal sites in Wales, and its occurrences and significance merit discussion.

Of the types of objects described above as characterising the Irish Sea Complex, the 'Larne Pick', so far as we know, is not represented among the material from Welsh sites, the 'Bann Flake' occurs on scattered sites ranging from Pembrokeshire to North Wales, and the 'Limpet Scoop' is apparently restricted to the south coast of Pembrokeshire and a single site in Glamorgan. Most of the sites on which this material occurs are now in coastal locations (fig. 2). The thin scatter of sites in North Wales, with their considerable variety of mostly poor industries, suggests that many of these sites may represent sporadic inland penetrations of a scattered population, perhaps differing widely in date and cultural origins, most of whose activities centred in areas now submerged by the Irish Sea. We may note in passing that the typically Sauveterrian industries found in Wales, at Prestatyn and Aberystwyth, show an equally scattered distribution and that the size and character of the Prestatyn industry (Clark, 1938, 330–2) offer a striking contrast with the other industries of the area; it is evident that, in this case at least, indifferent raw material did not prevent men from making microlithic implements.

The stratigraphy of coastal sites is notoriously unreliable: even where the material has been methodically collected or excavated and the associated deposits analysed, we have no proof that any single group of artefacts from a single site is the product of a single group of people. Even less can we be sure that any such group of objects must be contemporary, for individual objects found in the same climatic horizon may differ in date by some centuries.

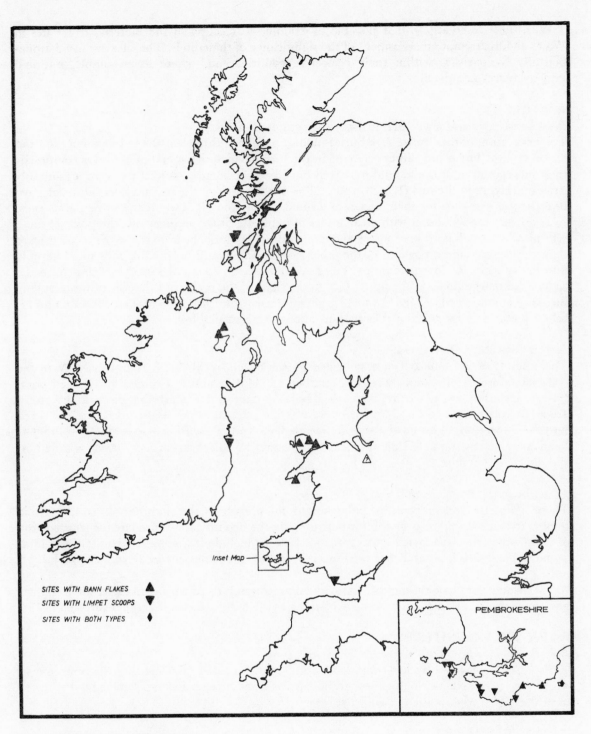

SITES WITH BANN FLAKES ▲
SITES WITH LIMPET SCOOPS ▼
SITES WITH BOTH TYPES ◆

PEMBROKESHIRE

Inset Map

fig. 2 Irish Sea Mesolithic Group

With these reservations, it is possible to examine a selection of the material from sites in Wales and to attempt an assessment of the significance of these finds. The sites are listed alphabetically by parishes within their respective counties and, where ascertainable, national grid references are given.

ANGLESEY

Bedd Branwen, Llanddeusant (SH/361850) (fig. 3, nos. 1–3)

The excavation of the Bronze Age burial-mound produced three leaf-shaped flakes of flint and one microlith. These four pieces occurred in the turf of which the actual mound was composed; their incorporation in the mound may well have been accidental, since they were presumably stray finds lying in the turf (Lynch, 1966). The construction of the mound does, however, give us a *terminus ante quem* for these pieces of around 1500–1400 BC. Two of the three points (nos. 1, 2) are leaf-shaped, no. 2 with clear traces of battering at the bulbar end; the point of no. 2 is formed by a small portion of cortex and is accordingly blunt. The bulbar end of no. 3 is thicker than the corresponding portions of the other two specimens and it probably falls more happily into the category of core-trimmings; there are, however, two small sectors of retouch on the right-hand margin, one on the upper face to the right of the point and the other on the bulbar surface. I am indebted to Miss Frances Lynch for drawing my attention to these hitherto unpublished pieces and for making information about them available.

Penmon (SH/8063) (fig. 3, nos. 4–7)

This small clutch of flint artefacts, collected on the beach by Mr W. J. Hemp and now in the National Museum of Wales (accession number 34. 659), contains a single, leaf-shaped point (no. 4) which shows signs of trimming at the basal end of the upper face. Other pieces in this group are a lanceolate flake (no. 5) blunted by microlithic retouch at the left-hand side of the tip, a button-scraper (no. 6) and a sizeable *dos rabattu* flake (no. 7), with coarse retouch on the left-hand margin. It is notable that *dos rabattu* flakes and button-scrapers have been recorded on sites in Pembrokeshire.

Lligwy Cromlech, Penrhoslligwy (SH/501860) (fig. 3, no. 8)

There is a single, leaf-shaped flint point among the finds from the chamber of this megalithic tomb[1]; its context is unrecorded, but its inclusion in the deposit cannot predate the construction of the monument. Miss Lynch (1969, 157–9) did not include it among her study of the finds from the site, but it is notable that the flints also include a button-scraper (Lynch, 1969, fig. 57, no. 14).

The point seems to be a highly characteristic example: a simple, prismatic-sectioned piece has been reduced in thickness by resolved flaking at the bulbar end of the upper surface.

CAERNARVONSHIRE

Bryn Refail, Llanengan (SH/305272) (fig. 3, nos. 9–10)

The industry excavated by Ridgway and Leach (1946) included two leaf-shaped points, one of which (no. 10) is reduced in thickness at the basal end by the removal of a resolved flake, struck from the upper edge of the striking platform.

DENBIGHSHIRE

Wrexham Area (?) (fig. 3, no. 11)

This piece was retrieved from a load of soil deposited by contractors on the new playing-fields for St Joseph's School, Wrexham.[2] Inquiries failed to establish the origins of the soil with any

---

[1] Information from Miss Frances Lynch.　　[2] Information from Mr J. M. Cleary.

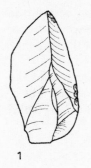

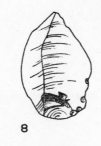

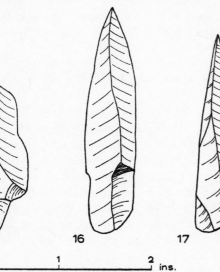
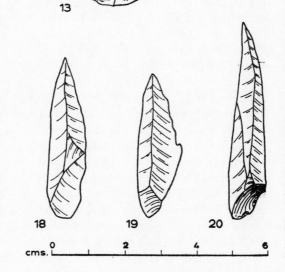

1–3 Bedd Branwen, Anglesey;
4–7 Penmon, Anglesey;
8 Lligwy, Anglesey;
9–10 Bryn Refail, Caernarvonshire;
11 Wrexham (?), Denbighshire;
12 Nanna's Cave, Caldey, Pembrokeshire;
13 Freshwater East, Pembrokeshire;
14 Short Point Gully, Pembrokeshire;
15 West Moor, Pembrokeshire;
16–20 Nab Head, Pembrokeshire

fig. 3 Mesolithic flints from Wales

certainty, but it seems, on balance, improbable that it could have originated far outside the Wrexham area. If it did originate in this part of eastern Denbighshire, the piece would be an isolated find and might serve to emphasise the scattered and fragmentary nature of the evidence from North Wales.

However dubious its origins, the piece is a very good specimen, with its leaf-shape and the resolved flaking of the butt-end; there is a small zone of microlithic trimming on the right of the tip. This hitherto unpublished piece has now been presented to the Museum of Welsh Antiquities, University College, Bangor.

GLAMORGAN
Merthyr Mawr Warren, Candleston (SS/8576)
A total of six 'Limpet Scoops' is recorded from this extensive and prolific sand-dune site (Grimes, 1951, 167).

PEMBROKESHIRE
Stackpole Warren, Bosherston (SR/9894)
The Rev. J. P. Gordon-Williams (1926, 106) notes: 'a felsite long bladescraper . . . , 27 battered back pen-knives, etc. . . . , a small indeterminate scraper . . . , one scoop.'

Nanna's Cave, Caldey Island (SS/967146) (fig. 3, no. 12)
The objects excavated from the red loam stratum within the cave include two 'Limpet Scoops', one of bone and the other of stone (Lacaille, 1955, 116–17); the stone specimen, as Mr Lacaille notes, is slightly atypical, but the one made of bone is the only example made of this material yet reported from Wales. This is presumably owing to the destruction of organic material on open sites; many examples made of bone are known from Scotland, notably the Risga site (Lacaille, 1954, 231), where the conditions for preservation were exceptionally good. The flint industry from the stratum contains a single leaf-shaped point and a number of pieces with secondary, microlithic retouch.

The precise date of the deposition of the red loam stratum is not clear: taken in conjunction with the underlying silty sand, it represents a climatic fluctuation from Continental to Oceanic conditions, and the layer, as well as the industry contained within it, compares with certain aspects noted at Freshwater West (Wainwright, 1959). The absence of any overlying deposits (apart from disturbed material) argues against a glacial date for these strata, but our knowledge of the climatic history of South Wales does not at present permit us to be more precise.

Frainslake, Castlemartin (SR/8898)
Gordon-Williams (1926, 108) notes: 'six scoops from the submerged forest'.

Freshwater West, Castlemartin (SR/886994)
The industry excavated on this site and published by Dr Wainwright (1959) contains, *inter alia*, button-scrapers, a poor microlithic element (one hollow-based point and four microburins) and 'Limpet Scoops'. The comparative frequency of 'Limpet Scoops' is noteworthy: there were eleven examples out of a total of thirty recognisable stone artefacts recovered.

A possible synchronism between the red loam layer, in which this industry occurred, and the similar layer in Nanna's Cave, Caldey, was noted by Dr I. W. Cornwall (Wainwright, 1959, 205). The button-scrapers in this industry afford a point of contact with finds from Penmon.

Little Castle Point, Dale (SM/796038)
T. C. Cantrill (1915, 179) reports two 'Limpet Scoops' among a small miscellany of flint flakes and cores.

Longlands Farm, Dale (SM/7907)
T. C. Cantrill (1915, 176) reports two 'Limpet Scoops'.

Short Point Gully, Dale (SN/799045) (fig. 3, no. 14)
Among the finds from this site, reported by T. C. Cantrill (1915, 184) are 28 'Limpet Scoops' and an 'arrowhead', of which the lower face is a simple flake-surface and the upper consists mainly of six elongated flake-scars with resolved flaking at the bulbar end. The piece has no true secondary trimming. The point differs from the majority of 'Bann Flakes' in the multiple faceting of the upper face. The edges near the point show slight signs of wear, suggesting that this piece is not merely a core-trimming. It appears most nearly to resemble the 'Bann Flakes' which are reduced in thickness and not in width by flaking at the bulbar end of the upper face.

Freshwater East, Lamphey (SS/0197) (fig. 3, no. 13)
A thin, leaf-shaped flake, with a slight retouch on the left side of the basal end, was found with traces of a good blade industry, two steep scrapers and many waste fragments, in a soil-drift deposit. Leach (1913, 399) drew attention to the epi-Palaeolithic aspect of this assemblage and established that the soil-drifts 'may be grouped with deposits which pass under and antedate the submerged forest'.

West Moor, Manorbier (SS/0398) (fig. 3, no. 15)
Finds from this site (Leach, 1913, 391–432) include industrial waste, a large end-scraper, two ridge-backed scrapers, one side-scraper, and a tanged flake which is the best example of the tanged type of 'Bann Flake' yet found in Wales. No environmental evidence was obtained.

Ramaskell, Marloes (SM/777077)
T. C. Cantrill (1915, 179) reports six 'Limpet Scoops'.

Nab Head, St Bride's (SM/789112) (fig. 3, nos. 16–20)
The large amount of material from this site includes five flint points, of which one (no. 16) has been reduced in thickness at the base (Leach, 1933, 235). The other four specimens are similar and it is possible that no. 20, which has a deep flake-scar at the right-hand side of the basal end, is a poor attempt to form a tanged flake. These flakes differ from the typical 'Bann Flakes' in their elongated, lanceolate form. Leach has also observed (1933, 234) that these flakes all have a certain amount of burnishing at the tips; the origins of this are a mystery, but since it occurs on all five specimens, it can hardly be fortuitous.

Leach (1933, 231) also describes and illustrates an elongated sandstone pebble with marked faceting at one end; this could well fall into the 'Limpet Scoop' category.

Longstone, Warren (SR/9398)
Gordon-Williams (1926, 106) reports: 'a flint flaker, a *rabattu* chip, a round scraper and four scoops'.

OBSERVATIONS ON DISTRIBUTION AND CHRONOLOGY

The characteristic types of the suggested Irish Sea Complex fall into a different category from the normal content of British Mesolithic industries, which have normally been analysed either from the point of view of their microlithic content or from that of possible Upper Palaeolithic survivals. It is perhaps significant that the 'Limpet Scoop' was first detected as a recognisable implement on Obanian sites, where it occurs in prodigious numbers and where flint is rare. Such implements are likely to be overlooked by surface-collectors searching specifically for flints. I have suggested above that environmental factors may have been responsible for some Mesolithic communities developing distinctive equipment, and this possibility is emphasised by the distribution of 'Limpet Scoops' and 'Bann Flakes' in Wales (fig. 2). As Gordon-Williams (1926) noted, these implements are unknown from Pembrokeshire north of St David's (Grimes, 1932), nor have they been noted from the many shell-mounds on the shore of Carmarthen Bay (Cantrill, 1909). These blanks on the map are not due to the lack of investigation nor to the accidents of preservation.

As noted above, the scattered nature and distribution of Mesolithic material in North Wales suggests the presence of man at a date prior to the submergence of the bed of the Irish Sea; on the assumption that the submergence was a single (if prolonged) event, which was responsible for the inundation of the Pembrokeshire submerged forest (North, 1955, 67), this suggestion may be underlined by Leach's observations at Freshwater East. Our knowledge of the environmental conditions in which these objects occur is scanty: it has been summarised by Leach (1913, 396–8), Cantrill (1915, 194–6) and, more recently, by Dr Wainwright (1963, 127–9). On all too many sites, no environmental evidence survives. While it may be tempting to associate the red loam layers at Freshwater West and Nanna's Cave, Caldey, with the same climatic phenomenon, our knowledge is far too scanty for any complete certainty and, at present, neither of these layers can be assigned to an absolute date, nor can the climatic fluctuations which they reflect be related to the movements of the land and water bodies in the Irish Sea area.

Of the two characteristic types of implement found in Wales, the 'Limpet Scoop' may be more narrowly bracketed than the 'Bann Flake'. In Scotland examples occur in the early post-transgression deposits in the Oban caves, and in Wales some examples have been shown to predate the inundation of the submerged forest; the Frainslake find may argue for their being contemporary with the submergence phase. At the other end of the scale, 'Limpet Scoops' have not been recorded in association with any demonstrably post-Mesolithic material in Britain; the date of the Thinic examples is uncertain.

The possibility that 'Limpet Scoops' are to be dated to a relatively early phase is emphasised by the evidence from the Carmarthen Bay area (Cantrill, 1909), where the various shell-mounds appear to post-date the submergence phase; certainly they are all above the present high-water mark. The inference is that the 'Limpet Scoop' had gone out of use before the submergence was completed and the shell-mounds formed. The absence of 'Larne Picks' from Wales must, however, be susceptible of a different explanation: no known cultural or chronological differences can account for it, and a more plausible explanation is that some unidentified difference of environment lies behind their absence.

This suggested Irish Sea Complex is of interest in that, almost alone among British material of the Mesolithic phase, the microlithic element is not the characteristic, unifying factor. The origins of the complex are obscure: like all Mesolithic groups (in the European sense of the term, at least), it must ultimately derive from the Upper Palaeolithic tradition. In the present state of our knowledge, it seems idle to speculate about which strand of that tradition lies behind this particular group and about how many metamorphoses it underwent before emerging into our ken as the earliest known group of material to have a distinctively western British, or Irish Sea, personality.

BIBLIOGRAPHY

Bishop, A. H., 1914. 'An Oransay Shell-Mound – A Scottish Pre-Neolithic Site', *Proc. Soc. Antiq. Scot.*, XLVIII, 52–108.

Breuil, H., 1922. 'Observations on the Pre-Neolithic Industries of Scotland', *Proc. Soc. Antiq. Scot.*, LVI, 261–81.

Cantrill, T. C., 1909. 'The Shell Mounds on Laugharne Burrows, Carms.', *Archaeol. Cambrensis*, 6th Ser., IX, 433–72.

—— 1915. 'Flint Chipping Floors in South-West Pembrokeshire', *Archaeol. Cambrensis*, 6th Ser., XV, 157–210.

Clark, J. G. D., 1935. 'The Prehistory of the Isle of Man', *Proc. Prehist. Soc.*, I, 70–92.

—— 1938. 'Microlithic Industries from Tufa Deposits at Prestatyn, Flintshire and Blashenwell, Dorset', *Proc. Prehist. Soc.*, IV, 330–2.

—— 1955. 'A Microlithic Industry from the Cambridgeshire Fenland', *Proc. Prehist. Soc.*, XXI, 3–20.

—— 1957. 'Notes on the Obanian', *Proc. Soc. Antiq. Scot.*, LXXXIX, 91–106.

Davidson, J. M., Phemister, J. and Lacaille, A. D., 1949. 'A Stone Age Site at Woodend Loch, near Coatbridge', *Proc. Soc. Antiq. Scot.*, LXXXIII, 77–98.

Donner, J. J., 1963. 'The Late- and Post-Glacial Raised Beaches in Scotland', *Ann. Acad. Scient. Fennicae* VIII, 53, 5–25.

Evans, J., 1867. 'Some Discoveries . . . in Lough Neagh, Ireland', *Archaeologia*, LXI, 2, 397.

Gordon-Williams, J. P., 1926. 'The Nab Head Chipping Floor', *Archaeol. Cambrensis*, LXXXI, 86–110.

Grimes, W. F., 1932. 'Surface Flint Industries around Solva, Pembrokeshire', *Archaeol. Cambrensis*, LXXXVII, 179–92.

—— 1951. *The Prehistory of Wales*. National Museum of Wales, Cardiff.

Jacq. M., ?1942. *Catalogue du Musée Archéologique James Miln–Zacharie Le Rouzic*, Impr. Lafolye et J. de Lamarzelle, Vannes.

Knowles, W. J., 1912. 'Prehistoric Stone Implements from the River Bann', *Proc. Roy. Irish Acad.*, 30 (C), 195–222.

Lacaille, A. D., 1954. *The Stone Age in Scotland*. Oxford.

—— 1955. 'The Prehistory of Caldey', *Archaeol. Cambrensis*, CIV, 85–165.

Leach, A. L., 1913. 'Stone Implements from Soil Drifts and Chipping Floors in South Pembroke', *Archaeol. Cambrensis*, 6th Ser., XIII, 391–432.

—— 1933. 'Stone Implements from the Nab Head, St Bride's, Pembrokeshire', *Archaeol. Cambrensis*, LXXXVIII, 229–36.

Livens, R. G., 1956. 'Excavations at Terally, Wigtownshire, 1956', *Trans. Dumfriesshire Galloway Natur. Hist. Antiq. Soc.*, XXXV, 85–102.

—— 1957. 'Three Tanged Flint Points from Scotland', *Proc. Soc. Antiq. Scot.*, LXXXIX, 438–43.

Liversage, G. D., 1968. 'Excavations at Dalkey Island', *Proc. Roy. Irish Acad.*, 66 (C), 53–233.

Lynch, Frances, 1966. 'Report on the Excavations at Bedd Branwen, Anglesey', *Trans. Anglesey Antiq. Soc. Fld. Club*, 1966, 1–37.

—— 1969. 'The contents of excavated tombs in North Wales', in T. G. E. Powell *et al.*, *Megalithic Enquiries in the West of Britain*, Liverpool, 149–74.

McBurney, C. B. M., 1959. 'Report on . . . the British Upper Palaeolithic Cave Deposits', *Proc. Prehist. Soc.*, XXV, 260–9.

Mitchell, G. F., 1947. 'An Early Kitchen-Midden in County Louth', *County Louth Archaeol. J.*, XI, 169–74.

Movius, H. L. Jr., 1942. *The Irish Stone Age*. Cambridge.

North, F. J., 1955. *The Evolution of the Bristol Channel*. Cardiff.

Rankine, W. F., 1952. 'A Mesolithic Chipping Floor at The Warren, Oakhanger, Selborne, Hants.', *Proc. Prehist. Soc.*, XVIII, 21–35.

Ridgway, M. H. & Leach, G. B., 1946. 'Prehistoric Flint Workshop Site near Abersoch, Caernarvonshire', *Archaeol. Cambrensis*, XCIX, 78–84.

Wainwright, G. J., 1959. 'The Excavation of a Mesolithic Site at Freshwater West, Pembrokeshire', *Bull. Board Celtic Stud.*, XVIII, 196–205.

—— 1963. 'A Reinterpretation of the Microlithic Industries of Wales', *Proc. Prehist. Soc.*, XXIX, 99–132.

Whelan, C. B., 1934. 'Studies in the Significance of the Irish Stone Age', *Proc. Roy. Irish Acad.*, 43 (C), 121–43.

Multi-Period Construction and the Origins of the Chambered Long Cairn in Western Britain and Ireland

J. X. W. P. Corcoran

Evidence derived from a number of excavations undertaken from 1961 onwards has emphasised that the final form of some chambered tombs in Britain and Ireland resulted from one or more additions to an earlier structure. This conclusion in itself is not remarkable, and had been suggested earlier as, for example, in the report of the excavation of Wayland's Smithy (BRK 1)[1] (Peers & Smith, 1921). The implications for megalithic studies resulting from more recent excavation, however, are not inconsiderable, not only for the evidence they may offer for prehistoric building skills, and perhaps for cult-practices, but also for some broader considerations of cultural diffusion. Not the least important of these last considerations are those concerned with the origin and development of what were to become morphologically well-defined regional groups of tombs in these islands, particularly those enclosed in long cairns. As this evidence of multi-period construction is derived from structures of varied plan, scattered widely from the north of Scotland to southern England, from Wales and from Ireland, it seems an appropriate time at which to summarise some of the data presently available, and to discuss some of their implications.

This essay is divided into three sections. The first summarises some of the evidence of multi-period construction derived from recent excavation. This is followed by an overall consideration of such evidence and its potential significance to the study of chambered tombs generally. The third section comprises a discussion, in the context of multi-period construction, of certain factors which appear relevant to the origins of the chambered long cairns of Britain and Ireland, and more particularly of those of the Carlingford group.

---

[1] Letters and figures in parentheses refer, as far as Great Britain is concerned, to inventories published in Powell *et al.*, 1969, for tombs of the Clyde and Cotswold–Severn groups and for those of North Wales, and to Henshall, 1963, for tombs in the north of Scotland. An explanation of the code-letters denoting counties in Britain is given in Powell *et al.*, 1969, xix–xxi. A three-letter code denotes a tomb in Britain, and a two-letter code a tomb in Ireland. For Ireland the system used is that of de Valéra, 1960, 12–13, with the exception of tombs in Counties Clare (CL) and Mayo (MA), regarding which reference is made respectively to de Valéra & Ó Nualláin, 1961, and to de Valéra & Ó Nualláin, 1964. Full bibliographical references to individual tombs are given in the respective inventories, with the exception, of course, of papers published since the publication of these inventories.

1 EVIDENCE DERIVED FROM EXCAVATION

Tulach an t-Sionnaich, Caithness.   A beginning may be made with Tulach an t-Sionnaich (CAT 58) (fig. 1*a,b*), situated five miles from the northern coast of Scotland (Corcoran, 1966, 5–22). It was during the excavation of this cairn in 1961 that the writer first encountered in person a chambered cairn of more than one period of construction. Before excavation Tulach an t-Sionnaich could be seen to be a long cairn, orientated approximately north–south, with the broader and higher end towards the south. There were no obvious surface indications of a burial chamber, but a prominent feature was a longitudinal hollow some 15·25 m. (50 ft) from the southern end, a distance equivalent to approximately one-quarter of the total length of the cairn viewed from the south. An early description referred to this hollow as a 'trench', which, it was believed, had been dug across the cairn.

As had been anticipated, a chambered structure was found to have opened from the southern end of the cairn. The alignment of this simple Passage Grave, some 15 degrees to the west of the apparently longitudinal axis of the cairn at first seemed unexceptional. Excavation of the south-eastern area of the cairn revealed revetment-walls, apparently built parallel to the Passage Grave. This seemed similarly unremarkable, although the identification of what appeared to be at least three revetment-walls was unexpected. Excavation of the south-western area of the cairn, however, showed that the revetment in that area also lay parallel to the Passage Grave, and therefore to the eastern revetment. At this stage of excavation it was obvious that if the revetment-walls on each side of the cairn were to continue on a straight alignment, the revetment on the western side would seem to project beyond what appeared to be the limits of the body of the cairn. It was not until trial cuttings had been made in the area of the transverse hollow referred to that this apparent anomaly was resolved, allowing a proper appreciation of certain other structural features previously uncovered at the southern end of the cairn.

The southernmost quarter of the total structure originally had been an independent tomb, a Heel-shaped Cairn, a type which at that time had rarely been recognised on the mainland of Scotland, although it was well attested in Shetland (Henshall, 1963, 135–53). To the north of the transverse hollow a long, low cairn had been built. Its composition and method of construction differed from those of the Heel-shaped Cairn, and its alignment did not continue on that of the latter, but followed the line of a low ridge, at the southern end of which the Heel-shaped Cairn had been built. Although it was not possible to examine the whole of the cairn, it seems probable that it did not enclose a chamber. The southern end of the long cairn appeared to have a distinct edge, formed of small orthostats, a 'pseudo-façade', built a short distance from the rear of the Heel-shaped Cairn. The two structures, however, were joined by an extension of the dry-stone revetment along the sides of the long cairn so as to enclose all but the south-western corner of the Heel-shaped Cairn. It was apparent that this had occurred some time after the construction of the latter, as at the southern end the outer wall which formed part of the revetment of the composite structure overlay some 0·35 m. (12 in.) of slip from the Heel-shaped Cairn.

In the final excavation report the writer hinted at the possibility that the Heel-shaped Cairn itself may have been of multi-period construction, although the argument was not pursued further (Corcoran, 1966, 16). With the support of evidence derived from subsequent excavation elsewhere, it now seems probable that what was described as the 'outer curved wall' (*ibid.*, figs. 5, 6) was originally the outer revetment of a circular cairn, some 10·7 m. (35 ft) in diameter, which curved inwards to the entrance to the Passage Grave and was bonded into the outer limits of the dry-stone-built passage (fig. 1*a*). This interpretation is further supported by the blocking found *in situ* at the entrance to the passage. The rather more roughly built 'inner curved wall' was probably intended to absorb some of the thrust from the apparently corbelled chamber. In brief, it seems that the original structure was a simple Passage Grave, enclosed in a

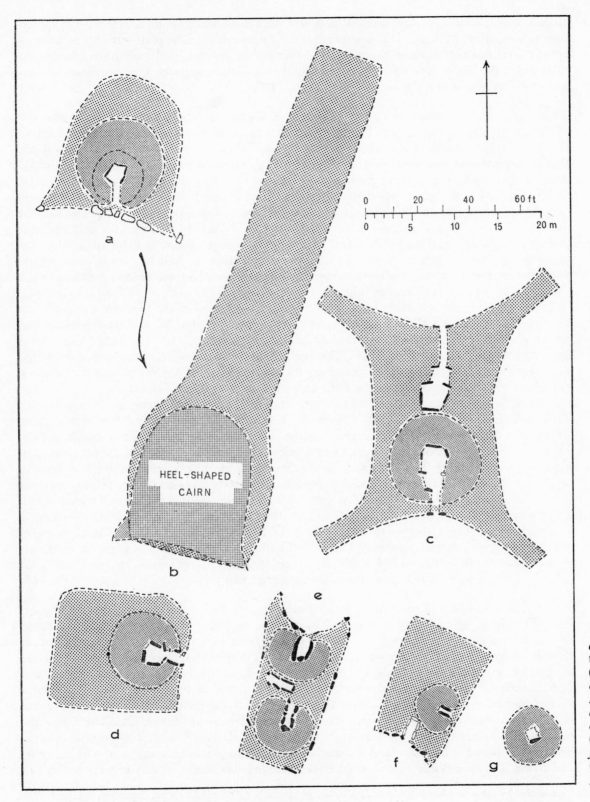

HEEL-SHAPED
CAIRN

a and b Tulach an
t-Sionnaich
(CAT 58),
c Tulloch of
Assery A,
d Balvraid,
e Mid Gleniron I
(WIG 1),
f Mid Gleniron II
(WIG 2),
g Mid Gleniron B

fig. 1 *Excavated multi-period chambered cairns in Scotland*

circular cairn, to which a heel-shaped 'platform' had been added, comparable with the structure at Vementry (SHE 45). It is possible that the construction of the platform with its uninterrupted façade which blocked access to the chamber at ground level may have marked the final use of the tomb. Alternatively, as Henshall (1963, 142) suggests, subsequent access may have been by means of a 'drop-entry' behind the façade.

Tulloch of Assery A, Caithness.   This short-horned cairn lay some 213·5 m. (700 ft) to the west of Tulach an t-Sionnaich. It is so far unique in that there are two Passage Graves set back-to-back (fig. 1*c*). In the final excavation report the writer made no reference to the possibility that it may have been of multi-period construction, primarily on account of extensive disturbance in the southern, and more particularly the south-western, part of the cairn (Corcoran, 1966, 22–34). In retrospect, however, supported again by evidence derived from subsequent excavation elsewhere, an alternative hypothesis involving multi-period construction may be offered. What was termed a massive 'core' enclosing the southern chamber may perhaps more properly be interpreted as the remains of a circular cairn enclosing a bipartite chamber and passage, the original entrance to which may have been marked by a pair of transverse portal stones, the western one only surviving. Such a cairn would appear to have measured more than 9·15 m. (30 ft) in diameter. The distance between the end-stones of the two chambers was such that it may reasonably be suggested that the end-stone of the northern chamber was built close to the edge of the earlier cairn. As it seems probable that the northern chamber had been corbelled, some internal support would have been necessary, and this would seem to have been provided by the northern 'core'. The horn-shaped outer revetment may have delimited little more than a low platform surrounding the central mass enclosing the burial chambers, comparable with the heel-shaped platform suggested at Tulach an t-Sionnaich.

Two further comments may be made in support of this revised interpretation. First, although both chambers in Tulloch of Assery A were of bipartite construction, they differ on plan, particularly in the length of their respective passages. Had the cairn been built as a unit, a more symmetrical arrangement might have been expected. The greater length of the northern passage, unique in its north-facing entrance, may have resulted from a desire to maintain symmetry of plan in the overall layout of the outer revetment. Second, it is germane to refer to circular walls which were found to surround the chamber of the short-horned cairn at Ormiegill (CAT 42), and apparently at Garrywhin (CAT 26). Anderson noted that the wall of the former was built of heavy blocks, rather more massive than the stone used in the construction of the outer walls, a feature comparable with that found at Tulloch of Assery A. It is possible, therefore, that originally both Ormiegill and Garrywhin were bipartite Passage Graves enclosed in circular cairns, to which were added platforms of short-horned plan.

Balvraid, Inverness-shire.   This cairn is situated some three miles from the west coast of the mainland of Scotland, near Glenelg.[1] A simple Passage Grave is entered from the east and is enclosed within a circular revetment, some 9·15 m. (30 ft) in diameter (fig. 1*d*). The latter would appear to be too large and too distant from the chamber to be interpreted merely as a structural feature designed to support stress from the chamber, particularly as the latter does not appear to have been corbelled. The revetment therefore may be interpreted as the outer limits of a circular cairn which originally enclosed a simple Passage Grave. Subsequently the entire structure was enclosed in a square cairn which had a slightly concave façade at the east side. The axis of the square cairn differs by some 15 degrees from that of the Passage Grave. The outer revetment was built of rounded boulders, and although it survived in places to a height of 0·61 m. (2 ft) and more, it is improbable that it could have exceeded this height by any great amount. On

---

[1] Excavated by the writer in 1965. Unpublished, but preliminary note in *Discovery and Excavation*, Scotland 1965. (1966), 20.

account of extensive disturbance to the body of the cairn, its original appearance cannot be reconstructed, but it might be suggested that a square 'platform' had been built to enclose a circular cairn.

If the hypothesis that a relatively low platform had been built around the cairns at Tulach an t-Sionnaich, Tulloch of Assery A and Balvraid is accepted, it may contribute something to knowledge of the means by which these localised types of cairn evolved in northern Scotland. In each case the earlier structure, whether it was a simple Passage Grave of widespread type, or the more localised bipartite Passage Grave, appears to have been enclosed in a conventional circular cairn. In northern Scotland there are several examples of bipartite Passage Graves enclosed in circular cairns, without the addition of platforms (Henshall, 1963, *passim*).

In offering the suggestion that these tombs may have been of multi-period construction, it is not implied that any extended period of time elapsed between the building of the Passage Graves and their respective enclosing platforms. The possibility may be allowed that the latter operation formed part of ritual activity consequent on the final use of the tomb, in a manner comparable with that suggested for some of the long cairns of the Cotswold–Severn region (Corcoran, 1969, 76, 91–2). This might apply more particularly in the case of Heel-shaped Cairns in which an uninterrupted façade was built across the entrance to the Passage Grave. On present evidence it would seem reasonable to distinguish on the one hand between those cairns, such as the two at Mid Gleniron discussed below, the final form of which involved the construction of a chamber or chambers subsequent to the primary tomb and the final enclosure of the whole complex within an outer cairn, and those just described, in which a platform was added to a circular cairn which contained a single burial chamber. The latter may not have implied anything more than embellishment as part of the concluding ritual activity. Although Tulloch of Assery A does not fit comfortably in the latter category, its affinities lie rather with the putative platform-cairns than with monuments such as those at Mid Gleniron, the final form of which appears to have owed something to traditions foreign to those of the builders of the earliest tombs in these composite structures.

Mid Gleniron, Wigtownshire.   Two further cairns in which the writer has found evidence of multi-period construction are Mid Gleniron I and II (WIG 1 and 2) in the south-west of Scotland (Corcoran, 1970a). Among several reasons for choosing to excavate was that Mid Gleniron I was a straight-sided and apparently long cairn across which there was a prominent transverse hollow which, by analogy with Tulach an t-Sionnaich, seemingly indicated the junction between an earlier and a later structure. At an early stage of the first season's excavation, however, it was found that, although the hollow did mark the limits of an earlier and a later structure, the two were not joined in any way (Corcoran, 1970a, 35). It was shown subsequently that the smaller of the two parts was a burial cairn of Bronze Age date, the builders of which apparently wished to place it as closely as possible to the earlier chambered cairn, but without connecting the two structurally. This demonstrates that only by excavation is it possible to be certain of the full significance of lateral hollows such as those at Tulach an t-Sionnaich and Mid Gleniron I. There was nevertheless a contrast between these two cairns in their external appearance before excavation. At Mid Gleniron I the smaller southern cairn to the south of the hollow was lower than the larger portion to the north, even allowing for a slope in ground level from north to south. In this it differed from the more prominent southern end of Tulach an t-Sionnaich. Of greater potential significance was the evidence before excavation at Mid Gleniron I of a crescentic façade at the northern end and, apparently set in the body of the mound, of a chamber (one of three visible) which certainly was closed to the south. If this was not a closed chamber, the inference is that it must have opened from the north. As its putative entrance faced into the body of the cairn and towards the rear of a second chamber to the north, which presumably opened from the façade, it seemed possible before excavation that, whatever might be the relationship of the two stone-built mounds lying each side of the transverse hollow, the mound to the north with its three visible chambers was itself of multi-period construction. This was subsequently verified.

The chambered cairn of Mid Gleniron I (fig. 1*e*) comprised two small ovate stone-built mounds arranged in tandem, each containing a rectangular chamber entered from the north, which had subsequently been incorporated in a short, straight-sided cairn with a megalithic façade at the northern end. A third chamber, set between the ovate cairns, was entered from the western side of the cairn, and appears to have been built contemporaneously with the straight-sided cairn. The neighbouring cairn of Mid Gleniron II (WIG 2) (fig. 1*f*), although less complex, was also of multi-period construction. A small ovate mound, containing a very small rectangular chamber, was incorporated in a straight-sided cairn, having a north–south orientation, in such a manner that access to the original chamber was gained from the eastern side of the later cairn. The latter also enclosed a larger rectangular chamber set on the longitudinal axis and entered from the south through a shallow orthostatic façade.

At both Mid Gleniron I and II the construction of the 'inner' cairns – those which originally had been freestanding mounds enclosing rectangular chambers – differed from that of the respective straight-sided mounds which subsequently enclosed them. It might be argued that these inner cairns were merely structural devices built to withstand structural stresses exerted from the chambers, analogues, for example, of that built around the transepted terminal chamber at Nympsfield (GLO 13). The inner structure at Nympsfield, however, was built much closer to the chamber than it was in any of the three chambers at Mid Gleniron. There would have been no structural necessity at Mid Gleniron for internal support, as the individual chambers were of simple construction. Two were rectangular chambers each built of two side orthostats and either an end-stone or dry-stone walling, that in Mid Gleniron II measuring internally little more than 1·22 m. (4 ft) by 0·46 m. (1 ft 6 in.). Although the side walls of the southern chamber in Mid Gleniron I were each built of several orthostats, these were small and little more than 0·91 m. (3 ft) high. In each instance the orthostats chosen were squat and flat-based, and therefore relatively stable without recourse to elaborate external support. Further evidence from excavation suggests that the roofing stones of each chamber were set directly on the orthostats, without corbelling, the use of which might have required some external support. Finally, the outer limits of the three inner cairns curve inwards as if to provide formal access to the chamber proper. Had these inner cairns been intended simply as support for their respective chambers, it would have been more effective structurally to have built the outer limits up against the sides of the orthostats. It is of interest that a short distance to the south of Mid Gleniron II there is a small circular cairn, Mid Gleniron B, which in its dimensions and method of construction, including a well-defined outer edge, resembles the inner cairns of Mid Gleniron I and II (fig. 1*g*). However, the chamber, in part orthostatic, is closed (Corcoran, 1970, *b*, 94–8).

Achnacreebeag, Argyll. This is a monument of particular interest, in that it differs from the other tombs described in the first part of this essay.[1] Although it was much disturbed prior to excavation, there can be little doubt that it was of multi-period construction (fig. 2*a*). The earlier part of the two tombs appears to have been a small, possibly closed, burial chamber, built of rounded boulders. In this it resembles some of the apparently early, and possibly indigenous, tombs of northern Europe, such as the *dysser* of Denmark. The resemblance is strengthened by the large capstone which covered the chamber, although large capstones of comparable type

[1] I am grateful to Dr J. N. G. Ritchie for giving me details of this tomb and allowing me to refer to them prior to the publication of his excavation report, and to the Royal Commission on Ancient and Historical Monuments of Scotland for permission to base fig. 2*a* on its Crown Copyright plan. The interpretation set forward in the text, however, is mine alone.

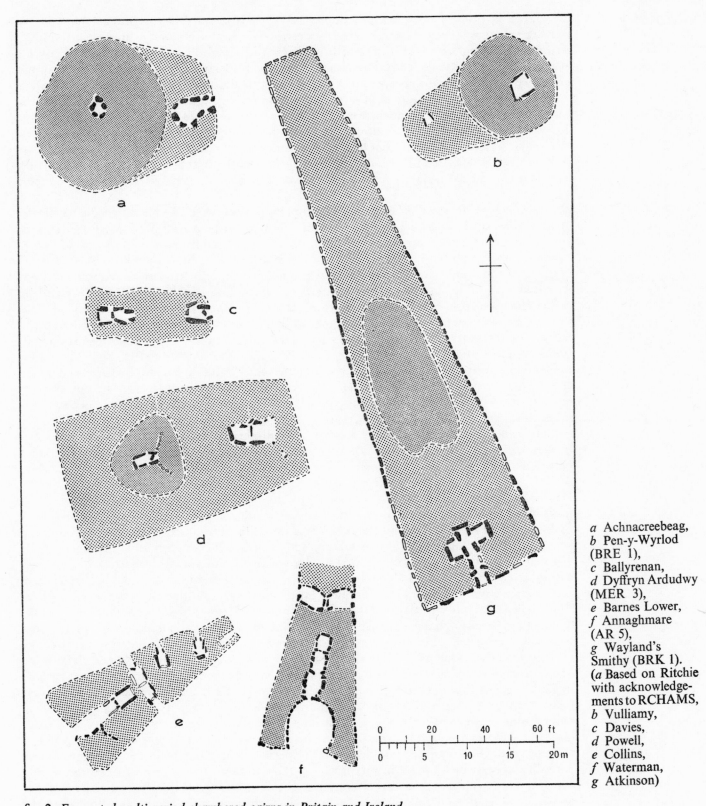

a Achnacreebeag,
b Pen-y-Wyrlod
(BRE 1),
c Ballyrenan,
d Dyffryn Ardudwy
(MER 3),
e Barnes Lower,
f Annaghmare
(AR 5),
g Wayland's
Smithy (BRK 1).
(*a* Based on Ritchie
with acknowledge-
ments to RCHAMS,
b Vulliamy,
c Davies,
d Powell,
e Collins,
f Waterman,
g Atkinson)

fig. 2 *Excavated multi-period chambered cairns in Britain and Ireland*

are known in Britain, as at Arthur's Stone (GLA 3). It seems that the primary chamber of Achnacreebeag was enclosed within a circular cairn, comparable not only with that surrounding Arthur's Stone but also with that which encloses Mid Gleniron B (Corcoran, 1970*b*, 94–8), although it seems that the cairn at Achnacreebeag is proportionately larger than those of the other two tombs cited. It appears that subsequently a small, simple Passage Grave, constructed also of rounded boulders, was built close to the eastern edge of the circular cairn. Additional cairn material was built up against the circular cairn in order to enclose the Passage Grave. There appears to have been no attempt to make the composite structure either straight-sided or circular in plan. The final plan of the cairn is apparently pear-shaped, reminiscent of that of Pen y Wyrlod (BRE 1) in which additional cairn material appears to have been built up against a circular cairn simply in order to enclose a small secondary burial chamber (fig. 2*b*).

Dyffryn Ardudwy, Merioneth.   The arrangement in tandem of two of the chambers demonstrated at Mid Gleniron I is paralleled in north-west Wales at Dyffryn Ardudwy (MER 3) (Powell, 1963). An earlier ovate cairn encloses a Portal Dolmen entered from the east. A second, larger chamber, also apparently in the Portal Dolmen tradition, was subsequently built to the east of the first, and both chambers were enclosed in a short, straight-sided cairn (fig. 2*d*). Dyffryn Ardudwy is of added interest in that pottery recovered from the pit in the forecourt of the earlier chamber appears to date from early in the Neolithic period of Britain and Ireland. This in some measure modifies a common hypothesis which tends to regard Portal Dolmens as being late within the series of Hiberno-British chambered cairns and derived, it has been suggested, from the larger and more complex long Court Cairns of Ireland (de Valéra, 1960, 64). That the tandem setting of two relatively simple chambers may be less uncommon is suggested by the chambered cairn of Presaddfed (ANG 2) in Anglesey, and Ballyrenan, Co. Tyrone (fig. 2*c*) in the north of Ireland. The latter comprises a Portal Dolmen set at the eastern end of a straight-sided cairn, and a chamber of two segments at the western end but originally open from the east. It seems possible that this was a cairn of multi-period construction. This was suggested by the excavator (Davies, 1937, 96), who considered that the western segmented chamber post-dated the eastern Portal Dolmen.

Wayland's Smithy, Berkshire. In this composite structure (BRK 1) excavation has revealed a conjunction of two different structural and presumably cultural traditions, one represented by a timber-built burial chamber and the other by a megalithic burial chamber set at one end of a long trapezoidal mound (fig. 2*g*) (Atkinson, 1965). Although the megalithic chamber only is properly the concern of this essay, its juxtaposition with a timber-built burial chamber enclosed within a mound of chalk is also relevant to the present discussion. Indeed, the sequence of construction is not dissimilar to that adduced for the entirely megalithic tombs already described. The earlier structure at Wayland's Smithy comprised a timber-built chamber of tent-like, 'pitched', or 'lean-to' shape, enclosed in a small but elongated oval mound of chalk lying on a basal layer of sarsen which was revetted by upright sarsens. It is orientated approximately north–south. This is the type of burial mound which in the past has commonly been referred to as an 'unchambered long barrow', but examination of earlier excavation reports of comparable mounds suggests that some may have enclosed timber-built chambers similar to that at Wayland's Smithy (Ashbee, 1966, 75–80). A little more than 6·10 m. (20 ft) to the south of the oval mound a megalithic chamber of cruciform plan was built and apparently enclosed in a cairn of sarsen boulders. It is not known, owing to disturbance, whether or not this chamber and its cairn originally had been freestanding. Had this been so, it might explain the pair of transverse jamb-like stones which are set in the passage a short distance from the present entrance, and which might have defined an earlier entrance. It might be argued that the outer pair of side orthostats were added to link the original entrance with the straight façade at a time when the composite structure was enclosed in the long cairn. Be that as it may, there is no doubt that the megalithic chamber and the earlier oval mound were incorporated within an elongated mound which tapers from a broad southern to a narrower northern end. As evidence suggests that a relatively short period of time separated the construction of the earlier and the later mound, any freestanding sarsen cairn built around the megalithic chamber would have been short-lived. In its final form Wayland's Smithy displays many of the characteristics of a terminally transepted terminal-chambered cairn of the Cotswold–Severn Group, having a single pair of transepts.

Annaghmare, Co. Armagh.   Another trapezoidal mound, but enclosing chambers belonging to a different cultural tradition, also appears as a result of excavation to have been of multi-period construction. This is the cairn at Annaghmare (AR 5) (Waterman, 1965). The structural enlargement again differed from those already described, as it involved the construction of two additional chambers at the rear of the cairn, together with an extension of the body of the cairn itself (fig. 2*f*). The earlier structure comprised a burial chamber of three segments entered through a deep, horseshoe-shaped forecourt at the southern end of a trapezoidal cairn. In comparison with some cognate cairns in the north of Ireland, the length of that at Annaghmare was small in that its apparent rear-end was built relatively close to the end-stone of the chamber. The additional chambers were built close to the revetment at the rear of the original cairn. They were irregular, somewhat oval on plan, set back-to-back with a gap of 8 inches between the respective end-stones and entered from the long sides of the cairn. Excavation of the chambered cairn at Annaghmare provides a further *caveat* in attempting to interpret visible features prior to excavation. To the writer (Corcoran, 1960, 104, 141) and to Evans (whose sketch-plan is reproduced *ibid.*, fig. 9*c*) what have been revealed as a pair of lateral chambers appeared from surface indications to represent the remains of a passage opening from the west, although de Valéra (1960, 124) more correctly interpreted these remains as lateral chambers opening from the sides.

Barnes Lower, Co. Tyrone.   Also in Ireland, excavation of a badly disturbed trapezoidal cairn at Barnes Lower has revealed evidence of apparently multi-period construction (Collins, 1966). This was a complex structure which comprised a long chamber of possibly four segments, entered from the south-west through a relatively flat orthostatic façade (fig. 2*e*). A short distance behind the end-stone of this terminal chamber was a pair of rectangular chambers set back-to-back, sharing a common end-stone, and entered from the sides of the cairn. To the north of these, two further box-like chambers entered from the west, and it seems possible that a smaller chamber also may have lain beyond them and was entered from the narrow north-eastern end of the cairn. Owing to very considerable disturbance, problems remain in the interpretation of this complex structure, such as that of deciding whether the smaller chambers had originally been independent tombs. There can be little doubt, however, that the chamber of four segments had not been built as a unit. Although the outer two segments were largely destroyed, sufficient remained to indicate that in contrast to the relatively large orthostatic construction of the inner two segments, and particularly the innermost, the outer appear to have been built of smaller orthostats with panels of dry-stone walling. Further, in the body of the cairn to the south of the chamber there was a curved setting of orthostats, the inner end of which may have been aligned on the junction between the inner and outer pairs of segments. Had this setting continued on its original curve, it would have projected beyond the limits of the later trapezoidal cairn. It nevertheless seems possible, as the excavator suggests, that these orthostats may have marked the edge of a cairn enclosing a chamber of two segments. In this context it may be significant that the revetment of the trapezoidal cairn in this area did not lie on the original ground surface, as did that on the opposite side, but lay on a confused mass of cairn stones. It seems possible that this may have represented the remains of an earlier, and perhaps more circular, cairn which originally had enclosed the chamber of two segments, and, in part at least, had been demolished in order to build the revetment of the trapezoidal cairn. A further detail of potential significance emerged from the excavation of Barnes Lower. The innermost segment of the long terminal chamber was separated from the neighbouring segment by a tall septal slab which would have prevented access, once the roof was in position. This compares with the inner closed segments at Cairnholy I and II (KRK 2, 3), referred to below (p. 43).

2 GENERAL CONSIDERATIONS

Excavation of the ten chambered cairns described has revealed from widely separated locations in Britain and Ireland evidence of structural additions to existing chambered burial mounds. In this it compares with the architectural history of many types of building, secular and ritual, in later times and in many places. It is generally possible in the case of buildings dating from historic times to assign motives and reasons for successive alterations, enlargements and embellishments. It is not possible, of course, to assign motives to prehistoric peoples, but in some instances it may be permissible to speculate on possible reasons which may have contributed to a decision to modify or enlarge a chambered cairn. One example may suffice, that of enclosing an earlier tomb within a long, trapezoidal mound. It seems possible that mounds of this plan may have acquired a particular ritual significance to such an extent that it was adopted widely by peoples already possessing varied traditions of chambered tomb design, without significantly altering the form of their burial chambers. Such peoples may have wished to adopt a ritual concept which possibly may have transcended – but which certainly was added to – their own localised traditions of funerary architecture, without abandoning those traditions. Whatever else is implied in the adoption of the long trapezoidal mound, it was not merely a structural device, since the size of these mounds is commonly greatly in excess of that necessary merely to enclose burial chambers. Considerations such as these must remain hypothetical. The interpretation of the structural sequence of an excavated chambered cairn, however, need not be hypothetical provided that it is undertaken critically in a manner comparable with that employed by architectural historians generally.

It must be emphasised that excavation alone is likely to reveal details of a structural sequence. Surface indications before excavation may be either misleading or misinterpreted, as has been demonstrated above in the case of Mid Gleniron I and Annaghmare. Yet in any attempt to study and interpret meaningfully the 2,000 or more chambered cairns which survive in varied degrees of preservation in these islands, it is necessary to consider unexcavated as well as excavated structures, since for many generations to come excavated tombs are likely to form but a small proportion of the whole. For some time it has been possible from a study of both unexcavated and excavated tombs to identify well-defined regional groups, such as those in the Cotswold–Severn region in England and Wales, cairns of the Clyde area and the Clava group in Scotland, and the Carlingford and Boyne tombs in Ireland (Piggott, 1954, *passim*). Obvious morphological features may be identified in many disturbed but unexcavated structures, and these have properly been compared with those examined in detail in the course of excavation. Were this not so, and were currently available evidence based only on the results of excavation, it would not have been possible to have attained the present state of knowledge and hypothesis. With the evidence of multi-period construction presently available from excavation, it may be inquired whether or not a more thorough examination of structural features visible in unexcavated cairns may reveal possible indications of comparable data and so permit the presentation of additional hypotheses, to be tested eventually by excavation. To this may be added a reconsideration of certain chambered cairns excavated in the past, as has been undertaken by Ashbee (1966, 75–80) in the comparable context of the study of earth and timber burial mounds.

The results of excavation described in the first part of this paper have revealed that structural additions took several forms and, perhaps more significantly in the present context, that some slight indication of structural complexity might in certain instances be identified before excavation, even if at that time its significance could not properly be appreciated.

One feature is the regularly shaped hollow extending across the full width of a long cairn. This should not be confused with more irregularly shaped hollows which may have been caused by stone-robbing or other interference in the body of the mound. At Tulach an t-Sionnaich a transverse hollow marked the junction of two structural units. Here there was little apparent difference in height between the two parts of the composite structure, as the builders of the long cairn seem to have taken advantage of a low sloping ridge to give it added elevation. Had both parts been built on level ground to the same respective heights, the southern end would have appeared as a more prominent mound, and cairn material to the north as a lower extension. Such is the appearance of Cnoc Freiceadain (CAT 18) and Na Tri Shean (CAT 41), two long cairns some four miles to the north-west of Tulach an t-Sionnaich. Henshall (1963, 75) has grouped together cairns of this type in the north of Scotland, and refers to them as the Na Tri Shean type. They commonly comprise a large, circular mound at the more easterly end, some 2·50–3·70 m. (8–12 ft) high, the remainder of the long cairn rarely exceeding a few feet in height. The long-horned cairn at Head of Work (ORK 18) in Orkney is similar. Allowing for the misinterpretation of an apparently comparable feature at Mid Gleniron I, a regular transverse depression therefore may indicate the junction between an earlier and an added structure, particularly when, as in the Na Tri Shean type, there is a contrast in height, and sometimes in width, between the two components.

One further possible example of multi-period construction of comparable type may be cited, again from the north of Scotland. In profile the long cairn at Camster (CAT 12) reveals two depressions across the width of the cairn. The more easterly end of the cairn is both higher and broader than the remainder, and has the appearance of originally having been an independent cairn. The depressions have not been made in recent years; they are shown in a woodcut published more than a century ago. While not pressing the suggestion that the cairn may have had three periods of construction, although this is not improbable, it does seem possible that the eastern chamber, a simple Passage Grave, was enclosed originally in its own cairn. Alongside this may have been built a more elaborate Passage Grave of Camster type, perhaps also contained within a circular cairn, the revetment of which may have been identified during a mid-nineteenth-century excavation (fig. 3d). Both chambers and their cairns, if the latter existed, were enclosed in a long-horned cairn in such a way that they were entered from one of the long sides of the cairn, unlike the remaining known long-horned cairns in the north of Scotland in which the chamber was entered from the broader end. It might be suggested that the long cairn was built to enclose two existing cairns, in response perhaps to a desire to conform to a convention of building long cairns which was reaching eastern Caithness at that time and is best exemplified at South Yarrows North and South (CAT 54, 55). Further reference to Camster Long is made below (p. 43).

In fieldwork generally, it may be advantageous not only to examine in plan view the outline of the mound, but also to record the profile wherever there are suggestions of either a lateral hollow or a prominent mound and associated 'tail'. It is possible that these features may not be confined to Scotland, as is suggested by the occurrence of comparable hollows in some mounds in the Cotswold–Severn group (Corcoran, 1969, 33–5). Within this group there is also one long cairn, Camp Barrow North (GLO 11), which has a prominent mound towards the south, with a considerably lower 'tail' extending towards the north. The long low mound attached to the circular chambered cairn of Bryn yr Hen Bobl (ANG 8) in Anglesey also suggests multi-period construction, although the exceptional length, c. 99 m. (c. 325 ft), is without known parallel. One further detail may be relevant in the examination of the body of unexcavated cairns. The

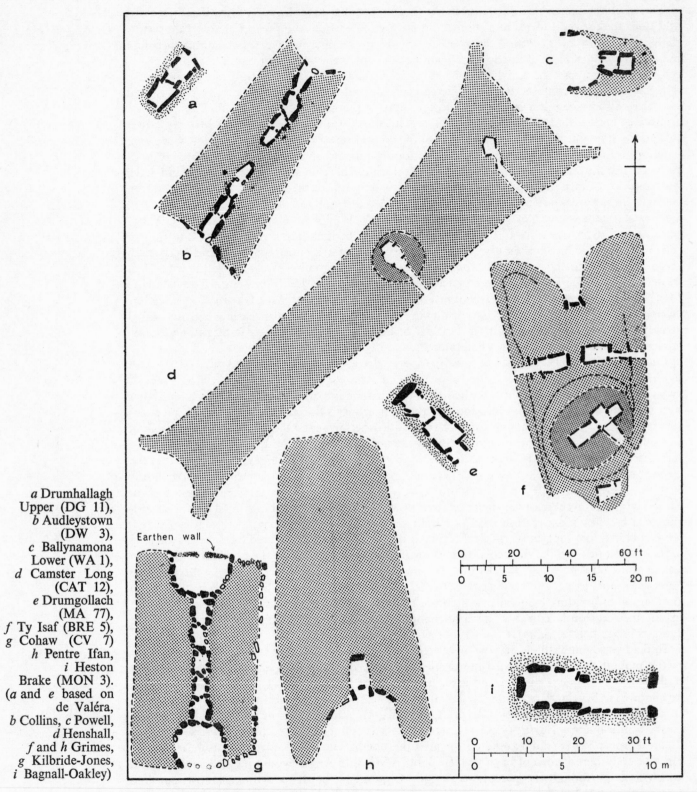

a Drumhallagh
Upper (DG 11),
b Audleystown
(DW 3),
c Ballynamona
Lower (WA 1),
d Camster Long
(CAT 12),
e Drumgollach
(MA 77),
f Ty Isaf (BRE 5),
g Cohaw (CV 7)
h Pentre Ifan,
i Heston
Brake (MON 3).
(*a* and *e* based on
de Valéra,
b Collins, *c* Powell,
d Henshall,
f and *h* Grimes,
g Kilbride-Jones,
i Bagnall-Oakley)

Earthen wall

0   20   40   60 ft

0   5   10   15   20 m

0   10   20   30 ft

0   5   10 m

fig. 3 *Chambered cairns referred to in text*

writer has found on two occasions that a contour plan may reveal before excavation some indication, not only of the shape of the mound as delimited by a revetment, which may be partially or completely obscured, but also some hint of multi-period construction. In the first instance the contour plan of a much disturbed cairn of indeterminate plan at Balvraid fore-shadowed the unexpected square plan subsequently revealed by excavation (fig. 1*d*). The second instance was Mid Gleniron I, the cairn of which was also much disturbed, where the contour lines indicated the separation between the two earlier circular cairns (fig. 1*e*).

Multi-period construction may also involve the chamber, as was demonstrated at Barnes Lower where it appears that two outer segments were added to an inner pair (fig. 2*e*). This was suggested by a pronounced difference in size between the orthostats used in each component, and the additional use of dry-stone walling in the outer segments alone. There was also some support for this interpretation in the curved setting of upright stones, which may have formed part of the revetment of a cairn originally enclosing what were to become the inner two segments of the composite structure. If it were to be accepted that a marked difference in method of construction between two parts of a chamber may sometimes indicate an extension to an earlier structure, then it should be possible to identify comparable features both in unexcavated cairns in which a chamber is visible, and perhaps in earlier excavation reports. Such appears to be the case at Heston Brake (MON 3), where there is not only a difference between the large orthostats forming the walls of the inner section and the smaller orthostats of the outer section of this long gallery (excluding the tall portals at the entrance) but also a break in the alignment of the walls at the point at which the junction occurs (fig. 3*i*). The inner section by itself would form a simple box-like chamber. In this it compares with the *protomegalith* defined by Scott (1969, 181), in his discussion of the Clyde cairns of south-western Scotland. Scott (1969, 193–8) has also argued that the chambers, each of two segments, of Cairnholy I and II (KRK 2, 3) resulted from successive additions to what originally were *protomegaliths* – in this case, closed chambers. The first stage may have been the erection of a pair of tall portal stones, form-ing a 'porch' which subsequently was enlarged to form a second segment by the addition of a pair of orthostats serving as side-walls, and a second pair of portals at the new entrance. A hypothesis such as this contributes something to the understanding of the manner in which the chamber of two segments, an important feature in the development of the mature Clyde cairn, may have evolved. The closed inner segment resembles that of Barnes Lower in Co. Tyrone described above (p. 39).

It also seems possible that a distinct break in the straight alignment of a passage or chamber, whether or not it is accompanied by a change in the method of construction, may also indicate a structural addition, although this has yet to be proved by excavation. This hypothesis may be demonstrated by reference again to Camster Long (CAT 12). It has been suggested that the more easterly of the two lateral chambers originally was enclosed in its own cairn (see above, p. 41). The chamber is a simple Passage Grave, but the present length of the passage is considerably greater than that normal for conventional tombs of this type in Britain (fig. 3*d*). The total length of the passage is approximately 7·30 m. (24 ft), but at a point some 5·20 m. (17 ft) in from the entrance there is a marked turn to the right. From the outer revetment of the long cairn the passage is straight, but the inner part is slightly curved on plan. The junction between the straight and curved sectors is marked by a pair of orthostats, and the walls of the inner sector of the passage are dry-stone-built. It seems possible that these orthostats may mark the original outer limits of the passage, serving perhaps as a pair of portals. It further seems possible, although there is no visible evidence of this, that the kerb of the putative circular cairn may have abutted on these stones. Were such a cairn to have been enclosed in the long cairn, and had access still been required, it would have been necessary to extend the passage to the line of the new outer revetment. A similar sequence might also be argued for the second visible chamber, in this instance of Camster type, although here the passage maintains a straight alignment, perhaps because the long cairn had been laid out at right angles to this chamber in preference to the simple Passage Grave. During excavations in the nineteenth century some evidence was found which suggested that a circular mound had enclosed the Camster-type chamber. It is perhaps significant that at the point at which this inner wall meets the passage, there is a break in the line of the western wall of the passage, suggesting that the outer part of the passage at this point had been built up against the inner cairn. It must be admitted, however, that the dimensions of this alleged inner cairn seem a little small to have enclosed a corbelled chamber of Camster type. Were these dimensions to be proved accurate, it would suggest that this inner cairn was more of a retaining feature, and that the Camster-type Passage Grave may have been built as part of the plan which also involved the long-horned cairn. Apart from this, the lengthening of the passage would, as in the case of the simple Passage Grave, be consistent with the hypothesis that two originally independent chambered cairns were enclosed in a long cairn. It is to be remembered that Camster Long differs in its lateral chambers from other known long-horned cairns, and the hypothesis of multi-period construction seems to provide the most satisfactory reason for its final plan.

Certain structural features in the large tomb of Knowth, Co. Meath, in Ireland may best be interpreted in the context of multi-period construction, as has been suggested by its excavator (Eogan, 1968, 354). This large circular cairn encloses two Passage Graves, set back-to-back. The eastern is a corbelled, cruciform Passage Grave, comparable with that at Newgrange (Eogan, 1969). The western, however, is of simpler design, comprising a chamber, almost square on plan, and apparently not corbelled. It is approached by a passage some 34·5 m. (113 ft) long, one of the longest known passages of its type (Eogan, 1967). Indeed, the overall length of the passage is quite out of proportion to the size of the chamber, and in this it differs from passages leading to comparable chambers which are also represented at Knowth in the smaller 'satellite' cairns surrounding the larger tomb (Eogan, 1968). The passage leading to the western chamber does not maintain a straight alignment. Some 26·2 m. (86 ft) from the entrance there is a break in the alignment, suggesting perhaps that the longer outer section had been added to an earlier passage and one which was more in keeping with the proportions of the chamber. The inner section of the passage and chamber together resemble simple Passage Graves included among the associated satellite cairns, such as Site 2 (Eogan, 1968, 305–9). It is relevant also to refer to cairn 3, which is earlier than the body of the large cairn at Knowth, as there is a break in the otherwise regular circumference of the latter in order to avoid the smaller cairn (Eogan, 1968, 354).

A possible sequence of construction for the large cairn may therefore be proposed. The earlier structure may be represented by the western chamber and the inner sector of the passage, from the break in alignment inwards. In other words, this may have been a simple Passage Grave, comparable with some of the satellites. It is possible that this Passage Grave may have been enclosed in a small circular cairn. For some reason, perhaps, this particular Passage Grave may have acquired some special significance, so much so that when the more elaborate cruciform Passage Grave was built, it was decided that the former also should be incorporated. That this may not have been determined simply by factors such as shortage of space for building and the like, is apparent in that access to the simple Passage Grave was maintained. The latter was not merely engulfed within the later structure in a manner comparable, for example, with the closed chamber in its circular cairn at Notgrove (GLO 4). In order to maintain symmetry of plan, and to incorporate both chambers within a circular cairn, it would have been necessary, according to this hypothesis, to have added an outer section to the passage of the earlier Passage Grave.

Another factor which appears relevant – and reference is made to this below – is the orientation of the entrance to a chambered tomb. Many Passage Graves are entered from the southeast, particularly in the case of monumental tombs such as Newgrange. This may have become part of accepted ritual practice at a relatively mature stage. Prior to this it seems that at Knowth, for example, the orientation of the passage was random (Eogan, 1968, *passim*). The western orientation of the rectangular Passage Grave, particularly in view of its length, is not typical of more monumental structures, which again might be considered an argument in favour of the incorporation of an earlier structure within a later cairn. A further detail of potential significance in the study of Passage Graves and the possibility of multi-period construction is the relationship of the plan of the passage and chamber to the enclosing cairn. It seems probable that tombs in which the rear of the chamber is positioned in such a way that it is set either close to the centre of the enclosing mound or beyond the centre, when viewed from the entrance, were planned and built as structural entities. The corollary is that some cairns containing Passage Graves in which the rear of the chamber is positioned on the near side of the centre of the cairn, as viewed from the entrance, may enclose a second chambered structure. This was demonstrated in Caithness where, at Tulloch of Assery A, a short-horned cairn of local type enclosed two Passage Graves set back-to-back (fig. 1c, see above, p. 34).

Reverting to the monumental tombs of the Boyne Culture in Ireland, and in particular to the group in the bend of the River Boyne itself, it may be significant that the inner end of the cruciform Passage Grave at Newgrange lies on the near side of the centre of the mound, viewed from its entrance (O'Kelly, 1967, 12). As at Knowth, the entrance is marked by a kerbstone, the decoration of which is more elaborate than the remaining stones of the kerb. Diametrically opposite is stone K.52 (O'Kelly, 1967, 29, pl. 6), decorated with motifs considerably more elaborate than that to be seen on the remaining kerbstones, apart from the entrance stone. It is tempting to speculate whether this might mark the entrance to an earlier chambered structure.

A distinct break in the alignment of a passage is not difficult to identify. It might appear that a comparable break in the alignment of either a Gallery Grave or a segmented chamber might be more difficult to recognise. In so far as the former type is concerned, reference to Heston Brake (MON 3) (fig. 3i and p. 43 above) suggests that such a break may be indicated by either a change in the method of construction, or at least in a difference in the size and relative proportions of the orthostats used in each of the separate parts. A difference in the method of construction between the two components of the segmented terminal chamber at Barnes Lower has been mentioned (see above, p. 39), although on account of destruction there is no evidence of any break in alignment. Excavation of the chambered cairn at Audleystown (DW 3) in the north of Ireland, however, revealed a number of potentially significant features (Collins, 1954). The enclosing mound is trapezoidal on plan, the wider end facing towards the south-west. Such an orientation is atypical among cairns of this type, and further reference to this is made below (p. 55). The chambers, each of four segments, are set back-to-back, and separated by a gap of little more than 2·40 m. (8 ft). Examination of the overall plan reveals that all four segments of the south-western chamber are symmetrically arranged on each side of its longitudinal axis, whereas there is a break in the alignment of the north-eastern chamber between the inner two segments and the outer two. It may also be significant that the inner two segments of the north-eastern chamber preserve a regularity of plan not maintained by the outer pair. It may reasonably be argued that opinions such as these are subjective, yet examination of the overall plan of the cairn at Audleystown cannot but reveal some difference in the layout of the two chambers. It might further be argued that the less regular plan of the north-eastern chamber resulted simply from inability or inattention on the part of those who originally planned the tomb. The writer believes, however, that in tombs planned and built as entities some symmetry of plan was intended and frequently achieved within the limits imposed by contemporary knowledge and practice of elementary survey. At Audleystown the symmetry of plan of the south-western chamber as a whole and that of the trapezoidal mound differ from the less regular disposition of orthostats forming the side-walls of the north-eastern chamber. A post-hole identified during excavation beyond the north-eastern forecourt (Collins, 1954, 15) may be relevant. A line drawn between this socket and the mid-point of the septal slab at the entrance to the south-western chamber would coincide with the longitudinal axis of the cairn as a whole. This line crosses approximately the mid-point of the entrance to the north-eastern chamber, but is not central to the four segments of that chamber, as it is to those of the south-western chamber. The apparently symmetrical relationship of the latter to the trapezoidal mound seems to indicate that the two were set out and built as part of one design. It would seem, with the limited knowledge and equipment then available, that any structural addition to an earlier structure might lack something of the regularity of plan frequently attained in structures built as part of an overall design. Pursuing the hypothesis offered in respect of the large cairn at Knowth, it would seem that the inner pair of segments of the north-eastern chamber at Audleystown may have comprised part of an earlier tomb, perhaps enclosed within a small, possibly circular or oval, mound. The gap between the end-stones of the north-eastern and south-western chambers is sufficient to have accommodated an approximately circular cairn enclosing the two inner segments of the north-eastern chamber. Reference to Mid Gleniron II (see above, p. 36) suggests that in some instances a later chamber was built as close as possible to the revetment of an earlier structure. With this, the arrangement at Notgrove (GLO 4) appears to be comparable.

Another potentially significant detail is the relationship of the axis of a chamber to that of an enclosing long cairn. It has been shown that in Tulach an t-Sionnaich the axis of the Passage Grave differed by some 15 degrees from that of the long cairn (see above, p. 32). This apparent anomaly was resolved after excavation had revealed that a long mound had been added to an earlier Heel-shaped Cairn, and that the builders of the former chose to make use of a low ridge, the alignment of which differed from that of the existing cairn. A similar feature may be identified in some unexcavated cairns. The alignment of the eastern chamber of Tulach Buaile Assery (CAT 59), an outstanding example of the Na Tri Shean type, differs by about 45 degrees from the longitudinal axis of the long cairn (see above, p. 41). The alignment of the chamber of Coille Na Borgie South (SUT 23) similarly differs from the longitudinal axis of its cairn. This feature is not confined to the north of Scotland, as may be seen at the Lang Cairn on Dumbarton Muir (DNB 3). By analogy with Tulach an t-Sionnaich, it would seem that a pronounced departure in the axis of a chamber from either the longitudinal or lateral axis of a long cairn may indicate multi-period construction, particularly when, as in the case of the Na Tri Shean type, it is associated with a transverse hollow across the body of the cairn. In a different context this would seem to apply in the case of Ty Isaf (BRE 5), where the axis of a transepted chamber enclosed in an inner circular cairn differs from that of an outer trapezoidal cairn which also encloses lateral chambers set at right angles to it (Corcoran, 1969, 84–6) (fig. 3*f*).

It seems possible, therefore, that a more detailed examination of structural features in the field, and some reconsideration of certain earlier excavation reports, may reveal indications of multi-period construction. This is not meant to imply that all or even a majority of chambered cairns necessarily resulted from an addition of one or more structural features to an earlier tomb. Truly monumental tombs such as Maes Howe (ORK 36) and Carn Ban (ARN 10), which exhibit a regularity of plan and construction, must surely have been planned and built to an overall design not modified by subsequent structural alteration or addition. At the time of their construction it might be argued that certain features of plan and construction had become accepted by, and acceptable to, local tradition, affected to a certain extent, perhaps, by the potentiality of stone available locally. The result would appear to have produced localised classes of tomb which eventually became the accepted type, although in some areas there may have been some subsequent minor local development. This may be seen in the Orkneys in the apparent development of the Maes Howe type (Piggott, 1954, 244–5). Although some additional influences may be suspected, it would seem that Maes Howe itself was derived from cruciform Passage Graves in Ireland. At least it seems permissible to consider the Boyne Culture of Ireland as partially ancestral to tombs of the Maes Howe type in Orkney.

It is not possible to identify an analogue beyond Britain and Ireland for the type of tomb represented by Carn Ban. Were it to be accepted that the broadly comparable type of tomb found in Ireland was ancestral to that of Scotland, or *vice versa*, it still would be desirable, if at all possible, to identify a potential ancestral form outside these islands. The monumental tombs of the Boyne Culture, for example, appear to belong to a generalised tradition which may be identified in Brittany and farther south along the Atlantic coastland of Europe as far as Iberia. Comparable evidence is available neither for possible antecedents of the Clyde tomb, the type to which Carn Ban belongs, nor for those of the Carlingford or Cotswold–Severn groups. Some attempt may now be made to resolve these difficulties against the background of multi-period construction.

3 THE ORIGINS OF THE CHAMBERED LONG CAIRNS OF BRITAIN AND IRELAND

It would seem that one of the most potentially valuable applications of the study of chambered tombs of multi-period construction is that concerned with the origins of localised traditions of funerary architecture. In discussing the origins of the long cairns of the Carlingford Culture in the north of Ireland, the writer in 1960 concluded:

It is not possible from present evidence to offer a convincing prototype in Europe for either the horned-cairn or the associated artifacts which make up the Carlingford Culture. . . . Each of the individual constructional details of the Carlingford cairns may be found in the European megalithic tradition, yet they are nowhere else found in exactly the same combination as in Ireland and it is impossible to point to a single European prototype. Throughout the megalithic cultures of the Mediterranean and Europe individual constructional details appear to have been adopted or discarded in different permutations according to the ritual and architectural dictates of their several cults. . . . Less certain are the means by which this fusion took place, but in the midst of constant sea-borne cultural interpenetration in Atlantic Europe, fusion could have taken place without leaving precisely identifiable traces in the archaeological record. A new culture would not become readily discernible until all its discrete elements had been brought together within a given area and allowed to develop (Corcoran, 1960, 136–7).

Ten years later the facts would appear to remain valid, but the hypotheses based on them are less acceptable. It no longer seems necessary to refer vaguely to the possibility of cultural fusion having taken place in Atlantic Europe. The archaeological record in these islands now appears to offer some evidence of the means by which this fusion may have occurred locally, in so far as 'individual constructional details appear to have been adopted or discarded in different permutations'. In particular, it is possible to offer a modified hypothesis as to the origins, not only of the Carlingford cairn, but also of the other two main types of chambered long cairn in these islands, those of the Clyde and Cotswold–Severn areas.

The study of chambered tombs naturally must be considered in relation to the Neolithic period generally. Presently available radiocarbon assays suggest that the Neolithic extended over a period of at least 1,500 years, perhaps as much as two millennia. It might therefore be assumed that considerably more insular development had taken place than had been envisaged at a time when a much shorter chronology was accepted. Few scholars today would believe that truly monumental tombs had been built by immigrant farmers immediately on arrival in these islands, yet this is what appears to have been implied, particularly by those writers who argued that the earliest builders of chambered tombs were the first Neolithic colonists to settle in specific areas. A further hindrance to fresh thought has been the concept of 'degeneration', the belief that the descendants of people who had built large and impressive tombs were themselves capable only of constructing small, simple tombs. Certainly, some 'degeneracy' might be argued from the plan of a tomb such as Pipton (BRE 8), but neither the technique of construction, nor the overall size of this tomb are inferior to comparable, but more regularly planned, tombs of this particular form within the Cotswold–Severn series. A similar 'weakening' of plan, but not of construction, may be argued in the development of the Maes Howe type in Orkney (Piggott, 1954, 244–5, fig. 37).

It is reasonable to assume, by analogy with ritual structures in other places and at other times, that simple architectural forms should have been built earlier than more complex, from which the former may have evolved. It would be difficult to argue, for example, that Salisbury cathedral was the prototype from which a simple chapel 'degenerated'. Yet that is the sort of thesis offered by those who would envisage some simple forms of burial chamber as having degenerated from a tomb of more complex plan. This is not meant to imply that simple tombs were not built subsequent to the development of more elaborate forms. A more meaningful analogy, taken from the context of the British Neolithic, may also be cited. It is now recognised that the Windmill Hill Culture of southern England did not arrive ready formed, as the several types of structure and artefacts involved are not found elsewhere in precisely the same association (Piggott, 1954, 97–101; 1955). Continental analogues may be identified for some of its separate components, and it would appear that new ideas were adopted as knowledge of them was brought to England and added to local cultural tradition. Furthermore, the culture once formed appears to have undergone further devolution.

It is relevant also to recognise the effect of Britain's insular position. Whereas it is apparent that in continental Europe there might have been opportunity for continuous contact with several neighbouring cultural traditions, those available to the peoples of prehistoric Britain and Ireland were more limited, in that voyages to the Continent by considerable numbers of people appear to have been exceptional. This implies that at times other than those at which migration took place, the insular peoples were less likely than their contemporaries on the Continent to have been stimulated by contact, frequent or occasional, with peoples of differing cultural backgrounds. That this need not imply cultural stagnation is shown in the Bronze Age, for example, by the manner in which insular schools of metallurgy were aware of contemporary developments in Europe, and were able to absorb new ideas and techniques into their distinctively local tradition. The peoples of prehistoric Britain and Ireland did not stagnate. They continued to develop ideas derived from abroad. This is illustrated to a remarkable degree by the chambered tombs of these islands, for within the small area consisting of Britain and Ireland there is a variety without parallel in any area of comparable extent elsewhere in Europe. This variety may be seen in the far north, for example, where tombs of the Orkney–Cromarty Group are not only diverse on plan, but include forms not found outside the area. This at least demonstrates the vigour of the cult or cults involved, and shows that there was no lack of inventiveness in the development of megalithic architecture as one of the outer limits of the distribution pattern of chambered tombs in Europe was reached.

The origins of the Clyde, Carlingford and Cotswold–Severn tombs may now be considered.

Clyde Tombs.[1]   Reference has been made to Scott's interpretation of the structural sequence at Cairnholy I and II (KRK 2 and 3) in which he traces the development of a chamber of two segments from a *protomegalith* (Scott, 1969, 193–7). It seems possible that developments comparable with this may have taken place, not only in south-western Scotland, but also in all those parts of Europe in which segmented chambers are found. Had it been necessary, as seems prob-

---

[1] This section is not intended as a précis of Scott's recent study (Scott, 1969), to which reference should be made, but offers some additional comment on the possible origins of the three structural components of Clyde tombs: chamber, long cairn, and façade.

able, for additional space to be made available for burial, a simple and obvious solution would have been provided by the construction of a second tomb, as appears to have occurred at Mid Gleniron I (WIG 1). The second of the two simple tombs in this composite structure was built as closely as possible to the earlier cairn. It has been admitted that any attempt to attribute motives to prehistoric peoples may be misleading, but it does seem possible that in certain instances there may have been a wish not merely to build a second structure close to an earlier one, but also to increase the space available for burial in such a manner that the original structure continued in use. Whether this had been influenced by a sense of *pietas* or by a more mundane wish to economise in labour and building materials may never be determined. It does seem possible, however, that a segmented chamber of two segments in south-western Scotland such as Clachaig (ARN 16), for example, became an accepted form relatively early within the period of use of megalithic tombs.

Such a simple development may reasonably be accepted as having occurred locally, and may equally reasonably be considered to have formed the basis from which chambers of more than two segments were evolved. It is not implied that all segmented chambers were of multi-period construction, but that the idea of building such chambers arose from the addition of a second segment to an existing chamber, as appears to have occurred at Cairnholy I and II. Long cairns and façades in south-western Scotland, such as Carn Ban (ARN 10) and East Bennan (ARN 14), are commonly associated with chambers of more than two segments. Whereas the simpler form of chamber is of megalithic construction only, dry-stone walling also is used in the construction of the larger tombs, including the 'post-and-panel' technique – upright megalithic orthostats linked by intercalary panels of dry-stone walling.

Although it might be argued that these features, long cairn, façade and post-and-panel construction, might have been developed locally, it is more probable that they were brought into the region from outside, and adopted eventually to form part of accepted local tradition. The long, straight-sided cairn, frequently of trapezoidal plan, is common not only to the developed Clyde cairn, but also to tombs of the Carlingford and Cotswold–Severn groups. One possible source for the long cairn of south-western Scotland is north Wales where Capel Garmon (DEN 3) is clearly an outlier of the Cotswold–Severn group, with its trapezoidal cairn and post-and-panel construction. In addition, Carnedd Hengwm North (MER 5) is a long cairn with a dry-stone revetment comparable with that commonly found in the Cotswolds. On the other hand, it is possible, as far as Cairnholy I is concerned, that the idea of the long cairn may have derived from the long barrow of Yorkshire, a suggestion reinforced by the resemblance between the undecorated carinated bowl at Cairnholy and comparable pottery in Yorkshire.[1] It may be significant that in Galloway, as opposed to the wider area of south-western Scotland in which Clyde tombs are found, Cairnholy I is the only cairn which is truly long, in that the mound is of a size considerably in excess of that necessary simply to enclose the chamber adequately. Cairnholy lies towards the eastern limit of distribution of chambered cairns in Galloway, and it is possible that the idea of the long cairn came from the east, by a route suggested by the long mounds found in Dumfriesshire (Scott, 1969, 321–2). For the majority of long cairns in the Clyde area, excluding Galloway, an origin in the Irish Sea area seems preferable. It is possible that Galloway, like the peninsulas of Cornwall and of south-western and north-western Wales, although open to influences coming from the south, did not produce distinctively local types of tomb, comparable with those farther away from the coastal areas of western Britain.

It is less easy to pin-point an origin for the façade of the developed Clyde tomb. The type of concave forecourt common to both Clyde and Carlingford tombs differs from the cuspate forecourts of the Cotswold–Severn group, so that it is improbable that the former derived from

[1] Personal communication from Mr T. G. Manby.

the latter. The provision of a façade which both flanked the entrance to, and delimited a forecourt area in front of, a burial chamber is widespread from the Mediterranean to Britain and Ireland. This is not to imply that all belonged to a common cultural, ritual or architectural tradition. Scott (1969, 210) has suggested Irish influence in the evolution of the forecourts in the Clyde area, but an alternative source of influence is possible.

Within Britain, for example, a simple façade at Dyffryn Ardudwy (MER 3) was defined by a retaining wall of horizontally laid stones, a rudimentary form of dry-stone walling (fig. 2d). Of greater relevance, perhaps, are those Portal Dolmens with orthostatic façades, such as Pentre Ifan, situated a few miles from the shores of the Irish Sea in Pembrokeshire in south-western Wales (fig. 3h). The portals are flanked by a shallow orthostatic façade set at the southern end of a long mound (Grimes, 1948). An orthostatic façade, rather more V-shaped in plan, appears to flank the entrance to the Portal Dolmen of Garn Turne in the same county (Grimes, 1932, 91). This suggests that in the southern part of the Irish Sea littoral some simple tombs such as the Portal Dolmen, which may be relatively early within the sequence as a whole, were provided with façades. The apparently simple terminal chamber of 'The Grey Mare and her Colts' at Gorwell in Dorset appears to be flanked by a small orthostatic façade (Piggott, 1946). Similar evidence is available from Ireland, and is referred to below. This might be taken to imply that in this respect tombs of both Clyde and Carlingford type were influenced from a common source.

Evidence that a façade was not associated invariably with a truly long mound is provided at both Mid Gleniron I and II (WIG 1 and 2), although the technique of post-and-panel was used. Mid Gleniron I is particularly instructive in that excavation revealed that the façade was added to the northern inner cairn, probably as part of the constructional phase which produced the short, straight-sided cairn. Scott (1969, 183–90) has traced the probable development of the façade of the Clyde tombs generally, and has convincingly suggested that prior to its acceptance as part of local megalithic tradition, façades were added to existing structures, as indicated by his 'complex entrances'.

Carlingford Cairns. If it may be accepted that the mature Clyde tomb derived its chamber from a simple type introduced into south-western Scotland early in the local Neolithic, and later adopted the long, sometimes trapezoidal, mound and dry-stone walling (perhaps from the Cotswolds by way of North Wales) and the orthostatic façade (perhaps from the Irish Sea littoral) then it seems possible that a comparable development may have taken place in the north of Ireland. It might further be suggested that the mature Carlingford tradition had been influenced at least in part from similar sources to those which affected the Clyde area.

An important structural distinction between Clyde and Carlingford tombs is the manner in which the chamber is divided into segments. In the former, septal slabs only were normally used, but in the Carlingford chambers the septal commonly is flanked by a pair of tall jamb-stones. According to Scott's derivation of the Scottish segmented chamber from the simple, box-like *protomegalith*, the septal slab set between contiguous segments might be considered to represent a survival of the closing slab of the *protomegalith*, although in many instances it was reduced in height to allow access to the inner segments. The arrangement of jambs separated by a transverse orthostat resembles that at the entrance to a Portal Dolmen, although the closing slab of many Portal Dolmens is considerably taller than the septal of a segmented chamber. It has been accepted that the two types of tomb were related in some way, but opinion has tended to favour the derivation of the Portal Dolmen from the segmented chamber (de Valéra, 1960, 64). Evans (1961, 231), however, has hinted at the opposite.

Excavation of Dyffryn Ardudwy (MER 3), in addition to the evidence it provided of multi-period construction (fig. 2d), also yielded from the small forecourt fronting the Portal Dolmen, which was the earlier structure, undecorated, round-based pottery 'of a type as early as any yet found in a megalithic tomb in the Irish Sea zone' (Powell, 1963, 23). Although this dating is not supported by any radiocarbon assay, it would appear legitimate to accept the probability that the origins of the Portal Dolmen belong to an early phase of the Hiberno-British Neolithic. In a sense it might be considered as a slightly more evolved type of *protomegalith*, graced by a pair of tall portal-stones. The arrangement of the two chambers at Dyffryn Ardudwy may be compared with that at Mid Gleniron I (WIG 1). The sequence of construction probably was similar in that a second, but independent, chamber was set close to an earlier. But in the north of Ireland, as in south-western Scotland, an earlier preference for small simple chambers seems to have been succeeded by segmented chambers. Prior to this, however, it seems possible that in parts of Ireland the idea of building a second or subsequent tomb relatively close to an earlier tomb may have been maintained for a period somewhat longer than seems to have occurred in western Britain. At Malin More, Co. Donegal, six Portal Dolmens are set in an almost straight line extending over a distance of more than 91·5 m. (100 yds) (Borlase, 1897, I, 240). It is probable that they may have been enclosed in one long cairn. At least three Portal Dolmens may be identified among a collection of six lateral chambers which lie in the south-western sector of a long cairn at Tullyskeherny (LE 9), at the opposite end of which is a segmented chamber, apparently approached through a forecourt (fig. 4*d*). The anomalous cairn B at Aghnaskeagh, Co. Louth, enclosed at least four chambers (fig. 4*c*), two of which certainly are in the Portal Dolmen tradition (Evans, 1938). It seems reasonable to suggest that monuments such as these may have been of multi-period construction, and built perhaps at a time prior to local acceptance and possible appreciation of the advantages of a segmented chamber. Lack of symmetry in the disposition of the chambers, which is apparent at Aghnaskeagh B, perhaps supports this hypothesis.

Before examining the means by which the Irish type of segmented chamber may have evolved from the Portal Dolmen, it is relevant to discuss certain aspects of Portal Dolmens generally, in so far as they affect the present argument. In the first place they are relatively numerous – more than 150 are known – and they are widely distributed not only in the northern counties of Ireland but also on both sides of the Irish Sea and as far inland in southern Britain as Oxfordshire (Corcoran, 1969, 38). Second, they are essentially simple tombs in a general, although not specific, manner analogous to the *dysser* of Denmark, and such tombs as Arthur's Stone (GLA 3), particularly in their frequently massive capstones. Third, reference has been made to the low-lying situation of many Portal Dolmens, and their proximity to expanses of open water. This has been interpreted as evidence of a greater penetration of wooded country-side by builders of Portal Dolmens than by builders of Court Cairns (de Valéra, 1960, 69). Current palaeo-botanical research relevant to the penetration of Britain and Ireland by early farmers during the late fourth and early third millennia BC, however, suggests that forest cover prior to disturbance by agriculture may have been more extensive than hitherto had been believed, and that it may have extended to an altitude of more than 305 m. (1,000 ft) above sea-level. In conditions of extensive forest cover it would seem reasonable to suppose that early agriculturalists would have sought breaks in this cover in order to establish their initial settlements, and to secure a base from which to begin clearance of the virgin forest. These breaks would most readily have been found in water-side locations, such as river-banks and lake-shores (Powell, 1969, 247–52). It is not unreasonable to suppose that relatively small and simple tombs found in such positions may more convincingly be attributed to an early rather than to a late stage of land-winning (*landnam*). An increase of population, consequent on more extensive and perhaps more competent exploitation of the environment for agriculture, may eventually have led to a situation conducive to the development and construction of chambered tombs more complex than the simple Portal Dolmen. It is perhaps not without significance that many of the more developed forms of localised tombs are to be found in areas of Britain and Ireland some distance from putative landfalls. Scott (1969, 190–1), for example, in pursuing ideas

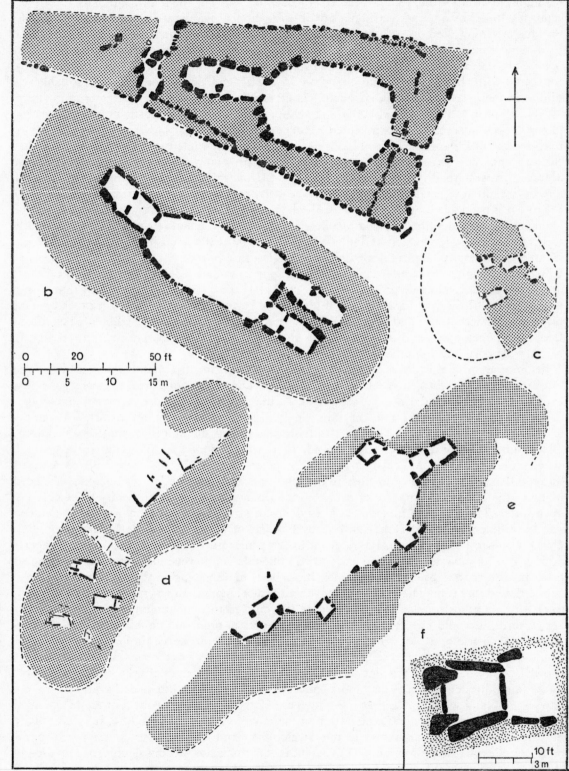

a Creevykeel (SL 2),
b Deerpark
(Magheraghanrush)
(SL 9),
c Aghnaskeagh B,
d Tullyskeherny
(LE 9),
e Farranmacbride
(DG 17),
Brennanstown.
(*a* Based on
Hencken,
b, *d* and *e*
de Valéra,
c Evans, *f* Powell)

fig. 4 *Chambered cairns referred to in text*

first set forward by Childe (1934), has demonstrated that the more developed form of Clyde cairn is not uncommonly to be found not only at some distance from the coasts of the estuaries and islands of the Firth of Clyde, but also at an altitude frequently above that of many of the simpler forms of tomb.

As with Scott's *protomegalith*, it is not difficult to visualise that the Portal Dolmen may have provided a structural unit suitable for enlargement by setting two such chambers contiguously and in tandem within a single mound. It might further be suggested that the inner pair of jambs and its septal slab represent the idea of original portals and closing slab of a Portal Dolmen. The septal, of course, would be necessarily lower in height than most closing slabs so as to allow access from one segment to the other. This must remain hypothetical until it is either proved or disproved by excavation.

There is evidence, however, from some few unexcavated monuments to support such an hypothesis. The inner segment of the chamber at Drumhallagh Upper (DG 11) is separated from the outer by jambs and a tall septal. As de Valéra (1960, 106, 67) remarks, 'The rear chamber is identical in all respects with a Portal Dolmen, with a three-quarter closure slab', and 'so extraordinarily like a Portal Dolmen as to suggest a direct influence from the Portal Dolmen'. It may also be significant that the outer segment is narrower than the inner, the side-walls of the former being aligned on what are the jambs, but which originally may have been the portals of a Portal Dolmen (fig. 3*a*). At Drumgollagh (MA 77), too, the outer segment is separated from the inner by jambs and a high septal. The segments again are of unequal width (fig. 3*e*). There also appears to be a second inner chamber separated from what otherwise is a conventional Portal Dolmen at Brennanstown, Co. Dublin (Powell, 1941, 17) (fig. 4*f*). The innermost segment at Barnes Lower was separated from its neighbour by a septal which would have prevented access once the roof was in position (see above, p. 40). This suggests comparison with Drumhallagh Upper and Drumgollagh, but at Barnes Lower two further segments seem to have been added to the inner two. If so, they probably were accompanied by a progressive enlargement of the enclosing cairn, as is suggested by the curved setting of orthostats which may originally have formed part of the revetment of a cairn enclosing a chamber of two segments. A similar duplication of a chamber originally of two segments has been suggested at Audleystown (DW 3) in view of the break in alignment between the inner and outer pairs (see above, p. 45).

The long cairn at Ballyrenan, Co. Tyrone (fig. 2*c*), encloses a Portal Dolmen set on the longitudinal axis at the eastern end, and a chamber of two segments at the western (Davies, 1937). The latter resembles that at Brennanstown in that an inner segment is separated by a septal slab from what would otherwise be a simple Portal Dolmen. As the entrance to the western chamber faces into the body of the mound, it seems probable that, as at Mid Gleniron I (WIG 1) and Dyffryn Ardudwy (MER 3), this monument was of multi-period construction. This was suggested by the excavator (Davies, 1937, 96), who concluded that the western segmented chamber was built later than the eastern Portal Dolmen, but there is no evidence to determine whether either of the chambers had been enclosed in an earlier, smaller cairn. The monument nevertheless provides evidence within a composite structure of one conventional Portal Dolmen and a second with an additional segment. As the interval between the erection of each chamber may not have been long, it is possible that the final stage of construction occurred at a time during which both conventional Portal Dolmens and chambers of two segments were being built locally. This hypothesis is strengthened by the tomb at Ballywholan in the same county, where a Portal Dolmen is set centrally at the eastern end of a long cairn, and a chamber of two segments near the western end (Wulff, 1923). The latter chamber, however, is set laterally with access from the southern side of the cairn. The cairn is considerably longer than that of Ballyrenan.

A main chamber of two segments, which is the commonest unit found in cairns of the

53

Carlingford Culture (de Valéra, 1960, 23), may therefore have resulted in part at least from a desire to increase space available for burial with a minimum of structural elaboration, while still retaining a common entrance and yet perhaps owing something to that feeling of *pietas*, already adduced, of incorporating an earlier burial chamber within a later cairn. Duplication of the two-segmented chamber subsequently may have become an accepted device in north-eastern Ireland, in order to accommodate an increased funerary population, as appears to be demonstrated at Audleystown (DW 3). It may not be without significance that the distribution pattern of chambers of four segments is largely concentrated in the north-east (de Valéra, 1960, pl. xxxiii) in the area most open to infiltration from the Irish Sea littoral, and therefore perhaps subject to a greater influx of population than that experienced by the west of Ireland. In this context, too, may be sought some explanation for the existence of some, relatively few, chambers of three segments (de Valéra, 1960, 23–4). There is a contrast, for example, in the small outermost segment at Ballymacdermot (AR 3) and the two larger inner segments (Collins & Wilson, 1964). As so little is known of potentially significant structural details within the body of the trapezoidal enclosing cairn, it is not relevant to speculate further on any possible structural sequence. Yet enclosed in the trapezoidal cairn at Goward (DW 7), there is a chamber of three segments, the outer one of which differs in size and construction from the inner two (fig. 5*e*). The end-stone of the innermost segment is flanked by a pair of jambs, curiously reminiscent of the putative origin of the sill-and-jamb segmentation typical of Carlingford cairns in general (see above, p. 50).

The segmented chamber of the devolved cairn of Carlingford type, however, is but one of the structural elements concerned. There remains the problem of origin of both the long cairn and the concave forecourt. With regard to the latter, it is perhaps germane to revert to evidence of forecourts within the Irish Sea littoral to the south of the Carlingford province (see above, p. 50). In Ireland itself orthostats may be identified which flank the entrance to Portal Dolmens. Glaskenny, Co. Wicklow (Powell, 1941, 17, but *cf.* de Valéra, 1960, 64, fn. 175), Kiltiernan and Larch Hill, Co. Dublin (Borlase, 1897, II, 393), and Tirnony, Co. Derry (Evans, 1966, 154) may be cited. Remains of an apparently crescentic orthostatic façade survive in a similar position at Goward, Co. Down, where the Portal Dolmen may have been enclosed in a circular mound (*Co. Down*, 1966, 79–80). The much disturbed chamber tomb at Ticloy, Co. Antrim, also appears to have been a Portal Dolmen flanked by a façade of low orthostats, set at the eastern end of a long cairn (Evans & Watson, 1942). A much disturbed structure at Ballygraffan, Co. Down, also appears to incorporate a Portal Dolmen with an associated orthostatic façade, possibly set laterally in a long cairn (*Co. Down*, 1966, 78–9). In the absence of a representative sample of excavated Portal Dolmens it is not known to what extent these may be considered typical. Monuments in which the remains of cairn material extend forward of the entrance to the chamber suggest that some form of forecourt may have been a more common attribute of Portal Dolmens than has hitherto been recognised, as may have been the case at Moyree Commons (CL 71), Ballyknock (MA 11, 12) and possibly Kilfeaghan, Co. Down (Collins, 1959). The evidence at least suggests that in Ireland façades, some certainly orthostatic, may have flanked the entrance to some Portal Dolmens, set either in round mounds or at one end, and possibly laterally, in long mounds. It is germane to recall the long cairn of Pentre Ifan in Pembrokeshire (see above, p. 50), for this may also be relevant to the origin of the orthostatic façades of both Clyde and Carlingford cairns.

Influences comparable with those which may have contributed to the adoption of long, frequently trapezoidal, cairns in south-western Scotland possibly affected developments in the north of Ireland, if it were to be accepted that the former derived ultimately from Cotswold traditions by way of North Wales. It is possible that certain cairns, such as Tan-y-Muriau (CRN 13) in the Lleyn peninsula, are of multi-period construction. Of more relevance are the two Carneddau Hengwm. A Portal Dolmen is set on the longitudinal axis at the eastern end of Carnedd Hengwm South (MER 6), and a lateral chamber, possibly a Passage Grave, opens from the northern side. The lateral chamber and certain structures in the body of the cairn resemble some in the Cotswolds. Carnedd Hengwm North (MER 5) apparently encloses at least two lateral chambers, but the cairn itself offers additional comparisons with some tombs of the Cotswold–Severn region. It is trapezoidal on plan, is orientated so that the wider end faces east, and is revetted by a dry-stone revetment of flat slabs (Bowen & Gresham, 1967, 9–15).

Many tombs in north-west Wales, including the Carneddau Hengwm, are situated within sight of the Irish Sea, in areas from which Ireland, particularly the higher ground, is visible in conditions of clear visibility. To experienced seafarers of the third millennium BC a crossing of the Irish Sea from North Wales to Ireland would have offered few problems, particularly if a mountainous hinterland, visible at the beginning of the voyage, may have indicated a suitable landfall. It is possible that the idea of building a trapezoidal mound may have reached the north of Ireland from North Wales. This is not meant to imply that other routes may not have been used, as the existence of long cairns in south-western Britain might suggest points of departure other than those in North Wales. The relatively small number of such cairns (as opposed to Irish Wedged-shaped Cairns) in the south of Ireland nevertheless suggests that more northerly crossings had been undertaken. This is perhaps demonstrated by the tomb of Ballynamona Lower (WA 1) in Co. Waterford, which lies within 92.5 m. (100 yds) of the sea (Powell, 1938). An apparently short mound encloses a chamber of two segments, approached from the west through a small semicircular forecourt flanked by a partially orthostatic façade (fig. 3*c*). Although the tomb lies outside the distribution area of Carlingford tombs generally, it might well be considered a representative of a stage of development within Ireland between the Portal Dolmen and the emergence of the Carlingford cairn proper. In other words, the third element, the long trapezoidal mound with its emphasis on the more easterly end, does not appear to have been adopted in the south of Ireland. The chambered cairn at Shanballyedmond, Co. Tipperary, has features comparable with some of those of Ballynamona Lower (O'Kelly, 1958).

In contrast, the cairn at Audleystown (DW 3), situated within some 185 m. (200 yds) of the shores of Strangford Lough, is trapezoidal on plan (fig. 3*b*). More important, the revetment is dry-stone-built, and compares closely with that of Carnedd North (MER 5) on the opposite shore of the Irish Sea, and indeed with those of many Cotswold cairns. The coastal position of Audleystown, its trapezoidal plan and dry-stone revetment together support the hypothesis of derivation from North Wales. It has been suggested that certain features may indicate multi-period construction (see above, p. 45). Were this so, it would seem that the trapezoidal cairn had been built to enclose an earlier chambered structure. Although the trapezoidal mound was adopted in the north of Ireland, dry-stone construction appears to have been employed less commonly, possibly owing to shortage of suitable stone. Dry-stone construction, however, is known in the far west, at Behy (MA 3) (de Valéra, 1965, 6–7).

De Valéra (1960, 29–31, 43–4, pls XXXV–XXXVI) has demonstrated that adherence to an east–west orientation in the laying out of long cairns appears to have been followed more commonly in the western than in the eastern counties of Ireland. This is to be expected, for a more consistent response to a preference for such an orientation is unlikely to have been achieved until the three principal structural components – segmented chamber, façade, and long cairn – had been adopted as essential features of the developed Carlingford cairn. If it is accepted that each of these three components derived from a separate source, then it is probable that the majority of monuments in which they occur consistently as part of a single unified plan and construction will have been built in areas some distance away from initial points of entry. It is obvious, of course, that each of the three characteristics are to be found together in tombs nearer to the eastern coast of Ireland, but, as has been suggested at Audleystown (DW 3), such tombs also may reveal evidence of multi-period construction. The fact that the wider end of Audleystown faces south-west is surely significant. This does not imply that all tombs in the hinterland will display each of the characteristics of the developed Carlingford type. The Court Cairn at Bavan (DG 23) was apparently enclosed in a short, polygonal cairn, not a long cairn (Flanagan & Flanagan, 1966).

It is also significant that within the Carlingford province, as in western Britain, some Portal Dolmens are set at the end of a long cairn, as at Ballykeel, Co. Armagh (Collins, 1965) and Kilfeaghan, Co. Down (Collins, 1959). Although it is uncertain whether these long cairns were trapezoidal on plan, their length suggests that an external tradition had been adopted, perhaps the same as that which may have contributed to the development of the mature Carlingford cairn. It is possible that excavation may reveal that some such monuments are of multi-period construction, and may show that long mounds had been added to existing Portal Dolmens. This might explain the orientation of Ballykeel, in which the chamber opens from the south, and Kilfeaghan, in which it opens from the north. In each instance the chamber faces uphill, a characteristic of many Portal Dolmens (Powell, 1963, 20). Had it been intended to enclose an existing Portal Dolmen within a long cairn, it would have been necessary to retain the orientation of the original chamber, provided that the latter was to be positioned in such a manner that access was to be gained from one end of the cairn. Portal Dolmens, however, were not invariably set at one end of a long cairn, as is shown at Ballygraffan, Co. Down, where the chamber, apparently flanked by an orthostatic façade, is set laterally (*Co. Down*, 1966, 78–9).

It would appear therefore, following the hypotheses set out in the preceding paragraphs, that the development of the Carlingford cairn compares closely with that of the Clyde tomb. Both types may have drawn upon common sources for their respective façades and long, often trapezoidal, cairns (see above, p. 54). This is not to deny the possibility suggested by Scott (1969, 215–17) that the construction of some cairns in the westerly and northerly peripheries of the Clyde province had been influenced in late Neolithic times by traditions emanating from the Carlingford province. In particular, the use of jamb-and-septal construction, foreign to the majority of Clyde tombs, is best explained by influences, if not by immigration, from Ireland, which is suggested further by the discovery in a settlement site at Auchategan in Glendaruel, Argyll, of pottery displaying characteristics similar to some in the north of Ireland.[1] The writer, however, has reservations concerning Scott's hypothesis that the deeply concave and semi-circular façade necessarily resulted from influences coming from Ireland (Scott, 1969, 210). It seems equally possible that this type of façade may have developed locally (see above, p. 50). It would be difficult, for example, to argue that influences from Ireland had affected the plan of the façade at Mid Gleniron I (Corcoran, 1970a, 75). The conclusion which appears to be particularly significant in this discussion is that local traditions affecting the design of burial chambers were retained in both areas. A similar situation appears to have obtained in the Cotswold–Severn region, but before the tombs of this area are discussed, brief reference may be made to the subsequent development of Carlingford cairns in the west of Ireland.

In contrast to the tombs of the Clyde area, some of those of the Carlingford tradition incorporate *courts* as opposed to *forecourts*; that is, enclosed areas fronting the entrance to burial chambers rather than open, concave forecourts. It is relevant to inquire whether the former derived from any external influences which may have affected Ireland, or whether they were a product of insular development. The distribution pattern of closed courts in the west of the country, particularly in coastal areas from Co. Mayo to Co. Donegal, might suggest that external influences were involved (de Valéra, 1960, pl. xxxii, 1). It is not improbable in prehistoric times that movements of peoples or ideas reached the west of Ireland by sea directly from continental Europe. This would seem to apply in the case of the Wedge-shaped Gallery Graves of the country which are not represented in Britain, and which appear to have a possible

---

[1] Unpublished. Preliminary note in *Discovery and Excavation, Scotland 1968*, (1969), 5.

ancestry among the Gallery Graves of Brittany. In the present context it is more germane to refer to the few transepted chambers recognised in the west of Ireland (de Valéra, 1965). Although these may reasonably be compared with those of the Cotswolds, there would seem to be less justification for arguing a derivation of the Irish examples from Britain, in view of the apparent absence of cognate structures in the eastern and central areas of the Carlingford province. Such doubts would seem to remain valid despite the use of dry-stone walling, comparable with that of the Cotswolds, in the revetment of the trapezoidal cairn enclosing the transepted chamber at Behy (MA 3), the court of which also is of dry-stone construction. In so far as the transepted chamber in the west of Ireland is concerned, it seems reasonable to suggest that the impetus which prompted their construction was derived from north-western France, an impetus comparable with that which appears, independently, to have introduced the transepted chamber to the Costwold–Severn region. In parenthesis, it may be germane to remark that transepted chambers comprise but a small proportion of known chambers in the long cairns of both the Carlingford and Cotswold–Severn regions.

Reverting to the origin of closed courts, it is not possible on available evidence to offer analogues either in Britain or continental Europe for those in the west of Ireland. It is necessary therefore to seek evidence which might suggest that the closed court developed in Ireland. While yet again it is to be admitted that any attribution of motives to prehistoric peoples must at best be hypothetical, it seems not unreasonable to assume that the forecourt fronting the entry to a burial chamber may have possessed some particular ritual significance. In certain contexts, other than those of Neolithic chambered tombs, it is possible to cite evidence which suggests that 'sacred' areas were delimited in such a manner that those who were not entitled to enter such areas were warned of potential trespass by some visible device, be it a fence, bank or ditch. Such a device need not necessarily have been difficult to surmount physically. It could have been more in the nature of a ritual boundary, comparable with the *temenos* of Greek tradition.

Excavation of two chambered tombs belonging to the Carlingford tradition has shown that access to what otherwise would have been an open forecourt had been checked by a barrier, perhaps more of a ritual than of a physical nature. At Cohaw (CV 7) the northern forecourt was closed by what appears to have been an earthen bank which incorporated four wooden posts. A narrow gap allowed access to the forecourt. Three postholes in a comparable position in the southern forecourt may represent the remains of a similar barrier (fig. 3g). At Aghanaglack (FE 11), the western of two forecourts was closed by three long, low orthostats, also apparently forming some kind of barrier (fig. 5d). Devices such as these might be considered as ancestral to structures such as the closed court at Creevykeel (SL 2), in which there appears to be a distinction between taller orthostats which flank the entrance to the chamber – orthostats comparable with those of the façade of an open forecourt – and shorter orthostats which form the remainder of the wall of the forecourt (Corcoran, 1960, 113). It must be admitted that there is as yet no evidence of any possible development from the situation represented by Cohaw and Aghanaglack on the one hand, and Creevykeel on the other.

The fact that relatively few tombs have been excavated in the western part of the Carlingford region probably has contributed to this lacuna, for it seems possible that any evidence of development towards the full court is more likely to be recovered from the centre than from the west of the province. It would certainly be relevant to know whether or not an open forecourt had been converted into a closed court by the erection of additional orthostats or dry-stone walling.

In this context, as in other aspects of megalithic inquiry, however, it may be possible to glean some hint of multi-period construction from the examination of the visible features of unexcavated Court Cairns. Although Creevykeel has been excavated, the excavator was unable to satisfy himself as to 'whether the whole monument represents one or more periods of construction' (Hencken, 1939, 54). In view of evidence derived from recent excavation, it would seem that certain features of layout and construction at Creevykeel are best interpreted as the result of multi-period construction. It is not proposed to attempt a reconstruction of any possible sequence, but merely to observe that the layout of the monument as a whole is not symmetrical (fig. 4a). In particular, the longitudinal axis of the segmented chamber differs by several degrees from that of both the court and the trapezoidal cairn, so that the entrance to the court is not aligned on the longitudinal axis of the chamber. If it were assumed that the cairn had been of unitary construction, any departure from a common alignment might be interpreted simply as the result of inaccuracies or inattention which had developed during the laying out and building of the monument. To the writer it seems equally possible that it resulted from inaccuracies of layout occasioned by the addition of later structural features. As Hencken himself (1939, 54) remarked, lengths of double revetment are suggestive of some alteration to the original structure. If the possibility of any structural addition is allowed, then it seems permissible to speculate whether this might also have involved the conversion of an open forecourt to a closed court, which is suggested by the difference in size between the orthostats of the façade proper and those of the wall of the court. But this must remain a matter of speculation.

Reference to the plan of certain other courts, however, reveals that in some there are breaks in what otherwise would be a regular layout. At Lecarrowtemple (MA 16), for example, the two halves of the court are not symmetrically arranged in relation to each other (fig. 5b). At Ballybeg (MA 31) there is a contrast between the more regularly semicircular plan of the eastern half of the court and the less even setting of the western (fig. 5c). This should not be taken to imply that all Court Cairns necessarily were of multi-period construction. Reference to the plan of a tomb such as Ballyboe (DG 6), for example, reveals a court of circular, regular plan, set symmetrically in relation to the chamber (fig. 5g). It does seem possible, however, that some courts originally may have been open forecourts, subsequently modified.

The hypothesis implied in this discussion derives from the assumption, prompted by evidence from Cohaw and Aghanaglack, that access to what otherwise would have been an open forecourt may sometimes have been restricted by the erection of a fence or wall across the open end of the forecourt. It is assumed further that the closed court subsequently may have become accepted as a regular feature of architectural and ritual practice, and that some existing forecourts may have been converted into closed courts. Following any general acceptance of the closed court as part of megalithic tradition, tombs built subsequently may have incorporated a closed court as part of the original plan. This is but one hypothesis, although it seems relevant in the context of a tomb such as Creevykeel, in which the court is set towards one end of the cairn, and in which the burial chamber or chambers open from one end only of the court.

A second class of tomb is known, however, in which the court is set in the centre of the cairn, with access from one side of the mound. In tombs of this type, a chamber or chambers open from each end of the court. This situation is comparable with that of Double-horned or Dual-court Cairns in that more than one structurally independent burial chamber are enclosed within a single cairn. Whereas in a Double-horned or Dual-court Cairn the chambers are set back-to-back, the second class of Court Cairn resembles two chambered tombs, each with an open forecourt, set face-to-face. It has been suggested that the Double-horned Cairn at Audleys-town (DW 3) may have been of multi-period construction (see above, p. 45). There is no evidence at present derived from excavation that any Median-court Cairn is of multi-period construction, although, as in the case of Terminal-court Cairns, certain details of construction and layout hint that this is not impossible. Reference to the plan of the court of Deerpark (Maghera-ghanrush) (SL 9) suggests that it may not have been planned as a unit (fig. 4b). There is, for example, a break in the otherwise regular setting of the northern wall, and to a lesser extent in the southern wall, of the court. The break in both walls occurs to the east of two orthostats,

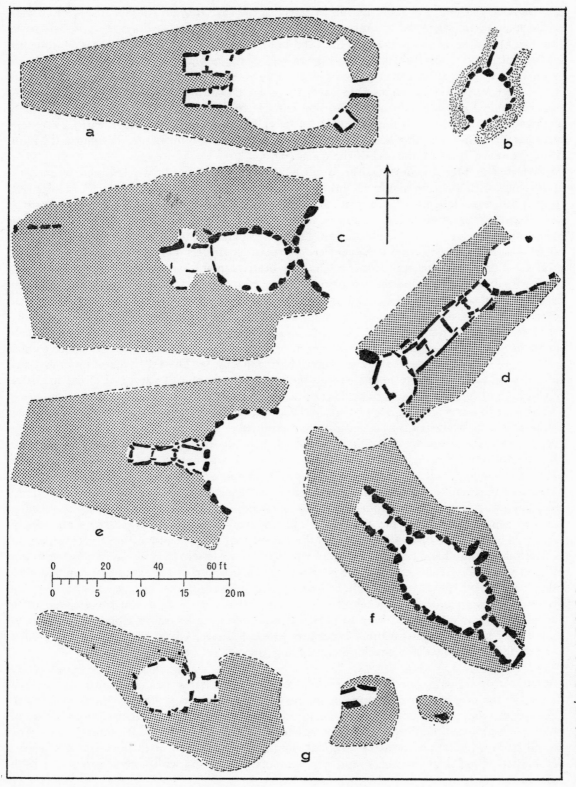

a Malinmore
(DG 19),
b Lecarrowtemple
(MA 16),
c Ballybeg (MA 31)
d Aghanaglack
(FE 11),
e Goward (DW 7),
f Ballyglass
(MA 13),
g Ballyboe (DG 6).
(a, b, c, f and g
based on de Valéra,
d Davies,
e Davies and Evans)

fig. 5 *Chambered cairns referred to in text*

each relatively larger than those set immediately to the east of them. In fact, the western half of the monument resembles a conventional chambered cairn of Carlingford type, having a chamber of two segments approached from the east through an open forecourt. It is not difficult to speculate on the possibility that the eastern half of the monument may have been built on to an earlier tomb. The parallel arrangement of two segmented chambers from the eastern end of the court, while not unique, is rarely found in the Carlingford tradition, and may represent a limited development unique to the west of Ireland. The overall irregularity of plan of Deer Park contrasts with that of Malin More (DG 19) in which two segmented chambers built parallel with each other are set symmetrically in relation to the court. The court at Malin More, however, is set at one end of the cairn (fig. 5a).

Reverting to Median-court Cairns, a certain parallel may be drawn between Deer Park and Ballyglass (MA 13) in that in each there is some irregularity of layout (fig. 5f). It might be supposed that at Ballyglass the western half of the court maintains a regular curve, almost a perfect semicircle, whereas the eastern gives the appearance of having been laid out in order to accommodate an existing structure. Its somewhat 'pinched' plan contrasts with the semicircle of the western. It may not be irrelevant to note that, as at Deer Park, the western half of the total structure gives the appearance of having been planned as a conventional chambered tomb with open forecourt, access being from the more easterly end. Without excavation, it must be admitted that considerations such as those set out in the preceding paragraphs are at best subjective. The writer is conscious that the plan of Ballyglass might be interpreted otherwise, for in general this is a monument notable for its regularity of plan, despite those features which might be adduced as evidence of multi-period construction. Reference may be made to one further monument possessing a median court, Farranmacbride (DG 17). Even without excavation, it would be difficult to maintain that its complexity of plan, so atypical of the majority of Carlingford tombs, was part of an overall design (fig. 4e).

This excursus into possible antecedents of the closed courts is offered as a further contribution to the relevance of the concept of multi-period construction. It cannot be claimed that such a concept necessarily solves outstanding problems relevant to the origins of certain classes of chambered tombs seemingly unknown beyond these islands; but in the apparent absence of external analogues, it does seem to offer a possible line of argument for insular development. Whereas it may not answer all or any outstanding problems, such an hypothesis may contribute something to present understanding. In so far as closed courts are concerned, it seems possible that two separate developments took place. The first would seem to be associated with a desire to restrict access to an open forecourt, and the second may have resulted from the construction of a second burial chamber and associated forecourt immediately in front of an existing tomb. Whatever may have contributed to the genesis of the closed court in Ireland, such a contribution must have originated in Ireland itself. Otherwise, how is the apparent absence of courts outside Ireland to be explained? Open forecourts are known in Europe from the Mediterranean to Orkney, and would therefore seem to have offered either a structural or ritual embellishment which may have been drawn upon according to local choice. Given the idea of a forecourt, it is not difficult to visualise a development leading towards a closed court.

Cotswold–Severn Cairns.   The writer has discussed recently what appear to him to be relevant factors in the origins and development of the Cotswold–Severn group of chambered tombs (Corcoran, 1969). This discussion may be summarised briefly. Three principal types of burial chamber have been identified, commonly enclosed in long, frequently trapezoidal cairns. The chambers are: (a) simple, box-like terminal chambers, comparable with Scott's *protomegaliths*; (b) transepted terminal chambers; and (c) chambers set laterally with access from one or both sides of the cairn.

External analogues for the transepted and lateral chambers are proposed. The former are paralleled in north-western France, and this probable connection has been discussed frequently (*e.g.* Daniel, 1950, 157–9; Piggott, 1962, 59–63). The latter appear to have been influenced from two sources. Both, like the transepted chamber, appear to belong to the Passage Grave tradition. One, as at Belas Knap (GLO 1), has affinities with polygonal Passage Graves, widespread in Europe generally. Analogues for the second type may be identified among Passage Graves in Hérault in the south of France (Arnal, 1963), although the means by which such traditions may have been transmitted to western Britain, without leaving any apparent evidence of their passage, remains unknown (Corcoran, 1969, 93–5). It is unnecessary to seek external analogues for a structure so widespread as the box-like simple terminal chamber.

To date there is little evidence for the existence of multi-period chambered tombs in the Cotswold–Severn region. This contrasts with the situation in both the Clyde and Carlingford regions in which there is some evidence of chambers, both simple and segmented, enclosed within mounds other than those of trapezoidal plan, and which lack the orthostatic façade considered distinctive of the fully developed chambered tombs of their respective areas. There does exist, however, a little evidence which suggests that each of the three types of chamber in the Cotswold–Severn region may in some instances originally have been enclosed within cairns of a plan other than trapezoidal. At Pen-y-Wyrlod (BRE 1), a simple box-like chamber is contained within a small cairn, to which appears to have been added a short 'tail' in order to incorporate a second very small chamber (fig. 2*b*) (Corcoran, 1969, 43). A nineteenth-century account of the excavation of the laterally chambered cairn of Belas Knap (GLO 1) refers to evidence which suggests that each of the chambers originally was enclosed within its own cairn (Corcoran, 1969, 89–90). The simple Passage Grave enclosed in a circular cairn at Broadsands in Devon is relevant in that it demonstrates that such structures were built in southern England (Radford, 1958). Comparable evidence of a transepted chambered tomb enclosed in other than a truly long cairn is not available, although the writer has argued (Corcoran, 1969, 276) that the tomb in Penmaen Burrows (GLA 5) may have been contained in a shorter cairn. The only monument so far known which appears to offer some relevant data is Ty Isaf (BRE 5). Whatever may have been the sequence of construction – and it would seem impossible to escape the conclusion that this had been a tomb of multi-period construction – the similarity between the transepted chamber and its circular revetment within this composite monument (fig. 3*f*) and those of certain Breton tombs is sufficiently close to be more than coincidental (Radford, 1958, 86). The difference in orientation between the axis of the transepted chamber and that of the trapezoidal cairn at Ty Isaf also seems relevant (see above, p. 46).

While emphasising that irrefutable evidence of multi-period construction is not so far available, the writer believes that a situation may have existed in the Cotswold–Severn region, comparable with that which has been postulated for the tombs of the Clyde and Carlingford areas. In other words, the long and frequently trapezoidal mound appears to have been adopted in each of the three areas by groups of people who already possessed locally established traditions of chambered tomb construction. It is irrelevant in the present context to rehearse the hypotheses which have been offered as to the possible derivation of the stone-built long cairns of the Cotswold–Severn region from the chalk-built mounds of the neighbouring and at least partially contemporary Windmill Hill culture, and from comparable mounds in north-eastern England (Corcoran, 1969, 75–9, 97–9). It is perhaps relevant only to refer to the hypothesis that the trapezoidal plan of such mounds may have derived from long houses known in parts of continental Europe to have been built during the Neolithic period (Piggott, 1966, 388–9), although houses of comparable design are so far unknown in Britain.

Recognition that multi-period construction may have contributed something to the development of each of the three well-defined groups of chambered long cairns in Britain and Ireland may help to resolve some of the problems of interpretation which remained unsolved in earlier studies. Were it accepted that the origins of the respective chambers of the Clyde and Carlingford groups might be identified in Scott's *protomegalith* and the Portal Dolmen respectively, then the former concept of a unified 'Clyde-Carlingford Culture' would appear to retain less validity, notwithstanding Scott's hypothesis that some of the later Clyde tombs may have been influenced from traditions derived from Ireland (see above, p. 56). Still less would it be relevant to argue that the presence of a long mound, whether of earth, chalk or stone, implies cultural unity, still less a diffusion *in toto* of funerary architecture and its associated ritual across Britain and Ireland, from whatever points of origin such a movement might be envisaged (de Valéra, 1961, 237–40, 251–2). On the one hand, data derived from evidence of multi-period construction would appear to complicate hypotheses appropriate to the origins of local traditions of funerary architecture, but on the other hand such complications paradoxically may simplify these hypotheses.

BIBLIOGRAPHY

Arnal, J., 1963. 'Les Dolmens du Département de l'Hérault', *Préhistoire*, XV (entire volume).

Ashbee, P., 1966. 'The Fussell's Lodge Long Barrow Excavations 1957', *Archaeologia*, C, 1–80.

Atkinson, R. J. C., 1965. 'Wayland's Smithy', *Antiquity*, XXXIX, 126–33.

Borlase, W. C., 1897. *The Dolmens of Ireland* (three volumes). London.

Bowen, E. G. & Gresham, C. A., 1967. *History of Merioneth*, Vol. I. Dolgellau.

Childe, V. G., 1934. 'Neolithic Settlement in the West of Scotland', *Scot. Geogr. Mag.*, I., 18–25.

Co. Down, 1966. *An Archaeological Survey of County Down*, edited by E. M. Jope. Belfast.

Collins, A. E. P., 1954. 'The excavation of a Double Horned Cairn at Audleystown, Co. Down', *Ulster J. Archaeol.*, XVII, 7–56.

—— 1959. 'Kilfeaghan Dolmen, Co. Down', *Ulster J. Archaeol.*, XXII, 31–2.

—— 1965. 'Ballykeel Dolmen and Cairn', *Ulster J. Archaeol.*, XXVIII, 47–70.

—— 1966. 'Barnes Lower Court Cairn, Co. Tyrone', *Ulster J. Archaeol.*, XXIX, 43–75.

Collins, A. E. P. & Wilson, B. C. S., 1964. 'The excavation of a Court Cairn at Ballymacdermot, Co. Armagh', *Ulster J. Archaeol.*, XXVII, 3–22.

Corcoran, J. X. W. P., 1960. 'The Carlingford Culture', *Proc. Prehist. Soc.*, XXVI, 98–148.

—— 1966. 'Excavation of three Chambered Cairns at Loch Calder, Caithness', *Proc. Soc. Antiq. Scot.*, XCVIII, 1–75.

—— 1969. 'The Cotswold–Severn Group' in Powell *et al.*, 1969, 13–104, 273–95.

—— 1970a. 'Excavation of two Chambered Cairns at Mid Gleniron Farm, Glenluce, Wigtownshire', *Trans. Dumfriesshire Galloway Natur. Hist. Antiq. Soc.*, XLVI, 29–90.

—— 1970b. 'Excavation of two Burial Cairns at Mid Gleniron Farm, Glenluce, Wigtownshire', *Trans. Dumfriesshire Galloway Natur. Hist. Antiq. Soc.*, XLVI, 91–9.

Daniel, G. E., 1950. *The Prehistoric Chamber Tombs of England and Wales*. Cambridge.

Davies, O., 1937. 'Excavations at Ballyrenan, Co. Tyrone', *J. Roy. Soc. Antiq. Ireland*, LXVII, 89–100.

de Valéra, R., 1960. 'The Court Cairns of Ireland', *Proc. Roy. Irish Acad.*, 60 (C), 9–140.

—— 1961. 'The "Carlingford Culture", the Long Barrow and the Neolithic of Great Britain and Ireland', *Proc. Prehist. Soc.*, XXVII, 234–52.

—— 1965. 'Transeptal Court Cairns', *J. Roy. Soc. Antiq. Ireland*, XCV, 5–37.

de Valéra, R. & Ó Nualláin, S., 1961. *Survey of the Megalithic Tombs of Ireland, Vol. I, County Clare*. Dublin.

—— 1964. *Survey of the Megalithic Tombs of Ireland, Vol. II, County Mayo*. Dublin.

Eogan, G., 1967. 'The Knowth (Co. Meath) Excavations', *Antiquity*, XLI, 302–4.

—— 1968. 'Excavations at Knowth, Co. Meath, 1962–1965', *Proc. Roy. Irish Acad.*, 66 (C), 299–400.

—— 1969. 'Excavations at Knowth, Co. Meath, 1968', *Antiquity*, XLIII, 8–14.

Evans, E. E., 1938. 'Aghnaskeagh Cairn B, Co. Louth', *County Louth Archaeol. J.*, IX, 1–18.

—— 1961. Review of de Valéra, 1960, *Studia Hibernica*, I, 228–32.

—— 1966. *Prehistoric and Early Christian Ireland: A Guide*. London.

Evans, E. E. & Watson, E., 1942. ' "The Stone Houses", Ticloy, Co. Antrim', *Ulster J. Archaeol.*, V, 62–5.

Flanagan, L. N. W. & Flanagan, D. E., 1966. 'The Excavation of a Court Cairn at Bavan, Co. Donegal', *Ulster J. Archaeol.*, XXIX, 16–38.

Grimes, W. F., 1932. 'Prehistoric Archaeology in Wales since 1925', *Proc. Prehist. Soc. East Anglia*, VII, 82–106.

—— 1948. 'Pentre Ifan Burial Chamber, Pembrokeshire', *Archaeol. Cambrensis*, C, 2–23.

Hencken, H. O'N., 1939. 'A Long Cairn at Creevykeel, Co. Sligo', *J. Roy. Soc. Antiq. Ireland*, LXIX, 53–98.

Henshall, A. S., 1963. *The Chambered Tombs of Scotland, Vol. I.* Edinburgh.

O'Kelly, C., 1967. *Guide to Newgrange.* Wexford.

O'Kelly, M. J., 1958. 'A Horned-Cairn at Shanballyedmond, Co. Tipperary', *J. Cork Hist. Archaeol. Soc.*, LXIII, 37–72.

Peers, C. R. & Smith, R. A., 1921. 'Wayland's Smithy, Berkshire', *Antiq. J.*, I, 183–98.

Piggott, S., 1946. 'The Chambered Cairn of "The Grey Mare and Colts"', *Proc. Dorset Natur. Hist. Archaeol. Soc.*, LXVII, 30–3.

—— 1954. *The Neolithic Cultures of the British Isles.* Cambridge.

—— 1955. 'Windmill Hill – East or West?', *Proc. Prehist. Soc.*, XXI, 96–101.

—— 1962. *The West Kennet Long Barrow.* London.

—— 1966. ' "Unchambered" Long Barrows in Neolithic Britain', *Palaeohistoria*, XII, 381–93.

Powell, T. G. E., 1938. 'Excavation of a Megalithic Tomb at Ballynamona Lower, Co. Waterford', *J. Roy. Soc. Antiq. Ireland*, LXVIII, 260–71.

—— 1941. 'Megalithic Tombs in south-eastern Ireland', *J. Roy. Soc. Antiq. Ireland*, LXXI, 9–23.

—— 1963. 'The Chambered Cairn at Dyffryn Ardudwy', *Antiquity*, XXXVII, 19–24.

—— 1969. 'The Neolithic in the West of Europe and Megalithic Sepulture: some points and problems', in Powell *et al.*, 1969, 247–72.

—— *et al.*, 1969. *Megalithic Enquiries in the West of Britain.* Liverpool.

Radford, C. A. R., 1958. 'The Chambered Tomb at Broadsands, Paignton', *Proc. Devon Arch. Exploration Soc.*, V, 147–66.

Scott, J. G., 1969. 'The Clyde Cairns of Scotland', in Powell *et al.*, 1969, 175–222, 309–28.

Waterman, D. M., 1965. 'The Court Cairn at Annaghmare, Co. Armagh', *Ulster J. Archaeol.*, XXXVIII, 3–46.

Wulff, W., 1923. 'Carnfadrig', *J. Roy. Soc. Antiq. Ireland*, LIII, 190–5.

ACKNOWLEDGEMENTS

In writing this essay I recalled with pleasure the many discussions concerning megalithic inquiry which I have enjoyed over the past few years with Dr T. G. E. Powell, Mr J. G. Scott, Miss A. S. Henshall and Miss Frances Lynch. I wish to acknowledge with thanks the stimulus which these discussions have given me, without of course committing my colleagues to the views set forward.

It was during the period when I was fortunate enough to live and work in the Marcher Country on the borders of Wales and England that I first saw a Cotswold–Severn tomb and first met Miss Chitty. Both pleasurable occasions also provided some of the stimulus which has contributed to the present study.

Burials in Megalithic Chambered Tombs

Colin A. Gresham

The problems raised by the quantity, disposition and condition of the skeletal remains found in the chambers of megalithic tombs have been discussed in many contexts (for a useful summary with references see Piggott, 1962, 65–8). Usually the suggestions put forward to account for the bones being scattered and the skeletons often incomplete are based on the unstated assumption that the builders of these tombs regarded the grave as a last resting-place for the dead. For this reason the disturbance of the remains and the absence of bones are attributed to three main causes: to the activities of persons introducing successive burials into the tomb; to the practice of keeping bodies elsewhere before relegating them to their final home; or to the depredations of tomb-robbers – including the removal of bones (particularly skulls) for ritual purposes.

The mind of primitive man does not always work in the straightforward and rational way that might be expected, and there are races which consider the tomb as the house of the dead who in certain ways are still sentient and can still take an interest in the affairs of the living. This belief is not the same as that of a soul which leaves the body at death, or some time later, and can return to the tomb; it is the actual corpse which is thought to retain some form of consciousness. Those who hold this belief of the 'living dead' bury in vaults which can easily be opened, and they regularly carry out from them the bodies there deposited. This they do at special festivals held at regular intervals for the purpose of entertaining the dead persons by means of processions, singing and dancing; a film of this ritual was shown on television a few years ago. After being given an airing in this way the bodies are returned to the tomb for another dull spell away from the world.

In this particular cult the dead are placed in leather bags to make handling easy. As the bodies decay the bags deteriorate and have to be renewed; at each repacking the bundle is reduced in size until it becomes no more than a bolster of dry bones, which remains fairly stable. When this final state is arrived at, it can be compared to the practice used in the Coptic churches in Egypt, where the bones of saints and martyrs are preserved in leather bags, which can be brought out and held by the persons wishing to venerate them.

It is an axiom of archaeological research that findings cannot be pressed very far, if at all, to elucidate the concepts behind ritual practices, and there is no intention here of suggesting that the builders of chambered tombs practised the cult of the 'living dead'; nor is it thought that they may have preserved bodies in any form of wrapping, for no excavator seems to have noted the possibility of this (although it is a point that might be looked for in the future). Bodies could be moved without wrappings, for instance if they were laid flat on a skin, which could be carried by two men like a stretcher. Attention has been called to this one particular ritual because, since certain prehistoric chambered tombs were designed so that they could be easily opened, it is not unreasonable to suggest that the persons using them did, at intervals, carry forth all or some of the dead bodies for unspecified ritual purposes, afterwards putting them back.

If this assumption be accepted as not too improbable, then certain deductions can be made as to the results that could follow. When decaying bodies were lifted for removal from the tomb, some small bones, particularly those of the hands and feet, could fall off; if unnoticed in the darkness, these could be kicked into corners or trodden into the floor, or they might later be picked up and put with the wrong body. When the bodies were being carried about outside the tomb similar bones could be lost in the forecourt, or even at some distance from it, and left there in the ground. The remains of the most ancient inhabitants of the tomb would be reduced to dust by centuries of handling – a not unusual fate of over-venerated relics. Families leaving the district might take away with them what little was left of their ancestors (particularly the skulls), and perhaps place them in other tombs.

It is natural to expect that a communal tomb used for successive burials over a very long period of time would become filled with bodies, but this is not in accordance with the facts as revealed by excavation. If some sort of ritual as is here suggested was in use, this could account for the relatively small number of bodies found, as well as for their condition.

Unlike a closed grave, a tomb which is the centre of an active ritual must at some point in time cease to be used in the way intended by its builders. Its functions are likely to come to a sudden rather than a gradual end, either because the people using it change their beliefs, or because they die out, or leave the district. It is therefore improbable that such a tomb would be found in full working order, for if it were abandoned in that condition it would before long be rifled. The tomb might be ceremonially closed, and the blocking of chambered tombs designed and used for successive burials over long periods is a problem closely related to that of the condition of the human remains found sealed in. The act of filling the chambers to the roof with material carried in for that purpose can have no connection with the intended use of the structure under the conditions here suggested; it would mark the final abandonment of any ritual involving the movement of the dead bodies, and might well be intended to prevent any further continuation of such ceremonies. The filling would hardly be placed over bodies disposed in the manner required by the ritual which was being terminated, and the scattered and incomplete remains found under such blocking material are probably no more than the *disjecta membra* of an abandoned cult.

These tentative suggestions are not intended to replace current theories, but they may be of use with them in the assessment of the problems of relevant sites.

BIBLIOGRAPHY

Piggott, Stuart, 1962. *The West Kennet Long Barrow. Excavations 1955–56.* Ministry of Works Archaeological Reports No. 4. London.

Portal Dolmens in the Nevern Valley, Pembrokeshire

Frances Lynch

The object of this short essay is to publish new plans and sections of the tombs in the Newport area of Pembrokeshire, some of which have never been published before, and to provide some discussion of their cultural background, which I believe to have been more uniform than has been previously suggested. It gives me much pleasure to offer this work to Miss Chitty, not only in gratitude for her great kindness to me, but also in the hope that she may enjoy reading it, so firmly, I feel, is the understanding of this particular group of tombs based on the geographical aspects of prehistory which she herself has always stressed so brilliantly.

The tombs in question are Carreg Coitan, Cerrig y Gof, Trellyffaint and Llech y Dribedd – all scattered along the coastal strip surrounding Newport Bay – and Pentre Ifan, which must be the result of inland penetration up the river. Movement still further eastwards to the head of the valley is attested by the ruined monument at Mynachlog Ddu, by the suggestive farm name, Cromlech, at Eglwyswrw (SN/135381), and by field names at Parke, Moylgrove (SN/128427) and Monington.[1]

The concentration of tombs in this area was first pointed out by Professor Grimes in his important paper on Welsh megalithic tombs in which he commented upon their relationship to the river Nyfer (Grimes, 1936, 113–14; fig. 5). The valley of the Nyfer is a broad, open, fertile area. The slopes are for the most part easy, though there are some precipitous cliffs in the vicinity of Nevern where the river has cut deeply. The mouth of the river forms an enclosed sandy bay protected by Dinas Head from the worst of the south-westerly winds. Between this headland and Newport are a few small coves, such as that just below Cerrig y Gof, which might have provided landing-places, but to the north the cliffs are high and the coastline inhospitable. The valley at Moylgrove is extremely steep and narrow, as is that of the Teifi at Cardigan and there is no other really convenient landing-place with easy access to the interior in this southern part of Cardigan Bay.

To the south the valley is cut off from the rest of Pembrokeshire, with its numerous megalithic tombs, by the somewhat forbidding mass of the Preselau mountains which provides a natural barrier to easy communication although there are two passes, at Bryn Berian and Mynachlog Ddu, which were certainly used by prehistoric man. Thus the area is suitable for early settle-

---

[1] There are two large stones in the hedge at Parke to add support to the name (RCAM, 1925, no. 719; Daniel, 1950, 204). Nothing now remains at Monington (RCAM, 1925, no. 705; Daniel, 1950, 206). I would agree with Daniel (1950, 206) that the rocks at Carnedd Meibion Owen, Nevern, are entirely natural in origin.

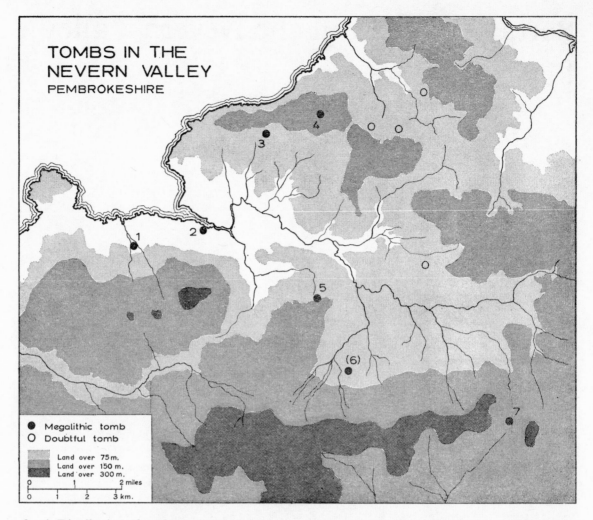

fig. 1 Distribution of tombs in the Nevern Valley: 1 Cerrig y Gof; 2 Carreg Coitan; 3 Trellyffaint; 4 Llech y Dribedd; 5 Pentre Ifan; 6 Bedd yr Afanc; 7 Mountain

ment, but its inhabitants, once settled, would inevitably tend to be isolated from their more immediate neighbours. The easiest contacts would be by sea, but these might be only occasional and from quite distant areas.

A comparable situation of geographical unity and isolation may be seen in the Conway Valley in North Wales, where there is a similar group of interrelated tombs whose distribution seems to represent the spread up the valley of a single group of people who retained their original tradition unaltered, probably over many centuries (Lynch, 1969, 124–43). The sideways spread from a single point of entry can, however, be better paralleled in the Ardudwy area of Merioneth, where again there is a single tomb-building tradition which undergoes an internal development, with later adaptations under the stimulus of new external contacts.

In each of these areas, therefore – Ardudwy, the Conway and the Nevern Valleys – there seems to have been an initial landing by people who subscribed to a particular tomb-building tradition. Whether they were also the first farmers in these areas is not known, but in any case they, or their ideas, became locally established and must have developed for many centuries without further interference. Changes can be seen in the tomb architecture, but the essential characteristics remain recognisable. However, certain sites reveal additions and alterations which suggest that new ideas from outside had begun to impinge upon these communities.[1] Although much more excavation is needed to bring precision to this picture, it seems likely that the spread of new ideas from one area to another took place during the Middle Neolithic period, which appears to have been a time of expansion and enterprise in most parts of these islands.[2]

It is intended in the following discussion to try to substantiate this theory in relation to the tombs of the Nevern Valley, where I believe one can see the threefold division of classic tombs, internally devolved types, and tombs which show contact with entirely new ideas.

As in Ardudwy and the Conway Valley, the main, unifying tradition of tomb-building in the Newport area is that represented by the Portal Dolmen. The antecedents of this very clearly defined type of tomb remain obscure. The Continent has nothing which appears ancestral to it, and it therefore seems probable that it developed somewhere in the Irish Sea area. Possibly the very early versions are simpler, more box-like and less easily recognisable than the classic type exemplified by the West Chamber at Dyffryn Ardudwy (MER 3).[3] Such simple rectangular chambers do exist in various parts of Wales, but none has been excavated, and most are badly ruined; it would thus be premature to make any definite suggestions about their relationship to the Portal Dolmens. My personal opinion, however, is that many of them must be later, locally devolved Portal Dolmens, and not prototypes. This is because in Ardudwy where settlement would logically progress up the hills away from the coast, the simpler chambers are found on the higher slopes (Lynch, 1969, 124–9). This postulate has guided my thinking in relation to the Nevern Valley tombs, but any such chronological scheme should not be over-emphasised; in fact, caution is suggested by the presence of a very classic Portal Dolmen on the high moorland at Carnedd Hengwm South, revealing how little we understand of the dynamics of architectural change within a stable tradition.

The most classic of all the Portal Dolmens in the Nevern Valley is Carreg Coitan or Pen y Bonc, just outside the town of Newport (SN/062394) (Grimes, 1936, 132, 134; fig. 25; Daniel, 1950, 199). It is situated on gently rising land no more than 100 metres from the south bank of the river and only about 10 metres above sea level. For most types of megalithic tomb a low-lying position is unusual, but Portal Dolmens are frequently found in such situations, which may, in fact, be considered characteristic of the group.[4] Carreg Coitan is placed at the end of the Nyfer estuary where the river begins to narrow and can be easily crossed. This may suggest a relatively early date among the Nevern Valley tombs but, as has already been said, too much emphasis should not be placed on this.

The surviving stones are part of a small, single-chambered Portal Dolmen with all the typical features (de Valéra & Ó'Nualláin, 1961, xiii). The H-shaped front, two tall portal stones with a high closing slab between them, clearly existed at this site, though unfortunately the eastern portal stone has been removed. The extra height of the portal area, slight but noticeable, is enhanced by the shape of the capstone. A massive, wedge-shaped capstone is another characteristic of this type of monument.

The chamber behind the portal is small and rectangular. The western side stone is missing and there is a gap between the back stone and the eastern side stone. This gap is unusual but may be compared to the small low stone at Maen y Bardd, Roewen (CRN 3), or to the gap

[1] One of the best examples is at Carneddau Hengwm where ideas from the Cotswold–Severn tradition cause alterations in the existing Portal Dolmen (Lynch, 1969, 136–9).

[2] The widespread distribution of Abingdon ware in southern England, the beginning of a far-flung export trade in stone axes, the appearance of Beacharra Ware (or Ballyalton Bowls) in Scotland and Ireland, the building of façades on Scottish tombs, are all indicative of this expansive phase.

[3] The reference number refers to the inventory in Powell *et al.*, 1969, 296–308; see Scott (1969, 175–82) for a discussion of the possible sequence in Scotland, though there are admittedly no classic Portal Dolmens in that area.

[4] For instance, Twlc y Filiast, Llangynog, Carms.; Porth Lwyd (CRN 4), Brennanstown, Co. Dublin; Haroldstown, Co. Carlow and others.

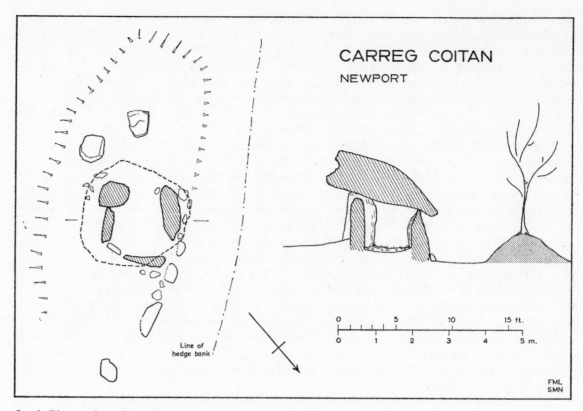

fig. 2 Plan and section: Carreg Coitan, Newport

filled with dry-stone walling in the East Chamber at Dyffryn Ardudwy (MER 3) (Lynch, 1969, 141–2, 134–5). These small informal entries may have been necessary for the introduction of burials, since the formal entrance at the front was always closed (the three stones there being a structural unity). Since it is not definitely proved, however, that successive burial took place in this type of tomb, the interpretation of such gaps as arrangements for re-entry must remain tentative.

The tomb is set in agricultural land and the cairn does not survive. There is a very slight rise in the ground some 2 metres in front of the portal which may cover blocking material, and there are some large boulders in the general vicinity. The proximity of the hedge has caused a path to be sunk between it and the back stone, and beyond the hedge there is no significant variation in the level field.

The front of the tomb faces south-east. Such a generally easterly orientation is usual amongst megalithic tombs of most kinds. However, in Portal Dolmens the practice of facing up the slope of the hill or up the valley often seems to have been more important than the compass direction (Powell, 1963, 20; Grimes, 1936, 122). This feature is not particularly marked among the Nevern Valley tombs, few of which are on sloping ground, but Carreg Coitan does face up the valley, though not towards Carn Ingli, the nearest mountain.

Pentre Ifan (SN/099370) on the southern side of the valley is one of the few Nevern sites where this detail of orientation is clear. It stands at about 150 m. (500 ft) above sea level on the western side of a spur jutting northwards from the main mass of the Preselau mountains. The portal faces up the slope towards the south.

The site was fully excavated in 1936–7 by Professor Grimes, who cleared not only the chamber and façade but a good deal of the cairn as well (Grimes, 1949, 3–23).[1] The monument is an impressive one and justly well-known. It consists of a single large chamber having a high closed portal with a semi-circular setting of large stones on either side. It is this façade which makes the site unique among Welsh megalithic tombs.[2] Professor Grimes considered that the entire monument was a structural unity, a variant of the well-known group of tombs with façades in the north of Ireland. I would agree that the façade at Pentre Ifan must be the result of contacts with Ireland, but I believe it is arguable that these new ideas impinge upon Pentre Ifan, or rather upon the community who built and maintained it, at a late stage in the tomb's history.

The evidence for two-period construction at any site is bound to be elusive and will not always carry complete conviction because the arguments are so often dependent upon the survival of an adequate quantity of cairn material. At Pentre Ifan the cairn had been badly denuded, especially in the area immediately surrounding the chamber and the façade; I must stress therefore that my reinterpretation of the sequence of building must necessarily be tentative. I believe that certain features revealed by Professor Grimes's excavation support my view, but I readily admit that these hints do not amount to incontrovertible proof.

Briefly, my belief is that the monument in its original form was a large, single-chambered Portal Dolmen, set in the southern end of a short cairn, roughly square in plan and having some sort of non-megalithic forecourt area in front of the portal, perhaps similar to that at Dyffryn Ardudwy (Powell, 1963, 19–24; pl. II, b). The later adaptation involved the addition of the high façade stones and the lengthening and regularisation of the cairn. No further burial chambers were added, so presumably these changes were simply designed to up-date the appearance of the original tomb which may still have been in use or, more probably, was still the venue for regular ceremonies.

Pentre Ifan I was a large Portal Dolmen entirely typical of the type. The portal is very splendid, with the classic H-plan and a high closing slab. It supports a large wedge-shaped capstone, 1·41 m. (4 ft 7 in.) thick at the front. At the back the capstone rests on a pointed, or gabled, back-stone. Stones of this shape were often used in this position by the builders of both Portal Dolmens and Court Cairns (Collins, 1954, 18, 31–2). George Owen in 1603 described four side stones none of which supported the capstone (Grimes, 1949, 6–8; pl. 3). In 1936 Professor Grimes found evidence for two stones on the west side, but found no holes on the east and suggested that this side may have been closed by dry-stone walling (Grimes, 1949, 12–13). Since these side stones, however, were not load-bearing, stone-holes would not be strictly necessary and I see no reason to doubt Owen's statement.[3] The use of two side stones is unusual, but then the chamber is larger than average: 5·22 sq. m. (60 sq. ft).

The chamber is built in a shallow pit. This may be a purely functional feature, dug to level the floor, or perhaps to obtain stone. It extends some distance beyond the portal and the side of it was cut by stone-hole D of the façade. It is not possible to say that this hole cut through the *filling* of the pit, because the upper levels had been badly disturbed.

The original arrangements at the front of the cairn are difficult to establish because it is here that the alterations have been greatest. Stone-holes which probably marked the edge of the early cairn (East 2, 3, 4, 5; West 2, 3) occur forward of the portal, so it must be assumed that

[1] I am most grateful to Professor Grimes for the generous assistance that he has given me in the writing of this note. It should perhaps be said that he is not convinced by the reinterpretation offered here, but is prepared to admit that nothing found during the excavation actually disproves it.

[2] I believe the authenticity of the façade at Garn Turne, Pembs. is doubtful. The stones may well be a natural feature since the area is strewn with fallen and upright blocks from a near-by outcrop (Daniel, 1950, 90; fig. 27, no.2).

[3] Recent excavations at Din Dryfol (ANG 5) have shown that even structurally important stones may have been simply stood on the old ground surface without any hole.

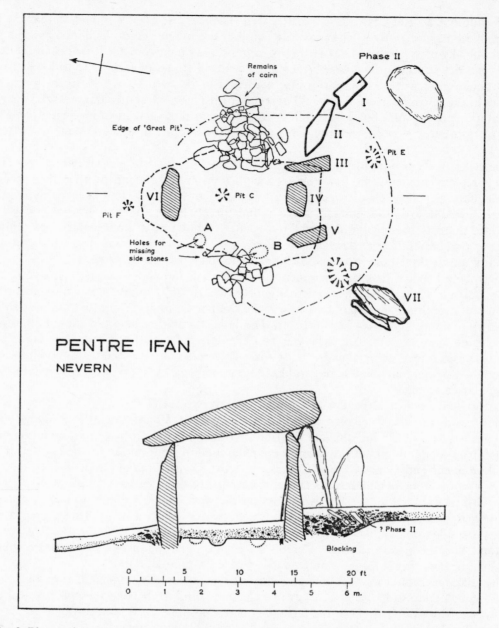

PENTRE IFAN

NEVERN

fig. 3 Plan and section of the megalithic structure: Pentre Ifan, Nevern (after W. F. Grimes)

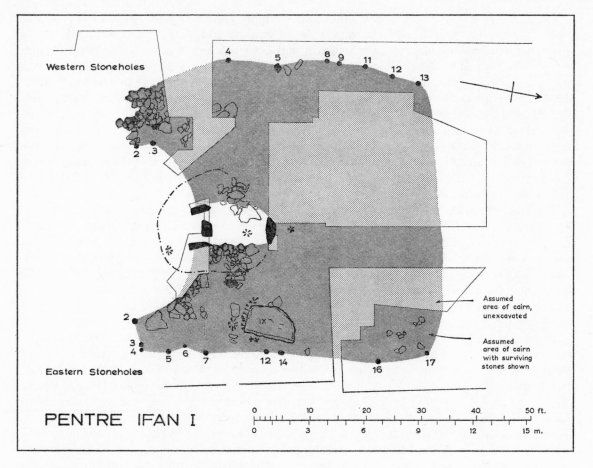

fig. 4 Pentre Ifan I (after W. F. Grimes)

there was some forecourt area at this stage. It may have been much the same shape and size as the inner half of the later version, with a chord of 8·3 m. (27 ft 3 in.) and a depth of 3 m. (9 ft 10 in.). The forecourt area at Dyffryn Ardudwy where the cairn was held back by rudimentary dry-stone walling might serve as a model for Pentre Ifan I. Such a wall would have provided a good edge against which to lean the façade stones, as the excavator in fact suggested they had been leant (Grimes, 1949, 14–15). But so little of the cairn survived that there is no real evidence on this point and in any case the position of stone II, set back from the portal, suggests that the earlier wall may have been demolished.

Another point of similarity between the forecourt area of Pentre Ifan I and Dyffryn Ardudwy West Chamber is the presence of a small pit to the right of the entrance. At Dyffryn Ardudwy this pit contained a great deal of pottery, whereas the one at Pentre Ifan was empty except for a soft filling. It is difficult to say whether there was any blocking material in the forecourt at this stage. The section down the centre shows the lowest level, in the great pit and against the closing slab, as a rather irregular mass without the consistent sloped arrangement clearly seen in the upper level. This apparent division between an upper and lower blocking may be fortuitous and restricted only to this spot, but it is worth noting that the blocking in front of the portal of the West Chamber at Dyffryn Ardudwy was tightly wedged, as here, but without any consistent arrangement, whereas the blocking of the later East Chamber was very definitely sloped.

The cairn which surrounded Pentre Ifan I was roughly square, 15·6 m. (51 ft 2 in.) long and 15 m. (49 ft 3 in.) wide. It covered some areas of burning and a large prostrate stone (IX) of unknown significance. The sides of this cairn had been marked by a wavering line of stones set into shallow holes. None of these stones survive, but the holes were revealed by excavation and provide one of the most important clues to the alterations undergone by the monument; for they are often duplicated by other rows of holes, or surviving stones, set a short distance outside them in a straighter line extending for a distance of 38 m. (64 ft 8 in.). For instance, on the west there is clear duplication between holes 8 and 7, and 9 and 10, while on the east stone VIII duplicates hole 7, and holes 12 and 13, and 14 and 15, are paired. No holes were found to mark the end of the cairn between holes E 17 and W 13 but as they are very irregularly spaced along the sides and only just over a third of the area here was excavated, their absence should not be considered certain.

The small size of the cairn and its lack of regularity are both features which, as far as we know, are characteristic of Portal Dolmens. The wavering edge can be paralleled at both periods at Dyffryn Ardudwy where the builders' lack of interest in the formal shape of their cairn is apparent and contrasts strongly with, for instance, the practice of the Cotswold–Severn cairn builders. The insistence on a neat edge to the cairn is less marked in Ireland where the normal cairn is, like Pentre Ifan II, straight, but not absolutely so.

The finds from the site were meagre. The pottery, sherds from the neck of a shouldered bowl, and the triangular flint arrowhead must date from the earlier phase. Neither are especially distinctive but are not inappropriate to a Portal Dolmen (Herity, 1964). The pottery may be compared to that from Dyffryn Ardudwy and to the larger range from the settlement at Clegyr Boia, Pembrokeshire, where the rather coarse paste would be more at home (Williams, 1953).

It is impossible to guess at the interval of time which elapsed between the building of Pentre Ifan I and the alterations which produced the monument which we see today. Comparisons have been made between Pentre Ifan I and Dyffryn Ardudwy West Chamber, but this is inevitable because Dyffryn is the only other excavated example in Wales. It should not necessarily imply that both must be equally early, for we do not know the rate at which this very persistent style changed. Evidence from south-west Scotland, however, does suggest that the horizon at which façades appear there is the Middle Neolithic (Scott, 1969, 175–222). In fact the situation outlined by Mr J. G. Scott for Kintyre is closely akin to that at Pentre Ifan. He demonstrates the development of a local tomb type without megalithic façade, on to which the idea of a more impressive forecourt is grafted. He sees this change as resulting from contacts with Ireland, where the façade was already well-established. For his area these contacts are clearly confirmed by the distribution of Beacharra and Ballyalton pottery and the Lyles Hill style of shouldered bowls. This comparison would suggest a date somewhere between 2700 BC and 2500 BC for Pentre Ifan II, in terms of conventional dating.

The origin of the megalithic façade in the Irish Sea area remains obscure, as do the beginnings of the Court Cairns with which it is normally associated. Dr Corcoran, in a recent paper as yet unpublished (Corcoran, 1969, 21), argues that the two-chambered Court Cairns with their jamb and sill divisions may represent a development from the Portal Dolmens, which in Ireland occasionally have a double chamber. These double chambers were presumably built in response to a need for extra burial space: a need met in the Nevern Valley and in Wales generally by the duplication of separate chambers. He also looks to the Portal Dolmen for the origin of the façade but suggests that the trapezoid cairn was adopted from the early earthen Long Barrows of southern England, perhaps via the Cotswold–Severn group.

His theory that the monumental façade, which becomes absolutely standard in one form or another on the Court Cairns, is part of the original Portal Dolmen tradition seems to me to lack substance. It is true that supposedly early Portal Dolmens such as Dyffryn Ardudwy do have some practical forecourt arrangements in the front, but the progression by which this develops into the monumental type seen at Pentre Ifan is dubious. My personal opinion, though for the present it must remain little more than a guess, is that, like the trapezoid cairn, the monumental stone façade was an idea borrowed from the Long Barrows which quite commonly covered huge wooden structures. Such an addition might well be eagerly adopted by a group who already laid great architectural emphasis on the entrance to their tombs.

Nevertheless, whatever the rights and wrongs of this argument – and at the moment the question cannot be adequately discussed because the tombs in question, such as Goward, Co. Down (*Co. Down*, 1966, 79–80), Tircony, Co. Derry, Browne's Hill, Co. Carlow (Evans, 1966, 154, 64) and Ticloy, Co. Antrim (Evans & Watson, 1942, 62–5) are unexcavated – the development of the façade, on Portal Dolmens or on Court Cairns, seems to have taken place in Ireland. Though there are many Portal Dolmens in Wales, spanning between them a considerable period, only Pentre Ifan has a monumental façade. At all the others the forecourt edging must have remained as insignificant as those on the Western and Eastern Chambers at Dyffryn Ardudwy. I am aware that this may be arguing in a circle, but I think the whole group of Welsh Portal Dolmens should be taken into account when considering this question of whether the Portal Dolmen with façade is a natural, native development.

Though Pentre Ifan is unique in Wales, yet it does not give the impression of an experimental or tentative style. The combination of such a classic Portal Dolmen with such a well-developed façade does not occur in Ireland. With such a façade one would expect a Court Cairn chamber, if the monument had been built as a single unit under stimulus from Ireland at this stage. Therefore I believe that the adoption of the façade only, grafted on to an existing tomb, is historically the most plausible explanation of the peculiarities of design found at Pentre Ifan.

The chamber of Pentre Ifan I remained untouched during the alterations; the façade stones were simply added on either side of the portal, either in front of, or replacing, the original edge of the cairn. These stones were not deeply set, as they would have to have been if they were to withstand pressure from a newly-built cairn, but seem to have been erected leaning slightly back against the cairn. The new forecourt was very much deeper (8 m.) than the old one if the ends of the cairn extended as far as stones x and xi, but the functional area, where the tall stones and blocking are, may have remained much the same. There were probably only four or five uprights; which means that the rest of the area must have been enclosed by smaller stones, or perhaps walling.[1] This would be in line with similar forecourts in Ireland. There is one major difference, however, between this and the normal Court Cairn forecourt, necessitated by the pre-existence of the Portal Dolmen; this is the treatment of the tomb entrance. It is usual for the entrance stones and the façade stones to form a continuous line, the entrance stones being set at right angles to the chamber. Here, of course, the portal has not been altered and it breaks the smooth line of the façade.

It is reasonable to suppose that the alterations to the cairn were made at the same time. The enlargement of the forecourt and the extension of the 'horns' meant that additional material would have to be added to the front of the cairn and the opportunity could well have been taken to improve the alignment of the sides (on the west, holes 1, 6, 7, 10 and stone xiii; on the east, holes 1, 8, 9, 13, 15 and stones viii and xii). The cairn must also have been more than doubled in size by the addition of an entirely new area at the back marked out by stones xii, xiv, xv, xvi and xiii (some may have been missed along the west side where the excavation did not extend much beyond the surviving cairn stones). The addition of a solid mass of cairn material without any new burial chambers is not unique (Corcoran, 1964–6, 18–22). It would seem that the length of the cairn became an important factor in its own right, regardless of what it covered. This trend may be linked with the emphasis on trapezoid shape and neat

[1] I think it is possible that the large fallen stone to the east of stone 1 may have formed part of the façade. It had presumably fallen before the blocking was built. (Compare Ballymacdermot, Co. Armagh [Collins & Wilson, 1964, 10] and Annaghmare, Co. Armagh [Waterman, 1965, 13].)

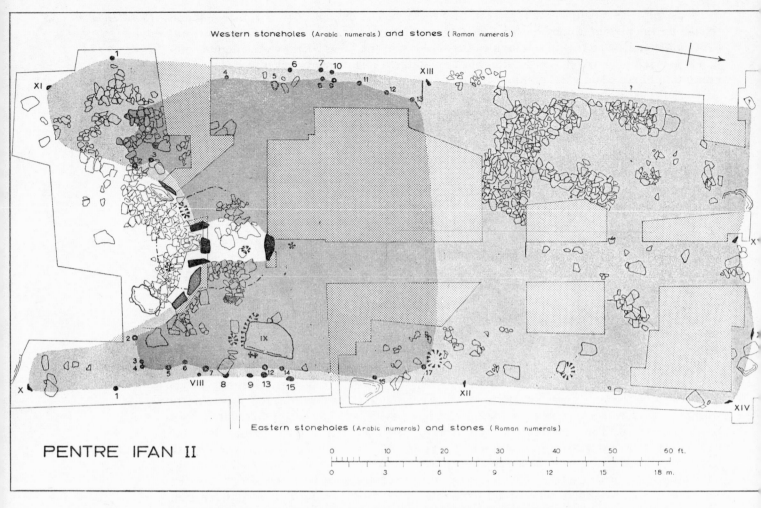

Western stoneholes (Arabic numerals) and stones (Roman numerals)

Eastern stoneholes (Arabic numerals) and stones (Roman numerals)

PENTRE IFAN II

| 0 | 10 | 20 | 30 | 40 | 50 | 60 ft. |
| 0 | 3 | 6 | 9 | 12 | 15 | 18 m. |

fig. 5 Pentre Ifan II with extent of earlier cairn indicated (after W. F. Grimes)

edges which is seen in some tomb-building traditions. Interest in the external appearance of the monument is not surprising for the outside was always visible, while only a few people may have seen the inside, and that infrequently.

The final blocking of the forecourt must belong to this phase, whether or not this covered any blocking belonging to the earlier structure. A double layer of blocking is not inconceivable; it is well documented, for instance, at Monamore, Arran (Mackie, 1963–4, 4–7).[1] The upper layers of the blocking found by Professor Grimes in the area of the portal and against the façade stones were carefully laid, sloped and overlapped for a considerable distance. This distinctive sloped blocking was found in front of the later chamber at Dyffryn Ardudwy and is frequently found in front of Court Cairns.[2] Its absence at the West Chamber at Dyffryn Ardudwy might suggest that it is a system evolved at a later date. Such a theory would fit the situation at Pentre Ifan well, but it should not be stressed until much more evidence has been assembled.

[1] Again, it is only the upper blocking which is sloped. There are also two levels of fill in the forecourt of Annagh-mare, Co. Armagh (Waterman, 1965, 11–13; fig. 5).
[2] Few Portal Dolmens have been adequately excavated in this respect. It is interesting, however, that there is no blocking in front of the portal at Ballykeel, Co. Armagh (Collins, 1965, 52–6; fig. 3).

The only find possibly associated with this phase is a roughly-made hollow scraper. It was found somewhere beneath the cairn to the east of stone IX. The hollow scraper is commonly found in Irish tombs of most kinds, but is surprisingly rare on the eastern side of the Irish Sea.

Llech y Dribedd (SN/101433) is the only other single chamber in the valley (Grimes, 1936, 139; Daniel, 1950, 198; pl. 1). It clearly belongs to the Portal Dolmen tradition but it is not an entirely classic example. Situated on the highest point of the plateau surface north-west of Nevern, it is close to the sea, but stands at a height of 182 m. (596 ft) above it, and so is more likely to have been built by people moving up from the valley than by direct coastal penetration. This coastal area, exposed as it is to very high winds, is unlikely ever to have been heavily wooded, and was therefore possibly attractive to early man.

The tomb is built of extremely massive and unwieldy stones, and this may explain some of its peculiarities, notably the odd angle at which the portal stones are set, neither well-aligned to the chamber, nor parallel to one another. The most remarkable feature of the portal here, however, is that it lacks a closing slab, the absence of which is almost certainly original since

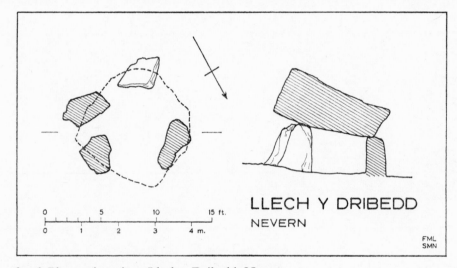

fig. 6 Plan and section: Llech y Dribedd, Nevern

the technique of building wedges the closing slab very tightly between the portals. The open portal is frequently found among Portal Dolmens in the north of Ireland – perhaps the best-known one is Legananny, Co. Down – but is rare in Wales.[1] There is no evidence yet on which to assess the significance of this variation.

The portal stones are very slightly higher than the back-stone but the real impression of extra height in the front is produced by the enormous wedge-shaped capstone. The lifting of such unnecessarily huge stones must have been an achievement of special virtue to the builders of Portal Dolmens, since their capstones are always impressive and can sometimes weigh 50 tons or more.

Only the back-stone of the chamber survives, but there is a slab which might have been part of a side stone lying close by to the south. The loss of both side stones is not unusual – for instance, they have disappeared at Pentre Ifan – for in Portal Dolmens they do not normally support the capstone and so can be removed without danger. The chamber area must have been about 2·25 sq. m. (30 sq. ft), almost the same size as that at Carreg Coitan; it may have been slightly wedge-shaped in plan.

[1] All the Portal Dolmens in North Wales are closed, whereas the open portal seems to be fairly common among the less classic sites of South Wales.

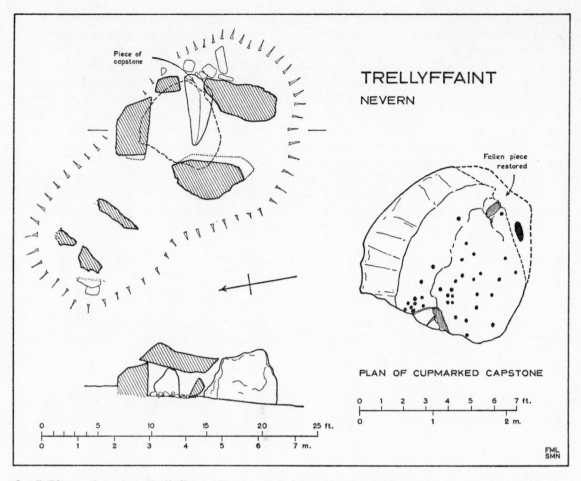

fig. 7 Plan and section: Trellyffaint, Nevern, with enlarged plan of capstone

The field in which the tomb stands has been cultivated for many years and nothing remains of the cairn. The complete absence of surviving cairn is common among Portal Dolmens. This may be due partly to their often low-lying situations, now heavily cultivated, but also to the fact that their cairns were not large in the first place. The portal faces south-east as at Carreg Coitan.

Two miles from Llech y Dribedd is the double-chambered tomb at Trellyffaint (SN/083425) (Grimes, 1936, 139; Daniel, 1950, 198–9, 90, 117).[1] It stands at the southern edge of the high coastal plateau. The site cannot be seen from below but it commands a magnificent view of the valley and of the entire Preselau range, and is visible for some distance to the north.

The monument consists of two megalithic structures set roughly side by side. One is much larger than the other and will be referred to as the main chamber. This main chamber appears to be bigger than Carreg Coitan or Llech y Dribedd because it is built of very thick split boulders, but in fact the area enclosed is not very much larger. Like Llech y Dribedd it is designed around three main stones: the portals and a large back-stone. Another similarity between the two sites is the absence of a closing slab, but at Trellyffaint the extra height of the portal stones is more marked, bringing it closer to the classic design.

The chamber is rectangular and, as in most Portal Dolmens, the side stones play an insig-

[1] Daniel's fig. 27, no. 4 does not show the second chamber.

nificant part. The one that survives on the east is small and does not adequately fill the space, which may originally have been closed with dry-stone walling. At present this gap is filled by a piece which has fallen from the capstone and now lies across the chamber.[1]

The capstone is relatively small and covers only the chamber area. Though it must have rested on the back of both portal stones it does not span the portal area. It is likely, therefore, that the monument originally had two capstones, an arrangement which can be seen on several Portal Dolmens, notably Knockeen, Co. Waterford. Carnedd Hengwm South and Hendre Waelod in North Wales were originally roofed in this way (Lynch, 1969, 138, 141). The missing front capstone would have lain like a lintel over the front of the portal stones, and would have rested at the back on top of the second capstone.

A remarkable feature of the surviving capstone is that its upper surface is covered with 35 cupmarks, each about 5 cms (2 in.) across, with one elongated hollow 25 cms (10 in.) long (on the fallen piece). There is no satisfactory explanation for these carvings. Cupmarks, frequently surrounded by rings, are normally found on living rock and traditionally assigned to the Bronze Age. Examples of this art style, however, have recently been found at Newgrange, Co. Meath, a Passage Grave with a conventional date of 2500 BC, so it is likely that its origin goes well back into the Neolithic (O'Kelly, 1964; 1969). Simple cupmarks are in several cases associated with Portal Dolmens; for instance Ballyrenan, Co. Tyrone (Davies, 1937, 89–100) and Bachwen (CRN 7) (Barnwell, 1867, 153), where, as here, they are on the capstone, and Cist Cerrig (CRN 10), where they are on a slab of living rock close to the tomb (Hemp, 1938, 141). There is a large tilted slab in a field at Trefaes, near Moylgrove, which has its upper surface covered with cupmarks (Grimes, 1929–31, 277). This might well have been the capstone of another Portal Dolmen and increases the possible additional sites in this Nevern/Moylgrove area to three.

Only three stones of the second chamber are visible. They are all rather slight, but rise to about the same height as the back-stone. The chamber must have been rectangular and seems to be entirely separate from the large one. The main chamber faces slightly west of south, looking out over the valley towards the mountains; the smaller one may have opened to the south-west. Both chambers must have been covered by the same cairn, the basal layers of which survive around the stones. This monument, however, like the others, is in agricultural land; the present shape of this raised area is thus no guide to the original extent or plan of the cairn.

Trellyffaint is an example of a recognisable Portal Dolmen with a subsidiary chamber without distinctive features. The building of multiple-chambered sites, or the addition of chambers to existing monuments, is a practice common to several tomb-building traditions. In the north of Ireland among the Court Cairns it is normal for the distinction between the main and subsidiary chambers to be obvious, from both size and position. In the Cotswold–Severn tradition the distinctive shape of the cairn usually gives cohesion to the plan of the chambers. Multiple-chambered sites, therefore, in which rectangular chambers of similar size are scattered somewhat haphazardly beneath a single cairn of variable shape, do not seem to belong to either of these traditions.

Portal Dolmens with more than one chamber are not very common, but they do occur in most areas where the more classic types are to be found. These may be the result of later addition as at Dyffryn Ardudwy (MER 3) (Powell, 1963) or may have been planned as one unit. In either case a frequent arrangement is to have the chambers set in a rough line in the centre of the cairn, sometimes facing in different directions.[2] When the cairn has been removed this can lead to an apparently confused plan. This is not to say that every site with small scattered chambers belongs indisputably to the Portal Dolmen tradition; Mid Gleniron I has shown that this is not so (Corcoran, 1962–3). But it does suggest that within a Portal Dolmen area such as the Nevern Valley it would not be surprising to find such sites.

[1] This is not a fallen supporter, as suggested by Daniel (1950, 199).
[2] For instance, Malin More, Co. Donegal, and other sites listed by de Valéra (1960, 135–6).

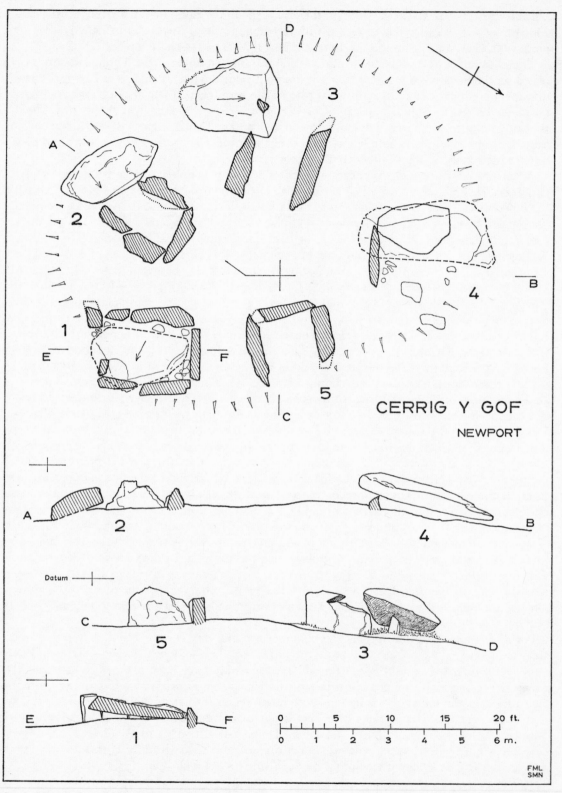

CERRIG Y GOF

NEWPORT

fig. 8 Plan and sections: Cerrig y Gof, Newport

Trellyffaint has clear Portal Dolmen affinities; Cerrig y Gof must be classified with far less certainty (Grimes, 1936, 132, 135; fig. 29; Daniel, 1950, 92, fig. 28; 141, 153–4, 199). The site is well known, lying very close to the main A487 road two miles west of Newport (SN/ 036389). It stands on gently sloping land between two small streams which converge and reach the sea at a narrow inlet about half a mile below the monument.

The site consists of five rectangular chambers set in a roughly radial arrangement. All the chambers are similar in size and each is approximately comparable in area to Carreg Coitan or Llech y Dribedd, but they are lower and have no high portal stones; nor would the flat capstones (mostly displaced) have given any extra emphasis to the entrances.

Only Chamber 1 appears to be complete. It is strictly rectangular, 2·5 m. by 1·5 m. (8 ft 2 in. by 4 ft 11 in.), with a single back-stone and four side stones. The back pair are larger than the front ones, a pattern which may have been repeated in the other chambers, for it is seen again in Chamber 2. The front of the chamber is open, but narrowed by two entrance stones set at right angles to its axis. The western one is slightly taller than the other orthostats and would have given an upward slope to the capstone, but it must be admitted that this is a very feeble echo of the classic, bold Portal Dolmen architecture.

Chamber 2 is relatively well preserved, but the capstone has been pulled off from the front; this suggests that the entrance area has been badly damaged and that some stones may have been removed. Chamber 3 has lost its back-stone. A small stone survives in the front here; it may be only a stump, but it is not obviously broken. Chamber 4 has collapsed to the west and the entire eastern side has gone. It may also have lost its entrance stones since the capstone is much longer than the surviving side stone. Chamber 5 has no capstone and the front may also have been destroyed, for the remaining stones look very much as if they had been saved from destruction by the presence of Chamber 1.

A good deal of cairn material survives between the chambers and just in front of them. The area is now approximately round, but this should not be taken as a guide to its original shape since it is almost certainly due to agricultural activity. Richard Fenton did a good deal of digging in and around the chambers at the beginning of the last century and found pottery, bones, charcoal and pebbles, none of which has survived (Fenton, 1811, 554–5).

Cerrig y Gof is a very good example of a multiple-chambered site without a main chamber; all the components are the same size, they face in all directions and they are set very close together. There is no room between them for individual cairns, so it is probable that they were all built at once. The radial arrangement is striking and is reminiscent of the circular site on Mull Hill in the Isle of Man. This site has double rectangular chambers approached by a single passage or porch, producing a T-shaped unit; six of these chambers are set on the circumference of a large circle (Piggott, 1932, 147; fig. 1). The monument has produced a well-known group of shouldered bowls which would be appropriate in the context of either a Portal Dolmen or a Court Cairn (Piggott, 1932, 146–7). The structure should probably be assigned to this same general context in spite of its passage-like entrances, although in fact the comparison with Cerrig y Gof is not especially close.[1]

Cerrig y Gof is a much less carefully organised monument, a haphazard agglomeration of chambers which must be the local answer to the need for more burial space within a tradition of single-compartment monuments, a trend which may be seen emerging at Trellyffaint. Cerrig y Gof may perhaps be more aptly (though unhelpfully) compared to the anomalous monument at Aghnaskeagh B, Co. Louth, which is only a few metres away from a good Portal Dolmen, Aghnaskeagh A (Evans, 1938, 1–8; de Valéra, 1960, pl. xxx, no. 27).

The site at Mountain, Mynachlog Ddu (SN/166328) is so ruined that nothing can be said about it beyond remarking on the size of the fallen supporters (Grimes, 1936, 139; Daniel,

Already stated by Grimes (1936, 132), though the analogy continues to be mentioned.

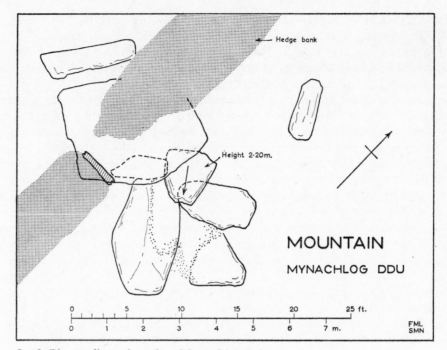

Hedge bank

Height 2·20m.

MOUNTAIN

MYNACHLOG DDU

0   5   10   15   20   25 ft.
0   1   2   3   4   5   6   7 m.

FML
SMN

fig. 9 Plan: collapsed tomb at Mynachlog Ddu

1950, 199). One of these is over 3 m. (9 ft 10 in.) long and three others are more than 2 m. (6 ft 6 in.); the tomb of which they formed a part must once have been very impressive. Such a size would be appropriate to a Portal Dolmen, but it is impossible to attempt any kind of reconstruction.

The site is on the saddle of a pass through the Preselau mountains. This is not the route taken by the modern road, but it was clearly used by prehistoric man, since it runs beneath the source of the Stonehenge Bluestones, and there are barrows, standing stones and stone circles in the valley.

Another tomb whose position may be dictated by a pass through the mountains is Bedd yr Afanc at Bryn Berian (SN/109346) (Grimes, 1936, 128, 130; fig. 2; Daniel, 1950, 90; fig. 27; 141, 203). This has a peculiar setting since it is built on a low island in an extensive area of raised bog. It is also a very peculiar tomb: a narrow, low gallery without apparent internal divisions. It appears to be a type unique in these islands and is certainly not a Portal Dolmen. It is therefore outside the main traditions of the valley and is very difficult to explain historically. It is hoped that the full publication of Professor Grimes's excavation may solve some of the problems associated with it (Grimes, 1939, 258).

The density of even those Portal Dolmens that survive in the Nevern area and the rather isolated position of the valley give this group the aspect of a concentration, but it is perhaps interesting to note that this pattern of distribution is not unique. In two areas of roughly comparable size, Ardudwy and the Conway Valley, where the historical situation was probably very similar to that in north Pembrokeshire, the number of surviving tombs is very much the same: six in the former, four in the latter. This similarity is interesting; perhaps in time it may be possible to interpret the distribution of tombs more clearly in terms of settlement and social grouping. A fairly standard area might emerge, which, it might be argued, could support a given number of people or family groups all served by (or serving) the one tomb. Possibly this goal may never be reached, but it is in such geographically restricted areas with a single dominant cultural tradition that a start might be made.

BIBLIOGRAPHY

Barnwell, E. L., 1867. 'Marked stones in Wales', *Archaeol. Cambrensis*, 3rd Ser. XIII, 150–6.

Collins, A. E. P., 1954. 'Excavation of a Double Horned Cairn at Audleystown, Co. Down', *Ulster J. Archaeol.*, XVII, 7–56.

—— 1965. 'Ballykeel Dolmen and Cairn, Co. Armagh.' *Ulster J. Archaeol.*, XXVIII, 47–70.

Collins, A. E. P. & Wilson, B. C. S., 1964. 'The excavation of a Court Cairn at Ballymacdermot, Co. Armagh', *Ulster J. Archaeol.*, XXVII, 2–22.

Corcoran, J. X. W. P., 1962–3. 'Excavation of a chambered cairn at Mid Gleniron Farm, Wigtownshire', *Trans. Dumfriesshire Galloway Natur. Hist. Antiq. Soc.*, XLI, 99–110.

—— 1964–6. 'Excavation of three chambered cairns at Loch Calder, Caithness', *Proc. Soc. Antiq. Scot.*, XCVIII, 1–34.

—— 1969. 'Chambered cairns of the Carlingford Culture, an enquiry into origins', Prepared for the third Atlantic Symposium, Arhus, May 1969.

Daniel, G. E., 1950. *The Prehistoric Chamber Tombs of England and Wales.* Cambridge.

Davies, O., 1937. 'Excavations at Ballyrenan, Co. Tyrone', *J. Roy. Soc. Antiq. Ireland*, LXXVII, 89–100.

de Valéra, R., 1960. 'The Court Cairns of Ireland', *Proc. Roy. Irish Acad.*, 60 (C), 9–140.

de Valéra, R. & Ó Nualláin, S., 1961. *Survey of the Megalithic Tombs of Ireland. Vol. I, Co. Clare.* Dublin.

Co. Down, 1966. *An Archaeological Survey of Co. Down.* N. Ireland Ministry of Finance.

Evans, E. E., 1938. 'Excavations at Aghnaskeagh, Co. Louth, Cairn B', *County Louth Archaeol. J.*, IX, 1–18.

—— 1966. *Prehistoric and Early Christian Ireland: A Guide.* London.

Evans, E. E. & Watson, E., 1942. 'The "Stone Houses", Ticloy, Co. Antrim', *Ulster J. Archaeol.*, V, 62–5.

Fenton, R., 1811. *Historical Tour through Pembrokeshire.* (1811 ed.)

Grimes, W. F., 1929–31. 'Pembrokeshire Survey', *Bull. Board Celtic Stud.* V, 277.

—— 1936. 'The Megalithic Monuments of Wales', *Proc. Prehist. Soc.*, II, 106–39.

—— 1939. 'Notes on Excavations'. *Proc. Prehist. Soc.*, V, 258.

—— 1949. 'Pentre Ifan Burial Chamber, Pembrokeshire', *Archaeol. Cambrensis*, C, 3–23.

Hemp, W. J., 1938. 'Cup-markings at Treflys, Caernarvonshire', *Archaeol. Cambrensis*, XCIII, 140–1.

Herity, M., 1964. 'The finds from the Irish Portal Dolmens', *J. Roy. Soc. Antiq. Ireland*, XCIV, 123–44.

Lynch, F. M., 1969. 'The Megalithic Tombs of North Wales', in T. G. E. Powell *et al.*, 1969, 107–48.

MacKie, E. W., 1963–4. 'New excavations on the Monamore Neolithic chambered cairn, Lamlash, Isle of Arran, in 1961', *Proc. Soc. Antiq. Scot.*, XCVII, 1–34.

O'Kelly, M. J., 1964. 'Newgrange, Co. Meath', *Antiquity*, XXXVIII, 288–90.

—— 1969. 'Radiocarbon dates for the Newgrange Passage Grave, Co. Meath', *Antiquity*, XLIII, 140–1.

Piggott, S., 1932. 'The Mull Hill Circle, Isle of Man, and its pottery', *Antiq. J.*, XII, 146–57.

Powell, T. G. E., 1963. 'The chambered cairn at Dyffryn Ardudwy', *Antiquity*, XXXVII, 19–24.

Powell, T. G. E., *et al.*, 1969. *Megalithic Enquiries in the West of Britain.* Liverpool.

RCAM, 1925. *An Inventory of the Ancient Monuments in Wales and Monmouthshire. VII. County of Pembroke.* Royal Commission on the Ancient and Historical Monuments in Wales and Monmouthshire. HMSO, 1925.

Scott, J. G., 1969. 'The Clyde Cairns of Scotland', in T. G. E. Powell *et al.*, 1969, 175–222.

Waterman, D. M., 1965. 'The Court Cairn at Annaghmare, Co. Armagh', *Ulster J. Archaeol.*, XXVIII, 3–46.

Williams, A., 1953. 'Clegyr Boia, St. David's, Pembs. Excavations in 1943', *Archaeol. Cambrensis*, CII, 20–47.

ACKNOWLEDGEMENTS

I am very grateful to Miss Susan Nicholson, MA, who surveyed these Pembrokeshire sites with me and cheerfully put up with some rather unpleasant weather. I am also grateful to Professor W. F. Grimes for discussing the problems of Pentre Ifan with me and for reading this article in typescript.

The Large Stone Axes Ascribed to North-West Pembrokeshire

F. W. Shotton

There have been sent to me from time to time, and mainly from the National Museum of Wales, a number of extremely large axes. They are very simple in form, with round-oval cross section and, with one exception (NMW 51.289), quite sharply pointed at the butt. They are usually completely smoothed, without traces of chipping or pecking scars, and above all are characterised by their massive character. The smallest I have seen has a length of 19·0 cms (7·5 in.), the largest complete one is 27·3 cms (10·75 in.) long, and an incomplete one may be estimated as originally 30 cms (11·8 in.) in length. Most of them are illustrated in fig. 1 and a schedule is given at the end of the paper.

At this point, it is necessary to state only that they are all fabricated from igneous rock, most of them being quartz-dolerite (or quartz-gabbro if coarseness of grain size is taken into consideration), but several are of more acid rock which may be called graphic granodiorite. I shall be discussing the petrological variation later.

Altogether about 16 of these axes are known to me, and their distribution is significant (fig. 2). Apart from two fragments from Dinedor Hill, Herefordshire, their occurrence seems to be entirely Welsh, though it is possible that some of the specimens referred to as 'quartz-gabbro' or 'quartz-dolerite' in the 4th report of the S.W. Group might prove to belong to Pembrokeshire (Evens et al., 1962). This is more likely because Group XIII, from the Preselau Hills, certainly occurs in the south-west, and No. 534 from Winchester, illustrated on fig. 7 of Stone & Wallis (1951), is in its form and great size (26 cms [10·25 in.]) exactly like the large axes now under discussion. In the Midlands two much smaller axes (Hardingstone, Northants. and Wa 6/c, Quinton, Meon Hill, S. Warwicks.) could be referred to XXIIIa and ?XXIIIa/b respectively, but I am reluctant to do this since similar rocks are known in North Wales.

It should be emphasised to the non-petrologist, however, that the term 'quartz-dolerite' can cover a widely ranging series of rock types, including, of course, Group XVIII, the Whin Sill, with which there is no possibility of confusing the rocks I am now describing. The largest number of large axe specimens, five, comes from Glamorgan, probably because of the high level of industrialisation, quarrying and ground disturbance, but they clearly do not originate in that county, which lacks igneous intrusions. I am convinced that they come from Pembrokeshire.

In the Cambrian and Lower Ordovician rocks of N.W. Pembrokeshire there are many sill-like intrusions which have in part been well described and located, though there are gaps in our knowledge. Fig. 3, which is certainly incomplete, particularly at the west end of the Preselau

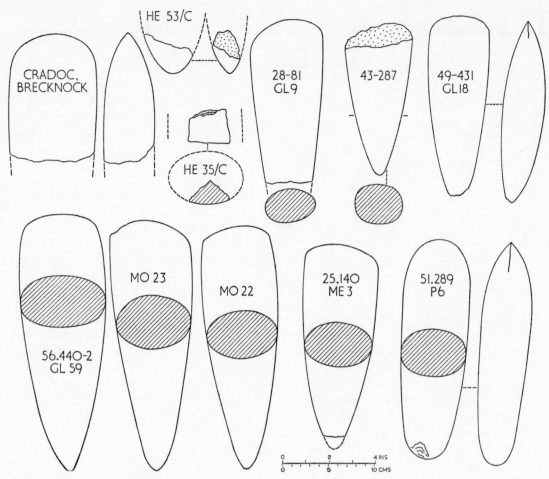

fig. 1 Axes of Group XXIII

Hills, purports to show the distribution of these rocks following the work of Pringle (1930), Cox, Green, Jones & Pringle (1930), Evans – now Lord Energlyn – (1945), Pringle & George (1948), Roach (1969), and Bates, Bromley & Jones (1969). These intrusions frequently result in high land with crags ('Carns') and from Carn Meini at the east end of the Preselau Hills originated the implements of 'spotted dolerite' or Preselite (Group XIII). This rock is not to be confused with the new group which I am now defining, but neither is the rock around Carn Meini exclusively spotted dolerite. It is therefore possible that this Carn could also have provided quartz-dolerite for some of the large axes.

These sill intrusions show considerable variation, even within one body, as has been shown conclusively by Roach (1969) in the case of the St David's Head and Carn Llidi sills. The most basic rock is an olivine gabbro, but this is rare and the overwhelmingly dominant type is a quartz-gabbro (or the 'quartz-dolerite' of most authors) which in itself, however, shows variations. By increase of silica content the rock passes into a pyroxene-granodiorite which is typical of the intrusions around the city of St David's. Lord Energlyn has also pointed out to me that at Carn Ingli, south of Newport, there is a range of type from granodiorite to normal quartz-dolerite in the one mass.

I am greatly indebted to Lord Energlyn for giving me the benefit of his personal knowledge of these intrusions. In some cases he has been able to suggest the Carn from which the raw

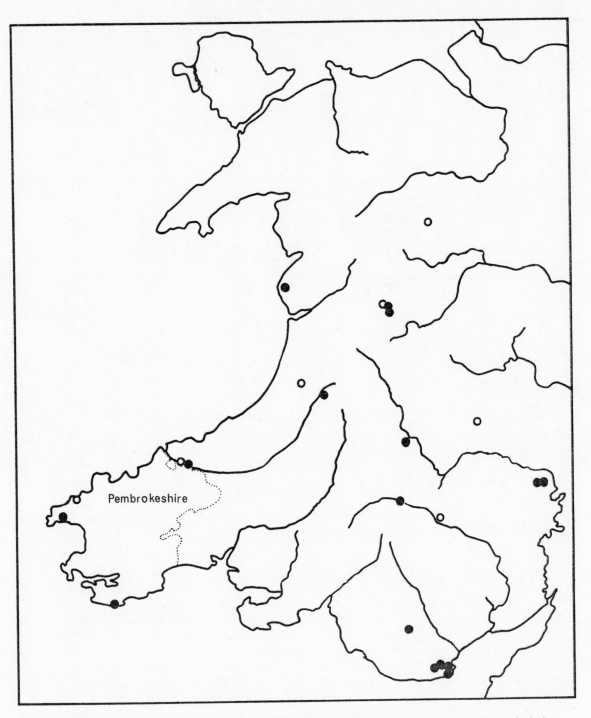

fig. 2 Distribution of Group XXIII axes (black spots) and perforated implements (open circles)

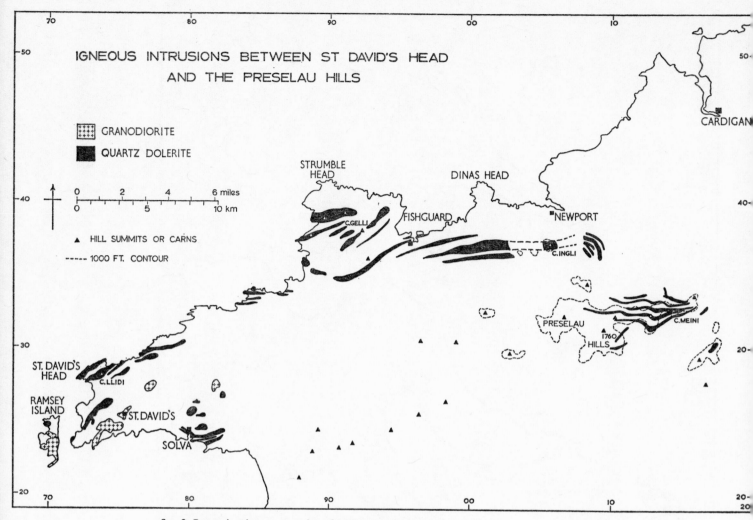

fig. 3 Intrusive igneous rocks of N.W. Pembrokeshire

material came – Carno (Mo 22) from Carn Ingli, Clegyr Boia (NMW 43.287) from Carn Llidi, and Dinas Powis (NMW 28.81) from Carn Meini or Moel Trigarn. In addition, he relates to Solva the axe-hammer from Teifi Side (NMW 47.164/131) which I list in a small schedule of perforated implements (Table 2), all of which may have come from the same source, even if they were not of the same date.

This assemblage of large axes is clearly entitled to be separated as a group; but it is not, in my opinion, a clearly-defined factory group nor yet an exact petrological group. In the petrological descriptions which follow I have described two types: XXIII a, a typical granodiorite, and XXIII b, a typical quartz-dolerite; but transitional types must be expected.

As for factory site or sites, Lord Energlyn has already expressed the view that three or four carns were involved, and I visualise that any carn which was made of suitable igneous rock and gave blocks on its screes of a foot or more in length was a potential source for an axe. Probably the spotted dolerite, Group XIII, of Carn Meini was used at the same time. On at least one specimen, from St Cyres, Penarth (NMW 56.440/2), polishing had not removed peck-marks. One would expect that in a coarse igneous rock, roughing-out would be done by pecking rather than by flaking. In such cases, the possibility of finding a working floor is remote.

A few perforated artefacts have also been found. These are not likely to be as old as the big axes, but are apparently of the same petrological type suggesting that exploitation of these rocks continued on a small scale into the Bronze Age or later. This is very probable since we know that Group XIII continued to be so used (Evens *et al.*, 1962), and I do not think that Preselite was regarded in any way differently from Groups XXIII a or b, with which it is mingled. These additional artefacts are listed in Table 2 (Schedule), and their distribution is shown on fig. 2. It will be noted that this distribution is much the same as that of the large axes, and is still essentially Welsh, though the perforated hammerstone from Llanrhaiadr ym Mochnant is sufficiently far north to raise the question of whether it derives from North Wales.

PETROLOGICAL DESCRIPTION

I have already stated that Group XXIII cannot be closely defined because there are transitional types between the two extremes of granodiorite and quartz-dolerite. What I propose to do is to describe the rock of the axe from Cradoc, Breconshire, as a typical example of the granodiorite (XXIII a), and that of the axe from St Cyres, Penarth (Gl 59), as an average quartz-dolerite. It is to be expected, and it will accord with the varied nature of the Pembrokeshire intrusions, that some axes will correctly be referred to XXIIIa/b.

The position of Group XIII presents some problems. The number was given to the 'spotted dolerite' of the Stonehenge Bluestones, and of a number of artefacts originating from Carn Meini in the east Preselau Hills. The light-coloured spots, which may be up to an inch in size, are due to crystal aggregates of oligoclase-albite feldspar, and the rock seems to be a variant restricted to Carn Meini and Cerrig Marchogion and easily recognised in large pieces by its spotted appearance. A thin petrological section and even a small tool may fail to show one of these spots. The rock, however, does contain a little (often very little indeed) interstitial quartz and, because of its main minerals, may therefore also be described as a quartz-dolerite even though it differs from the type XXIII b. It will be noted that in the Schedule below (Table 2) I list a small axe-hammer from Llanrhian (Pembs.) as XXIII b, though this one is described by Grimes (1951) as Preselite (XIII)—presumably then by visual inspection. This fact merely emphasises the impression that XIII, XXIIIa and XXIIIb, and all transitions between them, are really one group emanating from many different carns in Pembrokeshire, and perhaps they should all be considered together when dealing with the question of artefact dispersal. But since we must, for good historical reasons, retain XIII for the spotted dolerite and for that only, it becomes necessary to use a new number for the axes I have been discussing.

Group XXIIIa. Graphic Pyroxene Granodiorite

Coarse textured. *Feldspar* major constituent, considerably altered to micaceous products and zoisite/epidote. Little twinned, probably an acid plagioclase. *Clinopyroxene* important, ophitic, often altered marginally and sometimes largely to pale green hornblende. *Orthopyroxene* present but less than clinopyroxene, euhedral to ophitic, mainly unaltered. *Hornblende*, pale brown and probably original, in subordinate amounts. *Quartz* intersertal, frequently graphically intergrown with feldspar, irregularly distributed but 10–15%. *Iron ore* about 5%, magnetite or magnetite-ilmenite intergrowths with the ilmenite altered to leucoxene. *Apatite* is a minor constituent.

Group XXIIIb. Quartz-dolerite

Medium coarse texture, finer than granodiorite. *Feldspar* important, much altered to micaceous and zoisitic products, about andesine in composition. *Clinopyroxene* important, sub-ophitic, faintly pleochroic, altered marginally to pale hornblende. *Orthopyroxene* less important. *Quartz* less abundant than in XXIIIa, typically 5–10%, intersertal and sometimes in graphic intergrowth with feldspar. *Iron ore* frequent, magnetite or magnetite-ilmenite intergrowths, the ilmenite altered to leucoxene. *Apatite* as an accessory.

TABLE 1 SCHEDULE OF AXES

Type	Locality	National Grid Reference	Collection	Petrological Group	Remarks
Blunt-butted large axe	St Gowans Head, Pembs.	SR/9792	NMW 51.289	XXIII a	P.6
Butt half of large axe	Clegyr Boia, St. David's, Pembs.	SM/737251	NMW 43.287	XXIII b	Grimes (1951) No. 123 P.4
Large axe, butt missing	St Andrews Quarry, Dinas Powis, Glam.	ST/142714	NMW 28.81	XXIII b	*ibid.* No. 82: Gl 9
Large axe	St Andrews Quarry, Dinas Powis, Glam.	ST/1471	NMW 49.431	XXIII b	*Bull. B. Celt. Stud.* XIII, 245: Gl 18
Very large axe	St Cyres, Penarth, Glam.	ST/1871	NMW 56.440/2	XXIII b	Gl 59
Large axe	Talygarn, Llantrisant, Glam.	ST/027802	NMW 26.385	XXIII b	Grimes (1951) No. 81
Large axe	Lavernoch Road, Penarth, Glam.	ST/1869	Private	XXIII a	
Large axe	Teifi Side, Cards.	SN/2344	NMW 47.164/139	XXIII b	Grimes (1951) No. 354
Slender large cylindrical axe	Bwylch-y-ddwyallt, Pontrhydfendigaid, Cards.	SN/7063	NMW 47.164/101	XXIII b	*ibid.* No. 78
Blade half of large axe	Pennant Farm, Cradoc, Brecons.	SO/0130	NMW	XXIII b	
Large axe	Outskirts of Builth Wells, Brecons.	SO/0450	Private	XXIII a	Br 10
Very large axe	Tyn-yr-ytra, Carno, Mont.	SN/9696	Powysland Mus.	XXIII a/b	Mo 22
Very large axe	Tyn-yr-ytra, Carno, Mont.	SN/9696	Powysland Mus.	XXIII a/b	Mo 23
Large axe	Celmi, Merion.	SH/597047	NMW 25.140	XXIII b	Grimes (1951) No. 77. Me 3
Small fragment	Dinedor Hill, Herefords.	SO/536374	W. Nash, Dinedor	XXIII a	He 35/c
Small fragment butt end	Dinedor Hill, Herefords.	SO/541372	W. Nash, Dinedor	XXIII b	He 53/c

TABLE 2 SCHEDULE OF PERFORATED IMPLEMENTS

Type	Locality	National Grid Reference	Collection	Remarks
Small expanded battle-axe	Cist in the Beacon, Llanrhian, Pembs.	SM/832315	NMW 33.226	Grimes (1951) No. 560: XXIII b
Large crude axe-hammer	Teifi Side, Cards.	SN/2043	NMW 47.164/131	XXIII b
Small flat oval mace-head	Lower Lledrod, Cards.	SN/6673	NMW 47.164/146	Grimes (1951) No. 364: XXIII b
Perforated sub-oval disc.	Bwlch, Brecons.	SO/1422		XXIII b
Half axe-hammer	Kington Churchyard, Herefords.	SO/2956	Hereford Museum	XXIII b. He 1/ah
Coffin-shaped axe-hammer	Carno, Mont.	SN/9696	NMW 15.138-1	Grimes (1951) No. 341: XXIII b
Small perforated hammerstone	R. Iwrch, Llanrhaiadr-ym-Mochnant, Denb.	SJ/1226	Powysland Museum	XXIII b

BIBLIOGRAPHY

Bates, D. E. B., Bromley, A. V., & Jones, A. S. G., 1969. 'The Geology of the Bishops and Clerks Islands, Pembrokeshire', in *The Pre-Cambrian and Lower Palaeozoic Rocks of Wales*, Cardiff, 447–9.

Cox, A. H., Green, J. F. N., Jones, O. T., & Pringle, J., 1930. 'The Geology of the St. David's District, Pembrokeshire', *Proc. Geol. Assoc.*, XLI, 241–73.

Evans, W. D., 1945. 'The Geology of the Prescelly Hills, North Pembrokeshire', *Quart. J. Geol. Soc.*, CI, 89–107.

Evens, E. D., Grinsell, L. V., Piggott, S., & Wallis, F. S., 1962. 'Fourth Report of the Sub-Committee of the South-Western Group of Museums on the Petrological Identification of Stone Axes', *Proc. Prehist. Soc.*, XXVIII, 209–66.

Grimes, W. F., 1951. *The Prehistory of Wales*. Cardiff.

Pringle, J., 1930. 'The Geology of Ramsey Island (Pembrokeshire)', *Proc. Geol. Assoc.*, XLI, 1–37.

Pringle, J. & George, T. N., 1948. *British Regional Geology: South Wales*. H.M.S.O., London.

Roach, R. A., 1969. 'The Composite Nature of the St. David's Head and Carn Llidi intrusions of North Pembrokeshire', in *The Pre-Cambrian and Lower Palaeozoic Rocks of Wales*, Cardiff, 409–30.

Stone, J. F. S. & Wallis, F. S., 1951. 'Third Report of the Sub-Committee of the South-Western Group of Museums on the Petrological Identification of Stone Axes', *Proc. Prehist. Soc.*, XVII, 99–158.

The Problem of Iberian Affinities in Prehistoric Archaeology around the Irish Sea

T. G. E. Powell

The theme of this offering, laid before Miss Chitty with all affection and recognition, springs from a study of her own published in 1935. On that occasion she described, and proposed comparisons for, a fragmentary segmented bone object that had been found in a cremation cist-grave, with a Food Vessel and two flint implements, at Corrandrum, Co. Galway, in the west of Ireland (Chitty, 1934–5). For clarity of exposition, and impartial evaluation of the evidence as it then existed, Miss Chitty's paper reads as freshly today as it did more than three decades past. It is a measure of her work, and of her desire to share with others her harvest of accurate documentation, that younger generations now rise up to acknowledge their indebtedness not only for the printed word, but for her personal interest and encouragement. In the pages that follow, an attempt is made to survey the present situation regarding a number of matters that thirty years ago seemed, naturally enough, to be of fairly simple explanation in terms of direct relationship between the Iberian Peninsula and lands bordering the Irish Sea. There is no present need to trace to individual pioneers the first precise enunciation of hypotheses that led by the mid-thirties to a general attitude of mind in which the Peninsula played a dominant role in the formation of the Neolithic and Bronze Ages of Britain and Ireland. A bibliographical list of all the formative publications has been brought together (Daniel, 1958, 133–4), and this topic will doubtless yet be pursued by historians of the growth of archaeological ideas. It may be said at the outset that there has been a considerable shift of interpretation from Peninsular origins for aspects of material culture in Ireland and Britain to one in which both zones have more often drawn on common sources. General explanations of this kind must be reviewed, and have largely to do with greatly expanded concepts of the pattern of European prehistory. There remain, nevertheless, some few tangible pieces of evidence to support some kind of direct connection up and down the 'Atlantic Seaways', and these still deserve close scrutiny.

It will be well to begin with the 'Atlantic Seaways', and to be reminded that the general hypothesis for the spread of Neolithic economy throughout the western maritime provinces of Europe had involved a coastwise, if not altogether seaborne, opening up of lands from south to north. The impetus was accounted as West Mediterranean, if not in part African, and the frail remains of pioneer struggles by southerners in bleak and storm-tossed northern regions were more than offset by evidence of their elaborate concern for, and expenditure of energy on, the housing of the dead: megalithic tombs and kindred structures.

It had not yet become possible to distinguish between the characteristics of the oldest Neo-lithic settlement pattern throughout the western Mediterranean coastlands, today for the most part associated with Impressed Ware, and others, later in time and more diversified, with which megalithic and other built tombs could be connected. With a deeper appreciation of the role of environmental factors in determining the essentials of such lowly economies as that of the West Mediterranean Impressed Ware peoples, it has become ever more urgent to question whether they possessed either capability or need for such adjustments of life as would have led them into more northerly habitats. The conservatism of their pottery styles, and other durable equipment, spread over great distances and periods of time, would appear to reflect an attitude that was content with 'a cave-mouth in the sun', and a lowly husbandry of primitive cereals and ovicaprids. Donald F. Brown has given the best overall view to date (Brown, 1965), and there is a convenient summary and map of Impressed Ware by Piggott (1965, 57, & fig. 26), while Savory (1968) illustrates the wealth of available material in Spain and Portugal with reference to many select studies.

It would appear that the lands at the western extremity of the Mediterranean provided an ample fastness for archaic forms of livelihood in contrast to the situation in the northern Balkan region where outward-looking communities of the Starčevo-Körös Culture undertook the challenges of high forest, and winter snow, in the damper climate of the Danubian plain. The trend of archaeological evidence in recent years has moved substantially to support a view that the real initiators of Neolithic settlement in north-western Europe sprang mainly from mid-continental and south-eastern ancestors whose activities are traced in the Vinča-Lengyel complex and in its outliers. These people adjusted to temperate forest and lakeland habitats, across the northern skirtlands of the Alps and into France, as well as over the North European plain to the shores of the North Sea and the Baltic. In all this, there was provided a wider and more gradual environment, with more adequately equipped economies and cultures, to effect the earliest practice of farming in Britain and Ireland.

A number of studies brought together by van der Waals (ed. 1966/7) bear on this matter, and aspects of west-central, rather than south-western, origins for the Neolithic in the British Isles have been discussed by Powell (Powell *et al.*, 1969), and others in greater detail by Case (1969). From this standpoint it is no far step to a position where further dread questions must be faced. First, there is the question as to how many, if not possibly all, post-Impressed Ware Neolithic cultures in the Peninsula may not have been introduced from beyond the eastern end of the Pyrenees. Secondly, there is the question of who first found it worth-while to venture on the swell of the Atlantic Ocean, and whether the initiative may not have been undertaken by northerners rather than by southerners. Before attempting to sketch the nature of these problems it must be emphasised that there exist as yet no binding chronological conditions, neither in a sufficiency of adequately verified radiocarbon dates from the Peninsula, nor from correlations in exact archaeological comparisons, that forbid the possibility of examining in reverse every question to do with an early use of the 'Atlantic Seaways'. Such a stance in opposition to long accepted views is, indeed, further prompted by the body of radiocarbon dates for Neolithic farming enterprise, timber and stone tomb building, and early metallurgy *vis-à-vis* mid-continental developments. The troubled question as to which centuries are betokened in a calendrical sense is not relevant to the actual processes involved. The whole relative scheme for prehistoric Europe, in terms of interrelated farming and metal working population-groups, must move up or down the actual time-scale in one body.

The first question may now be taken up by pointing, in the writer's opinion, to one concrete example of an intrusive culture which had been carried around, or across, the Gulf of Lions, to develop its own regional characteristics in Catalonia. This was the Fossa Grave Culture (*Cultura de los sepulcros de fosa*) now admirably documented by Ana María Muñoz (1965). This culture seems best accounted for in terms of the outer periphery of the Vinča-Lengyel circle by means of connections across northern Italy, and sharing with the Chasséen of southern France some common elements (Brown, 1965, 326–8; Powell *et al.*, 1969, 257, with further references). Savory (1968, 83) prefers, however, to view the Catalonian Fossa Graves as derivative from within the Peninsula, and to see an extension of influence towards Italy. It is of no little interest that it was a leading Spanish archaeologist, Martín Almagro, who in 1961 first enunciated the case for Balkan-Danubian origins for the Neolithic cultures of the Peninsula, following after Impressed Ware, and this proposition would certainly reconcile many problems to do with Peninsular plain wares, including Almerian, and the related but independent styles of Portugal. Not only did the Fossa Grave Culture intrude, but so did elements recognised elsewhere as Chasséen and Lagozza, and these seem likely to signal populations which, reaching the sea, turned to building megalithic tombs – a response that was similarly met all along the 'Atlantic Façade', that highly perceptive concept put forward by Giot (1963, 3). At this point it is profitable to look ahead to the recurrent pattern of incomings in later times to the Peninsula and, excluding for the moment the question of Bell Beaker origins, to be reminded of the path of Urnfield and Hallstatt wanderings, and those of Teutonic invaders, Vandals, Goths, and others, in post-Roman times. In antiquity, the Peninsula could always absorb newcomers. There was no reverse pattern of overflow.

Leaving in fair doubt the likelihood that Peninsular Neolithic communities ever had reason to expand northwards, the second question, about navigation on the Atlantic, may now be outlined. A long-standing assumption has been that, following the gifts of Neolithic economy and skills in tomb-building, knowledge of metallurgy was also borne along the western seaways from south to north. On recent evidence, there appears to be much less to show for similarity, either in ores or products, between Peninsular metallurgy and that of Ireland and Britain, than between the latter group and mid-continental groups (Coghlan & Case, 1957; Case, 1967). Present evidence is of course strongest for regarding the earliest Irish and British copper artefacts as work of men of Rhineland Beaker Culture associations, but even if an earlier phase should prove distinguishable, is it not surprising that the insular industry should have shown such continued vitality while that in the Peninsula should have remained so conservative in perpetuation of archaic tools and weapons? This factor should be given some consideration in future deliberations on the problem of the origins of Peninsular metallurgy. If it was a spontaneous invention (Renfrew, 1967), might not more have been expected of its growth? If, on the other hand, it was an exotic introduction, among a largely unreceptive populace, its inert characteristics would be but part of that unfulfilment of endeavour seen at Los Millares and other incipient urban projects.

If there were at first no northward sea voyages, that does not mean that no opportunities opened up in one direction or another along the face of Giot's *façade atlantique* at a time when the north-western islands had become well-settled by farming, and perhaps metal-using, communities. It seems in fact that Neolithic peoples around the coastlands of north-western Europe had more probably need to develop ocean-going craft than those attached to the greater land-mass of the Peninsula. In a recent valuable study, examining restrictions that would have been imposed on intending Neolithic migrants wishing to cross only the narrow seas between the Continent and southern Britain, Case (1969) has shown how unlikely was the involvement of heavy timber-built boats, not only for constructional reasons, but for the economics of launching, crewing, and loading. Case has pointed to the advantages of skin-covered boats for ferrying families, food, and young livestock, apart from the whole environmental and cultural appositeness for their development in northern waters. P. Johnstone (1964) has done much to clarify issues for archaeologists in thinking about early western navigation, drawing attention to the evidence for large skin-covered boats and, perhaps most impressively, to a capacious sea-going Irish boat of a type that was still in use in the seventeenth century AD (Johnstone, 1964, pl. XLVIIa). It is of great interest that O. L. Filgueiras has drawn attention to traces of a meeting of northern and southern, skin and timber, boat-building traditions surviving in northern Portugal, where the skin-covered *pelota* has continued in use on the Douro, while the Galician *masseira* appears to be a light wooden adaptation of a skin prototype (Filgueiras, 1965, esp. 348, n. 14; figs. 2, 3). It may not be relevant to seek precedents, but southward navigation from Norway to Orkney and Shetland in skin boats was evidently undertaken by seafarers at home in the Circumpolar stone-using complex. In turn, may not Irish boatmen, seeking the sun, have first established contact with distant Lusitanian shores? There were surely, then as now, some enticements for not giving up after the initial discovery.

Before leaving the subject of boats, a technical point to do with the launching of timber-built Portuguese vessels of archaic character should perhaps be mentioned. Case (1969) has most recently given overall measurements for length and weight of the *saveiro*, the largest type of flat-bottomed fishing craft propelled with oars, and launched through surf from shelving beaches; also for the *meia lua*, a boat of smaller dimensions, but sharing with the *saveiro* a need for a proportionally large launching party using a timber slipway of some kind. Filgueiras illustrates the use of a timber launching-trolley (*jangada*), at least for the smaller vessels, and it is of interest that tripartite block wheels were employed (Filgueiras, 1965, figs. 4–7). In connection with the invention and practical use of block wheels, Piggott (1968) has stressed the importance of suitable metal tools for making dowels, and this lesson should apply equally to the first appearance of carvel-built boats on the Lusitanian coasts no less than to the provision of tripartite block wheels to assist in their launching, although no case could at present be sustained for simultaneous adoption in the far west. The matter should, however, be worth some exploration in terms of relative chronology, and the spread of advanced techniques in joining timber.

In megalithic architecture, the classification known as 'Passage Grave' is the most consistent, in terms of overall construction and appearance, of all types in western and northern Europe. Apart from some very minor groups of tombs utilising megalithic slabs, Passage Graves are the most predominant form in the Iberian Peninsula, and occur in select areas in great numbers. The position has been most recently summarised by Savory (1968), and the modern foundations of the study were laid by G. and V. Leisner (1943). The Passage Grave classification is based primarily on recognition of a well-defined chamber entered by an equally obvious passage, the whole usually covered by a tumulus that is circular in plan. It is well known that there exists a great range in style of construction, no less than in variation of ground plan of the chamber, and of relative size. Some tombs cannot be truly described as megalithic as they are built entirely of dry masonry with corbelled roofs, others are purely megalithic in construction both of walls and roof, while many incorporate elements of both building techniques on such a scale, and in so expert a manner, that no typological system can be deduced on style of building technique alone. The degree to which over the centuries such prominent monuments in the countryside, from Spain to Scotland and Sweden, have been the object of despoliation is well known. The result has been a great uncertainty as to the true relationship within the chambers of objects, even 'deposits', to the actual period and cultural context of construction. Doubts as to the adequacy of excavation technique, and the validity of interpretation, have further contributed to problems of any true assessment. The question of the origin of Passage Graves is too open and complex to warrant a firm statement at the present time and in a short space, but the interpretation most generally in favour supposes a spread of this tomb type from the Iberian Peninsula by various routes to Armorica and to Ireland, to mention only the two most important areas where Passage Graves occur in the north-west (fig. 1).

For present purposes it may be sufficient to point out that there is no evidence for a shared complex in material culture between the building communities in the major zones of dispersion,

fig. 1 Map of principal sites mentioned

97

and that the most ambitiously constructed tombs, in size and embellishment, diverge most between one group and another. A case would seem to exist for examining the possibility that instead of a highly skilled building technique having been initially spread northwards from the Peninsula, the greatest Passage Graves express, in each far distant zone, the optimum phase of economic prosperity and competence experienced by each building community. O'Kelly (1964; 1968) has inferred the complexity of resources and planning necessary for the building of Newgrange, and the long history of land clearance that made possible the vast provision of turves for use in the tumulus. Radiocarbon dates now published for the construction of the roof of Newgrange, in the order of 2500 BC (O'Kelly, 1969), establish a degree of architectural advancement in Ireland that has not been matched by radiocarbon assays yet available from the Peninsula. This matter, in addition to dates in the closing centuries of the fourth millennium BC for small dry-stone-built tombs, with chamber and passage, in Armorica (L'Helgouach, 1965; Powell *et al.*, 1969), well illustrates the open nature of the question of Passage Grave origins not only in chronological terms, but in geography and in architectural precocity. The question of direct seaborne intercommunication between the Iberian Peninsula and Ireland may be more significant, in terms of Passage Graves, for a phase in which maturity of architectural style, rather than early experiment, was being enjoyed in the groups of north-western Europe.

It would be tempting to take up special items in characteristics of building technique, and to suggest some possible interchanges of practice, given as much as received by the North-West, but space allows mention only of two different and rather more precise matters: stone basins, and mural art. For those who accepted a Peninsular origin for Passage Graves in Ireland, the carved stone block, *pila*, standing in the centre of the chamber of the Dolmen de Matarrubilla, Prov. Seville, has for long been regarded as explanatory of the presence of more rotund stone basins in a number of the Irish tombs. Obermaier's classic study in 1919 of the Dolmen de Matarrubilla was followed in description and discussion by the Leisners (1943, 195–6); and most recently F. Collantes de Terán (1969), in reporting on restoration of the tomb, has listed a few further blocks to those already known from tombs in the south of the Peninsula. When one moves from general comparison to particular analysis, it soon becomes apparent that the southern Peninsular *pila* bears little resemblance to the Irish stone basin. On the one hand is a small series of diversely constructed rectangular blocks with flat upper surfaces, and on the other a more uniform group of blocks or slabs with depressions cut into their upper surfaces, mainly, but not all, producing deep hemispherical basins. The *pila* in the Dolmen de Matarrubilla is an exception, even in its own territory, in that the large rectangular block shows an upper surface that has been cut down to form a trapezoidal depression 8–10 cms deep. The nearest comparison in Ireland known to the writer is the stone basin in Chamber I at Baltinglass, Co. Wicklow (Ó Nualláin, 1968, for consolidated references, and new map of Irish Passage Graves). Here the block is 1·83 m. (6 ft) long, 0·91 m. (3 ft) wide, and 0·61 m. (2 ft) high, figures which happen to compare closely with the dimensions of the Matarrubilla *pila*: 1·71 m. (5 ft 7 in.) long, 1·20 m. (3 ft 11 in.) wide, and 0·50 m. (1 ft 8 in.) high. The depth of the depression at Baltinglass is approximately 15 cms (6 in.), but the whole appearance of the stone basin block is very different from the carefully dressed Peninsular example. Another exceptional *pila* was uncovered in the Dolmen de San Bartolomé de la Torre, Prov. Huelva (Marquez & Leisner, 1952, 42), but this is a cist-like construction, being formed by a floor-stone set against the chamber wall, and with three low vertical slabs set against it to form the other sides. Despite the absence of any such feature in Armorican Passage Graves, it seems reasonable to deduce that somewhat similar ritual needs were felt to be met in certain, but not all, tombs in Andalusia and Ireland, by the use of upstanding blocks with or without depressions. If chronological considerations do not prove to stand in the way, the Irish basins, representing a more consistent phenomenon, might seem to claim priority, but it is beyond the

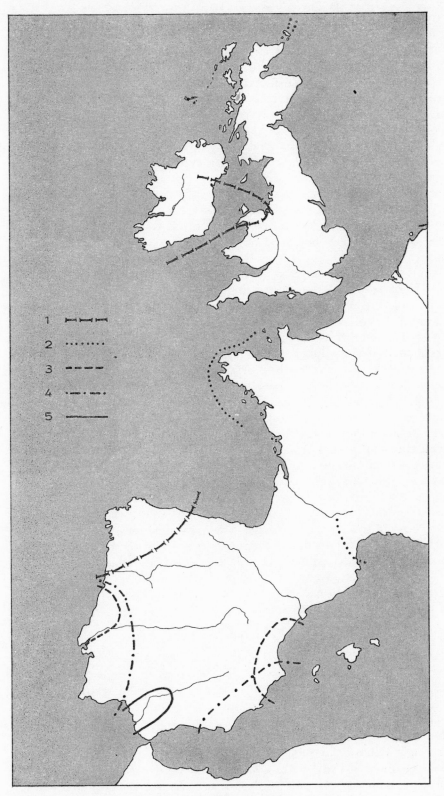

fig. 2 Zonation of certain phenomena discussed

1 area of occurrence of Irish and N.W. Peninsular megalithic tomb art (after Fleming, 1969)
2 area of occurrence of Armorican and related tomb-goddess art in France (after Fleming, 1969)
3 Area of occurrence of segmented bone pendants (after Savory, 1968)
4 Area of occurrence of segmented bone pin heads (after Savory, 1968)
5 Andalusian Passage Graves containing a *pila*

limits of archaeology to vouch for the influence of individuals in a matter about which ordinary seafarers are unlikely to have been concerned.

Turning to mural art, the whole subject has been so repeatedly reviewed in terms of attempting to explain the profuse, but different, Armorican and Irish styles as outcomes of sparse Peninsular exemplars, or as mural adaptations of Peninsular figurine styles, that it would be tedious to restate a well-known position. Miss Elizabeth Shee's comprehensive study of stone-cutting techniques, as well as of motifs, must be awaited before a sufficient foundation of fact is laid to allow further speculation. Meanwhile, attention should be given to a view expressed in a recent study of the decorated stones at Barclodiad y Gawres, Anglesey (Lynch, 1967). Miss Lynch makes the point that there is evidence in Armorica for a pre-Passage Grave usage of fairly simple stone-cut symbolism, and that such could have provided at least one initiative for the art resplendent in large Passage Graves yet to be built. A similar early element may have been present in Ireland, though it is not yet so demonstrable. On the other hand, Miss Lynch emphasises the vitality of designers operating around the Irish Sea, and suggests that their influence reached southward to Armorica to be seen especially at Le Petit Mont, and Gavrinis.

Irish influence in mural art reaching down to the north-west of the Iberian Peninsula has been put forward by A. Fleming (1969) in an interesting new approach to lithic funerary art as a whole in western Europe. Fleming distinguishes two iconographical provinces, one incorporating Armorica, the Paris Basin, and Languedoc, and concerned chiefly with stylistic portrayal of a tomb-goddess, and another incorporating the Passage Grave art of the Irish Sea zone together with that of north-western Spain and Portugal (fig. 2). This is Fleming's 'Atlantic Province', and the content of the art is much less certainly concerned with a tomb-goddess than with abstract designs, and in some of the best examples, a care for decorative effects enhancing the whole tomb. The case is attractive, and accords well with the trend of evidence that has appeared to emerge on other grounds in the foregoing pages. It is to be noted that the distribution of Fleming's Atlantic Province art in the Peninsula contrasts with the distribution of great Passage Graves, mainly in Andalusia. Detailed documentation of tomb forms in the north-west of the Peninsula is still awaited, but if the art reached down from Ireland to that quarter, it may be deduced from available information that the tombs in which it is found represent the end of a building tradition, though a tradition more probably Peninsular, and local, than brought from Ireland. This, at all events, is a point of much interest for future clarification. If, in conclusion of this sketch of Passage Grave interrelations, one may dare to relate such archaeological factors as have been brought together with the question of long-distance navigation in skin-boats, it will be observed that factors found in combination in Ireland occur in the Peninsula only in dispersed and variable form. All the evidence would seem to favour a reversal of direction for the first opening up of the Atlantic Seaways from that which has so long postulated northward-venturing oarsmen.

In face of the large range of linear and geometric motifs displayed in Passage Grave art in Ireland, and others again in Armorica, the question has been raised afresh as to designs borrowed from perishable materials. Fleming (1969) proposes ornamental textile hangings, and the idea is not so alarming as might have appeared a decade or more ago. Painted boards or skins, and basketry-woven screens, are also unlikely to progress beyond the status of archaeological possibilities, but that some motifs can have found repetition in humbler material, perhaps bespeaking a long familiarity, is suggested by the remarkable antler pin found in the southern recess of the chamber at Fourknocks I, Co. Meath (fig. 4). Hartnett (1957) gives a detailed description of the bold chevron pattern deeply cut over the smooth outer surface of this fashioned fragment of a split tine of Red Deer (*Cervus elaphus*). Enough has survived

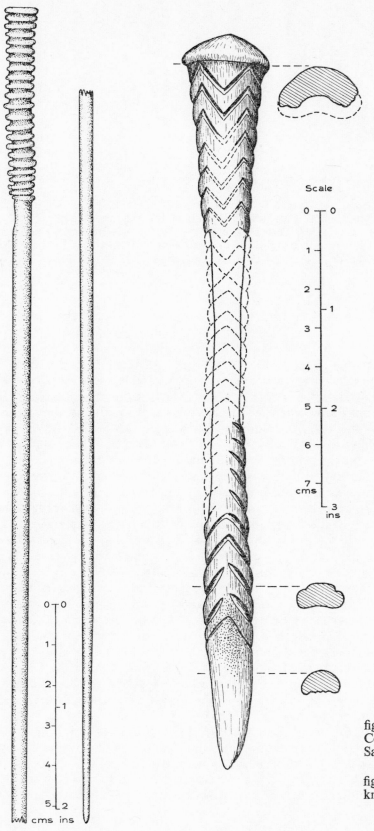

fig. 3 (left) Ribbed bronze pin from Le Combe Bernard, Côte d'Or (after Sandars, 1957)

fig. 4 Decorated antler pin from Fourknocks, Co. Meath (after Hartnett, 1957)

101

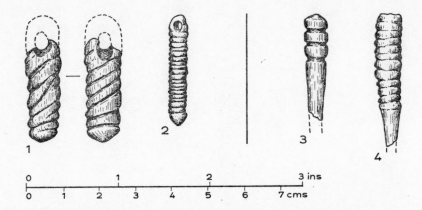

fig. 5 1. Limestone pendant from Carn G. Carrowkeel, Co. Sligo (after Hartnett, 1957)
2. Bone pendant from La Cueva de la Pastora, Alcoy, Alicante (after Nieto Gallo, 1959)
3–4. Segmented pin heads carved in one piece with shaft from: 3. Las Penicas 2, Nijar, Almería
4. La Cueva de la Pastora, Alcoy, Alicante (after Nieto Gallo)

from heat distortion, and breakage, to establish that the pin had been most carefully carved, and had been finished by fine polishing. The Fourknocks pin is eloquent for its time and place, it is complementary to the very fine mural art of the same tomb, and it is surely a pointer to the potentialities of further discovery in the 'Boyne province'. Hartnett, in the same report, drew attention to certain other, but less worthy, carved objects from Irish Passage Graves, and of these a broken pendant of limestone from Carn G, Carrowkeel, Co. Sligo, requires present attention (fig. 5.1). This object displays oblique incised lines, or shallow grooves, that cover the tapered surface from the broken perforation at one end to the low domical tip at the other – a simple enough neck ornament, but otherwise unknown as yet elsewhere in Ireland and Britain, and apparently also absent from tomb assemblages in Armorica.

For the Iberian Peninsula, groove-decorated pendants and pin-heads, all made of bone, have been studied by G. Nieto Gallo (1959), who has provided a useful map and list of find places. The pendants show an interestingly restricted distribution, being common in the province of Alicante and its borders, but not occurring elsewhere except for a small coastal group scattered north from the Tagus estuary to the vicinity of Coimbra (Da Veiga Ferreira, 1965, for additions in this area). Savory (1968, 94) notes a probable route from the Mediterranean coast to the Tagus that kept north of the Sierra Morena, and avoided the south-western culture-province in which lie the Dolmen de Matarrubilla and the other great Andalusian tombs (fig. 2). It should be noted that all the pendants from Peninsular sites show horizontal grooving, while on the Carrowkeel specimen spiral grooving was attempted. Otherwise all the pieces are alike in general characteristics and proportions, and the domical tip of the Carrowkeel specimen is closely matched from such sites as La Pastora, Alcoy, Alicante (Nieto Gallo, 1959, *fig.* 2, nos. 22, 23 and this paper, fig. 5.2), and, in Portugal, from the Gruta dos Salemas, Ponte de Lousa (Da Veiga Ferreira, 1965, fig. 1, no. 16).

Groove-decorated pendants are among characteristic objects found in multiple cave burials of Neolithic and early copper-using communities in the Alicante and Tagus estuary regions described (Savory, 1968, 90–6). To the same culture-complex belong bone pins with cylindrical heads decorated in a very similar manner (fig. 5.3 and 4). These pins with groove- or segmented decoration, show a similar distribution to the pendants, but also occur more widely, as at inland

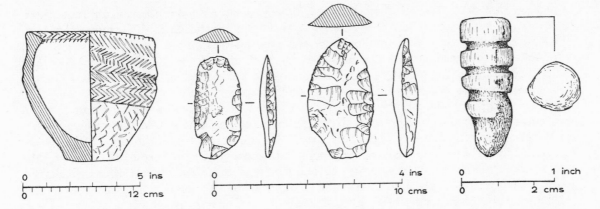

fig. 6 Grave group from Corrandrum, Co. Galway (from drawings supplied by the National Museum of Ireland)

sites in Almería, and scattered sparsely throughout Portugal south of the Tagus (Nieto Gallo, 1959; Savory, 1968, 94; figs 23, 39). The pins are not confined to cave burials, and have been found in a few megalithic tombs, but without as yet very precise implications of relationship. Miss Chitty (1934–5) recognised that among the Portuguese examples the grooved head might be a separate hollow piece surmounting the shaft, but that some pins were carved out of a single piece, the head being solid with the shaft (fig. 5.3 and 4). The Leisners (1943, 450–3), noting Miss Chitty's comments, discussed these pins in relation to a Copper Age first bone industry in the south of the Peninsula, and showed that pins with detachable heads were much more common than those made in one piece. Additions in Portugal to Nieto Gallo's list for the Peninsula are given by V. Leisner with a good photograph of a selection of pins that shows the generally fine carving of the heads with close-set grooves (V. Leisner, 1965, 184–8; pl. 146).

In dealing with the segmented bone fragment from Corrandrum, Co. Galway, Miss Chitty raised the question of a connection with Peninsular pins, but she was careful to point out the chronological difficulties as between Copper Age multiple burial deposits in the Iberian Peninsula, and a single cremation burial of the Irish Middle Bronze Age (fig. 6). Elucidation of the actual affinities of the Corrandrum object has not greatly improved since Miss Chitty wrote. If the Corrandrum object is the remains of a pin, it is of the solid one-piece type, and its carving is much cruder than apparent Peninsular exemplars. Apart from chronology, its uniqueness in Ireland must speak against its significance as representative of a sustained interconnection. Miss Chitty also drew attention to the possibility that the Corrandrum object was related to segmented bone beads found in Bronze Age associations in Britain, but as these latter were hollow, and different in function, a close connection could hardly be pressed. More recently, Piggott (1958), acknowledging Miss Chitty's pioneer observations on segmented beads, both bone and faience, has given fuller details of British finds, especially in connection with a small series of bone 'toggles', segmented objects very like beads, but with one or two lateral perforations, and, in a few examples, expanded ends. These are all hollow objects, and it is improbable, on practical grounds, that surface carving would have been attempted without first ensuring the success of longitudinal perforation. It seems unlikely, therefore, that the Corrandrum object should be regarded as an unperforated, unfinished, bead or toggle, although it has been taken as such by Simpson (1968, 198; fig. 49, no. 7). In view of the erosion of the Corrandrum object, it can hardly be insisted that a portion of shaft survives in extension of the ornamented part, but a narrowing of the object at this point might be one reason why the thicker segmented terminal alone survived. Another point is that Dr T. B. Costello, the original excavator, after the chance finding of the burial, reported the bone object as embedded in the mass of cremated bone fragments and earth within the cist (Costello, 1934–5). The accompanying Vase-type Food Vessel did not contain the cremation, so that a perishable container, a bag or cloth secured by a pin, might have been involved. On the other hand, Miss Lynch has shown reason for believing that fragments of plain pins found with cremation burials in some Irish Passage Graves, and at Barclodiad y Gawres, Anglesey, had been worn by the corpse, and burnt on the pyre (Lynch, 1969, 160). The same may be said for the Corrandrum object with the likelihood that the shaft was more prone to destruction in the heat than the more solid head.

The present writer inclines to an identification of the Corrandrum object as the remains of a pin with ornamental head, but believes that, in view of its simplicity and its cultural isolation, no wide-reaching issue is involved. It is, however, possible to offer another, very tentative, explanation of the shape of the segmented head. Eogan (1964, 270–2) has summarised the position of the Irish Middle Bronze Age in relation to the later part of the Wessex Culture and to the 'Tumulus Bronze' cultures of south-western Germany. Among diagnostic types are the small tanged bronze blades first defined as 'Class I Razors', and once believed to be of rather later cultural and chronological position (C. M. Piggott, 1946). Reference to Mrs Piggott's map and schedule shows authenticated associations of these razors with the cremation rite and with a variety of ceramic types that include Food Vessels. Two important burial associations of this razor type with Cordoned Urns, and cremations under tumuli, have been found in the same part of Co. Galway in which lies Corrandrum (see now Binchy, 1967). It is not impossible that the Corrandrum pin, if such it be, approximates to a bronze pin type of 'Tumulus Bronze' derivation. The fact that pins do not appear to have been normal to insular Bronze Age dress (Butler, 1963, 147) might favour a view that would find no special grounds for a heritage of pin wearing in Ireland after the proper use of Passage Graves, but could envisage the copying in bone of a rare exotic coming from a continental region to which other evidence points for connections at about the same time. The bronze pin type in question would most likely have been one of the ribbed forms (*Nadel mit geripptem Kopf*) well known from the Reinecke Bronze C grave at Askenhofen (Cowen, 1956, pl. 18), and illustrated with different bronze associations in a grave of the same period in the Köschinger Forst (Torbrügge & Uenze, 1968, pl. 123 with further refs.). Such pins reach as far west as the Upper Seine Tumulus group, and one is present in the important grave find from Le Comb Bernard (fig. 3) (Sandars, 1957, 103–8, 364).

The question of Iberian affinities around the Irish Sea during the period of development of Neolithic and Early Bronze cultures has been seen to narrow down to a few minor indications of contact during, but not necessarily at the beginning of, that period when Passage Graves were in use. The slight body of evidence that can as yet be marshalled is funerary in nature, and cannot be taken with any certainty as indicative of major directions of interest and endeavour in daily life. The discovery of new sites, and the improvement of techniques, may yet alter the whole concept as here put forward. For the succeeding periods of prehistory, the pattern of cultural relationships involving all the islands and coastal provinces of 'Atlantic Europe' is ever more certainly that of mutually independent reception of modes, and migrants, radiating from eastward of the great river lines of Rhône–Saône, and Seine. The present writer would not exclude the bearers of the Bell Beaker Culture from this rule although there is now no issue of Iberian styles being present in Britain or Ireland. The establishment of Tumulus Bronze communities in western France, fashioning their own highly distinctive bronze industry, with active trade up and down the Bay of Biscay, opened up an entirely more positive phase of sea-borne enterprise. The high point, so far as archaeology apprehends it, was reached in the eighth–seventh centuries BC with coastal trade going north and south, distributing bronze cauldrons and scrap, best exemplified in the remnants of cargo from Huelva with all the implicit demands of Tartessian markets (Hawkes & Smith, 1957; Hawkes, 1969).

BIBLIOGRAPHY

Binchy, E., 1967. 'Irish Razors and Razor Knives of the Middle Bronze Age', 42–60 in Rynne, E. ed., 1967.

Brown, D. F., 1965. 'The Chronology of the Northwestern Mediterranean', 321–42 in Erich, ed., 1965.

Butler, J. J., 1963. 'Bronze Age Connections across the North Sea', *Palaeohistoria*, IX (entire volume).

Butler, J. J. & van der Waals, J. D., 1967. 'Bell Beakers and Early Metal-Working in the Netherlands', *Palaeohistoria*, XII, 41–139.

Case, H. J., 1967. 'Were Beaker-people the First Metallurgists in Ireland?', *Palaeohistoria*, XII, 141–77.

—— 1969. 'Neolithic Explanations', *Antiquity*, XLIII, 176–86.

Chitty, L. F., 1934–5. 'Notes on Iberian affinities of a bone object found in County Galway', *J. Galway Archaeol. Hist. Soc.*, XVI, 125–33.

Coghlan, H. H. & Case, H., 1957. 'Early Metallurgy of Copper in Ireland and Britain', *Proc. Prehist. Soc.*, XXIII, 91–123.

Coles, J. M. & Simpson, D. D. A., eds, 1968. *Studies in Ancient Europe: Essays presented to Stuart Piggott*. Leicester.

Collantes de Terán, F., 1969. 'El Dolmen de Matarrubilla', 47–61 in Maluquer de Motes, ed., 1969.

Costello, T. B., 1934–5. 'Discovery of Bronze Age Burial with cremated remains', *J. Galway Archaeol. Hist. Soc.*, XVI, 63–6.

Cowen, J. D., 1956. 'Eine Einführung in die Geschichte der bronzenen Griffzungenschwerter . . .', *36 Ber. Röm.–Germ. Komm.*, 1955 (1956), 52–155.

Daniel, G. E., 1958. *The Megalith Builders of Western Europe*. London.

Da Veiga Ferreira, O., 1965. 'Os pendentes de osso "canelados" do nivel I da Gruta dos Salemas (Ponte de Lousa)', *Revista de Guimarães*, LXXV, 73–81.

Eogan, G., 1964. 'The Later Bronze Age in Ireland in the light of recent research', *Proc. Prehist. Soc.*, XXX, 268–351.

—— 1969. 'Excavations at Knowth, County Meath 1968', *Antiquity*, XLIII, 8–14.

Erich, R. W., ed., 1965. *Chronologies in Old World Archaeology*. Chicago and London.

Filgueiras, O. L., 1965. 'Barcos da costa norte, sua contribuição no estudio de áreas culturais', *Lucerna*, IV, 341–52 (Actas do III colóquio portuense de arqueologia).

Fleming, A., 1969. 'The Myth of the mother-goddess', *World Archaeology*, I, 247–61.

Giot, P. R., ed. and contrib., 1963. *Les civilisations atlantiques du néolithique à l'âge du fer* (Actes du premier colloque atlantique, Brest, 1961). Rennes.

Hartnett, P. J., 1957. 'Excavation of a Passage Grave at Fourknocks, County Meath', *Proc. Roy. Irish Acad.*, 58 (C), 197–277.

Hawkes, C. F. C., 1969. 'Las relaciones atlanticas del mundo Tartésico', 185–97 in Maluquer de Motes, ed., 1969.

Hawkes, C. F. C. & Smith, M. A., 1957. 'On Some Buckets and Cauldrons of the Bronze and Early Iron Ages', *Antiq. J.*, XXXVII, 131–98.

Johnstone, P., 1964. 'The Bantry Boat', *Antiquity*, XXXVIII, 277–84.

Leisner, G. & V., 1943. 'Die Megalithgräber der Iberischen Halbinsel: Der Süden', *Röm.-Germ. Forsch. 17*.

—— 1956. 'Die Megalithgräber der Iberischen Halbinsel: Der Westen', *Madrider Forsch. I*.

—— 1959. 'Die Megalithgräber der Iberischen Halbinsel: Der Westen', *Madrider Forsch. I/2*.

Leisner, V., 1965. 'Die Megalithgräber der Iberischen Halbinsel: Der Westen', *Madrider Forsch. I/3*.

L'Helgouach, J., 1965. *Les sépultures mégalithiques en Armorique*. Rennes.

Lynch, F., 1967. 'Barclodiad y Gawres: Comparative Notes on the Decorated Stones', *Archaeol. Cambrensis*, CXVI, 1–22.

—— 1969. 'The Contents of Excavated Tombs in North Wales', 149–74 in Powell *et al.*, 1969.

Maluquer de Motes, J., ed., 1969. *Tartessos: V Symposium internacional de Prehistoria Peninsular*. Barcelona.

Marquez, C. C. & Leisner, G. & V., 1952. 'Los sepulchros megaliticos de Huelva', *Informes y Memorias*, 26. (Com. gen. de excav. arqueol. Madrid.)

Muñoz, A. M., 1965. *La cultura neolitica Catalána de los 'Sepulchros de fosa'*. Barcelona.

Nieto Gallo, G., 1959. 'Colgantes y cabezas de alfiler con decoración acanalada: Su distribucíon en la Península Ibérica', *Archivo de Prehistoria Levantina*, VIII, 125–44.

O'Kelly, C., 1967. *Guide to Newgrange*. Wexford.

O'Kelly, M. J., 1964. 'Newgrange, Co. Meath', *Antiquity*, XXXVIII, 288–90.

—— 1968. 'Excavations at Newgrange, Co. Meath', *Antiquity*, XLII, 40–2.

—— 1969. 'Radiocarbon Dates for the Newgrange Passage Grave, Co. Meath', *Antiquity*, XLIII, 140–1.

ÓNualláin, S., 1968. 'A Ruined Megalithic Cemetery in Co. Donegal, and its context in the Irish Passage Grave series', *J. Roy. Soc. Antiq. Ireland*, XCVIII, 1–29.

Piggott, C. M., 1946. 'The Late Bronze Age Razors of the British Isles', *Proc. Prehist. Soc.*, XII, 121–41.

Piggott, S., 1958. 'Segmented Bone Beads and Toggles in the British Early and Middle Bronze Age', *Proc. Prehist. Soc.*, XXIV, 227–9.

—— 1965. *Ancient Europe*. Edinburgh.

—— 1968. 'The Earliest Wheeled Vehicles and the Caucasian Evidence', *Proc. Prehist. Soc.*, XXXIV, 266–318.

Powell, T. G. E. *et al.*, 1969. *Megalithic Enquiries in the West of Britain*. Liverpool.

Renfrew, C., 1967. 'Colonialism and Megalithismus', *Antiquity*, XLI, 276–88.

Rynne, E., ed., 1967. *North Munster Studies. Essays in Commemoration of Monsignor Michael Moloney*. Limerick.

Sandars, N. K., 1957. *Bronze Age Cultures in France*. Cambridge.

Savory, H. N., 1968. *Spain and Portugal* (Ancient Peoples and Places, 61). London.

Simpson, D. D. A., 1968. 'Food Vessels: associations and chronology', 197–211 in Coles & Simpson, eds., 1968.

Torbrügge, W. & Uenze, H. P., 1968. *Bilder zur Vorgeschichte Bayerns*. Konstanz.

van der Waals, J. D., ed., 1966 (1967). 'Neolithic Studies in Atlantic Europe', *Palaeohistoria*, XII (entire volume).

ACKNOWLEDGEMENTS

My thanks are due to Prof. M. J. O'Kelly for the photograph of the Baltinglass stone basin. For the drawings of the Corrandrum grave-group I am indebted to Dr Joseph Raftery, Keeper of Irish Antiquities, National Museum of Ireland, and to Mr Brendan Ó Ríordáin of the same museum who executed the original drawings, and to Mr Etienne Rynne for helping me with inquiries. Miss N. K. Sandars has kindly permitted me to make use of her drawing of the pin from Combe St Bernard, and for the final preparation of the maps and other text-figures I am especially grateful to Miss Frances Lynch.

Burial and Population in the British Bronze Age

R. J. C. Atkinson

The purpose of this essay is to explore the distribution of burials in barrows and cairns in England and Wales, as a means of estimating the population. I offer it as a grateful tribute to Miss Lily Chitty, whose studies of prehistoric distributions have become woven into the very fabric of British archaeology.

Discussion or estimates of prehistoric populations are conspicuously rare in the literature, and doubtless for good reason; for there are inherent uncertainties in most of the evidence that can be used for this purpose, and many of the assumptions necessary for arriving at any numerical estimate are of their nature unverifiable. Yet this is a question to which the answers, however tentative, have an obvious relevance for more than one field of archaeological interpretation.

At the most basic level, we need to take account of the numerical size of the non-literate communities of prehistory. The communication of new ideas from one community to another, the imitation of unfamiliar but attractive patterns of behaviour, the acceptance of fashionable novelties – or, for that matter, the rejection of available innovation – are all processes of cultural change or conservation in which an essential factor is the frequency of contact between individuals, outside the bounds of close kinship; and this is, at least partly, determined by the size and density of contiguous population-groups. To the extent, therefore, that it is the prehistorian's business to identify and to interpret changes in material culture, the evidence for the size of the population inhabiting a specified territory is as relevant and as important as, say, the evidence for the contemporary 'natural' environment.

But it is not merely for this formal reason that estimates of prehistoric populations are desirable. I have long believed, for instance, that the main justification for excavating unique sites of great size or complexity, such as Stonehenge or Durrington Walls or Silbury Hill, is that it is these alone, in their period, that allow us to observe a whole society in action. Because the principles of mechanics, and the efficiency of the human body as a prime mover, are hardly likely to have altered during the last five or six millennia, we can say with qualified confidence that certain tasks in the building of some of these major sites required a minimum labour force of, say, 200 people. But if we are to assess the social significance of the concerted activity of a group of this or any other size on a single site, we must be able to compare it with the estimated population of the region concerned and, if need be, with those also of more distant areas. Clearly a labour force representing, say, one-quarter of the estimated total population within a radius of, say, 100 km. of the site in question gives that site an importance which it could not merit if the proportion, within the same radius, were only one-twentieth. Thus, in this sense, therefore, the population problem is involved in the interpretation of many of the best-known of our prehistoric sites.

I have tried elsewhere (Atkinson, 1968) to examine the numerical implications of burials in long barrows and in chambered tombs in lowland England, in so far as their number may serve as a basis for estimating the contemporary population of the area in which they occur. In that study I drew attention to the effect upon the interpretation of our Neolithic material of the drastic lengthening of the chronology imposed by the introduction of radiocarbon dating (Atkinson, 1968, 84). Now (1970), as a result of the further refinement of radiocarbon dating through the adoption of corrections based on the dendrochronology of bristlecone pines, we are faced with a further inflation of real dates, which affects the Bronze Age as well as the Neolithic period. Though the magnitude of the correction-factor is certainly much smaller than that imposed by the adoption of radiocarbon dates twenty years ago, it is none the less substantial. Where hitherto, for instance, we have made the equation Beaker/Early Bronze Age = 2000–1400 bc[1], we must now substitute, on the right-hand side, the period 2500–1700 BC, an increase in duration of one-third.

For the purpose of estimating prehistoric populations we have, unfortunately, only one kind of reliable evidence, namely that of burials; and even this is subject to severe restrictions. For population studies the data derived from settlements are unsuitable, partly because very few settlements of any period have been completely excavated; and in any case it is not always easy or even possible to distinguish dwellings from buildings used for other purposes, or to do more than guess at the number of inhabitants appropriate to each dwelling, at the average life of individual buildings, or at the number of buildings in use at any one time. Moreover, at least in the lowland zone of Britain, it is only defended settlements, surrounded by substantial earthworks, that allow one to arrive at any estimate of their original density on the ground. Open, undefended settlements cannot be counted with any reliability, simply because there is no means of knowing how many more await discovery in a given area.

The evidence from burials, on the other hand, though far from ideal, does not suffer from so great a degree of inherent unreliability, and is certainly more plentiful and widespread. Once we start counting burials, we are at least counting the remains of actual people, instead of estimating their numbers from the size of their houses, the capacity of their storage-pits or the areas of their hill forts or their fields. There remain, however, many difficulties, of which the principal one is that it is only one type of burial, that in a barrow or cairn, which stands up, as it were, to be counted.

A line drawn across England from the mouth of the Tees to the Mersey divides a southern British province in which barrow and cairn burial is markedly dominant from a northern province in which these raised monuments are in a minority. A quarter of a century ago Gordon Childe estimated that over 70% of all the Beaker burials then known in Scotland came from cists without any covering mound, and that at least 60% of all burials with cinerary urns occurred in cemeteries of flat graves (Childe, 1946, 43, 63). It is unlikely that more recent discoveries have significantly altered these proportions. A more recent list of Beaker burials in the counties of Northumberland and Durham again shows 70% to have come from cists and only 30% from barrows or cairns (Tait, 1965, 65–70).

In the quest for population statistics, the difference between these two provinces is obvious. In the south, even though many barrows have been destroyed by ploughing and afforestation, especially during the last thirty years, it is still possible to arrive at approximate estimates of the original density of barrows in various regions, with the help of intensive fieldwork, of air-

[1] I adopt here the convention of bc/BC for radiocarbon/solar years respectively.

photographs and of the Ordnance Survey maps and other records compiled before the recent intensification of mechanised agriculture and continuous cropping. In the north, however, the distribution of barrows and cairns, however completely known, tells less than half the story, for there is no way of finding out how many more cists and cemeteries of flat graves remain to be discovered in the future. These are not structures which will be revealed by air-photography, except occasionally and in wholly unusual conditions.

For this reason the present investigation has necessarily been confined to the southern province in which burial in a barrow or cairn appears to have been the dominant rite. It has been conducted by posing and answering, in turn, the following questions:

First, what is the distribution of barrows and cairns, and into what principal groups do they fall? Second, do any of these groups correspond to naturally defined regions which could be regarded as territories of discrete population-groups? Third, how many people, on average, were buried in a single barrow or cairn? Fourth, over how long a period did the practice of tumulus-burial last? Fifth, what densities of population do the answers to these questions imply?

It should be understood, of course, that these questions, and the answers to them, can be meaningful only if the prior assumption is made that tumulus-burial was the common rite accorded to all, or almost all, of the members of the societies concerned. The adoption of any other working hypothesis necessarily stultifies the whole concept of using barrows and cairns as a basis for estimates of population; for if we assume that those buried in barrows and cairns were only a fraction of the total population, we must also assume that the remainder were disposed of at death by some other rite which is at worst archaeologically unidentifiable, and at best uncountable in terms of original frequencies.

For the distribution of barrows and cairns in England and Wales no detailed map has hitherto been published; though for some areas, and in particular for the counties of southern and south-western England, detailed surveys already exist. It is a measure of Mr L. V. Grinsell's contribution to British archaeology that over the last forty years he has personally visited and documented between one-third and one-half of all the barrows surviving in England and Wales. Unfortunately, however, he has had few imitators; and perhaps for this reason the only large-scale map of barrows which has so far appeared (RCHM, 1960, 25) excludes Wales and presents only a generalised and qualitative picture of the density of barrow-burial in England.

I have therefore attempted, in fig. 1, the production of a relative-density map of barrows and cairns in England and Wales, which is offered merely as a first approximation. In constructing it, I have relied heavily on the published sources marked by an asterisk in the bibliography (pp. 115–16), and in particular on the work of Mr Grinsell, who has been kind enough to put at my disposal, in advance of publication, his map of barrows in North Devon and West Somerset (Grinsell, 1971).

For the areas not covered by published sources I have had recourse to the only other information available on a national scale, namely that contained in the maps of the Ordnance Survey. Ideally one should use for this purpose the plans at the larger scales of 1:2500, 1:10560 or 1:25000; but in practice it is only the 1-inch map (1:63360) that allows the scanning of so large an area in the available time. At this scale it is of course impracticable to mark every recorded barrow, especially in areas of high density; and it has therefore been necessary to estimate the factor by which the number of barrows marked on the 1-inch map in a given area (in practice, one 10 km. square of the National Grid) must be multiplied in order to give the best estimate of the number of barrows actually observable in the area concerned. A calculation based on 150 grid squares of this size, in which the density of barrows on the ground has been reliably recorded by critical field-workers, shows that for every 10 barrows on the map there are, on the average, 22 on the ground, giving a multiplying factor of 2·2.[1] On the local scale,

[1] For the mathematically-minded, the regression equation is $y = 2 \cdot 21x + 0 \cdot 44$, and the correlation-coefficient is $+0 \cdot 77$.

of course, the actual factor, where it is verifiable, will almost certainly differ from this figure (though the difference will probably not be significant in the statistical sense); but on a national scale, pending the publication of further barrow surveys to the standards set by Mr Grinsell or by the Royal Commissions, this factor may be accepted as adequate for a first approximation.

At the scale of reproduction used here it is not possible, of course, to represent each single barrow, whether real or estimated. Each dot on the map therefore stands for *five* barrows on the average, with a single dot denoting 3–7 barrows inclusive, two dots 8–12, three dots 13–17, and so on. Since from one 10 km. square to the next the errors will be positive or negative indifferently, they will tend to cancel out; and as the local densities increase, the residual errors become rapidly insignificant.

The adoption of this convention, unavoidable for technical reasons, means that densities of one or two barrows per 10 km. square are not shown at all, and that in consequence some 300 barrows, or 60 dots, have been omitted from the map. This is, however, less than 2% of the total; and the omission of these lowest densities serves merely to sharpen the contrast between the main regional concentrations and the almost blank areas which separate them, especially in the lowland zone.

The second question to be asked concerns the clustering of the distribution thus recorded, and the possible correspondence of individual clusters to territories definable in other terms. In the past, the distribution of barrows on a regional or county scale has usually been presented on a base-map showing either the solid geology or a reconstruction of the natural vegetation based thereon. For some areas this has worked well; for others, understandably, it has been less satisfactory, because locally the underlying rock is not necessarily related at all closely to the soil type, which is usually the main factor determining the nature of the habitat. Moreover, the human influence upon the landscape, even where soil and rock types are well correlated, cannot be expressed in geological terms alone.

As an experiment, therefore, the boundaries outlined on fig. 1 are taken selectively – that is, where there appears to be a significant correspondence with a regional concentration of barrows or cairns – from the vegetation map published by the Ordnance Survey in the National Planning Series at a scale of 1:625000 (about 10 miles to 1 inch). This is not, of course, a map of 'natural' vegetation, for with trivial exceptions no such thing now exists in Britain. It is a map of grassland types, the distribution of which is the combined result of natural factors such as soil type, rainfall, elevation and temperature on the one hand, and of prolonged human exploitation of the landscape on the other. In so far as it includes the effects of man himself as an agent of ecological change, a map of this kind is likely to provide a better basis for the study of archaeological distributions than one based on geology alone.

The vegetational regions outlined on the map are distinguished by letters. It wi llbe seen that the most marked correspondence with the distribution of barrows occurs in the principal regions of calcareous grassland, where the characteristic species are the fescues which predominate in downland turf, especially when grazed by sheep or, during the last two millennia only, by rabbits. These areas comprise the Yorkshire Wolds (B), the Cotswolds (K), and the chalk downlands of Wessex and Sussex (M). It is noticeable, however, that on two other extensive tracts of similar fescue grassland, namely the Lincolnshire Wolds (C) and the Chilterns (N), not only is the distribution of barrows sparse but it also conforms far less closely to the ecological boundaries. The reasons for these differences deserve further investigation; but it can be said straightaway that they cannot be accounted for by the differential effects of modern cultivation. The wholesale destruction of barrows by ploughing, all too evident today, dates only from the supplanting of the horse-drawn plough by the tractor.

There are two other areas of predominantly calcareous soils in England where the density of barrows is high but the correspondence with a particular type of vegetation is only partial. These are the limestone uplands of Derbyshire (D) and the Mendips (P). In both regions the

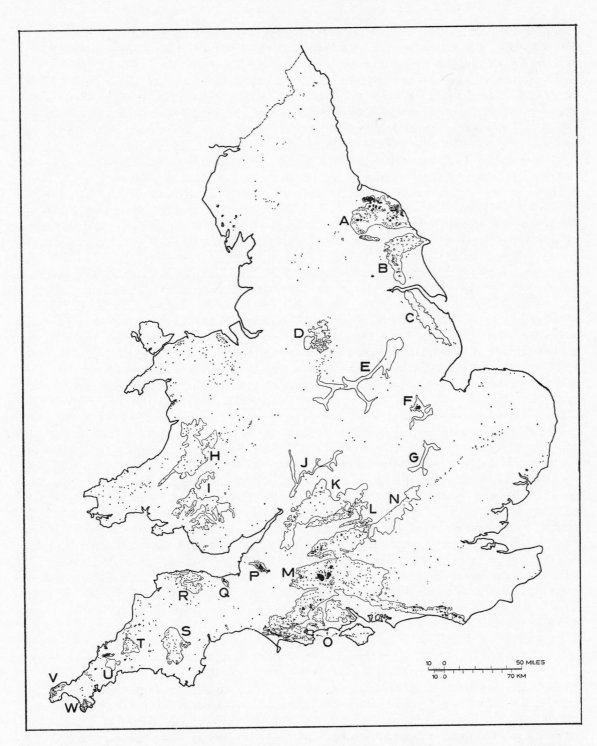

fig. 1 Relative density of round barrows and cairns in England and Wales. Each dot represents five barrows. The sources used in compiling this map are marked by an asterisk in the Bibliography.

composition of the grassland is variable, with patches of fescue intermixed with stretches, usually larger in extent, of the coarser *Agrostis* or Common Bent pasture which is characteristic of the unimproved upland grazing areas throughout Britain.

The second main group of territories outlined in fig. 1 comprises areas of upland heather moor and lowland heath, of which the most important, in terms of barrow distribution, are the moors of the North Riding of Yorkshire (A) and the heathlands of the New Forest and its westward extensions towards Dorchester (O). Elsewhere there are minor concentrations of barrows on the southern part of the Breckland, on the lower flanks of Dartmoor (S), on the Quantock Hills (Q) and on the outer parts of Exmoor (R), and in Penwith (V). It does not appear, however, that in other parts of the Highland Zone there is any marked correlation of barrows or cairns with the occurrence of heather moorland. In North Wales, for instance, the only area of heather moor to carry any substantial number of barrows is that of Eglwyseg Mountain, a few miles west of Wrexham; but this is only part of a more general distribution of barrows, denser towards the coast, which occupies the interior of Flintshire and south-eastern Denbighshire as far as the Dee.

In this connection it must be remembered, as Professor Dimbleby has convincingly demonstrated from the study of soils buried beneath barrows, that these moorland landscapes are far from being 'natural', and that the present heather vegetation has become dominant only as a result of human activity in prehistoric times (Dimbleby, 1962). Where therefore we have an association of a marked concentration of barrows with heather or heath, it is reasonable to assume that in part at least they are causally connected and that the moor now defines, broadly speaking, the area in which the barrow-builders were active. This is almost certainly the case on the limestone moors of the North Riding where, even if we leave out of account the still enigmatic fields of small cairns (Elgee, 1930, 121–2), the density of barrows and cairns is one of the highest in the country.

In the third place, the map shows a few small areas of wet peaty moorland in the South-West, on which the characteristic species is the Purple Moor Grass, *Molinia caerulea*. These include the central and higher parts of Dartmoor (S), Bodmin Moor (T), a small but densely occupied area between Wadebridge and St Columb Major and a larger area of the same character, on which barrows are conspicuously less dense, to the south of it (U), and finally a very dense concentration of barrows on the serpentine outcrop just inland from the Lizard (W). It is probable that in these areas also the present vegetation is the result of the activities of the barrow-builders or their predecessors. In such districts of locally high elevation and high rainfall, on impervious rocks, the removal of the natural forest may well have interfered irreversibly with the hydrological balance, so that rain which was formerly returned to the atmosphere through transpiration by the leaves of trees so saturated the soil that peat-formation was induced. The barrows in these areas may thus be the relics of a lost landscape of a quite different and more habitable kind.

In central and south Wales the boundaries marked H and I (in somewhat generalised form, as the distribution is locally discontinuous) are those of moorlands characterised by two principal grass types, the Purple Moor Grass being dominant in the wetter patches and the Mat-Grass (*Nardus stricta*) on the drier eminences and slopes. This is the vegetation-type most closely associated with the distribution of barrows and cairns; but it is evident that the degree of correlation is not high. In North Wales there appears to be no preferential association; but it must be borne in mind that the degree of generalisation that is unavoidable in a map published at a scale of about ten miles to the inch may obscure relationships that would be apparent at a larger scale.

In general, however, it seems clear that as an indicator of former territories the present-day distribution of vegetation types is much more efficient in the lowland than in the highland zone. This is understandable if during the Bronze Age there was the same pattern of contrasted economies that appears to have existed both in the preceding Neolithic period and in the subsequent pre-Roman Iron Age, with the growing of grain confined mainly to the lighter soils of southern and eastern England, and pastoralism being dominant elsewhere.

There remain on fig. 1 five marked areas whose boundaries are not reflected in the vegetation-types, namely the gravel terraces of the Trent (E), the Welland and the Nene (F), the Ouse (G), the Severn and the Warwickshire Avon (J), and the upper Thames (L). Of these it is only the last, probably, which has been explored and recorded, mainly from the air, for long enough and in sufficient detail to allow an estimate to be made of the original density and distribution of barrows (Riley, 1943–4, 66–72). For the extensive gravels of the Trent, an area larger than either the Yorkshire Wolds or the Wessex heathlands, systematic study is only just beginning; but there can be little doubt that in time this area, and that of the Severn-Avon gravels (Webster & Hobley, 1965), will prove to have had as dense a pattern of barrows as did the Thames valley between Lechlade and Goring. The work of the Royal Commission (England) has already shown the existence of comparable densities in the neighbourhoods of Maxey and Peterborough (RCHM, 1960, *fig.* 6; 1969, *figs.* 1, 2, 7, 9, 10). The Ouse gravels in the region of Bedford (G), however, remain still to be explored systematically by air-photography.

As a first approximation, therefore, the distribution recorded in fig. 1 may perhaps serve to give estimates of the relative density and of the absolute numbers of barrows in various regions of England and Wales. The question of the number of *individuals* represented can be answered fairly shortly; there is ample information, even if it is not all equally reliable.

For any of the territories outlined on fig. 1, the highest recorded figure for burials per barrow comes from a sample of rather more than 400 barrows on the Yorkshire Wolds (Greenwell, 1877, 458–71; Mortimer, 1905, 398–442). The statistics given by both excavators yield a figure very close to an average of three burials per barrow, and this is probably a little on the low side, since the usual practice of both was to drive a broad trench through the mound, comprising perhaps from two-thirds to three-quarters of its volume, but not to turn over the entire barrow.

A further 90 barrows excavated by Greenwell elsewhere in northern England (Greenwell, 1877, 471–8) give a substantially lower figure of about 1·9 persons per barrow. This too must be regarded as an underestimate.

In the south, the excavation of some 600 barrows in Wiltshire and Gloucestershire (V.C.H., 1957; O'Neil & Grinsell, 1961, 99–138) yielded a total of 760 burials attributable to the Bronze Age, or about 1·25 persons per barrow. Here the degree of underestimation is undoubtedly serious, because most of the excavations concerned were undertaken in the nineteenth century, and were confined to a central hole or shaft which left the major part of the barrow unexplored. It is perhaps more significant that a sample of about 40 Wiltshire barrow-excavations undertaken in the last fifteen years, in which all or nearly all of the mound was examined, yields an average of almost exactly three persons per barrow (Annable, 1958–65; Christie, 1964; Johnstone, 1963; Musty & Stone, 1956; Smith, 1965; Thomas, 1956; Thomas & Thomas, 1955; Vatcher, 1960, 1963).

The total sample that I have used here comprises 1,140 barrows excavated in varying degrees of completeness which yielded, in all, the burials of at least 2,300 persons, or an average of almost exactly 2 persons per barrow. For the reasons mentioned above, this is undoubtedly an underestimate; and in the calculations which follow a round figure of 3 burials per barrow has been adopted. The information available is not sufficient either to support or to cast doubt on the hypothesis that there were significant differences in the frequency of burials per barrow in different parts of the country.

The last of the initial questions to be asked is: how long did the practice of barrow-burial persist? This is an interesting and possibly contentious problem, which deserves closer attention than it has hitherto received. All that it is proposed to do here is to suggest the *minimum* period which seems possible, for it is this which governs the size of the maximum estimate of population to be deduced from the barrow map.

It will be generally agreed that the practice of burial in round barrows begins effectively in Britain with the arrival of Beaker people at a conventional date of 2000 bc or 2500 BC. Even if the known burials under round barrows with non-Beaker, and conventionally pre-Beaker, grave-goods (Piggott, 1954, 64, 111–12, 307, 354–8) could be shown conclusively to be earlier than this, their number is too small to make it necessary to qualify the foregoing statement.

There will be much less agreement, however, to the proposition that no barrow or cairn in Britain has yet produced grave-goods in a primary context that can be unequivocally assigned to any period later than the end of the Early Bronze Age, or, in conventional terms, 1400 bc; but this is, none the less, a statement extremely difficult to controvert. It is said, of course, that certain pottery types, such as Longworth's Secondary Series of Collared Urns, must belong to the Middle Bronze Age; but the arguments adduced are of an entirely typological kind, and cannot be supported at all widely either by associations with metal types or by radiocarbon dates. Fortunately it is not necessary to set out in detail here the basis for this contention, since this has recently been done most ably, for the relevant pottery types, by Burgess (Burgess, 1969); and since it is the pottery types alone that, in the conventional view, date any of the barrows to the Middle Bronze Age, the demonstration that these too do not substantially outlast the preceding period must apply equally to the barrows in which the pots occur.

In further support of this view, it is perhaps worth while to add that out of more than 550 excavated barrows in Wessex no more than 2% can be shown to contain a primary burial of Deverel-Rimbury type. It seems likely, therefore, that the practice of barrow-burial was already very rare at the beginning of this phase, conventionally dated to 1200 bc.

For present purposes, therefore, I assume that barrow-building lasted for some nine centuries, or from 2000 to 1300 bc (2500–1600 BC). In previous work on Neolithic populations I have assumed a crude death-rate of 40 per 1,000 or 4% per annum (Atkinson, Piggott & Sandars, 1951, 77–80; Atkinson, 1968, 87), which means that on the average a given population renews itself every 25 years, or four times a century. Since the present purpose is to estimate the *maximum* probable population during the succeeding Early Bronze Age, we may perhaps allow some improvement in this assumed crude death-rate; but certainly not beyond the limit of three renewals of population per century. For nine centuries this means twenty seven successive generations.

It is now possible to calculate, as a first approximation, the likely density of population during the Early Bronze Age for certain regions. This is done by taking the estimated number of barrows in the region and multiplying by 3 to obtain the estimated number of persons buried during the period concerned. This figure is then divided by 27 to give the population of the region (assumed to be constant over the period in question); and divided again by the size of the region to give the number of inhabitants per square mile.

The results of these calculations, based as they are on data of very different degrees of reliability and comprehensiveness, must be regarded as extremely tentative. For the Yorkshire Moors, for instance, they suggest an average population of about 300 people, or about 0·57 per square mile. The Mendips give the same density, and these are the highest apparent densities calculated. For the area of Wessex, including the heathlands, the average population works out at around 530 for some 2,260 square miles, or about one quarter of a person per square mile. For the Sussex chalk and for the gravel terraces of the upper Thames the density is about the same, with a population of about 50 for the latter area. In the highland zone it is obvious that the densities calculable would be even smaller than these; but the difficulty of defining adequately any territories makes even the most tentative calculation impossible.

By the standards of today in the same rural areas these densities are of course extremely low, and well below even the minimum densities recorded or deducible from historical records, such as the Domesday returns; but this is only to be expected, for even in Wessex it is likely that the areas cleared of forest after a millennium and a half of Neolithic settlement were substantially smaller than the deforested area of the eleventh century AD.

We may indeed ask whether the populations suggested above are not so ludicrously small that they *cannot* represent more than a small fraction of the actual population which was at the time, presumably by virtue of its high rank, alone accorded the honour of burial in a barrow or cairn. The necessary corollary of this view, of course, is that the remainder of the population was disposed of at death by some means which has left no archaeologically detectable trace; but there is no difficulty about this, since it is precisely what must have happened to almost the entire population of Britain during the Late Bronze Age and the earlier part of the pre-Roman Iron Age.

In the last resort, personal preference alone will decide whether the very tentative conclusions reached in this paper are acceptable or not; for there appears to be no satisfactory way of testing the hypothesis here advanced. My own view is that it is just possible that to the south of a line from the Tees to the Mersey the barrows and cairns of England and Wales *do* contain the remains of almost the whole of our Beaker and Early Bronze Age population, and that we do not *have* to suppose that these are the burial places of the aristocracy only. The total number of barrows and cairns in England and Wales is probably between 16,000 and 20,000, giving, on the assumptions that I have outlined above, an average population for the area of about 2,000. This is just, but only just, about enough for the successful completion of major works of civil engineering, such as the building of the third Stonehenge or of Avebury. If the labour for these was drawn from so small a population, then they are indeed national monuments.

BIBLIOGRAPHY

Annable, F. K., 1958–65. 'Excavation and Fieldwork in Wiltshire: 1957–64', *Wiltshire Archaeol. Natur. Hist. Mag.*, LVII, 5–9, 228–31, 393–5; LVIII, 30–1, 240–2, 467–8; LX, 132–4.

*Ashbee, P. & Dunning, G. C., 1961. 'The Round Barrows of East Kent', *Archaeol. Cantiana*, LXXIV, 48–57.

Atkinson, R. J. C., 1968. 'Old mortality: some aspects of burial and population in neolithic England', in Coles, J. M. & Simpson, D. D. A. (eds), *Studies in Ancient Europe*, 83–93.

Atkinson, R. J. C., Piggott, C. M., & Sandars, N. K., 1951. *Excavations at Dorchester, Oxon*.

*Bowen, E. G. & Gresham, C. A., 1967. *History of Merioneth*, vol. I. Dolgellau.

Burgess, C. B., 1969. 'Chronology and Terminology in the British Bronze Age', *Antiq. J.*, XLIX, 22–9.

Childe, V. G., 1946. *Scotland before the Scots*. London.

Christie, P. M., 1964. 'A Bronze Age Round Barrow on Earl's Farm Down, Amesbury', *Wiltshire Archaeol. Natur. Hist. Mag.*, LIX, 30–45.

*Davies, E., 1929. *The Prehistoric and Roman Remains of Denbighshire*. Cardiff.

*—— 1949. *The Prehistoric and Roman Remains of Flintshire*. Cardiff.

Dimbleby, G. W., 1962. *The Development of British Heathlands and their Soils*. Oxford.

*Dyer, J. F., 1961. 'Barrows of the Chilterns', *Archaeol. J.*, CXVI, 1–24.

Elgee, F., 1930. *Early Man in North-East Yorkshire*. Gloucester.

Greenwell, W., 1877. *British Barrows*. Oxford.

*Grimes, W. F., 1945. 'Early Man and the Soils of Anglesey', *Antiquity*, XIX, 169–74.

*Grinsell, L. V., 1934. 'An analysis and list of Surrey barrows', *Surrey Archaeol. Collect.*, XLII, 27–60.

*—— 1934a. 'Sussex Barrows', *Sussex Archaeol. Collect.*, LXXV, 217–75.

*—— 1938. 'Hampshire Barrows', *Proc. Hampshire Fld. Club Archaeol. Soc.*, XIV, 9–40.

*—— 1940. 'Sussex Barrows: Supplementary Paper', *Sussex Archaeol. Collect.*, LXXXI, 210–14.

*—— 1941. 'The Bronze Age Round Barrows of Wessex', *Proc. Prehist. Soc.*, VII, 73–113.

*Grinsell, L. V., 1959. *Dorset Barrows*. Dorchester.

*—— 1969. 'Somerset Barrows, Part I: West and South', *Proc. Somerset Archaeol. Natur. Hist. Soc.*, CXIII, 1–43 (separately paginated).

*—— 1971. 'The Barrows of North Devon', *Proc. Devon Archaeol. Soc.* (forthcoming).

*Grinsell, L. V. & Sherwin, G. A., 1941. 'Isle of Wight Barrows', *Proc. Isle of Wight Natur. Hist. Soc.*, III, 179–222.

Johnston, D. E., 1963. 'A group of barrows near Shalbourne, Wilts.', *Wiltshire Archaeol. Natur. Hist. Mag.*, LVIII, 362–9.

Mortimer, J. R., 1905. *Forty Years' Researches in the British and Saxon Burial Mounds of East Yorkshire*. London.

Musty, J. W. G. & Stone, J. F. S., 1956. 'An Early Bronze Age Barrow and Late Bronze Age Urnfield on Heale Hill, Middle Woodford', *Wiltshire Archaeol. Natur. Hist. Mag.*, LVI, 253–61.

*O'Neil, H. & Grinsell, L. V., 1961. 'Gloucestershire Barrows', *Trans. Bristol Gloucestershire Archaeol. Soc.*, LXXIX, 1–149.

Piggott, S., 1954. *Neolithic Cultures of the British Isles*. Cambridge.

*Riley, D. N., 1943–44. 'Archaeology from the Air in the Upper Thames Valley', *Oxoniensia*, VIII/IX, 64–101.

*RCHM, 1960. Royal Commission on Historical Monuments (England), *A Matter of Time: An Archaeological Survey of the River Gravels of England*.

RCHM, 1969. Royal Commission on Historical Monuments (England), *Peterborough New Town*.

Smith, I. F., 1965. 'Excavation of a Bell Barrow, Avebury G.55', *Wiltshire Archaeol. Natur. Hist. Mag.*, LX, 24–46.

Tait, J., 1965. *Beakers from Northumberland*. Newcastle-upon-Tyne.

Thomas, N., 1956. 'Excavation and Fieldwork in Wiltshire: 1956', *Wiltshire Archaeol. Natur. Hist. Mag.*, LVI, 237–40.

Thomas, N. & Thomas, A. C., 1955. 'Excavations at Snail Down, Everleigh: An Interim Report', *Wiltshire Archaeol. Natur. Hist. Mag.*, LVI, 127–48.

Vatcher, F. de M., 1960. 'The Excavation of a Group of Barrows at Down Farm, Pewsey, Wilts.', *Wiltshire Archaeol. Natur. Hist. Mag.*, LVII, 339–51.

—— 1963. 'The Excavation of the Barrows on Lamb Down, Codford St. Mary', *Wiltshire Archaeol. Natur. Hist. Mag.*, LVIII, 417–41.

*VCH, 1957. Victoria County History, *A History of Wiltshire*, vol. I, pt. I. London.

*Webster, G. & Hobley, B., 1965. 'Aerial Reconnaissance over the Warwickshire Avon', *Archaeol. J.*, CXXI, 1–22.

* Source used in compiling map in fig. 1 above.

Copper Age Cists and Cist-Cairns in Wales: with special reference to Newton, Swansea, and other 'Multiple-cist' Cairns

H. N. Savory

INTRODUCTION

Round cairns containing a single, usually central cist are a commonplace of Welsh Early Bronze Age archaeology, as they are of this period in various other regions of Britain. Less familiar in Wales are round cairns containing several well-built rectangular cists which, though they sometimes contain cremated burials, are of a size suitable for a contracted or, more rarely, an extended inhumation. These are, above all, an Irish, and to a lesser degree a Scottish or northern English, phenomenon. The frequency with which 'secondary' or 'satellite' burials occur in Welsh round cairns and barrows might, indeed, lead one to expect multiple cists in the same setting, but in fact the secondary burials in Wales take the shape of inhumations or, more frequently, cremations in pits or in coffers poorly constructed of small slabs packed round the cinerary urn to protect it. These may be found in any part of the mound or its underlying surface. Many secondary burials of this type may be interpreted as successive and should be contrasted with the groups of large and well-built cists which seem to have been placed in the cairn all at one time. It is these grouped cists which are the special concern of this paper.

'Multiple-cist' cairns, it has been said, are above all characteristic of Ireland (Macalister, 1928, 124; Ó Ríordáin, 1953, 76; Evans, 1966, 19) and it is here that the largest number of cists are found in one cairn; there are fewer examples in Scotland and northern England, especially of cairns with a large number of cists (fig. 1). There is no need for me to enter into any great detail in discussing the Irish cist cairns because Mr John Waddell, of the Department of Archaeology, University College, Galway, has already done so in a paper now in the press (Waddell, 1970).[1]

A special feature of some of these Irish 'multiple-cist' cairns is a symmetrical arrangement of a number of cists of normal size in relation to a large cist or megalithic structure, usually in a central position. Thus Cairn A at Aghnaskeagh, Co. Louth, contains on the east side the remains of a Portal Dolmen and on the west side six cists with cremations (Evans, 1966, 156). The well-known Mount Stewart Cairn, Co. Down, contained a large central cist and at least fifteen 'short cists' carefully grouped to the south of it (Evans & Megaw, 1937), and the

---

[1] I am greatly indebted to Mr Waddell for allowing me to consult this paper in typescript and draw upon the valuable list and bibliographies appended to it, both for the general observations that follow and for my distribution map.

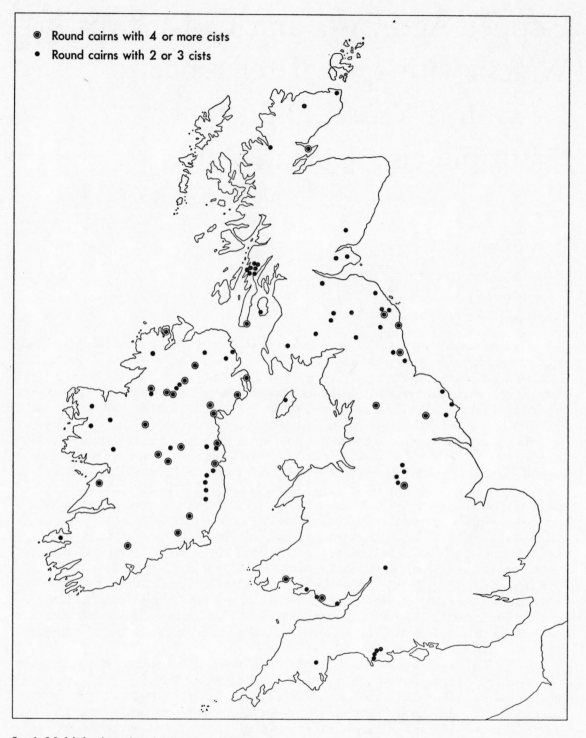

fig. 1 Multiple cist cairns in Britain and Ireland

Round cairns with 4 or more cists

Round cairns with 2 or 3 cists

cairn at Knockmaree, Co. Dublin, had four marginal cists arranged around a small central 'dolmen' (Ó Ríordáin, 1953, 76). At Mullingar, Co. Westmeath, five 'short cists' seem to have surrounded a larger central cist (Macalister, 1921, 343), and at Beihy, Co. Fermanagh, 'a large central megalithic cist' was encircled by a ring of more than seven 'short cists' (Evans, 1966, 113), while at Trillick, Co. Tyrone, a round cairn contained a ring of eight marginal cists (Evans, 1966, 205).

The suggestion that the Irish megalithic tradition of communal burial, or reburial, lives on in monuments of this sort is strengthened by consideration of the remarkable monument at Dun Ruadh, Co. Tyrone (Evans, 1966, 201), in which at least thirteen cists were set in a sort of ring-cairn enclosing a central courtyard, which might recall Professor de Valéra's Full Court Cairns (de Valéra, 1960). The symmetrical arrangement of cists in all the monuments mentioned above suggests adherence to a plan laid down by the original builders and carried out either at a single ceremony or at a succession of ceremonies held over a comparatively short period.

On the other hand the carefully excavated 'multiple-cist' cairn at Poulawack, Co. Clare, shows no such symmetry and several cists are clearly later additions, though even here the excavator felt that six of the cists were put into the cairn while it was being built (Hencken, 1935). The 'multiple-cremation' round cairn of Knockast, Co. Westmeath, contains a few cists, some of them very small, arranged in an unevenly spaced ring just within the foot of the cairn, but the majority of the forty-three burials are unprotected cremations placed haphazardly and are clearly successive. The associated finds, indeed, suggest that most of the burials in this cairn are of a later date in the Bronze Age than most of the sites we have been considering up to now, though it must be admitted that many of the minor 'multiple-cist' cairns listed by Waddell have a more or less haphazard arrangement and many contain numbers of cremation burials which are not protected by properly built cists, any more than are the typical secondary cremation deposits in Welsh cairns and barrows.

Waddell, in the study referred to, considers that Irish 'multiple-cist' cairns, and indeed Irish cist burials of all types, especially those which occur in flat cemeteries, represent a synthesis of two traditions – the Copper Age or Early Bronze Age single-grave, and the late Neolithic cremation cemetery. These cemeteries were originally 'flat' but in Ireland they frequently occupy the round cairns covering a megalithic Passage Grave – a local tradition which Waddell feels may have contributed to the development of the Bronze Age practice of 'multiple-cist' burial in round cairns. The single-grave and associated 'short cist' tradition in Ireland, where in fact over half the recorded cists occurred singly, must, he considers, have been introduced into Ireland from Britain by the users of the Food Vessel, a form which overwhelmingly predominates among the pottery associated with Irish cists.

Waddell's analysis serves to emphasise the contrast that exists, even here, between the contents and setting of Irish and British cists when studied as a whole. For he shows that, whereas roughly two out of three Irish cist burials seem to have been cremations (with inhumations relatively common only in the opening phase), a large majority of British 'short cists' contained inhumations, and very many of these were accompanied, not by Food Vessels, but by Beakers of various types – a class of ceramic which, to judge by Waddell's list, has so far not been reported from a single Irish cist, although it is now far better represented at other types of site in Ireland than it appeared to be twenty years ago. Even the Irish Food Vessels, as is well known, have for the most part a distinctively Hibernian character and only relate in broad outline, if at all, to typical British examples. Moreover, when one considers the setting in which cists occur, one finds that in Ireland there are very few examples of the cairn with the single, centrally sited cist which is so common in western parts of Britain such as Wales (see map, fig. 2), and that the 'flat' cists or cist-cemeteries commonly found in both Ireland and Scotland are, in Scotland, associated quite as often with short-necked Beakers as with Food Vessels.

The contrast which we have described between the cist burials of Britain and of Ireland can no doubt be partially explained by the assumption that the sum total of Irish cist burials embodies an evolution lasting several centuries and was carried out, in increasing isolation, after an initial phase of colonisation from Britain. Moreover the divergence in pottery styles might be due to the fact that the colonisation which implanted cist burial in Ireland occurred after the development of the Food Vase form in Britain. This would suggest an Early Bronze Age horizon, the evidence for which has been most recently summarised by Simpson (1968).

The picture is complicated here, however, by the fact that Irish Food Vessels have long been classified into two main groups: Vases and Bowls; of which the latter group is so characteristic of Ireland that it is generally held to have originated there. ApSimon, indeed, has emphasised this duality by arguing, very plausibly, that the Irish Vases owe much to northern British Beakers as well as Yorkshire Vases, whereas the Bowls are derived from southern British Long-necked Beakers (ApSimon, 1958) – a theory which has lately been strengthened by the publication of the important site on Dalkey Island, Co. Dublin, which has yielded transitional forms (Liversage, 1968).

The effect of this is to suggest that Irish Food Vessels may reflect two separate movements from Britain into Ireland which may not have occurred at the same time. ApSimon has in fact argued that the Irish Food Bowl form must have overlapped considerably in time with southern English Beakers since Beaker sherds, some of good quality, were found with fragments of Bowls on a hut floor sealed by a round barrow at Swarkeston in Derbyshire (ApSimon, 1958, 34; 1960). This association demonstrates the possible development of a 'reflux' movement of Irish forms of Vase or Bowl back into Britain, a development which is most marked in northern Britain where Food Vessels with Irish characteristics are strongly represented. This is especially so in south-west Scotland where there is also a concentration of 'multiple-cist' cairns; but it is perceptible also in South Wales and even, to a slight extent, in southern England.

It is tempting to see a relationship between this Early Bronze Age ceramic 'reflux' from Ireland and the dispersal of 'multiple-cist' cairns by the same routes through parts of Scotland and northern England on the one hand, and through South Wales and a limited area of southern England on the other (fig. 1). Further analysis, however, while supporting the idea of an Irish influence upon some builders of round cairns in the aforementioned areas of Britain, shows how complex were the cultural relationships in these islands at this time. The evidence from Wales, an area which had particularly close contacts with Ireland during the Bronze Age, helps to clarify these relationships, and knowledge of the small and ill-recorded group of 'multiple-cist' cairns on the South Wales seaboard has lately been increased by the re-excavation of the Newton cairn near Mumbles, undertaken by the writer in the summer of 1969. But before discussing the Welsh examples, the situation in northern England and Scotland should be briefly considered.

'MULTIPLE-CIST' CAIRNS IN SCOTLAND AND NORTHERN ENGLAND

The intrusive character of 'multiple-cist' cairns in northern Britain can be better appreciated when it is considered that the great majority of the sites shown on the map (fig. 1) lie to the north of Piggott's 'isotaph' line running from east to east along the valley of the Tees (Piggott, 1962, 76). To the north of this line 'flat' cist and pit burials predominate in the Copper and Early Bronze Age, while to the south of it barrow burials are more usual.

The 'flat' cist tradition in northern Britain is above all associated with Short-necked Beakers, the main concentration of which is in the region between the Moray Firth and the Firth of Tay, with another important group in south-east Scotland, Northumberland and Durham. The way in which the 'multiple-cist' cairns in Scotland avoid this primary Short-necked Beaker concentration is most striking. They skirt it, spreading on the one hand from Kintyre and the south-west towards the Firth of Forth, and on the other up the Great Glen to the far north of the country. Similarly the southward extension of the northern group of 'multiple-cist' cairns barely penetrates the main concentration of round barrows with pit-graves, normally containing Long-necked Beakers or Yorkshire Food Vases, to be found on the Wolds of the East Riding. In this area in particular the few Short-necked Beakers and the even more limited number of cists show up clearly in the records of Greenwell and Mortimer as culturally and stratigraphically intrusive.

If it were not for the contrasting distribution just noted, it would be natural to see the 'multiple-cist' cairns of northern Britain simply as a regional adaptation of a tradition of multiple burials, usually in pit graves, which is primarily characteristic of the localised southern British Bell Beaker (Wessex/Middle Rhine) and Cord-zoned Beaker groups and their successor, the Long-necked Beaker group. This element may be presumed to have spread from the south as far as Scotland by the same process as that which led to the appearance of a few examples of southern Beaker types (Piggott, 1962, fig. 10) on Scottish settlement and burial sites – not always in barrows – and to the production in Scotland of a number of hybrid Beakers, usually Short-necked in form but having Long-necked decorative features (Mitchell, 1933–4). In the same way the custom of building boat-shaped structures, or digging boat-shaped pits, in connection with barrow burials may have spread from south-western England and Wales to western and northern Scotland (Minnigaff, Eddertoun and Inverlael – see Appendix II) without causing much reaction in Ireland, so far as one can see as yet.[1]

It is equally true, of course, that Short-necked Beakers, mostly in a more or less debased form, spread southwards through Wales and the west Midlands as far as Somerset and Dorset, and, as we shall see later when considering Wales, this had the additional effect of extending southward the use of 'flat' cist burials. These two movements must be seen as parallel and complementary, in a cultural process which involves a great deal more than pots.[2] The occurrence of cairns with a central primary cist burial in the zone of overlap between northern and southern Beakers may be largely due to fusion between these two cultural groups. A recent radiocarbon date (1670 ± 50 bc) for an advanced stage of this southward spread of debased Short-necked Beakers is available at Chatton Sandyford, Northumberland (Jobey, 1968). But, as we shall see later when considering Wales, the process probably began a good deal earlier than this.

We noted at the beginning how the distributions of 'multiple-cist' cairns seemed to suggest the spread of a cultural trait from Ireland north-eastwards to the west coast of Scotland and south-eastwards to the South Wales seaboard. When, however, we analyse the associated grave goods in such cairns in northern England and Scotland (Appendix II), we encounter the awkward fact that a high proportion of them contain at least one cist burial with a Beaker. Such burials are mostly concentrated in the western and northern areas of Scotland, in Yorkshire and Derbyshire, while cairns containing nothing earlier than a Food Vessel predominate in south-east Scotland, Northumberland and Durham. Although one could try to explain this as due, at least in part, to an overlap between late Beakers on the west coast and early Food Vessels on the east coast, the replacement, at Cairnpapple, of a stone circle with Beaker burials of late date by a cairn with two primary cists with Food Vessels, points to a strong possibility that 'multiple-cist' cairns start rather earlier on the west coast than on the east. This conclusion might support the theory of Irish derivation, but by the same token we have

[1] There is one of Food Vessel date at Corrower, Co. Mayo (Raftery, 1960, 79–93), and one or two others which appear to belong to a fairly late date and constitute, with Corrower, a small group with a westerly distribution in Ireland.

[2] Indeed, concentration on ceramic typology and a wish to avoid finding an independent Continental origin for Long-necked Beakers beyond the Low Countries, has led Clarke to his quite unacceptable view that the latter developed out of late northern Beakers in the Fenland area and spread thence south-westwards (Clarke, 1966).

to admit that the west Scottish 'multiple-cist' cairns may also start earlier than such cairns in Ireland, where the predominant ceramic type is again the Food Vessel.

There is, indeed, a certain temptation to fall back on Kintyre and the area of the Crinan Canal as a primary centre from which impulses would have spread up the Great Glen to northern Scotland and southwards to the Cumbrian coast and thence to Yorkshire and Derbyshire: all areas with early 'multiple-cist' cairns. This Crinan region is a well-known economic and cultural focal point connected to south-western England by its rebated and decorated cist-slabs (Crawford, 1928; Craw, 1929–30; Campbell, Scott & Piggott, 1960–1) and by the bell-cairn and cist burial with southern English Beaker at Ballymeanoch, but it is difficult to include 'multiple-cist' burial among those influences derived originally from south-west England, for in the latter area such burials are few and undistinguished: the groupings are small and no cairns have symmetrically arranged cists.

Symmetry is the feature, we saw at the outset, which points particularly towards Ireland, and we have to admit that it is not too well represented on the eastern side of the Irish sea, even in northern Britain. The best example, Hedon Howe in the East Riding of Yorkshire, is peripheral. This site has a central cist with four marginal cists at the points of the compass, but unfortunately no grave goods have survived and the only chronological indication we have is the presence of a secondary inhumation with a Long-necked Beaker. In Argyllshire the best example of a symmetrical arrangement is that in the Achnamara cairn, Crinan, where cists were arranged in a peripheral ring. Three survive and probably there were originally one or two more. These arrangements, as we saw earlier, would have some parallels in Ireland, as would the scheme found both at Eddertoun, Ross and Cromarty, and at Blawearie, Northumberland, where there is a central, possibly primary, cist and several others in a group on one side of the cairn. Such a plan would indeed compare with the more magnificent cairn at Mount Stewart, Co. Down, where Food Bowls are the predominant ceramic form and no Beakers are present. At Eddertoun the Beaker – not, apparently, primary – belongs to the same stage of hybridisation as those at Chatton Sandyford, having decoration influenced by southern Bell Beakers or Long-necked Beakers. On the other hand, although the former begins with a Short-necked Beaker, the two cairns with the largest number of cists – Balnabraid, Argyll, and Amble, Northumberland – seem to have contained several cists which must represent successive burials during the local Food Vessel and Cinerary Urn phases. Moreover, no symmetrical arrangement can be detected at these sites.

It follows that 'multiple-cist' cairns in northern Britain cannot be treated as a unitary group. A first phase may be postulated in which a primary Beaker burial was succeeded by secondary cists, sometimes accompanied by enlargement of the cairn. This phase may be represented at Drumelzier, Peebles, and possibly at Auchencairn, Dumfries, and Low Trewhitt, Northumberland. Irish influence under which cairns were constructed with a symmetrical pattern of cists, all primary or some successive, may constitute a second phase and there may have been a third phase of degeneration in which a number of burials, in cists or pits, were inserted successively without regard for pattern. Paired primary cists, as at Rudstone, Yorkshire, and Cairnpapple, Lothian, should also perhaps be treated as a separate group. In support of this complexity of development one may note that Short-necked Beakers often occur in small cemeteries of cists, without trace of covering mounds, and this tradition could well have influenced the development of 'multiple-cist' cairns in Scotland.

We return to the south-west Scottish cairns where we noted an apparent association with an important concentration of Food Bowls of Irish type. Unfortunately it is difficult to work out this association in detail because many of the Argyllshire cairns were badly disturbed at the time of their exploration, and produced few, or even no, grave goods. In fact it is only at Dunchragaig that Food Bowls were directly associated (Craw, 1929–30, 134). They were in 'short cists', which were secondary to a massive cist with multiple cremations and an inhumation, apparently

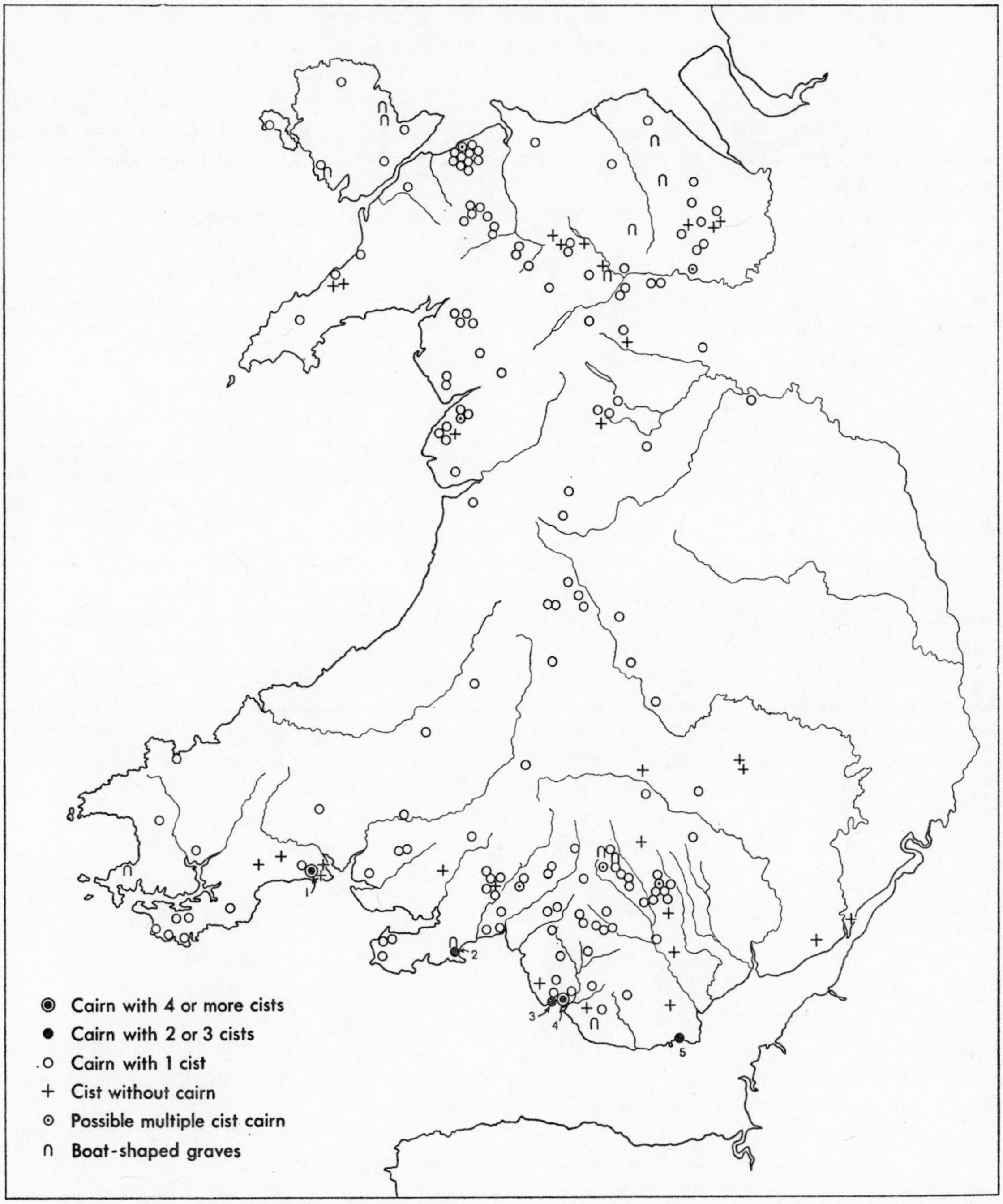
Cairn with 4 or more cists
Cairn with 2 or 3 cists
Cairn with 1 cist
Cist without cairn
Possible multiple cist cairn
Boat-shaped graves

fig. 2 Cists and Boat Graves in Wales: 1 Plashett, Laugharne; 2 Newton (Oystermouth); 3 Riley's Tumulus; 4 Pwll Swil; 5 Benricks

perpetuating late megalithic traditions. Thus the relationship between northern British 'multiple-cist' cairns and Food Bowls must remain theoretical. In view, however, of the evidence for Food Bowl/Beaker overlap at Swarkestone, it is always possible that the symmetrical layout of cists which predates the Long-necked Beaker burial at Hedon Howe, Yorkshire, and the 'multiple-cist' cairns with Long-necked Beakers in Derbyshire were due to Irish influence associated with early Food Bowls, spreading from south-west Scotland through the Pennine area of England.

At the same time we have to consider the possibility, suggested by the sequence at Dunchragaig and the evidence at Kintraw (Simpson, 1966–7), both in Argyll, that local megalithic traditions played a part, with the symmetrical arrangements of cists which are common to Ireland and northern Britain reflecting similar late megalithic trends found around the Irish Channel and represented particularly by monuments with chambers arranged radially. In south-west Scotland this late megalithic tradition of laterally chambered cairns can be seen developing in such long cairns as the Caves of Kilhern and Drannandow in Galloway (Piggott & Powell, 1948–9, fig. 16) and culminating in monuments like Cairnderry and High Gillespie in Galloway and Dunan Mor in Arran (Davies, 1945, fig. 4,10) in which radial chambers are set in round or oval cairns. In Ireland there is a parallel development, represented by such laterally chambered cairns as Aghnaskeagh B, Co. Louth (de Valéra, 1960, pl. xxx, 27) and Ballynoe, Co. Down (*Co. Down*, 1966, 87–9). In the Isle of Man the Mull Hill Circle (Piggott, 1932) with its ring of twelve paired cists with common entrance passages set in a sort of ring cairn, perhaps originally with a central cist, seems to represent the final stage along this line of evolution, a stage to which the monument at Cerrig y Gof, Pembrokeshire, with its radial arrangement of five megalithic cists, one with a surviving portal, comes close.

This late megalithic tradition of peripheral chambers seems to have developed more strongly on the eastern side of the northern Irish Channel than on the western and, if it really had some influence on the development of 'multiple-cist' cairns of Copper Age date, the case for regarding south-west Scotland as the primary centre of these cairns may be strengthened. If this were so, we should expect its ramifications to appear on the coast of North Wales, as with other north British cultural forms in this period; this seems, therefore, to be the appropriate point at which to examine more closely the Welsh manifestations of the 'multiple-cist' tradition.

'MULTIPLE-CIST' CAIRNS IN WALES

As the map (fig. 2) shows, it is in fact the southern, not the northern, seaboard of Wales which appears to have seen the main development of 'multiple-cist' cairns in this part of Britain. The few possible examples in North Wales listed in Appendix I are either no longer available for study or have not yet been examined sufficiently to determine the number and location of cists, so that there is nothing to show positively that these sites were anything more than cairns with a central primary and an additional secondary cist.

Similarly, the evidence from South Wales is not entirely satisfactory, since most of the sites are either destroyed and known only from brief descriptions in the literature, or are not yet fully explored. At least, however, we know that at Plashett, near Laugharne, there was once a cairn with seven or eight cists, arrangement unknown; that at Riley's Tumulus on Merthyr Mawr Warren there were two cists without grave goods, one of them probably primary, and three apparently secondary pit burials with Long-necked Beakers; while near by, at Pwll Swil, there is a possibility that there were at least three, originally perhaps four or five cists, arranged round a central, primary cist. Most other sites are of doubtful interpretation, though there seems to be good reason for believing in the existence of a 'multiple-cist' cairn of uncertain plan at the Bendricks, Sully, Glamorgan. Sites like South Hill, Templeton, Pembrokeshire (RCAM, 1925, 251) and Capel Cynon, Llandysiliogogo, Cardiganshire (Davies, 1905), seem to carry the

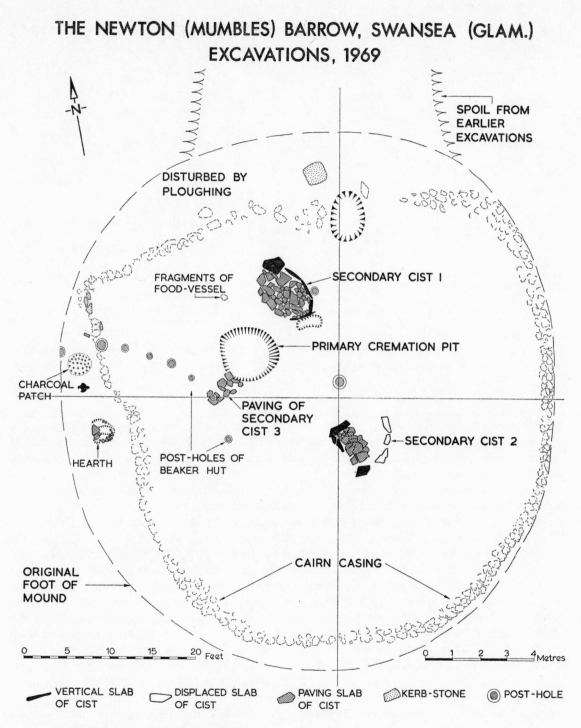

THE NEWTON (MUMBLES) BARROW, SWANSEA (GLAM.) EXCAVATIONS, 1969

SPOIL FROM EARLIER EXCAVATIONS

DISTURBED BY PLOUGHING

SECONDARY CIST I

FRAGMENTS OF FOOD-VESSEL

PRIMARY CREMATION PIT

CHARCOAL PATCH

PAVING OF SECONDARY CIST 3

SECONDARY CIST 2

HEARTH

POST-HOLES OF BEAKER HUT

CAIRN CASING

ORIGINAL FOOT OF MOUND

| 0 | 5 | 10 | 15 | 20 Feet |

| 0 | 1 | 2 | 3 | 4 Metres |

VERTICAL SLAB OF CIST   DISPLACED SLAB OF CIST   PAVING SLAB OF CIST   KERB-STONE   POST-HOLE

fig. 3 Newton, Oystermouth: plan of cairn

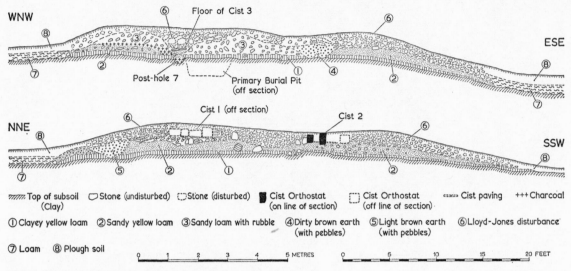

THE NEWTON (MUMBLES) BARROW, SWANSEA (GLAM.), 1969
SECTIONS

Key (legend):

Top of subsoil (Clay) · Stone (undisturbed) · Stone (disturbed) · Cist Orthostat (on line of section) · Cist Orthostat (off line of section) · Cist paving · Charcoal

① Clayey yellow loam ② Sandy yellow loam ③ Sandy loam with rubble ④ Dirty brown earth (with pebbles) ⑤ Light brown earth (with pebbles) ⑥ Lloyd-Jones disturbance

⑦ Loam ⑧ Plough soil

0 1 2 3 4 5 METRES   0 5 10 15 20 FEET

fig. 4 Newton, Oystermouth: sections through cairn

'multiple-cist' tradition down to a later horizon in the Early Bronze Age, but there is no very strong evidence that this tradition ever had much impact beyond the immediate seaboard of South Wales: possible inland sites are few and, with one exception, are not likely to prove to be true examples of the type.

The re-excavation of the Newton round cairn near Oystermouth carried out by the writer on behalf of the Ministry of Public Building and Works in 1969 has given us more exact knowledge of another coastal site which seems to belong to a very late horizon in the Copper Age. The barrow was a composite one, with an earthen core covered by a stone casing. At the base of this casing were three cists, most likely built at one time (figs. 3, 4). The earthen core covered an unaccompanied cremation deposit consisting of parts of the bones of two adults (one female) and a child scattered throughout the stony filling of a large D-shaped pit dug into subsoil. Recent disturbances of the cairn had destroyed much of the evidence for the stratigraphical position of this cremation deposit, but a broad scatter of charcoal running westward from the straight side of the pit over a low heap of spoil which probably represents the upcast from digging the pit, is likely to be connected with the burial ceremony and is definitely sealed by the cairn casing. The excavator therefore concludes that the deposit in the D-shaped pit is primary.

As there were no grave goods in this deposit and the three secondary cists had been previously cleared out, there was no direct evidence for the date of the burials, but a *terminus post quem* is provided by late Long-necked Beaker pottery (fig. 5) associated with a hearth and posthole system underlying the west side of the cairn. This pottery appears to be connected with a roughly circular hut about 7·40 m. (25 ft) in diameter, whereas part of a Food Vessel of a west Wales type (fig. 5, no. 13) found lying crushed at the base of the cairn-casing a short distance north-west of the primary pit is likely to have been connected with the ceremonial practised at the time of the latter's filling, or the closing of one of the cists.

These cists, at least the two relatively well-preserved examples, are large enough to have contained several lightly flexed, or even extended, inhumations, but the evidence of the long cist at Candleston, Merthyr Mawr Warren, not very far away, warns us that such cists may have contained cremations (Ward, 1919, 328–30). In fact there is, so far, no certain instance in Wales of a Food Vessel associated with anything but a cremation burial. A few specks of burnt bone, however, found during the recent exploration of cist No. 2 at Newton, cannot be decisive, for the area had been badly disturbed and the bone may have been redeposited from elsewhere in the cairn. In assessing the chronological position of the Newton cists it must be borne in mind that cremation was already being practised in South Wales by some Beaker-using communities. For instance, cremation was practised at Dolygaer, Breconshire (Ward, 1902, 25–8) and Eglwysilan, Glamorgan (Savory, 1948–50, 39); thus, in view of the evidence, already mentioned, for some overlap between Beakers and Food Vessels, the Newton cists may not be very much later in date than those at Riley's Tumulus, Merthyr Mawr Warren, which were apparently earlier than Beaker burials in pit-graves. Indeed the cists from the two sites are very similar in their mode of construction (figs. 3, 6), with a tendency to adopt a non-rectangular outline and the use of a comparatively large number of small side-slabs. This must represent a different structural tradition from the box-like cists with four relatively tall side-slabs that are commonly found in the 'flat' cist burials of the northern Beaker Culture and also among its outliers in Wales.

It can now be seen that there is in South Wales a small coastal group of true 'multiple-cist' cairns which belongs to the end of the Beaker phase, to a time when some fusion between inhuming Beaker and cremating Late Neolithic communities had been effected, and when Food Vessels of local types, probably originating independently of those in Yorkshire (Savory, 1957, 205–8), were being made alongside Long-necked Beakers – a time, in fact, which probably covers at least parts of the eighteenth and seventeenth centuries BC. This group includes at least two sites with a tendency towards a radial or peripheral arrangement of cists: Pwll Swil, where a probable ring of cists surrounded a central one, and Newton, where previous disturbance of the cairn may well have entirely removed one or two cists from a roughly radial arrangement.

Since the rest of Wales appears to offer no more than an array of 'flat' cist burials or cairns with a central cist and additional, secondary cists in one or two cases, it is hard to resist the conclusion that the South Welsh 'multiple-cist' cairns represent influence from some other area. That area is most probably Ireland, where symmetrical arrangements of cists most commonly occur. Moreover a glance in the other direction, towards Dorset, reveals nothing but a small group of cairns with two cists. One of these is the Bincombe Barrow with its cairn-ring and multiple secondary burials, of which only some are in cists (Payne, 1943). The grave goods probably represent an even later horizon in the Beaker phase than Riley's Tumulus. Two other Dorset sites contain paired cists with Beaker inhumations (at least one a Short-necked Beaker). It seems much more likely, therefore, that these, like the Northfield barrow, Cheltenham (Hill, 1930) and the single pair of cists on Dartmoor, represent not the beginning, but the end of a line of diffusion. This line would seem to run either through South Wales from Ireland or through the west Midlands from northern Britain (since the specifically Irish property of symmetry is lacking in the south-west).

Yet, if Ireland is to be considered the source of the 'multiple-cist' tradition in Wales, certain difficulties remain; namely, the absence of Beakers from 'multiple-cist' cairns in Ireland, and the failure of these cairns to spread through the northern seaboard of Wales. North Wales is an area where both Irish contacts and the influence of the strong tradition of peripherally-set megalithic chambers found, as we have seen, in the northern part of the Irish Sea area, especially south-west Scotland, might be expected. The answer no doubt depends on future archaeological discovery but, in so far as one can attempt some tentative suggestions now, the clues are probably provided by an analysis of the pottery and a study of the diffusion of the various types of associated grave structure found in Wales and Ireland during the Copper Age.

We have already seen that the pottery associated with 'multiple-cist' cairns in South Wales is Long-necked Beaker and a local type of Food Vase. In Scotland and northern England, on the other hand, it is Short-necked Beaker and Food Vase, usually of northern British type, together with the Irish Food Bowl. Waddell's study makes it clear that in Ireland the type of Food Vessel most closely associated with 'multiple-cist' cairns is the Bowl, an Irish invention which is well represented in south-west Scotland, but not in Wales. It is difficult therefore to visualise the symmetrical 'multiple-cist' cairn being introduced to South Wales by actual makers of Irish Food Bowls at a time when late types of Long-necked Beakers were still being made locally.

Some time ago I pointed out (Savory, 1957, 205–7) that those Welsh Food Vessels which seem to have some degree of Irish affinity can be separated into two groups with wellnigh exclusive distributions, one in North Wales, the other almost confined to West Wales. The first might be described as not so much 'Irish Vases' as northern British Vases evolving in an Irish direction; while the second group is much more markedly Irish in character, but still not quite typically so, and it does not include the true 'Irish Bowl' form. In any case there is no point of contact between these West Wales Food Vases and the 'multiple-cist' cairn group, except possibly in the case of the rather marginal Food Vase from the Newton cairn. The relationship between the grave-form in Ireland and South Wales in the late Copper Age is, therefore, perhaps best seen as the result of cultural contacts between communities of Secondary Neolithic origin served by potters whose styles, after the initial late Bell Beaker and Long-necked Beaker movement through Wales into Ireland, were rapidly diverging.

It should be noted that there is in Anglesey and at Llandegai, Caernarvonshire, a Long-necked Beaker group which forms a connecting link between those of the Bristol Channel area and of Scotland and may provide the true answer to the question of how the tradition of symmetrically arranged cists spread from the northern part of the Irish Channel area to South Wales without affecting North Wales as a whole or the Marches. Their movements may have been coastal, affecting Ireland and Scotland as well as Anglesey, and have involved a 'reflux' to South Wales.

At the same time one must not lose sight of the morphological relationship between Cerrig y Gof in Pembrokeshire with peripheral megalithic cists, and the group of late megalithic monuments with lateral chambers and sometimes a circular plan which are found to the north and west of the north Irish Channel. This relationship may reflect cultural contacts that followed the eastern Irish seaboard rather than the coasts of Liverpool Bay, a route which might explain the absence of evidence in North Wales. These contacts must have survived into the period after the first movement of Beaker-making people from the Bristol Channel area to Wales and Ireland. This move had taken place at a time when the custom of using 'flat' burial cists had been spread among single-grave communities by the makers of Short-necked Beakers, who had come from the eastern side of Britain.

In Wales the period of overlap between Long-necked and Short-necked Beakers during which cists, with or without covering mounds, were being constructed, must have been fairly long, extending over much of the eighteenth and seventeenth centuries BC. Such a span would allow time for the idea of symmetrically arranged multiple cists in round cairns to spread among communities using Long-necked Beakers in South Wales, Short-necked Beakers in Scotland, and Food Bowls in Ireland. That this was so is suggested by the numbers of such burials in Wales which can be marked on the map (fig. 2).[1] It can be gathered from a study of the published lists that, though apparent 'flat' cists have most frequently contained Short-necked Beakers, some have contained Long-necked Beakers and several contained no pottery of any kind, while

---

[1] The map is based on Bowen & Gresham, 1967; the County Inventories of the Royal Commission on Ancient Monuments; Savory, 1955, 1957, 1959; Griffiths, 1957; Livens, 1965, with the addition of some recent discoveries of 'short cists' without pottery near Chepstow and Caldicot in Monmouthshire (Barnett & Savory, 1961–4) and near Brecon (unpublished).

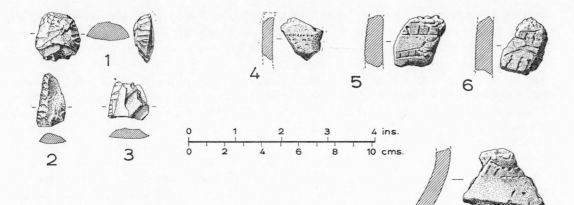

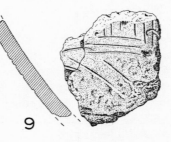

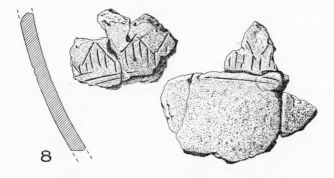

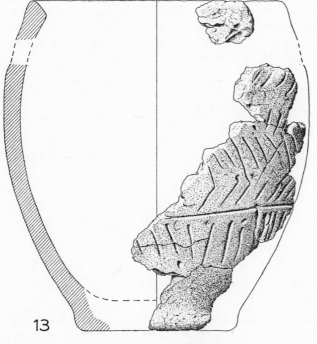

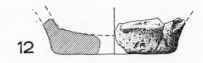

fig. 5 Flints and pottery from the Newton cairn

two in the Olchon Valley, Herefordshire, actually contained debased Bell Beakers (Marshall, 1930–2). Burials in central cists in cairns are mostly associated with Long-necked Beakers, although a debased Short-necked Beaker occurred in such a setting at Clynnog, Caernarvonshire (Roberts, 1910).

The use of 'flat' cists in Wales, in fact, began well before the phase of hybridisation between Long- and Short-necked Beakers because the Beaker found in such a cist at Brymbo, Denbighshire, was one of the purest and presumably earliest examples of the Short-necked form known in Britain (Savory, 1959). One must envisage therefore an early movement of such Beakers from the east coast of England during the early phase of Beaker settlement, as well as a later spread into Wales from Scotland and Cumbria. In return the 'boat grave' tradition, identified in Wales initially with debased Bell Beakers and Long-necked Beakers,[1] was carried north into Scotland, reaching the far north at Eddertoun in company with a debased Short-necked Beaker and multiple cists in a cairn. The spread of the English Food Vase tradition into Wales from the east still retained some association with central cists in barrows, but clearly did not involve the spread of 'multiple-cist' cairns, any more than did the spread of Short-necked Beakers at an earlier date.

CONCLUSIONS

The practice of constructing 'multiple-cist' cairns with a symmetrical arrangement of cists laid out at one time, or at any rate with some continuity of plan, probably first arose in areas to the north and west of the Irish Channel through the influence of local megalithic traditions on single-grave communities. These had already adopted cists from the Northern Beaker group, and cairns from the southern. This tradition was probably transmitted to the South Wales coast via the eastern seaboard of Ireland in the eighteenth or early seventeenth century BC, without affecting the ceramic styles that had by then become established locally: Food Bowls in Ireland and late Long-necked Beakers in South Wales and the Peak District. It is possible that paired primary cists, associated with Short-necked Beakers and English Food Vases, had spread independently from northern Britain via the west Midlands to Dorset at a somewhat earlier date. In a modest form the 'multiple-cist' tradition survived in West Wales, and possibly also elsewhere in Wales, on the Food Vase and, occasionally, even the Cinerary Urn and Pygmy Cup horizon of the Early Bronze Age.

[1] e.g. Talbenny, Pembs. (Fox, 1959, 44–6); Nant Maden, Brecs. ('Notes on excavations', *Proc. Prehist. Soc.*, XXVI, 1960, 349; XXVII, 1961, 351); Twyn-bryn-glas, Brecs. (Webley, 1960); Llandow, Glam. (Fox, 1959, 54–70) and Pant y Saer, Anglesey (Williams, 1875).

APPENDIX I

Welsh Round Cairns with two or more 'Short Cists'. (Very small cists protecting cinerary urns are omitted.)

(a) Certain or probable examples

Plashett Chapel, Llansadyrnin (Carms.) SN/282096
What seems to have been a damaged round cairn with multiple cists was destroyed here in 1875. According to Curtis (1880, 136–8) in that year Mr Raymond of Honeycourse Farm found a number of human skeletons, adult and immature, together with some large slabs, while ploughing a field about a quarter of a mile east of the chapel. They were in a stony patch about 9·20 m. (30 ft) across. A representative of the Royal Commission on Ancient Monuments (Wales) who visited the site in 1912 found no trace of the slabs, but was told by Mr Raymond's son that seven or eight separate 'graves' or 'cists' had been found, each about 1·22 m. (4 ft) by 0·91 m. (3 ft), covered by a single slab and containing a crouched skeleton. The bones had been reburied on the spot, under the slabs, after those obstructing the plough had been removed (RCAM, 1917, No. 558).

Newton Cairn, West Cross, Oystermouth, Swansea (Glam.) SS/605887
The cairn is a composite one, 15·40 m. (50 ft) in diameter, surviving to a height of 0·91 m. (3 ft). The central core is of earth covered by a casing of stones. The earth core covered a primary cremation pit. This pit was north-west of the centre, D-shaped in outline (about 1·65 m. [5 ft 6 in.] across), and contained the burnt bones of two adults and a child scattered throughout the fill. Three large stone cists were added to this mound: they were built on top of the earth core and were covered by the stone casing. All three were badly disturbed and no burials were found, though all would have been large enough for several flexed inhumations (the largest about 1·70 m. [5 ft 6 in.] by 1·25 m. [4 ft]). The cists are symmetrically arranged and it is possible that the pattern was originally completed by a fourth cist on the east side. The cairn overlay a settlement area associated with late Long-necked Beakers while a few sherds of Food Vessel were found beneath the stone casing. These may be connected with the primary burial. The cairn was already disturbed when it was dug into in 1928 by Lt.-Col. A. Lloyd-Jones. These excavations were never adequately published but there are accounts of what was found in the *Mumbles Press* for October 1929. The site was re-excavated in 1969 by the writer (publication pending).

Riley's Tumulus, Merthyr Mawr (Glam.)
SS/850771
Excavated by Mr W. Riley in 1904 without proper record: the scanty details recorded by John Ward (1919, 336–46) were collected after the destruction, and a proper plan could not be made. According to Riley the mound had been 16 m. (54 ft) in diameter and 6·4 m. (21 ft) high and consisted of sand, with a stony casing 1·25 m. (4 ft) thick. The mound covered six skeletons. On the north side three crouched inhumations, in pits dug in the sand of the tumulus without protective stones, were accompanied by Long-necked Beakers. Two of these are preserved in the National Museum (Grimes, 1951, No. 595, fig. 73, 2–3) and one is preserved in the Royal Institution of South Wales, Swansea (Williams, 1939, 21, fig. 1. 1). Ward states (1919, 345) that these inhumations were secondary, in the sense that they had been inserted into the mound, several feet above the original surface. He goes on to say (1919, 346) that two large stone cists found in the mound were at a lower level and that the larger of the two rested on the original surface near the centre and was probably primary. This cist was roughly circular, 0·91 m. (3 ft) in diameter, with nine side-slabs and covered by a single capstone; it contained the crouched skeleton of a man lying on the left side and with the head to the north. The smaller cist lay 4·27 m. (14 ft) to the east and was an elongated hexagon in shape, 0·76 m. (2 ft 6 in.) in length north to south and 0·48 m. (19 in.) wide; it had three small upright slabs on the west side and one on the north side. It contained the bodies of two children buried successively. Sketches of these two cists, made by J. M. Staniforth and published by J. W. Rodger in his obituary of Riley (Rodger, 1914) are reproduced (fig. 6) because their mode of construction, with numerous small slabs not to a simple rectangular plan, resembles that of the Newton (Swansea) cists. They contained no grave goods, but the skeletons, like those in the three pit graves, were all of the brachycephalic Beaker type (Hepburn, 1904).

Pwll Swil Tumulus, Merthyr Mawr (Glam.)
SS/856769
Excavated in 1901, when already in a wrecked condition, by Mr W. Riley, with help from

J. Ward. No plan survives, but Ward's account, written long afterwards, contains a drawing by Mr R. Morton Nance of a vertical view of one of the cists (that to the north-west) which held the crouched skeleton of a youth (Ward, 1919, 330–6). The mound appeared to have been of sand, with a stony casing, and was about 7·65 m. (25 ft) in diameter with traces of a kerb of upright slabs on the west side. One cist, to the north-west, was slightly rhomboidal in shape, 0·74 m. (2 ft 5 in.) in length, 0·51 m. (1 ft 8 in.) in width, and 0·30 m. (1 ft) in height, internally, and its longer axis was north-north-west and south-south-east. The side-slabs were single on three sides but on the fourth side were doubled. There was a single cover slab. This cist was erected on the old land surface and had stones piled against it, like those in Riley's Tumulus. A second, larger cist, containing the poorly preserved crouched skeleton of an adult, was also erected on the old land surface, near the centre, and may have been primary. A third lay to the south of the second and was small (0·56 m. [1 ft 10 in.] by 0·38 m. [1 ft 3 in.] internally) but neatly constructed of six slabs, one forming the cover: it contained the crouched skeleton of a child. A fourth cist was found on the west side, 4·51 m. (15 ft) south-west of the first and larger than any of the others, being 1·25 m. (4 ft 1 in.) long (north–south), 0·71 m. (2 ft 4 in.) in width, and 0·61 m. (2 ft) high. It was of rounded oblong shape, with sides constructed of many narrow slabs let into the natural soil and covered with two large overlapping slabs. It contained the crouched skeleton of a powerfully built man, lying on his left side with his head to the north and face to the east. Ward considered this burial to be a secondary one. None of the Pwll Swil burials was accompanied by any grave goods, but Hepburn's (1904) report on the skeletal material makes its Beaker character reasonably clear. There is a strong suggestion that the cists in this tumulus, before its disturbance, had been arranged in a widely spaced circle round a central primary cist.

Bendricks, Sully (Glam.) ST/131674

A small round barrow survives just within the western limits of a former Government Storage Depot, close to the head of the creek which is now enclosed by the breakwaters flanking the entrance to Barry Docks. It appears now as a low mound about 7·65 m. (25 ft) in diameter.

Square Cist

After J.M. Staniforth

Circular Cist (Capstone off)

fig. 6 Riley's Tumulus, Merthyr Mawr Warren (Glam.) 1904 (from Rodger 1914)

According to a personal report made to the writer in 1963 by Mr S. J. Strong of Cadoxton this mound was disturbed by the laying of a pipe line in which Mr Strong was concerned, when the Storage Depot was being constructed for the War Department early in World War II. Four skeletons were found, separated from one another by vertical slabs, which had no covering stones but otherwise resembled the reconstructed Brymbo Cist which Mr Strong had just seen in the Museum's Prehistoric Gallery. A passage lined with dry-stone walling covered by slabs resting on corbel stones ('cantilevered') ran from the burials towards the seashore about 45 m. (50 yds) away. The engineer in charge of the work had the burials covered over immediately for security reasons and the trench filled in without resort to archaeological advice. A further report, made to the writer in 1965 by Mr G. Dowdell of Barry, based on information supplied by Mr C. Wakeham of Cadoxton, indicates that the find was made in 1942 and involved three – not four – skeletons, thought to be a man, woman and child, each in a separate cist, and that the filling-in was indeed carried out at once without examination of the contents.

A visit to the site made by the writer in 1966 in the company of Mr Jeremy Knight of the Ministry of Public Building and Works verified the present surface appearance of the site; there appeared to be a shallow ditch around the mound. The reference in Mr Strong's account to a dry-stone passage might suggest a complex chamber relating to one element in the Cotswold–Severn long cairn tradition, but the mound to be seen on the spot now is definitely circular and too small to support interpretation as a chambered cairn; moreover, it would be unusual for the contents of a chamber in a Cotswold–Severn cairn to be immediately identifiable as the separate crouched burials of three individuals.

(b) Doubtful examples

Mynydd March Hywel, Dylais Higher (Glam.) SN/772047
A cairn close to bench-mark 1162 on the Ordnance Survey 6-inch sheet is stated in the field note-books of Sir Cyril and Lady Fox, now deposited in the National Museum of Wales, to have several orthostats projecting from its badly wrecked foundations. These might represent the remnants of several cists. A visit by the writer, in April 1970, confirmed the general terms of the statement: the cairn, about 9·20 m. (30 ft) in diameter and 0·60 m. (2 ft) high, seems to have been little,

if at all, disturbed during the last thirty years; but it is grassed over and it is impossible to say, without excavation, how many cists there were and how large. Probably there were not more than three, but most of the slabs seem to be out of position and all are tilted, so that it is uncertain whether they were more than small coffers protecting urns, like those of Templeton (Pembs.) and Capel Cynon (Cards.) which have been omitted from the list.

Mynydd y Glôg, Penderyn (Brecons.) SN/974090
A record of fieldwork by the late Mr P. Murray-Threipland, entered on the Ordnance Survey 6-inch sheet kept for record purposes in the National Museum of Wales, refers to four 'built cists' in a partially wrecked cairn on the western summit of Mynydd y Glôg. The writer visited this cairn in April 1970 but found no trace of orthostatically built cists in the hollowed centre of the cairn, which is about 12·25 m. (40 ft) in diameter and 1·25 m. (4 ft) high in its present condition. It is possible that small sub-rectangular recesses in the rubble core of the cairn may have seemed thirty years ago to have been lined with dry-stone walling.

Carn Bugail, Gelligaer (Glam.) ST/100036
According to J. W. Lukis (1875) this round cairn appeared at that time to contain three long cists, all aligned parallel to each other, north and south, and occupying a large part of the cairn. This, at any rate, is what is suggested by the plan (Lukis, 1875, 183) of this and adjoining cairns which Lukis published, but as he gives the dimensions of the cairn as 17·13 m. (56 ft) by 16·20 m. (53 ft), the cists as drawn must be completely out of scale, since if they were to scale they would be between 7.70 m. (25 ft) and 9.20 m. (30 ft) long. The plan, in fact, can hardly be based upon actual measurements of the cists, as these are not given for this particular cairn. It is perhaps not surprising, therefore, that the Royal Commission on Ancient Monuments in Wales, when they examined this cairn, only found traces of a single central cist (*Archaeology in Wales*, 5 [1965], 9).

Eglwyseg Rocks, Llangollen Rural (Denb.) SJ/222443
The late Canon Ellis Davies states that this round cairn, which is about 36 paces in circumference and 0·60 m. (2 ft) high, has the remains of stone cists, one of which, near the centre, is 1·25 m. by 0·91 m. by 0·61 m. (4 ft by 3 ft by 2 ft) (Davies, 1929, 260). The writer has not been able to visit this site.

Hafotty fach, Brithdir (Mer.) SH/662137
This cairn, now largely destroyed (Bowen & Gresham, 1967, 95, 106) is probably the one which is said to have contained two cists when it was opened in 1853.

Ty'n-y-llwyfan, Llanfairfechan (Caern.) SH/696740
This cairn, excavated in 1886 (*Archaeol. Cambrensis* 1888, 168–70), is said to have contained a central 'short cist' in which were traces of a cremation and a pot (not preserved) decorated with lines and chevrons. A second cist, only 'about a foot across', was found 0·61 m. (2 ft) south of the central one, and yielded more fragments of pottery. The contemporary description of the decoration of the lost pottery suggests that this may have been of Beaker type, in spite of the presence of a cremation. The cists have since been destroyed (RCAM 1956, 126).

APPENDIX II
'Multiple-cist' Cairns in Britain outside Wales, shown on the Distribution Map, fig. 1.
(For Irish 'Multiple-cist' Cairns, see Waddell, 1970.)

Scotland
Achnamara (Seafield), Crinan, Argyll (Childe, 1936–7)
At least three cists arranged in an arc, on the line of their major axes, immediately within an inner circular setting of blocks. No grave goods.
Auchencairn, Closeburn, Dumfries (RCAHM, 1920, I, 35; *Proc. Soc. Antiq. Scot.*, L [1915–16], 152)
Three cists: one yielded an atypical northern Beaker with an inhumation; two held cremations, without grave goods.
Ballymeanoch, Crinan, Argyll (Greenwell, 1864–6)
Two cists under a bell cairn, one large and nearly central (robbed), the other small peripheral, with southern (Long-necked) Beaker.
Balnabraid, Campbeltown, Argyll (Galloway, 1919–20; *Discovery and Excavation*, 1966, 46).
At least twelve cists, mostly with cremations but some inhumations, as well as secondary inhumations not in cists. Short-necked Beaker, two Food Vases and Cinerary Urn with fragments of bronze sheeting with geometrical designs in repoussé.
Brouch an Drummin, Kilmartin, Argyll (*Discovery and Excavation*, 1961, 11–12)
Three cists: one with a Beaker, another with a Food-Vessel (inhumations and cremations).

Cairnpapple, Torphichen, W. Lothian (Piggott, 1947–8)
Two primary cists in a large cairn within kerb, replacing stone circle with Beaker burials. One had an inhumation with a Food Vase; the other an unaccompanied cremation.
Drumelzier, Peebles (Craw, 1930–1, 363–72; RCAHM, 1967, 53, fig. 5)
Central cist with Cord-zoned Beaker under primary cairn, two large peripheral cists (empty) and four smaller cists (empty), added in secondary cairn. There are also traces of secondary cremations with Cordoned Urns, not in cists.
Dunchragaig, Kilmartin, Argyll (Craw, 1929–30, 134 f.).
Three cists: one large, with multiple cremations and an inhumation, no grave goods; others with one Food Bowl, accompanying cremations.
Eddertoun, Ross and Cromarty (Joass, 1866–8)
Six cists: one central, four others grouped in a bunch to the south (one of these had an inhumation with a typical northern Beaker [Abercromby, 1912, 289], the rest contained cremations). The sixth contained a cremation and was enclosed by a D-shaped structure.
Foulden, Cairn I, Berwickshire (Craw, 1913–14)
Three cists: two close together at centre with Food Vase in each, one with inhumation, the other with cremation; third cist at higher level, disturbed. Also primary pit grave with inhumation (two-period cairn) and isolated deposit of early-type stone battle-axe.
Gallows Knowe, Lintrathen, Angus (Fenton, 1939–40)
At least three cists, no grave goods, cremation in one cist.
Hare Law, Lochore, Fife (Constable, 1890–1; 1891–2; Feachem, 1963, 77)
At least three cists with inhumations, and two Food Vases. One of the cists which was at the centre, without a pot but with a metal object (lost), may have been a raised primary burial.
Inverlael, Inverbroom, Ross and Cromarty (Cree, 1913–14)
Two cists inside a D-structure: the larger (primary) was disturbed, the smaller (secondary) contained a cremation, barbed and tanged arrowhead and two scrapers.
Kalemouth, Roxburgh (Richardson & Lindsay 1951–2)
Two cists: one nearly central, with inhumation and Food Vessel, the other just inside kerb (empty).
Lady's Seat, Slockavullin, Kilmartin, Argyll (Craw, 1929–30, 143)

Two cists, one with rebated slabs, with an inhumation (possibly in a derived position) between them. No grave goods.

Minnigaff (Drannandow), Kirkcudbright (Edwards, 1922–3)

Two cists: one central, with inhumation and Food Vase, surrounded by a D-shaped structure; the other secondary, outside D-structure, with inhumation and fragmentary Food Vessel.

Nether Largie mid-cairn, Kilmartin, Argyll (Craw, 1929–30, 127–30),

At least two cists, one with rebated and grooved slabs. No grave goods.

Norrie's Law, Kirkton of Largo, Fife (RCAHM, 1933, 185; Feachem, 1963, 77)

Uncertain number of small cists, with cremations and at least one Food Vessel.

Rhudil Mill, Kilmartin, Argyll (Craw, 1929–30, 138)

Three cists: one with a Food Vase, one with an Urn and an inhumation, one empty.

Ri Cruin, Poltalloch, Argyll (Craw, 1929–30, 131–4)

Three cists with rebated side-slabs, one of them with carvings (splayed flat axes and [?] boat) on two of these slabs.

Strathnaver, Sutherland (Stevenson, 1938–9)

Two cists, one containing a jet necklace and a V-perforated button.

Warth Hill, Canisbay, Caithness (Feachem, 1963, 71)

Central cist with inhumation, no grave goods; secondary cist with inhumation, no grave goods.

Woodend, Tweedsmuir, Peebles (Stevenson 1939–40; RCAHM, 1967, 59)

A cairn with an uncertain number of cists. One central cist is still visible.

Isle of Man
Bishopscourt Farm, Micheal

Cairn containing two longish stone cists: one with a crouched inhumation and a Bowl Food Vessel, the other with a cremation and a Bowl Food Vessel. Excavated in 1953. Unpublished, Manx Museum.

Northern England
Amble, Northumberland (Greenwell, 1890, 66–70)

Central cist with inhumation, Food Vase, bronze knife-dagger with three rivets; about twenty other cists, one of them 1·80 m. (6 ft) long with inhumation; another 1·22 m. (4 ft) long with Food Vase and inhumation; others, small, with inhumations or cremations and Food Vases in some cases.

Bee Low Youlgreave, Derbyshire (Bateman, 1848, 35; Bateman, 1861, 71–4)

Built cist with reburied inhumation; two slab-lined pits with inhumations accompanied by a Long-necked Beaker and fragmentary Beaker (Short-necked?) respectively.

Blawearie, Eglingham, Northumberland (Greenwell, 1877, 418–21)

Four cists: one central (robbed); three grouped on west side, with inhumations, Food Vase, necklace and flint knife.

Fatfield, Sunderland, Durham (Trechmann, 1914, 169)

Three cists with inhumations, one with a Food Vessel.

Giants' Graves, Penygent, West Riding (Bennett, 1936–8)

Uncertain number of cists in wrecked cairn; two peripheral cists preserved, with traces of inhumations; also several hollows indicating the position of wrecked cists.

Gristhorpe, North Riding (Greenwell, 1890, 38)

Primary central cist with inhumation (robbed); small secondary cist south-south-east of centre, with cremation.

Hasting Hill, Offerton, Durham (Trechmann, 1914, 135–57)

Primary cist with inhumation and Food Vase; three other cists with two inhumations, one cremation, two Food Vases and flint saw; several secondary cremations without cists, with Food Vessels or Enlarged Food Vessels.

Hay Top, Monsal Dale, Derbyshire (Bateman, 1861, 74–7)

Built cist with inhumation of child and Food Vase; partly slab-lined cist with inhumation Food Vase and pin; pit grave with adult inhumation in stone setting; inhumation of child and two skulls with Long-necked Beaker.

Hedon Howe, Langton, East Riding (Mortimer, 1905, 346–50)

Five cists: one central, with three inhumations; others placed radially at the points of the compass near the edge of the mound. Two contained inhumations, all disturbed. There was also a secondary inhumation with Long-necked Beaker and secondary cremation with Food Vase.

Hepburn Moor, Northumberland (Thomas, 1960, 161)

Two cists, unexcavated.

Low Trewhitt, Coquetdale, Northumberland (Bate, 1911–12)

Three cists, all secondary: one central with Short-necked Beaker and two peripheral, one of the latter containing fragments of Short-necked Beaker and inhumation.

Lythe, North Riding (Greenwell, 1890, 43–5)

Primary central cist with inhumation and Food Vase; one secondary cist (robbed).

North Charlton, Northumberland (Tait, 1965, 32)

Three cists, one containing an inhumation with a bronze knife dagger.

Rudstone, East Riding (Greenwell, 1877, 234–45)

Two secondary cists placed at the bottom of the same intrusive shaft, with three inhumations and three cremations and three northern (Short-necked) Beakers.

Shield Knowe, Bewcastle, Cumberland (Hodgson, 1940)

Large primary cist with inhumation and two Food Vases; small secondary cist with inhumation and Food Vase; pit grave with cremation; no grave goods.

The Cops, Calton, Staffordshire (Bateman, 1861, 129–30)

Three cists with inhumations, no significant grave goods.

Top Low, Swinscoe, Staffordshire (Bateman, 1861, 133–8)

Six rock-cut graves: two wholly and four partly lined with vertical slabs. Long-necked Beaker (Abercromby, 1912, vol. I, 59) in one of the cists.

Wetton-near-Hill, Staffordshire (Bateman, 1861, 139–40)

Two cists, each with an inhumation, one of them accompanied by a Food Vase.

Southern England

Bincombe, Ridgeway Hill, Barrow XI, Dorset (Payne, 1943)

Multiple inhumations, of which seven were Early Bronze Age, with in a cairn ring. Two were in cists in a secondary position, one of them (No. 3) above an unprotected inhumation (No. 6) which adjoined another inhumation (No. 7), the latter accompanied by a Beaker bowl. Secondary inhumation (No. 5) (uncisted) was accompanied by a handled Beaker.

Bincombe Ridgeway, Dorset SY/674858 (MPBW *Excavations Annual Report*, 1963, 7)

(1) Bell barrow with primary cist containing the inhumation of an adult female with Short-necked Beaker and bronze awl; a satellite cist with an inhumation of a child; and a satellite cremation burial in a pit. There were also five secondary cremations, one with an Enlarged Food Vessel.

(2) Bowl barrow with primary cist containing inhumation with a Beaker, and a satellite cist with an inhumation of a child without grave goods; a secondary cist, disturbing primary cist, contained an inhumation with a Food Vase. There were two other secondary inhumations in pit graves.

Cosdon Beacon, Dartmoor, Devon (Worth, 1953, 171; Thomas, 1960, 76)

Cairn with peristalith and two cists.

Northfield Barrow, Charlton Kings, Cheltenham, Gloucestershire (Hill, 1930)

Three cists on east side of barrow with inhumations, two pins, flint knife, saw and fabricator.

Weymouth, Ridgeway Hill, Barrow X, Dorset (Grinsell, 1959, 141)

Two 'stone-lined chalk-cut graves (? both primary)' with an inhumation in each, accompanied by Food Vessels (?), were surrounded by a circle of twenty-two stones, 3·05 m. (10 ft) in diameter, with an entrance gap.

BIBLIOGRAPHY

Abercromby, J., 1912. *A Study of the Bronze Age Pottery of Great Britain and Ireland*. Oxford.

ApSimon, A. M., 1958. 'Food Vessels', *Univ. London Inst. Archaeol. Bull.*, I, 24–36.

—— 1960. 'Report on Flints and Neolithic and Bronze Age Pottery from Barrow 4 at Swarkeston', *J. Derbyshire Archaeol. N.H. Soc.*, LXXX, 19–41.

Barnett & Savory, 1961–4. 'A Beaker cist at Beachley', *Monmouthshire Antiq.*, I, 112–16.

Bate, D. M. A., 1911–12. 'On a North Northumberland Barrow and its Contents', *Proc. Soc. Antiq. Scot.*, XLVI, 15–26.

Bateman, T., 1848. *Vestiges of the Antiquities of Derbyshire*. London.

—— 1861. *Ten Years Diggings*. London.

Bennett, W., 1936–8. 'Giants' Graves, Penygent', *Yorkshire Archaeol. J.*, XXXIII, 318 f.

Bowen, E. G. & Gresham, C. A., 1967. *History of Merioneth*. Vol. I. Dolgellau.

Campbell, M., Scott, J. G., & Piggott, S., 1960–1. 'The Badden Cist Slab', *Proc. Soc. Antiq. Scot.*, XCIV, 46–61.

Childe, V. G., 1936–7. 'A round cairn at Achnamara, Loch Sween, Argyll', *Proc. Soc. Antiq. Scot.*, LXXI, 84–9.

Clarke, D. L., 1966. 'A Tentative Reclassification of British Beaker Pottery in the Light of Recent Research', *Palaeohistoria*, XII, 179–98.

Co. Down, 1966. *An Archaeological Survey of Co. Down.* E. M. Jope, ed. Belfast.

Constable, G. W., 1890–1. 'Notice of the Excavation of Harelaw Cairn on the Estate of Glencraig, Fifeshire', *Proc. Soc. Antiq. Scot.*, XXV, 69–72.

—— 1891–2. 'Notice of further excavations at Harelaw Cairn, Fifeshire', *Proc. Soc. Antiq. Scot.*, XXVI, 114–17.

Craw, J. H., 1913–14. 'Account of the Excavation of two Bronze Age cairns in the parish of Foulden', *Proc. Soc. Antiq. Scot.*, XLVIII, 316–30.

—— 1929–30. 'Excavations at Dunadd and other sites on the Poltalloch Estates, Argyll', *Proc. Soc. Antiq. Scot.*, LXIV, 111–46.

—— 1930–1. 'An underground building at Midhouse, Orkney, two urns found at Lintlaw, Berwickshire; and the excavation of a cairn at Drumelzier, Peeblesshire', *Proc. Soc. Antiq. Scot.*, LXV, 357–72.

Crawford, O. G. S., 1928. 'Stone Cists', *Antiquity* II, 418–22.

Cree, J. E., 1913–14. 'Notice of the Excavation of a Cairn at Inverlael, Inverbroom, Ross-shire', *Proc. Soc. Antiq. Scot.*, XLVIII, 112–24.

Curtis, M., 1880. *Antiquities of Laugharne and Pendine.* London.

Davies, E., 1929. *Prehistoric and Roman Remains of Denbighshire.* Cardiff.

Davies, J., 1905. 'The Find of British Urns near Capel Cynon in Cardiganshire', *Archaeol. Cambrensis*, 6 ser. V, 62–72.

Davies, M., 1945. 'Types of Megalithic Monuments of the Irish Sea and North Channel Coastland: a Study in Distributions', *Antiq. J.*, XXV, 125–44.

de Valéra, R., 1960. 'The Court Cairns of Ireland', *Proc. Roy. Irish Acad.*, 60 (C), 9–140.

Edwards, A. J. H., 1922–3. 'Report on the Excavation of a Bronze Age Cairn in the parish of Minnigaff, Stewartry of Kirkcudbright', *Proc. Soc. Antiq. Scot.*, LVII, 65–70.

Evans, E. E., 1966. *Prehistoric and Early Christian Ireland: A Guide.* London.

Evans, E. E. & Megaw, B. R. S., 1937. 'The Multiple-cist Cairn at Mount Stewart, Co. Down, Northern Ireland', *Proc. Prehist. Soc.*, III, 29–42.

Feachem, R., 1963. *A Guide to Prehistoric Scotland.* London.

Fenton, W., 1939–40. 'A Short Cist recently exposed in the Gallows Knowe, Lintrathen, Angus', *Proc. Soc. Antiq. Scot.*, LXXIV, 135 f.

Fox, C., 1938. 'Two Bronze Age Cairns in South Wales: Simondston and Pond Cairns, Coity Higher parish, Bridgend', *Archaeologia*, LXXXVII, 129–80.

—— 1959. *Life and Death in the Bronze Age.* London.

Galloway, T. L., 1919–20. 'Report on the Exploration of a Burial Cairn at Balnabraid, Kintyre', *Proc. Soc. Antiq. Scot.*, LIV, 172–91.

Greenwell, W., 1864–6. 'An Account of Excavations in Cairns near Crinan', *Proc. Soc. Antiq. Scot.*, VI, 336–51.

—— 1877. *British Barrows.* Oxford.

—— 1890. 'Recent Researches in Barrows in Yorkshire, Wiltshire, Berkshire, etc.', *Archaeologia*, LII, 1–72.

Griffiths, W. E., 1957. 'The Typology and Origins of Beakers in Wales', *Proc. Prehist. Soc.*, XXIII, 57–90.

Grimes, W. F., 1951. *The Prehistory of Wales.* Cardiff.

Grinsell, L. V., 1959. *Dorset Barrows.* Dorchester.

Hencken, H. O'N., 1935. 'A Cairn at Poulawack, Co. Clare', *J. Roy. Soc. Antiq. Ireland*, LXV, 191–222.

Hencken, H. O'N & Movius, H. L., 1932–4. 'The Cemetery-Cairn of Knockast', *Proc. Roy. Irish Acad.*, 41 (C), 232–84.

Hepburn, D., 1904. 'On prehistoric human skeletons found at Merthyr Mawr, Glamorganshire', *Trans. Cardiff Natur. Soc.*, XXXVII, 31–54.

Hill, H. C., 1930. 'Northfield Tumulus, Cheltenham', *Trans. Bristol Gloucestershire Archaeol. Soc.*, LII, 305–8.

Hodgson, K. S., 1940. 'Some Excavations in the Bewcastle District. I. A Bronze Age Tumulus on the Shield Knowe', *Trans. Cumberland Westmorland Antiq. Archaeol. Soc.*, n.s. XL, 154–62.

Joass, J. M., 1866–8. 'Note of Five Kists found under a Tumulus on the Glebe of the parish of Eddertoun, Ross-shire etc.', *Proc. Soc. Antiq. Scot.*, VII, 268 f.

Jobey, G., 1968. 'Excavations of Cairns at Chatton, Sandyford, Northumberland', *Archaeol. Aeliana*, 4 ser., XLVI, 5–50.

Livens, R. G., 1965. 'A Beaker find from Denbighshire and its significance', *Archaeol. Cambrensis*, CXIV, 112–19.

Liversage, G. D., 1968. 'Excavations at Dalkey Island, Co. Dublin', *Proc. Roy. Irish Acad.*, LXVI (C), 53–234.

Lukis, J. W., 1875. 'On the St Lythan's and St Nicholas' Cromlechs and other remains near Cardiff', *Archaeol. Cambrensis*, 4 ser., VI, 171–85.

Macalister, R. A. S., 1921. *Ireland in Pre-Celtic Times*. Dublin.

—— 1928. *The Archaeology of Ireland*, 1st edn. London.

Marshall, G., 1930–2. 'Report on the Discovery of two Bronze Age cists in the Olchon Valley, Herefordshire', *Trans. Woolhope Natur. Fld. Club*, 1930–2, 147–53.

Mitchell, M. E. C., 1933–4. 'A new Analysis of the Early Bronze Age Beaker Pottery of Scotland', *Proc. Soc. Antiq. Scot.*, LXVIII, 132–89.

Mortimer, J. R., 1905. *Forty Years' Researches in the British and Saxon Burial Mounds of East Yorkshire.* London.

Ó Ríordáin, S. P., 1953. *Antiquities of the Irish Countryside*, 3rd edn. London.

Payne, E. H., 1943. 'The Bincombe Barrow, Ridgeway Hill, Dorset', *Proc. Dorset Natur. Hist. Archaeol. Soc.*, LXV, 38–52.

Piggott, S., 1932. 'The Mull Hill Circle, Isle of Man and its Pottery', *Antiq. J.*, XII, 146–57.

—— 1947–8. 'The Excavation at Cairnpapple Hill, West Lothian, 1947–8', *Proc. Soc. Antiq. Scot.*, LXXXII, 68–123.

—— 1962. 'Traders and Metal-workers', in *The Prehistoric Peoples of Scotland*, Piggott, S. (ed.), London, 73–103.

Piggott, S. & Powell, T. G. E., 1948–9. 'The Excavation of Three Neolithic Chambered Tombs in Galloway, 1949', *Proc. Soc. Antiq. Scot.*, LXXXIII, 103–61.

RCAHM. Royal Commission on the Ancient and Historical Monuments of Scotland; Inventories: 1920 Dumfries; 1933 Fife; 1967 Peeblesshire.

RCAM. Royal Commission on Ancient Monuments in Wales and Monmouthshire; Inventories: 1917 Carmarthenshire; 1925 Pembrokeshire; 1956 Caernarvonshire, I, East.

Raftery, J., 1960. 'A Bronze Age Tumulus at Corrower, Co. Mayo', *Proc. Roy. Irish Acad.*, 61 (C), 79–93.

Richardson, J. S. & Lindsay, I. G., 1951–2. 'Excavation of the Kalemouth Cairn, Roxburghshire', *Proc. Soc. Antiq. Scot.*, LXXXVI, 200.

Roberts, E., 1910. 'Recent finds in Caernarvonshire', *Archaeol. Cambrensis*, 6 ser., X, 399–402.

Rodger, J. W., 1914. 'William Riley, J.P.' *Trans. Cardiff Natur. Soc.*, XLVIII, 9–12.

Savory, H. N., 1948–50. 'A Bronze Age Beaker from near Caerphilly', *Trans. Cardiff Natur. Soc.*, LXXX, 39 f.

—— 1955. 'A Corpus of Welsh Bronze Age Pottery. Part I: Beakers', *Bull. Board Celtic Stud.*, XVI, part iii, 215–41.

—— 1957. 'A Corpus of Welsh Bronze Age Pottery. Part II: Food Vessels and Enlarged Food Vessels', *Bull. Board Celtic Stud.*, XVII, part iii, 196–233.

—— 1959. 'A Beaker Cist at Brymbo', *Trans. Denbighshire Hist. Soc.*, VIII, 1–7.

Simpson, D. D. A., 1966–7. 'Excavations at Kintraw, Argyll', *Proc. Soc. Antiq. Scot.*, 54–9.

—— 1968. 'Food Vessels: associations and chronology', in *Studies in Ancient Europe: Essays presented to Stuart Piggott* (ed. Coles, J. M. & Simpson, D. D. A.). Leicester, 197–211.

Stevenson, R. B. K., 1938–9. 'Jet Necklace from a cist in Strathnaver', *Proc. Soc. Antiq. Scot.*, LXXIII (1938–9), 325 f.

—— 1939–40. 'Cists near Tweedsmuir', *Proc. Soc. Antiq. Scot.*, LXXIV, 145 f.

Tait, J., 1965. *Beakers from Northumberland*. Newcastle.

Thomas, N., 1960. *A Guide to Prehistoric England*. London.

Trechmann, C. T. , 1914. 'Prehistoric Burials in the County of Durham', *Archaeol. Aeliana*, 3 ser., XI, 119–76.

Waddell, J., 1970. 'Irish Bronze Age Cists: A Survey', *J. Roy. Soc. Antiq. Ireland*, C, 91–139.

Ward, J., 1902. 'Prehistoric Interments near Cardiff', *Archaeol. Cambrensis*, 6 ser., II, 25–32.

—— 1919. 'Prehistoric Burials, Merthyr Mawr Warren, Glamorgan', *Archaeol. Cambrensis*, 6 ser., XIX, 323–52.

Webley, D. P., 1960. 'Twyn Bryn Glas: the excavation of a round cairn at Cwm Cadlan, Breconshire', *Bull. Board Celtic Stud.*, XIX, part i, 56–71.

Williams, A., 1939. 'Prehistoric and Roman Pottery in the Museum of the Royal Institution of South Wales, Swansea', *Archaeol. Cambrensis*, XCIV, 21–9.

Williams, W. Wynn, 1875. 'Excavations at Pant y Saer Cromlech, Anglesey', *Archaeol. Cambrensis*, 4 ser., VI, 341–8.

Worth, R. H., 1953. *Dartmoor*. Plymouth.

Biconical Urns outside Wessex

A. M. ApSimon

This essay is really concerned with one aspect of the relationships between the Highland and Lowland zones of the British Isles in the Bronze Age. Though little Welsh archaeology comes directly into this, the theme is one through which Lily Chitty's work, particularly in her collaboration with Sir Cyril Fox, helped to shape the archaeological thinking of a whole generation. When I first began seriously to teach myself some archaeology, Cyril Fox's *The Personality of Britain* and Gordon Childe's *Prehistoric Communities of the British Isles* were the books in which I immersed myself. Miss Chitty's factual contribution to the first of these books remains, after more than thirty years, as valuable as ever. The annotated and amended maps in my own battered copy of *Personality* are a constant resource for archaeological teaching and for starting lines of thought in research.

When as a raw student I attempted my first original work, the publication of a decorated bronze dagger from the Thames, it was natural for me to turn for help with comparative material to the omniscient Miss Chitty. It is a pleasure to acknowledge such help, given freely and generously both then and later, which has enrolled me among her many friends. I am equally delighted to have this opportunity to pay a small tribute to one whose personal modesty fortunately fails to obscure the solid importance of her work.

THE DEVELOPMENT OF THOUGHT ON BICONICAL URNS

Recent interest in the subject of Biconical Urns was aroused by Glasbergen's study (1954) of Hilversum and Drakenstein urns. The British affinities of the urns from Marquise and Hilversum had been recognised by Dunning (1936), and Glasbergen's contribution was to show that Hilversum Urns were more numerous and earlier in date than had been thought. In fact, Thurnam (1873) was the first to distinguish these urns, calling them 'urns with border in place of rim'. Abercromby (1912) placed those urns with applied arc-shaped, 'horseshoe' handles in his Type III, Group 2. These 'Biconical' Urns, and indeed almost all urns except some Collared Urns, came to be attributed to the Late Bronze Age. This was partly due to an uncritical use of Abercromby's chronological scheme, partly because the idea of Late Bronze Age invasions found support in the idea suggested by Doppelfeld (1930) of Rhenish sources for 'Deverel-Rimbury' pottery, and partly from an understandable tendency to equate British urn-cremation cemeteries with continental 'Urnfields'. Thus the Biconical Urn from Tynings Farm, Cheddar,

Somerset, which became widely known through its publication by Kendrick and Hawkes (1932), was thought to be a hybrid between the native Middle Bronze Age Collared Urn tradition and an intrusive Late Bronze Age element.

These views did not go entirely unquestioned. In 1933 Hawkes (Hawkes & Preston, 1933) noted that the widely distributed horseshoe-shaped handles were evidently not an intrusive trait, while the common solid lug handles of Wessex might be derived from Cornish pottery. Three years later Leeds (1936) published a Biconical Urn from a ring-ditch grave at Radley, Berkshire. He equated the ring-ditch with Wessex disc barrows, whose grave goods included faience beads, from which he deduced that the Radley burial was probably older than the Late Bronze Age urnfields and the 'Rimbury' pottery discussed by Hawkes.

The first real advance, however, was due to Glasbergen. Piggott in his review (1955) of that work stressed that the necessity of looking for the British prototypes of Hilversum Urns in the Middle, and not the Late, Bronze Age would require considerable readjustment of ideas based on the orthodox Abercromby scheme. The challenge was taken up first by Isobel Smith (Butler & Smith, 1956). She argued that the Hilversum Urns did not derive directly from British Collared Urns as Glasbergen had thought, but from a southern English group of what she called 'relief-decorated urns'. This category included horseshoe-handled and other Biconical Urns, 'South Lodge'-type Barrel Urns and many 'Deverel-Rimbury' urns, Abercromby's Type IV. Dr Smith suggested that some features of these urns, particularly those of the Barrel Urns, might have antecedents in Late Neolithic Rinyo-Clacton pottery. She also suggested that the Cordoned and Encrusted Urns of the Highland Zone could be grouped together as an equivalent northern group of 'relief-decorated' urns, and that these also were derived from native Neolithic pottery. The theory, due to Childe (1940, 150), that Encrusted Urns developed basically from Skara Brae and Rinyo-style pottery, encouraged the idea of parallel development in the south. Butler and Smith were able to show quite conclusively that all these types of urns had appeared by the Middle Bronze Age at least.

One element of older ideas survived. Dr Smith suggested that a number of Biconical Urns were hybrids, decorated with impressed patterns which were simply imitations approximating to those used on collared urns.

Dr Smith devoted a later paper (Smith, 1961) to illustrating the British forerunners of Hilversum Urns and to discussing their associations, their probable chronology and their cultural significance. She suggested that because burials with Biconical Urns in Wessex were generally lacking in other grave offerings, the majority of these urns might be later than the richly furnished graves constituting the Wessex horizon, though a small minority of Biconical Urn burials with offerings showed that there was some overlap. In that paper she partly withdrew the idea of Rinyo-Clacton origins and, apart from noting the probability of a contribution from the handled urns of the Trevisker series of south-west England, she deferred further discussion of the origins and history of Biconical Urns.

The most recent and most comprehensive study of these urns is by Calkin (1964). That paper, although primarily concerned with the Bournemouth area, gave a complete descriptive catalogue of 71 urns from Dorset, south-west Hampshire and Wiltshire. The point of departure for Calkin's discussion of the origins of these urns was Hawkes's remarks (Hawkes & Preston, 1933) about possible Cornish connections. Calkin observed that the two main concentrations of Biconical Urns in Wessex, round Bere Regis in Dorset and Amesbury in Wiltshire, seemed to relate to finds of early-style Trevisker series urns from Sturminster Marshall, Dorset, and from Winterslow, Wiltshire. He compared three main variants, true 'truncated biconical' urns, urns with rounded 'biconvex' profile, and urns with concave or hollow necks, to similar varieties of shape in the Trevisker series. He traced the lug handles of these urns to the same source, beginning with large horizontally pierced handles and going on to a series of unpierced lugs, some with vestigial dimples in their ends. He thought that some details, including rims with concave internal bevels and ribs applied inside pot bottoms, might also be derived from the Trevisker series.

For the source of the second element in these urns, that responsible for applied cordons and finger-printing, or fingernail nicking, Calkin followed Dr Smith in turning to the Late Neolithic Rinyo-Clacton group, though he considered also the possibility of contribution by local Early Bronze Age rusticated wares. Calkin, like Dr Smith, doubted whether the 'horseshoe' handles found on 23 Wessex Biconical Urns were originally functional. He suggested that they might have arisen either as *skeuomorphs* of loops of a carrying rope, or as a relief version of a cord-impressed chevron pattern. The resultant more or less continuous curving strip, or series of contiguous loops, might by reduction or separation give the appearance of handles. Calkin admitted that cord decoration on some of these 'horseshoes' suggested that they were thought of as handles, but linked this with the use of cord decoration on handles of pots belonging to the Trevisker series. He suggested, on the basis of their relative frequency and of their position, on or above the shoulder of the pot, that these horseshoe handles originated in the Amesbury region and spread from there.

My own interest in the problems of Biconical Urns stems from work on the pottery of the Trevisker series (ApSimon, 1959a, 1969, 1970 – in Pollard & Russell, 1970) and on the pottery from Shearplace Hill, Dorset (Rahtz & ApSimon, 1962). Shearplace Hill brought me into close contact with John Calkin. Discussion and exchange of ideas led to general harmony between our views. We were agreed that the influence of the Trevisker series was dominant in most, though not all, Dorset Biconical Urns. With Wiltshire urns doubts arose, shapes could be derived from the Trevisker series, but only very few of these urns possessed detailed features, such as lugs, which could not but be derived from that series. The features which seemed unlikely to derive from the Trevisker series included fingertip decoration on rims and applied cordons, horseshoe handles, lugs with vertical piercings, certain rim forms, and distinctive kinds of cord-impressed decoration.

My attempts to tackle the problems of Biconical Urn relationships were in response to a query from Professor C. F. C. Hawkes, and were spread over the years 1961–66. Isobel Smith and John Calkin had examined the problem in Wessex, so I was led to look elsewhere, in particular for analogies to the cord-impressed decoration on these urns. Dr Smith had cited examples of Biconical Urns outside southern England and a further stimulus came from Calkin's allusion to some 39 urns showing features comparable to the Biconical Urns from Wessex, but scattered widely over the rest of the British Isles. Calkin had observed that urns with the most distinctive features, fingerprinting, lugs and horseshoe handles, were only found south of a line from the Humber to South Wales, whereas cord-impressed decoration was prevalent north of that line. In the section that follows I shall discuss a number of pots from this northern area to see what light they have to shed on our problem.

SKARA BRAE–RINYO, FOOD VESSELS AND ENCRUSTED URNS

The discussion begins with two urns found together at Uddingston, Lanarkshire (Morrison, 1968). The first of these (fig. 1.1;[1] Abercromby, 1912, vol. 2, pl. 101. 528a) has a biconical profile and a bevelled rim and is decorated with impressions of plaited cord. The fabric of this urn, dark inside, the outer third reddish, with smooth brown exterior, is quite exceptional among the urns in the National Museum of Scotland and strongly reminiscent of sherds attributed to Biconical Urns from Brean Down, Somerset (ApSimon, Donovan & Taylor, 1961, *fig.* 27, 23–25). The shape of this urn is closely comparable to that of a Biconical Urn from

---

[1] 'fig.' indicates an illustration in the present chapter; '*fig.*' indicates an illustration in the article referred to.

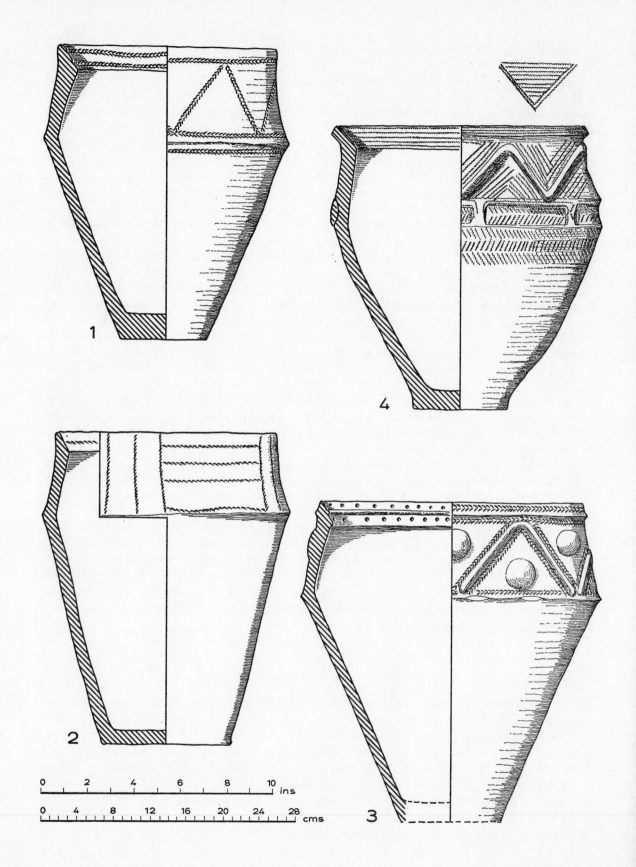

Ringwold, Kent (Smith, 1961, *fig.* 1.1; fig. 1.2). The decoration can be compared to that on another of the Ringwold urns (Smith, 1961, *fig.* 1.3) on which the lines are doubled. A third urn from Ringwold is said to have combined the shape of the first with the decoration of the second.

The second of the Uddingston urns (Abercromby, 1912, vol. 2, pl. 100.528; Fox, 1927, pl. 23, *fig.* 2; fig. 1.3), though very like the first, is in a different fabric. It has narrow raised ribs inside and outside the rim and the neck carries applied relief decoration in the form of a running chevron, balanced by circular bosses in the triangular spaces. It would of course be called an 'encrusted urn', although its only important point of difference from its companion is the relief decoration, carefully integrated with the impressed decoration, giving emphasis to the pattern.

Sir Cyril Fox (1927) suggested that Encrusted Urns were simply Food Vessel Urns with relief decoration added, citing in support of this these urns from Uddingston. He observed that the basic Food Vessel form could still be traced in very evolved examples and that associated impressed decoration was frequently of Food Vessel style. Fox clinched his argument by illustrating urns which carried on their shoulders the 'groove and stops' device characteristic of many Yorkshire Vase Food Vessels. These stops were in their turn derived from pierced shoulder lugs found on Food Vessels, so that it was clear that the development proceeded from Food Vessel to urn with relief decoration and not vice versa.

Not all urns with similar applied relief decoration are Food Vessel Urns. In Ireland there is an extensive series of urns belonging to what I have called the Irish-Scottish Vase or *Drumnakilly* series (ApSimon, 1970). On these the relief decoration is clearly a borrowing from Food Vessel Urns. A unique Collared Urn bearing applied relief decoration from Plas Penrhyn, Llangeinwen in Anglesey (RCAM, 1937, lviii, *fig.* 7) points the moral: 'Encrusted Urns' are not an entity. Instead we have urns belonging to quite different traditions to which relief decoration may be applied.

Criticism of Fox's ideas came from Childe. Childe was at great pains in his publication of the Skara Brae excavations (Childe, 1931) to establish the date of the site. He came down in favour of a Bronze Age date, suggesting that the relief decoration of Skara Brae pottery derived from that of Encrusted Urns. When later a Beaker was found in a desertion level of the similar settlement at Rinyo (Childe & Grant, 1939, 30–1), some adjustment to this idea was required. Accordingly, in his book, *Prehistoric Communities of the British Isles* (Childe, 1940, 150), Childe accepted Fox's contention that elements of Encrusted Urn shape and decoration were derived from Food Vessel pottery, but went on to argue that contact with and incorporation of Skara Brae–Rinyo traditions was basically responsible for the appearance of these urns. Childe's argument was based on urns with profuse applied relief decoration and covered with incisions, grooves, stabs, or impressions, found mainly in Ireland, some belonging to the Food Vessel and some to the Drumnakilly series. Fox's arguments, however, had already taken these urns into account. All their features can be explained by internal development within the two series. In particular, the replacement of cord impressions by a variety of impressed, scratched or fingernail decoration is a familiar development in the Food Vessel series. It is well illustrated by comparison of the urn with incised decoration from Lyle's Hill (Evans, 1953, pl. 6.1; ApSimon, 1970, *fig.* 6.1) with the cord-decorated urn from Bedrule, Roxburgh (Anderson, 1886; Fox, 1927, pl. 20, *fig.* 3; fig. 1.4). These reasons appear to justify the rejection of Childe's argument.

fig. 1 1. Food Vessel Urn, Uddingston, Lanarkshire; 2. Biconical Urn, Ringwold, Kent (after Smith, 1961); 3. Food Vessel Urn with relief decoration, Uddingston, Lanarkshire; 4. Food Vessel Urn with relief decoration, Bedrule, Roxburghshire

Any return to Childe's original hypothesis would involve serious chronological difficulties, for the relevant relief-decorated urns in Ireland appear to be substantially later, perhaps several centuries later, than Bell Beakers. In this connection I must disagree with Dr Michael Herity's suggestion (Herity, 1969) that the Skara Brae type of side-looped bone pin might be derived from side-looped bronze pins of central European origin. The resemblance between the two series does not seem to be sufficient to establish a connection for which there is no other evidence. My own view is that the Skara Brae pottery is truly Neolithic, a conclusion supported by the find from Townhead, Rothesay (Robertson-Mackay, 1952), of Grooved Ware and Western Neolithic pottery apparently associated on the same site and uncontaminated by Bronze Age material. In default of radiocarbon dating evidence it is possible that Skara Brae pottery is centuries older than urns with relief decoration, with no connection between the two.

Childe later criticised Fox's view of the origin of the relief chevrons (Childe, 1943). I think the criticism was just; Fox's explanation for these, as for the relief bosses, or 'rosettes', seems too mechanical. Food Vessel potters already used relief decoration in applying non-functional unpierced lugs, and I see no reason why elaboration to intensify the effect of impressed decoration should not have taken place without any call for outside influences. Fox's central idea seems to me to survive all these criticisms.

In casting doubt on the idea of a Skara Brae origin for 'Encrusted Urns', this discussion has in effect also cast further doubt on the idea that Biconical Urns might derive from 'Rinyo-Clacton' pottery. It has raised instead the interesting possibility of a Food Vessel contribution. At first sight this is an attractive proposition, for as far as form is concerned, a Biconical Urn such as that from Amesbury, G. 71, Wiltshire (Butler & Smith, 1956, *fig.* 6; Smith, 1961, *fig.* 1.4) might be regarded, if stripped of its arc handles, as no more than a larger version of an Abercromby type-3 Food Vessel, with everted rim, sharp-shouldered 'biconical' profile and well-defined foot, like that from Treneglos, Cornwall (Ashbee, 1958). This proposition would render significant the presence of earlier Food Vessel burials in the Amesbury barrow (Christie, 1968). Other vessels which might then be cited as comparative material would include Food Vessels and Food Vessel Urns from Muirkirk, Ayrshire (Simpson, 1965; fig. 3.1), Lyne, Peeblesshire (Stevenson, 1951), Cross Low, Parwich, Derbyshire (Abercromby, 1912, Vol. 1, pl. 32.65), Llanrwst and Glyn Trean, Denbighshire (Savory, 1957, *fig.* 5.2; fig. 4.6). I have chosen to illustrate another Food Vessel, from Stanton Park, Derbyshire (Bateman, 1848, 85; fig. 3.2) because of the decoration on its shoulder.

This decoration consists of short lengths of twisted cord impressions notching the shoulder. It is not uncommon on Food Vessels and Food Vessel Urns in northern Britain and is sometimes replaced by fingernail marks or by incisions. Similar decoration occurs on Food Vessels in southern England. Here most Food Vessels and Food Vessel Urns lack the richer cord-impressed decoration common in the north, and decoration tends to be restricted to nicking, fingertipping, stitch and stab marking of rims, shoulders or ridges and, sometimes, of applied cordons. An example of this is found on the Food Vessel from Fargo Plantation, Amesbury, Wiltshire (Stone, 1938).[1] This might then suggest a source for the distinctive fingernail, fingertip or nicked decoration of the rims, shoulders and applied cordons of Biconical Urns. This kind of decoration may well imitate the stitching of leather containers.

For comparison with the Stanton Park Food Vessel, I illustrate an urn from Alstonefield, Staffordshire (Bateman, 1848, 97–8; fig. 2.1). This might be called a Food Vessel Urn, but it clearly has resemblances to the Biconical Urn series. These comparisons can be extended to the patterns of impressed decoration. I have already commented on the running chevron decoration of the Uddingston and Ringwold urns. The hurdle pattern of the first Ringwold urn is equally at home on Food Vessels, whatever its ultimate origin. The cord decoration on the

---

[1] With comparative material cited by Miss Chitty.

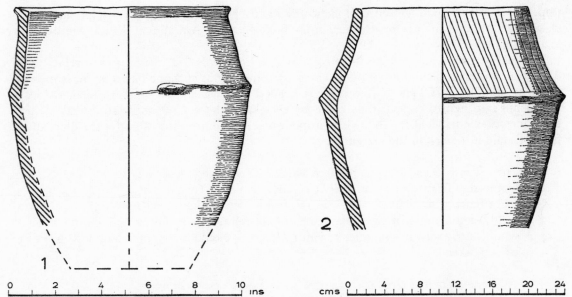

fig. 2 1. Food Vessel Urn (?), Alstonefield, Staffordshire; 2. Urn, Kintore, Aberdeenshire

fig. 3 1. Food Vessel, Muirkirk, Ayrshire; 2. Food Vessel, Stanton Park, Derbyshire; 3. Food Vessel, Pencaitland, East Lothian; 4. Cordoned Urn, Drumelzier, Peebleshire; 5. Cordoned Urn, Garrowby Wold, B.169, Bishop Wilton, Yorkshire; 6. Urn, Ballingry, Fife

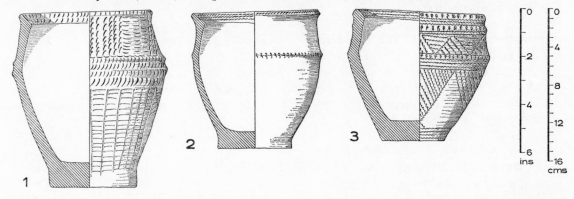

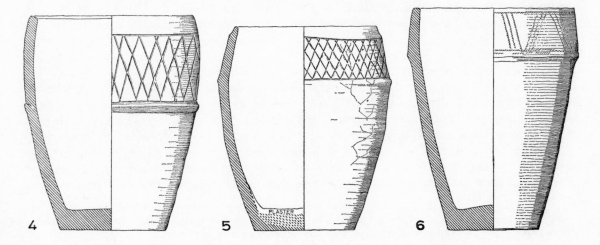

147

upper part of the Food Vessel from Pencaitland, E. Lothian (Callander, 1932; fig. 3.3), is closely comparable to that on the urn from Bush Barrow, Amesbury, Wilts. (Smith, 1961, *fig.* 2.6).

It would be premature to take these comparisons for proof of identity, or even relationship. They can, however, be usefully supplemented by comparisons of shape based on measurements made on sample sets of Type 3–4 Food Vessels, Food Vessel Urns and southern Biconical Urns, which put into figures comparisons made by eye. With the aid of simple statistical methods these measurements yield the following propositions, which are illustrated by the diagrams in fig. 4. Details are given in the appendix.

A   Nineteen Food Vessel Urns compared with 21 Food Vessels show:
1 A highly significant *increase* in height relative to width ($p < 0.001$).[1]
2 A slight but not significant *increase* in relative height of shoulder ($p > 0.05$).
3 A highly significant *decrease* in diameter of base relative to shoulder ($p < 0.001$).
4 A significant *increase* in diameter of rim relative to shoulder, i.e. pots look less 'biconical' ($0.01 > p > 0.001$).

B Twenty-three Biconical Urns compared with 21 Food Vessels show:
1 A highly significant *increase* in height relative to width ($p < 0.001$).
2 A significant *increase* in relative height of shoulder ($0.01 > p > 0.001$).
3 No significant difference in relative diameter of base.
4 A highly significant *decrease* in diameter of rim relative to shoulder, i.e. pots look more 'biconical' ($p < 0.001$).

C Twenty-three Biconical Urns compared with 19 Food Vessel Urns show:
1 No significant difference in relative height.
2 A significant *increase* in relative height of shoulder ($0.01 > p > 0.001$).
3 A highly significant *increase* in relative diameter of base ($p < 0.001$).
4 A highly significant *decrease* in diameter of rim relative to shoulder, i.e. pots look more 'biconical' ($p < 0.001$).

From these we may make the following points:
1 The conventional distinctions made between Food Vessels, Food Vessel Urns and Biconical Urns appear both justifiable and useful.
2 The differences between Food Vessels and Food Vessel Urns are of the same order of magnitude as those between these classes and Biconical Urns.
3 In some respects Food Vessels and Food Vessel Urns appear complementary (this is best appreciated by superimposing some of the diagrams for the same ratios in fig. 4). Thus when the actual heights of pots of these two classes are plotted on the same diagram, two well-marked peaks appear, one at about 150 mm. (Food Vessels) and one at about 300 mm. (Food Vessel Urns). This simple 1 : 2 relationship looks like a functional one and suggests that the hypothetical (or nearly hypothetical) domestic Food Vessel assemblage may normally have included both small and large pots. Either form, or both, might be selected for burial use. The bias of selection seems to have changed with time from burial with accessory vessels, towards urn burial.
4 The relatively and absolutely small bases of Food Vessel Urns are striking; even quite large urns may be built up on bases scarcely bigger than those of some Food Vessels. The relative diameter of these bases is significantly less than that of the control sample of Primary Series

---

[1] '$p < 0.001$' means that the given result would occur by chance less than once in a thousand times; '$p > 0.05$' means that the given result would occur by chance more than once in twenty times.

Collared Urns. This may perhaps be thought to throw some doubt on the idea that Collared Urns trigger off the development of Food Vessel Urns, as opposed to their selection for burial.

5 The comparisons do not suggest that southern Biconical Urns develop out of Food Vessel Urns. This might have been guessed from the failure of relief chevrons to appear in the south, except on Barrel Urns, which are another story. They do, however, allow for both series developing divergently from similar sources.

6 The general comparisons suggest that Food Vessels might be this source. Comparisons of the proportions of individual pots confirm the previous suggestion of the Treneglos Food Vessel as an example of a suitable prototype for some Biconical Urns.

7 Though some Biconical Urns have fairly narrow, footed bases that might relate to those of the Food Vessel family, their bases are generally wider and thinner, as on the pots from Ringwold and Bulford (Smith, 1961, *fig.* 1.1, 3, *fig.* 3.1, 2). This suggests the possibility that the development of Biconical Urns was partly the result of Food Vessel influence on another group. This possibility is explored in the next section. The conclusion of this section is that in the light of these comparisons it would be very unwise to dismiss the idea of a strong Food Vessel component in Biconical Urn development.

CORDONED URNS

Calkin's '39 urns with "biconical" features from outside Wessex' included one urn from Northern Ireland and one from Scotland. The Irish urn is that from Gortfad, Derry (Collins & May, 1959, Urn 2), found with a quite normal Cordoned Urn (Urn 1). Urn 2 has a convex profile, with a shoulder cordon, stabbed impressions on rim and cordon and traces of cord decoration. It is comparable in form to urns figured by Dr Smith (1961, *fig.* 2.3, 5) from Cherhill and Winterbourne Monkton, Wiltshire. The Scottish urn, from Seggiecrook, Kennethmont,

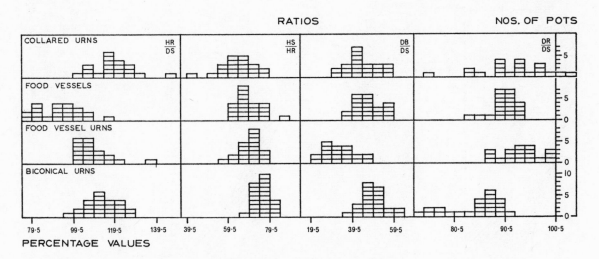

fig. 4 Diagrams illustrating comparisons between proportions of Biconical Urns and other pottery. H Height; D Diameter; R Rim; S Shoulder; B Base

149

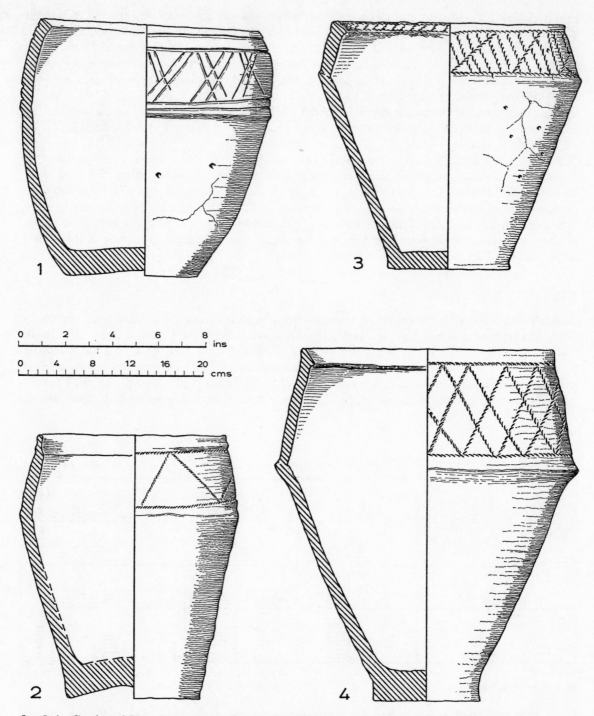

fig. 5 1. Cordoned Urn, Riggs, B.35, Thixendale, Yorkshire; 2, 3. Cordoned Urns, Pickering Moor (?), Yorkshire; 4. Urn, Acklam Wold, B.7, Yorkshire

Aberdeenshire (Callander, 1905, Urn 1), has a convex profile above the single shoulder-cordon and bears lattice-pattern decoration on the neck and rim bevel. It was found upright, containing a cremation, and associated with a slate pendant, along with two Cordoned Urns with lattice decoration and a third fragmentary urn (Callander, 1905, 1908).

These two urns suggested that Dr Smith's original idea of relationship between Biconical and Cordoned Urns might bear further examination. In this section I shall discuss a number of pots, mostly attributable to the Cordoned Urn group, to see what light they may shed on our problem.

The first of these is from Drumelzier, Peeblesshire (Craw, 1930–1, Urn 1) (fig. 3.4). This has a convex upper part with incised lattice-pattern decoration and a single shoulder-cordon. It was found inside a stone setting within a cairn. Fragments of a second urn were similar in shape and were decorated above the cordon with a zone of cord-impressed hatched triangles between horizontal lines (this urn has deteriorated so as to be no longer worth drawing). The first urn can be compared to a 'biconvex' urn from Bloxworth Down, Dorset (Calkin, 1964, *fig.* 14.4), decorated with cord-impressed lattice pattern, although the rim and the proportions of this urn are different.

There are three more 'convex' Cordoned Urns from Yorkshire. These are the urns from Garrowby Wold, B. 169, Bishop Wilton (Mortimer, 1905, pl. 44, *fig.* 367; fig. 3.5), from Riggs B. 35, Thixendale (Mortimer, 1905, pl. 59, *fig.* 543; fig. 5.1), and, a more recent find, from East Moor, Welburn (Manby, 1958). This urn was found with a bronze awl and has a sharply everted rim, while the part above the cordon is decorated with round impressions. The first two urns are of brown pitted ware, with shrinkage cracks and both may have stone and potsherds in the fabric.

Comparisons similar to those previously made, between the forms of these six Cordoned Urns with convex profiles and three southern 'Biconvex' urns, show no statistically significant differences in their proportions, although the numbers of pots used in these comparisons are of course very small.

Next we have a group from a cemetery at Ballingry, Fife (Lacaille, 1931). This includes two fragmentary Cordoned Urns (Urns 1 and 2) in a poor, coarse, shaly fabric with grits visible on the outer surface. Another (Urn 6, fig. 3.6) is of quite different fabric, hard brown ware, well finished. It has a ridged rather than cordoned shoulder and the neck is decorated with cord impressions. Except that it lacks the finger-printing of rims and shoulder cordons, this urn has a distinct resemblance to the urns from Tynings Farm and Toterfout-Halve Mijl chosen by Butler and Smith (1956, *fig.* 7) to illustrate their original comparison between the Hilversum and Wessex urns. This urn from Ballingry is clearly related to the series of 16 urns from Ardeer Cairn, Stevenston, Ayrshire (Mann, 1906; Abercromby, 1912, vol. 2, pl. 101. 535; Morrison, 1968). Most of these urns are plain but some have cord-impressed decoration like the Ballingry urn. There are some similar urns in Northern Ireland, as for example an urn from Doonan, Antrim (Abercromby, 1912, vol. 2, pl. 103, 549). Though Morrison (1968) calls these 'bucket urns', the treatment of rims and shoulders suggests that they are variants within the Cordoned Urn family. Similar cord decoration is common in the Cordoned Urn group.

The next two urns are from a barrow '6 miles north of Pickering' in the North Riding (Bateman, 1861, 205; Abercromby, 1912, vol. 2, pl. 96. 489,489a). Both are of rather flaky coarse brown ware and are badly cracked and warped. Urn 1 (fig. 5.2) has cord-impressed decoration arranged in the same pattern as the Uddingston urns, but the pattern and the hollow bevel to the rim are common on cordoned urns. Urn 2 (fig. 5.3) is quite markedly biconical in shape, with a distinct foot. The cord-impressed decoration was meant to be alternately hatched triangles, but only in one case did the potter get the pattern right. Neither of these urns has an applied cordon.

These comparisons reveal similarities between urns belonging to the Cordoned Urn and Biconical Urn series. Cordons are present on both. Cordoned Urns, though often smaller than Biconical Urns from southern England, resemble them in being built up on relatively wide, thin bases. All the patterns of cord-impressed decoration found on Biconical Urns are also found on Cordoned Urns and might be derived from them.

I conclude this part of the discussion with two Biconical Urns whose affinities require some thought. The first is from Acklam Wold, Barrow 7, East Riding (Abercromby, 1912, vol. 2, pl. 97. 491; fig. 5.4) and is one of those noted by Dr Smith in her first paper as possible 'hybrids'. This urn is made from coarse dark gritty ware, unevenly finished, and has some similarities, particularly in the form of the rim and the ring join at the prominent shoulder, to the second of the 'Pickering' urns. Lattice decoration is common on Cordoned Urns, but the base of the Acklam urn is much narrower than is usual in that series. The proportions of this urn are in fact almost identical to those of the Uddingston Food Vessel Urn, and its narrow base would be at home in that series. The treatment of the rim bevel and the cord-impressed lattice decoration are not characteristic of Food Vessel Urns. Narrow bases and lattice decoration occur on Collared Urns, though cord-impressed lattice pattern is not very common on Primary Series Urns (Longworth, 1961). There seems no reason to dispute the opinion, kindly expressed by Dr Longworth, that it would be difficult to accommodate the Acklam urn in the Collared Urn series.

The second of these simulated biconical urns is from Broomend of Crichie, Kintore, Aberdeen (Coles, 1901, *fig.* 31; fig. 2.2). This is made of hard brown ware, containing some coarse stone grit, but well finished, and decorated with fine incised lines reminiscent of those on Drumnakilly series urns (ApSimon, 1970) in Ireland. That series also produces biconical urns, apparently quite independently, but I would hesitate to connect the Crichie urn with them. Another urn from Broomend of Crichie (Coles, 1901, *fig.* 30 – urn 1; Abercromby, 1912, vol. 2, pl. 100.522) has a bevelled rim and a shoulder cordon and is decorated with plaited cord impressions arranged in chevron and trellis patterns. This has been called a Food Vessel Urn, but I do not know of any closely comparable vessels.

The moral of this section is that disparate sources may well produce superficially similar 'biconical' urns and that where we lack associations for our urns it may be difficult to identify the particular sources involved. The main trend of this discussion has, however, been to lend support to the idea of a close relationship between Cordoned and southern Biconical Urns, as suggested by Isobel Smith (Butler & Smith, 1956, 48). The distribution of these latter is almost precisely complementary to that of Cordoned Urns, for which Miss Chitty's 1938 map (Fox, 1947, pl. VIII) still displays the essential picture. Nevertheless caution is required here: Biconical Urns are not Cordoned Urns; had they been, we may be sure that Miss Chitty would have mapped them as such. We have already noted some differences of detail, a glaringly conspicuous difference being the absence of fingertip and fingernail decoration from Cordoned Urns.

Our next section, then, must discuss some of these differences and some of the cautions required in assessing the relationship. Waterman (Pollock & Waterman, 1964) has pointed out that the cordons have the function of covering and strengthening ring-joins in the pot wall. Many pots clearly belonging to the Cordoned Urn group are without cordons. Conversely, such cordons, being functional, may well have developed independently in other unrelated pottery traditions, and cannot be taken by themselves as a sure index of relationship. Some urns from southern England have a second cordon placed just below the rim. This feature, which tends to make them look rather like barrel urns, is reminiscent of many northern Cordoned Urns. Once again, however, the probability of simple functional convergence of form has to be considered.

Two urns from southern England have cordons on the lower body, as do some Cordoned Urns. The first of these, from Oliver's Camp, Bromham, Wilts. (Cunnington, 1930), has three finger-printed cordons below its shoulder, but is otherwise of normal 'biconical' form, except for having a rather small base and a pair of horizontally pierced handles on its shoulder. The only reasonable derivation for these would seem to be handles of the Trevisker series pottery of south-west England, and the form of the Bromham urn would be equally at home in that series. The second of these urns is that from Nether Swell, Gloucestershire (Greenwell, 1877, 446; Abercromby, 1912, vol. 2, pl. LXXXVI. 376). This has been described as a Cordoned Urn (British Museum, 1953, 26, *fig.* 6.3), and has a shoulder and a body cordon, from which, however, spring two sets of horseshoe-shaped handles. The register between rim and upper cordon has impressed cord decoration in nested running chevron pattern. The handles were put on after the cord decoration but were part of the scheme planned, since the spaces within them are filled by lattice pattern. These horseshoe-shaped handles are entirely absent from the northern Cordoned Urn series. In view of the cautions about the significance attached to cordons, here perhaps representing a translation of a functional carrying device, I hesitate to call this isolated example a 'Cordoned Urn' in the strict sense.

These horseshoe handles are perhaps the most intriguing feature of the Biconical Urn series. Both Dr Smith and Mr Calkin were reluctant to see them as real handles. This is a minor point, but it does relate to a more important issue, that of their origins. Calkin may perhaps be wrong in regarding as derivative the horseshoe handles on the Collared Urns from South Afflington (Calkin, 1964, pl. 1a) and Worgret (Abercromby, 1912, vol. 2, pl. 64. 23), Dorset,[1] which, as he rightly observes, show the nearest approach to functional handles. My opinion is that in the case of the Afflington urn we are very close to the moment of translation of this device from another material.

On the Afflington urn the handles rise from the upper of two shoulder ridges decorated with round stamped impressions. Horizontal lines of cord impressions, arranged in a band, link the handles and run round over their tops. Short lengths of cord impressions notch the edges of the handles and are set vertically across their bases in a manner suggestive of stitching or binding. The Worgret urn has its handles linked by a rather muddled incised version of this band, combining chevrons with the stamped impressions. A third fragmentary urn of uncertain type from Morvah, Cornwall (Abercromby, 1912, vol. 2, pl. 94. 467), has horseshoe handles incorporated in a double band of decoration, combining stamped impressions with a running chevron pattern like that on the Ringwold horseshoe-handled urn. Finally, the urn from between Budel and Weert (Butler & Smith, 1956, *fig.* 8) has simple linear bands of cord impressions linking the handles and connecting their tops with the rim.

These patterns suggest translation from some form of carrying net or frame, perhaps with wicker- or leather-covered handles. My feeling is that the handles on the pots were also meant to be used, and that the representation of the band linking them was added for the same psychological reasons as imitation casting seams on stone copies of metal battle-axes. It is important for our discussion to note that Longworth (1961, 285) cited the Afflington urn as an outstanding example of the permeation of the Collared Urn pottery of Wessex by influences from the Food Vessel series, and in fact classed it as a hybrid between Collared Urn and southern ridged Food Vessel Urn traditions. A Food Vessel Urn from Clocaenog, Denbighshire (Savory, 1961), has a row of pendent arcs in relief below its rim, which Savory interpreted as a representation of loop handles attached to a rope below the rim. This would suggest that a carrying device of this kind was used by the Food Vessel people, though perhaps not very widely. This

---

[1] Mr Calkin has kindly informed me that the reconstruction of the horseshoe-handled urn from Capel-le-Ferne, Kent (Ashbee & Dunning, 1961), as a Collared Urn is incorrect.

is perhaps as far as we can pursue this problem at present, but the suggestion of a connection with Food Vessels is clearly not without value for our general discussion.

BEAKER AND CONTINENTAL RELATIONSHIPS

Two further possibilities must be mentioned. The first is the suggestion by Miss S. Gerloff that pottery with fingertip decoration of applied strips, including Biconical Urns, was introduced to southern England by a folk movement from the continent during the 'Wessex' Bronze Age. I would consider this hypothesis only when all other explanations were exhausted, a position which I think has not yet been reached. A fatal objection to the general idea is the virtual absence of rich 'Wessex type' grave offerings from the Biconical Urn graves. The presence of bronze razors of class 1b in such graves is economically accounted for by the known links with the Hilversum Urn series in the Low Countries and the cross-channel movements which these imply.

The second is the question of whether the basic substratum in the Biconical Urn tradition might derive from the coarse pottery of the Beaker cultures. This seems fairly obvious in the case of the heavily rusticated urns of the Mildenhall–Ardleigh group in eastern England and this area may yet turn out to have played a more important role than Wessex. I have also considered this possibility for 'biconical' pottery from Devon (ApSimon, in Pollard & Russell, 1970) in which I saw influence from Trevisker, Collared Urn and perhaps some other undetermined tradition. The same question arose in considering a plain jar from a Bell Beaker cremation grave at Chew Stoke, Somerset (M.W.P.B. excavations, still unpublished). This is an idea which I am certainly not able to press on the evidence available to me.[1]

CONCLUSIONS

Apart then from these special cases and additional possibilities, our discussion as a whole has raised the question of participation by Food Vessel Urn and Cordoned Urn elements in the development of the Biconical Urn series. This brings us back to a question posed by Sir Cyril Fox (1947, 41): 'It may be asked whether the culture of the Highland Zone ever developed sufficient vigour to impose itself on the Lowland Zone.' Fox thought that the answer was probably 'No'; now we may not be so sure. Recent studies by D. D. A. Simpson (1965) tend to confirm what Miss Chitty's map (Fox, 1947, pl. IV) suggests, that the primary focus of the Food Vessel culture (in the strict sense) was in north-east England, between Humber and Tweed, in which region it succeeded Bell Beaker cultures in the funerary record. There may have been a later expansion covering a large part of the British Isles in which Food Vessels and Food Vessel Urns spread to southern England. Recent finds in this region suggest that its importance there may have been underestimated (Smith, I. F., in Christie, 1968, 353). The features of this southern English Food Vessel and Food Vessel Urn pottery seem compatible with the idea of southerly spread; and it seems wrong to separate this pottery from the northern series as sharply as I did in 1959 (ApSimon, 1959b). The features include a tendency towards simplification of form and decoration, and a shift away from cord-impressed patterns. These changes can all be documented from northern examples. Such expansion is, however, not presently demonstrable on the basis of available radiocarbon dates, and it would require many dates on carefully controlled material before it could be confirmed or denied, even assuming that the necessary precision in dating could be achieved.

If this expansion were to be confirmed, and the idea of Food Vessel influence on the Biconical Urn series in southern England accepted, then we would have gone far towards answering

---

[1] Except that what appears to be Beaker coarse ware with fingertip decoration on shoulders has now (1970) been found at Ballynagilly, Co. Tyrone.

'Yes' to Sir Cyril's question. The question of Cordoned Urn participation is somewhat obscured by the possibility of parallel development from related sources. It does not seem that we are dealing here with 'influences' which could be accepted or rejected. Dr Longworth has discussed the question of Cordoned Urn origins, showing quite clearly the strong influence of the Southern British Beaker tradition upon the decoration of Cordoned Urns, though the predominant use of cord impressions shows that other groups were also involved. Cordons are of course found on pottery of various Beaker groups, and the relationship can scarcely be doubted in the face of so explicit a Beaker derivative as the Cordoned Urn from Garrowby Wold, Barrow 169 (Mortimer, 1905, 138–40, pl. 44, *fig.* 368). Its companion, figured here (fig. 3.5), patently derives from the same tradition, though more distantly. The problems of Cordoned Urn origins, which I have touched on elsewhere (ApSimon, 1970), take us beyond the limits of this paper, but I would not like to rule out the possibility of parallel development. The effective absence of fingerprinting and horseshoe-shaped handles from the northern province shows that if 'trait flow' took place, its direction was from north to south and not vice versa. The presence of bronze razors of class 1 in Cordoned Urn and Biconical Urn graves links the two provinces, as already noted by Butler & Smith (1956) and by Ó Ríordáin (1967).

I do not pretend that this paper has solved the problems raised by Biconical Urns, either inside or outside Wessex. I hope that it has shown that 'biconical urns', developed within various traditions in our northern province, can be used to shed light on the problems of the southern province. The development of Biconical Urns can be thought of as a mosaic process with regional variations, both in substratum and in explicit elements. The essentially Highland Zone traditions of Food Vessel and Cordoned Urn groups play a very important role in this process, although the distinctive pottery of the Trevisker series of south-west England, itself a Highland Zone development, is seen to have had a dominating influence in Dorset and immediately adjacent areas. The association of a class 1 razor with an early Trevisker series urn at Winterslow (Stevens & Stone, 1938) strengthens the case for thinking in terms of such interactions between pot-making traditions. It must be said, however, that despite Miss Patchett (1952) and Butler & Smith (1956, 44), all the features of the Winterslow urn can be closely paralleled on normal Trevisker series pots from south-west England.

Mariette's find of Cornish-made Trevisker series pots in the Pas-de-Calais (Mariette, 1961) serves to remind us that in all this we must not forget those other 'urns outside Wessex', the Hilversum Urns. In particular, the urn from Vorstenbosch (Modderman, 1960) is of value as showing how local traditions, in this case those of the 'barbed-wire' Beaker group, may be absorbed by the Hilversum–Biconical Urn tradition. Our Dutch colleagues' insistence that the appearance of the Hilversum Urns and certain specialized burial customs in the Netherlands imply a migration from Britain of people with an individual material culture, also has a valuable moral for us. Thanks to this we can have more confidence that the disparate pottery traditions which we have come to distinguish within the once inchoate mass of 'Cinerary Urns' do have the significance, in human terms, so often denied them by British archaeologists.

APPENDIX

Comparison of the shapes of Biconical Urns and other pottery

Measurements made were: height of rim (HR), height of shoulder (HS), diameter of rim (DR), diameter of shoulder (DS), diameter of base (DB). On hollow-necked vessels DR was measured on top of the rim; on vessels with inbent neck and everted rim, DR is the minimum external diameter close below the rim. DS ignores applied cordons. These measurements were used to calculate the following ratios: height relative to diameter (HR/DS), relative height of shoulder (HS/HR), diameter of base relative to shoulder (DB/DS), diameter of rim relative to shoulder (DR/DS).

Using these ratios, comparisons were made between:

1. 21 Food Vessels, 19 Food Vessel Urns and 23 Biconical Urns. 20 Primary Series Collared Urns were used as a control.
2. 6 convex Cordoned Urns and 3 'Biconvex' Urns.

Means, variance, and Standard Deviations were calculated for each set and the significance of the differences between the sets assessed using Snedecor's *F* test and 'Student's' *t*. Details are given below; the results have been discussed in the main text. Frequency histograms of the ratios of the first group of sets are plotted in fig. 4. No correction has been made for skew distributions visible in some histograms.

For the sample set of Biconical Urns, correlation between certain of the ratios, and between the height (HR) and some of the ratios, was tested. The product moment correlation coefficients (*r*) obtained have been converted into percentage correlations. They are in no case significant. Such very low correlations confirm expectations, based on ordinary observation and common sense, that the shapes and proportions of these clay pots were determined within wide limits by the potters working within a ceramic tradition, rather than by the properties of the clay.

Correlation of variables in Biconical Urn shapes

Variates correlated	Percentage correlation
(DB/DS) : (DR/DS)	20%
(HR) : (DB/DS)	19%
(HR) : (DR/DS)	0·3%
(HR/DS) : (HS/HR)	8%
(HS/HR) : (DB/DS)	12%

SAMPLES

	Ratios and Standard Deviations (percentages)			
	(HR/DS)	(HS/HR)	(DB/DS)	(DR/DS)
21 Food Vessels	94 ± 11	70 ± 06	47 ± 06	90 ± 02
19 Food Vessel Urns	110 ± 09	70 ± 06	34 ± 07	94 ± 04
23 Biconical Urns	114 ± 08	75 ± 04	50 ± 06	84 ± 05
6 Convex Cordoned Urns	110 ± 10	67 ± 06	51 ± 09	88 ± 04
3 'Biconvex' Urns	103 ± 06	66 ± 10	52 ± 12	85 ± 05
20 Primary Series Collared Urns	119 ± 10	64 ± 10	45 ± 08	92 ± 07

COMPARISONS

F.V.s : F.V.U.s				
Variance ratio, *F*	26.4	0.1	44.2	10.1
Degrees freedom, Greater/Lesser estimates	1:38	38:1	1:38	1:38
t, 38 degrees freedom	5.1	—	6.6	3.1
F.V.s : Biconicals				
Variance Ratio, *F*	54.1	10.7	2.5	20.6
Degrees freedom, Greater/Lesser estimates	1:42	1:42	1:42	1:42
t, 42 degrees freedom	7.3	3.3	—	4.5
F.V.U.s : Biconicals				
Variance Ratio, *F*	2.5	14.9	64.3	31.4
Degrees freedom, Greater/Lesser estimates	1:40	1:40	1:40	1:40
t, 40 degrees freedom	—	3.3	7.9	5.6

	(HR/DS)	(HS/HR)	(DB/DS)	(DR/DS)
Food Vessels				
Treneglos, Cornwall	118	76	56	85
Muirkirk, Ayrshire	109	66	55	84
Lyne, Peeblesshire	104	69	47	87
Parwich, Derbyshire	99	72	55	89
Stanton Park, Derbyshire	101	68	56	93
Food Vessel Urns				
Uddingston, Lanark, Urn 1	110	68	36	87
Uddingston, Lanark, Urn 2	103	70	36	88
Bedrule, Roxburgh	102	64	34	90
Biconical Urns				
Ringwold, Kent, Urn 1	119	74	51	89
Amesbury, G.71, Wilts.	121	82	51	74
Bulford, G.47, Wilts. Urn 1	99	76	49	86
Bulford, G.47, Wilts. Urn 2	102	70	54	78
Bromham, Wilts.	113	75	36	88
Tynings Farm, Cheddar, Somerset	123	75	48	86
Convex Cordoned Urns				
Bishop Wilton, Garrowby Wold B.169, Yorks, Urn A	113	73	58	81
Thixendale, Riggs B.35, Yorks.	98	65	53	88
Welburn, Yorks.	104	63	42	89
Seggiecrook, Kennethmont, Aberdeen, Urn 1	124	71	56	91
Drumelzier, Peeblesshire	117	58	59	89
Gortfad, Co. Derry, Urn 2	101	71	37	91
'Biconvex' Urns				
Bloxworth, B.1, Dorset	102	55	66	89
Cherhill, B.1, Wilts.	110	72	44	86
Winterbourne Monkton, B.2	98	71	47	79
Cordoned Urns and Varia				
'Pickering', Yorks., Urn 1	115	69	56	85
'Pickering', Yorks., Urn 2	91	78	46	87
Ballingry, Fife, Urn 5	124	79	54	94
Acklam Wold B.7, Yorks.	112	75	35	82
Kintore, Broomend of Crichie, Aberdeen, Urn 2	—	—	—	—

The sample of Food Vessels used came mostly from Yorkshire and deliberately included 'biconical'-looking Food Vessels. The sample of Food Vessel Urns used was from the Highland Zone and was also deliberately biased in the same way. The sample of Primary Series Collared Urns was taken from urns figured by Longworth (1961) and Calkin (1964) and was not biased consciously, except that urns classed by them as 'hybrids' or as strongly influenced by the Food Vessel Urn series were not included. The series of Biconical Urns included as far as possible urns about whose classification there was no doubt. It omits therefore urns with lugs, for which a Trevisker affiliation might be claimed (except Bromham, Wilts.) and urns described by Calkin (1964) as 'sub-biconical'. It includes the following urns additional to those listed already below: *Dorset*, Bere Regis, B.1 (British Museum, Durden Colln. 245), Bloxworth (BMD 256), Dewlish, B.33, Roke Down (BMD 221), Thickthorn Down (Calkin, 1964); *Suffolk*, Hollesley, Leiston, Semer (Smedley & Owles, 1964); *Surrey*, Wonersh, 1892 (Mus., Birchington); *Sussex*, Charmandean, South Heighton (Musson, 1954); *Wiltshire*, Amesbury, G.77, Urns 1 and 2, Amesbury G.68, Bulford G.45–48, Shrewton, G.1–3, Winterslow, G.3 (Calkin, 1964).

BIBLIOGRAPHY

Abercromby, J., 1912. *A Study of the Bronze Age Pottery of Great Britain and Ireland*, 2 vols. Oxford.

Anderson, J., 1886. 'Notices of Recent Discoveries of Cists or Burials with Urns', *Proc. Soc. Antiq. Scot.*, XX, 97–101.

ApSimon, A. M., 1959a. 'Cornish Bronze Age Pottery', *Proc. W. Cornwall Fld. Club*, II, no. 2, 36–46.

—— 1959b. 'Food Vessels', *Univ. London Inst. Archaeol. Bull.*, I, 24–36.

—— 1969. 'The Bronze Age Pottery from Ash Hole, Brixham, Devon', *Proc. Devon Archaeol. Soc.*, XXVI, 21–30.

—— 1970. 'The Earlier Bronze Age in the North of Ireland', *Ulster J. Archaeol.*, XXXII, 28–72.

ApSimon, A. M., Donovan, D. T., & Taylor, H., 1961. 'The Stratigraphy and Archaeology of the Late-Glacial and Post-Glacial Deposits at Brean Down, Somerset', *Proc. Univ. Bristol Spelaeol. Soc.*, IX, 67–136.

Ashbee, P., 1958. 'The Excavation of Tregulland Barrow, Treneglos Parish, Cornwall', *Antiq. J.*, XXXVIII, 174–96.

Ashbee, P. & Dunning, G. C., 1961. 'The Round Barrows of East Kent', *Archaeol. Cantiana*, LXXIV, 48–57.

Bateman, T., 1848. *Vestiges of the Antiquities of Derbyshire*. London.

—— 1861. *Ten Years' Diggings in Celtic and Saxon Grave Hills in the Counties of Derby, Stafford and York, from 1848 to 1858*. London.

British Museum, 1953. *Later Prehistoric Antiquities of the British Isles*. London.

Butler, J. J. & Smith, I. F., 1956. 'Razors, Urns and the British Middle Bronze Age', *Univ. London Inst. Archaeol. Ann. Rep.*, XII, 20–52.

Calkin, J. B., 1964. 'The Bournemouth area in the Middle Bronze and Late Bronze Age, with the "Deverel-Rimbury" problem reconsidered', *Archaeol. J.*, CXIX, 1–65.

Callander, J. G., 1905. 'Notice of Two Cinerary Urns and a Pendant of Slate, found at Seggiecrook in the parish of Kennethmont, Aberdeenshire', *Proc. Soc. Antiq. Scot.*, XXXIX, 184–9.

—— 1908. 'Discovery of a fourth Cinerary Urn . . . at Seggiecrook, . . . Aberdeenshire', *Proc. Soc. Antiq. Scot.*, XLII, 212–22.

—— 1932. 'Unrecorded urns from different parts of Scotland', *Proc. Soc. Antiq. Scot.*, LXVI, 401–8.

Childe, V. G., 1931. *Skara Brae*. London.

—— 1940. *Prehistoric Communities of the British Isles*, London.

—— 1943. 'An Encrusted Urn from Aberlemno, Angus', *Proc. Soc. Antiq. Scot.*, LXXI, 189–91.

Childe, V. G. & Grant, W. G., 1939. 'A Stone-age Settlement at the Braes of Rinyo, Rousay, Orkney (First Report)', *Proc. Soc. Antiq. Scot.*, LXXIII, 6–31.

Christie, P. M., 1968. 'A Barrow-cemetery of the Second Millennium B.C. in Wiltshire', *Proc. Prehist. Soc.*, XXXIII, 336–66.

Coles, F. R., 1901. '. . . Report on Stone Circles of the North-east of Scotland, Inverurie district . . .', *Proc. Soc. Antiq. Scot.*, XXXV, 187–248.

Collins, A. E. P. & May, A. McL., 1959. 'Cremation Burials at Gortfad, Co. Londonderry, with some remarks on Cordoned Urns', *Ulster J. Archaeol.*, XXII, 33–41.

Craw, J. H., 1930–1. 'The Excavation of a Cairn at Drumelzier, Peeblesshire', *Proc. Soc. Antiq. Scot.*, LXV, 363–72.

Cunnington, M. E., 1930. 'Cinerary Urn and Bronze Dagger from Barrow on Roundway Down, near Devizes', *Wiltshire Archaeol. Natur. Hist. Mag.*, XLV, 82–3.

Doppelfeld, O., 1930. 'Die Herkunft der Deverel-Urnen', *Prähistorische Zeitschrift*, XXI, 161–75.

Dunning, G. C., 1936. 'Two Urns of Overhanging-rim Type found abroad', *Antiq. J.*, XVI, 160–4.

Evans, E. E., 1953. *Lyles Hill, a Late Neolithic site in County Antrim*. Archaeol. Res. Pubs. (Northern Ireland), Belfast HMSO.

Fox, C., 1927. 'An Encrusted Urn of the Bronze Age from Wales: with notes on the Origin and Distribution of the Type', *Antiq. J.*, VII, 115–33.

—— 1947. *The Personality of Britain*, 4th Ed. Cardiff.

Glasbergen, W., 1954. 'Barrow Excavations in the Eight Beatitudes. The Bronze Age Cemetery between Toterfout and Halve Mijl, North Brabant, II. The Implications', *Palaeohistoria*, III, 1–204.

Greenwell, W., 1877. *British Barrows*. Oxford.

Hawkes, C. F. C. & Preston, J. P., 1933. 'Three Late Bronze Age Barrows on the Cloven Way', *Antiq. J.*, XIII, 414–54.

Herity, M., 1969. 'Early Finds of Irish Antiquities', *Antiq. J.*, XLIX, 1–21.

Kendrick, T. D. & Hawkes, C. F. C., 1932. *Archaeology in England and Wales, 1914-1931*. London.

Lacaille, A. D., 1931. 'A Bronze Age cemetery near Cowdenbeath, Fife', *Proc. Soc. Antiq. Scot.*, LXV, 261–9.

Leeds, E. T., 1936. 'Round Barrows and Ring-Ditches in Berkshire and Oxfordshire', *Oxoniensia*, I, 7–23.

Longworth, I. H., 1961. 'The Origins and Development of the Primary Series in the Collared Urn Tradition in England and Wales', *Proc. Prehist. Soc.*, XXVII, 263–306.

Manby, T. G., 1958. 'A Cinerary Urn from Welburn, N.R.', *Yorkshire Archaeol. J.*, XXXIX, 395–6.

Mann, L. McL., 1906. 'Notes on . . . a Group of (at least) Sixteen Cinerary Urns found . . . at Stevenston, Ayrshire', *Proc. Soc. Antiq. Scot.*, XL, 378–96.

Mariette, H., 1961. 'Une Urne de l'Âge du Bronze à Hardelot (Pas-de-Calais)', *Helinium*, I, 229–32.

Modderman, P. J. R., 1960. 'Een "Hilversum" pot met wikkeldraadstempel versied en een bronzen naald uit Vorstenbosch (Noord-Brabant)', *Ber. v.d. rijksdienst voor het oudheidkundig bodemonderzoek*, IX, 288–9.

Mortimer, J. R., 1905. *Forty Years' Researches in British and Saxon Burial Mounds of East Yorkshire*. London.

Morrison, A., 1968. 'Cinerary Urns and Pygmy Vessels in South-West Scotland', *Trans. Dumfriesshire Galloway Natur. Hist. Antiq. Soc.*, 3 ser., XLV, 80–140.

Musson, R. C., 1954. 'An Illustrated Catalogue of Sussex Beaker and Bronze Age Pottery', *Sussex Archaeol. Collect.*, XCII, 106–25.

Ó Ríordáin, A. B., 1967. 'Cordoned Urn Burial at Laheen, Co. Donegal', *J. Roy. Soc. Antiq. Ireland*, XCVII, 39–44.

Patchett, F. M., 1952. 'Cornish Bronze Age Pottery, II', *Archaeol. J.*, CVII, 44–65.

Piggott, S., 1955. Review of W. Glasbergen, 'Barrow Excavations in the Eight Beatitudes', *Antiq. J.*, XXV, 235–7.

Pollard, S. H. M. & Russell, P. M. G., 1970. 'Excavation of Round Barrow 248b, Upton Pyne, Exeter', *Proc. Devon Archaeol. Soc.*, XXVII, 49–78.

Pollock, A. J. & Waterman, D. M., 1964. 'A Bronze Age Habitation Site at Downpatrick', *Ulster J. Archaeol.*, XXVII, 31–58.

Rahtz, P. A. & ApSimon, A. M., 1962. 'Excavations at Shearplace Hill, Sydling St Nicholas, Dorset', *Proc. Prehist. Soc.*, XXVIII, 289–328.

RCAM, 1937. Royal Commission on Ancient Monuments in Wales and Monmouthshire. *Anglesey Inventory*. London.

Robertson-Mackay, R., 1952. 'Grooved Ware from Knappers Farm near Glasgow and from Townhead, Rothesay', *Proc. Soc. Antiq. Scot.*, LXXXIV, 180–4.

Savory, H. N., 1957. 'A Corpus of Welsh Bronze Age Pottery: Part II: Food-vessels and enlarged Food-vessels', *Bull. Board Celtic Stud.*, XVII, 196–233.

—— 1961. 'Bronze Age Burials at Clocaenog (Denbighshire)', *Bull. Board Celtic Stud.*, XIX, 171–2; and 'Bronze Age burials near Bedd Emlyn, Clocaenog', *Trans. Denbighshire Hist. Soc.*, X, 7–22.

Simpson, D. D. A., 1965. 'Food Vessels in South West Scotland', *Trans. Dumfriesshire Galloway Natur. Hist. Antiq. Soc.*, 3 ser., XLII, 25–50.

Smedley, N. & Owles, E., 1964. 'Pottery of the Early and early Middle Bronze Age in Suffolk', *Proc. Suffolk Inst. Archaeol.*, XXIX, 174–97.

Smith, I. F., 1961. 'An Essay towards the Reformation of the British Bronze Age', *Helinium*, I, 97–118.

Stevens, F. & Stone, J. F. S., 1938. 'The Barrows of Winterslow', *Wiltshire Archaeol. Natur. Hist. Mag.*, XLVIII, 174–82.

Stevenson, R. B. K., 1951. 'Urn Burial near Lyne', *Proc. Soc. Antiq. Scot.*, LXXXIII, 231–2.

Stone, J. F. S., 1938. 'An Early Bronze Age Grave in Fargo Plantation near Stonehenge', *Wiltshire Archaeol. Natur. Hist. Mag.*, XLVIII, 357–70.

Thurnam, J., 1873. 'On Ancient British Barrows, especially those of Wiltshire and the adjoining counties (II: Round Barrows)', *Archaeologia*, XLIII, 285–544.

ACKNOWLEDGEMENTS

I hope Miss Chitty will enjoy reading this and that it will serve to convey some of the gratitude, respect and affection which we feel for her. It only remains to acknowledge my great indebtedness to Christopher Hawkes who set me off on the inquiry and vigorously criticised its progress, to my colleague Dr David Peacock for much patient daily discussion, and to my friends and fellow researchers, Isobel Smith, John Calkin and Ian Longworth. Mr Calkin lent me his dossier on Biconical Urns, and all have been most generous with facts and ideas. My thanks for facilitating my study of pottery in their charge and for permission to publish it are due to the officers of the following museums: National Museum of Antiquities of Scotland, Edinburgh; Kirkcaldy Museum; Glasgow Museum; Hull Municipal Museum; City Museum, Sheffield; Yorkshire Museum, York; Ulster Museum, Belfast. Among them I must mention, for their personal kindness to me, Mr J. G. Scott (Glasgow) and Mr R. B. K. Stevenson (Edinburgh).

An Early Bronze Age Stone Axe-Mould from the Walleybourne below Longden Common, Shropshire

Nicholas Thomas[1]

Publication of this fine mould for flat bronze axes allows the writer and a group of West Midland colleagues the opportunity to pay their tribute to one whose contribution to archaeology goes very far beyond the borders of Shropshire, but whose work in the West Midlands has been to them a particular inspiration.

The mould was found in 1961 less than three miles from Miss Chitty's home by Master Robert Blazey, of Brookfield, Longden Common.[2] It lay more or less in mid-stream in the Walleybourne Brook, a small tributary of the Cound Brook which flows into the River Severn at Cound, a few miles below Shrewsbury. It occurred just over 300 ft upstream from the bridge beneath which the Walleybourne crosses the Longden–Pulverbatch Road (SJ/435043). This stream marks the boundary between the parishes of Pontesbury and Church Pulverbatch.

The site of the find is a miniature gorge, densely overgrown and inaccessible. In Bronze Age times the immediate locality would have been wooded but pleasant and accessible. The mould could have been there for a considerable time without discovery and only someone like a child paddling in the brook near his home would have noticed it. Just above its confluence with another stream near the find-spot, however, the Walleybourne contains a considerable amount of flood debris. December 1960 saw extensive flooding all over Shropshire and it is possible that the mould may have been washed down from a higher point at that time, or dislodged from the bank. Stones in both streams at this point are stained a deep black by a substance identified by Professor Shotton as a form of algae. The staining on this mould is not as extensive as that on stones taken from the stream, and clearly it had not lain there for very long before discovery. Unfortunately this discolouring now makes it difficult to see whether the matrices of the mould show the blackening noticed on other moulds and attributed to remains of a dressing which would have been applied to the matrices before casting, to protect their surfaces (Britton, 1963, 276).

The mould (fig. 1, pl. III) was sliced by Professor F. W. Shotton (Sh 1/M) and found to be made of a grit with felspar fragments (plagioclase and microcline) and some muscovite (white mica). It is almost certainly a Carboniferous grit, but this type of rock is so widespread in

---

[1] This note combines the work of Dr E. T. Hall, Mrs E. E. Richards, Prof. F. W. Shotton and Messrs P.A. Barker, H. W. M. Hodges and R. E. James with that of the writer. It owes most, however, to Miss Chitty herself.
[2] It has been presented by him to the Shrewsbury Museum, inventory number M1. A facsimile in crystic resin was prepared by H. W. M. Hodges and is now at the Birmingham City Museum, no. A417'62.

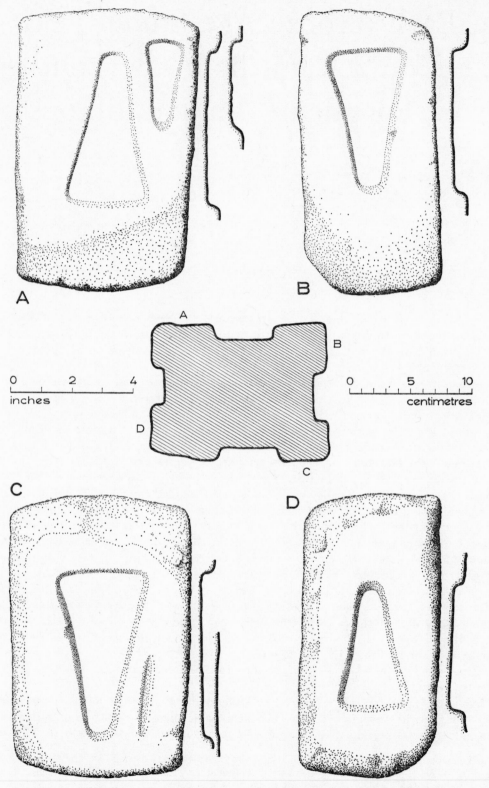

A

B

C

D

0   2   4
inches

0   5   10
centimetres

fig. 1 Axe-mould from the Walleybourne, Longden Common, Shropshire

England and east Wales, as well as in Ireland, that it is unlikely that its precise source could ever be located.

In shape, the mould is a four-sided block, rectangular in cross-section, measuring overall 22·6 × 14·9 × 11·2 cms (c. 10·5 × 5·875 × 4·375 in.) and weighing 6·9 kg. (15·25 lb). Surface markings suggest the probability that the block was artificially shaped by pecking, followed presumably by grinding of the four long sides, so that only the merest traces of the pecking process survive. The ends, however, which are irregular and convex, retain more noticeable peck marks and they contrast strongly with the flat sides.

Matrices for axes of five different sizes have been carved into the four sides and there is in addition a hollow for a small rod or awl. Dimensions of the axe-blanks which could have been cast from the mould, measured on the floors of the matrices, are as follows:

face	length of axe	width of blade	average depth
A1	11·8 cms	6·5 cms	1·2 cms
A2	6·35 cms	2·6 cms	0·95 cms
B	10·7 cms	5·9 cms	1·2 cms
C	12·7 cms	7·1 cms	1·1 cms
D	9·3 cms	4·9 cms	1·1 cms

Face C, rod or awl, length 6·35 cms, width, 0·55 cms, depth 0·25 cms.

Britton has remarked (1963, 265 ff.) upon the skill and patience lavished on these early moulds by their makers. The Walleybourne mould shows this to a marked degree. As we have already suggested, the craftsman began by preparing a neat, symmetrical block of convenient size and provided with four almost perfectly smooth, flat surfaces for matrices. Into these he has carved and ground hollows astonishingly regular in outline, with surfaces almost glassy smooth.[1] The upper edges of the matrices are rounded, but none shows the bevelling recorded on some moulds. It is noticeable that whereas the sides and blade end of the matrices are almost vertical and make a sharp angle with the floors, the butt end slopes more noticeably in each matrix, a small detail which can be seen in the majority of British open moulds and which would have allowed the blank to be removed more easily after casting. The requirements of even the early British bronze-smiths were exact, and evidently the tools of their trade included precise specifications such as this. Cross-sections of the axes in the Migdale hoard, for example, show these sloping edges not eliminated by subsequent working-up of the axe-blank (Britton, 1963, fig. 4). Surprisingly, only a very few of the flat bronze axes from Ireland show this feature (Harbison, 1969, pl. 11, nos. 5, 23).

The faces of the mould are so flat that, with the exception of Face A, a cover of wood or stone could have been placed over each matrix to seal it at all points, a technique to prevent oxidisation of the upper surface of the molten metal which is generally assumed in the foundry process with these early moulds. For Face A it would not have been difficult to cut lids for the two matrices, since this face is only slightly uneven at two points.

Surface scrapings were taken from matrices A1 and D, and from an exterior surface, for submission to the Research Laboratory for Archaeology and the History of Art at Oxford, and were examined by Mrs E. E. Richards. Five mg. of these scrapings were mixed with an equal weight of carbon powder and the mixture burnt in a D.C. arc. A spectrum was taken using a Hilger large spectrograph with quartz crystal.

The resulting spectrums of three specimens from both outside and inside were compared. In particular, suitable copper and tin lines were examined. The intensity of both the copper and tin lines from those specimens taken from the matrices were considerably greater than the same lines of the 'external' scrapings. Since all three pairs of specimens showed this differentiation,

[1] Considerably smoother than the four main surfaces of the mould. Grinding of the latter after preliminary pecking seems to have been less rigorous, although we are sure it was carried out.

it would seem highly likely that the matrices had been used for casting bronze. The small traces of copper and tin to be found on the outside of the mould are probably due to inclusions in the stone from which the mould was manufactured.

The Walleybourne mould is the twentieth certain example of its class to be published from Britain and the only one so far known to include as many as five axe matrices: eleven recorded British moulds have one matrix, and only the mould from Foudland, Aberdeen, has as many as four (Britton, 1963, 299, Table 3).

Britton has attributed these stone moulds to his Migdale-Marnoch tradition, to which they are linked by their geographical distribution in the highland zone of Britain – the Walleybourne mould falls just within this region – and by the restricted series of simple but distinctive tools and ornaments for which they provided blanks. The Walleybourne mould generally compares closely with the others in its class, the wide range of axe-sizes in the matrices being a typical feature. It is noticeable, however, that the sides and particularly the blades of the Walleybourne matrices are generally a little straighter than those in most of the other examples.

About ten Marnoch moulds include matrices for rods or awls. Lengths of the rods usually exceed 10 cms, while those of the two possible awls are less than 4 cms. The matrix in face C on the Walleybourne mould provides a casting rather larger than the usual awl of this period, but on average so much smaller than the typical bar castings that it seems best to regard it as for an awl.

Miss Chitty has suggested (Chitty, 1961–7, 60) that the Walleybourne mould may be Irish, on the grounds of its resemblance to the mould from Ballyglisheen, Co. Carlow (Prendergast, 1958, 139 ff., summarised in Coghlan & Raftery, 1961, 226, fig. 3). This piece has no less than eight axe matrices, arranged wherever they could be fitted on four surfaces of an irregular block. The material of the mould, moreover, was millstone grit. Some of the matrices of the Ballyglisheen mould show the same more gradual slope of the butt-end of the matrix, two of them having a step in addition. In shape, however, the Ballyglisheen matrices have deeper, almost straight butts and the blades are on the whole wider and more curved than those on the Walleybourne mould. Nevertheless, the possibility should not be overlooked that the smith who lost his mould, or left it beside this little Shropshire stream, may originally have come with the tools of his trade from Ireland.

The place of discovery of the Walleybourne mould is of great significance in the history of the Early Bronze Age metal industry in the West Midlands.[1] It is perhaps not generally realised by archaeologists that Shrewsbury is situated centrally between two series of copper veins: these occur south of the Severn in the Pre-Cambrian rocks from Linley and Norbury north-east to Lyth Hill; others are found in the sandstone ridges that rise from the Triassic Plain of northern Shropshire – Pim Hill, Grinshill and Hawkstone – and elsewhere in the Keuper Beds. In both groups copper was found in sufficient quantity to be worth mining in the nineteenth century and even earlier. Disused mines south-west of Shrewsbury occur in the areas of Cothercott, Westcott, Ratlinghope, Wentnor, Norbury and Linley (Dewey, Eastwood *et al.*, 1925, 18–21, N. Shropshire; 28–9, Llanymynech Hill; 56–9, S. Shropshire). A thriving prehistoric bronze industry here would lack only tin, but the presence in the West Midlands of a significant number of stone axes of Group I and allied rocks from Cornwall suggests that tin was probably being imported to the region at this time.[2] In Shropshire, for example, Group I axes and a small perforated hammer have been recorded from Buildwas (Sh 4/c), Clun (Sh 55 a/h), Kinlet (Sh 47/c) and Shrewsbury (Sh 3/c), and from Longdon Marsh (Wo 4/c) and Lower Hagley (Wo 1/c) in Worcestershire (Chitty, 1951–2, 112; also Chitty, 1957–60, 34, 50), while an

---

[1] This section summarises Miss Chitty's very important work on the movement of stone implements and metal across this part of Shropshire, and the writer is indebted to her for allowing him access to her notes and for discussing it with him.

[2] Information from Miss Chitty and Professor Shotton, mainly unpublished.

axe of material similar to Group I has come from the parish of Cound (Sh 5/c: Chitty, 1951–2, *loc. cit.*). The distribution of implements of Cornish rock farther south suggests that contacts with the south-west peninsula came across the Cotswolds and up the Severn and Avon.

More locally, it seems clear that the massive axe-hammers made of Picrite at the Hyssington (Group XII) axe factory (Shotton, Chitty & Seaby, 1951, 159 ff.) played a part in the metal industry, acting no doubt as highly efficient rock and ore breakers. Finds of implements of such material near these copper outcrops have been recorded by Miss Chitty at Wentnor Prolley Moor (Chitty, 1927, 75 ff., fig. no. 27; Sh 38/ah) and at Bayston Hill (Chitty, 1949, 34, fig. 8; Sh 40/ah).

The particularly valuable contribution made by Miss Chitty to the study of this local pre-historic bronze industry concerns her tracing of the route into Wales taken by Neolithic and Early Bronze Age peoples from the West Midlands along her Clun–Clee ridgeway (Chitty, 1963, 171 ff.), and her recognition of the highly important route from the Clun district to the Portway crossing the Long Mynd (Cobbold, 1904, 50–1, map, fig. 19, p. 36; tumuli, pp. 34–50)[1], then by its western branch to Cothercott Hill (Chitty, 1949, 25, 27–31), where it follows a ridge of the West Longmyndian rocks (Whitehead, 1955, 465–470) by Castle Pulverbatch, Longden Common, Exford's Green, Lyth Hill, Bayston Hill and the Sharpstones to the River Severn beyond Weeping Cross[2] on the south-eastern outskirts of Shrewsbury. The antiquity of this route is indicated by the distribution along it of flint and stone implements between the Severn at Weeping Cross and the northern end of the Portway traversing the Long Mynd, and by barrows on the Long Mynd itself. Some of the principal copper outcrops in this region occur along the line of the route. The Walleybourne mould also fits into this suggestive distribution and its discovery has provided Miss Chitty with a key piece in her establishment of a route which thus combines, directly or indirectly, an effective land bridge from Clun to Severn with a concentration of Late Neolithic–Early Bronze Age antiquities and barrows and outcrops of copper ore. The tin necessary to the industry was probably brought up the Severn.

Miss Chitty has described the Walleybourne multiple axe-mould as the most important prehistoric antiquity yet found in Shropshire, and it is fitting that an extended note about it should be included in a volume of essays written in her honour. Moreover the most original part of this note, in which the mould has been shown to fit into a local distribution which establishes the existence of a land route from the Severn deep into Wales, intimately connected with the stone axe trade and Early Bronze Age metal-working, is her discovery. That it has been no more than sketched in here is because only Miss Chitty is capable of setting it out fully; it is our hope that such an opportunity may occur when the combined research of Miss Chitty and Professor Shotton upon the West Midland stone axe trade is published in the not too distant future.

[1] This was 'the King's Highway over Longemunede' of Cantilupe's Register (Eyton, 1860, 199). The route was used for example in the trade from Graig Lwyd of axes of Group VII. I am grateful to Miss Chitty for this information and references.

[2] A substantial burial and settlement site from Late Neolithic to Iron Age times, now covered by the Sutton Farm Estate. It was excavated in advance of building, from 1965 onwards, by P. A. Barker, W. E. Jenks and R. G. Livens but has not yet been published.

BIBLIOGRAPHY

Britton, D., 1963. 'Traditions of metal-working in the later Neolithic and Early Bronze Age of Britain: Part I', *Proc. Prehist. Soc.*, XXIX, 258–325.

Chitty, L. F., 1927. 'Perforated Stone Axe-hammers found in Shropshire', *Bull. Board Celtic Stud.*, IV, 74–91.

—— 1949. 'Flint Implements recently found in Shropshire south of the Severn', *Trans. Shropshire Archaeol. Soc.*, LIII, 24–36.

—— 1951–2. 'Prehistoric and other Early Finds in the Borough of Shrewsbury', *Trans. Shropshire Archaeol. Soc.*, LIV, 105–44.

—— 1957–60. 'Recorder's Report for Archaeology', *Trans. Caradoc Severn Valley Field Club*, XV, 31–84.

—— 1961–7. 'Recorder's Account for Archaeology', *Trans. Caradoc Severn Valley Field Club*, XVI, 43–84.

—— 1963. 'The Clun–Clee Ridgeway: a Prehistoric Trackway across South Shropshire', in Foster, I. Ll. & Alcock, L. (eds), *Culture and Environment, Essays in Honour of Sir Cyril Fox*. London. 171–92.

Cobbold, E. S., 1904. 'Barrows and Tumuli: Portway', *Church Stretton: Some Results of Local Scientific Research*. III, 34–54.

Coghlan, H. H. & Raftery, J., 1961. 'Irish Prehistoric Casting Moulds', *Sibrium*, VI, 223–44.

Dewey, H., Eastwood, T. *et al.*, 1925. 'Copper Ores of the Midlands, Wales, Lake District and the Isle of Man', *Mem. Geol. Survey*, XXX.

Eyton, Rev. R. W., 1860. 'Manor of Lydbury North', *Antiquities of Shropshire*, XI, 194–224.

Harbison, P., 1969. *The Axes of the Early Bronze Age in Ireland (Prähistoriche Bronzefunde, Abf. IX. I Band)*. Munich.

Prendergast, E., 1958. 'National Museum of Ireland Archaeological Acquisitions in the Year 1957', *J. Roy. Soc. Antiq. Ireland*, 88, 139–43.

Shotton, F. W., Chitty, L. F., & Seaby, W. A., 1951. 'A New Centre of Stone Axe Dispersal on the Welsh Border', *Proc. Prehist. Soc.*, XVII, 159–67.

Whitehead, T. H., 1955. 'The West Longmyndian Rocks of the Shrewsbury District', *Geol. Mag.*, XCII, No. 6, 465–70.

The Ebnal Hoard and Early Bronze Age Metal-working Traditions

Colin Burgess and John D. Cowen

(1) ALBERT WAY'S DRAWINGS

The Ebnal hoard of bronze weapons and tools has not lacked for chroniclers, though most of their notices are slight indeed. Suffice it to say that the *locus classicus* on its history and contents was published by our good friend and general benefactress Miss Lily Chitty, when in 1940 she drew together and analysed the whole of the available evidence (Chitty, 1940). An admirable summary, with a figure showing four of the pieces, has since been published by Dennis Britton (1963).

Her presentation of the events, which I accept as secure and take as read, showed that the hoard was found in 1848 or 1849, 'in the bank of a ditch at Ebnall, near Oswestry', and consisted of at least eight pieces, as follows:

two ogival daggers of the Camerton-Snowshill type;

one end-looped spearhead;

two tools described as 'punches', one of shouldered, and one of lugged form;

a cast-flanged axe of the form characteristic of the Arreton tradition; and two more, reasonably supposed to be of the same type.

Of these only two pieces have survived, one of the daggers and one axe, both now in the National Museum of Wales. In addition sound drawings exist of the second dagger, the spearhead, and the shouldered 'punch'.[1] The type of the second and third axes rests on a natural (but unconfirmed) assumption. The form of the lugged 'punch' has remained till now unknown.

Over the years the two surviving pieces, and the three available drawings, have been reproduced on a number of occasions, and in a variety of combinations; but never, to my knowledge, all at the same time and place to illustrate the hoard, so far as may be, as a whole. Only once have photographs of the two surviving originals been published, again by Miss Chitty (1940).

In the library of the Society of Antiquaries at Burlington House there is a set of half-a-dozen large quarto portfolios filled with loose drawings of antiquities, given or bequeathed by Albert Way (1805–74). These volumes contain material sorted into broad categories, and among them

---

[1] As the true character of both these pieces is still far from certain, we shall generally refer to them from now on simply as 'tools'. There is no more assurance that the shouldered piece is a 'punch' than that the lugged piece is a 'trunnion stake', though either or both of these statements could be true.

one is entitled 'Metalwork of Bronze Age and Early Iron Age' (Soc. Ant. MS. no. 700). Into these containers it is clear that Way (or his executors) threw the vast mass of drawings of archaeological objects that he had himself made, or received from friends, wherever he went over a period of some 30–40 years in the middle of the nineteenth century, whether as a leading spirit in the newly-formed Archaeological Institute, or as a devoted supporter of the Cambrian Archaeological Association – for Wales and the Marches are well represented in this accumulation.

Some while ago, in looking over this material, not all of which is any longer serviceable (for want of annotation), and much of which has long since been published, the writer happened upon Way's collection of drawings of the Ebnal hoard. And here at last is a figure of the second 'punch', and one which shows it to be substantially different from the first (pl. VI, 3). The fact of the discovery has been briefly noted by Colin Burgess (1969, 25–6, n. 2).

The drawings are on six separate pieces of paper; they are of very varied quality and finish, and they must derive from at least three distinct sources.[1] The most attractive are three admirable life-size water-colour drawings (on two sheets), in which some care has been taken to catch the quality of the surfaces and colouring.[2] They show the spearhead (pl. IV), the shouldered tool, and a flanged axe very like that now at Cardiff (pl. V, 1, 2); and though I find it impossible to assert that it actually must be the same piece, the resemblance is certainly close enough to constitute strong confirmation (if any were still needed) of the attribution of the Cardiff axe to the Ebnal hoard (Chitty, 1940).

On a further sheet we have three careful pencil drawings showing the two daggers, neatly and accurately executed (pl. VI, 1, 2), and now, for the first time, the lugged tool (pl. VI, 3). A fourth sheet shows the shouldered tool alone, *en suite* with the drawings on the preceding sheet, and, but for the difference in technique, very closely resembling the water-colour version on pl. II. It suggests that this version (in which two apparently independent sources coincide) may well be more accurate than the not very convincing block made for the Society of Antiquaries in 1865, and adopted by John Evans in 1881 (Evans, 1881, 186–7, fig. 222). The above three drawings of the two 'punches' show clearly that they must have been plain, simple things, and for that very reason, perhaps, not easy to portray convincingly.

A fifth sheet shows simple pencil outlines of one of the daggers and both 'punches', clearly made by tracing round the objects; against each of the 'punches' is noted: 'about $\frac{3}{8}$ of an inch thick'. Lastly a half-sheet of paper, inscribed in a different hand, shows the smaller 'punch' in three aspects – on plan, in section, and in perspective. This is rather rough, but it tells the same story as the others. Most of the drawings are inscribed with some particulars of the discovery, but nothing not already covered by Miss Chitty.

The contents of the hoard show clearly enough that it can be related to the well-known group of hoards generically bracketed with that from Arreton Down, and closely associated with the Wessex Culture, as first, to the best of my belief, pointed out by Miss Chitty in 1940. Following on the more recent subdivision of the Early Bronze Age in Britain, and therewith of the Wessex Culture also, into two phases, it is no less clear that this group of hoards must fall within the later of the two phases. So far as Ebnal is concerned, I have myself for some while believed, not only that the hoard must fall within the limits of British EBA 2/Wessex II, but that it must be one of the latest of this arresting series of hoards.

In this context the well-known shouldered tool, having as yet no parallel or analogue, is valueless as a chronological indicator. But the longer, lugged tool now revealed is another matter. Closest home, and long since familiar, though a little different in form, is that in the Westbury-on-Trym hoard (Piggott, 1938). And there are others of which to take account. Colin Burgess

---

[1] A selection of the best is here reproduced on pls I–III by kind permission of the Society of Antiquaries of London.
[2] Both sheets are marked at the foot: 'commd. by Mr. Wynne'.

has drawn attention to the grave at Balneil, Wigtownshire, which beside another lugged tool contained also *inter alia* a quoit-shaped faience bead, and a bone crutch-headed pin (Burgess, 1969). Others are known from Ireland and Holland; but discussion of the implications of the whole group is reserved for Mr Burgess himself in a later section of this paper.

The overall effect, however, of this nexus of similarities and links over a fairly wide area is securely to fix our lugged tool within the EBA 2/Wessex II bronze industry in Britain. And the position of the Voorhout hoard (Butler, 1963; and see Burgess below), which with its palstaves must come after, but not long after, the end of British EBA 2, is at least presumptive evidence that Ebnal falls well towards the end of the period, and may in any case serve as a characteristic example of the final phase of Early Bronze Age metal-working traditions in Britain. Immediately thereafter, over the greater part of the country, there follows a remarkable lacuna in the sequence of bronze hoards, which is not the least of the several factors that combine to give to the Ebnal hoard its quite special interest.

J. D. C.

(2) EBNAL AND EARLY BRONZE AGE METAL-WORKING

Thirty years ago Miss Chitty described the Ebnal hoard as 'comparable with the famous Arreton Down and Plymstock hoards, and the burial group in the Snowshill Barrow, Glos.' (Chitty, 1940, 29). The mass of new evidence that has accumulated since then has done nothing to upset this judgement, and the following notes are offered as a tribute to her percipience in this, as in so many other matters.

Of the eight or more implements originally in the Ebnal hoard, it is now possible to identify two daggers, one socketed spearhead, one shouldered 'punch', one lugged tool and a flanged axe. This last was one of three 'palstaves' found, the suggestion being that the three were of similar form, and therefore that the only two Ebnal implements not accounted for were also flanged axes. This cannot, however, be conclusively demonstrated at present.[1]

The daggers

The two daggers are typical of the Camerton-Snowshill form (ApSimon, 1954). These are characterised by an ogival, grooved blade with thickened centre or midrib, and generally have an arched butt with three thick rivets to secure the handle. Of the two Ebnal examples, the surviving one (fig. 1 : 2) is more characteristic in its butt form than the lost specimen (fig. 1 : 3). The straight-based butt of the latter, however, has excellent parallels – notably the Camerton dagger itself (Evans, 1881, 243, fig. 303), and one from Ibworth, Hants (Dale, 1909–11, 98). These belong to a small sub-group within the Camerton-Snowshill series, characterised by primitive trapezoid butts with two rivet holes, apparently anticipating the diagnostic butt shape of the post-Wessex dirks and rapiers (Burgess, 1968). The Camerton dagger has a notch in the middle of its butt end for a third rivet, like the lost Ebnal dagger.

Britton (1963, 286) has shown Camerton-Snowshill daggers to be an element in his Arreton metal-working tradition, contemporary with Wessex II.

[1] In her discussion of the Brogyntyn Collection, Miss Chitty (1940, 35, n.2.) noted a strongly shouldered haft-flanged axe there as similar in patina to the Ebnal implements, and wondered whether this might not be one of the missing Ebnal axes. In view of the disparate forms of the Ebnal 'punches', this remains a possibility, though one which is unlikely ever to be proved one way or the other. The Brogyntyn axe is strongly Sögel-influenced, and must therefore stand near the beginning of the haft-flanged series at the transition from Irish/British Early to Middle Bronze Age. This would certainly fit with the chronology for Ebnal suggested here.

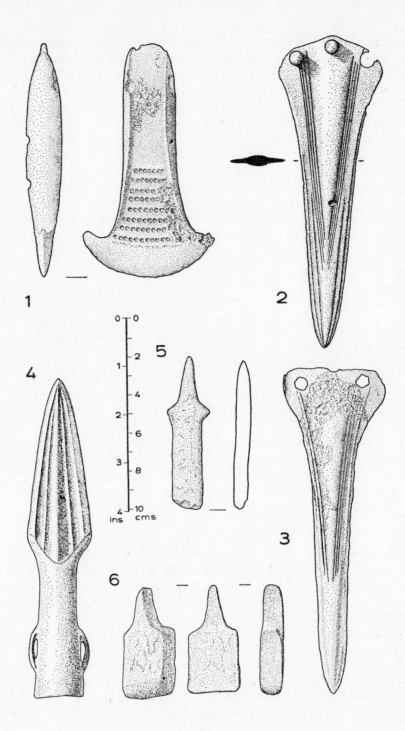

fig. 1 The Ebnal hoard reconstituted
fig. 2 Stone moulds from 1 Inch Island, Co. Donegal; (after Coghlan and Raftery, 1961) 2 Broughshane, Co. Antrim; (after Evans, 1881)
fig. 3 Stone mould from Bodwrdin, Anglesey (drawing: Frances Lynch)

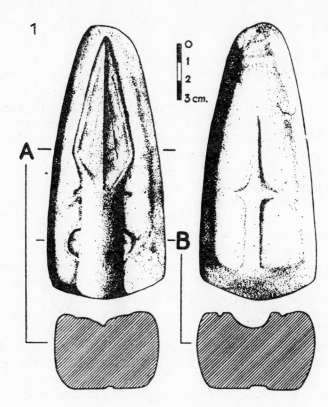

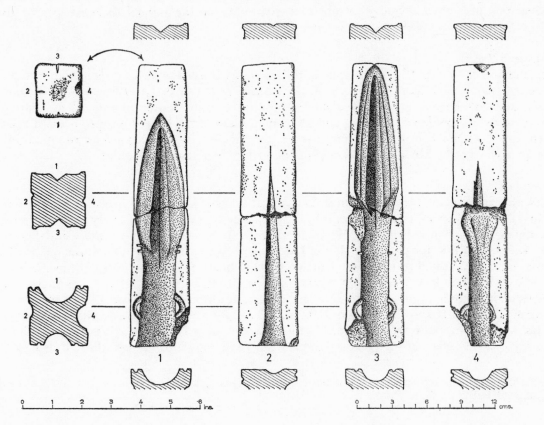

The spearhead

In the type of spearhead represented by the Ebnal example (fig. 1 : 4), the socket extends only to the base of the blade, from which it is divided by a curved or v-shaped line. The blade is solid cast, its edges of ogival outline or tapering to a rounded-off point, and it is of complex structure with varying arrangements of channels, grooves and ribs. The affinity with tanged, collared spearheads of Snowshill type is obvious, and the blade form is clearly linked to that of the ogival daggers and tanged spearheads of the Arreton tradition. Two shaft attachment methods are found on these early socketed spearheads, opposed holes in the socket to take a peg or pin, or loops, generally placed towards the end of the socket, to take a tie. The looped Ebnal spearhead belongs to the latter group, termed 'end-looped' by the present writer (Burgess, 1962, 85) in order to distinguish it from other looped spearhead groups. The pegged version is very rare, and apparently confined to southern and eastern England.[1] The looped form is very much more common, and is overwhelmingly concentrated in Ireland (fig. 6 : 4). Two stone moulds are also known from Ireland, from Lough Gur (Evans, 1881, 436) and from Inch Island, Co. Donegal (fig. 2 : 1) (Coghlan & Raftery, 1961, 234, fig. 22); there seems no doubt, therefore, that this may be regarded principally as an Irish type, a product of an Irish industry equivalent to the Arreton tradition. Another stone mould for the type, found at Bodwrdin, Anglesey (fig. 3) (Britton, 1963, 285, 291; Manby, 1966), was thought by Britton to be the only mould which could be assigned to the Arreton tradition, but this view must now clearly be re-examined. Wales and the Marches provide the largest concentration of end-looped spearheads outside Ireland (Burgess 1962, 85; Savory, 1966), and, in view of the Bodwrdin mould, some may have been manufactured there, but the type is almost unknown in the Arreton province (fig. 6 : 4). The examples from Wales and the Marches, geographically placed between the Arreton area and Ireland, can be interpreted in various ways. The most obvious explanation is that they represent an offshoot of the Irish industry. Alternatively they could be ancestral rather than derivative, a bridge in time and space between the pegged socketed spearheads of the Arreton area and the looped version of Ireland.

Shouldered 'punch'

The shouldered 'punch' (fig. 1 : 6) appears to be unique. It has a superficial resemblance to the socketed, shouldered 'hammers' of the Dowris phase of the Irish Late Bronze Age (Eogan, 1964) and may have been used for a similar purpose. It is interesting to note the association of one of these shouldered hammers and a trunnion stake in the Late Bronze Age hoard from Lusmagh, Co. Offaly (British Museum, 1953, 34, 37, fig. 12 : 6), which provides an interesting comparison with the Ebnal association of shouldered 'punch' and trunnion tool.

Lugged tool (fig. 1 : 5)

This appears similar to the trunnion stakes so well known from the Irish/British Bronze Age (Hemp, 1925; Maryon, 1938; Eogan, 1964, 274–6). The type was clearly a very long-lived one, examples being known from Middle Bronze Age contexts such as the Bishopsland hoard, Co. Kildare (Eogan, 1964, 275, fig. 5) and Late Bronze Age contexts, as in the Lusmagh hoard. Another important find is that in the Dutch Voorhout hoard (fig. 4) one of the Ilsmoor hoards of Early MII. This hoard has strong Welsh connections (Butler, 1959; 1960; 1963) and Butler regarded its trunnion tool as an Irish/British export, at a time which could hardly have been long after Wessex II and the Arreton tradition. The Early Bronze Age background of the type is less well-known, but is equally clear. The well-known lugged tool in the Westbury-on-Trym hoard (Britton, 1963, 286–9, 316, fig. 18) provides a starting-point, though this has its lugs at

---

[1] Although a mould for such spearheads is included in the remarkable group of moulds from Omagh, Co. Tyrone (Coghlan & Raftery, 1961, tav. XIII).

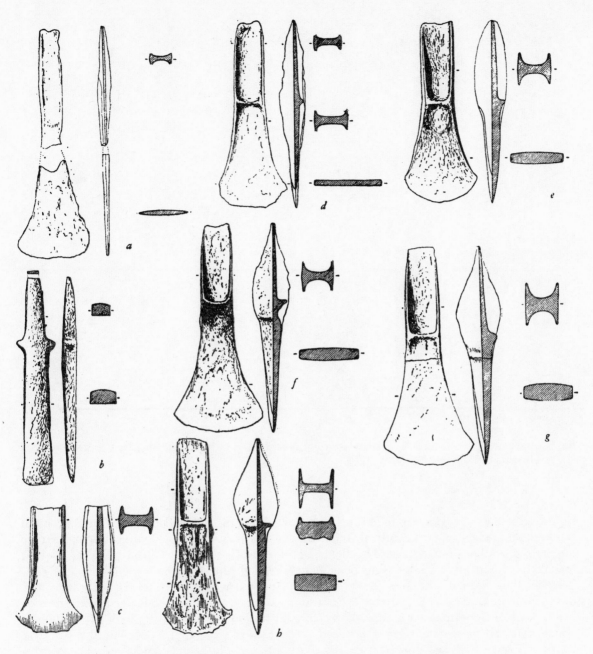

fig. 4 Implements from the Voorhout hoard, South Holland (after Butler, 1959)

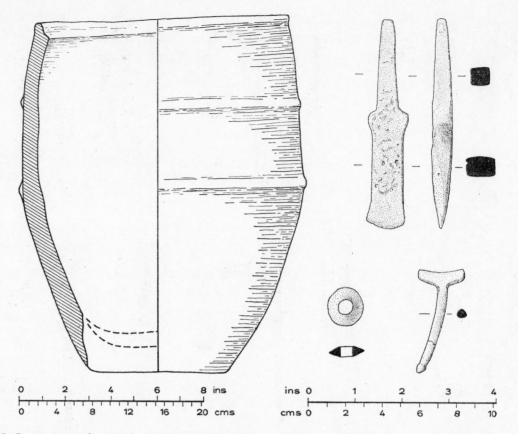

| 0 | 2 | 4 | 6 | 8 ins |
| 0 | 4 | 8 | 12 | 16 | 20 cms |

| ins 0 | 1 | 2 | 3 | 4 |
| cms 0 | 2 | 4 | 6 | 8 | 10 |

fig. 5 Grave group from Balneil, Wigtownshire (drawings of pot, bead and pin: D. Clarke, National Museum of Antiquities, Edinburgh)

right angles to its edge, instead of parallel to it. The closest of all parallels to the Ebnal example is that in the grave group from Balneil, Wigtowns. (fig. 5) (Curle, 1915–16) which, though rather larger, has similar stunted lugs. The Balneil group also included a Cordoned Urn, a quoit faience bead and a most interesting bone crutch-headed pin, apparently with a phallic end. The pin links Balneil with the Wessex Culture, and particularly Wessex II (Piggott, 1938, 85–7; Proudfoot, 1963, 414; Annable & Simpson, 1964, 26), and this is confirmed by the faience bead. Another important connection of the Ebnal trunnion tool is with the Inch Island mould, which not only has a matrix for end-looped spearheads like the Ebnal one, but also a matrix for small lugged tools of Ebnal size. Finally there is the mould from Broughshane, Co. Antrim (fig. 2 : 2) (Evans, 1881, 433), which had a matrix for a 'flat chisel with side stops', slightly smaller than the Ebnal tool. Other matrices on this mould were for 'a flat triangular celt-like tool', a flat ring, and a Group I dirk, the latter suggesting the transition period from Early to Middle Bronze Age (Burgess, 1968, 7–8).

The flanged axe (fig. 1 : 1)
This is a cast-flanged axe of the form typical of the Arreton tradition (Britton, 1963, 286). Characteristic is a slender body, with straight sides generally parallel or converging slightly to an arched butt end. The last feature results in a profile with a distinct spiked or tongued top. Usually there is a transverse bevel across the middle of each face between the flanges, but never

a true stop ridge. The blade is strongly expanded to a crescent shape, and the sides are either rounded or worked into flat, longitudinal facets. Decoration below the central bevel and on the sides is common, executed in punched, incised and hammered techniques, the last being by far the most common. Such axes were the main product of the Arreton tradition, and their distribution throughout southern and eastern England (fig. 6:2) outlines its sphere of influence. They are very rare beyond these areas.

Just as end-looped spearheads were an Irish counterpart of the Arreton pegged spearheads, so these flanged axes had an Irish equivalent. They are to be found in considerable numbers among the amorphous mass of flat and flanged axes grouped by Harbison into his 'Type Derryniggin' (Harbison, 1969a). They differ from the Arreton type in having a broader form, with greater tendency to parallel sides, and a straight, or only lightly arched, butt end. As a result, their profile does not usually have the Arreton spiked top. Their flanges are usually lower, and may sometimes have been hammered up rather than cast. The central bevel is often curved rather than straight, and the true stop ridge is sometimes found. Decoration is much more frequent and more varied than on the Arreton axes, and the emphasis is on incised and punched ornament. Flanged axes of the Derryniggin form seem to be fairly common in Scotland, Evans illustrating classic examples from Perth and Dams, Fifeshire (Evans, 1881, 60–1). The Gavel Moss hoard axes (Piggott & Stewart, 1958) are also of this type. There are several examples from northern England, Evans illustrating a fine example from Whittington Fell, Northumberland (Evans, 1881, 74, fig. 51: *not* 'Chollerford Bridge'), but the type is practically unknown over the rest of England and Wales.

The Ebnal implements thus show connections with the two major metal-working traditions of the later Early Bronze Age. The Camerton-Snowshill daggers and flanged axe can be related to the Arreton tradition of southern and eastern England, whereas the end-looped spearhead is a type at home in the Irish Inch Island–Derryniggin industry. The lugged tool would also seem to have a Hiberno-Scottish, rather than Arreton, background, in view of its relationship to the Balneil, Inch Island and Broughshane finds. The Ebnal find thus emerges as one of the really crucial hoards of the Irish/British Early Bronze Age, apparently the only one which links directly the two metal-working giants of the latter part of this period. It has less direct significance for events in Wales and the Marches, but before dealing with this, the Arreton and Inch Island–Derryniggin traditions should be considered more fully. The map, fig. 7, plots the distribution of main types in the Ebnal hoard, and shows the areas covered by the traditions they represent.

THE ARRETON TRADITION

Little can be added to Britton's detailed discussion of the Arreton tradition (Britton, 1963), but some of his conclusions must now be modified, since he did not attempt to take the Irish material into account. The three major products of this industry were the flanged axes and Camerton-Snowshill daggers discussed above, and tanged spearheads. There were, in addition, numbers of lesser products. Hitherto there has been only Britton's map of Arreton hoards to illustrate the distribution of this industry, and Britton was rightly cautious about basing too much significance on such fragmentary evidence. Further, certain of his hoard spots must now be removed – those for the Rodborough and Gavel Moss hoards, which will be considered with the Inch Island–Derryniggin tradition below, the find from Bracklesham Bay, Sussex, with its Derryniggin flanged axe and Group II dirk, and, of course, the Ebnal hoard, with its mixed background.

A more complete picture of the distribution of the Arreton tradition is provided by a map of its three main products, flanged axes, Camerton-Snowshill daggers and tanged spearheads (fig. 7). These make up the vast mass of Arreton material, and taken together they show that the Arreton

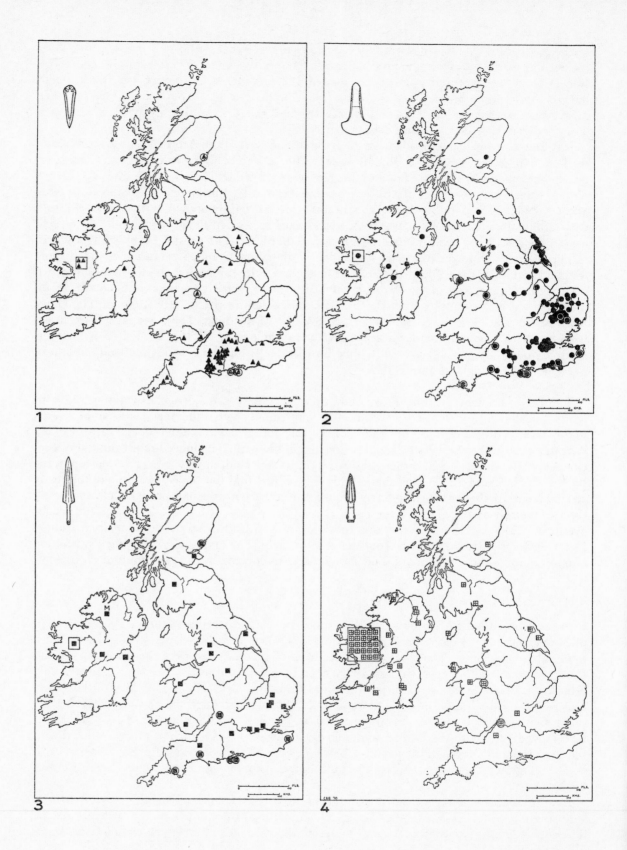

fig. 6 (left) Distribution maps of individual types in the Ebnal hoard, and of fanged spearheads
fig. 7 Distribution of the Arreton and Inch Island-Derryniggin traditions, as represented by types in the Ebnal hoard

sphere ran the whole length of southern England, from Cornwall to Kent, and extended throughout the eastern counties almost to the Tees. The main centres emerge as Hampshire–Sussex, the middle and upper Thames Basin and the Fens, but the importance of east Yorkshire and south Lancashire is also noteworthy. There are also notable gaps in the distribution – in particular, the Chilterns, Hertfordshire and Essex, and much of Kent and Surrey. Most significant is the fact that the main Wessex Culture area of Dorset and Wiltshire was not a major Arreton centre. In this region Camerton-Snowshill daggers from Wessex II graves provide the principal link with Arreton metal-working but other Arreton material is rare (fig. 7), and there are no hoards. Individual maps of these three main Arreton types show marked differences in distribution (fig. 6). The concentrations of Camerton-Snowshill daggers and Arreton flanged axes are largely mutually exclusive, the former in Wessex and the Upper Thames basin, the latter in the east; and, further, the daggers are mainly grave finds, the axes stray finds and from hoards. The widely scattered distribution of the tanged spearheads, with no marked concentrations, provides a further contrast. Most of our knowledge of the industry comes from stray finds and hoards. Only Camerton-Snowshill daggers were commonly deposited in graves, but the Snowshill burial included a tanged and collared spearhead (Greenwell & Brewis, 1909), and tanged spearheads were found in graves at Llanfachreth, Merion. with a ring (Chitty, 1926), and at Gilchorn, Angus, with a Camerton-Snowshill dagger (Henshall, 1968, 178, 180, 191, fig. 44:2).

Arreton material is largely unknown over much of central England, Wales, the Marches and north of the Tees, and is rare in Scotland. There is a scatter of finds from Ireland, and even a group of stone moulds, some for Arreton-type products, from Omagh, Co. Tyrone (Coffey, 1907; Greenwell & Brewis 1909, 446; Coghlan & Raftery, 1961), but any Arreton manufacture in Ireland is likely to have been brief and experimental (Flanagan, 1961, 287).

Arreton technology has been discussed at some length by Britton. No moulds for Arreton products are known, now that the Bodwrdin example is seen to be not relevant, and the Omagh moulds a peripheral flash-in-the-pan. Britton's suggestion that fragile clay moulds were normally used seems, therefore, even more likely (Britton, 1963, 296).

THE INCH ISLAND – DERRYNIGGIN TRADITION

With its wealth of grave and hoard associations, the Arreton tradition is more easily understood than its Irish equivalent. In Ireland, relevant associations are practically non-existent, and one has to lean heavily on typological comparisons. At present it is impossible to relate directly the end-looped spearheads and Derryniggin flanged axes that must have been the mainstays of this Irish industry. The axes have been found associated with a Ballyvalley-type flat axe at Bandon, Co. Cork, and with flint 'slug-knives' at Derryniggin, Co. Leitrim (Harbison, 1968, 43, 48, figs. 6, 16). In Scotland, similar flanged axes are associated at Gavel Moss with a large ribbed dagger, comparable with, though not identical to, one in the Arreton hoard (Britton, 1963, 286). This supports the probability that Derryniggin flanged axes were contemporary equivalents of the Arreton axes, as one might assume from comparing the two forms. End-looped spearheads in their turn are linked to the Ebnal hoard by the Inch Island spearhead and trunnion tool matrices, and thence to Arreton metal-working. This confirms the clear typological connection of these spearheads with the Arreton pegged type. Thus end-looped spearheads and Derryniggin flanged axes appear to have been contemporary, presumably products of an Irish industry equivalent to Arreton, one which also produced small trunnion tools. The latter provide a connection with the Broughshane mould, and what may have been another product of this industry in its final phases, Group I dirks and rapiers. These, with Group II weapons, were the primary forms in the Irish/British dirk and rapier series, and thus nominally Middle Bronze Age. Indeed, the available evidence clearly shows their place in the first phase of the Middle Bronze Age, surviving even later (Burgess, 1968, 7–10). At the same time they stand very close, typologically, to Camerton-Snowshill daggers, which must have been their direct ancestors, so that one would expect the earliest examples to span the transition from Early to Middle Bronze Age. Some of the simpler examples are in effect like Camerton-Snowshill daggers with trapezoid butts, and Harbison has no hesitation in assigning these to the Derryniggin phase (Harbison, 1969b).[1] The Broughshane mould, with its 'flat celt' and trunnion tool matrices, may have been significant here. On the other hand, the size and complexity of many Group I weapons, and above all the use of a two-rivet trapezoid butt, with all its Wöhlde connections, suggest that the type appeared late in the Derryniggin phase, and the relationship of the Inchnagree and Killymaddy moulds clearly places at least some of them in the Killymaddy, or first, phase of the Irish Middle Bronze Age (Burgess, 1968, 7–10).

Since so many Irish end-looped spearheads are unprovenanced, the map (fig. 6:4) can serve only as a rough guide to the distribution of the industry they represent. Harbison has mapped his Derryniggin axes (1969a, 76, fig. 3B), but it should be noted that by no means all of these are flanged axes and relevant here. There was clearly some related metal-working in Scotland, and the Gavel Moss hoard provides us with a convenient name for this.

EBNAL, WALES AND THE MARCHES

Only small numbers of implements of Arreton and Inch Island–Derryniggin types are known from Wales and the Marches, and the significance of these has been touched on elsewhere (Burgess, 1962, 82–94). This scarcity is paralleled in other regions, including much of northern England and parts of Ireland (Burgess, 1965, 74–5; 1968, 8), suggesting the survival in all these areas of earlier metal-working traditions, right to the end of the Early Bronze Age.

Arreton metalwork in Wales and the Marches is limited to one hoard from Menai Bridge, Anglesey (two, if one regards Westbury-on-Trym as part of the Marches), at least three pieces in a mixed hoard, Ebnal, two tanged spearheads from Llanfachreth and Blaenrhondda (Grimes, 1951, 250), Camerton-Snowshill daggers from St Brides Netherwent, Mon. and Crug-yr-Afan, Glam., the latter a non-metallic miniature copy (Burgess, 1962), and a possible flanged axe from Flintshire (Lort, 1779, 118, pl. ix:i). Clearly Arreton influence like Wessex Culture influence (Burgess, 1962), was hardly felt over most of the region. Signs of connections with Inch Island–Derryniggin metal-working are hardly more prominent, being restricted to end-looped spearheads in the Ebnal and Rodborough hoards, and possibly in the Kilcot Wood hoard, single finds from the Bristol area and Bala (Burgess, 1962, 85; Savory, 1966), and the Bodwrdin mould. There are also flanged axes of Derryniggin type from Titterstone Clee (Chitty, 1925–6, 235), Bryn Coch, Glam. (Savory, 1961), and Staunton, Glos. (Evans, 1881, 73). While the Irish industry can therefore have been no more influential in the region than the Arreton tradition, at least the Bodwrdin mould suggests some local manufacture. While the southern or eastern English background of local Arreton pieces seems secure, one cannot be so definite about the immediate source of the Bodwrdin industry. The obvious view is that it was an offshoot of the Inch Island–Derryniggin tradition, but the possibility that it reflects a stage in the spread of Arreton ideas to Ireland, developing *en route*, cannot be ruled out (Burgess, 1962, 85–6; Savory, 1966, 373).

CHRONOLOGY

In broad terms, the connections of the Ebnal hoard are with the Arreton and Inch Island–Derryniggin traditions, and thus with Wessex II, and with Reinecke A2–early B1 in central

---

[1] The bulk of Harbison's 'Offaly', 'Antrim' and 'Hill of Allen' type daggers falls within the present writer's Group I dirks and rapiers. Harbison assigns all three types to his Derryniggin period (Harbison, 1969b, 25–30).

Europe. Absolute dates are not so easy to fix in view of the recent severance of Wessex Culture/ Unetice links with the Shaft graves, and the bristlecone pine calibration of C14 dates (Renfrew, 1968). On the old scale, the period would have been *c.* 1500–1400 BC, but on the new bristlecone pine-corrected scale, this would be *c.* 1900–1700 BC (Burgess, 1970). There is no certain evidence at present which might be used to fix Ebnal more precisely within this background. To a certain extent it depends on whether the Bodwrdin industry was a development from Arreton and ancestral to Inch Island, in which case it would be earlier than if it was an offshoot of the Irish industry. In any case, since end-looped spearheads were developed from the Arreton socketed type, they are likely to have been later rather than earlier in the period. Furthermore, the near-trapezoid butt of the lost Ebnal dagger relates it to what should be a late group in the Camerton-Snowshill series, immediately ancestral to Group I dirks and rapiers. The connection with the Broughshane mould, with its matrix for fully developed Group I dirks, thus assumes added significance. All these clues, and the range of types represented in the Ebnal hoard, suggest that it was deposited in the latter part of the Arreton–Wessex II period, and probably near its end, not too far from the transition to the Middle Bronze Age and Acton Park metal-working.

C. B.

BIBLIOGRAPHY

Annable, F. K. & Simpson, D. D. A., 1964. *Guide Catalogue of the Neolithic and Bronze Age Collections in Devizes Museum*. Devizes.

ApSimon, A. M., 1954. 'Dagger graves in the "Wessex" Bronze Age', *Univ. London Inst. Archaeol. Ann. Rep.*, X, 37–62.

British Museum, 1953. *Later Prehistoric Antiquities of the British Isles*. London.

Britton, D., 1963. 'Traditions of metal-working in the later Neolithic and Early Bronze Age of Britain: Part I', *Proc. Prehist. Soc.*, XXIX, 258–325.

Burgess, C. B., 1962. 'Two grooved ogival daggers of the Early Bronze Age from South Wales', *Bull. Board Celtic Stud.*, XX, part I, 75–94.

—— 1965, in Jobey, G. *et al.*, 'An Early Bronze Age burial on Reaverhill Farm, Barrasford, Northumberland', *Archaeol. Aeliana*, 4 ser., XLIII, 65–75.

—— 1968. 'Bronze Age dirks and rapiers as illustrated by examples from Durham and Northumberland', *Trans. Archit. Archaeol. Soc. Durham Northumberland*, new ser., I, 3–26.

—— 1969. 'Chronology and terminology in the British Bronze Age', *Antiq. J.*, XLIX, 22–9.

—— 1970. 'The Bronze Age', *Current Archaeol.*, II, no. 8, 208–15.

Butler, J. J., 1959. 'Vergeten schatvondsten uit de Bronstijd', in *Honderd Eeuwen Nederland* (*Antiquity and Survival*, II, no. 5–6), 125–42.

—— 1960. 'A Bronze Age concentration at Bargeroosterveld . . .', *Palaeohistoria*, VIII, 101–26.

—— 1963. 'Bronze Age Connections across the North Sea', *Palaeohistoria*, IX (entire volume).

Chitty, L. F., 1925–6. 'Notes on Prehistoric implements', *Trans. Shropshire Archaeol. Soc.*, 4 ser., X, 233–46.

—— 1926. 'Bronze implement from Tyddyn Bach, Llanfachreth, Merioneth', *Archaeol. Cambrensis*, 7 ser., VI, 406–9.

—— 1940. 'Bronze implements from the Oswestry region of Shropshire', *Archaeol. Cambrensis*, XCV, 27—35.

Coffey, G., 1907. 'Moulds for primitive spear-heads found in the County Tyrone', *J. Roy. Soc. Antiq. Ireland*, XXXVII, 181–6.

Coghlan, H. H. & Raftery, J., 1961. 'Irish prehistoric casting moulds', *Sibrium*, VI, 223–44.

Curle, A. O., 1915–16. 'Notes on the discovery of a grave at Balneil, New Luce, Wigtownshire . . .', *Proc. Soc. Antiq. Scot.*, L, 302–5.

Dale, W., 1909–11. 'Report as Local Secretary for Hampshire', *Proc. Soc. Antiq. London*, 2 ser., XXIII, 96–100.

Eogan, G., 1964. 'The later Bronze Age in Ireland in the light of recent research', *Proc. Prehist. Soc.*, XXX, 268–351.

Evans, J., 1881. *The Ancient Bronze Implements, Weapons, and Ornaments, of Great Britain and Ireland.* London.

Flanagan, L. N. W., 1961. 'Wessex and Ireland in the Early and Middle Bronze Ages', *Bericht über den V. internationalen Kongress für Vor- und Frühgeschichte Hamburg 1958.* Berlin.

Greenwell, W. & Brewis, W. P., 1909. 'The origin, evolution, and classification of the bronze spearhead in Great Britain and Ireland', *Archaeologia*, LXI, 439–72.

Grimes, W. F., 1951. *The Prehistory of Wales*, 2nd ed. Cardiff.

Harbison, P., 1968. 'Catalogue of Irish Early Bronze Age associated finds containing copper or bronze', *Proc. Roy. Irish Acad.*, 67 (C), 35–91.

—— 1969a. *The Axes of the Early Bronze Age in Ireland (Prähistorische Bronzefunde*, Abt. IX, 1 Band). Munich.

—— 1969b. *The Daggers and the Halberds of the Early Bronze Age in Ireland (Prähistorische Bronzefunde*, Abt. VI, 1 Band). Munich.

Hemp, W. J., 1925. 'The trunnion celt in Britain', *Antiq. J.*, V, 51–4.

Henshall, A. S., 1968. 'Scottish dagger graves', in Coles, J. M. & Simpson, D. D. A. (eds), *Studies in Ancient Europe*, 173–95. Leicester.

Lort, Rev. Mr, 1779. 'Observations on celts', *Archaeologia*, V, 106–18.

Manby, T. G., 1966. 'The Bodwrdin mould, Anglesey', *Proc. Prehist. Soc.*, XXXII, 349.

Maryon, H., 1938. 'Some prehistoric metal workers' tools', *Antiq. J.*, XVIII, 241–50.

Piggott, S., 1938. 'The Early Bronze Age in Wessex', *Proc. Prehist. Soc.*, IV, 52–106.

Piggott, S. & Stewart, M., 1958. 'The Gavel Moss Hoard', GB.28 in 'Early and Middle Bronze Age grave groups and hoards from Scotland', *Inventaria Archaeologica*, GB.25–34, 5th set.

Proudfoot, E. V. W., 1963. 'Report on the excavation of a bell barrow in the parish of Edmondsham, Dorset, England, 1959', *Proc. Prehist. Soc.*, XXIX, 395–425.

Renfrew, C., 1968. 'Wessex without Mycenae', *Annual Brit. School Athens*, LXIII, 277–85.

Savory, H. N., 1961. 'Bronze flanged axe from West Glamorgan', *Bull. Board Celtic Stud.*, XIX, part 2, 172.

—— 1966. 'Bronze spearhead from Bala (Mer.)', *Bull. Board Celtic Stud.*, XXI, part 4, 371–3.

ACKNOWLEDGEMENTS

We are indebted to the curators and staff of many museums who readily made relevant material available for study; especially the British Museum (Dr I. H. Longworth), the National Museum of Wales, Cardiff (Dr H. N. Savory), the National Museum of Ireland, Dublin (Dr J. Raftery), and the National Museum of Antiquities, Edinburgh (Miss A. Henshall and Mr D. Clarke). Mr Clarke very kindly provided drawings of the Balneil urn, bead and pin. We are also grateful to the Society of Antiquaries of London, who allowed us to work on the Albert Way Papers, and to reproduce material from them here.

Three Unusual Implements in the Borough Museum, Newbury

H. H. Coghlan

In the course of microscopical examination of Bronze Age tools and weapons in the Borough of Newbury Museum, certain implements with western affinities were found to be unusual and interesting in that they presented marked differences from the familiar series of Bronze Age artefacts. These comprise a strange tool from Scotland, Argyllshire (museum number OA.229), which at first sight resembles a very crude form of flat axe; an unusually small palstave from Ireland (museum number S.504); and a miniature socketed axe, also from Ireland, Co. Carlow (museum number OA.83). The following reports throw light upon the mode of fabrication of the implements, but it must be stressed that the metallurgical work was limited by the number of sections which could be reasonably removed without damaging the objects for museum display.

FLAT AXE

From Argyllshire. Newbury Museum OA.229

At the butt-end of this axe (plate VIIa) the material has been fractured in antiquity. Below this fracture there is a large rivet hole approximately 12 mm. diameter, and above it an attempt has possibly been made to perforate another one. Large rivet holes are of course a feature of halberds, but the implement is certainly not a halberd. It is clearly an anomalous piece taking the form of a crude flat axe, and it could possibly be used as such. In its present condition the tool is very rough and poorly shaped, deeply pitted by corrosion upon both faces, with one of the very large corrosion pits at least 1 mm. in depth. The patination covering the metal is of very dark green colour, and superficially it appears to be in stable condition. In cross-section the axe is very slender, the maximum thickness being only 8 mm. One of the faces is nearly flat, and judging from its external appearance the object would seem to have been cast by the open-mould method. In its main plane the cutting-edge of the blade is of very rounded form, and while slightly blunted by use or hammering, it is still fairly well preserved. It is hardly possible to assign a date to such a strange implement but, since the analysis indicates a high content of arsenic and no tin, it was no doubt made within the well-defined period in which arsenical copper was characteristic (Coghlan & Case, 1957; Case, 1966). The total remaining length is 127 mm. and the width over the blade is 66 mm.

The analysis of the metal, expressed as percentage figures, is:

Cu 94*	Ag 0·3*	Au nd†	Zn 0·01	Cd nd†
Hg nd†	Sn –	Pb 0·005	As 4·8*	Sb 0·48*
Bi 0·003	Mo nd†	Mn < 0·01‡	Fe 0·3	Co nd†
Ni 0·04	Se 0·03	Te nd†	Ti nd†	V nd†
Be nd	Cr nd			

Other elements sought, but not detected, are: Ga In Ge Zr Nb Pt
* = chemical determination   † nd = not detected   ‡ < = less than
The analysis shows that the metal belongs to the well-known arsenical copper series, but the arsenic content is unusually high.

For the metallographic examination three sections were removed. Section A was taken through the cutting-edge, while section B was from the edge of the body well above the curve of the blade. Section C was taken through the rivet hole in a direction parallel to the main plane of the axe.

Upon examination of the polished metal of section A, it was seen that throughout the section, and particularly at the tip of the cutting-edge, the metal is porous (plate VIIb). In places, upon the edges of the specimen, corrosion has been severe, and in one position at about 3 mm. from the point, a band of corrosion has penetrated half-way through the metal (plate VIIc). The porosity at the cutting-edge is in places joined by what appears to be a grain boundary network of black material, and this is a form of intercrystalline corrosion rather similar to that often found in slightly cold-worked tin bronzes, but without the associated slip plane corrosion found in the latter (plate VIId). In section B, taken from the side of the axe, the metal is very poor and porous with, in places, severe corrosion penetration from the edges of the specimen. Small inclusions of dove-grey colour were observed, and these could be mixed oxides of arsenic and antimony (plate VIIe). In section C, taken from the rivet hole, the metal is highly porous throughout the section, and is so poor and brittle that fracture occurred before the cutting out of the section had been completed. At the edge of the rivet hole is a thick band of corrosion products, and there is no sound metal left at the edge of the hole, with the exception of a few very small spots.

With normal etching of section A, and viewed under low magnification, only the cored structure of the casting is seen. With deep etching and higher magnification, a structure of twinned crystals of low grain size can be seen superimposed upon the coring. There is a tendency for the microstructure to be elongated towards the cutting-edge, and a hardness figure of 94·9 HV_5, obtained in reasonably sound metal at 3 mm. from the point, shows that some cold work has been applied to the cutting-edge. It is just possible that there may be some increase in hardness at the extreme tip of the cutting-edge, although here the undeformed porosity does not suggest the likelihood of greater hardness. For section B, with normal etching and low magnification, only the cored dendritic structure of the casting is seen. Under higher power, and with some difficulty, a few isolated twinned crystals were detected at the edge of the section, but merely as a skin effect. In general, the metal in the whole of section B is substantially in the 'as cast' state, and unwrought. In a position where reasonably sound metal was found, a hardness value of 61·7 HV_5 was recorded, and this may well correspond to the copper-arsenic alloy in its softest condition.

Upon etching section C, again only the cored dendritic structure of the casting was seen (plate VIIf). No flowing of the structure was observed, and the metal here appears to be unworked and substantially in the 'as cast' state. In a few places, where small areas of uncorroded metal are left at the edge of the rivet hole, a few isolated twins could be seen under high power, and with very deep etching. Unfortunately, the thick band of corrosion at the edge of the rivet hole has destroyed any evidence which might suggest how the hole was perforated.

To sum up, it is difficult to account for this strange anomalous object. In its present form the piece bears no resemblance to a halberd or a dagger, and the only feature to suggest a connection with a halberd is the large-diameter rivet hole which is a characteristic of halberds. Had the object originally been a halberd, it would have been quite beyond the capacity of a prehistoric smith to forge it to its present shape. Also, since the sections examined show that, except for working at the cutting-edge, the tool is substantially in the 'as cast' state and unwrought, it cannot have started life as a halberd. If the outline of the broken butt is completed, it will be seen that the object can only be termed a poorly shaped flat axe. A possible explanation is that, starting with a very poor and brittle casting of a flat axe, full of pores and non-metallic inclusions, the smith began to make a halberd or dagger, but breaking-up occurred before he had completed the rivet hole. He then abandoned the work, leaving it in its present unfinished state. If this suggestion is correct, and in view of the substantially 'as cast' structures observed, it is just possible that we have an example of a flat axe which has been cast in a closed or bi-valve mould. Other examples so far known are a flat axe of copper from Ireland, Newbury Museum (number OA.228); and a flat axe of bronze from Cornwall, Newbury Museum (number OA.58). Alternatively this might be a deliberate attempt to provide a flat axe with holes for some reason, and one is reminded of the small, but well-known, group of flat axes of more sophisticated forms which is characterised by loops and holes (Coles, 1963–4).

PALSTAVE

From Ireland. Newbury Museum, S.504 (R.U.S.I. 1268 – 111)

This is a miniature palstave which is now in a very poor condition (plate VIIIa). The patination covering the metal is of a dark-green colour and appears to be stable, but a certain amount of superficial corrosion can be seen upon the surfaces. The median web of the implement ends in well-defined stop ridges. The side wings or flanges have been much damaged and large portions of these have been broken off, but undisturbed patination indicates that the flange fractures are not of recent date, and that they probably occurred in antiquity. It would appear either that the palstave has been very roughly treated, or that the flange metal is defective. A large void below the stop ridges certainly suggests defective metal. The cutting-edge of the blade is of very rounded contour in side view and is now blunt; indeed, from its appearance, one may question if it was ever really sharp. The finish of the palstave is rough, and most of the surfaces show ancient score markings and lines which suggest the use of a coarse gritted stone or hone having been used to clean or dress the casting. The total length of the palstave is only 77 mm. (3 in.), and the maximum width over the rounded blade is 25·5 mm. (1 in.). The wings or flanges were deep; one of these, which has not suffered fracture, has a depth of 6·55 mm. (0·26 in.) to the median web. The weight is 77 g. Two sections were removed for metallographic examination: section A, mount number one, from the cutting-edge; and section B, mount number two, from the median web at its outer end.

The analysis of the metal, by courtesy of the British Non-Ferrous Metals Research Association, and expressed as percentage figures, is:

Sn 12 (by chemical determination). Pb ~ 1.

Ni ~ 0·5	Fe 0·01	Al 0·02	Si. Tr < 0·02
Mn. nd. < 0·01 if any.		Bi 0·002	As 0·2
Sb 0·01	P ~ 0·01	Zn. nd 0·01 if any	
Au. nd < 0·001 if any.			

nd = not detected   Tr = trace   ~ = about   < = less than

The analysis shows that the metal is a tin-bronze, high in tin, also containing some lead and a somewhat unusually high content of nickel.

Examination of the polished but unetched metal of the cutting-edge section showed the metal to be poor with considerable porosity. Patination upon the edges of the specimen is thin, and there has been little build-up of external corrosion products. There is severe intercrystalline corrosion, particularly in the region of the cutting-edge, and non-metallic inclusions showing eutectic form are prevalent (plate VIIIb). Unexpectedly, $\alpha\delta$ eutectoid was not observed in the polished metal, although the chemical analysis indicates 12% of tin. In section B the metal is highly unsound with porosity and grain boundary films. The edges of the specimen have been quite severely attacked by corrosion, and in places what appear to be discrete particles of $\alpha\delta$ eutectoid may be seen embedded in the corrosion products. As in the case of section A, non-metallic inclusions showing eutectic form are prevalent (plate VIIIc & d).

Upon etching the cutting-edge section, a heavily cored structure is revealed. With some difficulty, equi-axed twinned crystals of medium grain size can be seen superimposed upon the coring, showing that the cutting-edge of the tool has been mechanically worked and partially annealed. Slip banding was not detected in the crystals. A hardness determination, taken near to the point of the cutting-edge, and in reasonably good metal, gave a value of 98 HV$_5$. Since approximately 85 HV$_5$ may be taken as the softest condition for a cast bronze of this composition, it appears that very little work-hardening had been applied to the cutting-edge.

Upon etching section B, only a few isolated twinned crystals could be detected in one place, and these twins are probably only the result of one or two accidental blows, rather than any intentional deformation. Hence, while the metal of this section has been heated after it was cast, it may be said that it has not been mechanically worked, and remains substantially in the 'as cast' state.

The purpose which this miniature palstave served is something of a mystery. Its very small size and highly rounded and obtuse blade suggest that it was not intended as a practical cutting tool, and that it may merely be a toy or model. In fact, upon technological grounds, it may be said with reason that this miniature palstave was not, and could hardly have been, used as a cutting tool in the modern sense. It will be noted from the report that the smith had gone to the trouble of partially annealing and working the cutting-edge of the blade. In this he was following established tradition for the larger palstaves, which were obviously working tools, but it will also be noticed that he did not devote time and labour to hardening the blade appreciably, although the technique was well-known, and generally applied to palstaves.

SOCKETED AXE

Late Bronze Age (Irish type). From Ireland. Co. Carlow. Newbury Museum. OA.83

This is a miniature socketed axe with a side loop. A plain moulding runs round the mouth or rim of the socket, and there is a second moulding below this at the level of the top of the side loop (plate IX). There is a good dark chocolate-coloured patina, and little corrosion attack can be seen by visual inspection. The axe has been cast in a conventional bi-valve mould, for casting flashes remain, and these also show that the side loop has been cast in one with the body of the axe. The blade is markedly crescentic. The walls of the socket are thin, in places no more than 1·5–2 mm. in thickness, and the socket cavity extends to approximately 36 mm. (1·436 in.) below the rim, leaving only about 9 mm. (0·375 in.) of solid metal between the bottom of the cavity and the cutting-edge of the blade. The total length of the axe is only 45 mm. (1·8 in.), and the width over the splayed blade is 44 mm. (1·8 in.).

The analysis of the metal, expressed as percentage figures, is:

Sn 6	Pb 2	As < 0·06	Sb < 0·06
Ni 1	Bi < 0·1	Fe –	Zn < 0·15
Ag < 0·06	Au –		

The composition of this metal is rather unusual. The tin content is low, as is the lead for a Late Bronze Age implement, while nickel, at 1%, is unusually high.

For metallographic examination three sections were removed. Section A was taken from the cutting-edge, section B through the mouth or rim of the socket, and section C from the wall of the socket at about the middle of the axe. Examination of section A in the polished state showed the interior metal to be very defective, and large areas of corrosion appear to have spread from isolated voids. The cutting-edge itself, however, and external regions of the bronze, appear to be sound. In section B, the metal is highly porous and unsound. Corrosion attack at the surfaces has not been severe, but in a few places there has been nodular penetration. In section C, the metal is unsound with gross areas of porosity, and in places corrosion attack upon the surface metal has been severe.

Upon etching section A, the microstructure revealed suggests that the cutting-edge has been work-hardened, but that the mass of the metal is in annealed state. Hardness determinations confirm that this is so, for a value of 121 HV_5 was recorded at the edge, whereas in the annealed metal further from the edge the hardness was only 88 HV_5. Upon etching sections B and C, the metal was found to be substantially in the 'as cast' state. As may be expected with so small a casting, heating has been of a general nature. The cutting-edge has been worked, and some cold hammering applied in order to harden it to some extent. The section taken near the middle of the axe shows that there has also been a certain amount of hammering here, while at the socket it may be said that the metal has not been worked. Hence, this miniature axe has been to some extent suitably prepared for use, and it has been carefully finished.

It is difficult to suggest any good reason for making so small an axe. If this is merely a case of a toy or model there would be no point in going to the trouble of working and hardening the cutting-edge. Again, these miniature axes are by no means uncommon in England and Ireland. Evans (1881, 135) states that socketed celts of not more than 0·75 in. in length have been found in Ireland, and that in these the sockets are large enough to take handles. Evans thought that they might possibly have been used as chisels. His remarks upon the small socketed tool from Reach Fen, Cambridge, are also of interest (Evans, 1881, 133). He rightly considered this to be far too light to serve as an axe, but said that it might safely be regarded as a chisel. Such a view may arise from confusion between an axe-edge and a chisel-edge, which are two very different things, and the suggestion seems unlikely to the present writer, who has never come across a small axe with a blade ground to a true chisel-edge. In view of the present report, however, and of the number of very small axes recorded, one may perhaps be justified in taking the view that they had some practical purpose. But if the purpose was that of an axe, one can only say that these miniatures must constitute a record for inefficient design.

BIBLIOGRAPHY

Case, H. J., 1966. 'Were Beaker-people the first metallurgists in Ireland?', *Palaeohistoria*, XII, 141–77.
Coghlan, H. H. & Case, H. J., 1957. 'Early metallurgy of copper in Ireland and Britain', *Proc. Prehist. Soc.*, XXIII, 91–123.
Coles, J. M., 1963–4. 'A flat axe from Chatteris Fen, Cambs.', *Proc. Cambridge Antiq. Soc.*, LVI–LVII, 5–8.
Evans, J., 1881. *The Ancient Bronze Implements, Weapons and Ornaments of Great Britain and Ireland.* London.

ACKNOWLEDGEMENTS

Our sincere thanks are due to the British Non-Ferrous Metals Research Association for the analysis of the palstave; to Mrs A. Millett for that of the socketed axe, which was carried out at the Oxford Laboratory for Archaeology and the History of Art; and to Dr George Parker who kindly took the photomicrographs for figures 2–6, and gave much valuable advice and consultation. All the Vickers hardness determinations were kindly supplied by Mr Ian Macphail of A.E.R.E., Harwell.

'Sleeve-Fasteners' of the Late Bronze Age

George Eogan

INTRODUCTION

This paper is a study of a group of gold ornaments that are distinctive of the Irish Late Bronze Age. About eighty-seven examples are known and all are fairly uniform in shape and similar in decoration. 'Sleeve-fasteners' are of interest because, as will be shown, they represent innovation by the Irish goldsmith. They may also represent an attempt to reproduce a button-type fastening but without the button (see below). Also included in the paper, but kept separately in the Schedule (p. 208), is a group *of small penannular rings with external longitudinal striations on the body and unexpanded ends.*

References to 'sleeve-fasteners' have been appearing in the literature since the eighteenth century. In 1773 the Rev. Richard Pococke, Bishop of Meath, published what seems to be a 'sleeve-fastener' from Co. Galway (Schedule, No. 18, and p. 195). Camden published two examples but he made no reference to find-places (Camden, 1789, 477, pl. 33, figs 3 and 4). In 1784 Charles Vallancey incorporated Camden's text and illustrations in Vol. 4 of his *Collectanea de Rebus Hibernicis*, p. 41, pl. 6, figs 3 and 4. Sir William Betham figured an example in 1842 (Betham, 1842, 112). The publication of the South of Ireland hoard (see p. 196) by Crofton Croker in 1854 included the 'sleeve-fastener' from that hoard as well as another example which, he stated, was then in his possession (Croker, 1854, 133–4). In 1862 Sir William Wilde (1862, 63–6, 68) published the group in the Collection of the Royal Irish Academy, and these, together with subsequent discoveries, were included by Armstrong in his *Catalogue of Irish Gold Ornaments* (Armstrong, 1933, 65–8).

Ornaments of this type are, of course, well known to Miss Chitty, and this paper is being offered to her in appreciation of her contributions to prehistoric archaeology and of the unselfish manner in which she has placed her vast knowledge of Bronze Age material at the disposal of research workers.

GENERAL DEFINITION

'Sleeve-fasteners' consist of a body and terminals. The decorated body approaches a semicircle in shape and it varies in external span from 33 mm. to 16 mm. It tends to have a rounded cross-section and it tapers from its maximum diameter in the centre to the terminals. The terminals are flat and disc-shaped. Most are circular in shape but some approach an oval. Generally the terminals are pronounced but in a small number of examples they expand only very slightly.

The well-defined examples are at an inclination to the plane of the body, and they are usually attached to it at a point off centre.

In the *small penannular rings with unexpanded ends* the body is of round cross-section. From a point of maximum diameter in the centre, the body tapers to the ends. They vary in diameter from 18 mm. to 12 mm. The large variety have blunted ends whereas the small ones have pointed ends. The smaller ones are by far the most common. Except for the absence of the disc terminals, these are similar to the 'sleeve-fastener' as had already been recognised by Wilde (1862, 65) and Armstrong (1933, 30).

FUNCTION

Despite some irrational explanations by writers such as Vallancey (1784, 96–7) and Crofton Croker (1854, 135) it may be said that a reasonable explanation for the use of the ornaments, for fastening garments, had been given in one of the earliest descriptions. Camden (1789, 477) wrote that 'these are evident fibulae. The circular ends passed through the button-holes and lay flat on the body, and the chased and ornamented part was turned to the eye'.

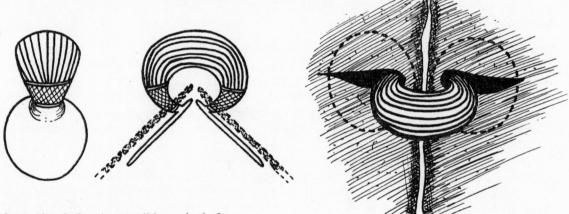

fig. 1 Sketch showing possible method of use

Wilde (1862, 65) offered a similar explanation and produced an illustration to show the manner in which the object could have been used. As Hawkes has already remarked, their function would thus have been in many ways similar to the 'dress-fastener' (Hawkes in Hawkes & Clarke, 1963, 223 with fig. 52:4). Utilised in that way, it would mean that when in use only the outer part of the body would be visible, or 'turned to the eye', as Camden so long ago thought. The term 'sleeve-fastener' has been gaining currency over the past few years (cf. Hawkes in Hawkes & Clarke, 1963, 223). Its use in this paper does not, however, mean that evidence is available to prove that these ornaments served as cuff-links. Their use as garment fasteners of some sort seems to be a reasonable interpretation, yet it should be remarked that in a number of examples the area between the inner edges of the terminals is very narrow and only the thinnest garment could pass through it.

When found in association with other objects, the number of 'sleeve-fasteners' varies; evidence from this source, therefore, does not help with interpretation of function. Three hoards (Gorteenreagh, Co. Galway, and South of Ireland) have one 'sleeve-fastener' each; two (Co. Mayo and Scotstown) have two each; one hoard (Belfast) has three and the Arboe-Killycolpy hoard has four 'sleeve-fasteners'. It appears that at Craighilly three 'sleeve-fasteners' were found together (nos. 6–8), and somewhere in Ireland (the provenance has not been recorded) 'several' were apparently found together (no. 83 in Schedule; Herity, 1969, 4). There is no mention of the presence of objects of other types in this find.

What function the *small striated penannular rings with unexpanded ends* served is not known unless that they were some sort of hair-ornament.

DISTRIBUTION (fig. 2)

There is no definite evidence for the discovery of a 'sleeve-fastener' or a small striated penannular ring outside Ireland.[1] In Ireland out of a total of eighty-seven examples only thirty-six or thirty-seven have a recorded find-place. The greatest number, nine, has been found in Co. Antrim. These come from five find-places. Co. Tyrone has two find-places: one, a single find; at the other, four were found together. Meath (all may be individual finds) and Monaghan (two find-places) have three objects each, while Counties Down, Fermanagh, Mayo (one find-place), Westmeath have two objects each. Counties Armagh, Clare, Donegal, Dublin, Galway, Louth, Sligo have produced one 'sleeve-fastener' each. A single specimen was also found somewhere in the south of Ireland, and another example may have been found in Co. Cork (No. 77).

Out of the fifteen *small penannular rings with unexpanded terminals* only four have a recorded find-place. These are single finds from Counties Antrim, Dublin, Fermanagh, Tyrone.

Taking both the 'sleeve-fasteners' and the small penannular rings with unexpanded terminals, it is clear that the distribution is markedly northern with a distinctive tendency to concentrate in the north-east. Out of the forty-one pieces with a recorded find-place, thirty-two are found north of a line from Dublin to Donegal Bay. South Leinster is devoid of finds and only seven finds are known from the provinces of Connaught and Munster.

ORIGIN

'Sleeve-fasteners' lack prototypes outside Ireland. They must, then, be taken as a creation of Irish goldsmiths to meet an exclusive need and market. But while lacking a prototype, the do have a model and this is the 'dress-fastener' as Hawkes (in Hawkes & Clarke, 1963, 223) has already shown. The 'dress-fasteners' represent an adaptation of the north European fibula of Period IV/V whereby the pin was rendered obsolete by Irish craftsmen in a land where the traditional method of fastening garments had been the button. While the Nordic fibula and the 'dress-fastener' served a similar function 'to fasten a cloak or cape across the chest', the Irish adaptation, resulting in the emergence of the 'dress-fastener', turned 'the Northern brooch form into that of a great inverted double button'. The 'sleeve-fasteners' represent a further development but on a smaller scale. 'They are', in the words of Professor Hawkes, 'more button-like in that the terminals are plain and flat, and were evidently for passing each beneath a button hole' (Hawkes & Clarke, 1963, 223, fig. 52.4).

The origin of the *small penannular rings with unexpanded ends* is not clear. In shape some resemble the round-sectioned 'hair-rings' (Armstrong, 1933, pl. 14:227–9). Of two objects, for instance, illustrated by Armstrong (1933, pl. 14: 171, 227) both are similar in shape, but the difference is that one (171, our no. 6) is decorated while the other (227) is plain. The body decoration, however, shows that they are related to the 'sleeve-fasteners'. Wilde (1862, 65) thought that they were unfinished 'sleeve-fasteners' and that it was intended to fit discs on to them, but this is not so, as the ends taper and the criss-cross hatching which is such a feature of the decoration on the 'sleeve-fastener' near the terminals is, except for no. 1, missing.

[1] It has been claimed that No. 75 was found with part of a lunula, 'lock-ring' and a plain 'hair-ring' on the Monzie Estate in Perthshire, but no definite proof has been put forward that the objects were discovered at Monzie or even in Scotland. Furthermore the presence of Early and Late Bronze Age types shows that one is not dealing with an associated find; there is moreover good evidence to indicate that the 'lock-ring' was of Irish manufacture (Eogan, *Proc. Roy. Irish Acad.*, 67 (1969), 118, No. 20 and 119 fn. 4). It seems reasonable to suggest that the presence in Scotland of the pieces from Monzie is likely due to the activities of collectors within fairly recent times.

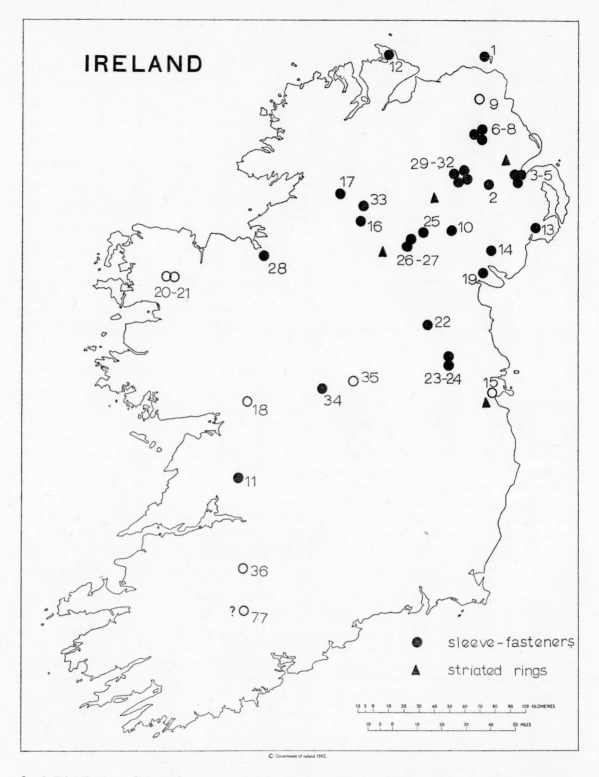

IRELAND

fig. 2 Distribution of sleeve-fasteners and striated rings. (Open symbols indicate that only a county provenance is known)

MANUFACTURE

Unless the body has been damaged it is not possible to say whether it is solid or hollow. The solid body could have been straightforwardly cast in a mould. Nos. 19, 73 and possibly 38 have a hollow body. According to Maryon (1938, 200) the body of No. 73 has been formed by bending sheet-metal round into a tube. The long edges were lapped and the joint was soldered. In what Maryon considers to be similarly made bodies, the joint is on the inner side, and it has always been finished off by soldering. Maryon believed that in general the terminals were soldered on to the body. On some examples (i.e. Nos. 1, 2, 13, 73) there is a spread of solder around the terminals but from a superficial examination it is not possible to say if these were soldered on. In some instances, however, it does appear that the body and terminals were cast at the same time and that the terminals were subsequently formed into a disc shape by hammering. This was the case with the Gorteenreagh example (No. 11) (Raftery, 1967, 66). Hammer marks occur on the upper surface of the terminals of No. 46 but there is no proof that these are original.

Regarding the small penannular rings with external striations on the body, No. 4 consists of a gold leaf over a (?) clay core. The body of No. 1 may be hollow.

DECORATION

Except for No. 11 (Gorteenreagh) the bodies are always decorated and this decoration is of a very standardised nature. On the body it is confined to the outer circumference, and consists of a series of parallel longitudinal striations. The standard of workmanship varies, but considerable skill is displayed on some examples, such as No. 31 where the striations are widest in the middle and taper to the ends. The striations end short of the terminals and the intervening space is decorated with a band of criss-cross hatching that forms a diaper pattern. This pattern is delimited on the top and bottom by parallel transverse lines, usually two or three in number. This band of decoration is formed from lightly incised lines in contrast to the deep scoring of the longitudinal lines and according to Maryon (1938, 200) this work was executed by a tracer. No. 47 has a diaper pattern on both sides of the body between the longitudinal striations and the undecorated undersurface. This band is bounded on the inside and on the outside by a fine groove.

Except for four examples (Nos. 15, 40, 59, 60) the terminals are undecorated. The exteriors of both terminals of Nos. 15 and 40 have almost identical decoration. This is a sort of herringbone pattern. No. 59 has a band of criss-cross hatching that is bounded on each side by a line. This band extends outwards from the base of the body almost to the edge. On No. 59 there is a short band of decoration on one terminal. This consists of two parallel grooves with oblique hatching in between. In all instances the decoration on the terminals consists of lightly incised lines.

A loop occurs on the terminals of Nos. 47, 84, 85.[1]

---

[1] There is a problem concerning the number of 'sleeve-fasteners' with loops. The only extant example known to me is No. 47. This weighs, according to Armstrong, 4 oz, 15 dwt, 19 gr. In National Library of Ireland MS. 4458, fol. 38, a 'sleeve-fastener' with loop is illustrated and its weight is given as 5 oz, 12 dwt. When compared, however, the illustration and the actual object seem similar, and on that account the illustration on MS. 4458, fol. 38 is considered to be that of No. 47 before its arrival in the collection of the Royal Irish Academy. If Pococke's illustration of No. 85 is correct, then that piece must also be considered separately. Its weight has been given as 5 oz, 15 dwt. Crofton Croker illustrated and briefly described No. 84. He gave its weight as 5 oz, 0 dwt, 18 gr. Its present whereabouts is not known. It appears that Crofton Croker's collection went to Lord Londesborough and at the sale of the Londesborough collection a number of Irish gold ornaments were purchased by General Pitt-Rivers. These were sold in the early 1930s and are now in the Detroit Institute of Arts, but the 'sleeve-fastener' in that collection (No. 77 in Schedule) is without loop. It appears, therefore, that the object illustrated by Crofton Croker should be treated separately.

(*Continued on page 194*)

The bodies of the *small penannular rings* also have parallel longitudinal striations on the outside, but the band of decoration near the ends usually consists of lightly incised, transverse parallel lines without the criss-cross hatching. Criss-cross hatching is, however, found on No. 1, but on other grounds, such as size, this is an unusual piece.

ASSOCIATIONS AND DATING

'Sleeve-fasteners' have been found with objects of another type on seven occasions. These associations are all hoards and their contents show that they can all be assigned with certainty to the final phase (the Dowris Phase) of the Late Bronze Age.

	Socketed axehead, bagshaped	Bronze ring, plain and solid	Bronze ring with two transverse perforations through the body	'Sleeve-fastener'	'Dress-fastener'	Penannular bracelet with evenly expanded hollow terminals	Gorget	'Lock-ring'	Sunflower Pin	Bulla
Co. Antrim, Belfast	1			3						
Co. Clare, Gorteenreagh				1		2	1	2		
Co. Galway				1	1					
Co. Mayo				2		11				
Co. Monaghan, Scotstown		16	1	2						
Co. Tyrone, Arboe/Killycolpy				4					2	1
South of Ireland				1				1	1	

The assumed origin of the 'sleeve-fastener' (p. 191) also helps with dating problems. In this, as has been pointed out above, the 'dress-fastener' plays a part, and some chronological priority must be given to its development. The 'sleeve-fastener' together with the penannular bracelet with hollow terminals that are set at a marked inclination to the line of the body (cf. Hawkes & Clarke, 1963, esp. pp. 196–7, 225 ff.) would then represent further insular development, but after the emergence in the first place of the 'dress-fastener'. As it was the influences or contacts stemming from the West Baltic area during Period IV/V that gave rise to the 'dress-fastener', its development must have taken place during the eighth century. It would then seem that the 'sleeve-fasteners' were emerging towards 700 BC. Their use must have extended over the seventh century; how much later is not at present known.

Further, regarding the piece illustrated in N.L.I. MS. 4458, fol. 38 (No. 47), written underneath are the words: 'found in Co. Mayo 2 together July 1829'. But this statement appears to be the result of confusion, for in the same MS., fol. 41, under the illustration of a gold penannular bracelet with evenly expanded hollow terminals, is written: "found in Co. Mayo with ten others, and two like that figured on page 38'. The object figured on fol. 38 is that already referred to above, the writing underneath it is in a different, possibly later, hand, and it appears that the writer misunderstood the statement on fol. 41 which clearly states that the Mayo pieces are 'like that figured on page 38'.

SUMMARY AND CONCLUSIONS

Eighty-seven 'sleeve-fasteners' have been recorded and these are confined exclusively to Ireland. The type developed in Ireland around 700 BC and its emergence clearly shows the ability of the goldsmith to adapt and thereby produce an ornament that was really a new type. The 'dress-fastener' played a part in their development, but they clearly demonstrate a further adaptation to produce a method of fastening a garment in a manner as close as possible to a button arrangement.

LIST OF ASSOCIATED FINDS OF 'SLEEVE-FASTENERS'

This list only includes the assemblages, all hoards, where 'sleeve-fasteners' are found in association with objects of another type.

CO. ANTRIM, BELFAST

1 *Publication:*
   None.
2 *Site and circumstances of discovery:*
   Nothing recorded.
3 *Collection:*
   Ashmolean Museum, Oxford (1927: 2936–9).
4 *List of objects:*
   1.   Bronze bag-shaped socketed axehead.
   2–3. 'Sleeve-fasteners', gold (Nos. 3–4).
   4.   'Sleeve-fastener' but the terminals are so small that its form is close to a small penannular ring with longitudinal striations on the outside of the body (No. 5).

CO. CLARE, GORTEENREAGH

1 *Publication:*
   Joseph Raftery, 'The Gorteenreagh Hoard', in *North Munster Studies* (ed. Etienne Rynne), Limerick 1967, 61–71.
2 *Site and circumstances of discovery:*
   Found under a flat stone about 20 cm. below the surface.
3 *Collection:*
   National Museum of Ireland (1948: 320–30).
4 *List of the objects (all gold):*
   1–2. Two penannular bracelets with evenly expanded hollow terminals.
   3.   'Sleeve-fastener' (No. 11).
   4.   Gorget.
   5–6. Two 'lock-rings'.

CO. GALWAY

1 *Publication:*
   Michael Herity, 'Early Finds of Irish Antiquities from the Minute-books of the Society of Antiquaries of London', *Antiq. J.*, XLIX (1969), 6–7, pl. 5.
   Richard Pococke, 'An Account of Some Antiquities found in Ireland', *Archaeologia* II (1773), 39–41.
   Charles Vallancey, *Collectanea de Rebus Hibernicis*, vol. IV (1774).
2 *Site and circumstances of discovery:*
   Nothing known except that both were found together in Co. Galway. The objects were melted down in Dublin in 1747.
4 *List of the objects (both gold):*
   1.   'Dress-fastener'.
   2.   Possibly a 'sleeve-fastener' (No. 18).

CO. MAYO

1 *Publication:*
   None.

2 *Site and circumstances of discovery:*
   Nothing recorded.

3 *Collection:*
   Not known if the objects survive. Data based on information in MS. 4458, fol. 41, in National Library of Ireland.

4 *List of the objects (all gold):*
   1–11.   Eleven penannular bracelets with hollowed evenly expanded terminals.
   12–13. Two 'sleeve-fasteners' (Nos. 20–21).

CO. MONAGHAN, SCOTSTOWN

1 *Publication:*
   E. C. R. Armstrong, 'Two Irish Bronze-Age Finds containing Rings', *Antiq. J.*, III (1923), 138.

2 *Site and circumstances of discovery:*
   Found near Scotstown while ploughing in a field.

3 *Collection:*
   National Museum of Ireland (1879: 6–25).

4 *List of objects:*
   1–2.   Two 'sleeve-fasteners' (Nos. 26–27).
   3–18. Sixteen plain solid bronze rings of varying sizes. Only two are complete.
   19.   Solid bronze ring with two plain transverse perforations through the body.

CO. TYRONE — ARBOE–KILLYCOLPY (The 'Lough Neagh hoard')

1 *Publication:*
   Joseph Raftery, 'Two Gold Hoards from Co. Tyrone', *J.R.S.A.I.*, 100 (1970), 169, 170–73.
   Messrs. Sotheby & Co., *Catalogue of Egyptian . . . Irish Bronze Age . . . Antiquities – Sold 27th November 1967* (London, 1967), 42, pl., and p. 91, exclude top ornament.

2 *Site and circumstances of discovery:*
   Nothing recorded except that the hoard was found between Killycolpy and Arboe. When the objects were sold at Sotheby's in 1967 it was then considered that they formed part of a hoard found at Killymoon.

3 *Collection:*
   National Museum of Ireland (1967: 235–8 'sleeve fasteners' only).

4 *List of objects (all gold):*
   1–4. Four 'sleeve-fasteners' (Nos. 29–32).
   5.   A 'bulla'.
   6–7. Two gold discs from heads of sunflower pins.

SOUTH OF IRELAND

1 *Publication:*
   Anonymous, *P.S.A.S.*, LXVIII (1933–4), 191–2, fig. 1.
   V. Gordon Childe, *The Prehistory of Scotland* (1935), 162, pl. XII.
   John M. Coles, 'Scottish Late Bronze Age Metalwork', *P.S.A.S.*, XCIII (1959–60), 93, pl. IV.
   T. Crofton Croker, 'Notes on various discoveries of Gold Plates, chiefly in the South of Ireland', *Collectanea Antiqua*, III (1854), 132–43.
   George Eogan, 'The Mull ("South of Ireland") Hoard', *Antiquity*, XLI (1967), 56–8, pl. VI.

2 *Site and circumstances of discovery:*
   Nothing known, the objects were bought by Crofton Croker in Cork in 1825. The following year Croker presented the group to Sir Walter Scott, and they remained at Abbotsford till 1934 when they were acquired by the National Museum of Scotland and were erroneously thought to have come from the Island of Mull.

3 *Collection:*
  National Museum of Antiquities of Scotland (FE 80–2).
4 *List of the objects:*
  1. 'Sleeve-fastener' (No. 36).
  2. 'Lock-ring'.
  3. Copper ornamented disc with gold foil covering now detached. (Head of sun-flower pin?).

SCHEDULE OF 'SLEEVE-FASTENERS'

The following abbreviations have been used:

Armstrong – E. C. R. Armstrong, *Catalogue of Irish Gold Ornaments in the Collection of the Royal Irish Academy*, 2nd ed., Dublin (1933).

Wilde – W. R. Wilde, *A Descriptive Catalogue of the Antiquities of Gold in the Museum of the Royal Irish Academy*, Dublin (1862).

N.M.I. – National Museum of Ireland.
N.M.A.S. – National Museum of Antiquities of Scotland.
B.M. – British Museum.
U.M. – Ulster Museum.
U.M.A.E.C. – University Museum of Archaeology and Ethnology, Cambridge.
Ash. O. – Ashmolean Museum, Oxford.

Some of the objects in the schedule may be duplicated. For instance, the pieces published by Camden (Nos 86–7) may have passed into a Museum.

The numbers in the Schedule correspond to those in the illustrations (figs. 3–8).

No.	County	Find-Place	Collection	References	Remarks
1	Antrim	Ballynagard Rathlin Island	U.M. L 1.1943	Evans, *Ulster J. Archaeol.*, VII (1944), 61–2, fig. 1.	
2	Antrim	Ballinderry	N.M.I. 1874:70	Armstrong, 67, No. 141, pl. 14; 165.	Dug up in a field
3	Antrim	Belfast	Ash.O. 1927:2937		Found with Nos 4 and 5, and all form part of a hoard, see p. 194.
4	Antrim	Belfast	Ash.O. 1927:2938		
5	Antrim	Belfast	Ash.O. 1927:2939		
6	Antrim	Craighilly	Ash.O. 1927:2940	J. Evans, *Ancient Bronze Implements . . .* (1881), 139.	
7	Antrim	Craighilly	Ash.O. 1927:2941		
8	Antrim	Craighilly	Ash.O. 1927:2942		
9	Antrim		B.M. 1942:5–5.1		Found around 1927 during ploughing.
10	Armagh	Caddy	B.M. 62.6–17.1		
11	Clare	Gorteenreagh	N.M.I. 1948:330	J. Raftery, *North Munster Studies* (ed. E. Rynne), 65–6, fig. 3:2.	
12	Donegal	Glengad	N.M.I. R.2604	Armstrong, 66, No. 125, pl. 14:150.	

No.	County	Find-Place	Collection	References	Remarks
13	Down	Downpatrick[1]	U.M. 206:1913	*Archaeological Survey, Co. Down*, 68, pl. 19 (No. 106). *Sale Catalogue of the Day Collection.* No. 424, pl. 20.	
14	Down	Tamary	N.M.I. 1931:333	*Archaeological Survey, Co. Down*, 68, pl. 19 (No. 105).	
15	Dublin		U.M. 207:1913	*Sale Catalogue of the Day Collection,* (1913), No. 425, pl. 20.	
16	Fermanagh	Inishmore	N.M.I. R.1859	Armstrong, 67, No. 140, pl. 14:155.	Found while digging in a potato field.
17	Fermanagh	Tallykeel	U.M. 26:1935	*Ulster J. Archaeol.,* I (1938), 204.	
18	Galway		Melted down	M. Herity, *Antiq. J.,* XLIX (1969), 6–7, pl. 5:5. *Pococke, Archaeologia* II (1773), 39–41.	Part of a hoard, see p. 194
19	Louth	nr Newry	N.M.I. 1876:19	Armstrong, 67, No. 142, pl. 14:163.	One terminal is missing.
20	Mayo		Not known	Information based on data in MS. 4458, fol. 41 in National Library of Ireland.	It appears that both Nos 20–1 were found together and that they formed part of a hoard, see p. 194.
21	Mayo		Not known	As for No. 20.	
22	Meath	Lawrencetown or Oakley Park	N.M.I. W.132	Armstrong, p. 66, No. 136, pl. 14:157.	
23	Meath	nr Tara Hill	B.M. 49.3–1.8		The Museum Register does not give the county in which Nos 23 and 24 were discovered but the Tara Hill referred to is likely to be the well-known Co. Meath site.
24	Meath	nr Tara Hill	B.M. 49.3–1.9	*Later Prehistoric Antiquities . . .* p. 36, fig. 14:4.	

[1] No. 13 was acquired by the Belfast Museum at the sale of the Day Collection. In this connection it may be noted that Evans in his *Ancient Bronze Implements . . .* (1881), p. 139, states that 'Mr Robert Day, FSA, has a specimen which also is one of three found together in the Co. Down'. Day does not appear to have acquired the other two pieces, and their present whereabouts is unknown to me. It has not been established that the object referred to by Evans is the Downpatrick piece, or that a hoard of three 'sleeve-fasteners' was found at some place in Co. Down.

No.	County	Find-Place	Collection	References	Remarks	
24 (cont.)					Both objects were acquired by the Museum at the same time but it has not been stated if the objects were found together.	*'Sleeve-fasteners' of the Late Bronze Age*
25	Monaghan	Drumbanagher	N.M.I. S.A.1928:716	*Annual Report N.M.I.*, 1928–9, p. 11.		
26	Monaghan	nr Scotstown	N.M.I. 1879:6	Armstrong, *Antiq. J.*, III (1923) 138. Armstrong, 67, No. 145, pl. 14:153.	Found with No. 27 and both form part of a hoard; see p. 194.	
27	Monaghan	nr Scotstown	N.M.I. 1879:7	As for No. 26.		
28	Sligo	Coloney	Purchased by Chicago Museum. A marginal note in the copy of the Day *Sale Catalogue* in the Irish Antiquities Division, National Museum of Ireland, states that the ornament was purchased by Chicago Museum. Information from Dr J. Raftery.	*Sale Catalogue of the Day Collection.* (1913), 63, No. 426, pl. 20. J. Raftery, *J.R.S.A.I.*, 100 (1970), 171–2, fig. 1		
29	Tyrone	Arboe-Killycolpy	N.M.I. 1967:235	Sotheby, *Catalogue of Egyptian . . . Irish Bronze Age . . . Antiquities, Sold 27th November 1967.* Illustrated opposite p. 43. Find-place incorrectly given as Killymoon.	Nos 29–31 were found together near the western shores of Lough Neagh between Arboe and Killycolpy.	
30	Tyrone	Arboe-Killycolpy	N.M.I. 1967:236			
31	Tyrone	Arboe-Killycolpy	N.M.I. 1967:237			
32	Tyrone	Arboe-Killycolpy	N.M.I. 1967:238			
33	Tyrone	Trillick	Ash.O. 1927:2935			
34	Westmeath	Athlone	B.M. W.G. 27			
35	Westmeath		Private			
36	South of Ireland		N.M.A.S. FE 81	Eogan, *Antiquity*, XLI (1967), 56–8, and references therein to previous publications.	Forms part of a hoard, see p. 190.	
37	Ireland		U.M. 3536			
38	Ireland		U.M. 1910:675			
39	Ireland		N.M.I. P.822	Armstrong, p. 67, No. 144, pl. 14:147.		
40	Ireland		N.M.I. P.823	Armstrong, p. 66, No. 124, pl. 14:152.		
41	Ireland		N.M.I. R.614	Armstrong, p. 67, No. 139, pl. 14:143.		
42	Ireland		N.M.I. R.4040	Armstrong, p. 66, No. 131, pl. 14:174.		
43	Ireland		N.M.I. 4042	Armstrong, p. 66, No. 130, pl. 14:162.		

	No.	County	Find-Place	Collection	References	Remarks
	44	Ireland		N.M.I. R.4043	Armstrong, p. 66, No. 129, pl. 14:158.	
	45	Ireland		N.M.I. R.4044	Armstrong, p. 66, No. 128, pl. 14:164.	
	46	Ireland		N.M.I. R.4045	Armstrong, p. 66, No. 127, pl. 14:156.	
	47	Ireland		N.M.I. W.123	Armstrong, p. 65, No. 121, pl. 14:151. Wilde, pp. 63–4, fig. 596.	
	48	Ireland		N.M.I. W.125	Armstrong, p. 67, No. 148, pl. 14:167. Wilde, pp. 63–4, fig. 596.	
	49	Ireland		N.M.I. W.126	Armstrong, p. 67, No. 149, pl. 14:169.	
	50	Ireland		N.M.I. W.127	Armstrong, p. 66, No. 137, pl. 14:161.	
	51	Ireland		N.M.I. W.128	Armstrong, p. 66, No. 132, pl. 14:146.	
	52	Ireland		N.M.I. W.129	Armstrong, p. 67, No. 138, pl. 14:166.	
	53	Ireland		N.M.I. W.130	Armstrong, p. 65, No. 123, pl. 14:141. Wilde, p. 65, fig. 598.	
	54	Ireland		N.M.I. W.131	Armstrong, p.66, No. 133, pl. 14:149.	
	55	Ireland		N.M.I. W.133	Armstrong, p. 67, No. 147, pl. 14:160. Wilde, pp. 63–4, fig. 595.	
	56	Ireland		N.M.I. W.134	Armstrong, p. 66, No. 134, pl. 14:154.	
	57	Ireland		N.M.I. W.135	Armstrong, p. 66, No. 135, pl. 14:159.	
	58	Ireland		N.M.I. W.136	Armstrong, p. 68, No. 150, pl. 14:173.	
	59	Ireland		N.M.I. 1874:2	Armstrong, p. 65, No. 122, pl. 14:144.	
	60	Ireland		N.M.I. 1881:106	Armstrong, p. 66, No. 126, pl. 14:142.	
	61	Ireland		N.M.I. 1892:31	Armstrong, p. 67, No. 143, pl. 14:145.	
	62	Ireland		N.M.I. 1946:395		
	63	Ireland		B.M. A.F. 409		
	64	Ireland		B.M. 39.1–25.1		
	65	Ireland		B.M. 47.11–26.5		
	66	Ireland		B.M. 71.4–1.7		
	67	Ireland		B.M. 71.4–1.8		
	68	Ireland		B.M. 74.3–3.6		
	69	Ireland		U.M.A.E.C. Z. 15080 *c*		
	70	Ireland		Ash.O. 1927:2943		

No.	County	Find-Place	Collection	References	Remarks	
71	Ireland		N.M.A.S. FF2			*'Sleeve-fasteners' of the Late Bronze Age*
72	Ireland		N.M.A.S. FF3			
73	Ireland		N.M.A.S. FF4			
74	Ireland		N.M.A.S. FF28			
75	Ireland		N.M.A.S. L 1963.31			
76	Ireland		Royal Ontario Mus. Toronto. 918.3.100			
77	Ireland		Detroit Institute of Arts. 54:240	Robinson, *Bull. Detroit Institute of Arts*, 33 (1953–4), 65.	Recent information from the Museum states that this piece was found in Co. Cork.	
78	Ireland		Metropolitan Museum, New York, 47.100.10. (139047 t f)			
79	Ireland		Private			
80	Ireland		Private			
81	Ireland		Collection not known	*Bull. Allen Memorial Art. Museum*, XVIII (1961), 159, No. 80.	Formerly in the Collection of Oberlyn College. Sold by auction 1969.	
82	Ireland		Collection not known		Information from MS. 4458, fol. 36, in National Library of Ireland.	
83	Ireland		Collection not known	M. J. Herity, *Antiq. J.*, XLIX (1969), 4, pl. 3a.	One of a hoard of similar objects.	
84	Ireland		Collection not known	Crofton Croker, *Collectanea Antiqua*, III (1854), 133–4.		
85	Ireland		Collection not known	Camden, *Britannia* (ed. Gough) vol. III (1789), 478, pl. 40: fig. 7. Herity, *Antiq. J.*, XLIX (1969), pl. 8b. Pococke, *Archaeologia*, II (1773), 39, pl. 1, fig. 6. Vallancey, *Collectanea*, IV, 97, pl. 14, fig. 7.		
86			Collection not known	Camden, *Britannia* (ed. Gough) (1789), vol. 3, 477, pl. 33: figs 3 and 4.		
87			Collection not known	Vallancey, *op. cit.*, vol. III, 16, Nos. 3 and 4.		
88				N.M.I. IA/L/1968		

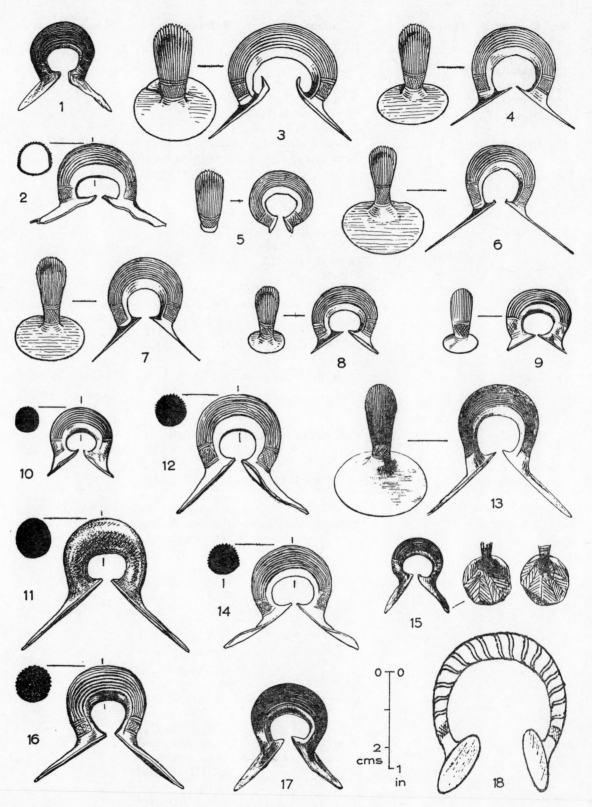

fig. 3 Sleeve-fasteners, corpus numbers 1–18 (18 after Pococke, 1773)

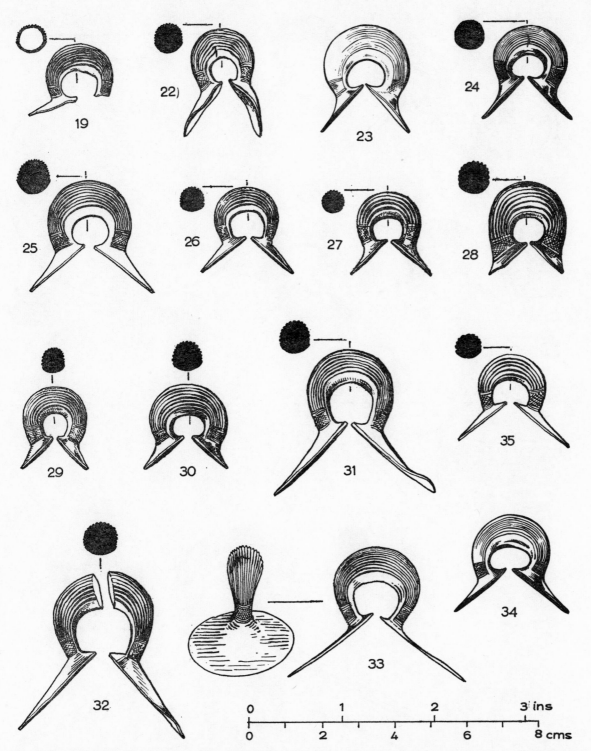

fig. 4 Sleeve-fasteners, corpus numbers 19–35 (nos. 20–21 are known only from manuscript references) (28 after *Sale Catalogue of the Day Coll.*, pl. xx)

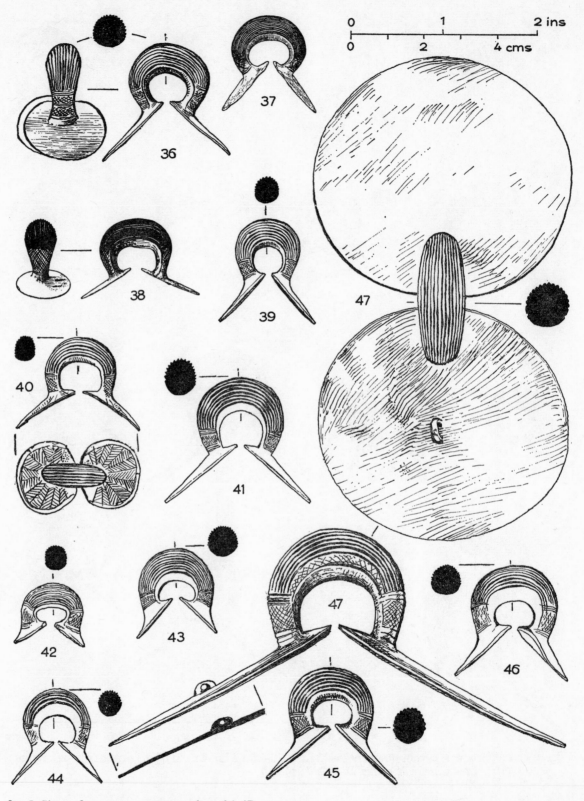

fig. 5 Sleeve-fasteners, corpus numbers 36–47

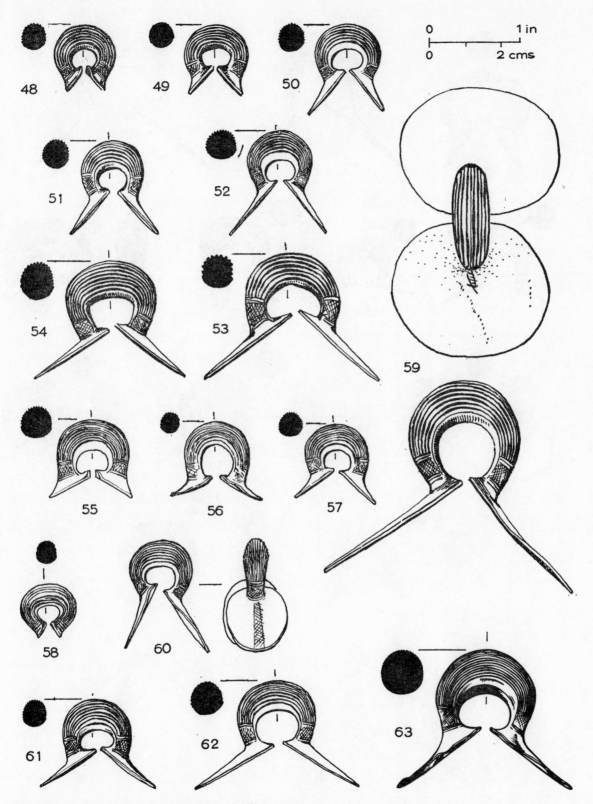

0 — 1 in

0 — 2 cms

48

49

50

51

52

59

54

53

55

56

57

58

60

61

62

63

fig. 6 Sleeve-fasteners, corpus numbers 48–63

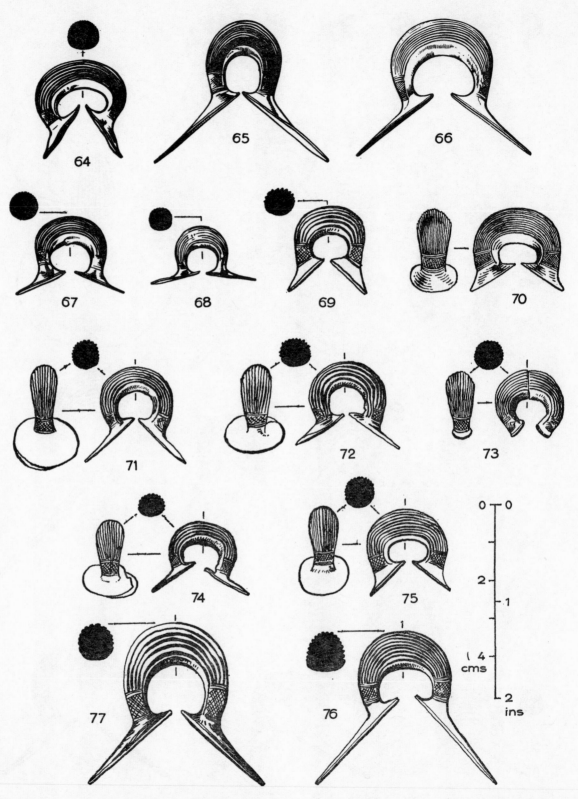

fig. 7 Sleeve-fasteners, corpus numbers 64–77

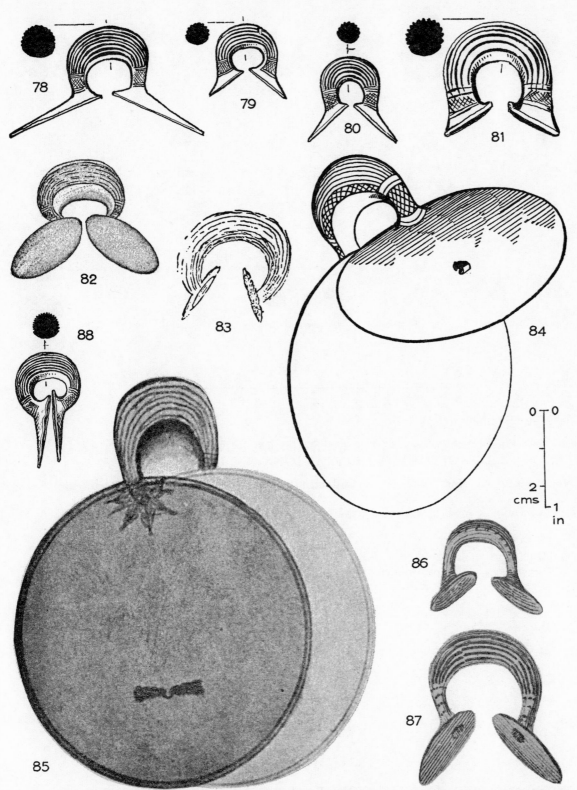

fig. 8 Sleeve-fasteners, corpus numbers 78–88 (82 after MS. 4458, fol. 36, Nat. Lib. Ireland; 83 after Herity, 1969; 84 after Croker, 1854; 85 after Pococke, 1773; 86 and 87 after Vallancey, 1784)

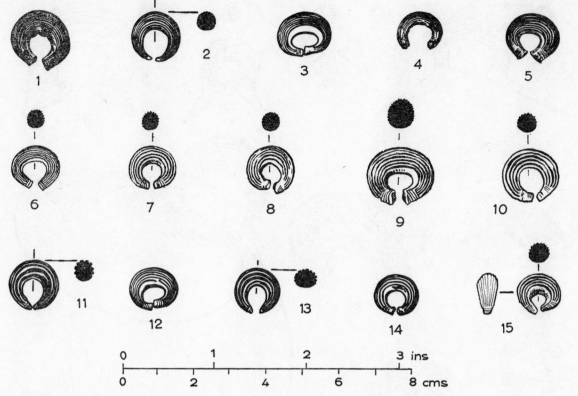

fig. 9 Striated rings

SCHEDULE OF SMALL PENANNULAR RINGS WITH EXTERNAL LONGITUDINAL STRIATIONS ON THE BODY (fig. 9)

No.	County	Find-Place	Collection	References	Remarks
1	Antrim	nr Belfast	U.M. 208:1913	*Sale Catalogue of the Day Collection,* No. 427, pl. 20.	
2	Dublin	nr Dublin	B.M. 49.3–1.18		
3	Fermanagh	Newtown Butler	B.M. 60.11–22.1		
4	Tyrone	Glenadrush	U.M. 281:1964	L. N. W. Flanagan, *Ulster J. Archaeol.,* XXIX (1966), 110, 113–14, pl. 17b, c.	Found in 1964 on the shore of Lough Eskragh. Damaged at ends but it would seem that this object did not have disc-shaped terminals.
5	Ireland		U.M. DF.3		
6	Ireland		N.M.I. W.124	Armstrong, p. 68, No. 151, pl. 14:171	
7	Ireland		N.M.I. W.137	Armstrong, p. 68, No. 152, pl. 14:170	
8	Ireland		N.M.I. R.4035	Armstrong, p. 68, No. 154, pl. 14:172	

No.	County	Find-Place	Collection	References	Remarks
9	Ireland		N.M.I. R.4036	Armstrong, p. 68, No. 153, pl. 14:168.	
10	Ireland		B.M. 38.7–18.5		
11	Ireland		B.M. 71.4–1.9		
12	Ireland		B.M. 74.3–3.3		
13	Ireland		B.M. 74.3–3.4		
14	Ireland		B.M. 74.3–3.5		
15	Ireland		N.M.A.S. FF.5		

'Sleeve-fasteners'
of the
Late Bronze Age

BIBLIOGRAPHY

Armstrong, E. C. R., 1933. *Catalogue of Irish Gold Ornaments in the Collection of the Royal Irish Academy*, 2nd ed. Dublin.

Betham, W., 1842. *Etruria-Celtica*, vol. II. Dublin.

Camden, W., 1789. *Britannia*, vol. III (ed. R. Gough from 3rd ed., 1607).

Croker, T. C., 1854. 'Notes on various discoveries of Gold Plates, chiefly in the south of Ireland', *Collectanea Antiqua*, III, 131–52.

Hawkes, C. F. C. & Clarke, R. R., 1963. 'Gahlstorf and Caistor-on-Sea', in *Culture and Environment: Essays in Honour of Sir Cyril Fox* (Foster, I. Ll. & Alcock, L., eds). London, 193–250.

Herity, M., 1969. 'Early Finds of Irish Antiquities', *Antiq. J.*, XLIX, 1–21.

Maryon, H., 1938. 'The technical methods of the Irish smiths in the Bronze and Early Iron Ages', *Proc. Roy. Irish Acad.*, 44 (C), 181–228.

Pococke, R., 1773. 'An account of some antiquities found in Ireland', *Archaeologia*, II, 32–41.

Raftery, J., 1967. 'The Gorteenreagh Hoard', in Rynne, E. (ed.), *North Munster Studies: Essays in commemoration of Monsignor Michael Moloney*. Limerick, 61–71.

Vallancey, C., 1784. *Collectanea de Rebus Hibernicis*, vol. IV.

Wilde, W. R., 1862. *A Descriptive Catalogue of the Antiquities of Gold in the Museum of the Royal Irish Academy*. Dublin.

ACKNOWLEDGEMENTS

For facilities to study and for permission to publish 'sleeve-fasteners' in their Collections, I wish to thank the authorities of the National Museum of Ireland; The Ulster Museum; The British Museum; The National Museum of Antiquities, Scotland; The Ashmolean Museum, Oxford; The University Museum of Archaeology and Ethnology, Cambridge; The Royal Ontario Museum, Toronto; The Metropolitan Museum, New York; the Detroit Institute of Arts; Mr Thomas Pakenham. I am especially grateful for assistance received, when working on the material, to Dr Joseph Raftery, Dublin; Mr L. N. W. Flanagan, Belfast; Dr Ian Longworth, London; Mr H. J. Case, Oxford; Miss M. Craster, Cambridge; Miss A. Henshall, Edinburgh; Miss P. Bolland, Toronto; Dr Helmut Nickel, New York.

Finally I wish to thank Dr Michael Herity for drawing my attention to the illustrations of 'sleeve-fasteners' in MS. 4458, National Library of Ireland.

A grant from University College financed the preparation of the illustrations.

The Broadward Complex and Barbed Spearheads

Colin Burgess, David Coombs and D. Gareth Davies

Lily Chitty's work over the years has been remarkable for its diversity, but the subject of **Bronze Age** metal-work has been the one with which she has perhaps been most closely associated. Her knowledge of these metal finds and their history may never be equalled. Her investigations of lost and doubtful material, particularly hoards from Wales and the Marches, have constituted masterpieces of archaeological detective work (e.g. Chitty, 1928; 1940; 1965; Chitty & Coombs, 1967–8). To offer some similar archaeological detection in her honour would be difficult if not impossible, because any such work would inevitably draw largely on her unique knowledge. We can at least offer her an illustrated account of one of the most important, but least adequately published, hoards from her own area, and attempt to set it in a wider context. Complete publication of the Broadward hoard is beyond the scope of this work, because Miss Chitty herself would have to be so closely involved, and because excavation of the site would clearly be desirable. As it is, in the writing of the summary account here, the authors had to approach her surreptitiously to clear up certain points relating to the hoard's history. Our paper is divided into four sections:

(i)   the history of the Broadward hoard;
(ii) the contents of the Broadward hoard and the background of the types represented;
(iii) the origins, background and function of barbed spearheads;
(iv) the place of the Broadward hoard and barbed spearheads in the British Late Bronze Age.

(i) THE HISTORY OF THE BROADWARD HOARD[1]

The Broadward hoard was found on 30 July 1867 in drainage operations in a marshy field called 'Lower Moor' nearly ¼ mile S.S.E. of Broadward Hall in the Clun valley (Jackman, 1868; Rocke & Barnwell, 1872; Barnwell, 1873; Banks, 1873).[2] The site is in an extension of Clungun-

---

[1] The authors are deeply indebted to Miss Chitty for all the help she has given them on this, as on so many other occasions.

[2] See also the British Museum registers relating to Broadward accessions.

ford parish, almost on the Herefordshire border, but actually just inside Shropshire, *c.* 2 miles N.W. of Leintwardine and 7 miles W. of Ludlow (SO/391762). Indeed, most writers have followed Evans (1881, 465, 500) in placing the find in Herefordshire.[1] The implements were found about 5–6 feet down, together with great quantities of animal bones, including whole skulls. It was noted that animal bones could be dug up in almost every part of the field. The implements were lying in a 'confused heap', and many were removed from the cutting 'cemented together with the gravel into large solid lumps' (Rocke & Barnwell, 1872, 343–4). Their generally corroded and oxidised state was commented on. Just how many pieces were found is not known. Certainly the 70+ Broadward implements and fragments preserved in the British Museum today (Appendix 1) can represent only a part of the original find, since it is recorded that the labourers took away many pieces, and a whole boxful of others was retained at Broadward Hall, from where they subsequently disappeared. Furthermore, the ditch filled with water so rapidly that the site could not be examined properly, and the cutting was not extended, so that it is not known how many pieces, if any, were not recovered. Clearly excavation of the site would now be desirable on many counts.

Also found 'in the same hole' as the bronzes was a Romano-British lattice-decorated pot, a record which might have caused trouble for subsequent generations of scholars. The exact relationship of the pot to the bronzes was never described, however, and it could well have been at a different level. Moreover, a possible explanation of its presence is provided by Banks (1873), who noted that a tumulus adjoining the site had previously been levelled, spoil from it being thrown into the morass in order to improve the ground. If it was not actually deposited with this tumulus material, the pot could reflect some previous dumping to consolidate the area.

Apart from the pieces carried off by labourers, and the boxful retained at Broadward Hall, others were obtained by the antiquaries and collectors who abounded in Victorian England. It was three of these who provided the British Museum with its Broadward material. As early as 1872 A. W. Franks presented an assortment to the Museum (nos. 1872, 3–29, 1–10), and a larger collection was given by C. H. Read in 1902 (1902, 5–15, 1–22). Finally, more pieces were acquired as part of the Greenwell Collection (WG 2203–2232).

There is some evidence for a second discovery of bronze implements near Broadward Hall about 1912–13, and we are grateful to Miss Chitty for letting us see her notes on the subject. The evidence is slight, however: basically, information gleaned from people in the area by local antiquaries, and, quite possibly, a folk memory, blurred by time, of the original discovery. Nevertheless it is certain that the then Herefordshire County Surveyor, G. H. Jack, FSA, a keen antiquary, was shown 'a good-sized heap' of bronzes at Broadward Hall about 1912–13, and allowed to take seven or eight pieces away. Whether this was the original find, or a new one, may never be known for certain. The fate of this 'heap' is not known, for the Hall has since changed hands many times.

C.B.

(ii) THE CONTENTS OF THE BROADWARD HOARD AND THE BACKGROUND OF THE TYPES REPRESENTED

All the original reports of the hoard describe it as consisting mainly of spearheads, together with a few ferrules, sword fragments and miscellaneous pieces. Many of the spearheads still had wood, apparently carbonised, in their sockets. The Broadward material in the British Museum includes many of the pieces figured by Rocke and Barnwell (1872), and there are no types described or illustrated in the original reports which are not represented in the surviving collection. The following are in the British Museum:

[1] Although Evans himself placed it in Shropshire in some of his text references, e.g. 1881, 168, 285.

20 barbed spearheads or fragments of barbed spearheads, four with lunate openings in their blades;

4 leaf-shaped spearheads with fillet-defined midribs;

3 lunate-opening spearheads;

9 spearheads with leaf-shaped blades of ogival outline, of which

   3 have midribs defined by simple, linear punched ornament,

   1 has a decorated blade,

   4 are plain,

   1 has a ribbed socket base;

10 leaf-shaped spearhead fragments of uncertain type;

7 fragments of spearhead sockets;

5 fragmentary spearshaft ferrules;

2 'bugle-shaped objects';

1 fragment of a tubular ring or armlet;

1 tanged chisel;

11 leaf-shaped sword fragments: eight are blade fragments, one is a complete hilt and upper blade of Ewart Park type, another is a much damaged lower hilt and upper blade, and there is a third hilt fragment;

1 short tongue chape;

1 carbonised point of a wooden spearshaft.

All the material is bright green in colour, badly corroded and broken, and there is much heavy encrustation. It has all received laboratory treatment.

In addition to the material surviving in the British Museum, Rocke and Barnwell (1872, no. 6, opp. p. 351 and no. 5, opp. p. 352) illustrate two spearheads which seem to have been lost. Both have sockets decorated with encircling grooves, but whereas one seems to have been a plain ogival spearhead, the other was a fine example of the type with fillet-defined midrib, the fillets extending down the sides of the socket to surround the rivet holes.

The barbed spearheads (figs. 4–5)

The origin and background of barbed spearheads will be considered in greater detail below.

The Broadward examples are of a peculiar short form (*c.* 150–165 mm., 6–6·5 in.) practically unknown outside the Broadward hoard. In other respects they are typical of the broad, parallel-sided variety of barbed spearhead (see below), with strong barbs. Some possess the long metal pins which are characteristic of barbed spearheads as a whole, and of no other spearhead type. While there are some complete or fairly complete examples, others are fragments, including pieces of blade, or just typical oval-sectioned sockets retaining long pins. A number have pieces of wooden shaft in their socket or midrib. Some of the smaller fragments may originally have come from one spearhead, so that there may have been fewer than the twenty specimens apparently represented today. Four have small lunate openings in their blades.

Spearheads with fillet-defined midribs (fig. 5).

Leaf-shaped spearheads with a midrib defined by a single, or more rarely double, pair of beadings or fillets seem to have been a peculiarly Irish/British phenomenon. The four Broadward specimens are all blades or blade fragments, representing fairly small examples of the type, and they have the usual single pair of beadings.

Spearheads with fillet-defined midribs appeared first in the Wilburton phase of the south English Late Bronze Age, as in such typical hoards as that from Nettleham, Lincs. (Trollope, 1861; Kendrick & Hawkes, 1932, 131) and Wilburton itself (Fox, 1923, 61, pl. x). Thereafter they became much more common and widespread, occurring from the eighth century in hoards throughout Britain.[1] In this respect they follow the familiar pattern set by other originally Wilburton types which became widely distributed beyond the Wilburton province only in the post-Wilburton era (Burgess, 1968a, 40). We propose to term this later period the Ewart Park phase, after the form of leaf-shaped sword which became the standard pattern throughout Britain and Ireland after the decline of Wilburton metal-working in the eighth century.

The flat fillet extensions on to the socket sides below the base of the blade strongly suggest a skeuomorphic reminiscence of the basal loops of some basal-looped spearheads. Fillet-defined spearheads may therefore have been yet another Late Bronze Age development from the long-established basal-looped tradition. Lunate-opening spearheads have always been regarded as such, and barbed spearheads may have been similarly affected (see below). An immediate connection may be seen in the basal-looped spearheads of Knockans type, which had a fillet-defined midrib. On these the fillets extend on to the sockets as loops, though in the case of the example in the Harrogate find, Yorks. (Coles, Coutts & Ryder, 1964), the loops are not perforated. The Knockans fillets in turn must have derived from the blade channels of the main stream of basal-looped spearhead development. It is known that basal-looped spearheads of all forms survived through the Wilburton-Wallington period (Burgess, 1968b, 38), so there is no chronological objection to their connection with the fillet-defined type. Indeed, in the Nettleham hoard, basal-looped and fillet-defined spearheads occur together.

Lunate-opening spearheads (fig. 6)

Lunate blade openings are found on leaf-shaped spearheads of a variety of forms,[2] as well as on barbed spearheads. The three Broadward examples all differ from one another. One (fig. 6:26) is of the type with fillet-defined midrib, the lunate openings themselves being edged by beadings. The second (fig. 6:25) has a plain blade, rounded midrib and simple lunates, while the third (fig. 6:27), very badly corroded, appears to have affinities with barbed spearheads. Its lunate openings are small, like those in the Broadward barbed spearheads, set in an oval-sectioned blade with obvious barbed spearhead affinities, and the base of this blade continues as short fillets down either side of the socket, ending in small but pronounced barbs.

Lunate-opening spearheads, like those with fillet-defined midribs, were developed first by the smiths of the southern Wilburton tradition, occurring in such typical hoards as those from Blackmoor, Hants (White, 1887, 451), Wilburton (Evans, 1885) and Guilsfield, Montgom. (Savory, 1965; Davies, 1967, fig. 2, c, e and p. 101). All of these are likely to have been deposited at the end of the Wilburton phase (Burgess, 1968b, 36–7), so that lunate-opening spearheads may have been a late Wilburton development. In the Ewart Park phase, they, like some other Wilburton types, were widely adopted outside the former Wilburton province,[3] and, indeed, in this later phase were more characteristic of the North and West than of the South.

Leaf-shaped spearheads with ogival blades (fig. 6)

The pegged, leaf-shaped spearheads of Britain and Ireland exhibit two main blade outlines.

[1] e.g. Auchtertyre, Morayshire, in Scotland (Evans, 1881, fig. 383); Heathery Burn in northern England (Britton & Longworth, 1968); and Bexley Heath, Kent, in southern England (Britton, 1960a, GB. 53).

[2] cf. Evans, 1881, 334–7: plain blade with rounded midrib (fig. 417), stepped blade (figs 418, 420), blade with fillet-defined midrib (fig. 419), and lozenge-sectioned blade (fig. 421). There are also some channelled blade spearheads of Eglwyseg-Rosnoën type (Burgess, 1968b, 8–9; fig. 5:4b, 5) which have lunate openings, e.g. from the Thames near Hampton Court (London Museum, A 27215), and several from 'Ireland' (National Museum, Dublin, W 30 (Eogan, 1964, fig. 1:4) and W 112; Ulster Museum, Belfast, 1911:163b).

[3] e.g. hoards from Glen Cova, Angus, and Ballimore, Argyllshire, in Scotland (Coles 1959–60, for full lists and refs.); Whittingham, Northumberland, Agelthorpe, Middleham, Yorkshire, and Winmarleigh, Lancashire, in northern England (*Northumberland County History*, XIV (1935), 28–9, pl. II; Evans, 1881, 334–5, figs 418–19; *VCH, Lancashire*); and Dowris, Co. Offaly, in Ireland (British Museum, 1953, pl. V:1).

Firstly, there is what may be termed the lanceolate outline, in which the curve of the edge, from base to maximum width to point, is continuously convex, though the widest part of the blade is below the middle (cf. Evans, 1881, figs 378, 379, 381, 384). There is a less common elliptic variant, broadest at the middle (Evans, 1881, fig. 385). Secondly, there is the 'waisted' or ogival outline, flame-shaped in its extreme form, with a distinct concavity or straightening of the curve above the point of maximum width, and a marked narrowing just before the point (e.g. Evans, 1881, figs 386, 388, 390, 391, 392). The size range of the lanceolate form is much greater than that of the ogival spearheads, which tend to be smaller and narrower. The lanceolate form appears to have been the earlier-developed. After an initial flash-in-the-pan appearance in the Early Bronze Age Arreton tradition (Britton, 1963, 288, fig. 19), it disappeared for much of the Middle Bronze Age. The looped, leaf-shaped spearheads of the Middle Bronze Age almost invariably have this lanceolate outline, and this may explain why, when pegged spearheads were reintroduced in the Penard phase (Burgess 1968a, 42, n. 35; 1968b, 34), their leaf-shaped blades were of the same form. In the succeeding Wilburton phase in southern England, pegged spearheads of various types rapidly ousted looped spearheads (which proved more durable in other regions), though the lanceolate/elliptic outline is still the one encountered. Its continuing domination is confirmed by the few plain, pegged leaf-shaped spearheads which turn up in the contemporary Wallington hoards of northern England: these too have lanceolate or elliptic outlines (Burgess, 1968a). Only in the Ewart Park phase, when pegged spearheads everywhere replaced looped types, did the ogival form appear in any numbers, becoming more popular than the lanceolate outline in some areas (e.g. in the Carp's tongue hoards of south-eastern England).

While spearheads with the ogival blade are generally plain, examples with decorated sockets are fairly numerous, especially in south-eastern England. The decoration is almost invariably linear or geometric, usually punched or incised, and simple encircling grooves are the commonest device. In some cases a similar effect is achieved by using ribbing rather than grooving (fig. 6:32). It is interesting to note the association of such decorated sockets with the waisted, and not the lanceolate/elliptic, blade outline.

There are nine spearheads with ogival blades in the Broadward hoard, and possibly fragments of others. The proportion of decorated examples is high, only four being completely plain. One has a familiar horizontally ribbed socket base, but the ornament on three others is not so common. These have their midribs edged by lines of punch marks, a feature which it is difficult to parallel closely, though one of the Guilsfield spearheads offers some comparison (Savory, 1965, fig. 2:1; Davies, 1967, fig. 2,c).[1] Finally, there is one example which has a blade decorated with hatched triangles, an extremely rare device found elsewhere only on spearheads in the hoards from Broadness, Kent (fig. 13), Willow Moor, Salop (Appendix 1) and Bilton, Yorks. (Howarth, 1899, 78). The connection is clearly important, and will be returned to later.

Fragmentary leaf-shaped spearheads of uncertain type (fig. 7)

Ten leaf-shaped spearheads are too fragmentary to permit identification, but the chances are that most, if not all, were of the pegged type with ogival blade.

Spearhead sockets (not illustrated)

Apart from identifiable sockets from barbed spearheads, there are seven small socket fragments, some of which might have belonged to spearheads discussed above, and about which little useful can be said. One crushed piece, either from a spearhead socket or ferrule (fig. 7:50), is the 'spud' which so exercised Barnwell (1873) in his supplementary note on the Broadward hoard.

---

[1] Since the above was written, D. C. has noted a spearhead in the Museum of Archaeology and Ethnology, Cambridge (no. Z.4301) with its midrib defined by punched or incised running chevrons.

Spearshaft ferrules (fig. 7)

The earliest spearshaft ferrules to appear in Britain and Ireland were the pointed ones introduced in the Penard phase (Burgess, 1968a, 5, 7, 8; 1968b, 5, 34). The idea seems to have come from central Germany, where such ferrules had an M.IV background (Sprockhoff, 1937, 30–1; Coles, 1959–60, 24; Butler, 1963, 133–4; Davies, 1967, 102–3).

In the succeeding Wilburton phase in south-eastern England, this pointed type gave way to long tubular forms, either tapering slightly and evenly from mouth to flat or rounded closed base, or with a slightly thickened middle. In some cases, as in the Guilsfield hoard (Savory, 1965, fig. 4: 7, 8, 9, 13; Davies, 1967, fig. 2, f, g, h), the closed end may be slightly expanded. There was a similar development of tubular ferrules in the St-Brieuc-des-Iffs industry of north-west France, which so closely paralleled the Wilburton tradition (Briard, 1965, 175–98; Burgess, 1968b, 9–17, 36–7), but they do not seem to have been used to any extent in other parts of Britain at this time. It is only in the Ewart Park phase, as in the case of so many other Wilburton fashions, that they seem to have spread outside the south-east, occurring, for example, in Scotland (Peelhill hoard, Coles & Scott, 1962–3), in the Midlands (Great Freeman Street, Nottingham hoard, M. A. Smith, 1957) and widely in the west, as will be seen below.

More typical of the Ewart Park phase, however, are short ferrules with a waisted or expanded foot, apparently a development from those Wilburton tubular ferrules with slightly expanded ends. Their expansion is generally moderate (figs 7, 20), but occasionally reaches extreme proportions in the well-known disc-foot ferrules (Coles, 1959–60, 24–5; Hawkes & Smith, 1955, G.B.12[3]). The latter need not have been a development from the basic expanded-foot type, since disc-foot examples are already present in two late Wilburton hoards, at Blackmoor and Fulbourn Common, in contexts transitional to the Ewart Park phase (see below, p. 218). The expanded-foot type does not seem to occur in these late Wilburton finds, but was widespread in the succeeding Ewart Park period. It occurs in Carp's tongue contexts (e.g. Wickham Park, Surrey, Smith, 1958, GB.39), but is more characteristic farther west, as will be seen.

There are four, possibly five, ferrules surviving from the Broadward hoard, one of which might be a fragmentary spearhead socket rather than a ferrule. Two are of the expanded-foot type (fig. 7:46–7), two others of the tubular form (fig. 7:48–9), one with surviving metal pin.

'Bugle-shaped objects' (fig. 7)

There are two looped tubes, variants on the familiar 'bugle-shaped objects' of the Carp's tongue complex. The Broadward examples have shorter tubes than the normal pattern, but there seems no reason why they should be regarded as anything other than 'bugles'.

'Bugle-shaped objects' were just one of the many types which went to make up the mass of bric-à-brac common to the Carp's tongue complex on both sides of the Channel (Burgess, 1968b, 17, 22–3, 38–9). In fact the term 'bugle-shaped object' covers two very different functional forms, similar in plan but not in section, which must have been used in completely different ways. The first has loop and tube of circular section, but the second is a flat casting, or of semi-circular section, with loop or loops at the back (Briard, 1965, fig. 77; Burgess 1968b, fig. 13:20, 21, 22). The tubular version may have served as a strap fastening, to judge from the wear on the remarkable two-piece 'bugle-shaped object' from Wayland's Smithy, Berks. (Atkinson, 1965, 132, with n. 19). The individual elements of this piece, a reel-shaped object and a looped ring, are representatives of two familiar types often found in hoards of the period, though not usually in association. Such objects could well provide a British prototype for 'bugle-shaped objects', as Atkinson has suggested, especially as they are almost unknown in France; but equally they could constitute local variations on an already existing fashion. In this context it may be significant that a majority of the known looped rings, and half the reel-shaped objects, come from areas outside the Carp's tongue lands of south-eastern England. It is this stumpy

Wayland's Smithy form of 'bugle-shaped object' which those from Broadward most closely resemble in their proportions.

Tubular ring (fig. 7)

Rings made of sheet metal bent into a tube are familiar from Carp's tongue contexts on both sides of the Channel, but particularly in France (Briard, 1965, 218–20, fig. 78). These are frequently filled with small pellets, and they tend to be much smaller than the Broadward ring, *c.* 30–35 mm. (*c.* 1·25 in.) against the 70–80 mm. (*c.* 3 in.) of the Broadward ring. In its size and proportions it is much more like the *bracelets creux à petits tampons* of the French Carp's tongue hoards, some of which are plain like the Broadward ring (Briard, 1966, pls 23, 24). However, both small rings and bracelets tend to have their joins logically concealed on the inside of the curve, whereas the Broadward piece has its join on one face of the ring.

Tanged chisel (fig. 7)

The tanged chisels of the Early and Middle Bronze Age in Britain and Ireland are of a simple rod or bar form without any stop between tang and blade, but often with an expanded blade. The same pattern is repeated from Early Bronze Age contexts (e.g. Llanddyfnan, Anglesey: Savory, 1957, 211; Arreton Down, I.O.W.: Alexander & Ozanne, 1960, 275) through the Middle Bronze Age (e.g. Sparkford, Somerset: Smith, 1959, GB.46; Bishopsland, Co. Kildare: Eogan, 1964, 275), and even into the Wilburton phase (e.g. Buttington Hall, Montgom.: Ward, 1934, 139, pls XIII, c, d, XVIIb). Stouter chisel-like implements with side stops were in use throughout this long period, the so-called trunnion celts or chisels (see Burgess & Cowen above, chapter 13), but these have been interpreted as metal-workers' stakes rather than chisels (Maryon, 1938).

The change to more sophisticated tanged chisels may have taken place in the Wilburton phase, though tools assignable to this period are generally very rare. A fragmentary chisel in the Wilburton hoard was at least shouldered, though it is broken off below the point at which any stop might have occurred. The find from Doncaster, Yorks., which can be assigned to the contemporary Wallington tradition (Burgess, 1968a, fig. 7:2) has a large tanged chisel with collared stop, though this tool, in its size and proportions, clearly owes much to the simple chisels and trunnion tools of the Early and Middle Bronze Age.

It is the centuries after Wilburton to which the small chisels with stops clearly belong, for the associations are then numerous and widespread (Eogan, 1964, 298). Nevertheless a late Wilburton origin cannot be ruled out in view of the slight evidence noted above, and of the presence of a chisel with stop in the Saint-Brieuc-des-Iffs hoard, I.-et-V., the type find of the French equivalent of Wilburton metal-working (Briard, 1965, fig. 59). After Wilburton such tools became a common feature of the Carp's tongue complex in Britain and France, but they are also numerous in the north and west of Britain, and in Ireland. Eogan has distinguished two main blade shapes: (1) straight-sided and roughly triangular, and (2) concave-sided with expanded edge (Eogan, 1964, 298). There would seem, however, to be at least four basic shapes: (1) narrow, straight-sided, truly chisel-like; (2) broad, straight-sided, triangular; (3) concave-sided with expanded edge; (4) convex curve, of 'crinoline' shape. On the basis of the chisels from Doncaster, Wilburton and Saint-Brieuc-des-Iffs, one must agree with Eogan that shape (1) developed earliest, but undoubtedly it persisted thereafter alongside the other shapes. There are in addition four types of stop to be considered: (a) collar stop (fig. 14:46); (b) side stops or lugs (fig. 18:42); (c) ledge stop (fig. 7:51) and (d) shoulder stop (as in the Booltiaghadine hoard, Co. Clare, Eogan, 1966). Any permutation of blade shape and stop form may be encountered, so that it is difficult to isolate valid chisel types. Blade shapes 2 (triangular) and 1 (narrow, merging at the extremes of their proportions) are the commonest, and collar stops by far the commonest form of stop. Blade shape 3 (concave-sided and expanded) seems best represented in Ireland, but other blade and collar forms seem to be widely distributed. The presence of tanged chisels in settlement sites at Staple Howe, Yorks. (Brewster, 1963), Scarborough, Yorks. (R. A. Smith, 1928), and Eldon's Seat, Dorset (Cunliffe, 1968), should be noted. These seem to belong to the seventh–sixth centuries.

The Broadward chisel presents an unusual combination of convex-sided blade, shape 4, and ledge stop, and it does not seem to have any exact parallels.

Leaf-shaped swords (fig. 8)

There are eleven fragments of leaf-shaped swords. Eight are pieces of blade, having the cross-section with swollen centre typical both of some Wilburton (Group IV) and of Ewart Park (Group V) swords (Cowen, 1933; Burgess, 1968b). Two fragments join to make an almost complete hilt and upper blade, pronounced unmistakably Ewart Park by the straight ricasso. The much-corroded lower hilt and upper blade of another sword, and the hilt end of a third, seem also best assigned to the Ewart Park series. The almost complete hilt is slotted, a fashion more characteristic of Wilburton swords, and rare among Ewart Park weapons (but cf. an unprovenanced example in the London Museum, O.1347; from the Thames at Hammersmith [Cambridge Mus. Arch. & Eth.]; in the Tarves hoard, Aberdeenshire [Coles, 1959–60, fig. 6] and several from Ireland [Eogan, 1965, fig. 62]. The other hilt end has the more usual Ewart Park rivet holes.

Ewart Park swords were first defined by Cowen (1933). They are characterised above all by their straight ricasso, contrasting with the curved ricassi of other native Irish/British sword types. Short, straight shoulders and straight ricasso together produce a distinctive biconical outline. This is not the place, however, to repeat Cowen's analysis of the other diagnostic features of this and other Irish/British sword types (Cowen, 1933; 1951; 1952). Ewart Park swords comprise Group V in the scheme of classification of swords in Britain and Ireland suggested by one of us elsewhere (Burgess, 1968b). They are by far the most common and widespread sword type in the Bronze Age of these islands. Their immediate forerunners seem to have been the Group IV Wilburton swords with curved ricassi, characteristic of the Wilburton phase. Their area of development was seemingly the Wilburton lands of south-eastern England, for in two late Wilburton hoards, from Blackmoor, Hants, and Fulbourn Common, Cambs. (Clarke, 1821), Ewart Park swords are associated with developed Wilburton swords. No other part of Britain or Ireland seems to have either such early associations of Ewart Park swords or such a long and varied tradition of sword development as the South-East. It appears, therefore, that the Ewart Park sword was developed when the Wilburton tradition was almost at an end, perhaps by the smiths who were initiating the industrial revolution which overtook Wilburton (Burgess, 1968b). Up to this point, in the eighth century, leaf-shaped swords, like socketed axes, and lead-bronze technology, were something of a south-eastern monopoly (Burgess, 1968a), but from this time such fashions seem to have ousted lingering Middle Bronze Age traditions over the rest of Britain and Ireland. The mechanics of this dissemination are far from clear, but suffice it to say that from the eighth century onwards the leaf-shaped sword became a common feature throughout these islands, and everywhere the Ewart Park form, or variants on it, was the one used (Eogan, 1965; Burgess, 1968b).

Short tongue chape (fig. 8)

There are three main types of scabbard chape known from the Late Bronze Age of Britain and Ireland: (1) tongue-shaped, (2) bag-shaped or purse-shaped, and (3) winged. They have recently been discussed in some detail by Eogan (1965, 168–71). A very rare fourth group consists of short, straight-sided 'pocket' chapes in the hoards from Guilsfield (Savory, 1965, fig. 5:6; Davies, 1967, fig. 1, r, p. 103), Stoke Ferry, Norfolk (Hawkes, 1955, GB.8.2) and Isleham, Cambs. (Britton, 1960; Edwardson, n.d.).

The tongue chape series includes the chapes of Eogan's Classes 1 and 2 (Eogan, 1965,

168–9). Tongue chapes occur in three main sizes, long, short and diminutive; but all share a basic tongued form, of lozenge section, with sides tapering from an open mouth to a narrow, closed foot.

(a) Long tongue chapes, the Wilburton type. This is the commonest form. The mouth may be straight or concave, the sides straight or ogival in outline, and the edges of the faces 'flanged' or simple. The central ridge sometimes supports a beading, and may be flanked by grooves. The foot is generally unexpanded, but may end in a small disc or rotating washer, or a downward projecting stud.

Long tongue chapes were developed and used on both sides of the Channel by the smiths of the closely related Wilburton and St-Brieuc-des-Iffs traditions (Eogan, 1964, 288–93; Briard, 1965, 177–9, 195–6, fig. 58; Burgess, 1968b, 9–17, 36–7). They do not seem to have outlasted this phase, being replaced subsequently, in non-Wilburton areas, by the shorter type (b).

(b) Short tongue chapes, the Stogursey type. These are similar to the basic form (a), but average only 120–180 mm. (4·75–7 in.) in length against the 255–380 mm. (10–15 in.) of type (a). Being shorter, they have a more squat appearance. Type (b) tongue chapes are first evident in late Wilburton hoards, as at Guilsfield (Savory, 1965, figs 5:4, 6:11) and Isleham (Edwardson, n.d., pl. v), but they were more characteristic of the subsequent phase, especially in northern and western Britain (Evans, 1881, 304; Coles, 1959–60, 24; Eogan, 1965, 169).

(c) Diminutive tongue chapes. There are two forms of tongue chapes which average about 50–80 mm. (2–3 in.) in length. The first, as represented in the Broadward hoard, is narrow, and has fairly straight sides tapering to the foot. The second form is more baggy, with deeply concave mouth and markedly ogival sides, the hoard from Pant-y-Maen, Pembs., providing the best-known example (Griffiths, 1957, fig. 1:9). Another occurs in the Broadness hoard (fig. 14:44). Both forms tend to have an expanded foot.

C.B.

(iii) THE ORIGINS, BACKGROUND AND FUNCTION OF BARBED SPEARHEADS

Classification

Very little work has been done in the past on the classification of barbed spearheads. Evans (1881, 337–8) distinguished two forms, the familiar large pattern with true barbs, obliquely angled, and a smaller form, as in the Broadward hoard, in which the base of the blade extends roughly at right angles from the socket. Greenwell and Brewis (1909, 454) and R. A. Smith (1909–11) also recognised these two main forms. Greenwell and Brewis grouped barbed spearheads into their Class VI. Smith drew attention to another barbed type in publishing a spearhead from the Hatfield Broad Oak hoard, Essex (Smith, 1909–11, 165–6, fig. 3; Davies forthcoming in *Inv. Arch.*). This is a rare form characterised by a narrow blade of flat lozenge or elliptical section, and rudimentary barbs. It may more easily be termed the Donington type after the example from Donington on Bain, Lincs., published by Thompson (1954). Evans (1933) took the matter of classification no further, and while Hawkes (in Bartlett & Hawkes, 1965) was concerned largely with the function of barbed spearheads, Burgess (1968b) confined himself largely to problems of distribution and background.

Study of extant barbed spearheads from 39 individual find-places in Britain (Appendix 3) (figs 4, 5, 9, 10–11, 15, 19, 21–24, 26–32) shows that there are four main forms. The old 'large' type can be subdivided into Type I, in which the blade is leaf-shaped and lozenge-sectioned and the barbs are short (e.g. figs 19, 22, 30:1), and Type II, the familiar broad form, with straight, roughly parallel sides, wide point and enormous barbs. Type III comprises the old short form of the Broadward hoard, broad and parallel-sided like Type II, but with less acutely angled barbs. Type IV consists of the small Donington-type spearheads with rudimentary barbs. Lunate openings may be found on examples of Types I, II and III, just as they are found on spearheads of a wide variety of other forms.

Type IV examples clearly stand apart from the more familiar weapons of Types I–III. The features which distinguish the latter have often been described. Apart from the obvious barbs and broad point, the following points are noteworthy. Firstly, there is a low, flat or lozengic cross-section, without the usual clearly defined rounded midrib. The wide, low centre is separated from the blade wings by a slight step or change in angle. The socket cavity through the blade is thus of a flattened elliptical or lozenge section. Secondly the socket, often oval-sectioned, is remarkably short and small for the size of the weapon. Thirdly the rivet holes are set high up on the socket, immediately beneath the barbs. Shaft attachment employed a stout metal peg projecting through these holes almost to the width of the barbs. These pegs often survive, and are characteristic of no other spearhead types in these islands. Finally the thinness of the casting is often noteworthy.

In addition to these four basic types of barbed spearhead, a wide variety of other spearheads occasionally have slightly barbed or squared-off blade bases. Some of these may have been significant for the development of barbed spearheads, and will be considered below.

Distribution (fig. 1)

The distribution of Type I, II and III barbed spearheads has been mapped by one of us elsewhere (Burgess, 1968b, 25, fig. 16). Apart from the one Scottish find from Duddingston Loch, Midlothian, one from Ferriby, Yorks., and a fragment from 'Yorkshire', all barbed spearheads have come from Britain south of the River Humber. The finds form two interesting linear concentrations, firstly along the Thames Valley as far west as Berkshire, with outliers in Berkshire and Hampshire; and secondly a line extending from Devon/Somerset northwards through South Wales and the Marches to Cheshire, branching off to Derbyshire and Yorkshire. The finds along the south coast, from East Anglia, and from Alderney seem to be offshoots of the main distribution. It is noticeable that the examples from these areas are only small fragments in scrap hoards, whereas most of those from the main concentrations in the Thames Valley, south-west England, the Marches and the north are complete or near-complete examples. The main distribution of Types I–III forms an arc around East Anglia and the south-east, the classic Carp's tongue area, with the Thames providing the line for the single major penetration into this region.

The distribution of the individual classes is worthy of further attention:

Type I, the leaf-shaped Bloody Pool type, is known definitely from only five widely scattered sites representing very varied contexts. Only one, from Moulsford, Berks. (fig. 30:1) is a single find. This and the examples in the Bloody Pool (Devon), Ashley (Hants) and Bishop's Castle

fig. 1 Distribution maps: hoards encircled; –¦– regional provenance only

   a Hollow, lozenge-sectioned spearheads of the Wilburton Complex: ◎ multiple find

   b Barbed spearheads

   c The Broadward complex
       ● barbed spearhead (Types I–III only)
       ◉ hoard with barbed spearhead
       ◎ other spearhead hoards
       ▲ barbed spearheads in Series 2 hoards

   d The distribution of spearhead and sword hoards
       ● spearhead hoard
       ⊞ sword hoard

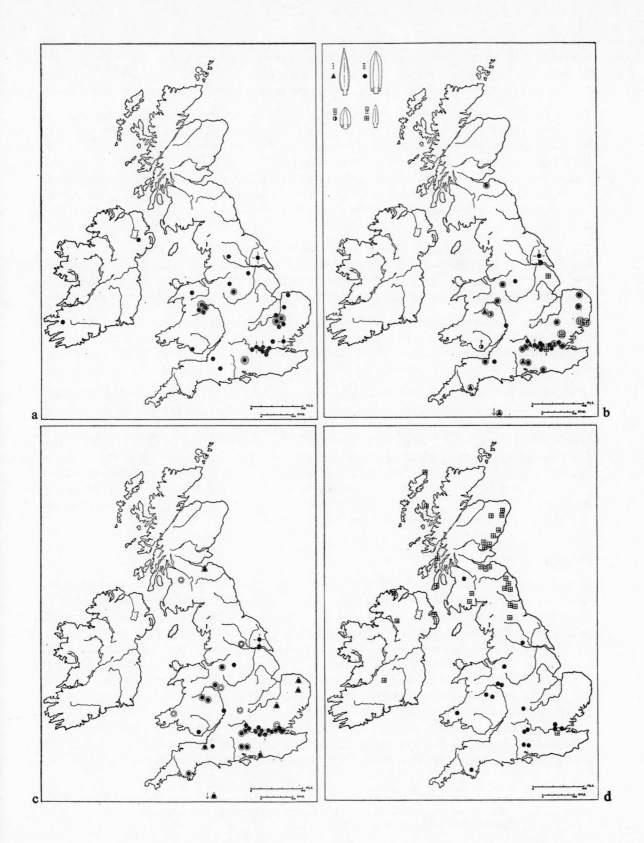

(Salop) hoards are all in the main areas of barbed spearhead concentration, and in contexts typical of these areas. The fifth occurrence, in the Longy Common hoard, Alderney, provides the exception in that it is both the only barbed spearhead to have been found outside mainland Britain, and the only Type I example to have come from a peripheral, Carp's tongue context.

Type II, the broad, parallel-sided Congleton type, is by far the commonest. It is interesting to note that the bulk of complete specimens are single finds, the large majority from rivers around the main arc of barbed spearhead distribution, especially the Thames. The Broadness hoard, Kent (figs 10–14), provides the only multiple association of complete and near-complete specimens, though the Congleton, Cheshire, and Speen, Berks., hoards (figs 23, 26) have single examples. Other hoard specimens are fragments, not surprisingly, since most of the hoards concerned are scrap finds. The bulk of the examples from the Carp's tongue south and east fall into this category.

Type III, the short Broadward type, is known only from the Broadward hoard itself, and, a single example, from the hoard of fused swords and spearheads from Thames Street, London (fig. 24). This is but one indication of Marches–Thames Valley connections which seem to have been important in the distribution of barbed spearheads (see below).

Type IV, the Donington type, has a markedly different distribution from the other three forms, coming mainly from those eastern regions in which classic barbed spearheads are rare. There is one from Lincolnshire, two from Suffolk, one from Essex and one from the Thames (figs 9, 27, 29).[1]

There are two general considerations to be noted about barbed spearhead distribution. Firstly, a minor point – the curious fact that all the barbed spearheads with lunate openings have come from hoards. No single finds have this feature. More important is the often noticed association of Type I–III barbed spearheads with watery environments. Of the 34 individual provenances, 22 are river, lake or bog sites. Of the rest, apart from those where the nature of the find-spot is uncertain, most are in the east and south-east, in those hoards where barbed spearheads seem to occur as intrusive scrap fragments. In the main areas of barbed spearhead distribution, practically all the find-spots are 'wet', and this has inevitably led to much speculation about the use of such distinctive implements (see below).

Origins

Barbed spearheads constitute a notably insular tradition. None have hitherto been found on the Continent, although the Alderney find suggests that isolated examples may have been carried across the Channel; but the total absence from Ireland is more puzzling. This insularity suggests origins lying wholly within the British spearhead series. Obviously possible lines of development are best sought in those areas where barbed spearheads are concentrated. The problem is to find potential starting-points for all the features which together characterise barbed spearheads: the barbs, the lozengic or flattened blade section and cavity, the short socket, the peg holes just beneath the blade, the big, projecting metal pin, and the thinness of the casting. Furthermore, such features must be sought among spearheads of a period prior to that when barbed spearheads were being made, which, broadly speaking, was the Ewart Park phase (see below).

This compels one to look among spearheads of the preceding Wilburton phase, and it is in the Wilburton tradition itself that most of the necessary spearhead features can be found. One

---

[1] Since the above was written, D. C. has identified another example in the Cumberlow Green hoard, Herts. (Clark, *Antiq. J.*, XX (1940), 61–2, pe. VII, shown as a hollow point). There is another possible fragment in the Green End Road hoard, Cambridge (*RCHM, Cambridge*, pl. 2).

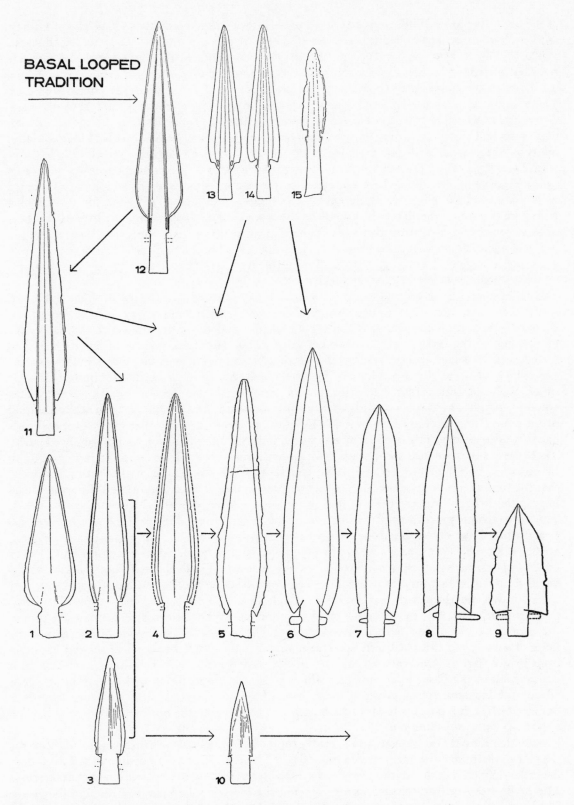

BASAL LOOPED
TRADITION

fig. 2 Theoretical development diagram for barbed spearheads

of the most diagnostic Wilburton spearhead types is the hollow-blade type, generally of lozenge section, but sometimes of elliptic section (Savory, 1958, 32; Butler, 1963, 106–8; Burgess, 1968a, 31, fig. 22:5–7; 1968b, 15, 36, fig. 9:14). These show a departure from the familiar rounded midrib of Bronze Age spearheads, and although many have a sharply ridged blade, others exhibit a comparatively flat section (figs 28:4; 29:3). The casting is remarkably thin. There is also a marked step separating the main, hollow blade from its solid bevelled edge. The socket is generally quite short, often of barbed spearhead proportions (figs. 28:3; 29:4), and, what is more, the peg holes are characteristically set high up, just below the blade base. Finally, many of these spearheads have slightly squared-off, and even slightly barbed, blade bases (figs 28:3; 29:1–3), a feature which is widespread among Wilburton spearheads generally. Quite clearly there is much here of relevance for barbed spearhead development: flattened section with hollow, elliptical blade cavity, the stepped blade/bevel division, the short socket with high peg holes, the thin metal, and the distinctive blade base treatment. Indeed it is possible to convert such spearheads to true barbed spearheads on paper merely by widening the bevelled edges, as the diagrams show (fig. 2), and as Greenwell and Brewis demonstrated sixty years ago (1909, pl. LXXV, fig. 58). R. A. Smith (1909–11, 164) also suggested this connection with hollow-bladed Wilburton spearheads.

It is thus easy to see a progression from these hollow-bladed spearheads to Type I barbed spearheads with their leaf-shaped blade of lozenge section (figs 2, 19, 20, 22, 27, 30:1, 9–10). More difficult to explain is the big metal pin, and the exaggeration of the barbs, the broadening of the blade, and the parallel sides which are characteristic of Type II barbed spearheads. In some respects Wilburton spearheads are useful here too. Some hollow-bladed examples have unusually broad blades (fig. 29:4), and these may be related to similarly shaped spearheads, but with rounded midribs, one of which, from the Thames at Kingston (Smith, 1909–11, 163, fig. 2), has a protruding metal pin. Some of the Blackmoor spearheads also had metal pins. These cases are very much in isolation, however, and another group of spearheads has to be called upon to provide a likely source both for the metal pin and pronounced barbs. These are the basal-looped spearheads, which have already been discussed as an influence upon fillet-defined and lunate-opening spearheads. It must be stressed from the outset, however, that the role of basal-looped spearheads is more problematical than that of the Wilburton spearheads, and is likely to have been of less importance, certainly in the development of Type I. The only obvious precursors of the large barbs of Type II weapons are the blade bases of the straight-based variety of basal-looped spearhead (Burgess, 1968a, 19, 22, 45, notes 93, 94; 1968b, 8, 35, 38, fig. 5), as R. A. Smith (1909–11, 164) noticed. Some examples have a very barbed appearance (fig. 28:5, 6). Basal-looped spearheads of both the leaf-shaped and straight-based forms provide a further possibility. The loops of these must often have broken off, and the result is a spearhead which is not only strongly barbed, but also has the stumps of its loops projecting on either side of the socket just below the blade. The effect is very much like that of the projecting pin of the barbed spearheads, and is illustrated here both by 'breaking' the loops of a complete straight-based specimen, and by an actual broken leaf-shaped example from Bristol (fig. 2). One can perhaps see in the configuration of projecting pin and barbs a new version of the basal loop, but one still serving the same function in shaft attachment (Bartlett & Hawkes, 1965). Given a large, broad basal-looped spearhead with torn loops and damaged edges, it is possible to produce something approaching the outline of a Type II barbed spearhead with projecting pin.

Attention should also be drawn to a small group of fillet-defined spearheads with slight barbs which can be termed the Staines type (fig. 28:1, 2). These weapons are distinguished from normal fillet-defined spearheads not only by their barbs, but also by their retention of characteristic Middle Bronze Age features such as a ridged midrib, or channelled blade. Although they have no associations, a Wilburton background seems likely on typological grounds, and they should occupy a position somewhere in the general interrelationship of basal-looped, fillet-defined, lunate-opening, Wilburton and barbed spearheads (fig. 2). A spearhead in the Broadness hoard is similar (fig. 12:12), but has the rounded midrib more appropriate to fillet-defined spearheads.

The chart (fig. 2) summarises the elements that may have influenced the development of barbed spearheads. Type III, the short Broadward form, may be seen as an individualistic local variation of Type II. Type IV seems to have been a separate, simpler development from Wilburton hollow spearheads with rudimentary barbs. Indeed, one of the latter, from the Guilsfield hoard (fig. 28:3), has a form very close to that of Type IV spearheads.

While Wilburton spearheads are ideally placed, chronologically, to have influenced barbed spearhead development, basal-looped spearheads, nominally Middle Bronze Age, might seem a different matter. Fortunately there is abundant evidence, as we have seen, for the survival of all forms of basal-looped spearhead right through the Wilburton phase into the beginning of the Ewart Park phase (Coles, Coutts & Ryder, 1964; Burgess, 1968a, 19, 22, 45, n. 94; 1968b, 38). This is best attested in the north and Ireland and, by analogy, in the west. The situation in the south-east is much less certain, for here the development of Wilburton metal-working brought Middle Bronze Age traditions to an end around the tenth century BC (Burgess, 1968a; 1968b, 9–17). But at least on the fringes of the Wilburton province, abutting on to lands which were still technologically Middle Bronze Age, basal-looped spearheads remained in use. In Lincolnshire, one was included in the Wilburton hoard from Nettleham (Trollope, 1861; Kendrick & Hawkes, 1932, 132, fig. 55), and in Berkshire one deposited with a barbed spearhead at Speen (fig. 23) shows survival into the Ewart Park phase. The Berkshire hoard of Yattendon, also deposited in this period, includes three examples (fig. 15:7–9), but as it contains many scrap survivals from earlier periods, this need not be significant.

Study of the distribution of Wilburton and basal-looped spearheads should enable one to determine the development area of barbed spearheads. It is clear that the main barbed spearhead areas (fig. 1b) overlapped only partly with the main Wilburton province (map, Burgess, 1968b, 12, fig. 8). This state of affairs is even more marked if one considers only complete and near-complete barbed spearheads of Types I–III. The main Wilburton lands were in the area from the Thames to Cambridgeshire, and in Hampshire. The most important areas of overlap with barbed spearheads are in the Thames Valley and Hampshire. If one narrows the search to Wilburton hollow spearheads, and Wilburton spearheads with slightly squared-off or barbed blade bases, the concentrations are seen to lie not only in the Cambridge region, the Thames Valley and Hampshire, but also in the upper Severn basin, in Shropshire and Montgomeryshire (fig. 1a). From the point of view of barbed spearhead development the Cambridge region can be ruled out, since barbed spearheads never became important there. One is left with the Thames Valley, Hampshire and the upper Severn Basin as areas in which both Wilburton and barbed spearheads are concentrated. If the Wilburton spearheads provided the main inspiration behind barbed spearheads then any of these regions could have been the area of inception. But if basal-looped influence was involved, then the field can be narrowed down.

The main concentrations of basal-looped spearheads, especially the straight-based form, are in the Thames Valley, the Fens, and Ireland. Again the Fens, like Ireland, must be ruled out as non-barbed spearhead areas. Basal-looped spearheads are almost wholly absent from Hampshire and the upper Severn region. One is left with the inescapable conclusion that if barbed spearheads reflect basal-looped influence to any great extent, then the Thames Valley is likely to have been the area of development, as the only region in which all the relevant Wilburton and basal-looped spearhead types and barbed spearheads were plentiful. Since barbed spearheads (apart from Type IV) seem to have had no place in the Carp's tongue complex, and the Thames Valley up to London was one of the most important Carp's tongue areas (map, Burgess, 1968b, 23, fig. 14), the Thames Valley above London may have been the area of inception. The vast concentration of Carp's tongue material peters out markedly beyond the Surrey border, and it is the Berkshire stretches of the river beyond, which have produced the greatest density of barbed spearheads. Of course a more complex evolution sequence is possible, with Type I barbed spearheads developing out of Wilburton forms in the Marches or in Hampshire, and in turn being converted into Type II under basal-looped influence in the Thames Valley. The available evidence admits no certain solution.

The chronology of barbed spearhead development seems fairly secure. There is not one scrap of a barbed spearhead in any of those late Wilburton hoards which seem to stand at the transition to the new metal-working of the Ewart Park phase in the eighth century: Isleham, Fulbourn Common, Blackmoor, Sturry (Jessup, 1943; Grace, 1943) and Guilsfield (Davies, 1967, 105–6; Burgess, 1962, 23–4; 1968b, 36–7). On the other hand three of these hoards contain spearheads of the types which contributed to barbed spearhead development. This process seems therefore to have taken place after the transitional period. A clue to the sequence is provided by the associations of barbed spearheads in their main areas of distribution. The Wilburton element is still very strong, although we have seen that the time must be post-Wilburton and, as we shall see, contemporary with the Carp's tongue complex. Now, it seems likely that the eighth century was an unsettled period for metal-workers in south-east England. The Wilburton tradition was under pressure from influences which eventually ushered in the industrial revolution of the Ewart Park phase (Burgess, 1968b, 17). There is some evidence for a movement of Wilburton smiths, or a traffic in outmoded Wilburton metalwork, to the west and north, for the main Wilburton finds of northern England, Wales, the Marches and Ireland all seem to have been deposited at this time (Burgess, 1968a, 40). A movement of metal-workers, not just metalwork, is suggested by the continuation of Wilburton traditions in the north and west, as we have noticed above, contrasting with their total eclipse by Carp's tongue metal-working in the south. This same late Wilburton movement may well have taken lead-bronze and the Ewart Park sword westwards and northwards, for these had been adopted throughout these islands by the end of the eighth century. In just such a climate of change, Thames Valley smiths could have developed barbed spearheads, which were subsequently carried up the Thames Valley and beyond in the general movement westwards. But this Thames–West axis must then have remained open, for the new Carp's tongue metal-working petered out beyond the Wey, while the connections between the Broadward, Broadness and Thames Street hoards (see below) betoken a continuing relationship, and a movement eastwards as well as westwards.

Function

Most writers since Evans have agreed that the barbs of these spearheads could not have served their obvious function of preventing dislodgement. Because of the length and breadth of such weapons, a tremendous thrust would have been required to achieve penetration beyond the barbs. Even then the projecting pin close up to the barbs would have rendered the effort useless. Early writers on the subject generally regarded them as fish spears or harpoons because of their association with rivers, lakes and bogs, and of the widespread use of barbs on fish hooks and fish spears among primitive communities. To be effective, however, the fish spear has to have barbs near the point even if they do extend down to the socket. Their use as fish spears was questioned by Evans (1881, 338), who suggested that they were far too big to have been used in the spearing of any British fish, observing they 'would have made sad havoc even of a forty-pound salmon'. He suggested instead that they might have been used in hunting large wild animals, though their restricted distribution would argue an importance beyond this.

The barbs could therefore hardly have served the normal function of weapon barbs. Their position is completely wrong. Nor is it likely that the spearheads themselves, at least Types II and III, could have been intended as weapons of penetration. Their shape is completely unsuitable, broad, parallel-sided with wide point, and they are generally flimsy objects, the casting much thinner than usual, as R. A. Smith observed (1909–11, 163). Their makers 'seem to have aimed at breadth rather than solidity', he went on. Nor was the socket and blade cavity conducive to normal, functional shaft attachment. The socket is remarkably short and small for such large implements, and it was not as if a shaft could be passed through the socket into the cavity beyond. The thickness of the middle of the implement lessens markedly above the socket, and the cavity within rapidly becomes a low ellipse, unsuitable for receiving a normal shaft. Furthermore, the cavity on many examples was never cleared of its clay core, and one finds them completely blocked beyond the external socket. The shaft attachment would thus have been limited to the length of the socket, and this was far too short to provide a conventional shafting strong and secure enough for either a throwing or a thrusting weapon. Hawkes (in Bartlett & Hawkes, 1965) suggested that this weakness could be overcome by using a less obvious shaft attachment method, and saw the barbed spearhead as the answer to the leather shield. The socket would be fitted with a separate small wooden butt-piece with projecting tongue, this to fit into a slot in the main shaft, the two being held together by a leather thong passing from the main shaft and round the metal pin. The spearhead and peg would be released on impact with the shield, but would still remain attached to the main shaft by the thong. The shaft then becomes an encumbrance hindering proper use of the shield. Hawkes compared this with the later Roman *pilum*, which employed the same encumbrance principle.

Without practical experiment it is difficult to gauge the feasibility of this suggestion, but work on leather shields by Coles (1966–7, 19) has shown that they were strong enough to withstand repeated blows from a specially sharpened bronze sword. Thus, it is difficult to imagine effective penetration by a large spearhead with a wide blunt point and parallel sides, especially if the weapon was thrown. Leather shields are so far known only from Ireland, yet barbed spearheads are not known there. If they were an effective answer to leather shields, one would have expected them to appear in Ireland. Used as an encumbrance weapon in this way, they may have been effective against big game rather than against shields, as Evans conceived (1881, 338). But the barbs still remain unaccounted for.

To suggest a practical use for a spearhead with broad parallel sides, wide blunt point, large barbs, short socket and projecting bronze pin is therefore difficult. They seem to have no particular advantages in hunting or fighting; in fact, they have serious disadvantages for both of these pursuits. In view of this, one cannot overlook their possible use as ceremonial and decorative weapons like the bronze shields of this period (Coles, 1962, 185) and the parade armour of the Iron Age and Romano-British periods. The idea of parade weapons in Britain can be taken back at least into the Middle Bronze Age, where very long basal-looped spearheads are known, far too big to have been used effectively, and far too grand for their owners to have risked actually using them (Coles, Coutts & Ryder, 1964, 191). Large ceremonial rapiers, copies of functional smaller ones, are also known from both sides of the Channel. In Ireland and Britain there are unpractically long and thin examples such as that from Lissane, Co. Derry (Evans, 1881, 252, fig. 318); and on the Continent there are the great ceremonial weapons from Ommerschans, Holland, and from Plougrescant, Côte du Nord, and Beaune, Côte d'Or, France (Butler & Bakker, 1961). Towards the end of the Wilburton phase it is noticeable that many objects, especially articles of horse gear, have elaborate decoration, and the emphasis seems to be on the visual effect of the warrior. This is a trend that became even more marked in the Ewart Park phase. Perhaps the barbed spearhead, elaborately lashed on to a wooden shaft with streamers hanging from the projecting pins, is part of the same tradition. Whatever the use of the spearhead itself, it does seem that the projecting pin may have been used for tying purposes, in which case the configuration of barbs, pin and the space between, can be seen as a version of the Middle Bronze Age basal loop. Without practical experiment who knows what other purpose may have been served, what sound-effect, for example, could have been produced by such an arrangement.

As well as being ceremonial weapons, barbed spearheads may have served a ritual or votive purpose. The Celtic tradition of depositing votive offerings in water is well known, and the fact that so much of the finest Bronze Age metalwork of Britain and Ireland has come from rivers and bogs may well indicate the same sort of thing. Coles, for example, recorded that 30 of the 36 bronze shields from Britain and Ireland have come from such contexts, and suggested they may have been deposited there as ritual objects (Coles, 1962, 185). Bronze shields, like barbed spearheads, seem designed to serve a ceremonial rather than a practical use. The Llynfawr find (Fox & Hyde, 1939) can be interpreted as a ritual water deposit, as can the Llyn Cerrig Bach find several centuries later (Fox, 1946). On the Continent the idea of ritual deposits in the Bronze Age has long been accepted (Hundt, 1955; Jacob-Friesen, 1968, 272–4), and Butler and Bakker (1961, 208) regarded the bog hoard from Ommerschans in the Netherland as a votive deposit. Lawrence (1929, 69) thought that some of the Thames bronzes might have been cast into the river as votive offerings, and Trump (1968, 222) has made the same suggestion to account for the great concentrations of rapiers from the Fens and the Thames. Eogan has also raised this possibility for Irish material (Eogan, 1964, 311–14).

Type IV weapons, not barbed spearheads in the classic sense, seem outside the main line of barbed spearhead development. R. A. Smith (1909–11, 166) figured and described the example from the Hatfield Broad Oak hoard as an embryonic barbed spearhead, and Thompson (1954) published the Donington specimen as cut down from a spearhead of Type I or II. Hawkes suggested that they could have served as core models for the more familiar types of barbed spearhead (Bartlett & Hawkes, 1965), but for various reasons we believe this unlikely. Firstly, the position of the peg-holes on all the five examples known is higher even than on Type I–III spearheads, right up at the barb roots. If one retained this placing from mould to final casting, the holes would be masked by the barbs, which would prevent insertion of the characteristic long pin. Secondly, although the blocked sockets of many barbed spearheads make it impossible to measure their core lengths, these would generally seem to have been either much longer or shorter than the Type IV implements. A third and most important point is the easterly distribution of Type IV, contrasting strongly with the pattern for Types I–III. What is more, three of the five came from Carp's tongue hoards, which suggests that they belong to a different tradition from classic barbed spearheads and are perhaps their eastern equivalents. Since they are altogether more functional than Types I–III, being slimmer, smaller and only slightly barbed, it is interesting that they apparently achieved no great success. Clearly, like Types I–III, they were a development from Wilburton spearheads, especially hollow-bladed types, but the development may well have been parallel to, and unconnected with, that of true barbed spearheads. Certainly, it is difficult to see them in any ancestral or derivative role.

C.B., D.C., D.G.D.

(iv) THE PLACE OF THE BROADWARD HOARD AND BARBED SPEARHEADS IN THE BRITISH LATE BRONZE AGE

Barbed spearheads have been found in a considerable number of hoards, and the contents of these, and of other relevant hoards, are shown as an association diagram in fig. 3. This reveals that one is dealing with two different series of hoards, series 1 in which the spearhead/ferrule element is overwhelmingly dominant, and series 2 in which the emphasis is on socketed axes, tools and ingot metal. There is also a distributional difference between the two, series 1 coming from central-southern England, the west and north, series 2 from the Carp's tongue lands of the south-east. There is inevitably some overlap in content: for example, Ewart Park swords and plain spearheads occur in both groups. Two hoards, from Yattendon and Stogursey, occupy an intermediate position in that they lie outside the series 2 area, and are strong in spearheads,

fig. 3 Association diagram for hoards with barbed spearheads (Types I-III), and spearhead hoards.

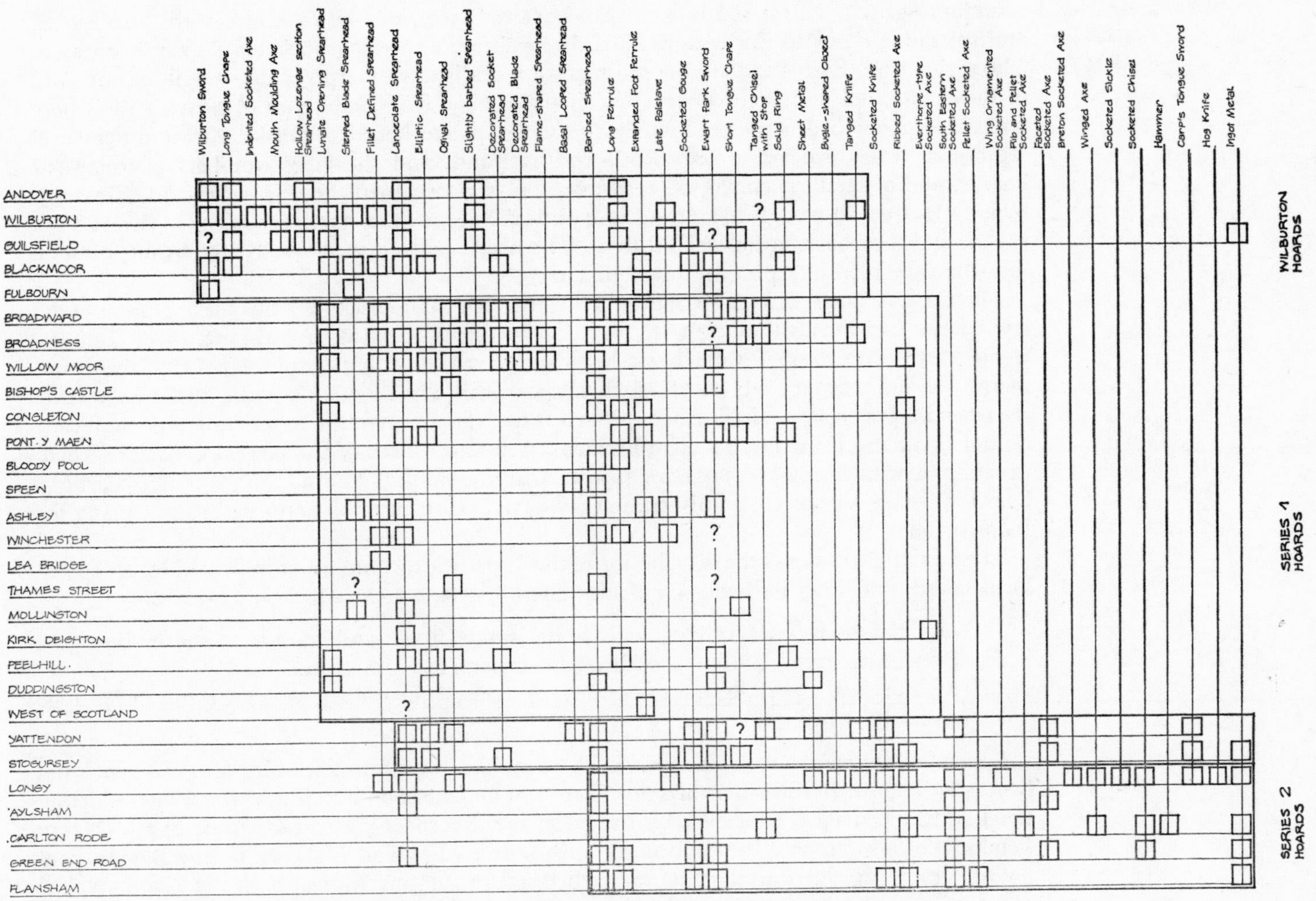

as well as in axes, tools and ingot metal. For the sake of comparison, some Wilburton hoards have also been added to the table.

The Broadward hoard clearly belongs to the remarkable group of spearhead hoards, and it is equally clear that the distribution of these corresponds closely with that of barbed spearheads. It has long been realised that metal-working in Britain and Ireland in the Ewart Park phase, from the eighth century, can be divided regionally on a basis of socketed axe types (Hodges, 1956, 31; Burgess 1968b, 17–26). It is also evident that regional hoard types can be distinguished, their differences suggesting all manner of social, cultural, technological and political variations, the nature of which can hardly be guessed at. Our two series of hoards suggest two very different states of affairs. The spearhead hoards, centred in the region from Cheshire to Devon and eastwards to the London basin, must be classed as warrior hoards, and, what is more, postulate a wide area in which spear warriors were dominant. Some of them had Ewart Park swords too, but socketed axes and tools are notably rare in these hoards. Contrast the situation in a northeastern region stretching from north Yorkshire up into eastern Scotland, where a very different type of warrior hoard predominates. These are smaller than the spearhead hoards, and consist instead of swords, generally two or three, with rings (for sword harness?) and chapes also

229

common (fig. 1d). To the south of this land of sword warriors, in Yorkshire and Lincolnshire, and spreading down to East Anglia, hoards consisting entirely of socketed axes are common. The region from East Anglia to the south coast is undisputed Carp's tongue territory, the land of those axe, tool and ingot hoards which make up our second series of hoards. Elsewhere notable regional hoard groups include the socketed axe hoards of the Llantwit province of south-east Wales, spreading into south-west England, and the large numbers of ornament hoards, and of small, personal socketed axe, tool and ornament hoards in Ireland. Clearly a region's hoards do not always reveal its political state, as the hundreds of stray Ewart Park swords and spearheads from Ireland show. The hoard pattern is obviously significant, but one must be careful in interpreting this significance.

The Carp's tongue series 2 hoards are less important than series 1 for this survey, because the few barbed spearheads they contain are scrap fragments, and apparently intrusive. Unifying trends clearly run through the series 1 hoards, and the association table shows that this is not merely the fact that they all consist largely of spearheads and ferrules, but also because the same spearhead types occur again and again. Barbed spearheads are but one unifying type, and they do not occur in all the hoards. The Broadward hoard, as one of the largest finds concerned, provides us with a suitable name for this spearhead complex. Hardly any of these spearhead hoards have been properly published, so they have been illustrated here (figs. 4–27), many for the first time.

The map (fig. 1c) shows the distribution of this Broadward complex, as indicated by the spearhead hoards and stray barbed spearheads. The important areas which emerge are:

1. The Thames–Kennet valleys, with many single finds, and hoards at the eastern and western extremities, and in a southward extension in Hampshire.
2. The Marches, especially the upper Severn area of Shropshire, which has produced four massive hoards.

Other finds show penetrations into Derbyshire and southern Yorkshire and even into the Scottish lowlands. In the other direction there was an extension into south-west Wales, skirting the Llantwit province, as shown by the large bog hoard of spearheads from Pant-y-Maen, Pembs. (Griffiths, 1957). Penetration of south-western England is shown by the Bloody Pool hoard, Devon (fig. 22), and the Godney barbed spearhead, but this was basically 'South-Welsh' axe territory, closely linked to the Llantwit province across the Bristol Channel (Burgess, 1968b, 19, 21).

Of all these spearhead hoards, that from Broadness most clearly resembles the Broadward find, a remarkable coincidence in view of their similar names and the fact that they lie at opposite ends of the Broadward territory. They share not only barbed, lunate-opening, fillet-defined and ogival spearheads, but also spearheads with decorated blades, long ferrules, sword fragments, diminutive chapes and tanged chisels. Broadward has in addition expanded-foot ferrules, Broadness elliptic, lanceolate and various, less familiar spearheads. Admittedly Broadward has Type III and Broadness Type II spearheads, but another Thames hoard, from Thames Street, London (fig. 24) has the only Type III barbed spearhead outside the Broadward hoard, and strongly reinforces this connection between Shropshire and the London area.

It is unfortunate that of the three other relevant Shropshire hoards, two, found at Willow Moor about 1790 and at Bishop's Castle in 1862, are completely lost, though drawings of a few pieces from the latter (which comprised hundreds of spearheads) do exist (fig. 27, Appendices 1 & 2). These show a fine Type I barbed spearhead with lunate-openings, lanceolate spearheads and Ewart Park sword fragments. The third hoard, found at Willow Moor in 1834, included about 150 spearheads, but it too has been largely dispersed. Miss Chitty's detective work (1928) has shown how close it must have been to Broadward and Broadness in its contents, including barbed, lunate, fillet-defined, decorated-blade, ogival, elliptic and lanceolate spearheads, as well as Ewart Park swords. The other hoard from the Marches, from Congleton, Cheshire (fig. 26) is very different, constituting a personal deposit of two spearheads, one barbed, one lunate-opening, two ferrules, including an expanded-foot specimen, and one socketed axe. The presence of the latter is significant, for to the north and west of Cheshire, axes become a more regular component in hoards. Shropshire has yielded another spearhead hoard, now lost, from Snead (Appendix 1), but nothing is known about the contents or relevance of this find.

The Broadness hoard is the most important of what may be termed a southern group of seven hoards. A fillet-defined spearhead is all that remains of a bucketful found at Lea Bridge, Walthamstow. The Thames Street hoard comprises six spearheads and two sword blade fragments very badly corroded, and fused together (fig. 24). Two ogival spearheads and the important Type III barbed spearhead noted above have become detached from the tangled mass. It is impossible to identify for certain the spearheads still fused together, but two seem to have had hollow blades (though with rounded midribs), and one of these may be of the stepped blade type found in other hoards of this group. The stepped blade spearhead is certainly represented in the hoard from Ashley Wood, Hants (fig. 19) together with Type I barbed, fillet-defined and lanceolate spearheads, mostly fragmentary, the bottom of an expanded-foot ferrule, Ewart Park sword fragments, and an element not encountered hitherto, a 'Late' palstave. The spearhead/ferrule element, though dominant, is not as completely so as in the hoards examined hitherto. The trend is repeated in both the 'Winchester' (fig. 21) and Yattendon hoards. The Winchester find has a tubular ferrule and large numbers of spearhead fragments, including Type II barbed, some with lunate openings, and fillet-defined examples; but it also has sword blade fragments, and pieces of both socketed axes and 'Late' palstaves. In the Yattendon hoard (figs 15–18) the proportion of spearheads has dropped to a half, 28 out of 59 pieces, and in addition to Ewart Park sword fragments, socketed axes and palstaves, there is a large tool element. Tanged and socketed knives, tanged chisels and socketed gouges are all strongly represented. The spearheads include, in addition to fragments of Type II barbed spearheads, ogival, lanceolate and elliptic forms, but basal-looped and side-looped specimens are also present, though whether as scrap survivors or contemporary pieces is impossible to say. There is some metallurgical evidence[1] for the local survival of side-looped spearheads through the Wilburton phase, and the Speen association of Type II barbed spearhead and basal-looped spearhead (fig. 23) suggests the same for basal-looped spearheads.

The increased proportion of implements other than spearheads in these Hampshire and Berkshire hoards presumably reflects their proximity to the Carp's tongue province, with its great emphasis on axe and tool hoards.

An unpublished hoard found between Mollington and Warmington on the Oxfordshire–Warwickshire border (fig. 25) serves, together with the Type II barbed spearhead from the Severn below Worcester, as a link between these two major groups of hoards. The Mollington hoard comprises lanceolate spearheads, a stepped blade spearhead, and a short tongue chape of Stogursey type.

Outside these two main hoard groups, spearhead hoards, like barbed spearheads, are widely scattered. They may best be dealt with on a regional basis:

[1] Unfortunately available analyses of Yattendon implements (Coghlan, 1970) do not cover definite basal-looped or side-looped specimens. Coghlan's Y.35 is probably a side-looped spearhead, however, and the metal of this is lead-bronze (2·8% lead). This supports earlier evidence for the survival, even in the south, of side-looped spearheads into a period when lead-bronze was used (Brown & Blin-Stoyle, 1959, 199; including a lead-bronze side-looped spearhead from Fyfield, Berkshire). There is another pointer to the contemporaneity of the Yattendon side-looped spearheads with at least some of the Late Bronze Age material in the hoard. This relates to the remarkable incidence of faceting among the Yattendon implements of surfaces which are normally smoothly curved. A pegged, leaf spearhead and two socketed gouges exhibit this most unusual feature – and so does the midrib of one of the side-looped spearheads.

Scotland The hoard of spearheads, Ewart Park swords and a bucket fragment from Duddings-ton Loch is well-known (Callander, 1921–2). In addition to its fine Type II barbed spearhead with lunate openings (fig. 31:54), it included lunate-opening and lanceolate spearheads. The hoard from Peelhill, Lanarks. (Coles & Scott, 1962–3) is more truly a spearhead hoard, with 28 spearheads and two ferrule fragments out of 36 pieces found. With lunate-opening, elliptic, lanceolate and ogival spearheads, and tubular ferrule fragments, this hoard looks very much out of place in Scotland, and would have seemed far more at home if found in the Marches. Its broad, lunate-opening spearhead is very similar to the one in the Broadness hoard, and its plain spearheads include examples with grooved socket bases. Three rings and Ewart Park sword fragments are more what one would expect of the Scottish sword hoard group. Another hoard, from the 'West of Scotland' (Coles, 1959–60, 134), comprising two plain leaf-shaped spearheads and a disc-foot ferrule, can also be related to this Broadward group.

Northern England From Congleton, single finds of Type II barbed spearheads from Cow Dale, Derbyshire (fig. 31:21) and the Humber bank at Ferriby (fig. 32:52), and the point of another from 'Yorkshire', lead to interesting hoards from Bilton and Kirk Deighton. The latter is a spearhead hoard of three lanceolate examples and a socketed axe (Radley, 1966). The Bilton find is a mixed hoard of seven spearheads and six socketed axes, together with two Ewart Park sword fragments (Howarth, 1899). Its main interest is a spearhead with blade decoration of hatched triangles, a rare parallel for the Broadward and Broadness examples. It also includes fillet-defined, lanceolate and elliptic spearheads.

Wales The lost Pendoylan barbed spearhead is the only sign of Broadward influence in the Llantwit province in south-east Wales, and evidence from North Wales is equally lacking. An important spearhead hoard from Pant-y-Maen, Pembs. (Griffiths, 1957) suggests penetration of south-west Wales, though this find is very much in isolation. The surviving material includes 17 spearheads and 5 ferrules out of 29 pieces. The spearheads are fragmentary, and all are plain lanceolate and elliptic examples. The ferrules comprise three expanded-foot and two tubular examples. Fragments of Ewart Park swords, a diminutive chape and three lost rings indicate a contrasting element in the find, though the chape is very similar to that in the Broadness hoard.

South-West England The territory to the south of the Bristol Channel was, by and large, related to the Llantwit province of south-east Wales. This is clear from the distribution of 'South-Welsh' and faceted socketed axes, and moulds for their manufacture, in the south-west (Burgess, 1968b, 19, 21). From Stogursey, Somerset, has come the largest single find of 'South-Welsh' socketed axes (pls X–XII), so that one can envisage a Llantwit-Stogursey metal-working province centred on both sides of the Bristol Channel.

The Stogursey hoard includes fragments of barbed spearheads, and is the only hoard which directly links this tradition with the Broadward complex. The only other evidence for Broad-ward penetration of the south-west is the Type II barbed spearhead from Godney, Somerset (fig. 32:44), and a typical spearhead hoard from Bloody Pool, Devon (fig. 22). This comprised a number of Type I barbed spearheads, a plain spearhead and tubular ferrules, but today only a few fragments survive.

Series 2 hoards Most of the finds discussed above have come from outside the well-defined Carp's tongue province of south-eastern England, but we have seen that there are a few typical scrap hoards from this area, series 2 hoards, which include barbed spearhead fragments. Three are from East Anglia – Aylsham and Carleton Rode in Norfolk (Norwich Castle Museum, 1966), and Green End Road, Cambridge (*RCHM, Cambridge*, I, pl. 2) – one from the south coast, Flansham, Sussex (Hearne, 1940), while there is a fifth relevant hoard from Longy Common, Alderney (Kendrick, 1928, pls VII, VIII). They show the emphasis on axes, tools and ingot metal so typical of Carp's tongue hoards, and have a correspondingly small spearhead/

ferrule element. Characteristic of French Carp's tongue hoards, but much less a feature of the English finds, is a great range of bric-à-brac (Burgess, 1968b, 17, 38-9). It is not surprising, therefore, that of these series 2 hoards, only that from Longy Common is strong in bric-à-brac (fig. 3). Carp's tongue hoards, however, on both sides of the Channel are clearly founders' deposits of scrap implements and ingot metal, occasionally incorporating exotic fragments. It therefore seems sensible to regard the few barbed spearhead fragments from these series 2 hoards firstly as scrap metal, and secondly as foreign scrap, since such spearheads are clearly not at home in Carp's tongue areas. Their paucity is surprising in view of the strong Wilburton traditions in East Anglia in particular. It reinforces the impression that true barbed spearheads served a very particular need, one which did not exist, or was not felt, in the east. This is further emphasised by the total absence of barbed spearheads in the Carp's tongue areas of France, so closely related to south-east England at this time. Yet other products from Western Britain found their way to Carp's tongue France in this period, notably a considerable number of 'South-Welsh' socketed axes (Savory, 1965, 187; Burgess, 1968b, 21 with n. 83). The situation is understandable, however, if one regards barbed spearheads as serving a ceremonial and religious need among the people of a restricted part of England.

The south-eastern Carp's tongue hoards do have their Type IV spearheads, but these are not barbed spearheads in the true sense. They are altogether more functional than the weapons of Types I–III, and it is therefore surprising that they achieved such little popularity. Although their associations are so very different from those of Type I–III spearheads, it is interesting to note that the Levington hoard provides one of the closest parallels for the exaggerated flame-shaped blade of the Broadness decorated spearhead (figs. 13:26; 27:10). The Levington hoard has additional interest in that, while it is a classic English Carp's tongue hoard, and thus totally different in its character from individual hoards of the Broadward group, yet so many of its constituents can be found in different Broadward contexts: ogival spearheads, including some with grooved sockets, tanged chisels, Ewart Park swords, ribbed socketed axes, and a bugle-shaped object. This should provide a pointer to the chronology of the Broadward complex.

Chronology

Just as the development of barbed spearheads owed much to the spearheads of the Wilburton tradition, so what may be called the Broadward complex clearly had Wilburton roots. The relationship was certainly more than an industrial one. Just as the Broadward complex has an essentially martial character, so the Wilburton tradition was basically warrior-orientated. Hoards of the Broadward complex consist largely of spearheads and ferrules and in this respect also they follow the Wilburton pattern. For Wilburton hoards also are strong in spearheads, though admittedly they have strong sword/chape elements as well and do not give such an impression of almost total reliance on the spear. In Wilburton, as in Broadward contexts, axes and tools are rare, though here too the trend is more marked in the Broadward hoards.

In industrial terms also the Broadward complex was the inheritor of Wilburton traditions, for it took over a considerable part of the Wilburton repertoire (fig. 3). Lunate-opening, fillet-defined, stepped blade and plain spearheads (including hollow blade forms), tubular and disc-foot ferrules, tongue chapes, and even Ewart Park swords, 'Late' palstaves and lead-bronze can be regarded as part of this Wilburton inheritance. With hoards of the Broadward group showing so much Wilburton material, it might be argued that they must have overlapped considerably with the Wilburton tradition. The evidence, however, is against this. We have seen that barbed spearheads are completely absent from the group of late Wilburton hoards – Wilburton itself, Isleham, Fulbourn Common, Blackmoor and Sturry – which mark the transition to the Ewart Park phase. But these hoards contain so many of the individual elements which went to make up barbed spearheads and the Broadward complex that the latter presumably represent the next stage of development.

Closer scrutiny of hoards in the Broadward group shows that, despite their large Wilburton content, they are demonstrably contemporary with the various regional metal-working traditions of the Ewart Park phase. These connections can best be taken by areas:

Connections with Carp's tongue metal-working

The bugle-shaped objects in the Broadward hoard are well-known, but there are other important links with the Carp's tongue complex. Even if one disregards the barbed spearheads in series 2 hoards as possible scrap survivals from an earlier period (and they could equally well be contemporary scrap) there still remain the Stogursey and Yattendon associations, both containing fragments of Carp's tongue swords.

The Llantwit-Stogursey tradition of the Bristol Channel region

The only direct association of 'South-Welsh' axes, the main Llantwit-Stogursey product, and barbed spearheads is in the Stogursey hoard itself. No hoards of the Broadward complex contain specifically Llantwit-Stogursey material or vice versa, though the Yattendon hoard includes a slender-faceted axe (fig. 17:40), a type characteristic of both Llantwit-Stogursey and Carp's tongue metal-working (Burgess, 1968b, 21, 38–9).

The Heathery Burn tradition

The 'Yorkshire' 3-ribbed socketed axe (Fox, 1933, 158, pl. ix, fig. 10B), the most diagnostic product of the north English Heathery Burn tradition (Burgess, 1968b, 19, 39–40) has only once been found associated with a barbed spearhead, in the Stogursey hoard. Two Yorkshire hoards provide evidence for Broadward–Heathery Burn connections, however. The Bilton hoard, related to the Broadward complex by its concentration of spearheads, notably one with decorated blade, includes among its socketed axes examples of two specifically Heathery Burn types. One is a Yorkshire 3-ribbed axe, and another is of the northern plain or Everthorpe type (Burgess, 1968b, 39–40, fig. 18:1, p. 29). The spearhead hoard from Kirk Deighton also includes one of these Everthorpe-type plain socketed axes. Finally the Broadness hoard includes a knife with ribbed tang, a type best represented in Heathery Burn contexts (Blundell & Longworth, 1967) and in the Dowris phase in Ireland (Eogan, 1964, 296).

The Duddingston phase of Scotland

The relationship of the Broadward complex to the Duddingston Loch find has already been discussed. This hoard, rich in spearheads, including a Type II barbed example, has given its name to the Duddingston phase of the Scottish Late Bronze Age (Coles, 1959–60). Two other Scottish spearhead hoards mentioned above can also be dated to this phase, that from the 'West of Scotland' (Coles, 1959–60, 24–5, 134), and the Peelhill hoard (Coles & Scott, 1962–3). The latter, while so closely related to the Broadward complex, also has the Ewart Park sword and ring combination characteristic of the sword hoards of eastern Scotland and north-east England (see above). These sword hoards clearly spanned the Duddingston/Heathery Burn phase (cf. Coles, 1959–60 for the dating of such hoards), lasting as late as the Tarves phase around 500 BC (Coles, 1959–60, 52–3). The Tarves hoard itself included a short tongue chape of Stogursey type. Another spearhead hoard of the Broadward group includes this sword/ring element, that from Pant-y-Maen.

Finally, it is possible to make more general observations about the dating of the hoards of the Broadward group, some of which contain implements referable to the Ewart Park phase, if not to a particular regional industry. This applies to the as yet undifferentiated 3-ribbed socketed axes in the Congleton and Willow Moor hoards, the Willow Moor socketed sword (Hartshorne,

1841; Brailsford, 1947), and the Broadward and Broadness tanged chisels. The fragments of distinctive fillet-defined spearheads with hollow heads in the Ashley and Winchester hoards (figs 20, 21) seem best paralleled in the Great Freeman Street, Nottingham, hoard (M. A. Smith, 1957, GB.22(2), 20, 21). This find has obvious Broadward affinities, with its range of spearheads and tubular ferrule, its ribbed 'Late' palstave like those in the Ashley and Winchester hoards, and a ribbed, tanged knife like that from Broadness. But it must have been deposited well within the Ewart Park phase on the evidence of its socketed axes, including Yorkshire 3-ribbed examples. The Broadness 'stud' (fig. 14:47) also demands a late date, for it represents a type common in both Carp's tongue and Hallstatt contexts, and is found in the Staple Howe palisade settlement.[1]

How long the Broadward complex survived in the Ewart Park phase is difficult to determine, since there are so few points of contact with Continental chronologies. It is a pity that the degree of contemporaneity of material in Carp's tongue hoards presents such a problem. For the Longy Common hoard combines barbed spearhead fragments with a Breton socketed axe, a type generally thought of as late seventh–sixth centuries and even later in date (Briard, 1965, 271–5). Similarly the short type of tongue chape present in the Stogursey and Mollington hoards also occurs in the Tarves hoard, as we have seen, which should date around 500 BC. One can only conclude that there seems no reason why the Broadward complex should not have survived throughout the Ewart Park phase until the coming of iron. Certainly there is nothing else from the areas over which it is distributed which could have succeeded it in the same phase.

Conclusions

Barbed spearheads developed out of the great wealth of spearheads which were such a prominent feature of the Wilburton tradition of south-east England. Hollow-blade spearheads with lozengic and elliptic sections were particularly important in this development, but rudimentary barbs occurred on a wide variety of Wilburton spearheads. Of the areas in which these ancestral spearheads are concentrated, the middle Thames Valley, Hampshire and the upper Severn basin are important in this context. The distribution in the Severn basin resulted from the late Wilburton movement northwards and westwards. Any of these regions could have been the area of inception if the Wilburton spearheads alone led to barbed spearheads. But if, as is likely, basal-looped spearheads also played a part, then the Thames Valley above London is the likely area. In any case strong connections between the Severn basin and the Thames Valley continued from the time of the late Wilburton movement, which took Late Bronze Age technology and fashions to the west and north. Wilburton traditions were submerged over much of their homeland, in East Anglia and the Fens in particular, by the rise of Carp's tongue metalworking. The consequent dissemination of Wilburton elements contributed to the rise of a new tradition in the middle Thames Valley, Berkshire, Hampshire and the Marches. This preserved many of the old Wilburton traditions, and can be termed the Broadward complex after one of its most important hoards. These hoards are very distinctive, strong in spearheads and ferrules and retaining many Wilburton fashions especially spearhead types. The most distinctive of its spearheads was a new development, however—the barbed type. This served no obvious utilitarian purpose, and was perhaps evolved purely for ceremonial and ritual purposes. The Broadward complex probably dominated much of the Marches, the Thames Valley and central southern England through the Ewart Park phase until the coming of iron.

C.B., D.C., D.G.D.

[1] e.g. in Carp's tongue hoards from La Prairie de Mauves, Nantes (Briard, 1966, pl. 14), Ile Nihen, Morbihan (Briard, 1961, 58), and Azay-le-Rideau, I.-et-L., (Cordier, Millotte & Riquet, 1959, pl. 5); in Hallstatt C contexts e.g. tombelle A, Court-Saint-Etienne, in Belgium (Mariën, 1958, fig. 4), and apparently at Staple Howe, Yorkshire (Brewster, 1963).

APPENDIX 1—SPEARHEAD HOARDS

1 Bibliography:
> Bunny, 1860.
> Evans, 1870–3; 1881, 330, 333, 337, fig. 422.
> *VCH, Berks. I* (1906), 180 (fig.), 195.

2 Site and circumstances of discovery:
> Found in peat on Speen Moor in the Kennet Valley, 1½ miles N.W. of Newbury.

3 Collection:
> Not known.

4 Contents (fig. 23):
> 1. Barbed spearhead, Type II.
> 2. Basal-looped spearhead, leaf-shaped.

5 Further information:
> Illustrations here (fig. 23) based on drawings in B.I.C., which provides another source of information.

YATTENDON BERKSHIRE
1 Bibliography:
> Evans, 1879; 1881, 169, 403, 466, fig. 196.
> *VCH, Berks. I* (1906), 182–3, 196.
> Roskill, 1938.
> Coghlan, 1970.

2 Site and circumstances of discovery:
> Found in the spring of 1878 ('1876' in Coghlan, 1970), in building Yattendon Court, on the top of a hill west of Yattendon village. The bronzes were discovered in preparing foundations for a terrace on the south side of the house. They were in a 'wet, drab clay', 18 in. down in a mass of gravel, and this was coloured red, purple and black by 'the action of fire'. The bronzes adjoined two great baulks of oak, placed crosswise, interpreted as the remains of a much later beacon.

3 Collection:
> Borough Museum, Newbury.

4 Contents (figs 15–18):
> 1–2. Two fragmentary barbed spearheads, Type II.
> 3–6. Four 'elliptical' leaf spearheads.
> 7–9. Three basal-looped spearheads.
> 10. Side-looped spearhead.
> 11–13. Three small leaf blades, probably of side-looped spearheads.
> 14. Leaf spearhead, with octagonal-faceted socket.
> 15–16. Two lanceolate leaf spearheads.
> 17. Ogival leaf spearhead.

> 18–25. Eight fragmentary leaf spearheads of uncertain type.
> 26–28. Three spearhead sockets.
> 29. Short, conical 'ferrule'.
> 30. Disc with necked perforation.
> 31–34. Four pieces of sheet metal.
> 35. Decorated flat axe.
> 36. Miniature low-flanged palstave.
> 37. Blade of low-flanged palstave.
> 38. Blade of 'transitional' palstave.
> 39. Socketed axe, 'South-eastern' plain type.
> 40. Socketed axe, slender faceted type.
> 41. Socketed axe, massive plain ('Sompting') type (Burgess, 1969).
> 42–44. Three tanged chisels.
> 45–50. Six socketed gouges.
> 51–52. Two socketed knives.
> 53. Knife with flanged tang.
> 54. Knife with riveted tang.
> 55–56. Two fragmentary sword hilts, Ewart Park type.
> 57. Upper blade of a leaf-shaped sword.
> 58. Carp's tongue sword blade fragment.
> 59. End of a tongue chape.

5 Further information:
> MS. on the find by H. Peake in the possession of the late Mr M. Waterhouse and Mrs Waterhouse at Yattendon, where the hoard was drawn by C.B., 1966. Hoard since deposited on loan at Newbury Museum.

CONGLETON CHESHIRE
1 Bibliography:
> Jackson, 1927.
> Varley & Jackson, 1940.
> Thompson, 1970.

2 Site and circumstances of discovery:
> Found 3–4 feet down in digging the foundations for a new school, New Street, Congleton, October, 1925.

3 Collection:
> Congleton Public Library (no. 4 lost).

4 Contents (fig. 26):
> 1. Barbed spearhead, Type II.
> 2. Lunate-opening spearhead.
> 3. Long tubular ferrule, with slightly dished closed end.
> 4. Short expanded-foot ferrule.
> 5. Socketed axe, three-ribbed.

5 Further information:
> None.

BLOODY POOL   DEVON

1 Bibliography:
   Tucker, 1855; 1867, 120–2.
   Rolls, 1861.
   Evans, 1881, 338–9, 465.
2 Site and circumstances of discovery:
   Found in a swampy hollow, formerly a pool,
   called 'Bloody Pool', at South Brent, on the
   edge of Dartmoor.
3 Collection:
   Royal Albert Memorial Museum, Exeter
   (survivors).
4 Contents (fig. 22):
   1–2. Two fragments of barbed spearheads,
       Type I.
   3–4. Two fragments of tubular ferrules.
   5. Lower part of plain leaf spearhead, of
       uncertain type.
5 Further information:
   6. Fragments of large Type I barbed spear-
       head, and
   7. Fragments of tubular ferrule drawn
       after Tucker, 1855, 1867. The hoard
       consisted of several spearheads, all
       except one barbed, and four ferrule
       fragments.

ASHLEY   HAMPSHIRE

1 Bibliography:
   None.
2 Site and circumstances of discovery:
   Found in ploughing up scrubland in Ashley
   Wood, 6 miles W. of Winchester.
3 Collection:
   Winchester City Museum.
4 Contents (figs 19, 20):
   1. Fragmentary barbed spearhead, Type I.
   2–3. Two points of barbed spearheads, Type
       I.
   4. Stepped-blade spearhead.
   5–7. Three lanceolate leaf spearheads.
   8–9. Two fragments of plain leaf spearheads
       of uncertain type.
   10–14. Five fragments of fillet-defined spear-
       heads.
   15. Base of expanded-foot ferrule.
   16–18. Three hilts of Ewart Park swords.
   19–21. Three sword blade fragments, much
       twisted.
   22. Palstave of 'Late' type.

5 Further information:
   The following fragments are not illustrated:
       Three fragments of fillet-defined spear-
       head.
       One piece of spearhead socket.
       Three fragments of plain leaf spear-
       heads of uncertain type.
       Three pieces of fused scrap.

WINCHESTER AREA   HAMPSHIRE

1 Bibliography:
   None.
2 Site and circumstances of discovery:
   Nothing known.
3 Collection:
   Winchester City Museum.
4 Contents (fig. 21):
   1. Four fragments, probably from one
       barbed spearhead, Type II.
   2. Tip of barbed spearhead, Type II.
   3–4. Two fragments of barbed spearheads,
       Type II.
   5–6. Two fragments of lunate-opening bar-
       bed spearheads, Type II.
   7–12. Six fragments of fillet-defined spear-
       heads.
   13. Two joining fragments of plain leaf
       spearhead of uncertain type.
   14–15. Two fragments of plain leaf spear-
       heads of uncertain type.
   16. Palstave of 'Late' type: butt probably
       from the same implement as blade.
   17. Palstave blade with decoration of three
       converging ribs, probably 'Late' type.
   18–20. Three blades of socketed axes of
       uncertain type.
5 Further information:
   The following fragments are not illustrated:
       21. Tip of tubular ferrule with rounded
           end.
       22. Tip of fillet-defined spearhead.
       23. Tip of leaf spearhead.
       24–26. Three pieces of leaf-shaped
           sword blade.
   Drawings based on preliminary sketches
   made by D.C., 1967, but the find was not
   available for further study in 1970, nor
   was any more information forthcoming.

BROADNESS   KENT
1 Bibliography:
   R. A. Smith, 1909–11.

2 Site and circumstances of discovery:
Dredged up off the west side of Broadness, between Greenhithe and Northfleet, in 1892. The implements came from the first few feet of deep ballast, below the superficial alluvial peat and clay deposits in the river bed.

3 Collections:
London Museum: mainly Lloyd and Corner collections. British Museum: mainly Greenwell collection.

4 Contents (figs 10–14):

1–5. Five complete barbed spearheads, Type II.
    1. L.M. C 886.
    2. L.M. C 880
    3. B.M. WG 1712, with lunate-openings.
    4. L.M. C 885.
    5. L.M. C 887.

6–10. Five fragments of barbed spearheads, Type II.
    6. L.M. C 898
    7. B.M. 1913,5–17,1
    8. L.M. C 897
    9. B.M. WG 1714
    10. B.M. WG 1713

11–17. Seven fillet-defined spearheads.
    11. L.M. C 879
    12. L.M. 49.107/836: slightly barbed. Grooved socket base. Fillets on socket sides decorated with lozenges bearing hatched feather pattern.
    13. L.M. 49.107/864
    14. L.M. C 901
    15. L.M. 49.107/854
    16. L.M. C 894: point of very large example.
    17. L.M. 49.107/846: fillets separated from midrib by narrow channel, in the manner of Knockans-type basal-looped spearheads, and they do not continue on to the sides of the socket.

18. Pegged spearhead with channelled, leaf blade:
Eglwyseg-Rosnoën type (Burgess, 1968b, 8–9, fig. 5:4b, 5). L.M. 49.107/843.

19–24. Lanceolate leaf spearheads.
    19. L.M. 49.107/848
    20. L.M. 49.107/847
    21. L.M. C 877
    22. L.M. 49.107/855

    23. L.M. 49.107/844: unusual ridged midrib.
    24. L.M. 49.107/842: bevel outlined by groove.

25. Broad elliptic leaf spearhead: L.M. C 895.

26. Flame-shaped spearhead, blade wings and socket decorated with hatched triangles and grooving: L.M. C 1138.

27. Ogival leaf spearhead, socket decorated with lines and arcs of short punch marks: B.M. WG 1717.

28–29. Two lunate-opening spearheads.
    28. B.M. WG 1718
    29. L.M. 49.107/865 and C 900: two joining pieces, an example of unusually broad form, with wide, flat mid-section and broad bevelled edges, suggesting strong barbed spearhead influence.

30–31. Two spearheads with leaf blades of rather kite-shaped outline.
    30. L.M. C 884
    31. B.M. WG 1716

32–33. Spearhead fragments.
    32. L.M. 49.107/859: upper part of a leaf blade.
    33. L.M. 49.107/874: socket only.

34–42 Nine tubular ferrules.
    34. B.M. WG 1721: complete long example with swollen centre.
    35. L.M. 49.107/867: tapering, ends broken.
    36. L.M. A 17579: tapering; closed flat end.
    37. L.M. 49.107/870: tapering; closed, flat, slightly expanded foot.
    38. L.M. C 904: mouth survives but foot gone. Head of fastening pin projects.
    39. L.M. 49.107/871: short; tapering to closed, flat foot.
    40. L.M. C 906: lower part only; closed, flat foot.
    41. L.M. C 903: broken at both ends; head of fastening pin projects.
    42. L.M. C 905: lower part; rather rounded, closed foot.

43. Point of leaf-shaped sword: L.M. 49.107/830.

44. Diminutive tongue chape: L.M. 49.107/868.

45. Knife with ribbed tang: B.M. WG 1720.

46. Tanged chisel: L.M. C 902.

47. Domed stud, bar at rear: L.M. C 1139.

5 Further information:
Validity as a closed find dealt with by R. A. Smith (1909–11). Hundreds of flints and a flanged axe, reputedly dredged up at the same time as the bronzes, were rejected by Smith as part of the hoard.

Specimens in the Lloyd Collection in the London Museum (49.107/ . . .) were originally described as 'part of a hoard found below Limehouse', but 49.107/865 joins to L.M. C 900, known to be from the Broadness find, to make a complete lunate-opening spearhead, which confirms that these 'Limehouse' implements are part of the Broadness material. It is known in any case that Lloyd acquired part of the Broadness find (R. A. Smith, 1909–11), and this is not otherwise accounted for. The 'Limehouse' implements added to the other known Broadness specimens make a total of 47 pieces, which is the number of Broadness implements recorded by Smith.

PEELHILL LANARKSHIRE
1 Bibliography:
Coles & Scott, 1962–3.
2 Site and circumstances of discovery:
A glacial moraine 300 yards N. of, and overlooking, Peelhill Farm, near Strathaven, Lanarkshire. Ploughed from a hollow in the moraine, a former bog, which was being drained and consolidated, in March 1961.
3 Collection:
Glasgow City Museum.
4 Contents (numbering from Coles & Scott, 1962–3):
1—3, 8, 11, 17, 18, 24, 25, 27: Eleven broad elliptic leaf spearheads, with 'thinned' midribs.
4. Plain, leaf spearhead with blade bases extending as wings down the socket sides to peg holes (cf. Broadward lunate-opening spearhead).
5, 10, 26. Three ogival leaf spearheads: 10 has grooved socket base.
6. Lanceolate leaf spearhead.
7. Lunate-opening spearhead, blade of broad, elliptic outline (cf. Broadness example).
9, 12, 13, 15, 16, 23, 28: Seven damaged leaf spearheads of uncertain type.
19–22. Four spearhead sockets: 19 is grooved.

29. Two fragments of tubular ferrule.
30. Socketed axe, plain, of rectangular section.
31. Leaf-shaped sword of Ewart Park type, in three pieces.
32–34. Three rings.
5 Further information:
None.

LEA BRIDGE LONDON
1 Bibliography:
Hatley, 1933, 13.
2 Site and circumstances of discovery:
In building the Lea Bridge waterworks, Walthamstow. Only one spearhead survives out of the 'bucketful' found, the rest being disposed of by workmen.
3 Collection:
Walthamstow Museum (survivor).
4 Contents:
1. Fillet-defined spearhead.
Remainder lost.
5 Further information:
Reputedly found with horse bones and fossil shark teeth.

THAMES STREET LONDON
1 Bibliography:
None.
2 Site and circumstances of discovery:
According to British Museum records, Thames Street, London, E.C.
3 Collection:
British Museum, 1868,75–2,1.
4 Contents (fig. 24):
1. Barbed spearhead, Type III.
2–3. Two damaged ogival leaf spearheads.
4–7. Twisted and fused together:
4. Leaf spearhead with hollow blade, possibly stepped-blade type.
5. Leaf spearhead with hollow blade, much damaged.
6–7. Two pieces of sword blade.
5 Further information:
Although reputedly from Thames Street, E.C., there is no Thames Street as such in London E.C., although there is a Lower Thames Street and an Upper Thames Street.

MOLLINGTON OXFORDSHIRE
1 Bibliography:
None.

2 Site and circumstances of discovery:
From Lower Farm, Mollington, between Mollington and Warmington on the Oxfordshire/Warwickshire border.

3 Collection:
County Museum, Warwick.

4 Contents (fig. 25):
1. Stepped blade spearhead.
2–4. Three lanceolate leaf spearheads.
5. Short tongue chape of Stogursey type, the foot having a disc terminal with central, downward-projecting boss. Fastening pin in position.

5 Further information:
None.

PANT-Y-MAEN   PEMBROKESHIRE

1 Bibliography:
Evans, 1881, 285, 304, 315, 340, 389, 464, figs 370, 425.
R.C.A.M. Pembrokeshire Inventory, no. 195, figs 333–4.
Griffiths, 1957 (including early references).

2 Site and circumstances of discovery:
Found in a 'pit of turbary peat about three feet deep' in 1859, in draining a bog on the boundary between Pant-y-Maen and Blaengilfach Farms, Henfeddau, Clydey parish, 6 miles S.W. of Newcastle Emlyn. The cut was made in deepening a tiny stream, 300 yards N.E. of Pant-y-Maen farm house.

3 Collection:
Mostly St David's College, Lampeter; some in Carmarthen Museum.

4 Contents:
1–2. Two large lanceolate leaf spearheads (one in Carmarthen).
3–6. Four short, squat elliptic leaf spearheads (one in Carmarthen).
7–14. Eight fragments of leaf spearheads of uncertain type.
15–19. Five spearhead sockets.
20–22. Three expanded-foot ferrules (one in Carmarthen).
23. One short, tapering ferrule.
24. Fragment of tubular ferrule.
25. Hilt of Ewart Park sword.
26. Four joining fragments making up most of a Ewart Park sword, lacking only the hilt tang.
27. Blade of a leaf-shaped sword.
28. Fragment of leaf-shaped sword blade.
29. Diminutive tongue chape.
30–32. Three small rings (lost).

5 Further information:
Also called the Glancych hoard. An earlier discovery of three spearheads and a 'piece of broken double-edged brass sword' was made at the same spot by the same man, Samuel Davies, in 1848, but these were lost. Davies became frightened when digging out the 1859 bronzes, thinking he had hit a burial place, so he turned a diverted brook back over the spot. It is therefore possible that not all of the hoard was recovered. Some of the 1859 bronzes may have passed into private hands.

BISHOP'S CASTLE   SHROPSHIRE

1 Bibliography:
Chitty, 1937, 131.

2 Site and circumstances of discovery:
Found in cutting a drain in the old Poolhole, the site of an old pool, in a field called 'The Bloody Romans', on Lydham Heath, near the Lea Farm, Bishop's Castle.

3 Collection:
All lost (mostly sold as old metal at 4d per lb) except one spearhead in the possession of Mr E. C. Edwards of Bishop's Castle.

4 Contents (fig. 27):
Early records speak of several hundred spearheads, a few broken swords and thousands of white stones. In addition to the surviving spearhead, drawings exist of a few pieces (see 5).
1. Barbed spearhead, Type I, with lunate-openings. Socket and barbs damaged (Mr Edwards).
2. Lanceolate leaf spearhead with 'thinned' midrib.
3. Ogival leaf spearhead.
4. Leaf spearhead with damaged edges. 'Thinned' midrib.
5. Twisted fragment of sword, shoulders and upper blade, probably of Ewart Park type.
6. Upper blade of a leaf-shaped sword, probably Ewart Park type.
7–8. Two pieces of sword blade.

5 Further information:
Illustrations of 2–8 based on drawings preserved in the Way Papers, Library of the Society of Antiquaries of London. See Appendix 2. Drawing of 1 based on drawing in B.I.C., which provides another source of information.

1 Bibliography:

Jackman, 1868.

Rocke & Barnwell, 1872.

Barnwell, 1873.

Banks, 1873.

Evans, 1881, 168, 285, 319–20, 336, 338, 340, 397, 465, fig. 495.

Burgess, 1968b, 24, 40–1, fig. 15.

2 Site and circumstances of discovery:

In draining a marshy field called 'Lower Moor', about ¼ mile S.S.E. of Broadward Hall, Clungunford parish, Shropshire, almost on the Herefordshire border, July 1867.

3 Collection:

British Museum.

4 Contents (figs 4–8):

1–8. Eight complete, or near complete, barbed spearheads, Type III:
- 1. 1902,5–15,1
- 2. 1902,5–15,3
- 3. 1872,3–29,1
- 4. 1872,3–29,2
- 5. 1902,5–15,14
- 6. WG 2205
- 7. WG 2208
- 8. 1872,3–29,3

9–14. Six fragmentary barbed spearheads, Type III:
- 9. WG 2210
- 10. WG 2210a
- 11. WG 2207
- 12. WG 2209
- 13. WG 2206
- 14. WG 2210b

15–16. Two barbed spearheads, Type III, with lunate-openings:
- 15. No number; two joining pieces.
- 16. 1902,5–15,14

17–18. Two fragments of barbed spearheads, Type III, with lunate-openings:
- 17. WG 2203
- 18. WG 2210c and d, two joining pieces.

19–20. Two sockets of barbed spearheads, with projecting pins:
- 19. 1902,5–15,2
- 20. WG 2217

21–24. Four broken fillet-defined spearheads:
- 21. 1872,3–29,5
- 22. WG 2222
- 23. WG 2215
- 24. 1902,5–15,16

25–27. Three broken lunate-opening spearheads:
- 25. 1902,5–15,5
- 26. 1902,5–15,18
- 27. WG 2204: very heavily encrusted; drawing is schematic.

28–30. Three ogival leaf spearheads, with punched decoration defining midrib:
- 28. WG 2216
- 29. WG 2213
- 30. WG 2214

31. Ogival leaf spearhead, with decorated blade:
- 1902,5–15,17

32. Ogival leaf spearhead with ribbed socket base:
- 1902,5–15,7

33–36. Four ogival leaf spearheads:
- 33. 1902,5–15,15
- 34. 1872,3–29,4
- 35. 1902,5–15,6
- 36. WG 2212

37–45. Nine fragments of leaf spearheads of uncertain type:
- 37. WG 2221
- 38. WG 2211
- 39. WG 2219
- 40. WG 2218
- 41. WG 2223
- 42. WG 2220
- 43. No number
- 44. 1872,3–29,7
- 45. 1872,3–29,6

46–47. Two expanded-foot ferrules:
- 46. 1872,3–29,8
- 47. WG 2225

48–49. Two broken tubular ferrules:
- 48. 1902,5–15,10: head of fixing pin projects
- 49. WG 2224

50. Crushed fragment of spearhead socket or ferrule:
- 1902,5–15,9

51. Tanged chisel: 1872,3–29,9

52. Part of a tubular ring: 1902,5–15,20

53–54. Two bugle-shaped objects:
- 53. 1902,5–15,11
- 54. WG 2226

55–62. Eight leaf-shaped sword fragments:
- 55. Two pieces, 1872,3–29,10 and 1902,5–15,19, join to make the hilt and upper blade of a Ewart Park sword.
- 56. WG 2232: hilt end, Ewart Park type.

57. WG 2231a: damaged shoulders and upper blade, Ewart Park type.
58. WG 2231b
59. WG 2229
60. WG 2231
61. WG 2230
62. 1902,5–15,8
63. Diminutive tongue chape: 1902,5–15,12.

5 Further information:
The following are not illustrated:
64. Small fragment of leaf spearhead of uncertain type, WG 2211a.
65–71. Seven small pieces of spearhead sockets.
72–74. Three pieces of sword blade.

SNEAD   SHROPSHIRE

1 Bibliography:
Chitty, 1937, 131.
2 Site and circumstances of discovery:
Reputedly dug up 'on the Shropshire side of Snead in a field near the Camlad containing a big stone'.
3 Collection:
Lost.
4 Contents:
'Bronze spearheads'. Nothing further known.
5 Further information:
Possibly a spearhead hoard of the Shropshire group, but no greater certainty seems possible, with such vague information.

WILLOW MOOR, 1834   SHROPSHIRE

1 Bibliography:
Hartshorne, 1841.
Chitty, 1928.
2 Site and circumstances of discovery:
Found during field draining in the spring of 1834 on Willow Moor at Willow Moor Farm, near the Wrekin, Little Wenlock. Two spearheads were found 3 feet down, then the main group of bronzes was found further into the morass. They formed a heap 'capable of being covered by a half bushel measure', and comprised *c.* 150 spearheads (some records speak of 200–300), a celt, a small number of swords, and three or four small whetstones.
3 Collection:
Mostly lost; survivors scattered, as below.
4 Contents:
Known pieces consist of one socketed axe, one Ewart Park sword, one sword blade, one socketed sword, one lunate-opening spearhead, six elliptic leaf spearheads, two ogival leaf spearheads, three lanceolate leaf spearheads, three fillet-defined spearheads, one barbed spearhead, four fragments of leaf spearheads, one decorated spearhead, and two spearhead sockets, scattered as follows:

Shrewsbury Museum
1. Three-ribbed socketed axe (casts in Hereford Mus. and Library of Soc. of Antiquaries of London).
2. Lunate-opening spearhead, cast only (other casts in Hereford Mus., Soc. of Antiquaries and National Museum, Cardiff).
3. Fragment of leaf spearhead, of uncertain type.
4. Broken elliptic leaf spearhead.
5. Fillet-defined spearhead, grooved socket.

Pritchard Collection
6–8. Three fragments of leaf spearheads, of uncertain type.

Lord Forester, Willey Park
9. Lower part of leaf-shaped sword blade.
10. Ogival leaf spearhead.
11. Fragment of leaf spearhead with ribbed socket.
12. Fragment of leaf spearhead, fillet on socket sides, but this does not extend on to blade. Ribbed socket base.
13–14. Two broad elliptic, leaf spearheads.

Windle Collection, Toronto
15. Lanceolate leaf spearhead.

Lukis Museum, Guernsey
16. Fillet-defined spearhead with grooved socket.

Society of Antiquaries of London
17. Ewart Park sword in three pieces, end of hilt missing.
18–19. Two lanceolate leaf spearheads.
20–21. Two slender elliptic leaf spearheads.
22. Broad elliptic leaf spearhead.
23. Point of barbed spearhead, Type II.
24–25. Two spearhead sockets, one with multiple grooves.

Lost (Hartshorne, 1841)

26. Fillet-defined spearhead, socket decorated with concentric circles between bands of horizontal ribbing; zigzag ornament on the fillets and on the blade (described but not figured by Hartshorne).

27. Part of a socketed sword (figured by Hartshorne).

Ludlow Museum

28–29. Two unprovenanced ogival leaf spearheads have the same distinctive patina and condition as surviving Willow Moor implements, and may well have belonged to the hoard.

5 Further information:
   This find was wrongly listed as two hoards by Evans (1881, 113, 234, 285, 314, 336, 338, 452, 465), under the names 'Little Wenlock' and Wrekin Tenement.

WILLOW MOOR, 1790   SHROPSHIRE

1 Bibliography:
   Hartshorne, 1841, 95.
   Chitty, 1928, 42.
2 Site and circumstances of discovery:
   On Willow Moor, near the Wrekin, Little Wenlock, *c.* 1790. Nothing more known.
3 Collection:
   Lost.
4 Contents:
   'A considerable number of broken weapons similar to those which were met with in the year 1835' (Hartshorne, 1841, 95; Hartshorne thought that the 1834 hoard had

been found in 1835). These implements had already been lost by Hartshorne's day.
5 Further information:
   None.

KIRK DEIGHTON   YORKSHIRE

1 Bibliography:
   Radley, 1966.
2 Site and circumstances of discovery:
   Found in a ploughed field at the north end of Kirk Deighton parish, *c.* 4 miles E. of Harrogate.
3 Collection:
   Harrogate, Royal Pump Room Museum.
4 Contents:
   1–3. Three lanceolate leaf spearheads.
   4. Socketed axe, plain, of Everthorpe type.
5 Further information:
   One spearhead found *c.* 1954. The other implements found at the same spot in 1955.

'WEST OF SCOTLAND'

1 Bibliography:
   Coles, 1959–60, 134.
2 Site and circumstances of discovery:
   Found in a cairn in the west of Scotland, some time before 1726.
3 Collection:
   National Museum of Antiquities, Edinburgh.
4 Contents:
   1–2. Two fragments of leaf spearhead.
   3. Disc-foot ferrule.
5 Further information:
   None.

APPENDIX 2 – ALBERT WAY AND THE BISHOP'S CASTLE HOARD

by John D. Cowen

The Albert Way papers in the Library of the Society of Antiquaries of London include illustrations of one sort or another of various hoards from Wales and the Marches. In addition to those of the Ebnal implements, recorded elsewhere in this volume, there are drawings of the Pant-y-Maen (Glancych), Guilsfield and Broadward hoards. Quite the most interesting, however, are drawings of some of the objects found 'near the Lea Farm, on the Oakeley Estate, near Bishop's Castle' in 1862; other sources add: 'from the site of a pool on Lydham Heath in a field called "The Bloody Romans"'.

Here again the only useful, and fully documented, account of this hoard we owe to Miss Chitty (1937). It must have been a very large hoard: the sources speak of 'many hundreds of spearheads', several broken swords, and many white stones. Of all this material only a single piece has survived – a large, but broken, lunate barbed spearhead; and when Miss Chitty drew it for the British Association Card Catalogue of bronzes it was still in private possession. In

August 1873, the Rev. T. Owen Rocke had been able to exhibit six spearheads and three sword fragments, apparently from this hoard, to the Knighton meeting of the Cambrian Archaeological Association (*Archaeol. Cambrensis*, 4 ser., IV (1873), 411–12).

The drawings, on which fig. 27:2–8 is based, were not, in this instance, originally by Way himself, but were copied by him from what he called 'sketches' made by the Rev. T. O. Rocke, and sent in May 1869 to the Rev. E. L. Barnwell, a well-known antiquary in his day, who will no doubt have made them available to Way. It must be added that, judging by Way's copy, Mr Rocke's 'sketches' must have been remarkably competent. They show three leaf-shaped spearheads (Class V), and four fragments representing at least two swords, unhappily too much broken for the type to be determinable. Their main interest lies in the fact that, so far as I can accurately determine, no figure of any piece from this apparently large hoard has ever been previously published.

APPENDIX 3 – LIST OF BARBED SPEARHEADS

Type I

1 Thames at Moulsford, Berkshire (fig. 30).
  Reading Museum, 63:48.
  VCH, Oxon, I (1939), 249, fig. 10.
2–4 Bloody Pool hoard, South Brent, Devon (fig. 22).
  Exeter Museum.
  Bibliography: see Appendix 1.
  Two fragmentary examples survive, and a third is illustrated in the published accounts, out of the several found originally.
5–7 Ashley hoard, Hampshire (fig. 19).
  Winchester Museum.
  Three fragmentary examples.
8 Bishop's Castle hoard, Shropshire (fig. 27).
  Private collection (Mr E. C. Edwards, Bishop's Castle).
  Bibliography: see Appendix 1.
  Complete example, with lunate openings: drawing after B.I.C.

9–10 Longy Common hoard, Alderney (fig. 30).
  Lukis Museum, Guernsey.
  Kendrick, 1928, pls. VII–VIII.
  Two fragmentary examples: drawings after B.I.C.

Type II

11 River Thames (fig. 30).
  London Museum.
  Point only.
12 Thames at Bray, Berkshire (fig. 31).
  Reading Museum, S 252:45/1.
  Berkshire Archaeol. J., XLIX (1946), pl. III.
13 Thames at Bray, Berkshire (fig. 30).
  Reading Museum, S 252:45/2.
  Berkshire Archaeol. J., XLIX (1946), pl. III.
14 Gravel pit at Monkey Island, Bray, Berkshire (fig. 30).
  Reading Museum, 42:53.
15 Thames at Maidenhead, Berkshire (fig. 30).
  Reading Museum, 68:52.

16 Speen, Berkshire (fig. 23).
   Present location unknown.
   Bibliography: see Appendix 1.
17 Thames at Wallingford, Berkshire (fig. 30).
   Reading Museum, 1091:64.
18–19 Yattendon hoard, Berkshire (fig. 15).
   Newbury Museum.
   Bibliography: see Appendix 1.
   One nearly complete blade, one blade fragment.
20 Green End Road hoard, Cambridge (fig. 31).
   Cambridge University Museum of Archaeology and Ethnology.
   RCHM, City of Cambridge Inventory, I, xxxiv, pl. 2.
   Lower part only.
21 Cow Dale, near Buxton, Derbyshire (fig. 31).
   Buxton Museum.
22 Congleton hoard, Cheshire (fig. 26).
   Congleton Public Library.
   Bibliography: see Appendix 1.
23 Plaistow Marshes, Essex (fig. 31).
   British Museum, 1865, 12–20,6.
   Franks, 1864–7.
24–28 Winchester area, hoard, Hampshire (fig. 21).
   Winchester Museum.
   Fragments of at least five examples, including one, probably two, with lunate openings.
29–38 Broadness hoard, Kent (figs 10–11).
   London Museum and British Museum.
   Bibliography: see Appendix 1.
   Five complete examples, including one with lunate-openings, and five broken examples.
39 Thames at Chiswick, London (fig. 32).
   Ashmolean Museum, Oxford, 1927:2557.
   Greenwell & Brewis, 1909, pl. LXXIV, fig. 54.
40 Thames at Wandsworth, London (fig. 31).
   Present whereabouts uncertain.
   Drawing after B.I.C.
41 Carlton Rode hoard, Norfolk (fig. 32).
   Norwich Castle Museum.
   Norwich Castle Museum, 1966, pl. VI.
   Fragment.
42 Aylsham hoard, Norfolk (fig. 32).
   Norwich Castle Museum.
   Fragment.
43 Willow Moor, 1834 hoard, Shropshire (fig. 31).
   Collection of the Society of Antiquaries of London.
   Bibliography: see Appendix 1.
   Point only.
44 Godney, Somerset (fig. 32).
   Glastonbury Museum.

45–49 Wick Park, Stogursey hoard, Somerset (pl. x).
   Taunton Museum.
   Fragments of five examples.
50 Flansham hoard, Sussex (fig. 32).
   Littlehampton Museum.
   Hearne, 1940.
   Fragment.
51 River Severn, half a mile below Diglis Lock, near Worcester (fig. 32).
   Cheltenham Museum.
   Archaeol. J., II (1846), 187.
52 North Ferriby, Yorkshire (fig. 32).
   British Museum, WG 2057.
   Bartlett & Hawkes, 1965.
53 'Yorkshire' (fig. 32).
   Yorkshire Museum, York, 1170/1948.
   Point only.
54 Duddingston Loch hoard, Midlothian (fig. 31).
   National Museum of Antiquities, Edinburgh.
   Callander, 1921–2.
   Broken example with lunate openings.

Type III

55 Thames Street hoard, London (fig. 24).
   British Museum, 1868, 75–2.
56–73 Broadward hoard, Shropshire (figs 4–5).
   British Museum (see Appendix 1).
   Bibliography: see Appendix 1.
   Eighteen complete and fragmentary examples, some with lunate openings.

Type IV

74 River Thames (fig. 29).
   Lost.
   Drawing based on one in Albert Way MSS., Library of Society of Antiquaries of London.
75 Hatfield Broad Oak hoard, Essex (fig. 29).
   Colchester Museum.
   R. A. Smith, 1909–11, 165–6, fig. 3.
   Colchester Museum, 1960, pl. VII.
   Davies, *Inventaria Archaeologica*, forthcoming.
76 Donington on Bain, Lincolnshire (fig. 29).
   Lincoln Museum.
   Thompson, 1954.
77 Felixstowe Railway Cutting hoard, Suffolk (fig. 9).
   Ipswich Museum.
78 Levington hoard, Suffolk (fig. 27).
   Ipswich Museum.

Type uncertain

79 Pendoylan, near Cardiff, Glamorgan.
  Lost.
  Rolls, 1861.
  Never illustrated: described as only 7 in.
  long and 3⅛ in. across the barbs, which
  strongly suggests this was another example
  of Type III.

Sockets

80–81 Broadward hoard, Shropshire (fig. 4).
  British Museum.
  Bibliography: see Appendix 1.
  Two sockets with long metal pins protruding.
82–83 Wick Park, Stogursey hoard, Somerset
  (pl. XII).
  Taunton Museum.
  Two typical short, oval-sectioned sockets.

NOTES ON THE TEXT AND DRAWINGS

Sections (i) and (ii) were written by C. B., who also undertook general correlation, and prepared the paper as a whole, using MSS. provided by D. C. and D. G. D. Appendix 1 is set out on the lines established by Coles, 1959–60, and Eogan, 1964. The abbreviation 'B.I.C.' refers to the Bronze Implements Card Catalogue, now housed in the British Museum.

The final drawings are all by Mrs Maureen Fadian, based on originals drawn as follows: C. B. drew the Broadward, Yattendon, Ashley, Bloody Pool and Mollington hoards, and some of the single finds on figs 28–32; D. C. dealt with the Winchester, Speen, Thames Street and Congleton material, and most of the single finds of barbed spearheads; and D. G. D. drew the Broadness, Felixstowe and Levington material, and many of the single finds on figs 28–29.

Sections of implements have been drawn where possible, but this was impossible in the case of many spearheads, which have sockets blocked by clay core, silt or wooden shaft fragments. In such cases only the external section can be given, and this is indicated by an outline containing a question mark. Where the position of the blocking is sufficiently definite, it is marked by the symbol ⌒, but in many cases the socket and midrib is partially blocked at various points. In some cases, as with many Broadward implements for example, corrosion and encrustation defeat any attempt to draw a meaningful section. The symbol ⊤⊤ indicates the limit of the midrib cavity. Broken lines by the sides of spearhead sockets indicate the position of the shaft peg.

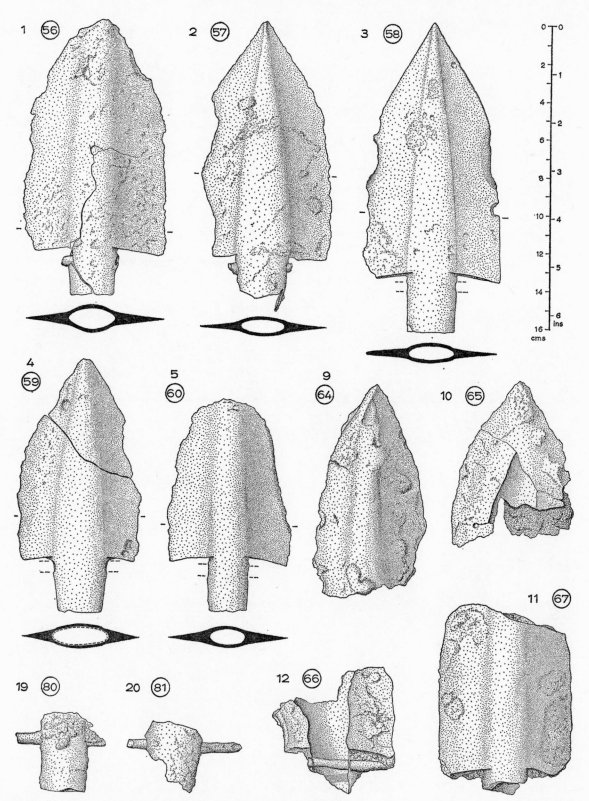

fig. 4 The Broadward hoard, Shropshire: barbed spearheads

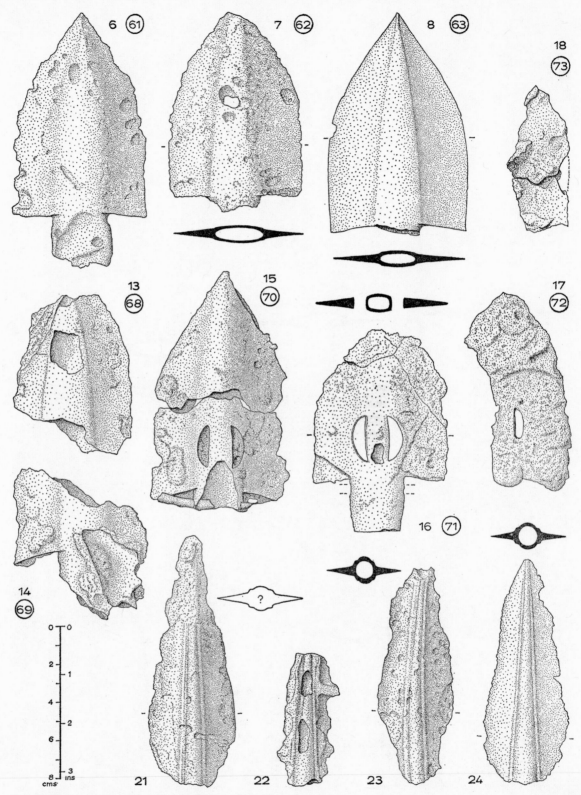

fig. 5 The Broadward hoard, Shropshire: spearheads

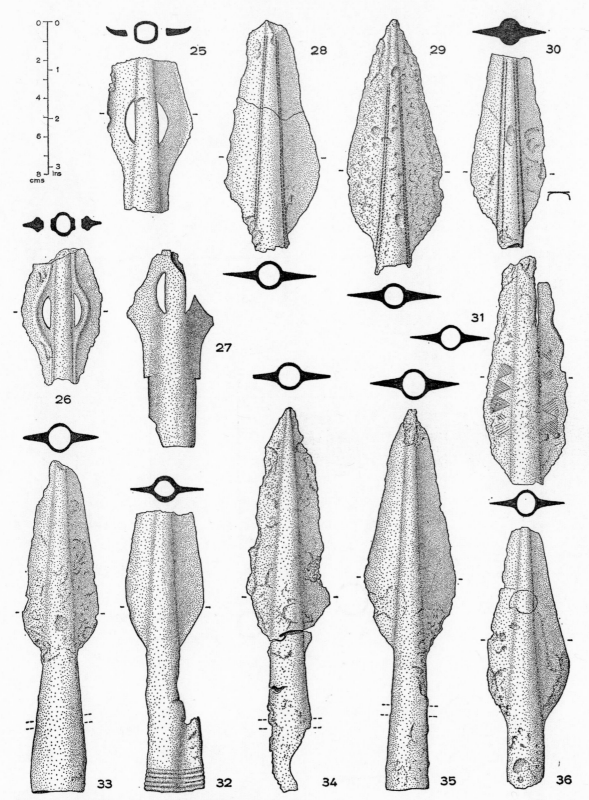

fig. 6 The Broadward hoard, Shropshire: spearheads

37

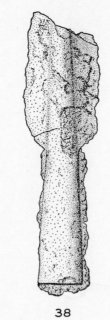

38

39

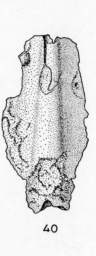

40

43

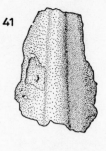

41

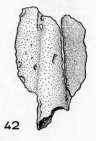

42

44

46

47

48

49

45

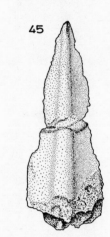

51

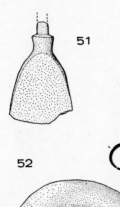

52

50

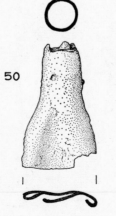

53

54

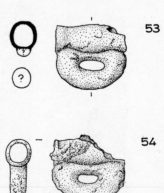

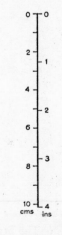

0
2
4
6
8
10
cms

0
1
2
3
4
ins

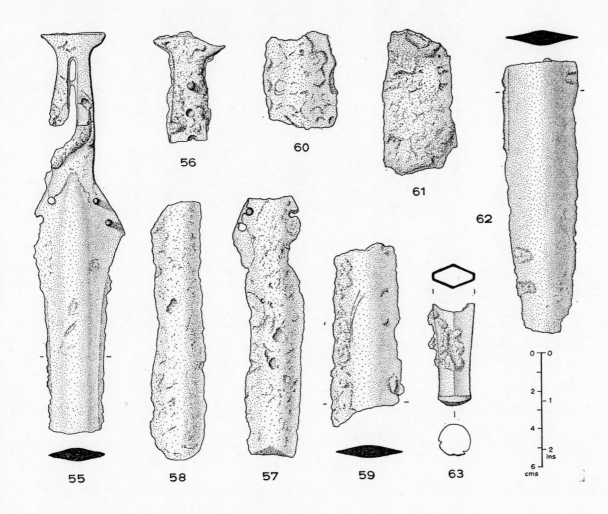

fig. 7 (*left*) The Broadward hoard, Shropshire: ferrules and miscellaneous
fig. 8 (*above*) The Broadward hoard, Shropshire: swords and chape

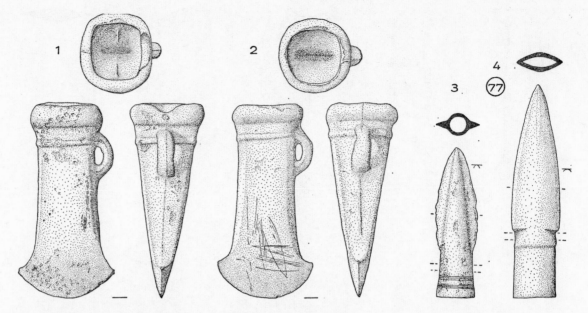

fig. 9 (*above*) The Felixstowe Railway Cutting hoard, Suffolk
fig. 10 (*right*) The Broadness hoard, Kent: barbed spearheads

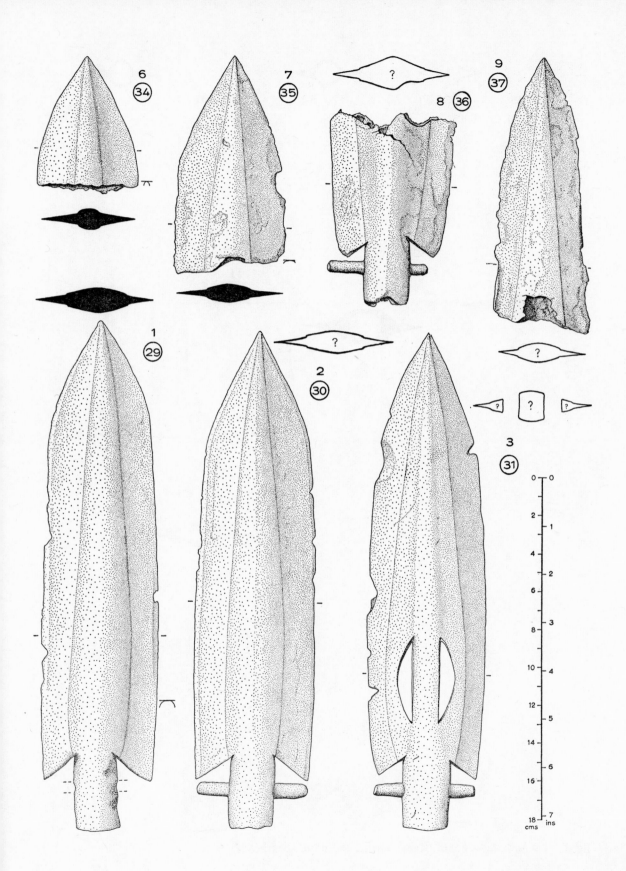

253

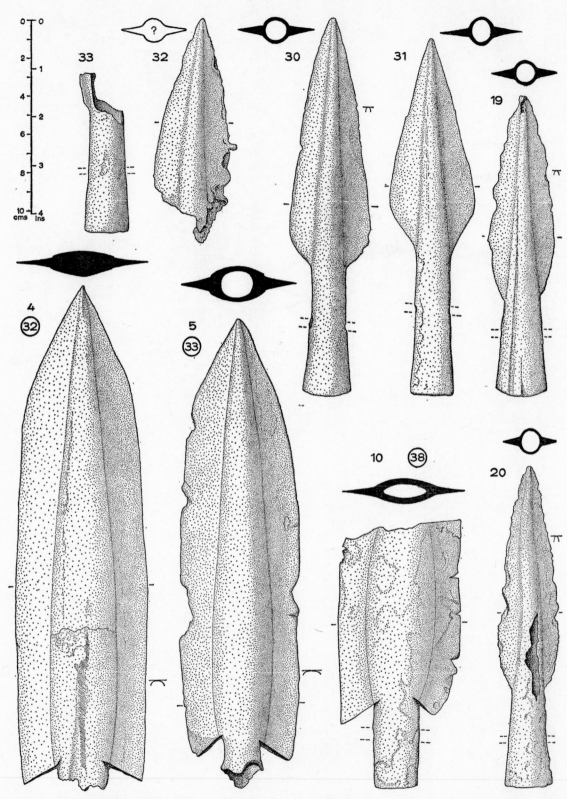

fig. 11 The Broadness hoard, Kent: barbed and other spearheads

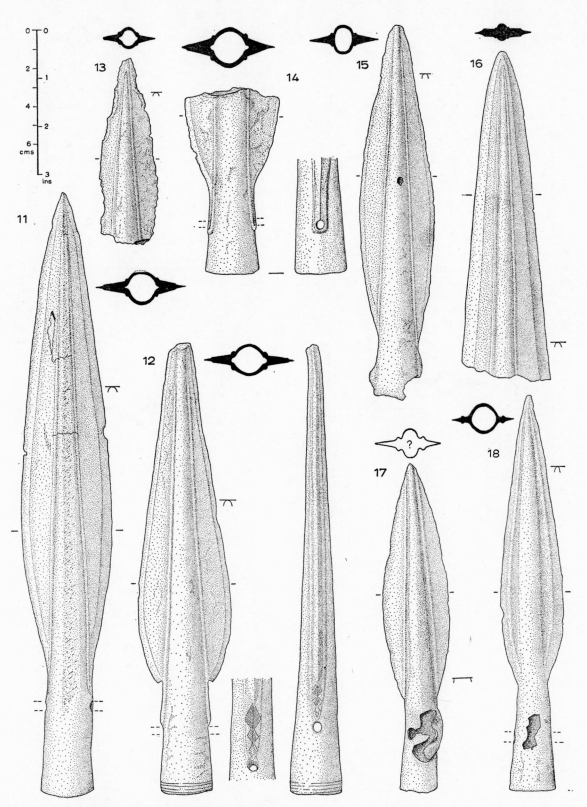

fig. 12 The Broadness hoard, Kent: spearheads

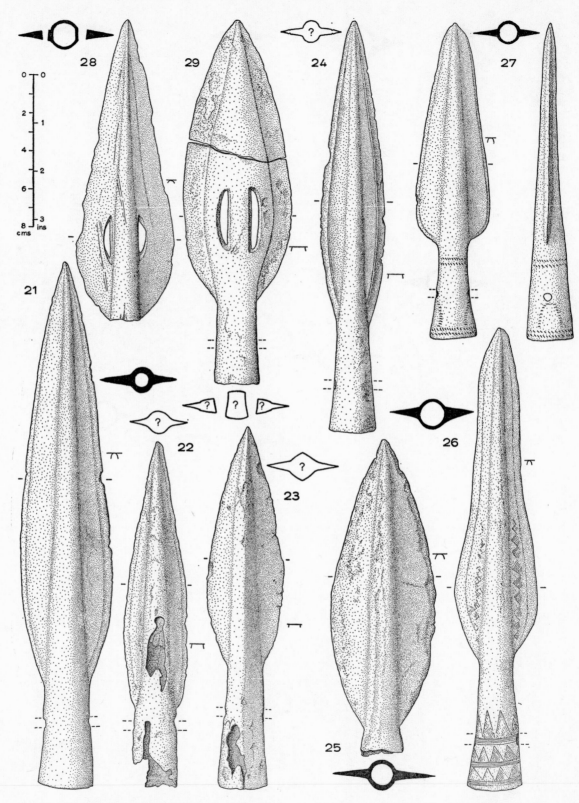

fig. 13 The Broadness hoard, Kent: spearheads

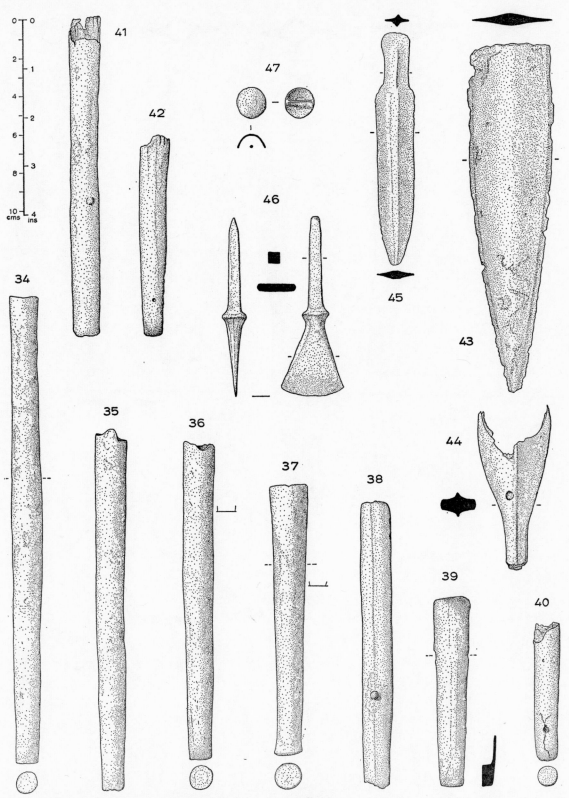

fig. 14 The Broadness hoard, Kent: ferrules and miscellaneous

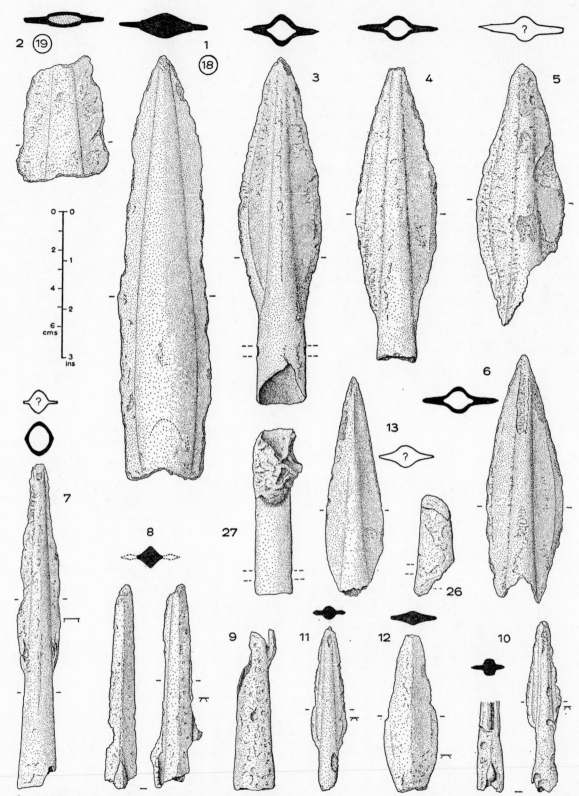

fig. 15 The Yattendon hoard, Berkshire: spearheads

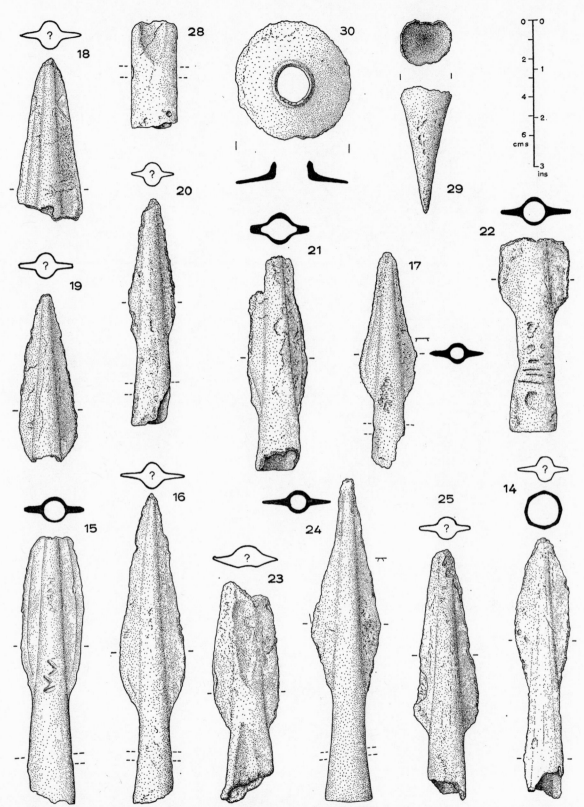

fig. 16 The Yattendon hoard, Berkshire: spearheads and miscellaneous

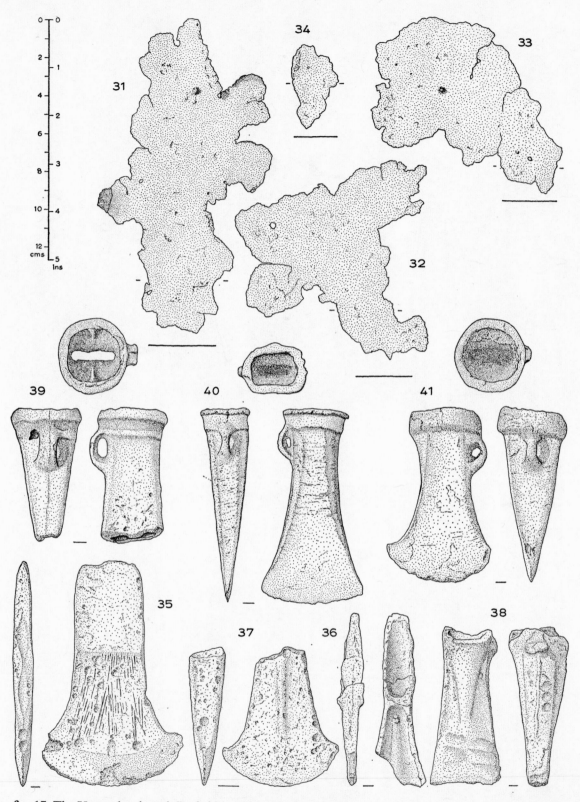

fig. 17 The Yattendon hoard, Berkshire: axes and sheet metal

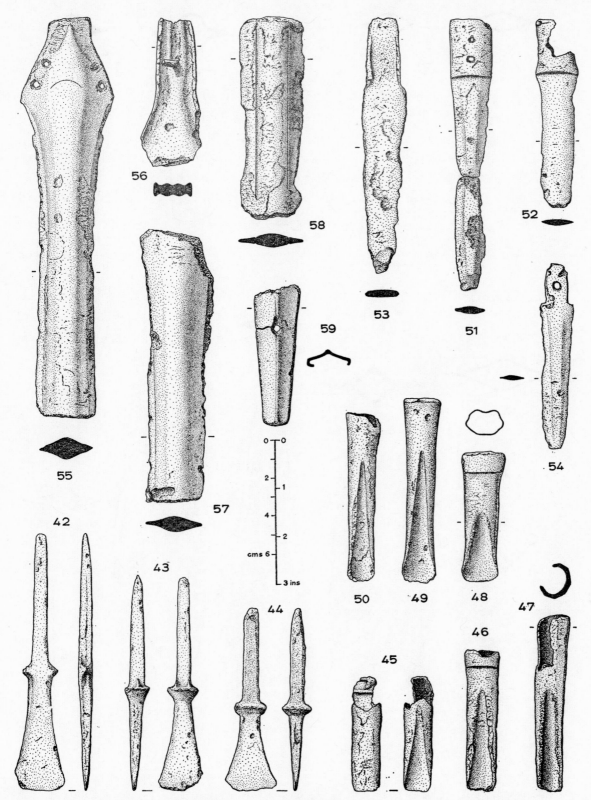

fig. 18 The Yattendon hoard, Berkshire: tools and swords

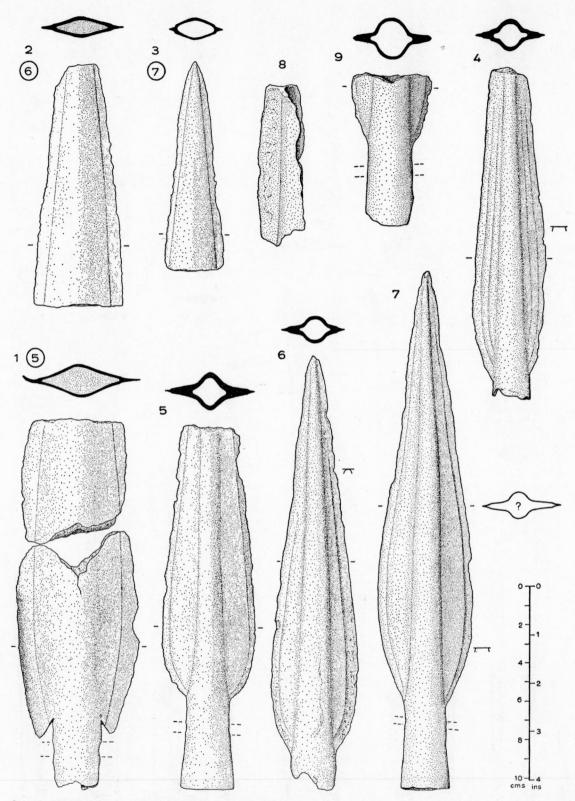

fig. 19 The Ashley hoard, Hampshire: spearheads

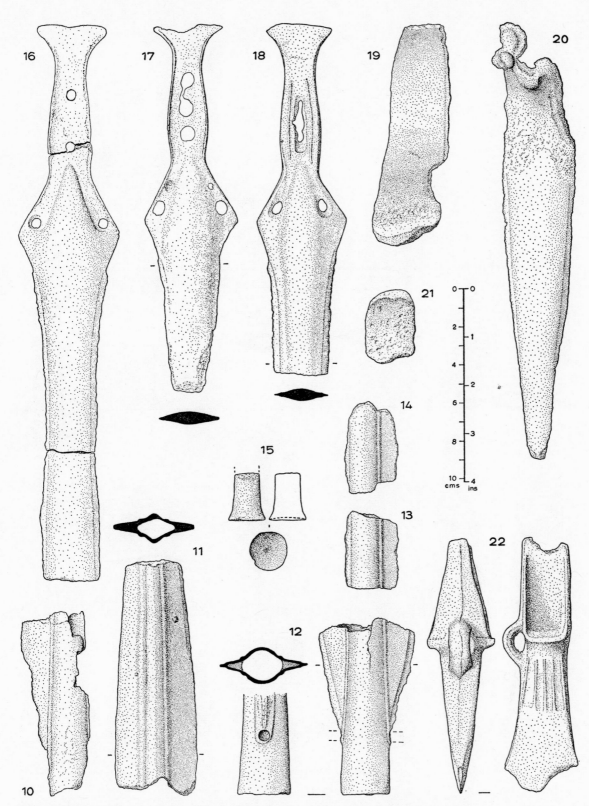

fig. 20 The Ashley hoard, Hampshire: spearheads, swords and miscellaneous

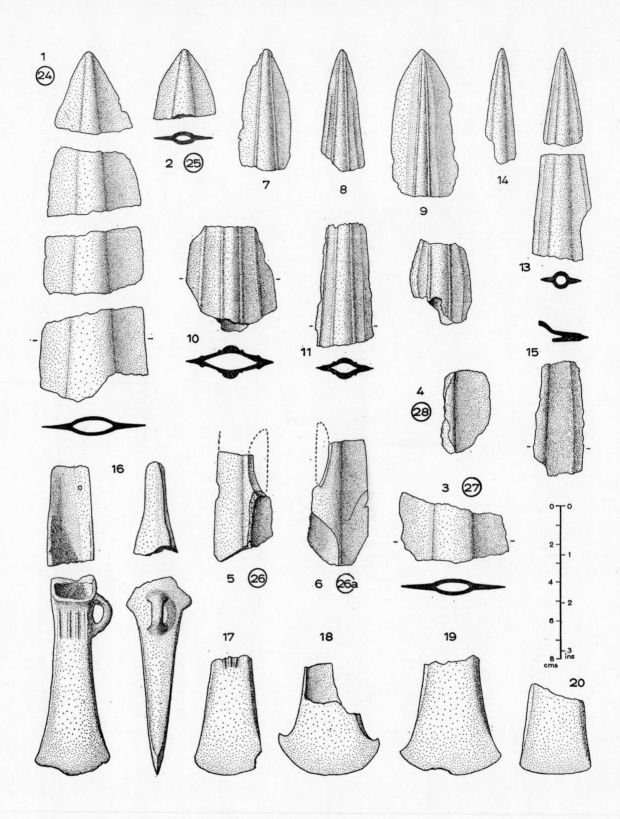

fig. 21 Hoard from the Winchester area, Hampshire

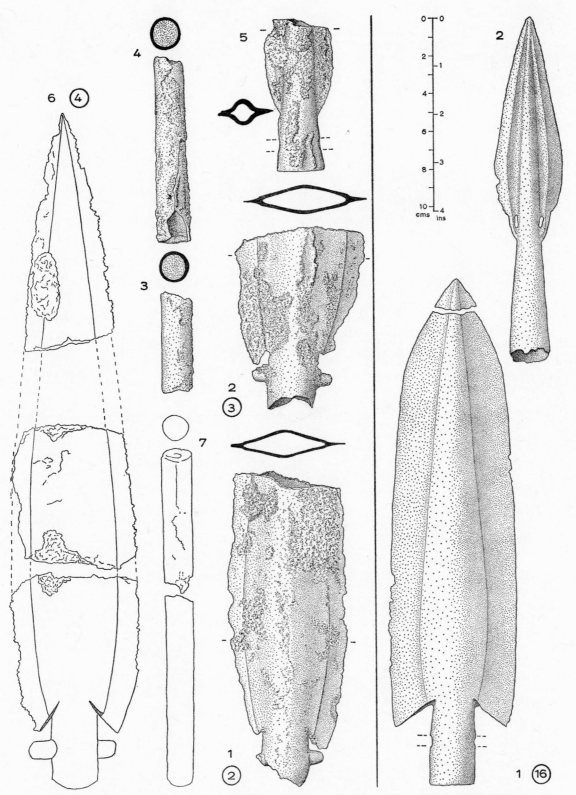

fig. 22 (*left*) The Bloody Pool hoard, South Brent, Devon (6 and 7 after Tucker, 1855, 1867)
fig. 23 (*right*) Spearheads from Speen, Berkshire (after B.I.C.)

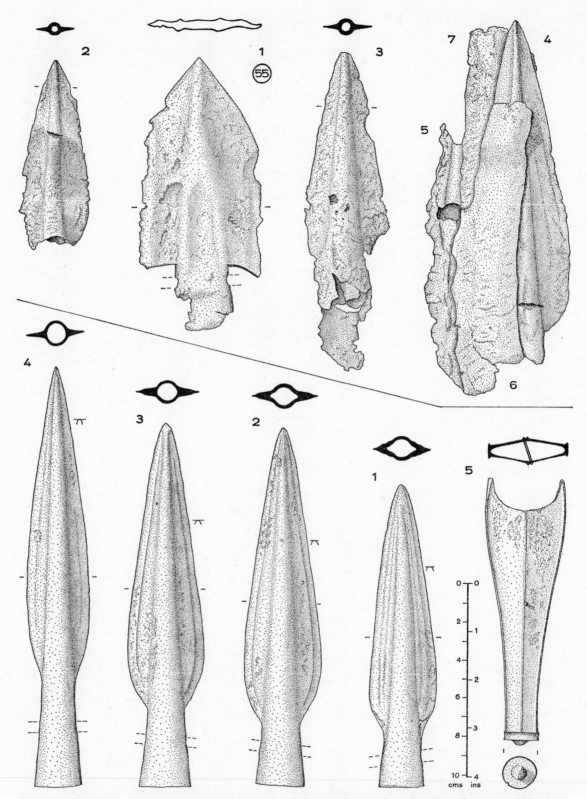

fig. 24 (*above*) The Thames Street hoard, London; fig. 25 (*below*) The Mollington hoard, Oxfordshire

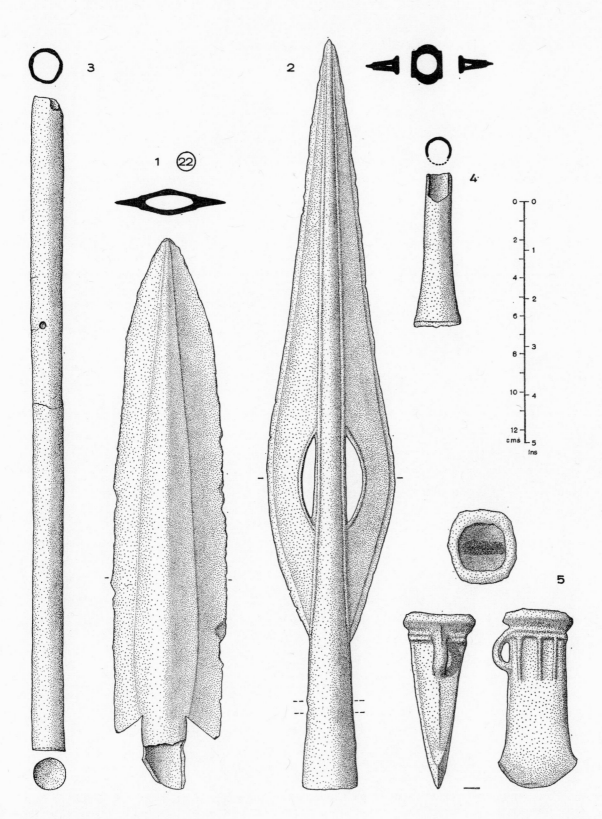

fig. 26 The Congleton hoard, Cheshire

fig. 27 1–8 Implements from the Bishop's Castle hoard, Shropshire (1 after drawing in B.I.C.; 2–8 after drawings in the Albert Way Papers, Society of Antiquaries of London); 9–10 From the Levington hoard, Suffolk

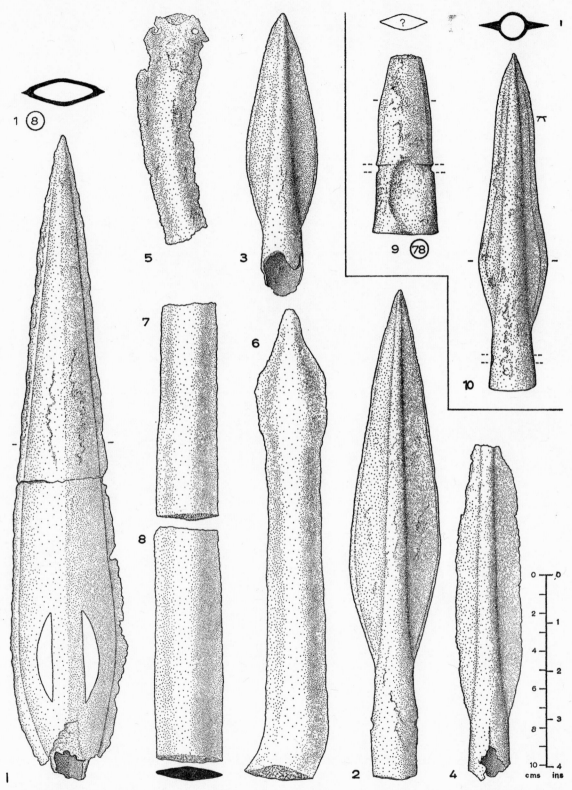

1 Ⓑ

5

3

7

6

2

8

9 ⓥ

10

4

0
2
4
6
8
10
cms

0
1
2
3
4
ins

fig. 28 1 Staines type spearhead from Quy Fen, Cambs.; 2 Staines type spearhead from the Thames at Staines (London Mus.); 3–4 Hollow spearheads from the Guilsfield hoard, Montgom. (Welshpool Mus. and National Mus., Cardiff); 5 Straight-based basal-looped spearhead, unprovenanced (London Mus.); 6 Straight-based basal-looped spearhead, unprovenanced (London Mus.)

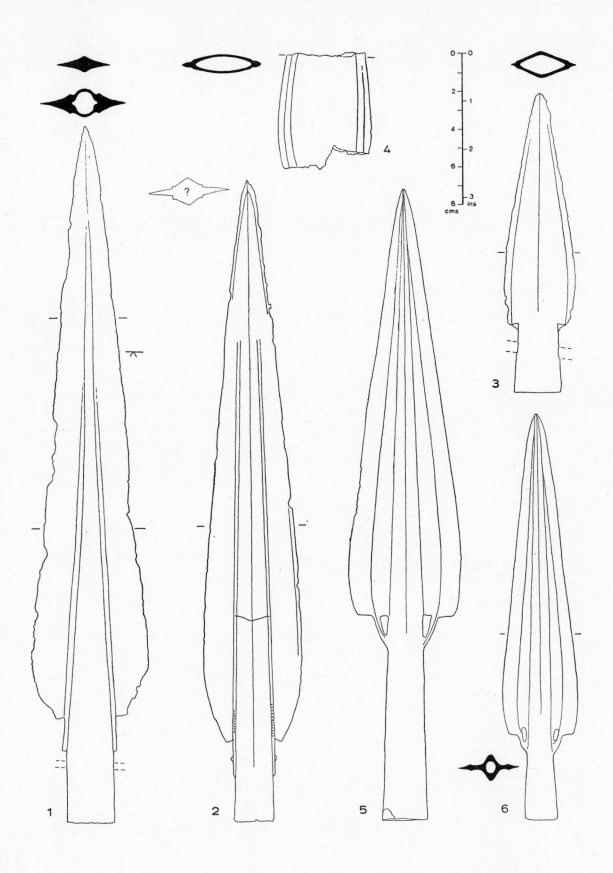

fig. 29 Hollow, lozenge-sectioned spearheads from: 1 Thames at Richmond (British Mus.); 2 River Thames (London Mus.); 3 Guilsfield hoard, Montgom. (National Mus., Cardiff); 4 Thames at Teddington (London Mus.)

Type IV barbed spearheads from: 74 River Thames (after drawing in Way Papers, Soc. of Antiquaries of London); 75 Hatfield Broad Oak hoard, Essex; 76 Donington on Bain, Lincolnshire (nos. 74–76 refer to Appendix 3)

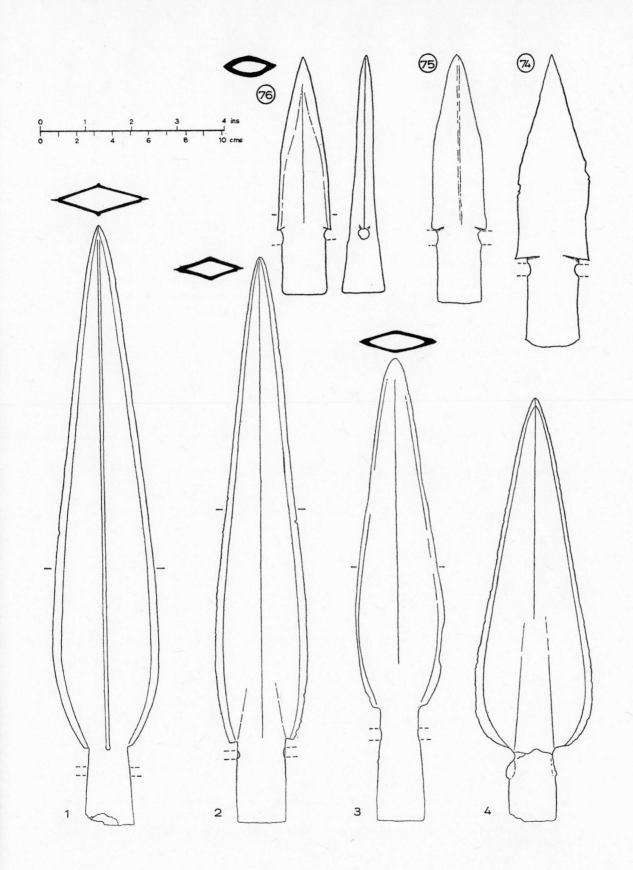

fig. 30 Type I barbed spearheads from: 1 Thames at Moulsford, Berkshire; 9–10 Longy Common hoard, Alderney. Type II barbed spearheads from 11 River Thames; 13 Thames at Bray, Berks; 14 Monkey Island, Bray; 15 Thames at Maidenhead, Berks; 17 Thames at Wallingford, Berks (numbers refer to Appendix 3)

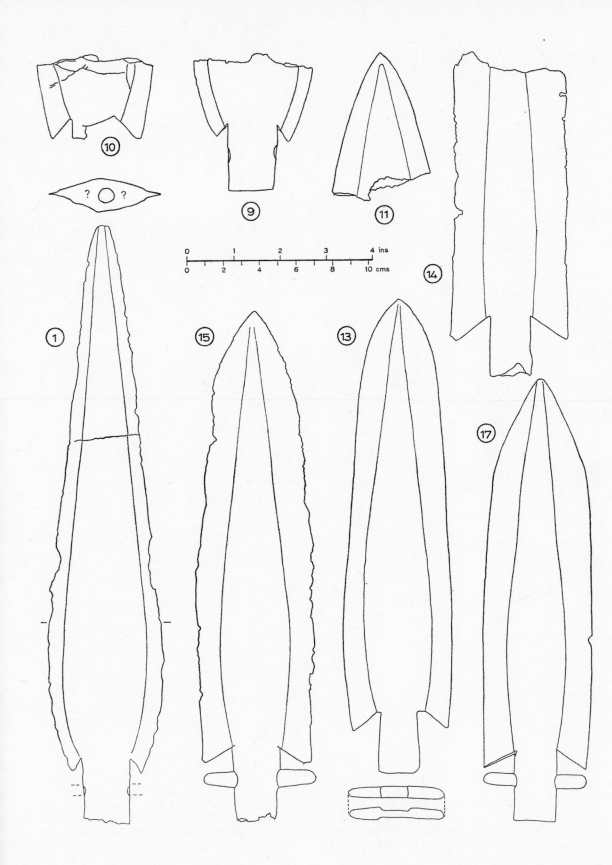

fig. 31 Type II barbed spearheads from: 12 Thames at Bray, Berks; 20 Green End Road hoard, Cambridge; 21 Cow Dale, near Buxton, Derbyshire; 23 Plaistow Marshes, Essex; 40 Thames at Wandsworth (after drawing in B.I.C.); 43 Willow Moor hoard, Shropshire; 54 Duddingston Loch hoard, Midlothian (numbers refer to Appendix 3)

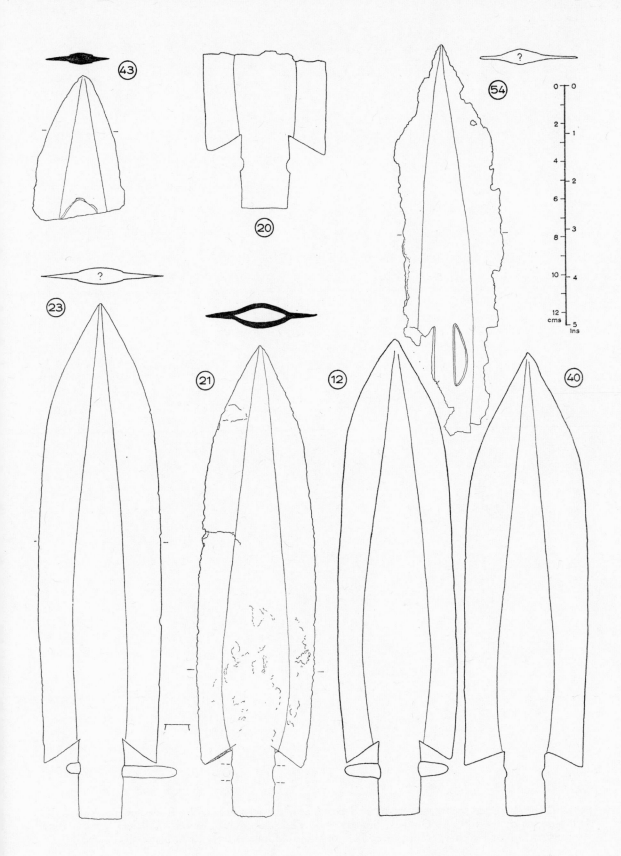

fig. 32 Type II barbed spearheads from: 39 Thames at Chiswick; 41 Carlton Rode hoard, Norfolk; 42 Aylsham hoard; Norfolk; 44 Godney, Somerset; 50 Flansham hoard, Sussex; 51 River Severn below Worcester; 52 North Ferriby, Yorkshire; 53 'Yorkshire' (numbers refer to Appendix 3)

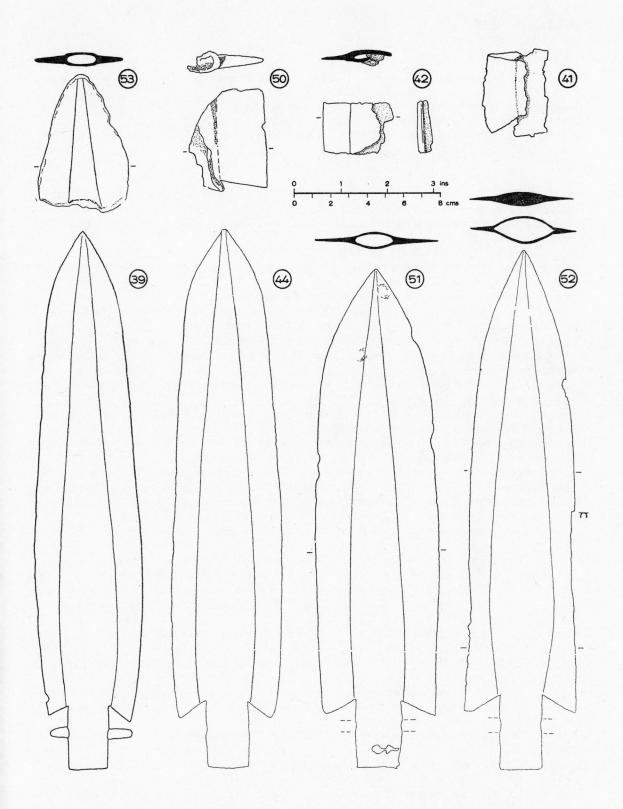

BIBLIOGRAPHY

Alexander, J. & Ozanne, P. C. and A., 1960. 'Report on the investigation of a round barrow on Arreton Down, Isle of Wight', *Proc. Prehist. Soc.*, XXVI, 263–302.

Atkinson, R. J. C., 1965. 'Wayland's Smithy', *Antiquity*, XXXIX, 126–33.

Banks, R. W., 1873. 'The Broadward find', *Archaeol. Cambrensis*, 4 ser., IV, 202–4.

Barnwell, E. L., 1873. 'The Broadward find – supplementary note', *Archaeol. Cambrensis*, 4 ser., IV, 80–3.

Bartlett, J. E. & Hawkes, C. F. C., 1965. 'A barbed bronze spearhead from North Ferriby, Yorkshire, England', *Proc. Prehist. Soc.*, XXXI, 370–3.

Blundell, J. D. & Longworth, I. H., 1967. 'A Bronze Age hoard from Portfield Farm, Whalley, Lancashire', *Brit. Mus. Quart.*, XXXII, 8–14.

Brailsford, J., 1947. 'A Founder's hoard from Dartford, Kent, with a note on socketed bronze swords', *Proc. Prehist. Soc.*, XIII, 175–7.

Brewster, T. C. M., 1963. *The Excavation of Staple Howe*. Wintringham, Yorks.

Briard, J., 1961. 'Dépôts de l'Age du Bronze de Bretagne', *Trav. du Lab. d'Anthropologie Préhist. de Rennes*, 1–82.

—— 1965. *Les Dépôts Bretons et l'Age du Bronze Atlantique*. Rennes.

—— 1966. 'La Praire de Mauves à Nantes', *Trav. du Lab. d'Anthropologie Préhist. de Rennes*, 1–60.

British Museum, 1953. *Later Prehistoric Antiquities of the British Isles*. London.

Britton, D., 1960. 'The Isleham hoard, Cambridgeshire', *Antiquity*, XXXIV, 279–82.

—— (ed.), 1960a. 'Bronze Age grave-group and hoards in the British Museum', *Inventaria Archaeologica*, 8th Set: GB. 48–54.

—— 1963. 'Traditions of metal-working in the late Neolithic and Early Bronze Age of Britain: Part I', *Proc. Prehist. Soc.*, XXIX, 258–325.

Britton, D. & Longworth, I. H. (eds), 1968. 'Late Bronze Age finds in the Heathery Burn Cave, Co. Durham', *Inventaria Archaeologica*, 9th Set: GB. 55.

Brown, M. A. & Blin-Stoyle, A. E., 1959. 'A sample analysis of British Middle and Late Bronze Age material, using optical spectrometry', *Proc. Prehist. Soc.*, XXV, 188–208.

Bunny, E. B., 1860. In 'Proceedings' (Speen Spearheads), *J. Brit. Archaeol. Assoc.*, XVI, 322–3, pl. 26.

Burgess, C. B., 1962. 'A Socketed axe from central Monmouthshire and its significance for the Bronze Age in Wales and the Marches', *Monmouthshire Antiq.*, I, part 2, 17—27.

—— 1968a. *Bronze Age Metalwork in Northern England c. 1000–700 BC*. Newcastle upon Tyne.

—— 1968b. 'The later Bronze Age in the British Isles and north-western France', *Archaeol. J.*, CXXV, 1–45.

—— 1969. 'Some decorated socketed axes in Canon Greenwell's Collection', in 'Studies in Commemoration of William Greenwell, 1820–1918', *Yorkshire Archaeol. J.*, XLII, 267–72.

Butler, J. J., 1963. 'Bronze Age Connections across the North Sea', *Palaeohistoria*, IX (entire volume).

Butler, J. J. & Bakker, J. A., 1961. 'A Forgotten Middle Bronze Age hoard with a Sicilian razor from Ommerschans (Overijssel)', *Helinium*, I, 193–209.

Callander, J. G., 1921–2. 'Three Bronze Age hoards recently added to the National Collection, with notes on the hoard from Duddingston Loch', *Proc. Soc. Antiq. Scot.*, LVI, 351–64.

Chitty, L. F., 1928. 'The Willow Moor bronze hoard, Little Wenlock, Shropshire', *Antiq. J.*, VIII, 30–47.

—— 1937. 'How did the hill-fort builders reach the Breiddin?', *Archaeol. Cambrensis*, XCII, 129–50.

—— 1940. 'Bronze implements from the Oswestry region of Shropshire', *Archaeol. Cambrensis*, XCV, 27–35.

—— 1965. 'Irish bronze axes assigned to the Guilsfield hoard, Montgomeryshire', *Archaeol. Cambrensis*, CXIV, 120–9.

Chitty, L. F. & Coombs, D., 1967–8. 'Bronze hoard and burial found at Greensborough Farm, Shenstone, Staffordshire, in 1824', *Trans. Lichfield S. Staffs. Archaeol. Hist. Soc.*, IX, 1–16.

Clarke, E. D., 1821. 'An account of some antiquities found at Fulbourn in Cambridgeshire . . .', *Archaeologia*, XIX, 56–61.

Coghlan, H. H., 1970. *A Report upon the Hoard of Bronze Age Tools and Weapons from Yattendon, near Newbury, Berkshire.* Newbury.

Colchester Museum, 1960. *Souvenir of the Centenary of the Colchester and Essex Museum.* Colchester.

Coles, J. M., 1959–60. 'Scottish Late Bronze Age metalwork . . .', *Proc. Soc. Antiq. Scot.,* XCIII, 16–134.

——1962. 'European Bronze Age shields', *Proc. Prehist. Soc.,* XXVIII, 156–90.

—— 1966–7. 'Experimental Archaeology', *Proc. Soc. Antiq. Scot.,* XCIX, 1–20.

Coles, J. M., Coutts, H., & Ryder, M. L., 1964. 'A Late Bronze Age find from Pyotdykes, Angus, Scotland, with associated gold, cloth, leather and wood remains', *Proc. Prehist. Soc.,* XXX, 186–98.

Coles, J. M. & Scott, J. G., 1962–3. 'The Late Bronze Age hoard from Peelhill, Strathaven, Lanarkshire', *Proc. Soc. Antiq. Scot.,* XCVI, 136–44.

Cordier, G., Millotte, J. P., & Riquet, R., 1959. 'La cachette de bronze d'Azay-le-Rideau (Indre-et-Loire)', *Gallia Préhist.,* II, 57–71.

Cowen, J. D., 1933. 'Two bronze swords from Ewart Park, Wooler', *Archaeol. Aeliana,* 4 ser., X, 185–98.

—— 1951. 'The earliest bronze swords in Britain and their origins on the Continent of Europe', *Proc. Prehist. Soc.,* XVII, 195–213.

—— 1952. 'Bronze swords in northern Europe: a reconsideration of Sprockhoff's *Griffzungenschwerter*', *Proc. Prehist. Soc.,* XVIII, 129–47.

Cunliffe, B., 1968. 'Excavations at Eldon's Seat, Encombe, Dorset', *Proc. Prehist. Soc.,* XXXIV, 191–237.

Davies, D. G., 1967. 'The Guilsfield hoard: a reconsideration', *Antiq. J.,* XLVII, 95–108.

Edwardson, A. R., n.d. *Bronze Age Metal Work in Moyses Hall Museum, Bury St. Edmunds, Suffolk.* Bury St Edmunds.

Eogan, G., 1964. 'The later Bronze Age in Ireland in the light of recent research',　*Proc. Prehist. Soc.,* XXX, 268–351.

—— 1965. *Catalogue of Irish Bronze Swords.* Dublin.

—— 1966. 'A hoard of bronze objects from Booltiaghadine, Co. Clare', *N. Munster Antiq. J.,* X, 67–9.

Evans, E. E., 1933. 'The bronze spearhead in Great Britain and Ireland', *Archaeologia,* LXXXIII, 187–202.

Evans, J., 1870–3. 'The Bronze Period', *Proc. Soc. Antiq. London,* 2 ser., V, 392–412.

—— 1879. 'A hoard of bronze antiquities found in Berkshire', *Proc. Soc. Antiq. London,* 2 ser., VII, 480–5.

—— 1881. *Ancient Bronze Implements, Weapons, and Ornaments, of Great Britain and Ireland.* London.

—— 1885. 'On a hoard of bronze objects found in Wilburton Fen, near Ely', *Archaeologia,* XLVIII, 106–14.

Fox, C., 1923. *The Archaeology of the Cambridge Region.* Cambridge.

—— 1933. 'The distribution of Man in East Anglia, c. 2300 B.C.–A.D. 50', *Proc. Prehist. Soc. E. Anglia,* VII, part ii, 149–64.

—— 1946. *A Find of the Early Iron Age from Llyn Cerrig Bach, Anglesey.* Cardiff.

Fox, C. & Hyde, H. A., 1939. 'A second cauldron and an iron sword from the Llyn Fawr hoard, Rhigos, Glamorganshire', *Antiq. J.,* XIX, 369–404.

Franks, A. W., 1864–7. In 'Proceedings' (Plaistow spearhead), *Proc. Soc. Antiq. London,* 2 ser., III, 165–6.

Grace, R., 1943. 'Additions to the Bronze Age hoard from Broadoak, Sturry, Kent', *Antiq. J.,* XXIII, 148–9.

Greenwell, W. & Brewis, W. P., 1909. 'The origin, evolution and classification of the bronze spear-head in Great Britain and Ireland', *Archaeologia,* LXI, 439–72.

Griffiths, W. E., 1957. 'The Pant-y-Maen bronze hoard', *Bull. Board Celtic Stud.,* XVII, 118–24.

Hartshorne, C. H., 1841. *Salopia Antiqua.* London.

Hatley, A. R., 1933. *Early Days in the Walthamstow District* (Walthamstow Antiq. Soc. Publ., XXVIII).

Hawkes, C. F. C. (ed.), 1955. 'Grave-groups and hoards of the British Bronze Age', *Inventaria Archaeologica,* 1st Set: GB. 1–8.

Hawkes, C. F. C. & Smith, M. A. (eds), 1955. 'Bronze Age hoards in the British Museum', *Inventaria Archaeologica*, 2nd Set: GB. 9–13.

Hearne, F., 1940. 'A bronze hoard from Flansham, near Middleton', *Sussex Archaeol. Collect.*, LXXXI, 205–9.

Hodges, H. W. M., 1956. 'Studies in the Late Bronze Age in Ireland II: the typology and distribution of bronze implements', *Ulster J. Archaeol.*, XIX, 29–56.

Howarth, E., 1899. *Catalogue of the Bateman Collection of Antiquities in the Sheffield Public Museum*. London.

Hundt, H.-J., 1955. 'Versuch zur Deutung der Depotfunde der Nordischen Jüngeren Bronzezeit unter besonderer Brücksichtigung Mecklenburgs', *Jahrbuch des Römisch-Germanischen Zentralmuseums Mainz*, II, 95–132.

Jackman, T., 1868. In 'Proceedings' (The Broadward hoard), *J. Brit. Archaeol. Assoc.*, XXIV, 64, 307.

Jackson, J. W., 1927. 'A Bronze Age find in Cheshire', *Antiq. J.*, VII, 62–4.

Jacob-Friesen, G., 1968. 'Ein Depotfund des Formenkreises um die "Karpfenzungenschwerter" aus der Normandie', *Germania*, XLVI, 248–74.

Jessup, R. F., 1943. 'A Bronze Age hoard from Sturry, Kent', *Antiq. J.*, XXIII, 55–6.

Kendrick, T. D., 1928. *The Archaeology of the Channel Islands, Vol. I: The Bailiwick of Guernsey*. London.

Kendrick, T. D. & Hawkes, C. F. C., 1932. *Archaeology in England and Wales 1914–31*. London.

Lawrence, G. F., 1929. 'Antiquities from the Middle Thames', *Archaeol. J.*, LXXXVI, 69–98.

Mariën, M.-E., 1958. *Trouvailles du Champ d'Urnes et des Tombelles hallstattiennes de Court-Saint-Etienne*. Brussels.

Maryon, H., 1938. 'Some prehistoric metalworkers' tools', *Antiq. J.*, XVIII, 241–50.

Norwich Castle Museum, 1966. *Bronze Age metalwork in Norwich Castle Museum*. Norwich.

Radley, J., 1966. 'New Bronze Age spearheads from Yorkshire, and a provisional list of Yorkshire spearheads', *Yorkshire Archaeol. J.*, XLII, part i, 15–19.

RCHM Cambridge. Royal Commission on Historical Monuments, England, 1959. *An Inventory of the Historical Monuments in the City of Cambridge*. Part I. London.

Rocke, T. O. & Barnwell, E. L., 1872. 'The bronze relics of Broadward, Shropshire: some details of the Broadward "find"', *Archaeol. Cambrensis*, 4 ser., III, 338–55.

Rolls, J. E., 1861. In 'Proceedings' (Pendoylan and Bloody Pool Finds), *Archaeol. J.*, XVIII, 161.

Roskill, V., 1938. 'Bronze implements of the Newbury region', *Trans. Newbury Dist. Fld. Club*, VIII.

Savory, H. N., 1957. 'A corpus of Welsh Bronze Age pottery, II: Food Vessels and Enlarged Food Vessels', *Bull. Board Celtic Stud.*, XVII, 196–233.

—— 1958. 'The Late Bronze Age in Wales: some new discoveries and new interpretations', *Archaeol. Cambrensis*, CVII, 3–63.

—— 1965. 'The Guilsfield hoard', *Bull. Board Celtic Stud.*, XXI, part ii, 179–206.

Smith, M. A. (ed.), 1957. 'Bronze Age hoards and grave-groups from the N.E. Midlands', *Inventaria Archaeologica*, 4th Set: GB.19–24.

—— (ed.), 1958. 'Late Bronze hoards in the British Museum', *Inventaria Archaeologica*, 6th Set: GB.35–41.

—— (ed.), 1959. 'Middle Bronze hoards from southern England', *Inventaria Archaeologica*, 7th Set: GB.42–7.

Smith, R. A., 1909–11. 'A Bronze Age hoard dredged from the Thames off Broadness', *Proc. Soc. Antiq. London*, 2 ser., XXIII, 160–71.

—— 1928. 'Pre-Roman remains at Scarborough', *Archaeologia*, LXXVII, 179–200.

Smith-Masters, J. E., 1929. *Yattendon and its Church*.

Sprockhoff, E., 1937. *Jungbronzezeitliche Hortfunde Norddeutschlands. Periode IV*. Mainz.

Thompson, F. H., 1954. 'A bronze spear-head from Donington on Bain, Lincolnshire', *Antiq. J.*, XXXIV, 238.

—— 1970. 'Archaeology of the Congleton area', in Stephens, W. B. (ed.), *History of Congleton*.

Trollope, A., 1861. In 'Proceedings' (Nettleham hoard), *Archaeol. J.*, XVIII, 159–60.

Trump, B. A. V., 1968. 'Fenland rapiers', in Coles, J. M. & Simpson, D. D. A. (eds), *Studies in Ancient Europe*, Leicester, 213–25.

Tucker, C., 1855. In 'Proceedings' (Bloody Pool hoard), *Archaeol. J.*, XII, 84–5.

—— 1867. 'Notices of antiquities of bronze found in Devonshire', *Archaeol. J.*, XXIV, 110–22.

Varley, W. J. & Jackson, J. W., 1940. *Prehistoric Cheshire*. Chester.
Ward, J., 1934. 'The Bronze Age in Montgomeryshire: Part II', *Montgomeryshire Collect.*, XLIII, 110–65.
White, G., 1887. *The Natural History and Antiquities of Selborne*. New ed. London.

ACKNOWLEDGEMENTS

We are grateful to the curators and staff of museums throughout Britain and Ireland who have given us every facility in our work on material in their collections for this survey; especially the British Museum and the London Museum, the Buxton, Exeter, Ipswich, Norwich Castle, Reading, Taunton, Warwick and Winchester Museums, Congleton Public Library, and the National Museums in Cardiff, Edinburgh and Dublin; to the Society of Antiquaries of London, for allowing us to work on material in their collections, including the Way Papers; to Dr J. D. Cowen for providing Appendix 2; to Mr R. A. Rutland for drawings of material in Reading Museum and to Mr D. V. Clarke of the National Museum of Antiquities, Edinburgh, for providing a drawing of the Duddingston Loch barbed spearhead. C. B. would like to record his debt to the late Mr M. Waterhouse, and Mrs Waterhouse, for all the help and hospitality he received when he drew the Yattendon hoard at Yattendon in 1966. The Trustees of the British Museum, the London Museum and the Ipswich Museum kindly allowed material to be deposited at Verulamium Museum, St Albans, so that D. G. D. could study and draw it. Above all, we are indebted to Mrs Maureen Fadian, who worked for so many months in preparing for publication our original pencil drawings, and helped to put the whole paper together.

The Hill-fort on South Barrule and its Position in the Manx Iron Age

Peter S. Gelling

The Iron Age in the Isle of Man was a lengthy period. Its beginning, as will be suggested in this paper, was at least not later than in most other parts of the British Isles; and as, firstly, there was no Roman invasion to interrupt it, and, secondly, the coming of Christianity left no mark that has yet been clearly identified on secular sites, the next unmistakable archaeological horizon is provided by the Viking burials of the ninth and tenth centuries AD, and by the houses which reflect Scandinavian traditions of building.

Three main types of site have to be fitted into this local Iron Age: the hill-forts, the promontory forts, and the circular rath-like sites of the kind excavated by the late Professor G. Bersu on the farms of Ballacagen and Ballanorris in the south of the island. There are only two hill-forts (of which South Barrule is one); thus, most of the sites which are known or believed to belong to the Iron Age fall into one or other of the second two categories.

It was the excavations on Ballacagen and Ballanorris which provided the first fixed point for the Manx Iron Age. Although they have not yet been fully published, the plan of the earliest phase of site A on Ballacagen has been in print for many years (Bersu, 1945–6) and illustrates the excavator's conclusion that these roughly circular sites, demarcated by low earth-banks, mark the positions of large timber houses as much as 26 m. (c. 85 ft 6 in.) in diameter. They could provide shelter for livestock as well as for the family, and could be regarded as an adaptation of the Little Woodbury plan to the wetter conditions of the north-west. Professor Bersu dated the occupation of the Ballacagen sites to the first–third centuries AD. They are undefended, as indeed are all the sites of this group, except in so far as some of them are situated in very marshy ground; and it is tempting to associate them with the period of *pax Romana* in the Irish Sea area. But they may not all belong to this period, and it has been suggested that at least one was still occupied as late as the Viking period (Gelling, 1964).

It was one of the promontory forts which provided the next relatively fixed point. This was Close ny chollagh, a coastal fort only about a mile away from Ballacagen. It has a dump rampart on the landward side, and a stone wall, faced with excellent dry masonry, on the other three. It contained four huts, which were probably occupied consecutively. The clearest indication of date was provided by a La Tène III brooch of Colchester type lying near the top of a thick deposit of midden material which covered all the huts but one. This was almost certainly lost well before the end of the first century AD, more probably in the first half of the century, and, on the evidence of its stratigraphical position, probably towards the end of the occupation of the site. It appears therefore that this small but quite strongly defended coastal fort preceded the establishment on Ballacagen of a large undefended homestead, and that the change from one to the other took place in the first century AD (Gelling, 1958).

It is unfortunately impossible to say how far this date can be applied to the other promontory forts, of which twenty-one examples are known round the coast, and three inland. Three other coastal forts have been excavated (Bersu, 1949; Gelling, 1952; 1959), but in all of them the principal remains belonged to the Norse period. Their defences were in one case demonstrably, and in the other two very probably, a good deal older than the Norse remains, but that is all that can be said. The only inland promontory fort that has been excavated is on Ballanicholas farm in the parish of Kirk Marown (Gelling, 1968). It is very small, and almost the whole of the defended area was occupied by a timber house about 9m. (30 ft) in diameter. This time the most valuable piece of dating evidence was a penannular brooch probably belonging to the first, or possibly the second, century AD. An earlier rather than a later date within this range is suggested by the fact that there was no trace of pottery on the site, and that pottery was similarly lacking at Close ny chollagh. At Ballacagen, on the other hand, a little coarse pottery was present even in the earliest phase. Iron Age pottery was totally absent at the other three excavated coastal forts.

It may be tentatively deduced from this evidence that there was a period in the early first century AD (and probably earlier still, since the promontory forts characteristically show two periods in their defences) when these forts were occupied by people who did not use pottery. Then there was a change to the undefended type of site represented by Ballacagen, and at this time a little rudimentary pottery was used. This phase lasted, according to Bersu, until at least the third century AD.

At this stage it was thought desirable to fit a hill-fort into the sequence, and South Barrule was chosen for excavation (fig. 1, pl. XIII). The mountain is 484m. (1585 ft) high, and the fort occupies the summit. There are two ramparts, roughly 30m. (100 ft) apart, and the inner one is now so slight, and in some places so difficult to follow, that it is hard to resist the conclusion that it was robbed to provide material for the outer one. This inner rampart appeared, when excavated, to have had an outer face of stone, made up of large slabs of slate laid as headers, backed by a turf bank. Within the area it encloses, the outlines of nearly eighty huts can be discerned on the surface, and of these, three were excavated in 1960 and 1961, and one more in 1968. It soon became clear in 1960 that pottery was relatively plentiful on the site, a most unexpected state of affairs in the Isle of Man. It was by no means a sophisticated ware, but it was nothing like as thick and coarse as the pottery from Ballacagen. It seemed, therefore, that the site must be either earlier than the pottery-less promontory forts, or later than Ballacagen; which means, in fact, either earlier than the first century AD, or later than the third. When the work of the first two years' digging was published (Gelling, 1963) a tentative preference was expressed for the later date, and the nature of the settlement was related to the disturbed conditions which seem to have prevailed in the Irish Sea during the later fourth century AD. As the two possibilities were quite widely separated in time, it was reasonable to hope that a radiocarbon date might come down decisively on one side or the other, so a further excavation was carried out in 1968 to secure a suitable sample.

That year the work was carried out in unusually fine weather, and there was no difficulty in showing that there had been two periods of occupation, apparently not very much separated in time, in the hut which was excavated. The carbon sample examined came from the upper of two closely superimposed hearths, and the date given for it by the Radiocarbon Dating Laboratory at Birmingham University (Birm–119) was 523 ± 84 BC (Libby half life). In view of the modifications recently suggested for radiocarbon dates based on this half life, the calendar date of the site is probably at least as early as 523 BC, and possibly appreciably earlier. This at least seems to dispose of the later date which was at first thought possible, and demands an explana-

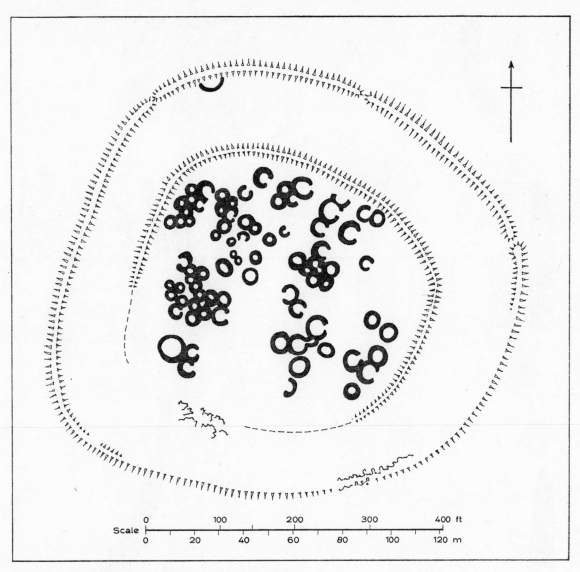

fig. 1 General plan of the hill-fort on South Barrule

tion in terms of a stage of the Iron Age which would, at least until recently, have been considered a very early one indeed.

The pottery found in 1968 was of the same kind as that found in the earlier excavations, but it included some larger pieces and some more significant shapes. As in the previous excavation, it was in a very soft condition, and had to be treated urgently before much could be done to clean it. This has contributed to the very dark colour of many of the sherds, originally discoloured by fire or peat-staining. None of the sherds appears to have been dark originally, and various shades from cream to pale buff seem to have predominated. The cream surface, which looks at first sight like a slip but may have been produced by levigation, occasionally has a faint pinkish tinge, and sometimes contrasts sharply with a dark core. The surface is sometimes smooth and regular, but it is more often irregular and undulating. The surface of fig. 2, no. 1, when all allowance has been made for deterioration, seems to indicate that this was one of the

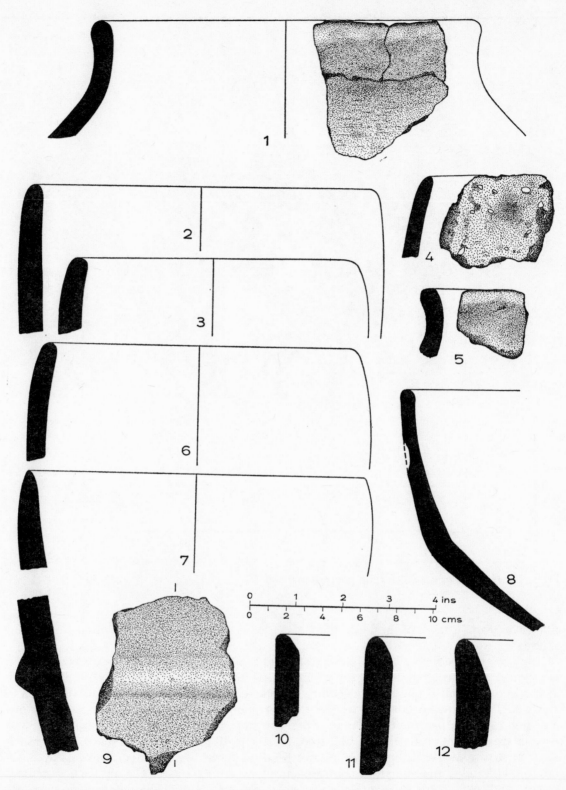

fig. 2 Pottery from the hill-fort on South Barrule ($\frac{1}{2}$)

cruder pots, and the better surfaces appear on the barrel-shapes. Fig. 2, no. 8, likewise, is of a very inferior ware. Most sherds are tempered with a coarse grit. On the surface of the more carefully made pots this scarcely shows, but at the other extreme (e.g. fig. 2, no. 4) no effort at all is made to conceal it. There are several intermediate varieties, and on many the tempering does show through the cream surface quite clearly, though the grits are relatively fine, seldom having a maximum dimension of more than 2 mm.

A cream surface, not unlike that found on many of these sherds, appears quite often on the Ballacagen pottery, which also sometimes has a pinkish tinge. But this is an altogether coarser ware, with grits up to 24 mm. in maximum dimensions. None of the sherds show anything like the finish of the better sherds from South Barrule, and, apart from the cream surface, the two groups differ so much in other respects that there is hardly likely to be any connection between them.

The predominant shape amongst the pottery is a plain barrel-type, with the rim either vertical or slightly inturned. This appears to be related to the plain shape which MacKie places at the beginning of his Hebridean Iron Age sequence. A very similar shape has recently been found at Skaill, Deerness, Orkney, in association with grass-tempered ware very like that which occurs in the earliest deposits at Jarlshof (Hamilton, 1956, p. 13). What distinguishes the South Barrule shapes is the absence of a flattened rim. Rims are normally rounded, one or two are almost pointed, and they often have a marked internal bevel. Local cinerary urns normally have just such a bevel on the rim, and their other characteristic feature, the cordon, is represented on one sherd from South Barrule (fig. 2, no. 9). It is tempting to interpret this as evidence for contact with the local Bronze Age potting tradition. A comparable continuity in potting has been suggested for the Ludlow area in south Shropshire, principally on the basis of the material used for tempering (Gelling & Peacock, 1968); and here also the relevant Iron Age sherds – from Caynham Camp – have a plain internally bevelled rim.

Two of the sherds (fig. 2, nos 1 and 8), provide a hint of external influence. They stand apart from the rest, and it is possible to see in them reflections of the situate jar and the carinated bowl which characterise Iron Age A in England. The reflections are admittedly rather faint, but one might, for instance, believe that no. 8 was connected with the type of carinated bowl found at Maiden Castle, in which the flaring rim begins immediately above the carination. But on neither of these two sherds is there a clearly articulated rim; if there is any Iron Age A tradition here, it is certainly rather devolved. A pot like no. 1 might have been expected to have some sort of finger-print ornament, but in fact it has not, nor has any other sherd from the site.

Who were the people who built the hill-fort? The plain barrel shape of most of the pottery belongs to a widespread group, but the absence of any flattening on the rim suggests that this was a separate variety which had evolved locally. So the fort-builders may simply have been the local Bronze Age population. There may have been amongst them a small external element who had some acquaintance with Iron Age A potting traditions, and it was possibly this group which was responsible for the idea of constructing a hill-fort. The defences are very simple, and do not make it necessary to postulate the arrival of outsiders with a tradition of this kind of building, with the possible exception of a modest timber *chevaux de frise* which was found at one point some 7 m. (24 ft) outside the inner rampart (Harbison, 1971, 206-8). This may represent something a little more specialised than the local population could have devised for themselves when they felt the need for defence.

The crisis which led to the building of the fort, and compelled people to live on an extremely bleak mountain-top, must have been a serious one, and it probably arose as early as the sixth century BC. A few years ago this date would have been regarded as surprisingly early, but today it can be related to even earlier dates for fortifications in Scotland (MacKie, 1965). At the moment it seems as if the general insecurity which characterises the Iron Age set in earlier in the

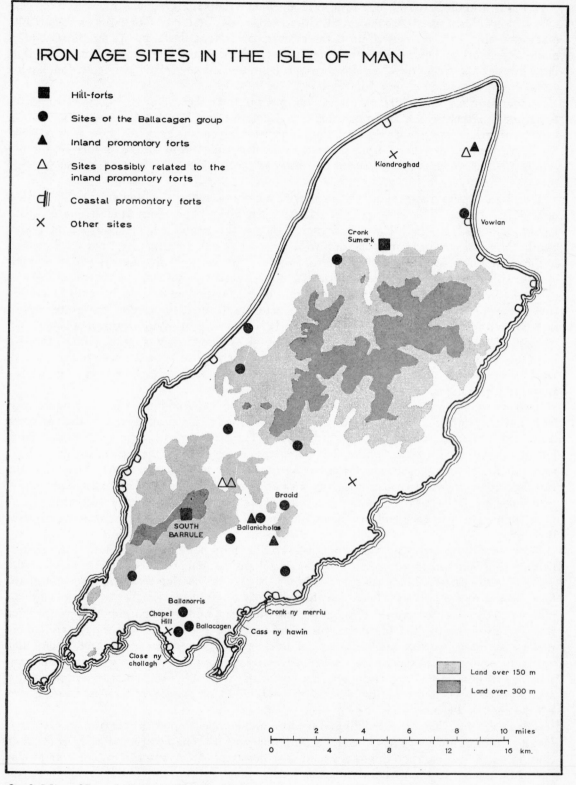

IRON AGE SITES IN THE ISLE OF MAN

- ■ Hill-forts
- ● Sites of the Ballacagen group
- ▲ Inland promontory forts
- △ Sites possibly related to the inland promontory forts
- ◁| Coastal promontory forts
- ✕ Other sites

Kiondroghad

Vowlan

Cronk Sumark

Braaid

South Barrule

Ballanicholas

Ballanorris

Chapel Hill

Ballacagen

Cronk ny merriu

Cass ny hawin

Close ny chollagh

Land over 150 m

Land over 300 m

| 0 | 2 | 4 | 6 | 8 | 10 miles |

| 0 | 4 | 8 | 12 | 16 km. |

fig. 3 Map of Iron Age sites in the Isle of Man

north and west than it did elsewhere in the British Isles. It is meaningless to describe the South Barrule hill-fort as Late Bronze Age or as Early Iron Age, but it does represent a type of settlement which became very common in England in the ensuing centuries. It would be interesting to know whether the island's other hill-fort, Cronk Sumark, which overlooks the northern plain, is as old as South Barrule. No excavation has been done there, but the inner of the two main ramparts has produced vitrified material, and although this does not provide much chronological guidance, at least it does not exclude an early date.

The small fortified site – a sort of family-size fortification – is much more characteristic of the Irish Sea–Western Scotland area than is the hill-fort. The coastal promontory fort of Close ny chollagh was occupied in the first century AD, and so, probably, was the inland fort on Ballanicholas. Both indicate a time of insecurity comparable to that which produced the South Barrule hill-fort, but they show a quite different kind of response. It was the family which at this stage protected itself, not the community as a whole. Naturally it cannot be said that none of the promontory forts is as old as the hill-fort on South Barrule, but such indications of date as we have suggest that they characterise a subsequent phase.

After them, in perhaps the late first century AD, we have the undefended round houses on Ballacagen, the latest of which was occupied until the third century AD. It is hard to say what happened after that, if indeed any changes took place at all. It has already been suggested that the circular house still formed part of the Manx scene when the Vikings arrived.

At some point the top of the South Barrule was re-fortified, this time with a more formidable rampart, which had a vertical outer face of stone. The fort was now much larger, but no huts seem to have been built in the extra space available. Unfortunately excavation threw no light whatsoever on the date of this later rampart. Between *c.* AD 300 and the Norse settlement the only secular site which is known to have been occupied is on Kiondroghad in the north of the island. This appeared before excavation to be a round house of the Ballacagen type, but it turned out to be a metal-working site of about the eighth century AD, and the only building which could be identified was a small oblong hut (Gelling, 1969). So it has to be admitted that the sites marked on fig. 3 as being of the Ballacagen type may not really form a homogeneous group.

In so far as a sequence can be proposed at the moment for the Manx Iron Age, it appears to be as follows: first, South Barrule hill-fort; then, the small promontory forts (Close ny chollagh and Ballanicholas); then, the large undefended circular house (fig. 3). There is one Iron Age site that has been partially excavated, which cannot yet be fitted into the sequence. This is the settlement on Chapel Hill, which is near to both Ballacagen and Close ny chollagh. The slight bank which surrounds it scarcely deserves to be called a defensive work, and it would be misleading to describe it as a hill-fort. When Dr Bersu excavated there he found signs of intensive occupation, including deeply cut postholes which indicated solid wooden buildings; but he found no dating evidence at all, and could only ascribe the site generally to the Iron Age. All one can say is that the absence of pottery makes it unlikely that the settlement was contemporary with either South Barrule or Ballacagen.

BIBLIOGRAPHY

Bersu, G., 1945–6. 'Celtic homesteads in the Isle of Man', *J. Manx Mus.*, 72–3, 177–82.

—— 1949. 'A promontory fort on the shore of Ramsey Bay, Isle of Man', *Antiq. J.*, XXIX, 62–79.

Gelling, P., 1952. 'Excavation of a promontory fort at Port Grenaugh, Isle of Man', *Proc. Isle Man Natur. Hist. Antiq. Soc.*, V, no. 3, 307–17.

—— 1958. 'Close ny chollagh: an Iron Age fort at Scarlett, Isle of Man', *Proc. Prehist. Soc.*, XXIV, 85–100.

—— 1959. 'Excavation of a promontory fort at Cass ny hawin, Malew, Isle of Man', *Proc. Isle Man Natur. Hist. Antiq. Soc.*, VI, no. 1, 28–38.

—— 1963. 'Excavations at the hill-fort on South Barrule', *Proc. Isle Man Natur. Hist. Antiq. Soc.*, VI, no. 3, 313–23.

—— 1964. 'The Braaid site', *J. Manx Mus.*, 80, 201–5.

—— 1968. 'Excavation of a promontory fort on Ballanicholas, Kirk Marown, Isle of Man', *Proc. Isle Man Natur. Hist. Antiq. Soc.*, VII, no. 2, 181–91.

—— 1969. 'A metalworking site at Kiondroghad, Kirk Andreas, Isle of Man', *Medieval Archaeol.*, XIII, 67–83.

Gelling, P. & Peacock, D. P. S., 1968. 'The pottery from Caynham Camp, near Ludlow', *Trans. Shropshire Archaeol. Soc.*, LVIII, part 2, 96–100.

Hamilton, J. R. C., 1956. *Excavations at Jarlshof, Shetland*. Edinburgh.

Harbison, P., 1971. 'Wooden and stone *chevaux-de-frise* in central and western Europe', *Proc. Prehist. Soc.*, XXXVII, part I, 195–225.

MacKie, E., 1965. 'Brochs and the Hebridean Iron Age', *Antiquity*, XXXIX, 266–78.

The Size-Distribution of Hill-Forts in Wales and the Marches

A. H. A. Hogg

SUMMARY

Classification of hill-forts by size makes it possible to identify several separate groups of small enclosures (under 0·7 hectare, 1·75 acres) which show a marked difference in distribution from the larger forts. The possible significance of these differences in terms of social function and the spread of hill-fort building is discussed.

INTRODUCTION

Since the Ordnance Survey in 1962 published the Map of Southern Britain in the Iron Age, it has been recognised that hill-forts[1] in that area show a tendency towards a western distribution, mainly owing to a preponderance of small forts. Subsequent examination of size-distribution in particular areas has shown striking differences between regions, even on the basis of very rough comparison.[2] It seemed therefore that a more thorough analysis covering the whole of Wales including the Marches might yield some interesting results.

In detail, the region studied is that between the Mersey and Severn estuaries, extending eastwards as far as the 60 km. line of the National Grid in squares SJ and SO. The area is approximately one-fifth of that covered by the Iron Age Map; but the number of sites known is just over 770, compared with less than 1,400 for the whole map. Rather less than a quarter have been the subjects of detailed and accurate surveys, though the enclosed areas of almost exactly 90% of these 770 sites have been at least roughly identified. But since this sample

[1] The term 'hill-forts' (sc. 'and related structures') is widely understood, and is more concise and generally less inaccurate than most alternatives which have been suggested. The purist who demands a precise definition may regard the term as covering classes A, B and H of the 'Scheme for Recording . . . Earthworks . . .' published in 1910 and later by the Congress of Archaeological Societies. These are:

A. Fortresses partly inaccessible by reason of precipices, cliffs, or water, defended in part only by artificial works.

B. Fortresses on hill-tops with artificial defences, following the natural line of the hill, or, though usually on high ground, less dependent on natural slopes for protection.

H. Ancient village sites protected by walls, ramparts, or fosses.

A few sites generally accepted as hill-forts may perhaps come into class X: Defensive or other works which fall under none of the above headings.

[2] During work for the RCAM Inventories of Caernarvonshire and Glamorgan, and on selected coastal areas to be published in the forthcoming report of the CBA Conference on the Iron Age in the Irish Sea Province.

might be taken as representative of British hill-forts in general, it must be emphasised at once that marked regional differences exist; such conclusions as are reached may suggest lines of inquiry appropriate to other areas, but without more detailed study they cannot safely be extended even to adjacent districts.

Investigation has been restricted to consideration of the enclosed area and the number of defensive ramparts. These are the only significant data[1] known for the whole region; area is probably the most important single characteristic. Various sources have been used,[2] but for many of the sites it has been necessary to depend on the 6-inch O.S. Map. There is thus a large uncertainty in area, perhaps as much as 0·1 hectare (·25 acre) either way even for the smallest enclosures, but, as will be seen, this does not invalidate most of the statistical deductions, though no doubt fine detail is obscured.

METHOD OF ANALYSIS

The initial hypothesis was that the total distribution of forts in Wales was made up from a number of distinct groups. Each group would be likely to display a preferred size, though with a wide range on either side of it; and each group would tend to occupy a particular district, though there might be a diffuse scatter of examples round the edges. The limits of size and district for different groups might overlap.

This hypothesis was suggested by the examination of limited areas mentioned above; the aim here has been to discover whether such groups exist, and to what extent they can be identified, working over a larger region. The approach adopted was to sort the forts by size, the limits of each class being initially rather close, in the ratio $\sqrt{2}:1$. Using as background a map showing all known forts, the separate classes were plotted. From this, groups were tentatively identified, and these were then re-examined, both on the map and by the size-distribution within the groups. For brevity, only the final results are given here; the stages leading to them are merely outlined.

Clearly this limitation to size and number of ramparts cuts out several important elements, but this disadvantage is to some extent counterbalanced, not only because the simplification makes the material more manageable, but because the assessment of the relations between forts on the evidence of such factors as rampart structure tends to be rather subjective. Even the two items considered cannot always be determined quite objectively. It is sometimes difficult to decide whether a fort is uni- or multi-vallate, or to estimate the area enclosed at a particular stage in the development of a multi-period site.

Many forts, of course, have been extensively altered during their existence. In the initial analysis, each phase was treated separately, so that one site might appear on several maps. This still occurs on those published, but where several phases occur within the limits of a single map the rule followed has been to plot the site as being of the largest size which it reached, within those limits; where the largest enclosure was at one stage uni- and at another multi-vallate, it is plotted as multivallate.

---

[1] The height above Ordnance Datum is also known, but seems to have little significance in detail.

[2] Apart from descriptions of a few individual sites, the best sources are the RCAM Inventories for Anglesey (1937 and reprints), Caernarvonshire (1956–64) and Glamorgan (in preparation), and Bowen & Gresham, 1967. County lists have been published in the *Bulletin of the Board of Celtic Studies* as follows: Brecknock (H. N. Savory) XIV, 66 ff. and XV, 230; Carmarthenshire (H.N.S.) XVI, 54 ff.; Glamorgan (H.N.S.) XIII, 142 ff. and XV, 229; Monmouthshire (H.N.S.) XIII, 231 ff. and XV, 229; Radnorshire (H.N.S.) XV, 73 ff.; Cardiganshire (A. H. A. Hogg) XIX, 354 ff.; Pembrokeshire (D. W. Crossley) XX, 171 ff. The last two give too little detail of areas.

*The Size-
Distribution of
Hill-forts in Wales
and the Marches*

THE AGE OF THE FORTS

The most important factor for understanding the evolution of hill-fort building is a knowledge of the dates of construction and occupation, and this is unfortunately almost entirely lacking, though a few sites in the Marches, such as Croft Ambrey, are now yielding some reliable evidence. Nevertheless, for the region as a whole, only the vaguest generalisations are possible. Casual finds of Roman pot, and the sparse results of excavation, suggest that most sites may have remained in occupation during the first century BC, whatever their type of construction; but where a structural sequence can be worked out, univallate forts are earlier than multivallate.

Thus it is probably legitimate to regard the total distribution of all types of fort as corresponding roughly to that of the fort-dwelling population at the time of the Roman invasions, while the univallate sites represent a generally earlier phase of settlement. It would be unsafe, though, to argue that any particular univallate enclosure was necessarily earlier than a multivallate one. There is a further difficulty in that some of the forts are certainly post-Roman. Where this has been proved by excavation, the site has been omitted, but the writer now considers it very doubtful whether all enclosures of similar form and construction must be placed so late. Doubtful sites have therefore been retained, except those which seem likely to represent twelfth-century earthwork castles.

IDENTIFICATION OF GROUPS

Considering the region as a whole, a marked change in the appearance of the distribution maps becomes noticeable when the areas of the sites plotted exceed 0·7 hectare (1·75 acres). Below that figure several groups can be more or less convincingly identified, so it seems justifiable to consider these small forts as a separate class.

It is doubtful whether the work involved in any sophisticated clustering technique would be justified by the quality of the results, but to give some sort of objective definition to the groups, envelopes have been sketched for all the positions of a 10 km. diameter circle enclosing five small forts, also for those enclosing four where the result differs significantly. These envelopes are shown on fig. 4, since to superimpose them on the map showing the small forts would make it more difficult for the reader to assess their validity for himself. In most cases, examination of the map suggested that these envelopes were too exclusive, so larger arbitrary boundaries have been added. As will be seen below, however, the subjectively chosen groups F and L show in their histograms a much less marked preference for a particular size of fort. This suggests that the forts included in them are less likely to belong to a single identifiable class.

Eleven separate groups of these small forts seem to be identifiable (figs 1, 4). Their histograms (fig. 5) show that they almost certainly include examples much larger than the assumed limit of 0·7 hectare, so attempts to separate out other groupings must start with the largest forts.

The next well-marked change in the distribution pattern (*cf.* figs 1, 3) occurs at about 2 hectares (5 acres). The histogram for all forts (fig. 5) shows a clear break in the size-distribution for multivallate sites at 12 hectares (30 acres), so although the division is not so definite for univallate enclosures it seems justifiable to separate out a small class of fort above that limit. Neither this nor the 2–12-hectare class can be subdivided on distributional evidence alone; no detailed attempt at classification by structure will be made here, though this would certainly be possible, given fuller knowledge of the remains.

The distribution of forts between 0·7 and 2 hectares supports the conclusion, reached by a study of the histograms and by *a priori* reasoning, that both the larger and smaller size-distributions spread over into this range. The map (fig. 2) therefore gives little useful informa-

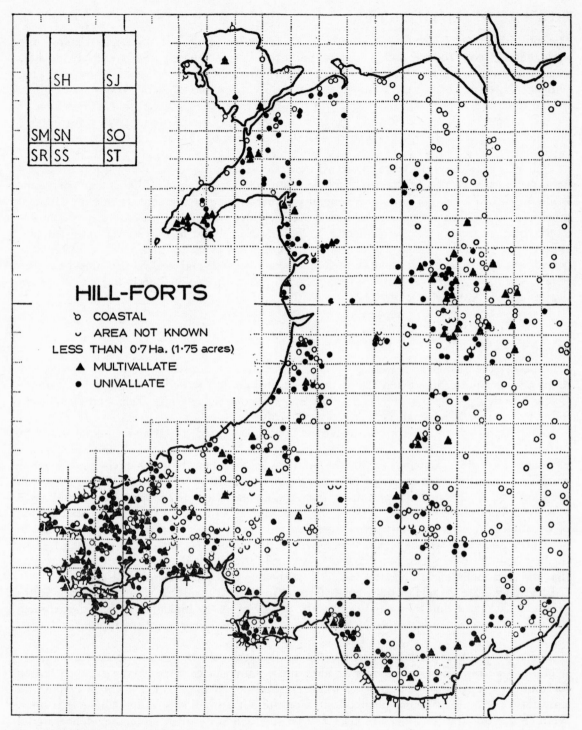

HILL-FORTS

ᓍ COASTAL
ᴗ AREA NOT KNOWN
LESS THAN 0·7 Ha. (1·75 acres)
▲ MULTIVALLATE
● UNIVALLATE

fig. 1 Small hill-forts in Wales

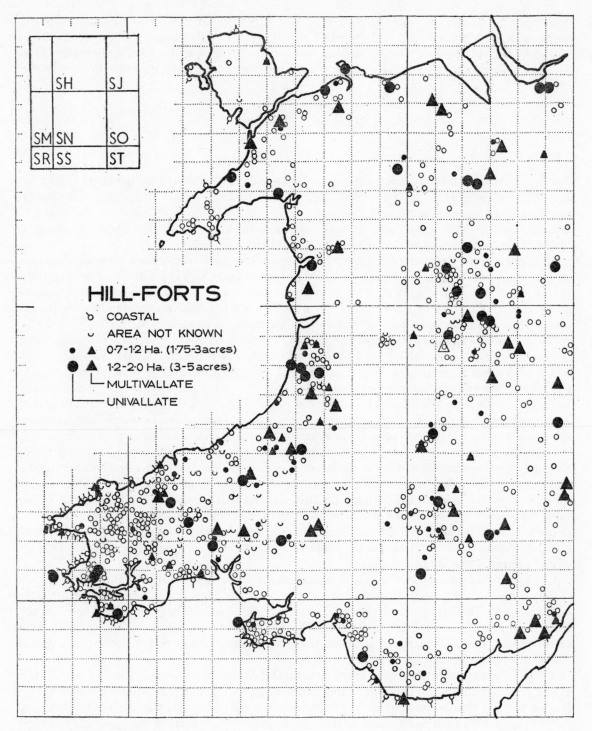

fig. 2 Medium-sized hill-forts in Wales

tion, but it is included for completeness. The 2-hectare forts are shown both on this map and on fig. 3. In both these maps, also, the size ranges have been subdivided, at 1·2 and 6 hectares (3 and 15 acres) respectively, to correspond to the divisions used on the Ordnance Survey Iron Age Map, though it is doubtful whether these sizes are of any particular significance in this region.

THE SEPARATE GROUPS OF SMALL FORTS

For the purpose of this discussion these groups are sufficiently defined by the maps (figs 1, 4) and the size-histograms (fig. 5). The Statistical Note forming an appendix to this discussion applies a rather more systematic analysis to some aspects of these, but the evidence from size alone is obviously not detailed enough to justify anything very refined. For the same reason, a rather more subjective approach seems legitimate here.

Statistically (*see* p. 303 and fig. 4), the eleven groups of small forts show a clear division into two sets: I, comprising D, E, F, G and L; and II, with A, B, C, H, J and K. It is interesting that these are not separated by the central mountain mass; set I includes the two Cardiganshire groups D and F. These two are statistically so different from their coastal neighbours that it can be regarded as wellnigh certain that they do not have the same origins.

The statistical evidence also demonstrates fairly conclusively that the small multivallate forts of Pembrokeshire (group H) are not in general merely representatives of the univallate type which have been strengthened by the addition of an extra rampart (as perhaps in group A, see below), but must be regarded as a separate class.

These are the only points which can be established by a strictly objective examination of size-distribution alone, but there is some other evidence which may be taken into account. Groups A and C, which have been fairly completely studied, will serve as examples.

Group A, in the western tip of Lleyn, comprises only 12 sites. All are very weakly defended, although seven are bivallate. One of the latter, Castell Odo, has been excavated (Alcock, 1960), and proved to be a development from a univallate enclosure similar to others in the group; it therefore appears twice in the histogram. This suggests that all the enclosures may be of the same type basically, only about half having received a second rampart. In all, the banks are of earth with stone facing and are little stronger than modern field-banks. The plans are almost circular, though not exactly so. No site exceeds 0·7 hectare in area, but there is no indication of any preferred size within that range.

Group C, in north Merioneth, also includes about a dozen small univallate enclosures, all closely similar to each other (Bowen & Gresham, 1967, nos. 250–80) but contrasting strongly with group A. They are defended by good dry-stone walls, and their plans are adapted to the sites chosen, which are naturally defensible. There seems to be a marked preference for an area of about 0·2 hectare (0·5 acre). Apart from the general similarity in size, therefore, the group differs from A in almost every visible detail.

There seem to be equally well-marked structural differences between A and J, B and J, and C and J, and probably also between G and its neighbours D, E, F and L, while a detailed examination of the Table accompanying the statistical note will show that members of one set may differ considerably from one another in their relationship to members of the other set, although the differences within the set are not statistically significant.

It seems likely, then, that most of the eleven groups do correspond to some extent to genuinely distinct cultural entities. The evidence is at least sufficient to show the need for a fuller examination of this possibility, and at the same time to demonstrate that results found in one district cannot safely be extended as a generalisation to others.

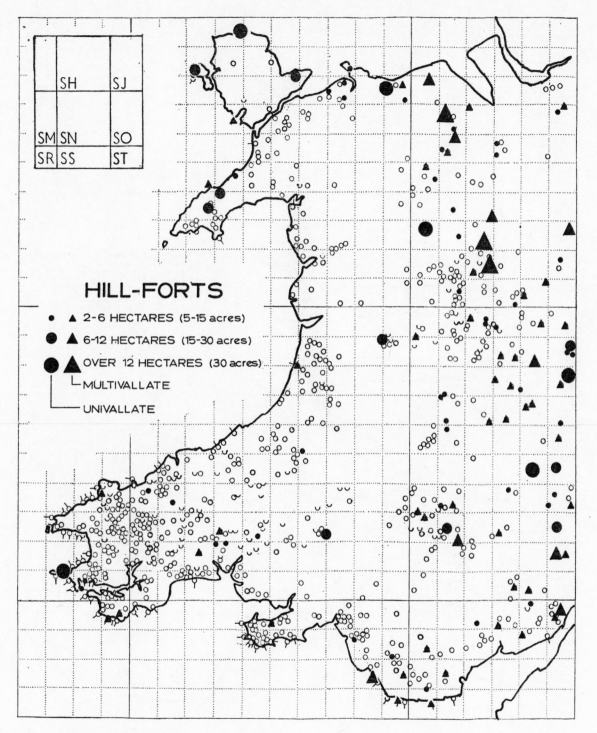

HILL-FORTS

• ▲	2-6 HECTARES (5-15 acres)	
● ▲	6-12 HECTARES (15-30 acres)	
● ▲	OVER 12 HECTARES (30 acres)	

└ MULTIVALLATE

── UNIVALLATE

	SH	SJ
SM	SN	SO
SR	SS	ST

fig. 3 Larger hill-forts in Wales

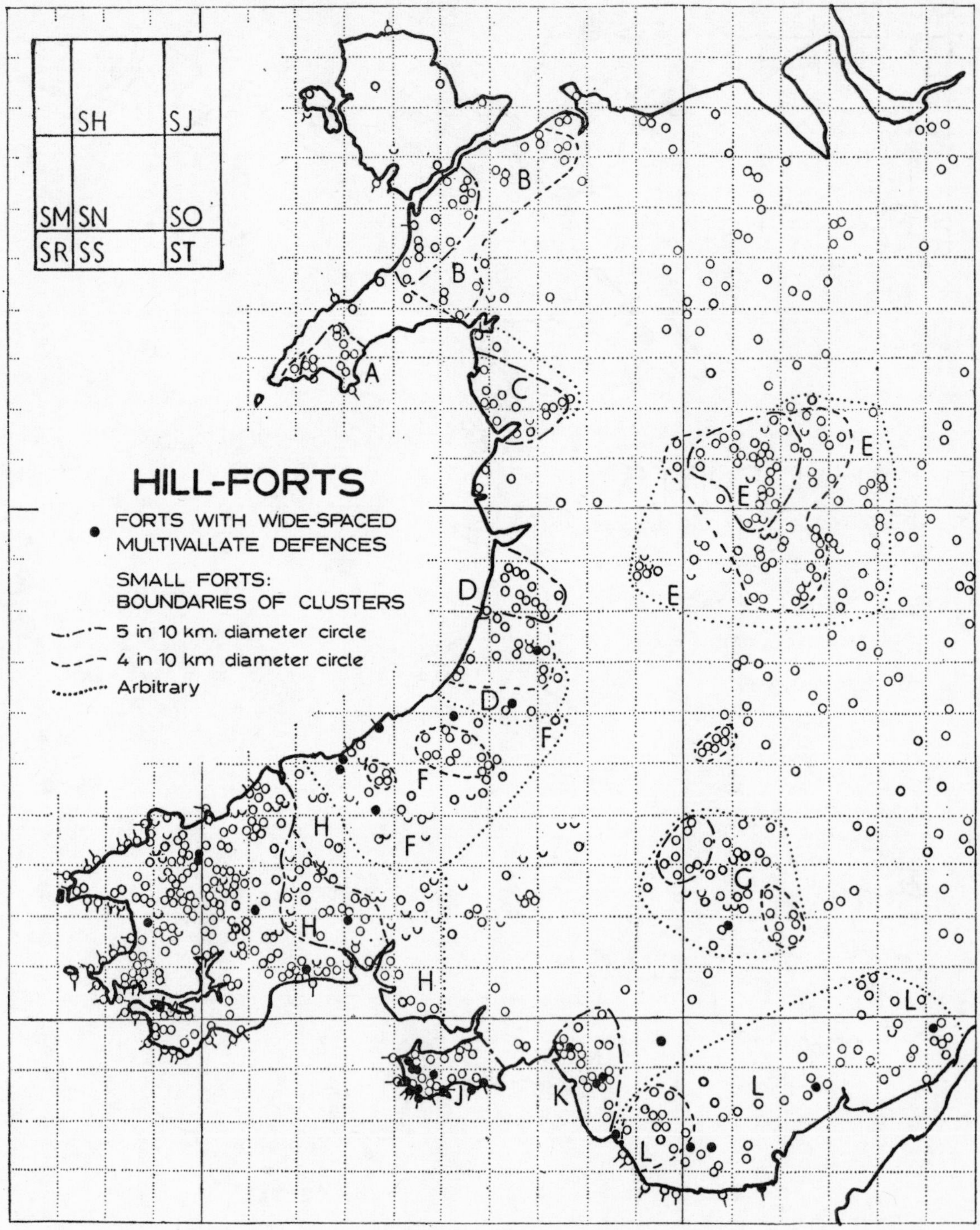
SH
SJ
SM
SN
SO
SR
SS
ST
HILL-FORTS
FORTS WITH WIDE-SPACED MULTIVALLATE DEFENCES
SMALL FORTS: BOUNDARIES OF CLUSTERS
5 in 10 km. diameter circle
4 in 10 km diameter circle
Arbitrary
A
B
C
D
E
F
G
H
J
K
L

fig. 4 Groupings of small hill-forts in Wales

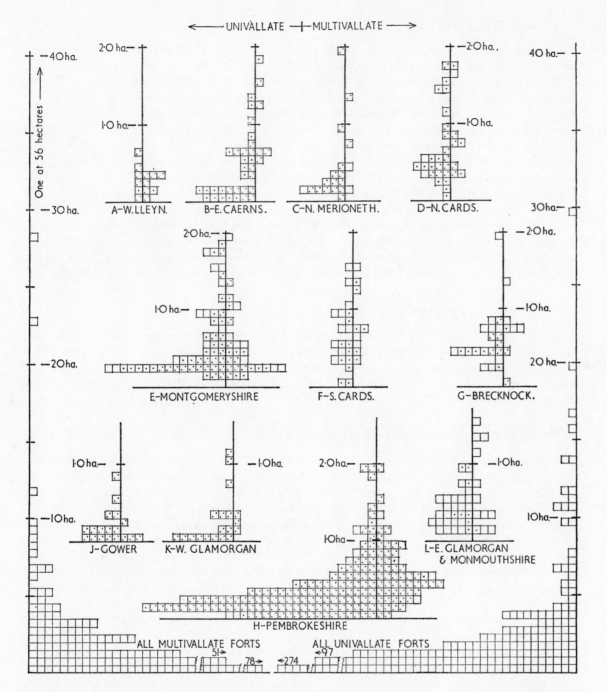

fig. 5 Size-distribution, for all forts by 0·5 ha. steps, and for selected groups by 0·1 ha. steps. The presence of one or two dots indicates that the fort lies within an envelope for circles of 10 km diameter containing respectively 4 or 5 forts. In the groups, those over 2 ha. are omitted, and those within the boundaries corresponding to 4 or 5 in a 10 km. circle are indicated by one or two dots respectively. Percentage probability of pairs of groups is derived from families having the same size distribution.

THE LARGE FORTS

Even when the evidence of size is considered alone, the contrast between the distribution shown in fig. 3 and that of the small forts is striking, but on structural evidence classification merely into uni- and multi-vallate is too simple. Among the univallate types, for example, defences formed by bank and ditch can be distinguished from those using a stone wall, and the latter class can again be divided into those which show stone-walled hut foundations and those which do not. Without further research, though, it is impossible to decide to what extent even this more elaborate classification is valid; the large stone forts in the south and east, such as Carn Goch or Titterstone Clee, are not necessarily closely related to those in Anglesey and Caernarvonshire, even though they show several similarities. Among the multivallate forts there is almost certainly a significant difference between those which contain round houses and those with rows of square buildings, but even their distribution cannot be known without excavation. At present, therefore, it is only possible to note the marked preference of these larger forts for the eastern part of the region considered, keeping in mind that they represent several groups which should ultimately be distinguishable. Further, it seems clear that, for a proper analysis of these groups, sites east of the present limits would need to be taken into account.

FORTS OF INTERMEDIATE SIZE

The distribution of these (fig. 3) can be accounted for completely on the assumption that they are all representatives either of the smaller or larger types which have been arbitrarily excluded by the limits chosen. They will therefore not be discussed in detail. It seems likely, though, that fuller investigation, taking structural features into consideration, would permit identification of distinct groups.

FORTS WITH WIDE-SPACED MULTIPLE DEFENCES

This type of fort has been studied in some detail by Lady Fox (1952; 1961). It is not amenable to investigation simply in terms of size or on map evidence, for not only does it include several sub-classes, but extension of a small fort can result in a structure very similar in plan but probably quite different in function. For completeness, however, sites which seem on the evidence of their plans on the 6-inch O.S. Map to belong to this class have been shown on fig. 4; no relation to the small-fort groups is implied. Promontory forts which seem to be of this kind are included, but not multivallate contour forts where the defences diverge in places; the addition of these latter has little effect on the distribution-pattern. For all enclosures likely to belong to this class, however, field investigation is essential, so they will not be discussed further.

PROMONTORY FORTS

Coastal promontories offer particularly convenient sites for defences, and this alone is often a sufficient explanation of their use. Some, however, were almost certainly chosen because of the proximity of good landing-places; several reasons are possible. But, again, site-investigation is essential for any useful discussion.

CONCLUSIONS

It must be repeated and emphasised that this study has been based on the evidence of size and distribution only, and that the data are imperfect and incomplete. Nevertheless some tentative conclusions can be reached, serving at least as bases for further investigation.

The most important result is the identification of separate elements in the hill-fort pattern.

The Size-
Distribution of
Hill-forts in Wales
and the Marches

The existence of several distinct groups of small forts seems to be established, though their precise limits both in size and location generally require further examination. These small groups also show a distribution which is markedly different from that of the large forts.

This separation into elements has an advantage for future research in that, at worst, only a hundred or so forts need to be considered at a time, instead of the whole set of 770; and when any attempt is made to advance beyond the rather elementary generalisations offered here, it becomes obvious how much more research is needed, both on the surface and by excavation.

In broad terms, the social interpretation of the evidence seems fairly clear. The small forts must for the most part be regarded as defended farms, occupied by a single family and its dependants; the more strongly fortified can perhaps be properly called castles. These nearly all form groups which are distinctive enough to suggest that they are either of different origins or have developed in isolation. Most of the large forts, especially when they contain visible hut-sites, were presumably small towns or villages; though some may have been occupied only seasonally, and others may have been no more than places of occasional refuge. On this view, towns and villages were the normal settlement type in the Marches, and separate farms near the west coast; but the two types of settlement overlap. On present evidence any attempt to determine the relationship between the 'villages' and 'farms' can be no more than guesswork; neither is it possible to point to any association of small forts which suggests that a single outstanding example in some way controlled a number of dependants, as the words 'castle' and 'farm' would imply if the analogy were fully valid.

For the temporal evolution of the settlement-pattern, however, several alternative explanations are possible. Marginally, the most satisfactory hypothesis is that the hill-forts were introduced to this region by successive landings, spread over several centuries, of small groups at different points along the coast. They established themselves first in small fortified farms, and as they became more numerous and more fully organised they expanded eastwards, in association with other groups, into areas capable of maintaining a larger density of population; villages or small towns thus became possible. This hypothesis accounts for the extreme rarity of pottery in most western sites, especially in the earlier levels, as well as for the differences in character which can be recognised even between neighbouring groups. The presence of some larger forts of types rarely found farther east can also be explained as having been built by the original inhabitants for defence against the invaders. Several alternative theories are possible, though, without doing much violence to the evidence, including an almost exact reversal of that set out above; it is unnecessary to describe them in detail.

Clearly, this crude analysis by size is no more than a first step towards an understanding of the problem. Much more excavation is needed, but logically this should be preceded by a careful objective survey of the visible remains. Defensive enclosures are artefacts which under sensitive examination may display as many characteristic details as pottery or metalwork; they have the further advantage of having been made where found. It is important that they should not be forced into arbitrary categories determined on the basis of incomplete knowledge; a careful analysis of all surface features with the meticulous attention given to museum objects should by itself help greatly towards an understanding of the Iron Age in the west, as well as providing a sound basis for planned research by excavation.

STATISTICAL NOTE

Although the data are probably too crude to justify any very elaborate statistical treatment, something rather better than mere subjective comparison seems desirable. For each pair of the groups A – L, Wilcoxon's Sum of Ranks test[1] was applied to all univallate forts of less than

[1] Langley, 1968, gives a clear account of the method, with the relevant tables and formulae.

1 hectare (2·5 acres). This test assigns a numbered rank, in order of size, to each fort in the two groups combined, and the rank-numbers are then separated out and totalled for each group; reference to tables then gives the probability (P) of the two groups being derived from the same 'family' of sizes. Some marginal cases were also tested by the Siegel-Tukey modification, the results of which give more weight to the spread of values than to their average, but B and D were the only pair for which this test gave a substantially lower value for P. Only values of P below 10% are shown, and for simplicity these have been interpolated between those of 10%, 5%, 1% and 0·2% given in the tables available; but no great stress should be placed on the precise value of any figure.

In attempting to interpret these results, it is important to realise their limitations. The test can give only *negative* information. Thus there is only a 0·2% probability, one chance in five hundred, that groups F and H belong to the same 'family', so it is fairly certain that they do not. On the other hand, the test merely shows that on the evidence of size there is a chance greater than one in ten that A and C both belong to another 'family'; this does not prove that they do so belong, and indeed structural evidence suggests that they do not. Also, the evidence applies to groups taken as a whole; although group H is so unlike group F, it does not follow that no typical example of the first group (assuming for the sake of illustration that such could be identified) can occur in the area covered by the second.

	F	L	D	E	G	C	H	K	J	B	A
F						1.0	0.2	1.0	3.0	4.5	9.3
L						0.1	0.1	0.2	4.0	5.0	
D					9.9	0.5	0.1	0.4	9.9	(2.3)	
E					5.0	0.2	0.1	0.3	5.0	3.1	
G			9.9	5.0		0.1	0.1	0.1	0.5	0.5	2.5
C	1.0	0.1	0.5	0.2	0.1						
H	0.2	0.1	0.1	0.1	0.1						
K	1.0	0.2	0.4	0.3	0.1						
J	3.0	4.0	9.9	5.0	0.5						
B	4.5	5.0	(2.3)	3.1	0.5						
A	9.3				2.5						

Even with these reservations in mind, it is clear that the groups fall into two sets. The table (or 'matrix') has been arranged to emphasise this, not geographically. One set comprises groups D, E, F, G and L; the other, A, B, C, H, J and K. Leaving out A, which contains only six forts and thus could not be expected to give a very well-marked statistical result, the chance that any member of one set derives from the same 'family' as any member of the other set is not greater than one in ten, and usually very much less; conversely, with one exception, the chance that any member of one set may be of the same 'family' as another member of the same set is greater than one in ten. The exception is G, compared with D and E, and even here the odds against are not statistically very significant.

The term 'family' here is of course used only with reference to size-distribution. Examples of structural differences have been mentioned in the general discussion. Detailed examination

*The Size-
Distribution of
Hill-forts in Wales
and the Marches*

of the Table, too, will suggest that there are differences between the groups composing each set. For example, the chances that group H derives from the same 'families' as D, E, F or L are, in order of magnitude, smaller than the corresponding chances for either B or J, which are themselves structurally different from each other.

Only groups E and H contain enough multivallate forts to justify detailed comparison, and the result was inconclusive, P being about 10%. Comparison of multivallate and univallate forts in H, however, gave a value for P of less than 0·2%, making it almost certain that they represent two distinct classes, not modifications of a single type.

BIBLIOGRAPHY

Alcock, L., 1960. 'Castell Odo: an embanked settlement on Mynydd Ystum, near Aberdaron, Caernarvonshire', *Archaeol. Cambrensis*, CIX, 78–135.

Bowen, E. G. & Gresham, C. A., 1967. *History of Merioneth*. Vol. I. Dolgellau.

Fox, A., 1952. 'Hill-slope forts and related earthworks in South-western England and South Wales', *Archaeol. J.*, CIX, 1–22.

—— 1961. 'South western hill-forts', in S. S. Frere (ed.), *Problems of the Iron Age in Southern Britain*. (Univ. London Inst. of Archaeol.) Occasional Paper No. 11. London.

Langley, R., 1968. *Practical Statistics (for non-mathematical people)*. London.

The Function and Population of Hill-forts in the Central Marches

S. C. Stanford

The writer will be but one of many whose excavation of settlement detail has been encouraged by Miss Chitty's intense interest in the people responsible for the prehistory that we try to reconstruct, and in so far as this essay attempts to number them in Herefordshire and Shropshire, he hopes she may consider it an appropriate offering. Our appreciation of societies must be incomplete unless we have some idea of population density and grouping; we cannot begin to appreciate the Iron Age unless we know whether we are dealing with densely settled populations or with isolated groups of refugees. The former assessment would imply jostling communities, busy on the land, whittling away the undeveloped areas that separated them; people organised for the large-scale communal efforts that could find expression in the great earthworks of the hill-forts and that would have been available for forest clearance as well as war. If, on the other hand, we assume scattered communities, thin on the ground and weak in organisation, who on some rare occasions made the supreme effort of erecting defences behind which to hide, our picture of the Iron Age will obviously be very different. The new evidence from the Border hill-forts leads the writer to the former interpretation for this area, but this does not necessarily apply to British hill-forts in general, which will vary in date and function from one region to another.

The map (fig. 1)[1] of hill-forts enclosing more than three acres (1.2 hectares) is probably almost complete, for few can have been completely obliterated. To those shown by the Ordnance Survey (1962) have been added Eaton Camp (RCHM, 1931, 61–2) and The Berth (Gelling & Stanford, 1965, 82–3), making a total of 54 sites whose ascription to the Iron Age can hardly be questioned. Thirteen smaller sites in Shropshire and two in Herefordshire have been excluded because the date of several of them is uncertain and none has been shown by excavation to have been constructed in the Iron Age. Their inclusion would not greatly alter any of the conclusions developed here, since their total enclosed area does not exceed that of a single large hill-fort such as Sutton Walls. The enclosed areas of the larger sites have been calculated mainly from the small-scale plans and dimensions in the Victoria County History for Shropshire (1908), and from the more detailed plans of the Royal Commission on Historical Monuments for Herefordshire (1931; 1932; 1934). If, as it appears, the hill-fort was virtually the only form of Iron Age settlement in Herefordshire and perhaps the main one in Shropshire,

[1] I am grateful to Miss Frances Lynch for re-drawing figs. 1–3.

it can provide a basis for assessing total population that is unparalleled in any pre-medieval period. The estimate made here depends on the following assumptions: (1) Most of the sites on fig. 1 were contemporary in the late Iron Age. (2) They functioned as settlements, not as refuges. (3) The population density within them was comparable with that estimated for Croft Ambrey in north Herefordshire, i.e. 70–100 per acre (180–240 per hectare). (4) In the later Iron Age there was little or no other form of settlement.

The first task is to decide how many of the hill-forts were contemporary. This is all the more necessary now since excavations at Caynham Camp, Croft Ambrey and Midsummer Hill between them suggest that hill-fort occupation hereabouts extended from the sixth century BC to the Roman conquest (Stanford, 1969). Radiocarbon dates for Midsummer Hill Camp have now indicated that the La Tène invasions were as early as perhaps *c.* 390 BC (Birm. 142, 420 ± 185 BC for small branches on the floor of the quarry-ditch), and imply that Croft Ambrey was founded *c.* 550 BC. Fortunately we do get some special help in this matter from two sources: (1) The identification of specialised professional potters who worked in the vicinity of the Malvern Hills and distributed their wares widely in these two counties (Peacock, 1968) has given pottery in this region a new value, minimising the arguments for cultural retardation and allowing similar forms of pottery tempered with similar grit to be accepted as contemporary. (2) Gateway sequences, yet to be published, show that certain types of gateway enjoyed a limited vogue. This evidence is detailed back to the early fourth century BC for Croft Ambrey and Midsummer Hill, and there are particular instances where sites far afield can be linked with these sequences (Stanford, 1969).

From this kind of evidence we may accept that a number of hill-forts were contemporary beyond doubt. At Croft Ambrey (Stanford, 1967), Credenhill (Stanford, 1971) and Sutton Walls (Kenyon, 1954), Dr Peacock's Group B1 (limestone-tempered) wares were succeeded late in the Iron Age by his Group A (Malvernian-tempered) wares which were distributed in areas north and west of the Malverns from the mid-first century BC. Group A continued to be made in the Roman period to form the basis of a Romanised Malvern pottery industry in the second century AD (Peacock, 1965–7, 15–18); thus, its products cannot by themselves date a site to the Iron Age, but since the Group B1 potters did not survive the Iron Age it seems reasonable to assume occupation in the late Iron Age when both groups are found, even unstratified, on sites far from the Malverns as at The Berth (Peacock, 1968, 427). Oldbury (Peacock, 1968, 427; Brown, 1961, 85), Dinedor (Peacock, 1968, 427; Kenyon, 1954, 57), and Poston (Peacock, 1968, 427; Anthony, 1958, 30) have produced Group B1 sherds, but although the samples do not apparently include Group A there is Roman material from each, so that it will be assumed that the occupation period included the later part of the Iron Age. Aconbury also produced a quantity of Iron Age and some Roman sherds (Kenyon, 1954, 25–6), and although the former have not been analysed the combination may be used to suggest that Aconbury too was occupied in the late Iron Age. One of the few sherds from Caynham Camp has been compared by Mr Gelling with material that is late in the sequence at Croft Ambrey (Gelling & Peacock, 1966, 96). On this ceramic basis alone contemporaneity may be inferred for nine hill-forts – Aconbury, The Berth, Caynham, Credenhill, Croft Ambrey, Dinedor, Oldbury, Poston and Sutton Walls.

At Midsummer Hill Group A potters became dominant at an earlier stage than they did to the west, but the close match of the gateway sequence with that of Croft Ambrey confirms that it too was occupied during the late Iron Age. Especially relevant here is the similarity of plans for the last ten gates, with 'bridges' employed at both sites for the last four (Stanford, 1969).

Included in this region is a great variety of defensive earthwork, much of it demonstrably contemporary, so that it seems unlikely that the earthworks alone will ever provide any finely graded sequence for dating purposes or neat groupings for cultural divisions (Varley, 1950, 43; Hogg, 1965). Thus, in Herefordshire, Sutton Walls had a dump rampart and single ditch for most of its occupation, whereas at Croft Ambrey there were two ditches with medial bank and counterscarp bank outside the main dump rampart before the site was abandoned. Dinedor and Midsummer Hill are mainly univallate, but the last-named had a stone revetment to its rampart. Credenhill had a single ditch and counterscarp bank. There is no reason to distinguish between these sites on the grounds of artefacts or chronology; the differences in defence reflect different problems of topography and geology. The distinction between cultures in the lower Severn valley on the basis of univallate or bivallate defences (Clifford, 1961, 31–2) has been rendered invalid by our new understanding of the pottery, and at Rainsborough in Northamptonshire a fifth-century date has been suggested for bivallate defences (Avery, Sutton & Banks, 1967, 291). Even if the guard-rooms associated with the latter example are approximately contemporary with those of Midsummer Hill they would, on our current reckoning, go back to the early fourth century. Although there is therefore little to be said for employing bivallation alone as a dating criterion after *c.* 390 BC there remains at least one class of earthwork which should be separated and may still be dated within a narrow bracket. This is the fully developed multivallation, with the defence zone approaching 100 yards (91·5 metres), as found in the final phase at Maiden Castle, Dorset (Wheeler, 1943, 48–51). It is unfortunate that the simple distinction between univallate and multivallate defences has often led to disregard of the great difference in scale between defences like that of Maiden Castle and the narrower defensive zones of most other multivallate sites. This distinction should be maintained and sites possessing the developed form of this defence should be recognised as achieving it in the late Iron Age. In Herefordshire and Shropshire this implies a late date for the final form of Risbury Camp, Wapley Camp, Bury Ditches and Old Oswestry.

Taken together, the sites which thus show evidence of occupation or reconstruction in the closing decades of the Iron Age are just sufficient to show a pattern emerging. Fortunately some are neighbours, and the distances between them prove to be comparable with the general spacing of hill-forts in their respective areas. Thus The Berth is 17 km. from Old Oswestry; Caynham, 12 km. from Croft Ambrey; Credenhill, 8 km. from Sutton Walls and 11 km. from Dinedor, which is itself 9 km. from Sutton Walls and 4 km. from Aconbury. As the total pattern of fig. 1 clearly reveals, the spacing is least in the Wye Valley and in the central hills of the upper Teme Valley, and greatest in the Severn Valley lowlands. Although the inquiry has so far been limited to evidence that is relatively specific for contemporaneous occupation in the late Iron Age, it has been sufficient to show that contemporary hill-forts could be spaced as closely as 4–17 km. The sample so far includes 14 of the 54 sites over three acres (1·2 hectares).

While recognising that we are now moving to include evidence that is less specific, an attempt may be made to see how many other sites were probably contemporary with those already listed at some time between *c.* 390 BC and AD 50. There are grounds for believing that the Group B1 pottery school was established *c.* 390 BC utilising stamped ornament derived from metal prototypes. To the published list of sites yielding this ware Midsummer Hill may now be added, but this does not at present extend our coverage in Herefordshire and Shropshire. Additional evidence for contemporaneity within the early part of this period is the presence of guard-rooms at Titterstone Clee (O'Neil, 1934), The Roveries (information from Mr N. Thomas) and The Wrekin (Kenyon, 1942), since the gateway stratigraphy of Croft Ambrey and Midsummer Hill shows that such structures were introduced late in the fourth century and were maintained for only about seventy years.

Dr Savory's difficulties with Dr Willoughby Gardner's evidence for a much later date at Dinorben cannot prevent the earlier date being more acceptable, since this is now supported by evidence from Northamptonshire, Herefordshire and Dorset (Gardner & Savory, 1964, 87–90). Brought together, these several criteria allow 17 sites (31%) to be recognised as broadly contemporary at some stage in the last 350 years of the Iron Age.

Is it possible to invoke evidence, however tentative, that even more of the hill-forts on fig. 1

were built or occupied in this same period? In 1937 Miss Chitty emphasised the unity of the Welsh Marches hill-fort province with her map showing inturned entrances which she regarded as having been introduced by hill-fort-building invaders (Chitty, 1937). With the recent questioning of the invasion hypothesis itself and with the increasing complexity of evidence regarding gateway structures, we may have come to overlook the implications of her map. At Rainsborough, and in 1968 at Midsummer Hill, inturned entrances about 15 m. long have been shown to have been constructed to accommodate guard-rooms in the thickness of the rampart terminals. At Croft Ambrey too, a straight-gap entrance of period IV was succeeded by a 14 m. inturn required for the stone guard-rooms of period V. Without overlooking the possibility of somewhat shorter inturns developing without guard-rooms, or the distinctive phenomenon of the very long inturn, the continental *zangentore* (Dehn, 1961, 393–4, and Avery, Sutton & Banks, 1967, 255), we may in the Welsh border proceed on the assumption that a marked inturn is most likely to reflect the presence of a guard-room at some stage, and so adopt as contemporary with our guard-roomed entrances those at Abdon Burf, Bach Camp, Backbury, Burrow Camp, Bury Walls, Calcot Camp, Caer Caradoc (Church Stretton), Caer Caradoc (Clun), Coxall Knoll, The Ditches, Earl's Hill, Haughmond Castle, Herefordshire Beacon, Ivington Camp, Little Doward Camp, Nordy Bank, Oliver's Point, Pyon Wood, Wall Hills (Ledbury) and Wall Hills (Thornbury). Only three of the sites previously listed did not appear in Miss Chitty's list – Dinedor, Poston and Oldbury; these are too mutilated for their entrance form to be known.

The map is now as complete as the present evidence will permit, encompassing 37 (69%) of the hill-forts. The new inclusions have not affected the general spacing of neighbours. In the Severn valley 11–15 km. is common and the average of nine measurements is 13 km. In the central hills the distance between neighbours rarely exceeds 10 km. and the average of fourteen measurements is 7 km. In the Lugg and Wye valleys the hill-forts are never more than 10 km. apart, and the average of fifteen measurements is 7 km. Overall, most sites are 7 km. apart and few are less than 5 km. Some of the latter might still be accepted as contemporary since they stand on opposite sides of major rivers – Little Doward and Symonds Yat (Glos.), Coxall Knoll and Brandon Camp – but there remain a few that appear to be inexplicably close – Nordy Bank and Abdon Burf, Pyon Wood and Croft Ambrey, Dinedor and Aconbury, Midsummer Hill and Herefordshire Beacon, all of which pairs are no more than 4 km. apart. With these exceptions the hill-forts are relatively evenly spaced, in a manner suggesting that they were sited as centres for the exploitation of the surrounding area rather than as frontier posts or simply as refuges upon the least accessible hill-top. In this case their enclosed areas might be expected to be related to their population, and this in turn to the territory they controlled; it should be possible to allocate territory proportionate to their size.

A first approximation may be made by tracing circles proportionate to the enclosed area about each hill-fort. If the right scale can be achieved we should have a clearer pointer to any sites which are superfluous to the 'village' hypothesis and for which some special reason, either of date or function, may have to be adduced. This has been done on fig. 2 for all hill-forts over 3 acres (1·2 hectares), whether or not there is any particular evidence for contemporaneity. It has not been considered necessary to have the hill-fort central to its territory, any more than the average Anglo-Saxon village was central to its parish in hilly country. For the latter, proximity to water-supply and the best arable land were the main localising factors; in the Iron Age on the Welsh border the chief requirement was a strong defensible position. Fig. 2 reveals that the differences in spacing are nearly everywhere compensated by the differences in hill-fort size. The circles cover most of the ground between the hill-forts without leaving wide gaps and without undue overlapping; and they show that many of the close neighbours can still obtain a fair share of territory. The only sites that still give some difficulty are Caplar and Cherry Hill Camps in the Woolhope Hills, Gadbury Bank (Glos.), just overlapped by the Midsummer Hill circle, and Pyon Wood whose territory has had to be extended south of the River

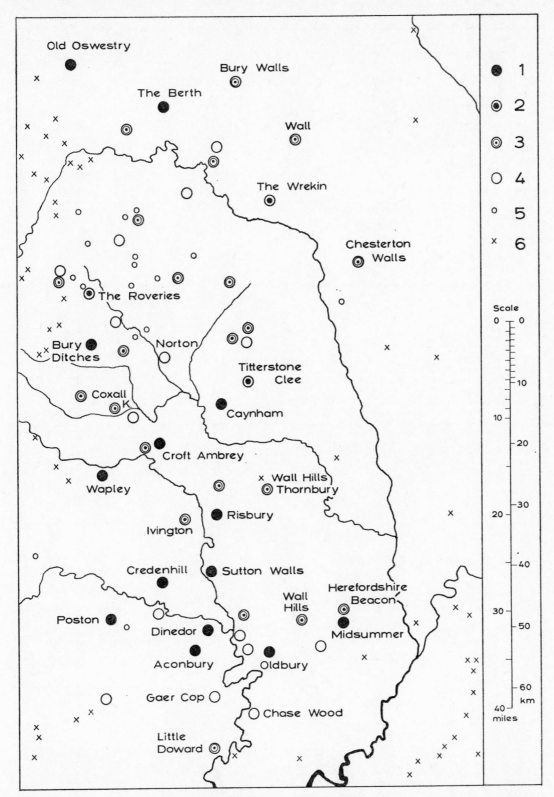

fig. 1 Hill-forts in Herefordshire and Shropshire: 1 with evidence for late Iron Age occupation or construction. 2 with evidence of occupation or construction after *c.* 390 BC. 3 with inturned entrances (excluding sites in categories 1 and 2). 4 other sites over three acres (1·2 hectares); 5 sites under three acres (1·2 hectares); 6 hill-forts in neighbouring counties

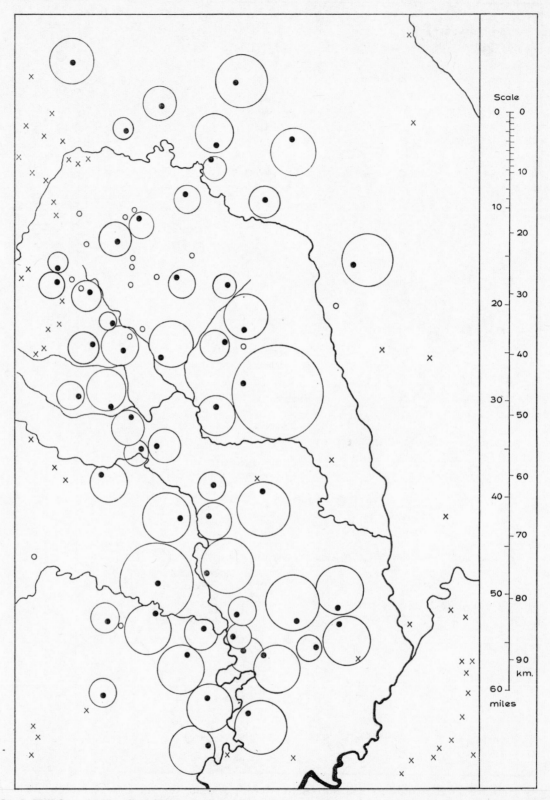

fig. 2 Hill-forts in Herefordshire and Shropshire. Sites over three acres (1.2 hectares) marked by circles proportionate in area to the enclosed area of the hill-fort)

Lugg in order to avoid overlapping Croft Ambrey or Brandon Camp. These cases are few enough to show that the great majority of the hill-forts could have been contemporary.

In the Severn valley the wider spacing is not equally matched by the size of the hill-forts. This may reflect a lower density of population resulting from an increased amount of low-lying poorly drained land, or the hill-fort may not be the only form of Iron Age settlement. It may be significant that the only Iron Age sites other than hill-forts to be recognised and excavated in the two counties are in the Severn valley at Sharpstones Hill and Weeping Cross (Jenks, 1966; 1968). Mr Jenks's report on these sites and their probable date will be awaited with great interest.

The exercise so far has worked so well that it seems worth offering fig. 3 as a more realistic interpretation of hill-fort territories. Here, the weight of territory has been shifted as necessary in order to remove any overlapping, to avoid any territory straddling a major river and to utilise any convenient streams as probable boundaries. The latter step may be justified not only on the grounds that a stream provides a ready-marked boundary, but because streams offered valuable resources in watering-places, rushes and a variety of riverside timber, and may be confidently regarded as desirable possessions by any Iron Age society. With this rearrangement the last obstacles to contemporary occupation of all the hill-forts over 3 acres (1·2 hectares) are removed. With their territories thus reorganised, Pyon Wood, Cherry Hill and Caplar Camp stand clear of their neighbours, and Gadbury Bank is no longer overlapped by Midsummer Hill.

If these hill-forts are to form the basis for a population estimate it must be shown that they were permanently occupied. The evidence at Croft Ambrey has been particularly specific on this point and it may be confidently asserted that there at least (no exceptional site in terms of size or position) occupation was permanent throughout the history of the hill-fort (Stanford, 1967). The evidence is in the renewal of gates at the entrances and of huts in the interior, while in the quarry-ditch there were numerous stand-still levels of trampled accumulation frequently cut by successive structures and holding at one point a succession of fifteen hearths. The acquisition of evidence of this order must necessarily be a very slow process, but Croft Ambrey points the way for the interpretation of occupation evidence from other sites. A frequent renewal of timber structures was demonstrated in the quarry-ditch at Credenhill (Stanford, 1971), and at Sutton Walls the occupation refuse and frequent hearth sites in the quarry scoops show that that site was also permanently occupied (Kenyon, 1954). At Midsummer Hill there was a repeated renewal of gates and internal buildings (recent excavations by the writer), and at Caynham Camp the one large area excavated in the interior was almost covered by postholes (Gelling, 1962–3, 98). Beyond these sites, where the structural evidence is firm, we have Dr Kenyon's conclusions that the occupation at Dinedor and Aconbury was similar to that at Sutton Walls (Kenyon, 1954, 25), and that The Wrekin was permanently occupied (Kenyon, 1942). Iron Age pottery and cooking stoves (VCP) from The Berth are consistent with occupation (Gelling & Stanford, 1965), and the numerous artefacts and defence reconstructions at Poston Camp show that it too was permanently occupied (Anthony, 1958). The later huts found within the rampart at Old Oswestry were provisionally dated to the Dark Ages on the basis of the associated crude pottery (Varley, 1950, 64), but since the parallels employed to support this dating have been held by others to be of Iron Age date (Alcock, 1960, 86; Gelling & Stanford, 1965, 83–6), these and the earlier Old Oswestry huts may yet prove to support a permanent Iron Age occupation. In conclusion we may note that no extensive excavation within a hill-fort in these two counties has failed to produce evidence of permanent occupation since G. H. Jack's trenching of Caplar Camp in 1926 (Jack & Hayter, 1924–6).

If permanently occupied, how closely were these hill-forts developed internally? At Croft Ambrey, wherever excavation has been undertaken, the pattern has been one of closely set rectangular huts arranged along the contours with paths only 3–4 m. wide between them. At

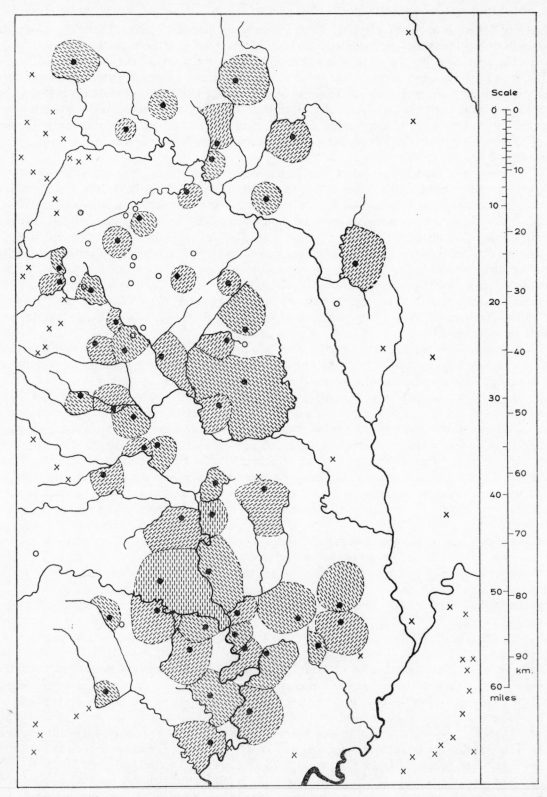

fig. 3 Hill-fort territories in Herefordshire and Shropshire. The shaded areas are proportionate to the size of the hill-fort enclosures

Credenhill a similar arrangement of rectangular buildings was found in two rows in the quarry-ditch, the only area extensively excavated. At Sutton Walls the rescue nature of the excavation prevented full exploration of the lower levels of the quarry-ditch and we are without a great deal of structural evidence. Nevertheless it would appear that two postholes recorded in Area 1, Pit 1, Trench B probably had their other two members under the baulk to the north (Kenyon, 1954, 15), indicating a small rectangular building like those at Credenhill, Croft Ambrey and Midsummer Hill. The interpretation of some of the larger examples of these buildings as dwellings has been questioned recently (Stead, 1968, 158), and pending the full publication of Croft Ambrey it is worth emphasising that these rectangular structures are the only types found so far in Herefordshire, and that their density at Croft Ambrey and Credenhill is quite different from that of four-post structures on published sites elsewhere, which have usually been interpreted as granaries. In one area at Croft Ambrey six such structures, with overall measurements ranging from 2·7 × 2·1 m. to 3·7 × 3·3 m. (9 ft × 7 ft to 12 ft × 11 ft), were completely excavated in a space of 276 sq. m. (332 sq. yds). At Grimthorpe (Yorks.) there were, by contrast, only eight four-post buildings in an area of approximately 1,670 sq. m. (2,006 sq. yds) and only four of these were as large as the smallest of the Croft examples in the sample just quoted. The plan of Tollard Royal (Wilts.) (Wainwright, 1968, 105) shows again the difference between the phenomena under discussion, with only four possible granaries in an enclosure of approximately 2,700 sq. m. (3,241 sq. yds). The Herefordshire sites are clearly in a quite different case, and we may proceed to hazard a guess at the density of population at Croft Ambrey on the assumption that half the buildings were dwellings, the remainder granaries or stores. Spaced on the basis of the sample already discussed, there would be room for 285 buildings within the 2·4 hectares (6 acres) of the original Plateau Camp at Croft. The enlargement of the camp to 3·2 hectares (8 acres) was primarily to allow the construction of a larger rampart but although the broken nature of the resulting quarry-ditch floor precluded for a time the same intensive development there, much of it was eventually built upon and structures were erected also over the demolished early rampart. It may not be too speculative to assume that the early density was eventually achieved over the whole interior of the enlarged Main Camp, i.e. approximately 118 buildings per hectare (47 per acre). If only half of these were dwellings holding, on average, families of four, the density of population would be 236 per hectare (94 per acre). If the full coverage of the Plateau Camp were regarded as being achieved only in the later years of the Iron Age and no allowance made for the buildings on the demolished rampart and in the quarry-ditch, the final density of buildings might come as low as 89 per hectare (35 per acre), and the population density down to 178 per hectare (70 per acre). On these assumptions the population density of Croft Ambrey may be regarded as 180–240 per hectare (70–100 per acre). This is admittedly very high compared with the estimate of 50–75 per hectare (20–30 per acre) for Caernarvonshire hill-forts (Hogg, 1960, 22), but there is supporting evidence for the contention that the Herefordshire sites were more closely developed than their Caernarvonshire counterparts. At Credenhill a small excavation showed that part of the quarry-ditch was occupied as densely as the sample quoted from Croft Ambrey, with four rectangular buildings in an area of 210 sq. m. (251 sq. yds). On the Malvern Hills both the Herefordshire Beacon (St Joseph, 1965) and Midsummer Hill camps exhibit numerous small terraces and scoops cut into the very steep slopes within the defences. At the latter site 244 such scoops with a diameter over 3·3 m. (11 ft) have been surveyed on about 50% of the interior, the remainder being overgrown or too level to show any terracing. If these are all building sites, as excavation so far indicates, and this density is maintained over the whole of the hill-fort, a total of at least 432 buildings may be deduced. If half were dwellings, the population density would be 114 per hectare (46 per acre), and even this preliminary estimate indicates a greater density than that estimated for Caernarvonshire. The comparison has been made elsewhere (Stanford, 1967, 32) between these Herefordshire patterns and densities and those implied for Castel Coz in Brittany where 113 rectangular hut platforms were recorded in two-thirds of the 0·9 hectare promontory fort (Le Men, 1872).

If we suppose that something like the Croft Ambrey density was eventually achieved on all the hill-forts of Herefordshire and Shropshire the total Iron Age population may be calculated by multiplying the mean of the Croft estimates, 210 per hectare, by the total enclosed area of the hill-forts over 1·2 hectares, i.e. 276 hectares, a population of nearly 58,000. The writer has recently suggested that the Iron Age population of this area was a combination of a surviving late Bronze Age population represented, for example, by the cemetery at Bromfield, near Ludlow, and at least two successive invasions by hill-fort-building overlords (Stanford, 1969). There is no need therefore to bring these many thousands into the Welsh Border in one brief episode, and although any attempt to apportion the increase between these three sources must be immensely speculative, the exercise may perhaps be justified to see whether the postulated invasions can be reduced to a reasonable level.

Since the period with which we are dealing is now seen to be a very long one (hardly less than 600, perhaps as much as 650 years) natural increase in population could be an important factor. The evidence bearing on this is extremely scanty but it may be noted that there is no sign in this area of any hill-fort being reduced, and that what earthwork evidence there is rather encourages the view that population increased. It has already been noted that at Croft Ambrey the extra space offered by the enlargement of the perimeter came to be utilised, showing a possible increase in population of the order of 33% between *c.* 390 BC and AD 50. At Caynham Camp the relative date of the rampart dividing the interior into two areas of about 3·2 and 0·8 hectares is uncertain. Although a limited excavation revealed walling similar to that used elsewhere in the final period (Gelling, 1960, 225), the plan suggests that this was an earlier defence, left behind when the camp was extended along the ridge. On this interpretation an extension of about 25% is implied. At Poston Camp a similar increase occurred between the uncertainly dated periods I and II (Anthony, 1958). On none of these sites is there any special evidence for a cultural change associated with the alteration of the enclosed area, and it will therefore be assumed that there was a natural increase of population of the order of 25% over perhaps 440 years, or 0·06% per annum. On other sites the evidence for this increase may be concealed through the destruction of earlier defences, as at Croft Ambrey and Poston, or the increase may have been accommodated without extending the defences. Even a small increase of this order means that the population in the early fourth century BC would have been only 80% of the total reached in the early first century AD – about 46,000.

There are several pointers to a major invasion in the early fourth century when the Group B1 pottery appears and timber guard-rooms and sleeper-built huts are introduced at Midsummer Hill. It is possible that the latter site was laid out afresh at this time, but if it was simply enlarged, the sharply defined topography makes it virtually certain that the original enclosure would have been only about 7·5 acres (3·0 hectares) on the western summit. Such an enlargement (to 19 acres [7·6 hectares]) is echoed on other Herefordshire sites where earthworks clearly reveal two phases of construction. Wall Hills, Ledbury, exhibits an original enclosure of 8 acres (3·6 hectares) with simple gap entrances, which was enlarged to 25 acres (10 hectares) within an extension rampart showing the eroded remains of deeply inturned entrances (RCHM, 1932, 117). Ivington Camp's inner univallate enclosure of 8 acres (3·2 hectares) with a simple entrance was subsequently contained within a bivallate defence with inturned entrances when the camp was enlarged to 20 acres (8·0 hectares) (RCHM, 1932, 132). Herefordshire Beacon camp was enlarged from 7 acres (2·8 hectares) to 19 acres (7·6 hectares) within defences pierced by inturned or overlapping entrances (RCHM, 1932, 56), and the Little Doward camp was enlarged from a cliff-top promontory fort of 6 acres (2·4 hectares) to one of 19 acres (7·6 hectares) (RCHM, 1932, 68). On a smaller scale, the original 6·5-acre (2·6-hectare) enclosure on Coxall Knoll was given a new southern rampart and an eastern extension bringing the enclosure to 11 acres (4·4 hectares); the new entrances were inturned (RCHM, 1932, 28). The phenomenon is consistent enough to raise the possibility that the new organisation favoured units of about 20 acres (8 hectares). If so, then the following sites may be candidates for enlargement or foundation at the same time: in Herefordshire, Aconbury (17 acres: 6·8 ha.), Chase Wood (22 acres: 8·8 ha.) Eaton (18 acres: 7·2 ha.), Gaer Cop (17 acres: 6·8 ha.), Oldbury (15 acres: 6·4 ha.), Sutton Walls (25 acres: 10·4 ha.) and Wall Hills, Thornbury (22 acres: 8·8 ha.); and in Shropshire, Bury Walls (21 acres: 8·4 ha.), Chesterton Walls (22 acres: 8·8 ha.), Norton (15 acres: 6·4 ha.), Old Oswestry (15 acres: 6·0 ha.), and Wall (16 acres: 6·4 ha.). Consideration must be given also to the two exceptionally large sites, Titterstone Clee (72 acres: 28·7 ha.) and Credenhill (50 acres: 20·0 ha.), both of which have excavated evidence for occupation after the arrival of Group B1 pottery (Credenhill) or the advent of stone guard-rooms (Titterstone Clee). If all these had been extended on the same scale as the other large Herefordshire sites (i.e. by 25·6%), the total enlargement would have amounted to 282·5 acres (113 hectares), raising an existing 402·5 acres (161 hectares) to 685 acres (274 hectares), an increase of 70%. Translated into population this means that about 19,000 of the estimated population of 46,000 in the early fourth century would have been intrusive. This is probably a generous estimate since it includes an allowance for so many sites for which there is no recorded evidence of enlargement at this time. The minimum figure, indicated by the population of the six sites on which this hypothesis was founded would be about 6,000, unduly small in proportion to the indigenous population.

At the same rate of increase as that postulated for the later centuries, the late fifth-century population of 27,000 could have been achieved from a sixth-century population of 24,000. If the sixth-century invasions had been on the same scale as those just deduced for the fourth century, there would be little need of any native Late Bronze Age complement, which would run against the strong arguments already noted above and elsewhere (Hogg, 1958; Gelling, 1962–3, 100; Gelling & Peacock, 1966, 97; Wainwright, 1967, 24). These earlier invasions must have been on a smaller scale, but at present there seems to be no evidence on which we can even hazard a guess at the proportion of invaders to natives. A force of about 10,000 dispersed in parties of about 200 to each of the 54 hill-forts might have achieved the conquest and control of the two counties, but the contrast between Croft Ambrey and Caynham Camp rather suggests that there were both intrusive and native hill-fort communities living side by side, the latter developed at the insistence of or by the example of the newcomers.

These speculations may be summarised as follows:

Hill-fort population in sixth century BC		24,000 (12 per sq. mile)
Natural increase at 0·06% per annum till *c.* 390 BC	3,000	
Total population in late fifth century BC		27,000 (13 per sq. mile)
Intrusive population *c.* 390 BC	19,000	
Total population *c.* 390 BC		46,000 (22 per sq. mile)
Natural increase at 0·06% per annum till AD 50	12,000	
Total population *c.* AD 50		58,000 (29 per sq. mile)

The population densities thus indicated may be compared with those estimated for Herefordshire (842 sq. miles) on the basis of the Domesday returns – 20,534, i.e. 24 per sq. mile; and on the Poll Tax returns of 1377 – 25,831, i.e. 31 per sq. mile (Russell, 1948). By 1801 the population of Herefordshire had risen to 88,436, i.e. 105 per sq. mile. Although the considerable change in population distribution which occurred with the collapse of the hill-fort communities at the Roman conquest prevents any attempt to link our Iron Age estimates with those of Domesday, the implications of the comparability of Iron Age populations with early Medieval populations in this area may provide us with food for thought regarding the role played by these hill-fort Celts in clearing the forest and so paving the way for future farmers.

It has been conjectured that the great increase in population in the course of the Iron Age was due in part to natural increase in a society which despite invasion seems to have achieved a remarkable stability, and in part to fairly sizeable invasions. If, further, these invaders are conjectured to have moved into this area from beach-head camps it may be noted that one of 225 acres (90 hectares) would hold the force envisaged for 390 BC at the same density as in their permanent quarters in the late Iron Age. Even if the force was enlarged to allow settlement of neighbouring counties the area of the beach-head would not be as much as double this size for, on the basis of sites enclosing 15 acres (6 hectares) or more, there is little to be added west of the Severn. With only one site of this size, Spital Meend, Monmouthshire appears to have escaped the attention of these colonists, as does Breconshire also. Only Burfa Camp in Radnorshire, and The Breiddin and Llanymynech in Montgomeryshire, appear to extend this territory into Wales. Half-a-dozen Cotswold-edge sites might be seen to complete the list that makes up the full complement of this invasion – 9 possible sites compared with the 20 conjectured for Herefordshire and Shropshire. The beach-head will not be as large as the great Wessex beach-head on Bindon Hill, Dorset, which encloses 300 acres (160 hectares) (Wheeler, 1953). If such a beach-head exists, the focus of these large hill-forts is on the lower Severn, the route of entry suggested by Miss Chitty for the builders of inturned entrances (Chitty, 1937) and emphasised by Dr Kenyon (1954, 28) as the entry for the stamped-ware group – her Bristol Channel B culture, re-designated Western Third B by Professor Hawkes (Frere, 1961, 15). Meanwhile Dr Peacock's work has reinforced this view with a pottery industry near the lower Severn, close to the Malvern Hills (Peacock, 1968, 424). This attempt to number the hill-fort population has focused our attention on the large hill-forts and emphasised that the great weight of the invasions of *c.* 390 BC fell upon the area that is now Herefordshire, creating thereby an Iron Age territory which corresponds broadly with a physiographical region and in which the Malvern potters were to distribute their wares. This is roughly region 21 of Professor Hawkes's map, the region in which he saw the Western Third B culture established. It still coincides with the area reached in quantity by Group B1 potters, whose field of activity should, as Professor Hawkes has pointed out to me, reflect something of the political or cultural map of the Welsh border. While we have a greater understanding of this area after the advent of these same potters, it is important to recall that our knowledge of the cultures and defences that preceded their arrival is most inadequate; indeed, in Herefordshire itself these are largely conjectural. Is this because the influence of the inturned-entrance builders led to extensive quarry-ditching of earlier sites, while their wealth in pottery has led to less well-endowed cultures being overlooked?

BIBLIOGRAPHY

Alcock, L., 1960. 'Castell Odo: an embanked settlement on Mynydd Ystum, near Aberdaron, Caernarvonshire', *Archaeol. Cambrensis*, CIX, 78–135.

Anthony, I. E., 1958. *The Iron Age Camp at Poston, Herefordshire*. Hereford.

Avery, M., Sutton, J. E. G., & Banks, J. W., 1967. 'Rainsborough, Northants, England, Excavations 1961–5', *Proc. Prehist. Soc.*, XXXIII, 207–306.

Brown, A. E., 1961. 'Records of surface finds in Herefordshire', *Trans. Woolhope Natur. Fld. Club*, XXXVII, 77–91.

Chitty, L. F., 1937. 'How did the hill-fort builders reach the Breiddin? A tentative explanation', *Archaeol. Cambrensis*, XCII, 129–50.

Clifford, E. M., 1961. *Bagendon: a Belgic oppidum*. Cambridge.

Dehn, W., 1961. 'Zangentore am spätkeltischen Oppida', *Pamatky Archeologicke*, LII, 390–6.

Frere, S. S. (ed.), 1961. *Problems of the Iron Age in Southern Britain*. Univ. London Inst. of Archaeol. Occasional Paper No. 11. London.

Gardner, W. & Savory, H. N., 1964. *Dinorben: A Hill-fort occupied in Early Iron Age and Roman times.* Cardiff.

Gelling, P. S., 1960. 'Excavations at Caynham Camp', *Trans. Shropshire Archaeol. Soc.*, LVI, 218–27.

—— 1962–3. 'Excavations at Caynham Camp', *Trans. Shropshire Archaeol. Soc.*, LVII, 91–100.

Gelling, P. S. & Peacock, D. P. S., 1966. 'The pottery from Caynham Camp', *Trans. Shropshire Archaeol. Soc.*, LVIII, 96–100.

Gelling, P. S. & Stanford, S. C., 1965. 'Dark Age Pottery or Iron Age Ovens?', *Trans. Proc. Birmingham Archaeol. Soc.*, LXXXII, 77–91.

Hogg, A. H. A., 1958. 'The Secondary Iron Age in Britain', *Antiquity*, XXXII, 189–90.

—— 1960. 'Garn Boduan and Tre'r Ceiri, excavations at two Caernarvonshire hill-forts', *Archaeol. J.*, CXVII, 1–39.

—— 1965. 'The Early Iron Age in Wales', ed. I. Ll. Foster & Glyn E. Daniel, *Prehistoric and Early Wales*, 109–50. London.

Jack, G. H. & Hayter, A. G. K., 1924–6. 'Excavations on the site of Caplar Camp', *Trans. Woolhope Natur. Fld. Club*, 83–8.

Jenks, W. E., 1966. *West Midlands Annual Archaeological News Sheet*, No. 9.

—— 1968. *West Midlands Annual Archaeological News Sheet*, No. 11.

Kenyon, K. M., 1942. 'Excavations at the Wrekin', *Archaeol. J.*, XCIX, 99–109.

—— 1954. 'Excavations at Sutton Walls Camp', *Archaeol. J.*, CX, 1–87.

Le Men, R. F., 1872. 'Gaulish fortresses on the coast of Brittany', *Archaeol. J.*, XXIX, 314–30.

O'Neil, B. St J., 1934. 'Excavations at Titterstone Clee Camp', *Antiq. J.*, XIV, 13–32.

Ordnance Survey, 1962. *Map of Southern Britain in the Iron Age*. Chessington.

Peacock, D. P. S., 1965–7. 'Romano-British pottery production in the Malvern District', *Trans. Worcestershire Archaeol. Soc.*, 3 ser., I, 15–28.

—— 1968. 'A petrological study of certain Iron Age pottery from Western England', *Proc. Prehist. Soc.*, XXXIV, 414–27.

RCHM, 1931. Royal Commission on Historical Monuments, *Herefordshire*, Vol. I. London.

—— 1932. Royal Commission on Historical Monuments, *Herefordshire*, Vol. II. London.

—— 1934. Royal Commission on Historical Monuments, *Herefordshire*, Vol. III. London.

Russell, J. C., 1948. *British Medieval Population*. London.

St Joseph, J. K., 1965. 'Air Reconnaissance, Recent results, 5', *Antiquity*, XXXIX, 223–4.

Stanford, S. C., 1967. 'Croft Ambrey – some interim conclusions', *Trans. Woolhope Natur. Fld. Club*, XXXIX, 31–9.

—— 1969. 'Welsh border hill-forts', *C.B.A. Conference on the Iron Age in the Irish Sea Province*, forthcoming.

—— 1971. 'Credenhill Camp, Herefordshire – An Iron Age Hill-fort Capital', *Archaeol. J.*, CXXVII, 81–127.

Stead, I. M., 1968. 'An Iron Age hill-fort at Grimthorpe', *Proc. Prehist. Soc.*, XXXIV, 148–90.

Varley, W. J., 1950. 'Hill-forts of the Welsh Marches', *Archaeol. J.*, CV, 41–66.

Victoria County History, 1908. *Shropshire*, I.

Wainwright, G. J., 1967. *Coygan Camp*. Cardiff.

—— 1968. 'The excavation of a Durotrigean farmstead near Tollard Royal in Cranbourne Chase', *Proc. Prehist. Soc.*, XXXIV, 102–47.

Wheeler, R. E. M., 1943. *Maiden Castle, Dorset*. Oxford.

—— 1953. 'An Early Iron Age "Beach-head" at Lulworth, Dorset', *Antiq. J.*, XXXIII, 1–13.

Enclosures of Iron Age Type in the Upper Severn Basin

C. J. Spurgeon

This field study is part of a wider investigation of earthwork enclosures of all periods in Montgomeryshire, undertaken under the guidance of Mr Leslie Alcock of University College, Cardiff, to whose help and encouragement I am much indebted, though he is in no way responsible for any errors of fact or interpretation.[1] Fieldwork on the sites covered here was undertaken from 1960 to 1964. It was a privilege, resulting from this work in her area, to meet Miss Chitty and enjoy her irrepressible energy, enthusiasm and endless store of information. Her unfailing interest and encouragement makes it a pleasure to dedicate this contribution to her.

INTRODUCTION

The area under consideration covers that part of Montgomeryshire drained by the Severn above its junction with the Vyrnwy, with the exception of one contributing river-system, namely that of the Camlad. This has been reluctantly excluded, so as not to increase unduly the number of sites involved. The first attempt to provide a descriptive list of these enclosures is embodied in the Montgomeryshire Inventory of 1911 (RCAM, 1911). The list by Dr V. E. Nash-Williams in 1933 (Nash-Williams, 1933, 321-3) was essentially based on the Inventory. The site lists accompanying the Ordnance Survey Map of Southern Britain in the Iron Age (1962), while admirable in so many ways, are none the less inadequate for a true appreciation of probable Iron Age sites in Montgomeryshire; only 48 sites are listed for the whole county, while the classification, which makes three acres the maximum enclosed by the smallest sites, fails to indicate the predominance of tiny sites of under one acre in the county (47 out of about 80).

The main purpose of this survey, therefore, is to provide a revised descriptive list of sites for a large part of the county. Four sites given in the Inventory have been rejected and eighteen added. The additions comprise eight sites discovered from the air by Dr St Joseph, eight otherwise classified in the Inventory, and two discovered by Mr W. G. Putnam.

[1] Warm thanks are also due to Mr W. G. Putnam who kindly informed me of his discovery of two sites during his Roman field researches (Nos. 26, 27); to Dr J. K. St Joseph of the Cambridge University Committee for Aerial Photography for his kind permission to describe and interpret information yielded by his air photographs, many of which show previously unrecorded sites; to Mr A. H. A. Hogg who read the text and assured the correction of several errors; and to Miss Dorothy Ward who undertook the task of typing.

THE CLASSIFICATION OF SITES

A total of 53 sites are described. Eight of these are not classified; for three probable sites (Nos. 46–8) information is insufficient, while five others are doubtful sites (Nos. 49–53) included for reasons given in descriptions. The remainder (Nos. 1–45) have been classified first by the area available for use within their defences, thereby including, for some sites, the ground between widely-spaced defences or within annexes. Their areas, thus defined, place them in one of four groups, the smallest being of 1 acre or less, the second of 1–3 acres, the third of 3–8 acres, and the largest of over 8 acres. This division appears sound, the groups above 1 acre averaging about 2, 5 and 15 acres respectively. The four groups are then subdivided into univallate sites and bi- or multi-vallate sites. A site with a minor counterscarp bank, with no evidence of a second ditch, is regarded as univallate. On this basis the 45 sites may be tabulated as follows:

1 acre (0·4 hectare) or less enclosed	univallate: 13 (Nos. 1–13) bi-/multi-vallate: 10 (Nos. 14–23)
1–3 acres (0·4–1·2 hectares) enclosed	univallate: 5 (Nos. 24–28) bi-/multi-vallate: 7 (Nos. 29–35)
3–8 acres (1·2–3·2 hectares) enclosed	univallate: 1 (No. 36) bi-/multi-vallate: 5 (Nos. 37–41)
Over 8 acres (3·2 hectares) enclosed	univallate: 0 bi-/multi-vallate: 4 (Nos. 42–45)

No provision has been made in the classification to indicate those sites possessing widely-spaced ramparts or other features reminiscent of Lady Fox's 'South-Western Hill-Forts' (Fox, 1952; 1961).[1] Such features are noted in the descriptions, but, in the absence of a single site of indisputably south-western type, they are too few to suggest south-western influences. For those who might dispute this, the relevant sites are those numbered 30, 31, 33, 37, 38, 40, 42, 47.

Stone ramparts are known at so few sites that it would have served little purpose to classify them separately. Furthermore, of three sites of this type, one, namely the Breiddin (No. 42), had sections of stone and of earth rampart apparently co-existing in the same line, and merely reflecting the nature of the ground traversed. The near-by site on New Pieces (No. 31) also combined the two, with an inner earthen bank and an outer stone wall. At Ffridd Faldwyn (No. 45) the defences of the third Iron Age period had an inner bank of earth revetted front and back in stone. A few other sites, such as Cefn y Castell (No. 25) and Pen y Clun (No. 33), have stony banks suggestive of revetments of this type, and excavation would probably show this to have been the most usual form of rampart. One site, however, our third with a true stone wall, does call for special mention. It is the small circular site at Pen y Gaer (No. 6), certainly a walled site, and without a ditch. Only this site suggests some influence from north-west Wales.

Only about a quarter of our sites were sufficiently large and well-defended to be termed hill-forts; and two of these have been excavated (The Breiddin, No. 42; Ffridd Faldwyn, No. 45). Among the other less demonstrably Early Iron Age sites only one, the two-acre site on New Pieces (No. 31), has been excavated, to produce only Romano-British dating evidence. Despite this it would seem reasonable to suppose that most of the sites included are of the Early Iron Age, with some continuing in use into the Roman period. Others may have been built under the Romans, but this cannot be shown without excavation, and when detected would probably illustrate the continuing Early Iron Age tradition exemplified by New Pieces. Romano-British date may be indicated by the partly angular layout displayed by the crop-mark sites of Hydan Fawr (No. 29) and Arddleen (No. 30).

---

[1] Inturned entrances are also not indicated. No additions can be made to Miss Chitty's list for the area (Chitty, 1937).

Any suggestion that some of our sites may be of Dark Age or Medieval date is more difficult to answer. Alcock (1963) has shown that small sites like Dinas Powis, Phase 4, Glamorgan, were built by the Welsh in the Dark Ages. One can only state that so far no archaeological or documentary evidence has suggested such a date for any site included, nor has any been excluded on such evidence. At this point a further word of caution is needed as to the probability of the existence of Mercian sites in the region. None has been identified west of Chirbury (Salop), which lies immediately east of our area. Fox (1929, 44–5) has suggested that the 1·25-acre (0·5-hectare) embanked enclosure of Caer Din, fig. 3 (SO/274898), also just east of our area, may be Mercian. Three other sites included here may merit consideration as Mercian works. They are Crosswood (No. 24), Beacon Ring, fig. 4 (No. 36), and Nantcribba Gaer (No. 50). Caer Din lies 1,600 yards east of Offa's Dyke, while our three also lie just east of the Dyke at 520, 1,680 and 100 yards respectively. The three, while admittedly larger and lacking the vague angularity noticed by Fox at Caer Din, are all roughly circular. Like Caer Din they all lie on fairly level ground with no natural defence. No other univallate ringworks have been noted in our area.

Turning to the possibility of a medieval date for some of our smaller sites, it should first be noticed that none of them displays the bold deep ditching or scarping characteristic of undisturbed medieval work. Furthermore, the study of known medieval earthwork castles in Montgomeryshire shows the motte to be the predominant type in the county. The medieval ringwork, precisely that class of site which can be mistaken for a small Early Iron Age site, is represented by a single example, as against 36 mottes (Spurgeon, 1965–6).

Despite the reservations it seems reasonable to regard the sites here included, except for the doubtful ones (Nos. 49–53), as being of the Early Iron Age until excavation can show otherwise. With only 3 of the 53 sites having been excavated, speculation is unavoidable.

SITING AND DISTRIBUTION

In general, the larger sites have stronger defences and occupy stronger natural positions. Individual altitudes are not very significant in such broken country where, for example, Beacon Ring at 403·5 m. (1,325 ft) is situated on a lofty plateau of good arable land. It should also be noted that the floor of the Severn Valley itself is at 60–152 m. (200–500 ft) in its course through the area. Since all types classified are widely inter-dispersed, the average altitudes are of interest. The two smaller categories of under 3 acres (0·4 hectare) enclosed show no difference, the larger ones of 1–3 acres (0·4–1·2 hectares), in fact, lying on average at 224·9 m. (739 ft) as against 229·8 m. (755 ft) for those of under 1 acre (0·4 hectare). The third group, however, of sites of 3–8 acres (1·2–3·2 hectares), lies at 259 m. (850 ft), while the largest, of over 8 acres (3·2 hectares), are at 314·25 m. (1,031 ft). Of our 48 sites, 35 lie on or between the 152 m. (500 ft) and 305 m. (1,000 ft) contours shown on the map (fig. 1). Only 9 lie above and 4 below this zone. There is no discernible difference in height between univallate and multivallate sites.

In considering altitude it should be noted that, with perhaps two exceptions, all are on or close to arable land. The two are Dinas (No. 43) and Pen y Gaer (No. 6), which stand apart in other ways. This avoidance of the bleak uplands is most noticeable to the north-west of our area where the high ground around the headwaters of the Carno and Rhiw is devoid of sites. It has recently been observed that the distribution of hill-forts in Wales and the Marches looks, on the whole, like that of '. . . communities interested not exclusively in pastoral farming but rather in mixed arable and stock-raising' (Alcock, 1965, 188). Our distribution would certainly fit this observation. Direct evidence for arable farming, however, is lacking, except for the field system apparently connected with New Pieces (No. 31), and dated with that site by O'Neil to Romano-British times (O'Neil, 1937, 89–90, 97, 112–13), and the strange pits dug within the

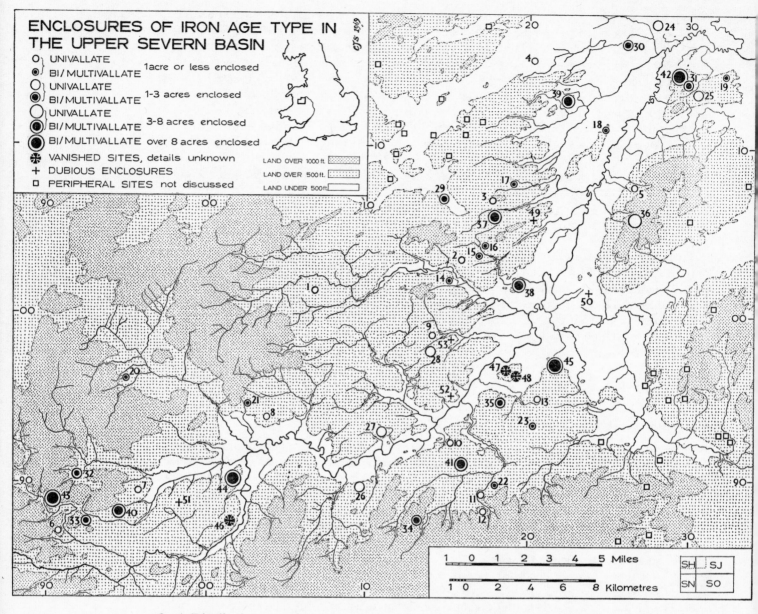

fig. 1 Distribution map of enclosures of Iron Age type in the Upper Severn Basin

old inner enclosure at Ffridd Faldwyn during a later phase (O'Neil, 1942, 18, 19, 42–3) and tentatively related to the grain-drying racks and granaries of Little Woodbury.

The minority of our sites which could reasonably be termed hill-forts includes the four of over 8 acres (3·2 hectares). Among smaller sites of under 8 acres (3·2 hectares), only Pen y Gaer (No. 6), Cefn y Castell (No. 25, pl. 1), Pen y Gaer (No. 28), Y Gaer (No. 32), Pen y Clun (No. 33), and Beacon Ring (No. 36), seem to be true hill-forts. The rest occupy sites of varying degrees of weakness on slightly raised hillocks or modest positions overlooked from adjacent high ground in at least one direction. A few are even on, or a little above, valley floors (e.g. Y Wern, No. 16, fig. 3; Crosswood, No. 24; Hydan Fawr, No. 29). These numerous weakly-defended and poorly-sited enclosures must have been occupied by small communities and in many cases by single families. Many more have probably been obliterated by the plough, like those discovered as crop-marks by Dr St Joseph. Their relationship to the hill-forts proper is uncertain, but in general they tend to cluster in the vicinity of these stronger sites which are themselves fairly evenly distributed over the area. This distribution does suggest they may have been the defended camps or homesteads of tribesmen who can be imagined resorting to the main forts for marketing or tribal rituals, or for refuge with their animals in troubled times (Hughes, 1922).[1]

CHRONOLOGY

The Breiddin provides us with our earliest evidence of Early Iron Age settlement represented by the Iron Age 'A' sherds found in association with objects of Late Bronze Age type. The discovery of a palisaded enclosure during the recent (1969) excavations on the site, seemingly connected with the same transitional Late Bronze Age–Iron Age 'A' community, may indicate the cultural context of the palisaded enclosure of the initial Iron Age phase at Ffridd Faldwyn. Iron Age 'A' settlers had probably reached the central Marches in the third century BC, and evidence elsewhere (Gardner & Savory, 1964, 75–8) suggests a movement up the Marches from southern England which is best exemplified by the haematite-coated carinated bowl of All Cannings Cross First 'A' type from Old Oswestry (Salop).

The long sequence of fortifications at Ffridd Faldwyn, punctuated by periods of neglect or abandonment, must imply a date not much after the third century BC for the timber-laced rampart built over the decayed remains of the initial palisaded enclosure. The subsequent enlargement and multiplication of the defences by 'B' settlers was the work of at least three phases, culminating in all probability in a final refurbishing under the threat of Roman attack. A similar phased enlargement and multiplication of defences is suggested by the remains at Cefn Carnedd (fig. 4 and pl. III) and Gaer Fawr.

It seems probable, though not yet tested by the spade, that the small multivallate sites are the work of 'B' settlers. The small univallate sites are so simple that it would be unwise to suggest that they are earlier, though the larger Beacon Ring may well be an Iron Age 'A' site.

TRANSITION TO THE ROMAN PERIOD

The tribesmen defending the area against the Romans were probably of the Cornovii, later to be centred on the Romanised capital at Viroconium Cornoviorum. The apparent lack of any significant differences between the Shropshire sites and those under consideration supports this, as does the Dark Age unity of the two areas, within the kingdom of Powys, before the Mercian coming. On considering the sites it seems possible to suggest that Cornovian territory may have reached as far as the Caersws area, with Cefn Carnedd possibly representing the westernmost citadel of the tribe. Beyond, to the west, clustered in isolation to the north of Llanidloes at an

[1] See Hughes (1922) for an earlier discussion of the distribution, siting and purpose of some of the sites.

average height of 327·7 m. (1,075 ft), is a small strangely assorted group of sites (Nos. 6, 7, 32, 33, 40, 43). It is by no means a homogeneous group. Two of the group are small univallate enclosures of under 1 acre (0·4 hectare), one being the stone-walled Pen y Gaer, the other the hill-slope ring-work of Dolgwden. The others are the sites with widely-spaced ramparts at Y Gaer (1·5 acres: 0·6 ha.), Pen y Clun (3 acres: 1·2 ha.) and Pen y Castell (fig. 4, 3·5 acres: 1·4 ha.), and finally the great, apparently unfinished, enclosure of about 18 acres (7·2 ha.) on Dinas. The small walled site of Pen y Gaer seems best paralleled in north-west Wales. It is tempting to wonder whether this isolated group, so diverse yet together so different from the rest of our sites, may be related to the Ordovices. It is very unlikely that this matter of tribal areas can ever be established, but since claims have been made for Cefn Carnedd as a possible site for the last stand of Caractacus in AD 51, and more recently for the area south-west of that fort (St Joseph, 1961, 267, 270–1), it seems worth noting that Dinas would, in some ways, fit the details better. Both Cefn Carnedd and an earlier claimant, the Breiddin, are sites with a long structural history, whereas Dinas is seemingly unfinished and therefore more akin to the hurriedly constructed fortification described by Tacitus, though its area of some 18 acres (7·2 ha.) may seem insufficient.

Following the Roman Conquest the evidence from the Breiddin and New Pieces suggests that the native population continued their way of life little changed. New Pieces, which O'Neil considered to have been built after the Conquest, contained a crude roughly circular hut of wattle-and-daub associated with Romano-British pottery. The crop-mark sites of Hydan Fawr and Arddleen show possible Romano-British influence in their partly angular form.

The re-occupation of some hill-forts during the Roman period is very probable but only proved at the Breiddin, where recent evidence suggests that the defences were in good condition when it was re-occupied in the late Roman period. It should be noted that the Roman forts at Caersws and Forden were two of the three largest forts in Wales, and were occupied almost continuously throughout the Roman period, which might suggest that our tribesmen were not quite so passive as those pictured by O'Neil at New Pieces.

Among the finds at Caersws were inscribed tiles, usually interpreted as evidence that the fort was at one time held by the First Cohort of Celtiberians. Professor Birley, however, has pointed out that the tiles may commemorate the First Cohort of Cornovii, who were raised in the early Principate, and may even have been used to garrison a fort on the borders of their territory (Birley, 1952, 15). Birley concludes in a way well suited to round off our tentative observations when he states: 'But we are obviously treading on very uncertain ground here, and it will be sufficient to have mentioned the possibility without committing ourselves further.'

PLANS AND SITE DESCRIPTIONS

The plans in figs 2 and 3 are original accurate surveys. Those on fig. 4, however, are based on the plans given by the 1/2500 O.S. maps with modifications and additions roughly taped or paced.

In the descriptions, only selected references to the *Montgomeryshire Collections* are given. Full references can be found in the index to these volumes published by the Powysland Club in 1962.

UNIVALLATE SITES WITH 1 ACRE OR LESS ENCLOSED (NOS 1–13)

(1) *Pen y Gaer*, Llanwyddelan (SJ/067014) (RCAM, 1911, no. 732). A small much eroded camp, roughly oval in shape, on the summit of a hill at 259 m. (850 ft). Faint remains of a single bank-and-ditch enclose an area of about 1 acre (0·4 ha.). Traces of a track up the hill on the W. suggest an entrance at that end.

(2) *Bank Farm*, Berriew (SJ/159033) (RCAM, 1911, no. 16). The O.S. map shows an oval univallate enclosure, its circuit marked by a scarp to N. and E. and by a bank-and-ditch to S. and W. It lies at 244 m. (800 ft) on the N. end of a low hill with modest slopes, except on the S.W., where the external ground is level. The site has recently been levelled, leaving only the faintest traces of the bank and ditch on the S.W.

(3) *Y Golfa*, Castle Caereinion, fig. 2 (SJ/178069) (RCAM, 1911, no. 91). A small pear-shaped enclosure at 305 m. (1,000 ft) on the tip of a sloping spur thrust out obliquely from Y Golfa hill. The ground falls abruptly on the S. and from the tip of the spur to the W., but to the N. the fall is modest to a wide but shallow natural gully with a marshy floor. To the E. the ground rises up to the main plateau. The defences consist of scarping around the tip of the spur and along the N. side, with an earthen bank-and-ditch across the neck on the E. The ditch is partly covered by a golf tee. The area is half an acre, measuring 55 m. (180 ft) E.–W. and 30·5 m. (100 ft) at its widest behind the bank on the E. No entrance is apparent.

(4) *Trefnanney Gaer*, Meifod, fig. 2 (SJ/204156) (RCAM, 1911, no. 762). A small oval enclosure at 122 m. (400 ft) on the W. end of a low hill with steep falls, except on the E. where the hill continues at the same level. Only isolated traces of the former bank-and-ditch of this univallate enclosure survive, and are best seen at the E. end, facing the line of easy approach. Elsewhere a scarp and berm mark the line. To the N.E. the scarp following the N. flank curves in a little across the ridge, but stops before linking with the N. end of the cross bank defining the E. side, which does not reach the steep natural slope. This gap probably marks the entrance. The area enclosed is about 1 acre (0·4 ha.).

(5) *Black Bank*, Cletterwood (now Trewern), fig. 2 (SJ/264076) (RCAM, 1911, no. 141). Sited at 274 m. (900 ft) on the tip of a sloping spur between two dingles on the W. flank of the Long Mountain. It is roughly oval, and defined by a scarp and berm along the flanks and around the tip of the spur. At the E. end, across the neck and facing rising ground, a ditch fronts the scarping. The sloping interior covers ¾ acre (0·3 ha.), measuring 73 m. (240 ft) along the spur by 39 m. (130 ft) across. The entrance was probably at the W. on the tip of the spur, where for about 5·5 m. (18 ft) there is a gap in the scarp.

(6) *Pen y Gaer*, Llanidloes Without (SN/908869) (RCAM, 1911, no. 593; Hamer, 1868, 219; 1873, 158). The construction of the road and viewing-point at the new Clywedog reservoir has made this remote site easily accessible. It consists of an unditched dry-walled enclosure of about three-quarters of an acre (0·3 ha.), on the summit of Pen y Gaer at 390 m. (1,280 ft). The collapsed wall has spilled downhill, but recent 'burrowing' by persons unknown has cleared the outer face in stretches of varying length around the S. side. The inner face is nowhere clear, but surface indications suggest a wall 3·5–4 m. (12–13 ft) thick. The outer face is set somewhat down the slope from the general

level of the summit, around which the inner face ran. The clearance at the gateway on the S. shows one arm of the wall turning inwards and still standing six courses high at one point, while the other arm, though more mutilated, appears to turn outwards to give an oblique passage through the wall. The interior is uneven, with a rocky rounded knoll occupying the S.W. quarter, below which, near the centre of the enclosure, the ground is marshy. The fall from the site is least on the S.W., where wall debris and natural scree litter the ground, giving the impression of a *chevaux de frise*. Some sharp stones are certainly earth-fast and dangerous in the tufty grass, but not enough to establish this rare form of outer defence.

In Montgomeryshire there are about 80 camps of Iron Age type, of which only two others, besides Pen y Gaer, have stone walls. These are the Breiddin (No. 42) and Craig Rhiwarth (SJ/057271) (Hogg, 1965, 138–9; RCAM, 1911, no. 633; Anon., 1938; Richards, 1938), both of which are at the other end of the county and on a massive scale. Pen y Gaer, therefore, is unique in the county, and the unofficial clearance and rough trenching at two points is regrettable.

(7) *Dolgwden*, Trefeglwys (SN/955892). A small circular univallate hill-slope enclosure recently discovered from the air by Dr St Joseph (AFB 73). The site lies at 252 m. (825 ft) on gently sloping ground with no natural protection. Most of its circuit has long been reduced to a barely perceptible hump by ploughing. On the upper (N.) quarter, however, its line is very well preserved in the hedge-line, which bows outwards to follow the top of its bank. Beyond the hedge is a fine rock-cut ditch 1·75 m. (5 ft 6 in.) deep. The area enclosed is about ¾ acre (0·3 ha.).

(8) *Gwynfynnydd*, Llanwnog, fig. 2 (SO/039936) (RCAM, 1911, no. 708; AP no. ADC 10). The passing of the north-bound Roman road from Caersws, immediately E. of Gwynfynnydd, no doubt encouraged its classification as a rectangular and Roman site. It is, in fact, as Pennant observed, an oval site. With no natural protection, it lies on a gentle slope from N.W. to S.E. at 183 m.

(600 ft). Surveyed in 1961, it has since been greatly reduced by ploughing. The area enclosed by its single bank-and-ditch is about 1 acre (0·4 ha.) and measures 81 by 61 m. (270 by 200 ft). The bank was well-marked except on the S., where a strong scarp was present. The external ditch was visible only on the N.E. for some 46 m. (150 ft) of the circumference. A slight lessening of the scarp at one point on the S. may have marked the entrance.

(9) *Lower Ucheldre*, Bettws Cedewain, fig. 2 (SO/141986) (RCAM, 1911, no. 32). A small camp enclosing ¾ acre (0·3 ha.) on a minor spur with a dingle to the N. and a slight, though marshy, gully to the S. Westwards the ground rises up beyond a well-preserved bank-and-ditch across the neck of the spur. At the S.W. corner the ditch merges with the natural gully, and the bank ends after turning sharply eastwards. The N. end of the crossbank probably ended on the steeper fall to the dingle in similar fashion, but a modern track has cut through it at this point. Behind the bank, which is 43 m. (140 ft) N.–S., the spur gradually tapers to a narrow point, and along the sides the scarping of the natural slopes was sufficient defence. A sloping entrance-way runs obliquely up the scarp to enter the camp 31 m. (100 ft) from the N.W. corner, the scarp swinging inwards at this point. An isolated stretch of berm runs around the tip of the spur with traces at one point of a ditch and counterscarp, above which is the corresponding bank. Along the spur the interior measures 97·5 m. (320 ft). Higher ground across the gully to the S. completely overlooks the camp.

(10) *Giant's Bank*, Llanmerewig, fig. 2 (SO/152923) (RCAM, 1911, no. 620). A small oval enclosure on the top of a modest hillock at 183 m. (600 ft). It measures internally some 84 m. (275 ft) E.–W. by 38 m. (125 ft) N.–S., and the area enclosed is about ¾ acre (0·3 ha.). Ploughing has reduced most of the defences to a scarp and berm. There is a trace of the ditch only around the W. end, above which are vague indications of a counterscarp bank which appears to continue as a line of scarping around the S.

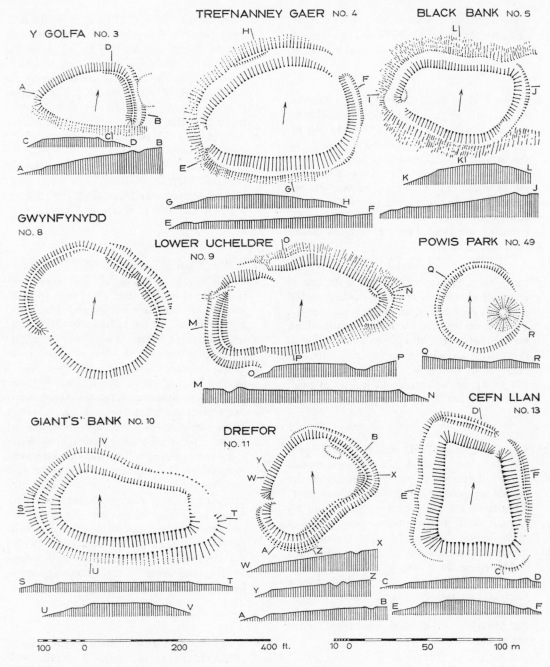

Y GOLFA NO. 3

TREFNANNEY GAER NO. 4

BLACK BANK NO. 5

GWYNFYNYDD NO. 8

LOWER UCHELDRE NO. 9

POWIS PARK NO. 49

GIANT'S BANK NO. 10

DREFOR NO. 11

CEFN LLAN NO. 13

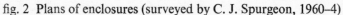

100   0   200   400 ft.   10 0   50   100 m

fig. 2 Plans of enclosures (surveyed by C. J. Spurgeon, 1960–4)

side. Sherds of 'ornamented pottery', recorded from the site in 1833 (Lewis, 1833, under Llanmerewig), have been too easily assumed to have been Samian.

(11) *Drefor*, Kerry, fig. 2 (SO/172889) (RCAM, 1911, no. 285). This tiny pear-shaped enclosure of ¾ acre lies on a slope at 259 m. (850 ft), its broadest end uphill facing E. A bank-and-ditch defines the enclosure, except for 39·5 m. (130 ft) of the N.W. side, which shows only a scarp. The defences are strongest facing the rising ground which completely overlooks the site. A simple entrance is placed near the narrow lower end, and faces W.

(12) *Cwm Golog*, Kerry (SO/176881). An arc of much eroded bank-and-ditch facing uphill on the E. slope of Bedran at 274.5 m. (900 ft). There is no trace of the lower circuit which was probably less strongly entrenched, as is commonly so with these minor hill-slope enclosures. This site was discovered from the air by Dr St Joseph (AUE 83). The full area could not have exceeded 1 acre (0·4 ha.).

(13) *Cefn Llan*, Llandyssil, fig. 2 (SO/206948) (RCAM, 1911, no. 385). Cefn Llan crowns a low hill at 213 m. (700 ft). The fall on the N. is very gentle, and higher ground overlooks the site from no great distance on all sides. A small stream curves around the foot of the hill on the S. and E. The enclosure, a tapering quadrilateral of ¾ acre (0·3 ha.) is defined on the S. and W. sides by a scarp and berm. On the N., the weakest side, a ditch and counterscarp bank front the scarp. A counterscarp bank also runs along the E. side but is less well-defined. A simple entrance lies at the N.E. corner.

BIVALLATE OR MULTIVALLATE SITES WITH 1 ACRE OR LESS ENCLOSED (NOS 14–23)

(14) *Cae Thygley*, Berriew (SJ/155020) (RCAM, 1911, no. 14). A small circular camp on sloping ground at the end of a spur above the Rhiw Valley. The inner line is marked by a scarp enclosing about ½ acre (0·2 ha.). There is a low outer bank with a faintly marked ditch to the W. facing up the slope.

(15) *Lower House*, Berriew (SJ/170035) (RCAM, 1911, no. 15).[1] A small oval enclosure at 214 m. (700 ft) on slightly raised ground at the top of the slope to the Luggy Brook, flowing by to the N.E. Across the brook the site overlooks Y Wern (No. 16). The position is not a strong one. On the S.W., after a slight fall, the ground rises to overlook the camp, and on this side the defences comprised three close-set earthen banks. The entrance was probably at the W. end. The area enclosed is only about ½ acre (0·2 ha.). Being subject to frequent ploughing, the defences are now reduced to scarps and berms.

(16) *Y Wern*, Castle Caereinion, fig. 3 (SJ/172041) (RCAM, 1911, no. 93).[2] This small hill-slope site is weakly sited at 167 m. (550 ft), just above the marshy ground beside the Luggy Brook. It is completely overlooked from the slope behind it and from the higher ground across the brook, on which lies Lower House Camp, 430 m. (500 yds) to the S.S.W. and 38 m. (125 ft) higher. Water erosion has distorted and confused the defences, especially on the upper (E.) side, though further erosion has recently been reduced at the expense of a deep drainage ditch dug right across the site. The remains indicate a roughly circular enclosure of about one acre, and some 61 m. (200 ft) in diameter, defended by two close-set ramparts on the upper side. The inner line alone, as little more than a scarp and ditch, continues down the slope on the N. side, and curves around the lower side to embrace a small annexe fronting the lower end of a corresponding line around the S. and W. sides.

(17) *Tan y Clawdd*, Castle Caereinion (SJ/189079) (RCAM, 1911, no. 90). A small, well-defended site enclosing ¾ acre (0·3 ha.), but now much mutilated by the farm and buildings upon it. It was defended by a double line of rampart and ditch with an outer counterscarp bank, though in places the line seems to have been reduced to two banks. The site is not in a strong natural position.

[1] St Joseph AP no. AOU 43.
[2] St Joseph AP nos. AOU 41, 43, 45.

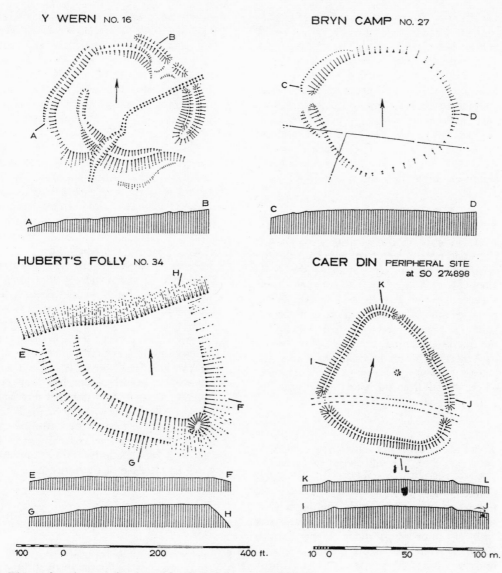

Y WERN NO. 16

BRYN CAMP NO. 27

HUBERT'S FOLLY NO. 34

CAER DIN PERIPHERAL SITE at SO 274898

100   0   200   400 ft.

10 0   50   100 m.

fig. 3 Plans of enclosures (surveyed by C. J. Spurgeon, 1960–4)

(18) *Crowther's Camp*, Welshpool (SJ/248113) (RCAM, 1911, no. 929; Lines, 1889, 334–5). Crowther's Camp lies at 152 m. (500 ft) on the N. end of a long hill on the W. side of the Severn, 4 km. (2½ miles) N.E. of Welshpool. It is now much mutilated and densely overgrown in places. It appears to have been a small D-shaped enclosure of about ¾ acre (0·3 ha.), defended by three close-set ramparts and ditches on all except the straight W. side, where the scarping of the steeper fall of the Severn was sufficient defence. The important Bronze Age 'Guilsfield' Hoard was found 90 m. (100 yds) S. along the ridge.

(19) *Castle Camp*, Bausley (SJ/322145) (RCAM, 1911, no. 12; Hughes, 1922, 88, 96). A small multivallate site on a spur thrust out to the N.E. from the greater height of Kempster's Hill. The steep fall on the S.E. side of the spur gave sufficient defence, but in other directions a circuit of from two to four ramparts defines an area of ¾ acre (0·3 ha.). In places these defences have been reduced to scarp and berms. The entrance was to the S.W., where the defences terminate before reaching the steep natural fall.

(20) *Castell Carno*, Carno (SN/949961) (RCAM, 1911, no. 46). At 312 m. (1,025 ft), Castell Carno occupies a slight eminence on the tip of a spur overlooking Carno to the N.E. About ½ acre (0·2 ha.) is enclosed by a curving bank to the N. and N.W., facing rising ground. Beyond a ditch is a second bank. A simple entrance gap faces W., the banks attaining their greatest height each side of it. There are no traces of artificial defences around the rest of the enclosure, where the fall from the spur was presumably sufficient protection.

(21) *Wyle Cop*, Llanwnog (SO/023945) (RCAM, 1911, no. 709). A hill-slope enclosure at 228 m. (750 ft), set beside a steep-sided dingle which bounds it on the W. Its full extent is uncertain, only the upper (N.) side surviving. This comprises two ramparts with an intervening ditch. These banks, springing from the dingle, follow a curving line for about 46 m. (150 ft) eastwards before dying out. The site is not likely to have exceeded 1 acre (0·4 ha.).

(22) *Clwt Camp*, Kerry (SO/180896) (RCAM, 1911, no. 284). This site lies in Sibwll Wood at 243·5 m. (800 ft) and about 1 km. (½ mile) N.E. of Drefor (No. 11). Like that site it is tiny and placed on a slope, the higher ground of which completely overlooks the site from the S.E. The slope continues below the site to the N.W., and on the S.W. a small but deep natural gully protects it. To the N.E. lies level ground along the slope. Enclosing a mere ⅓ acre (0·13 ha.), the defences consist of a bank-and-ditch outlining

a D-shaped area, the straight side facing N.E. An outer bank is present on the N.W. and N.E. sides. Both banks are now very indistinct on the straight N.E. side. There is a simple entrance on the N.W. The slope of the hill rises so steeply to the S.E. that the outer lip of the ditch is well above the top of the bank behind it.

(23) *Cefn y Coed*, Kerry (SO/204933) (RCAM, 1911, no. 287). A small multivallate camp on the slope a little below and S. of the ridge of Cefn y Coed, which bounds the parish. Overlooked from the N., with level ground to E. and W. and a modest fall away to the S., the site is very weak. The defences, however, were strong, especially since they enclose a mere ⅓ acre (0·13 ha.). They consisted of a double close-set line of bank-and-ditch, outlining a roughly square area of 46 m. (150 ft) E.–W. by 36·5 m. (120 ft) N.–S., measured internally. These defences are best preserved on the upper side. On the W. a field boundary runs along the inner bank, but ploughing has destroyed the two ditches and outer bank. A double scarp marks the lines to the S., but on the E., where the *Inventory* recorded an entrance gap of 6·5 m. (21 ft), the encroachment of farm-buildings has left only a slight and broken scarp on the line of the inner bank.

UNIVALLATE SITES WITH 1–3 ACRES ENCLOSED (NOS 24–28)

(24) *Crosswood*, Llandrinio (SJ/279175) (RCAM, 1911, no. 362; Thomas, 1894, 23–4). A circular univallate site on low-lying ground about a mile W. of Llandrinio. Its altitude is 61 m. (200 ft). Only the faintly discernible arc of the N. line of the rampart survives to the N. of the modern road, which cuts through the enclosure from E. to W. The greater part of the site lay S. of the road. About 2 acres (0·8 ha.) seem to have been enclosed. Offa's Dyke passes 550 m. (600 yds) W. of the site.

(25) *Cefn y Castell*, Middletown (SJ/306134, (pl. 1) (RCAM, 1911, no. 796; Lines, 1889, 335–6, 415–16; Hughes, 1922, 88, 98). A contour fort crowning Middletown Hill at

358 m. (1,175 ft), 1 mile S.E. of the Breiddin. An elongated oval enclosure covers about 2 acres (0·8 ha.) of the irregular domed hill-top. The enclosing rampart is of earth, with a strong stone content, and external berm. It breaks for entrances at the N.E. and S.W. ends, the rampart ends inturning sharply. A small annexe is formed beyond the S.W. gate by a slight bank thrown across the ridge, with its own centrally-placed entrance. There are quarry scoops behind the rampart of the main enclosure. Little trace is left of the ditch which survives mainly as a berm.

(26) *Castell y Dail*, Newtown (SO/095898). The name, but not the site, is mentioned in the *Inventory*. Although marked on the first O.S. 1-inch map, it has only recently been rediscovered by Mr W. G. Putnam. It lies at 183 m. (600 ft), about 185 m. (200 yds) S.W. of Castell y Dail farm, on a small rise on the slopes of the high ground S. of Newtown. The falls to the N., therefore, are steep, but southwards only a slight hollow separates it from the rising ground which overlooks it. It measures 149·5 m. (490 ft) by 46 m. (150 ft) internally. The defences are much eroded, leaving no more than a scarp and berm, with just a short stretch of bank-and-ditch barely visible near the S.E. corner. An entrance is suggested by the inturning of the scarp at the S.W. end. About 1½ acres (0·6 ha.) are enclosed.

(27) *Bryn Camp*, Llanllwchaiarn, fig. 3 (SO/110926). The faint remains of an oval enclosure, discovered by Mr W. G. Putnam, lie on a slightly projecting shelf of level ground thrust out from the rising ground about ½ mile N. of Newtown. It lies at 159 m. (525 ft) with falls away on all sides except the N. and N.E., where the ground rises gradually to over 181·75 m. (600 ft). Almost obliterated by ploughing, it is further obscured by the hedge-lines of three fields which meet in the enclosures. The single bank survives in a much eroded state on the W. for about 21·5 m. (70 ft), with a central entrance gap 3·75 m. (12 ft) wide. Short stretches of shallow ditch survive each side of the entrance, but continue as berms before

even they are gone, leaving the greater part of the enclosure outlined by a scarp. The area enclosed is about 1¼ acres (0·5 ha.) and measures 91·5 m. (300 ft) E.–W. by 76 m. (250 ft) N.–S.

(28) *Pen y Gaer* or *Y Pegwn*, Bettws Cedewain (SO/139976) (RCAM, 1911, no. 31). First recorded by Edward Lhwyd as '. . . a place called Pen y Gaire where formerly there hath been a beacon repayred in the memory of men now living and seems to be a place where some towne formerly stood by ye wayes to it and mounts in being' (Lhwyd, 1696, 71). Pennant, and Lewis in his *Topographical Dictionary of Wales*, both speak of triple defences, but the surviving remains suggest no more than a univallate site with vague traces of a counterscarp bank at the N.E. end and possibly on the S.W. also. It occupies a long isolated hill 297·5 m. (975 ft) high. A bank-and-ditch survives at the N.E. and S.W. ends, with a scarp and berm along the N.W. and a very eroded scarp to the S.E. The area enclosed was an elongated kidney shape and ridged along its length, covering some 3 acres (1·2 ha.). It measured 175 m. (190 yds) by 70 m. (80 yds) and had an entrance at each end.

BIVALLATE OR MULTIVALLATE SITES WITH 1–3 ACRES ENCLOSED (NOS 29–35)

(29) *Hydan Fawr*, Castle Caereinion (SJ/147068). No traces remain above ground of this site discovered from the air by Dr St Joseph (1961, 268, pl. XLIII a). It lies on a flat indefensible position between two minor brooks at 144·5 m. (475 ft). To the S. the ground rises steeply to overlook the site. The Llanfair Light Railway impinges on the N.E. side of the defences, which the aerial photographs show as two widely-spaced ditches with an outer third line visible only around the S.E. quarter. The most significant feature is the very angular shape of the inner enclosure, outlined by three straight sides which are closed on the N. by a curving line. The outer lines are less noticeably angular. The inner enclosure occupies about 1 acre (0·4 ha.), which, added to the area within the middle line, gives a total of about 3 acres (1·2 ha.).

(30) *Arddleen*, Llandrinio (SJ/259164). This bivallate D-shaped enclosure with widely-spaced defences lies at 76·2 m. (250 ft) on the low, gently-contoured ridge 370 m. (400 yds) N. of Arddleen on the A483 Welshpool–Oswestry road. Discovered from the air by Dr St Joseph (AP Nos ABP 88, 89), it has been ploughed out and shows as crop marks. The internal enclosure covers about ½ acre (0·2 ha.), while the outer line gives an overall area within it of little under 2 acres (0·8 ha.). The two lines are parallel and straight on the S.E. side and break centrally for the entrance; while closer together than elsewhere, they are still widely spaced.

(31) *New Pieces*, Criggion (SJ/298140). A little E. of the Breiddin (No. 42) a lesser hill rises to 320 m. (1,050 ft), in a weak position below the summit, and on its S. slopes, lies a small camp. It seems to have relied entirely on the gradual natural fall on the E. and S. sides. The W. and N. sides are protected by a double line of widely-spaced defences, which were investigated during the Breiddin excavations of 1933–5 (O'Neil, 1937, 90–1, 96–7, 107–12). The main line consisted of a strong rampart of earth and stones, revetted externally in stone, and internally in timber with posts set about 2·3 m. (7 ft 6 in.) apart. A narrow berm separated the stone revetment from a V-shaped ditch. Though well-preserved where sectioned on the W. side, this line was almost gone on the vulnerable N. side facing up the hill. An entrance was placed to the N.W., the rampart to the N. turning in, while that to the S. stopped 9 m. (30 ft) short of the gateway located against the N. inturn. The outer line was a stone wall 2·75 m. (9 ft) wide and without a ditch. Its entrance was to the N.W. and opposite that in the inner line. Between this camp and the Breiddin are traces of ancient fields which are probably related to the lesser camp. O'Neil cleared an oval hut, outlined by postholes, and lying just within the inner entrance. The finds, mainly associated with this hut, were all of the Roman period. O'Neil concluded that the site represented the resettlement of the native population following the Roman conquest and a forced evacuation of the strong Breiddin camp. Recently, however, it has been argued (Forde-Johnston, 1962, 79–81;

see also Alcock, 1965, 185) that the site was built in the pre-Roman Iron Age as a small satellite to the Breiddin, its function being to act as a strongpoint to cover ground hidden from the main camp by the lesser hill. While a pre-Roman foundation cannot be ruled out, it seems doubtful that New Pieces Camp could have served much purpose as a strong outpost, especially in view of its apparent lack of any artificial defences towards the gradual slopes to S. and E., precisely those slopes which were hidden from the main camp. Furthermore, while the choice of the hill-slope, rather than the summit, is said to indicate its function as a site viewing hidden ground, it should be noted that small, isolated hill-slope sites are not uncommon in this area.

(32) *Y Gaer*, Trefeglwys (SN/919903) (RCAM, 1911, no. 879; Hamer, 1868, 222; 1879, 19). Y Gaer, on the farm of Cefn Cloddiau (= 'the ridge of the ditches'), stands at the E. end of a spur at a height of 274·5 m. (900 ft). The ground rises gradually to the W.; but to the N.E., and especially to the S., the fall away was steep. The site is now divided unequally by a hedge running N. to S. Two-thirds of the site to the E. of the hedge are almost totally ploughed out, but the remainder, on the W., is better preserved and still retains slight banks. Sufficient remains to confirm Edward Lhwyd's description of it as a 'treble fortification', though in his time (c. 1696) it had 'extraordinary deep trenches' (Lhwyd, 1696, 40). An inner oval enclosure marked now by a scarp, except above the steep natural fall on the S., covers an area of about ¾ acre (0·3 ha.) of slightly raised ground at the end of the spur, all to the E. of the modern hedge. Beyond this, at a distance of 24·5 m. (80 ft) on the W. and 12 m. (40 ft) on the N., stood an outer line of two close-set ramparts with an intervening ditch, enclosing a further area of about ¾ acre (0·3 ha.). It is this double outer line which alone preserves traces of its ramparts to the W. of the hedge. Along the N. the outer works are set a little down the slope from the inner enclosure, and show only as scarps, the outer one converging with the passing road. Eastwards they are obliterated, but the direction of the middle line, where last perceptible, shows that they

continued widely-spaced from the inner enclosure on that side. 'Silver pieces' are said to have been found on the site (Hamer, 1879, 19).

(33) *Pen y Clun*, Llanidloes Without, fig. 4 (SN/926875) (RCAM, 1911, no. 595; Hamer, 1868, 218–19; 1873, 157–8; Savory, 1962, 22). Pen y Clun is a hill on the E. end of a ridge of high ground thrust out from the E. slope of Bryn y tail (403 m.) (1,321 ft). It has no level summit and the site lies on the rocky sloping ground towards the saddle between the two hills. The fall is steep to the south, while to the N. it is precipitous. To the E. the natural fall seems to have been defence enough, but to the N. and S. artificial defences follow the top of the steep natural falls to curve inwards to a central gateway and enclose an area of 1½ acres (0·6 ha.). On the N. this defence consists of a bank which gradually increases in size towards the gate, where it ends with traces of quarry scoops behind it. Its last 76 m. (250 ft) to the gate is fronted by a strong ditch and counterscarp bank. At the gate the main bank bifurcates, one arm turning inwards up the slope, the other at rather over 90 degrees turning outwards and shutting the ditch-end off from the entrance-way. On the S. the defence is a scarp, which becomes a bank with external ditch as it curves sharply in to flank the S. of the entrance, against the inturned arm to the N. Beyond the gate, some 41 m. (135 ft) farther down the slope, a second line runs N. to S. to enclose a further 1½ acres. This outer line is only preserved for about 27·5 m. (90 ft) at its S. extremity, where it ends abruptly without turning back to join the inner defences. A short stretch of external ditch is also visible at this end. To the N., ploughing has left only a slight scarp. Earlier plans and descriptions show it to have consisted of a rampart and ditch, which, like the inner line, had a counterscarp bank to the N. of its inturned entrance, which lay centrally opposite the inner entrance.

It should be noted that the straight trench of irregular depth, which runs along the top of the hill to the E., is a modern trial cut by lead prospectors. That it could not be the E. line of the inner enclosure, as had been suggested, is clear from its position below

the ridge and blind to the E. Its true nature is further indicated by its continuation beyond the fort and down the steep slopes to N. and S.

The surviving ramparts are of earth, but in places projecting stones suggest the probability of a stone revetment.

(34) *Hubert's Folly* or *Pen y Castell*, Kerry, fig. 3 (SO/134876) (RCAM, 1911, no. 296; Hughes, 1922, 88, 107; Morris, 1889, 353–69). N.E. of Cae-betin farm the northward-flowing Miheli brook is joined from the W. by the stream in the precipitous Cwm-y-ddalfa. In the angle formed by this confluence is a much eroded bivallate enclosure. The ravine along the N. side needed no artificial defences, but a double line curved around from it to face the gentle slopes on the W. and S. After some 91·5 m. (300 ft) the outer line fades out, but the inner one continues for a further 15 m. (50 ft) to end on a small modern quarry pit, beyond which it continues, having turned at right angles, to head N. and towards the ravine. This E. side faces the less precipitous fall to the Miheli. Only scarps are visible, and that to the E. is particularly indistinct and fades out 31 m. (100 ft) short of the ravine. A third line has been recorded on the W. side (Hughes, 1922, 107), but no traces of it are now visible. The area enclosed is 1¼ acres (0·5 ha.).

The site has been regarded by some as the abortive castle built in 1228 by Hubert de Burgh and known as 'Hubert's Folly'. The name is still used for this site, although it is clearly an earthwork of Iron Age type.[1]

(35) *Cuckoo Hall*, Llandyssil (SO/182947). A small multivallate enclosure at 183 m. (600 ft) on the summit of an unnamed hill, 275 m. (300 yds) S.E. of Cuckoo Hall. It was discovered from the air by Dr St Joseph, whose A P (no. ASQ 46) shows the defences of the W. half of the site as crop-marks. These defences consisted of two close-set banks with ditches and an external counterscarp bank. In the adjacent fields, which contain the E.

[1] For the probable site of the true Hubert's Folly, see Spurgeon, 1965–6, 44–7.

end of the site, nothing is visible. The area enclosed was probably between 1 and 2 acres (0·4–0·8 ha.).

UNIVALLATE SITE ENCLOSING 3–8 ACRES (NO. 36)

(36) *Beacon Ring* or *Caer Digoll*, Trelystan/ Leighton, fig. 4 (SJ/265058) (RCAM, 1911, no. 302; Hogg, 1962, 28). One of the finest sites in Montgomeryshire, consisting of a large oval enclosure of 5 acres on the highest part of the Long Mountain plateau at 408 m. (1,338 ft). It was shown on Speed's map of 1611 and marked 'Carlion Hill'. Though the slopes from the perimeter are very gentle, the single massive bank and its ditch provide a strong defence. On the W. the bank stands 6 m. (20 ft) above the ditch bottom, and falls 1·5 m. (5 ft) internally. There are clear, though intermittent, traces of a berm between bank and ditch, suggesting box-rampart construction. There are breaks in the defences to the N. and S. That to the S. is certainly an original entrance and consists of a simple gap of 15 m. (50 ft) between the rampart ends, which are not quite in line, that on the E. being somewhat in advance of the other. Air photographs taken before the unfortunate afforestation of the interior show traces of internal quarry scoops behind the rampart. In appearance the site is of Iron Age 'A' type, but little is known of the early phases of the Iron Age in the area, and there is no clear local parallel to Beacon Ring.

MULTIVALLATE SITES ENCLOSING 3–8 ACRES (NOS. 37–41)

(37) *Pen y Foel*, Castle Caereinion, fig. 4 (SJ/ 178059) (RCAM, 1911, no. 92; Thomas, 1902). This strong hill-fort, crowning the top of Pen y Foel[1] at 274 m. (900 ft), comprises a quadrangular main enclosure of about 3½ acres (1·4 ha.), with an annexe of about 1½ acres (0·6 ha.) on its W. side. Ramparts played less part in defending the site than the steep scarping of the natural fall on all sides. No rampart crowns this scarping above the very steep N. slope, nor above the slightly less steep fall to the E., though here a platform below the scarp

[1] Thomas (1902) regarded it as a twelfth-century castle.

indicates a ditch. This ditch survives only for a short distance at the N.E. angle, where it has a counterscarp bank, while beyond the platform towards the S.E. angle there are traces of a further scarped line in the dense undergrowth. An original track, still in use, follows the foot of the scarping along the S. side from the S.W. angle. At the angle the scarp is topped by a slight rampart which increases in strength westwards, and attains its greatest dimensions at the centre of the S. side, where it curves in slightly and ends, to allow the track to enter the enclosure. Beyond, a scarp alone completed the line on this side, and at the entrance curves outwards to flank the lower side of the entrance for some 31 m. (100 ft), showing traces of a bank. The W. fall from the site is less steep, and here the scarping was again surmounted by an earthen rampart, and fronted by a strong ditch. This line has been mutilated for about 31 m. (100 ft) on the S. side by the farmhouse and its garden. The slight inturning of the rampart-end immediately N. of the farmhouse suggests that a second gate existed here, giving access to the annexe. This annexe is outlined by a scarp, partly embanked and ditched, which runs across the ridge at an average distance of 38 m. (125 ft) from the W. side of the main enclosure. A central gap, though clearly disturbed, faces the suggested inner entrance near the farm. The gentle incurve of the scarp N. of this gap in the outer line increases the probability of an outer gate at this point. On the steep N. slope the annexe is closed by a scarped line, but there is no surviving trace of any southern return of the annexe defences to the main enclosure.

(38) *Cefn yr Allt*, Berriew, pl. XV (SJ/193019). Cefn yr Allt rises to 159·5 m. (525 ft) at its N. end, where there are steep falls to the Luggy Brook on the N. and to the Severn on the E. The angle between these steep slopes was enclosed by a triple line of widely-spaced defences. These are now totally ploughed away, and we are indebted to Dr St Joseph whose air photographs show them as crop-marks (AP nos. AGD 82–3). The site was still visible on the ground in 1833, when Lewis recorded a 'British encampment' on the hill (Lewis, 1833, under Berriew).

The inner line seems rather more angular than the others, and encloses about 3½ acres (1·4 ha.). The outer lines are curved throughout their course across the angle, and outside them the ground is almost level. The total area within the outermost line is about 7 acres (2·8 ha.).

(39) *Gaer Fawr*, Guilsfield (SJ/224130) (RCAM, 1911, no. 214; Lines, 1889, 336–40, 416; Jones & Owen, 1900, 165–8). This complicated multivallate site crowns a long hill lying N.E.–S.W. It would appear to have had a long structural history, similar to that known at Ffridd Faldwyn (no. 45), and indicated by surface remains at Cefn Carnedd (no. 44). The initial hill-fort, probably univallate, covered 3 acres (1·2 ha.) along the highest part of the hill, and was outlined by the innermost scarps along its flanks. Its entrances, presumably one at each end, have been masked by works of a later phase. At some stage it became necessary to enlarge the fort and this was done by enclosing an additional 3½ acres (1·4 ha.) below the main hilltop on the N.W. side. This new outer line was bivallate along the N.W., but as it curved in towards the entrances at each end of the hill this was increased to four ramparts. At the N.E. end the innermost rampart of this enlarged enclosure climbed up over the scarp of the earlier fort and turned in to flank an entrance. At the S.W. end, however, the new defences continued around well beyond the S.W. end of the old enclosure, to halt at a bank running down from the old enclosure and forming one side of an embanked entrance-way to the inner area. In the same way, on the S.E. side, the innermost line formed an inturn at the N.E. entrance, but continued outwards on the S. to flank the embanked entrance-way to the S.W. gate. A scarp marking a second defensive line on the S.E. side may also have been added at this time. The complication of the defences of this enlarged fort suggests that it was the product of several building phases, but this could only be proved by excavation.

(40) *Pen y Castell*, Llanidloes Without, fig. 4 (SN/946881) (RCAM, 1911, no. 594; Hamer, 1868, 216–18; 1872, 48; 1873, 155). The

hill on which this site lies rises 291·5 m. (956 ft) at its S. end, and along its S.E. side the fall is steep and seems to have required only scarping. To the W. and N.W. the fall away is quite gradual, and on this side a semicircular defensive line was built, its ends based on the naturally strong S.E. slopes. These curving defences consisted of a double, widely-spaced line which has been almost totally ploughed away. They survive only as scarps of varying strength, some followed by hedge-lines. They survived as banks and ditches in the 1860s, though ploughing had already begun to erode them (Hamer, 1872, 48). On the N. side the last 31 m. (100 ft) of the double line has entirely disappeared. Throughout most of their course the lines are about 18·5 m. (60 ft) apart, though towards their termination at the S. end the outer line diverges from this parallel course to form a blunt angle, widening the outer enclosure to 31 m. (100 ft), before resuming its original distance from the inner line at the termination above the E. hillside. The area of the inner enclosure is about 2½ acres (1·0 ha.), while that between the ramparts would have added about 1 acre (0·4 ha.). A track crossing the scarped lines on the W. probably indicates the site of the entrance.

(41) *Great Cloddiau*, Kerry (SO/159909) (RCAM, 1911, no. 283; Hughes, 1922, 88, 106). This large, roughly circular enclosure of about 4 acres (1·6 ha.) lies on ground sloping gently to the E. A farmhouse stands on the line of the ditch on the E. side, and the activities of generations of its occupants have left only intermittent traces of the defences. To the N.W., slight signs of an outer bank can be seen in a field which has long been under plough. Elsewhere the outer line has been erased.

BIVALLATE AND MULTIVALLATE SITES ENCLOSING OVER 8 ACRES (NOS. 42–45)

(42) *The Breiddin*, Criggion (SJ/292144) (RCAM, 1911, no. 149; O'Neil, 1937; Chitty, 1937; Lines, 1889, 327–34; Hughes, 1922, 88, 97). With O'Neil's excavation report available, a detailed description is not needed of this, the best known hill-fort in Montgomeryshire. It lies on a long hill with such steep falls

along the N.W. side that defences there were unnecessary. Along the S.E. side, facing New Pieces, was a triple fortification. An inner stone wall runs the full length of the hill to close on steep falls at each end. A second stone wall fronts the greater part of the inner line at some distance down the slope. Beyond these walls, and on level ground at the foot of the hill, an earthen rampart and ditch was built across the col between the Breiddin and New Pieces. This line was not necessarily of a different period since, as it curved up the hillside at its S. end to flank the approach to the main entrance through the walls, it became a stone wall identical to the inner defences. The main entrance was near the centre of the S.E. side, and was inturned.

O'Neil noted four periods: Period I (*c.* AD 1) was represented by a hut antedating the defences and thought to have been part of an undefended settlement. Associated finds included a small number of Late Bronze Age survivals, and later levels included some 'rubbish survivals' of pottery which has been more recently identified as of Iron Age 'A' type (Gardner & Savory, 1964, 77; Hogg, 1965, 135). It should be noted, however, that the sherds associated directly with O'Neil's Period I occupation were predominantly of the black vesicular ware now identified as typical of the Western 3rd 'B' pottery on the site. Period II (*c.* AD 50–75) saw the erection of the defences which O'Neil thought to be of one period. The absence of datable finds was taken to indicate the short duration of Period II. Period III (*c.* AD 75–fourth century) began with the burning of a hut of Period II and the dismantling of the defences at the entrance. This O'Neil took to be the work of Roman invaders. The main feature of this period, however, was what O'Neil regarded as the resettlement of the hill-fort survivors in the new, smaller and weaker enclosure on New Pieces (see no. 25). Finally, Period IV (*c.* AD 380, possibly continuing, despite the lack of positive evidence, until eighth century AD) saw the reoccupation of the main fort in the fourth century, though without the rebuilding of the defences.

Since O'Neil devised the above scheme for the phases found at the Breiddin, and partly as a result of his own subsequent work at Ffridd Faldwyn (no. 45), some doubts have been expressed about his dating. In particular it has been suggested that the destruction at the start of Period III may well have occurred long before the arrival of the Romans (Gardner & Savory, 1964, 193–4). The bearing this would have on the interpretation of the defences is obvious. It is fortunate that we may now look forward to some clarification of these problems. Recently (late 1969) a rescue excavation at the S. end of the site was begun under the direction of Mr C. R. Musson, who has most generously given details of his provisional conclusions. It can now be seen that, at this point at least, there was a pre-rampart palisade roughly following the line of the inner stone wall. Within the rampart were wattle and daub huts, probably all circular; one has produced 3rd 'B' pottery from its floor, but others have still to produce datable finds. Prior to or associated with the palisaded settlement is the rim of a situlate jar of 'A' type, together with sherds which some would regard as being in Late Bronze Age tradition. The hint of a transitional Late Bronze Age–Iron Age phase, previously suggested by the finds in O'Neil's Period I, is further strengthened by the find of a bronze disc-headed pin of Late Bronze Age type known from Heathery Burn Cave. Stamped Western 3rd 'B' ware and the crude ware termed 'VCP' is associated with the stone rampart. O'Neil's belief that the defences were not rebuilt following the late Roman reoccupation (Period IV) is thrown into some doubt by the recovery of a sherd of 'imitation Samian' ware at the foot of the front revetment and buried by the collapse, while the late Roman pottery in general tends to come from low rather than high in this collapse.[1]

(43) *Dinas*, Llanidloes Without/Trefeglwys (SN/906891) (RCAM, 1911, no. 599 [name only]; Hamer, 1868, 219–20; 1879, 17–18). This strange site lies on Dinas Hill, which rises to

---

[1] I am most grateful to Mr Musson for sending these details within weeks of the end of the first phase of the excavation, and for reading and greatly improving my draft on the Breiddin. While much of the recent material and recording had not been worked through, the great interest of these provisional conclusions makes them a very welcome addition.

445 m. (1,461 ft) at its highest (S.) end and is clasped within a loop in the Clywedog river, flowing around at the foot of precipitous slopes to the E., W. and S. The top of the hill slopes gently from S. to N., at which end the hillside slopes away far less steeply than elsewhere. The site occupies the sloping N. end of the hill, so that its S. line crosses the hill 135 m. (150 yds) from and rather below the summit. At the N. end the line is drawn around the foot of the hill, some 540 m. (700 yds) from, and about 76 m. (250 ft) lower than, the S. end of the enclosure. On the E. side of the hill the fall is so steep that no defence was needed except for some scarping towards the N. On the W. a line, showing variously as a bank or scarp, runs along the side of the hill at a short distance down the slope. In places an external ditch is visible, and in several places the line is broken. Neither the W. line, nor the scarping on the E., continues around the N. end of the hill. Instead, at some 31 m. (100 ft) farther down the slope, a boldly curving rampart, now much eroded in places, clasps the base of the N. end of the hill. The gap between the W. end of this curving rampart and N. end of the W. line is occupied by a very marshy area on the hillside, while the steepness of the slope on the N.E. was probably sufficient there for a simple palisade to have been adequate for closing the gap. A further line of rampart and ditch fronted the central part of the curving line on the N. This lay some distance beyond and below it, but its features are unclear owing to ploughing and traffic hollows across the ridge.

Being in many ways unique, one might doubt that it is of the Iron Age. It has been suggested that it is a Neolithic causewayed camp (Hemp, 1929); but its vast size, its situation and even its name, seem to justify its classification as an Iron Age site. There are certainly indications that it was never completed, and these are particularly clear at the higher S. end where a 15 m. (50 ft) gap separates the end of the cross bank from the precipitous fall to the E., and a further gap of 39·5 m. (130 ft) is left at the S.W. angle.

(44) *Cefn Carnedd*, Llandinam, fig. 4, pl. XVI (SO/017900) (RCAM, 1911, no. 334; Davies, 1857, 167; Anon., 1866; Hamer, 1868, 210–14; *Transactions of Cedewain Field Club*, 1910–11, 24–5; St Joseph, 1961, 267, 270–1).[1] The elongated hill of Cefn Carnedd dominates the convergence of valleys at Caersws, and along its summit lies one of the finest hill-forts in Montgomeryshire. The summit is at 274 m. (900 ft), and the flanks of the hill are steep on all sides, particularly to the S.E. towards Llandinam, where defences were not necessary. Around the ends of the hill and along the N.W. flank three banks and ditches were made. They ranged down the slopes and enclosed about 8 acres (3·2 ha.). Recent ploughing has reduced these defences to scarps and berms on the N.W. side, but they are better preserved around the ends, where entrances were placed. The entrance at the S.W. end was protected by the merging and incurving of the middle and outer banks, which swing inwards to join the scarp of the inner line on the N.W. side. At the N.E. entrance the ditch-ends flanking the entrance are impressive, and on the N.W. side the outer rampart curves inwards on the line of the entrance. Beyond the N.E. entrance, some 40 m. (45 yds) down the slope, a further line of scarp and intermittent ditch crosses the end of the hill and returns to the main flanks to annexe a further acre to the fort. An annexe of similar type may have existed beyond the S.W. gate, but the vagueness of the indications precludes certainty. Returning to the N.E. end, one should note the line of scarp and ditch running down, and then along, the hill from the N. end of the annexe. Its curving line takes it some 90 m. (100 yds) below the defences, and sets it in a line along the N.W. side of the hill, though it terminates at a hedge before going far, and is no longer visible beyond.

The features described, though doubtless of several structural phases, represent the greatest development of the site, and cover an overall area of some 15 acres (6 ha.). The most interesting aspect of the site, however, is the slight but undeniable evidence for an earlier less extensive phase. This phase is suggested by the illogical kink in the inner scarp about half-way along the N.W. flank. On the line of the incurve of this kink the air photographs (nos. AQD 92, 94; AUF 10) show clearly the faint traces of a

[1] St Joseph AP nos. AQD 92, 94; AUF 10; SN 45, 46; AEU 78; AJF 73, 76.

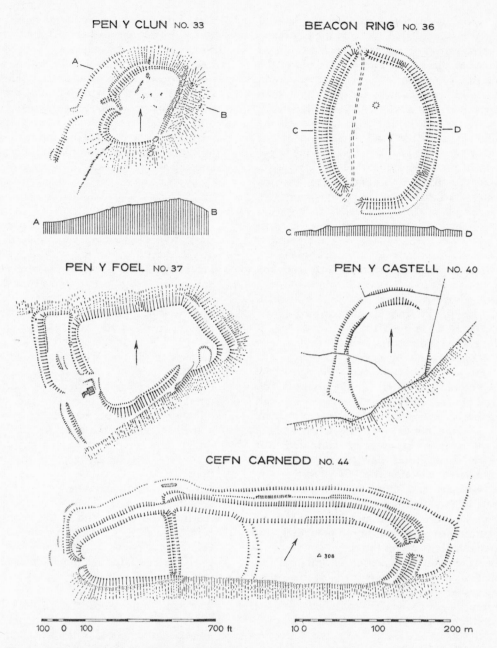

PEN Y CLUN NO. 33

BEACON RING NO. 36

PEN Y FOEL NO. 37

PEN Y CASTELL NO. 40

CEFN CARNEDD NO. 44

100 0 100   700 ft   10 0   100   200 m

fig. 4 Plans of larger enclosures (based on OS. 25 in. plans, modifications and additions by C. J.
Spurgeon, 1960–3, not accurately surveyed)

slighted bank-and-ditch crossing the hill to
define an enclosure of about 4 acres (1·6 ha.)
at the S.W. end. This early line across the
hill seems to have had a counterscarp bank,
and this, together with the closer spacing of
the inner two lines of the larger fort at the
S.W. end, suggests that the earlier enclosure
may have been, or have become, bivallate.

The defences across the hill at the N.E. end
of this smaller site were slighted when the
fort attained its greater extent.
The final phase of occupation recognisable
in the remains is represented by the hitherto
unmentioned cross-bank and ditch running
over the hill in a straight line about 120 m.
(130 yds) from the S.W. end. Its straightness,

comparative freshness, and above all its lack of any gap allowing access to the rest of the main fort enclosure, all show it to represent an ultimate phase of occupation confined to 1¾ acres (0·7 ha.) at the S.W. end. It probably dated to Romano-British or Dark Age times.

(45) *Ffridd Faldwyn*, Montgomery (SO/217969) (RCAM, 1911, no. 802; O'Neil, 1942; Hogg, 1965, 140; Gardner & Savory, 1964, 72, 76, 81, 86; Kenyon, 1956, 40–2). This fine hill-fort was excavated, with significant results, in 1937–9 by the late B. H. St J. O'Neil. It was shown that the Early Iron Age occupation began with a double palisaded enclosure, with no bank or ditch, and covering about 3 acres on the highest part of the hill at about 243·5 m. (800 ft). The entrance through the palisade was inturned. No datable finds were associated with this period, but analogies suggest it was of 'A' type and possibly as early as the third century BC. The use of a simple timber palisade as an initial phase is known in south Britain at the Iron Age 'A' sites at Quarley Hill (Hampshire) and Hollingbury Hill (Sussex). In the west it has also been recorded in an initial 'A' context at Old Oswestry (Salop), Eddisbury (Cheshire) and at Castell Odo (Caernarvonshire). The recent indications that the Breiddin (see no. 42) seems to have begun with a palisaded enclosure associated with 'A' pottery should also be noticed.

The next period of the fort saw the refortification of the enclosure on the lines of the palisade after a period of inactivity during which the palisade decayed *in situ*. The new defences consisted of a timber-laced rampart with ditch beyond a narrow berm. The entrance was inturned and may have been spanned by a bridge over the gate. About 15 m. (50 ft) in advance of the entrance, which lay over the earlier entrance at the S. end, were traces of an outer double line of bank-and-ditch, but their context is uncertain. The second period ended with a fire, probably caused by an assault on the fort, which resulted in the vitrification of parts of the timber-laced rampart.

Following the fire there was a further period of decay before a third fort was built incorporating the old site, but on the N.W.

and S. sides its defences were placed much farther down the hillside and enclosed about 9 acres (3·6 ha.). These defences consisted of a massive stone-revetted rampart with ditch and counterscarp bank. Later an annexe was added at the S. end. O'Neil suggested that at least three structural periods were represented in this large outer camp, all of the pre-Roman Iron Age. At some time during the course of these multivallate phases the old inner enclosure had its ditch re-cut and its interior covered with a maze of large pits, the purpose of which is far from clear.

Finally, after the defences had begun to fall into disrepair, an apparently hurried re-fortification occurred, probably in response to the coming of the Romans.

SITES OF UNKNOWN SIZE AND CHARACTERISTICS (NOS. 46–48)

(46) *Caer Fechan*, Llandinam (SO/015877) (RCAM, 1911, no. 332). Insufficient remains are left of this site to show its size or features. Pennant (1778, iii, 184) noted that it was 'surrounded with a number of fosses, from one to five, according as the strength or weakness of the parts required'. These multivallate defences were still in evidence a century ago (Hamer, 1868, 214–15). The site lies at 297·5 m. (975 ft) near the N. end of a ridge of high ground above the Severn. An isolated fragment of rampart close to Y Gaer farm is all that now remains.

(47) *Goron-ddu*, Llandyssil (SO/186966). A small defended enclosure, discovered from the air by Dr St Joseph (1961, 268) at 190 m. (625 ft) on the top of the ridge called Goron-ddu. Crop-marks showed an irregular quadrilateral enclosure with rounded corners. Nothing is visible on the ground. This was presumably one of the 'several ancient British encampments in a greater or lesser degree of preservation' noticed on the hill by Lewis (1833, under Llandyssil; another was presumably the near-by site at Henfron, see below, no. 48). The air photograph shows signs of an outer line which, Dr St Joseph suggests, is unrelated to the enclosure.

(48) *Henfron*, Llandyssil (SO/192962). At 183 m. (600 ft) on the same high ground as Goron-

ddu (no. 47), and some 820 m. (900 yds) S.E. of that site, Dr St Joseph noticed another defended enclosure from the air (St Joseph, 1961, 268). Again the site showed as a crop-mark, and nothing is to be seen on foot. It lies on Henfron farm beside a steep natural fall towards the S., but with gently rising ground to the N. The air photograph shows a small, single-ditched enclosure.

POSSIBLE SITES (NOS 49–53)

(49) *Powys Park Ring*, Welshpool, fig. 2 (SJ/ 202058). A curious site comprising a per-fectly circular enclosure 49 m. (160 ft) in internal diameter. Sited on a sloping shelf and overlooked from the N.W., it is defended by a well-preserved scarp and ditch, a slight bank existing only to the vulnerable N.W. side. Just within the enclosure above the steep fall to the S.E. is a low circular mound with a diameter of 23 m. (75 ft). This mound stands 1·25 m. (4 ft) high, is unditched, and has the appearance of a round barrow. Its position within the enclosure has led to the unlikely classification of the site as a motte and bailey. It would seem more probable that it is a defensive enclosure, of Iron Age or later date, which was built around an earlier sepulchral monument. The enclosed area is about ¾ acre (0·3 ha.) and lies at 243·5 m. (800 ft).

(50) *Nantcribba Gaer*, Forden (SJ/237014) (RCAM, 1911, no. 175). About 120 m. (130 yds) E. of Offa's Dyke, on the wide plateau thrust out from the S. slopes of the Long Mountain, stands an impressive and isolated boss of rock which appears to have been utilised as a motte and was later surmounted by a small masonry castle (Spurgeon, 1961–2; 1965–6, 35–6). Sur-rounding this rock and its castle, at a distance which varies from 61 m. (200 ft) on the E. to 18·5 m. (60 ft) on the S., is a roughly oval enclosure. It is outlined by a ditch and counterscarp bank. In the absence of a bank within the ditch one might suspect that it once possessed a medieval curtain wall which has been robbed. This, however, is unlikely since there is no trace whatsoever of such a wall, and in any case it would have enclosed an area far too large, about 4 acres

(1·6 ha.), for an outer ward of the castle on the rock. There is also no historical evidence for a village or town at the site. It seems more probable that an earlier defended site was built here, and that its main bank provided the material which was used by the early Normans who produced a superb motte by the addition of earth to parts of the great rock. If this suggestion is correct, it is possible that the earlier site was a large plateau-sited Iron Age ringwork similar to Beacon Ring, which lies a few miles N.E. On the other hand, its position immediately behind Offa's Dyke makes it unwise to ignore the possibility that it was a Mercian fort.

(51) *Pen y Castell*, Llanidloes Without (SN/ 982886) (RCAM, 1911, no. 596; Spurgeon, 1965–6, 27–8). A motte and bailey on the summit of a hill at 274 m. (900 ft). The motte lies at the end of an oval bailey, but the relationship between the two is such that the bailey may well have been an earlier enclosure, the motte overlying its defences at the S. end.

(52) *Dolforwyn Castle*, Bettws Cedewain (SO/ 152950) (RCAM, 1911, no. 34; Spurgeon, 1965–6, 39–42). It is possible that this castle, begun in 1273 by Llywelyn ap Gruf-fydd, was built over an Iron Age hill-fort. The castle stands at 213 m. (700 ft) on a ridge across which vast medieval ditches were cut to the N.E. and S.W. Beyond the outer lip of the N.E. cross-ditch is a bowed-out bank-and-ditch of unimpressive pro-portions, and the ends of which have been severed by the later ditch. Its appearance suggests it might be the only remaining trace of a hill-fort on the site.

(53) *Pentre Llifior*, Berriew (SO/157984). Mr W. G. Putnam has kindly reported his discovery of the traces of a small defended enclosure at the above location but this has not yet been visited by the writer.

(i) *Cwm*, Castle Caereinion (SJ/166059). Curving line of ditch showing as crop-mark from the air (St Joseph, AP no. AOU 38).

(ii) *Tomen*, Llandrinio (SJ/256176). Medieval ringwork classified as hill-fort in RCAM, 1911 (no. 360).

(iii) *Fan Camp*, Llanidloes Without (SN/931884). Natural feature still termed 'camp' on some maps (RCAM, 1911, no. 597).

(iv) *Lletty Earthwork*, Llandinam (SO/007840). Arc of low bank 49 m. (160 ft) long with central break. Lies on low marshy ground (RCAM, 1911, no. 333, under Hill-forts).

(v) *Y Foel*, Llandinam (SO/019841). St Joseph's air photographs (AKM 102, 103) show a convincing univallate contour fort, but on the ground it is seen to be a natural feature.

(vi) *Llanmerewig Churchyard* (SO/158932). Bank around churchyard once suggested as possible hill-fort (RCAM, 1911, no. 621).

(vii) *Red House* (SO/174973). Interesting scarps on the low hill probably represent earlier field boundaries.

(viii) *Town Hill*, Montgomery (SO/218954). Faint indications of an earthwork of uncertain character.

(ix) *Old Hall Camp*, Kerry (SO/207897). Classified as hill-fort in RCAM, 1911, no. 286. A medieval earthwork, almost certainly the true Hubert's Folly (see No. 34).

BIBLIOGRAPHY

Alcock, L., 1963. *Dinas Powis, an Iron Age, Dark Age and Early Medieval Settlement in Glamorgan.* Cardiff.

—— 1965. 'Hillforts in Wales and the Marches', *Antiquity*, XXXIX, 184–95.

Anon., 1866. 'Machynlleth Meeting Report', *Archaeol. Cambrensis*, 3 ser., III, 540.

—— 1938. 'The Stone Rings on Craig Rhiwarth', *Montgomeryshire Collect.*, XLV, 104–21.

Birley, E., 1952. 'Roman Garrisons in Wales', *Archaeol. Cambrensis*, CII, 9–19.

Chitty, L. F., 1937. 'How did the hill-fort builders reach the Breiddin? A tentative explanation', *Archaeol. Cambrensis*, XCII, 129–50.

Davies, D., 1857. 'Caersws. Roman Remains discovered and described', *Archaeol. Cambrensis*, 2 ser., III, 151–72.

Forde-Johnston, J., 1962. 'Earl's Hill, Pontesbury and related Hillforts in England and Wales', *Archaeol. J.*, CXIX, 66–91.

Fox, A., 1952. 'Hillslope Forts and related earthworks in South West England and South Wales', *Archaeol. J.*, CIX, 1–22.

—— 1961. 'South Western Hillforts', in Frere, S. S. (ed.), *Problems of the Iron Age in Southern Britain.* Univ. London Inst. Archaeol. Occasional Paper No. 11, 35–60.

Fox, C. F., 1929. 'Offa's Dyke: A Field Survey. 4th Report. Montgomeryshire', *Archaeol. Cambrensis*, LXXXIV, 1–60.

Gardner, W. & Savory, H. N., 1964. *Dinorben, a hill-fort occupied in early Iron Age and Roman times.* Cardiff.

Hamer, E., 1868. 'Ancient Arwystli; its earthworks and other Ancient Remains', *Montgomeryshire Collect.*, I, 207–32. (Reproduced from *Archaeol. Cambrensis*, 3 ser., XIV [1868], 1–23.)

—— 1872. 'A Parochial Account of Llanidloes', *Montgomeryshire Collect.*, V, 1–48.

—— 1873. 'A Parochial Account of Llanidloes', *Montgomeryshire Collect.*, VI, 155–96.

—— 1879. 'A Parochial Account of Trefeglwys', *Montgomeryshire Collect.*, XII, 1–28.

Hemp, W. J., 1929. 'A "Neolithic Camp" in Wales', *Archaeol. Cambrensis*, LXXXIV, 145.

Hogg, A. H. A., 1962. *Newtown Meeting Programme.* Cambrian Archaeol. Assoc., 1962.

—— 1965. 'Early Iron Age Wales', in Foster, I. Ll. & Daniel, G. E. (eds), *Prehistoric and Early Wales.* London. 109–50.

Hughes, I. T., 1922. 'The Hill Camps of Montgomeryshire', *Montgomeryshire Collect.*, XL, 85–108.

Jones, T. S. & Owen, R., 1900. 'A History of the Parish of Guilsfield (Cegidva)', *Montgomeryshire Collect.*, XXXI, 129–200.

Kenyon, K., 1956. *Roy. Archaeol. Inst. Church Stretton Meeting Programme.* Roy. Archaeol. Inst., 1956.

Lewis, S., 1833. *A Topographical Dictionary of Wales*. London.

Lhwyd, E., 1696. 'Parochialia', Part III, published as a supplement to *Archaeol. Cambrensis*, 6 ser., XI (1911).

Lines, H. H., 1889. 'Breiddin Hill Camp and others in the Vicinity', *Montgomeryshire Collect.*, XXIII, 321–44, and supplementary notes, 413–16.

Morris, E. R., 1889. 'History of the Parish of Kerry', *Montgomeryshire Collect.*, XXIII, 81–120 and 345–70.

Nash-Williams, V. E., 1933. 'An Early Iron Age Hillfort at Llanmelin near Caerwent, Mon.', *Archaeol. Cambrensis*, LXXXVIII, 237–346.

O'Neil, B. H. St J., 1937. 'Excavations at Breiddin Hill Camp, Montgomeryshire 1933–5', *Archaeol. Cambrensis*, XCII, 86–128.

—— 1942. 'Excavations at Ffridd Faldwyn Camp, Montgomery, 1937–9', *Archaeol. Cambrensis*, XCVII, 1–57.

Pennant, T., 1778. *Tours in Wales*. References are to the edition of 1883, edited by J. Rhys.

RCAM, 1911. Roy. Commission on Ancient Monuments in Wales and Monmouthshire. *Montgomeryshire Inventory*. The references are to inventory numbers, not pages.

Richards, R., 1938. 'Craig Rhiwarth', *Montgomeryshire Collect.*, XLV, 196–200.

Savory, H. N., 1962. *Newtown Meeting Programme*. Cambrian Archaeol. Assoc., 1962.

Spurgeon, C. J., 1961–2. 'Gwyddgrug Castle, Forden and the Gorddwr Dispute', *Montgomeryshire Collect.*, LVII, 125–36.

—— 1965–6. 'The Castles of Montgomeryshire', *Montgomeryshire Collect.*, LIX, 1–59.

St Joseph, J. K., 1961. 'Aerial Reconnaissance in Wales', *Antiquity*, XXXV, 263–75.

Thomas, D. R., 1894. 'History of the Parish of Llandrinio', *Montgomeryshire Collect.*, XXVIII, 17–80.

—— 1902. 'The Castle of Caereinion', *Montgomeryshire Collect.*, XXXII, 223–6.

An Emergency Excavation on Pontesford Hill Camp, 1963

Philip Barker

I am doubly delighted to be able to offer Miss Chitty this excavation report, firstly as thanks for the unstinting encouragement and friendship she has always given me, and many others beginning in archaeology, and secondly, because Pontesford Hill, a towering landmark overlooking her house, has become part of her life, and just as it was a great pleasure to show her the excavation in progress it is now a greater pleasure to offer her the results as a tribute.

This short excavation on one of the outer ramparts of the small multivallate lower fort on Pontesford Hill showed that there had been pre-rampart occupation of at least three phases, the first associated with Neolithic flint implements, the second and third with pebble floors, probably of huts. There was evidence that the rampart which overlay these had been crowned with a palisade. Apart from the flint implements there were no finds except one pig's tooth.

The Site (figs 1, 2)

Pontesford Hill is a massive outcrop of pre-Cambrian rocks on the northern edge of the Shropshire hill country overlooking the plain in which Shrewsbury lies.

The highest part of the hill, properly called Earl's Hill, carries a large fort with an extension, perhaps later in date, along a spur to the south. The main entrance, which is at the northern end of the camp, is inturned and is approached by a winding track leading from the line of dying trees which runs like the crest of a boar down the ridge northwards toward the lower camp. There are outworks which guard this road and form additional defences to the entrance above. The main camp is separated from the extension along the spur by a rampart and a deep ditch without a defended entrance. The defences of the extension are slighter, with a narrow entrance approached by a steep track at the south-western end, where there are three banks and ditches across the tip of the spur. Little is known about this camp; no extensive excavation or significant finds have been made there, and its dates, phases and intensity of occupation remain conjectural.

The hill-forts on Pontesford Hill have been described and illustrated in the *Victoria County History of Shropshire* (i, 368–9) and by Forde-Johnston (1962). Neither camp, however, has been fully surveyed.

The short excavation of 1963 was sited outside the main entrance of the lower camp, a much smaller, though multivallate, fort on the northern flank of the hill. Although heavily defended it is curiously vulnerable, being dominated by the main hill which rises above it to the south.

PONTESFORD HILL CAMP : 1963
THE TWO FORTS

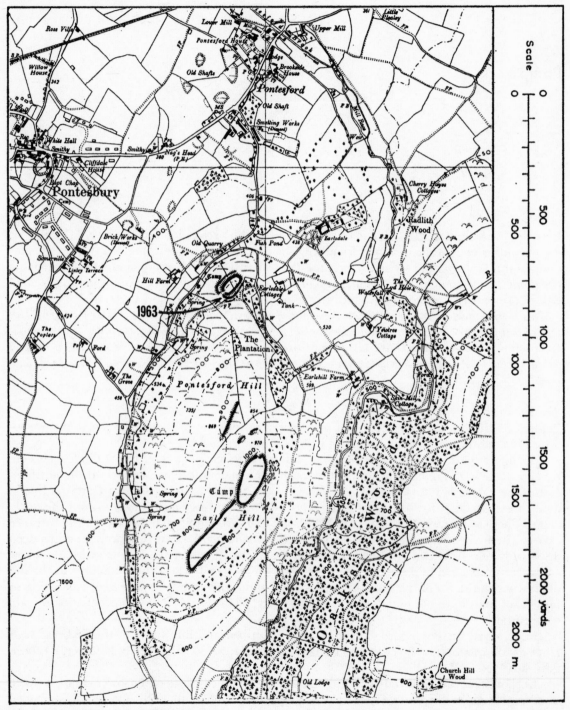

fig. 1 Plan of Pontesford Hill (OS map)

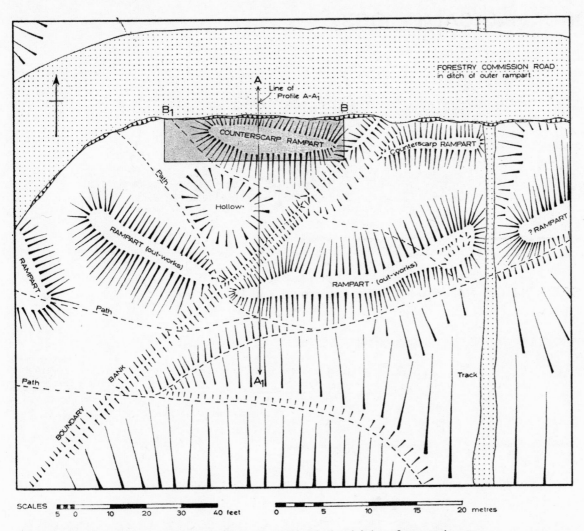

Inside the figure:

FORESTRY COMMISSION ROAD
in ditch of outer rampart

A
Line of
Profile A-A₁

B₁   B
COUNTERSCARP RAMPART
Counterscarp RAMPART

Path

Hollow

RAMPART (out-works)

RAMPART

? RAMPART

RAMPART (out-works)

Path

Path

BANK

BOUNDARY

A₁

Track

SCALES
5 0   10   20   30   40 feet   0   5   10   15   20 metres

fig. 2 Pontesford Hill: Lower Camp. Plan of earthworks in vicinity of excavation area

The earthworks on the col between the lower camp and the main hill are very complicated, being confused by a boundary bank and by paths which criss-cross the area. They have never been surveyed in detail and fig. 2 represents only part of the complex. The purpose of the lower camp has been the subject of a good deal of speculation (Forde-Johnston, 1962), which only extensive excavation of this and the upper camp will solve.

The subsoil of the excavated area was presumed to be the boulder clay into which the earliest features were cut, a glacial deposit lying in the col between the hills.

THE EXCAVATION (plates XVII–XVIII)

An access road, built by the Forestry Commission to enable them to deal with fires on the hill, had been sited along the main ditch of the lower camp and had sliced off the front edge of the counterscarp of the outer rampart. This exposed a long section (fig. 3, section B–B₁) which showed that a thick layer of dark earth and charcoal (layer 3) and some pits and other features (F6, 7, 8, 21, 22) were sealed by the rampart material (layer 2). The writer, on discovering these

347

PONTESFORD HILL CAMP 1963

PROFILE A-A₁

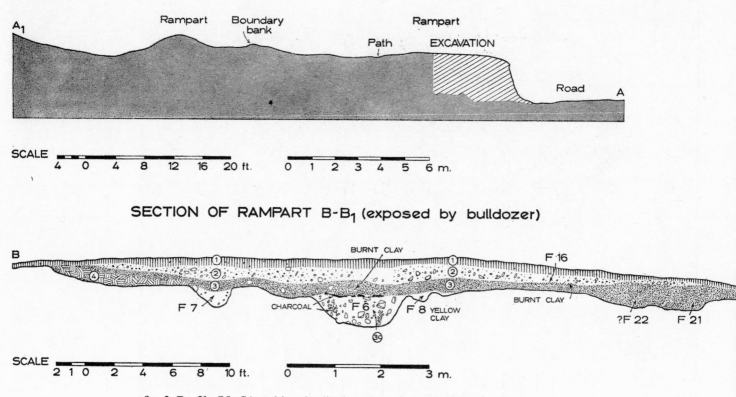

SCALE

4 0 4 8 12 16 20 ft.   0 1 2 3 4 5 6 m.

SECTION OF RAMPART B-B₁ (exposed by bulldozer)

SCALE

2 1 0 2 4 6 8 10 ft.   0   1   2   3 m.

fig. 3 Profile (N.-S.) and longitudinal section of counterscarp-rampart

features in the spring of 1963, removed a pig's tooth from the layer (3) of dark earth. This tooth proved subsequently to be the only find from the whole excavation, apart from the flint implements of layer 4.

Since the rampart and the underlying occupation layers, whose extent was unknown, were being destroyed by erosion, a short emergency excavation was arranged with the aid of a grant from the Ministry of Public Building and Works. The excavation was carried out by members of the Shrewsbury Archaeological Research Group of the Shropshire Archaeological Society on 1–9 June 1963.

METHOD

Since there was a possibility that a palisade might be found on the crest of the rampart and that timber structures might be buried by it, an area 13 feet wide and 50 feet long was stripped. The bases of three large postholes were found immediately under the turf on the rampart; they were preserved and the excavation continued in the areas between them. In this way the postholes have been left so that a future investigation can be keyed precisely into the 1963 excavation. In addition, since the underlying structures need eventually to be seen as completely as possible if they are to be understood, only small portions, sufficient to demonstrate their nature, have been destroyed. It will be seen from the discussion below that the whole of the col between the smaller fort and the main hill will repay large-scale area excavation in the future.

THE SEQUENCE OF STRUCTURES

The natural boulder clay was reached in only three places (shown on fig. 4, *Plan of earliest excavated features*). In the south-east corner of the excavated area gullies had been cut into the natural clay and had become filled with soft brown stone-free clay (layer 4). This clay, which was confined to this small area, contained the flints described and illustrated below. No flints were found at any higher levels.

These gullies are the earliest features and may perhaps be dated by the flints in their fill to the Neolithic period. Their relationship with pebble surface F20 and post sockets F16a–19 cannot be demonstrated. The four post sockets are grouped a little beyond the edge of pebble surface F20 and it is tempting to see F20 as a hut floor with the post sockets as part of the hut structure. Since all these features remain undisturbed, it should be possible to show their function in a future excavation.

The clay-filled gullies were sealed by a stone arrangement enclosing an area of charcoal (F14a) close to two postholes F13 and F14 which were cut into the clay and the underlying subsoil, but were sealed by layer 3. The filling of PH F14 was very similar to the soft brown clay which filled the gullies, but the filling of PH F13 was quite different (see section h–h₁). In addition it will be observed that layer 3 sags into the filling of F13, but not into that of F14 (fig. 5, sections a–a₁ and h–h₁). It appears likely therefore that F13 and F14 are not contemporary and that F14 is perhaps earlier than F13. It is not possible to demonstrate the relationship of either of them to pebble floor F15. F6, on the edge of the area, was a clay-filled pit with burning and charcoal in its upper levels and was perhaps a rubbish pit in which a fire had been made. It contained no finds. F16 was a layer of clay, burnt red, and may have been a small hearth, though since there were no finds it is impossible to be sure. Pebble surface F22 had a small pit F21 cut into it. Though the interpretation of these features is unsatisfactory, it is clear that they represent timber structures probably associated with pebble floors, and that the burnt areas and pits, even without finds, imply occupation.

All these earlier features were sealed by layer 3 which was continuous over the whole area. This layer of dark earth with stones and much charcoal seems to represent a build-up of occupation material after the pebble surface and their associated features had gone out of use. As so often occurs, these thin pebble surfaces could not be seen in the sections (d–d₁, f–f₁) (fig. 5).

THE RAMPART

The rampart (layers 2, 2a, 2b, 2c, 2d) was a dump of yellow boulder clay. There were three very shallow postholes of large diameter along its crest (F4, F9, F10). It is clear that these are simply the bottoms of postholes which were originally much deeper, the rampart having lost through weathering a good deal of its former height. This view is reinforced by the way in which layers 2a and 2b (fig. 5, section a–a₁) slope upwards to the present surface, where they have been truncated by erosion.

The distance between PHs F9 and F10 is exactly twice that between PHs F4 and F9 and it seems reasonable to postulate a lost posthole halfway between F9 and F10, a posthole that was originally a few inches shallower than the others and therefore did not survive.

These three postholes, together with PH F2, did not have construction pits, the rampart material having been piled round the standing posts. PH F3, on the other hand, appears to be later than the rampart since a hole, F3a, had to be dug to receive it.

PHs F2 and F3, together with pebble surface F5, may be part of a fenced entrance leading to

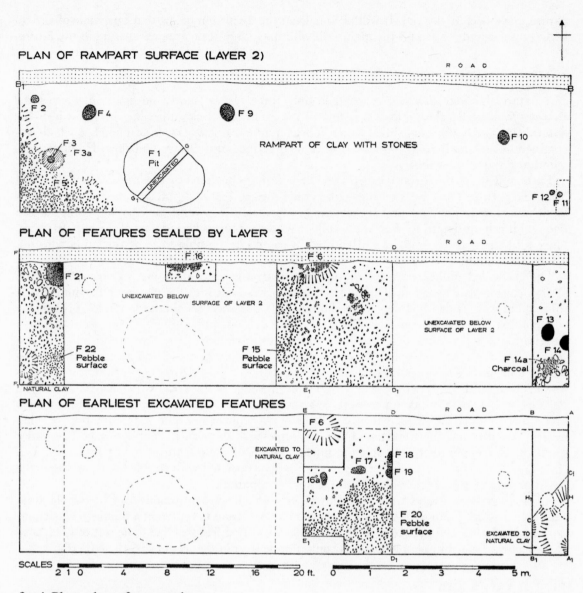

PLAN OF RAMPART SURFACE (LAYER 2)

ROAD

F 2
F 4
F 9
RAMPART OF CLAY WITH STONES
F 10
F 3
F 3a
F 1
Pit
F 5
F 12
F 11

PLAN OF FEATURES SEALED BY LAYER 3

ROAD

F 16
F 6
F 21
UNEXCAVATED BELOW
SURFACE OF LAYER 2
UNEXCAVATED BELOW
SURFACE OF LAYER 2
F 13
F 22
Pebble
surface
F 15
Pebble
surface
F 14
NATURAL CLAY
F 14a
Charcoal

PLAN OF EARLIEST EXCAVATED FEATURES

ROAD

F 6
EXCAVATED TO
NATURAL CLAY
F 18
F 17
F 19
F 16a
F 20
Pebble
surface
EXCAVATED TO
NATURAL CLAY

SCALES
2 1 0   4   8   12   16   20 ft.   0   1   2   3   4   5 m.

fig. 4 Phase plans of excavated area

the main entrance of the camp, though the evidence is too slight for more than conjecture. The purpose of PHs F11 and F12, which were not contemporary, is unknown. At some comparatively recent but unknown date, a large pit F1 (fig. 5, section g–g₁) had been cut into the rampart and backfilled. This pit contained no bones or other finds. Since the acid soil had not permitted the survival of any bones (except the pig's tooth mentioned) the pit had possibly contained an animal burial of which even the teeth had disappeared.

The eastern end of the excavation cut into a boundary bank (see fig. 2 and sections a–a₁, a₁–b) which continues northwards to bisect the interior of the camp.

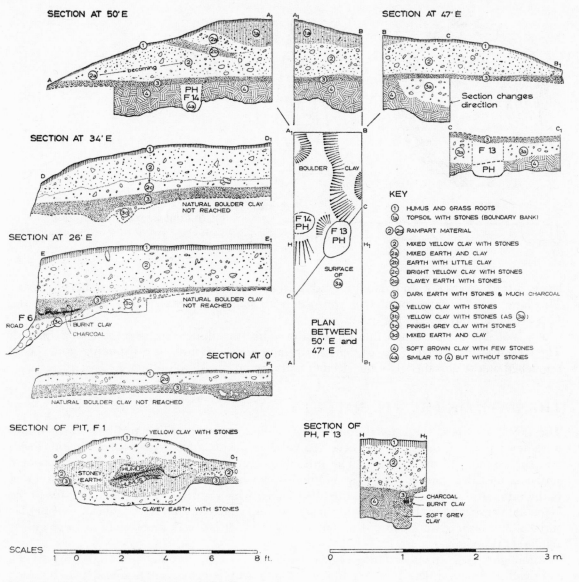

SECTION AT 50' E

SECTION AT 47' E

SECTION AT 34' E

SECTION AT 26' E

F 6
ROAD
BURNT CLAY
CHARCOAL
NATURAL BOULDER CLAY NOT REACHED

SECTION AT 0'

NATURAL BOULDER CLAY NOT REACHED

NATURAL BOULDER CLAY NOT REACHED

PLAN
BETWEEN
50' E and
47' E

BOULDER CLAY

F 14
PH

F 13
PH

SURFACE
OF
③a

F 13
PH

Section changes
direction

KEY

① HUMUS AND GRASS ROOTS
①a TOPSOIL WITH STONES (BOUNDARY BANK)
②-②d RAMPART MATERIAL
② MIXED YELLOW CLAY WITH STONES
②a MIXED EARTH AND CLAY
②b EARTH WITH LITTLE CLAY
②c BRIGHT YELLOW CLAY WITH STONES
②d CLAYEY EARTH WITH STONES
③ DARK EARTH WITH STONES & MUCH CHARCOAL
③a YELLOW CLAY WITH STONES
③b YELLOW CLAY WITH STONES (AS ③a)
③c PINKISH GREY CLAY WITH STONES
③d MIXED EARTH AND CLAY
④ SOFT BROWN CLAY WITH FEW STONES
④a SIMILAR TO ④ BUT WITHOUT STONES

SECTION OF PIT, F 1

YELLOW CLAY WITH STONES

STONEY
EARTH

HUMUS

CLAYEY EARTH WITH STONES

SECTION OF
PH, F 13

CHARCOAL
BURNT CLAY

SOFT GREY
CLAY

SCALES

1 0   2   4   6   8 ft.

0   1   2   3 m.

fig. 5 Sections across excavated area (N-S)

THE FLINTS

The writer is most indebted to Miss Chitty and Mr Nicholas Thomas for the following account.

1 (fig. 6). A large steep-ended round scraper of opaque pale grey flint, plano-convex, worked all round to give sharp edges and leaving a plain, slightly concave, sloping area on the back; the end is strongly overhung, with flaking nearly vertical. There is a fleck of gloss on the face. The type and size are exceptional for Shropshire but can be paralleled by scrapers from the earliest levels at Windmill Hill (Keiller, 1965; e.g. fig. F7 and fig. 40, F32 and F33 from primary

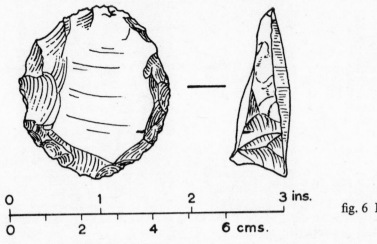

fig. 6 Flint scraper from layer 4

levels of the Causeway Camp dated by radiocarbon methods to the mid-third millennium BC).
This large, round, steep-ended type contrasts with smaller scrapers with scale flaking of the
Late Neolithic and Beaker periods.

2–5 (not illustrated). Small thin pieces of grey lustrous flint, translucent and unpatinated.
The largest of these flakes (No. 2), length 19 mm., width 10 mm., is a trimming from a core
retouched on the dorsal edge of the striking platform, and with a bulb on the face.

THE DATE OF THE STRUCTURES

The rampart material lay directly on layer 3 without the intervening turf-line which would
have developed if a time-lapse had occurred between the abandonment of the occupation levels
and the building of the rampart. The preceding occupation levels, particularly the pebble
surfaces, must therefore be part of a continuous sequence which ended with the construction
of the rampart. On the other hand, the silted gullies which contained the flints, datable to the
Neolithic period and probably early in that period, may have been filled long before the pebble
surfaces and layer 3 were laid down. The fact that the flints were found only in these gullies
reinforces this view.

Although there is no direct dating evidence it seems probable that the rampart, being part of a
multivallate system, is late Iron Age in date, and that therefore occupation of the col between
the main hill and its outlier began in Neolithic times and continued, though perhaps inter-
mittently, until the late Iron Age. There was no evidence of occupation later than this.

DISCUSSION

It is now clear that the outer ramparts of this small multivallate fort are only the last of a series
of developments affecting the col. There is evidence of Neolithic activity, and probably occupation, here, and later at least two periods of undefended, presumably Iron Age, occupation
before expansion of the defences obliterated the extra-vallate buildings. The rampart (the
counterscarp rampart of the main ditch) was crowned by a palisade with major postholes
twelve feet apart. Erosion of the top of the rampart was sufficient to remove traces of the structure between the main posts. It is clear even from these fragments of evidence that any theory
of the purpose of this lower fort must take into account permanent or semi-permanent occupation of the col, perhaps for a very long time before the camp's final heavily defended form.

Since the col, from its situation below the hills, will have received downwash from them, there is every possibility that the Neolithic occupation levels have been preserved. This may therefore be one of the very few sites in the region where there is a real chance of excavating Neolithic structures. It is very much to be hoped that the chance will one day be taken on an adequate scale and with full scientific facilities.

BIBLIOGRAPHY

Forde-Johnston, J., 1962. 'Earl's Hill, Pontesbury and related hillforts in England and Wales', *Archaeol. J.*, CXIX, 66–91.
Keiller, A., 1965. *Windmill Hill and Avebury*. Oxford.

ACKNOWLEDGEMENTS

Thanks are due to all those who took part in the work, to the Ministry of Public Buildings and Works whose grant made the excavation possible, to Mr Stokoe, of the Forestry Commission, for his continuous help, and to Miss Chitty and Mr Nicholas Thomas for their comments on the flint implements.

BIBLIOGRAPHY OF THE WORKS OF LILY F. CHITTY

Donald Moore

1913

'Hanwood monumental inscriptions', *Trans. Shropshire Archaeol. Soc.*, XXXVI, 1913, Misc., VII, xv–xxx.

1914

'Report of annual excursion' (of Shropshire Archaeological Society to Alveley and district), *Trans. Shropshire Archaeol. Soc.*, XXXVII, 1914, ix–xiv.

1919

'Elizabethan coins found at Hanwood', *Trans. Shropshire Archaeol. Soc.*, X (part 1), 1918–19, Misc., V, vii.

1920

'Proceedings of the Shrewsbury Congress of the British Archaeological Association, 13–17 July 1920', *J. Brit. Archaeol. Assoc.*, New series, XXVI, 111–89.

1923–4

'The Bronze Age in Shropshire', *Shropshire Notes & Queries*, 3, IV, 1922–4.

1924

Transcript of 'The earliest book of the Drapers' Company, Shrewsbury', *Trans. Shropshire Archaeol. Soc.*, XLII, 258–77.

1925

'Three bronze implements from the Edgebold Brickyard, Meole Brace', *Antiq. J.*, V, 409–14, figs.
'Bronze spear-head found near the Day House, Cherrington', *Trans. Shropshire Archaeol. Soc.*, XLIII (part 1), Misc., V, vii–viii.
'Bronze implements from the Edgebold Brickfield, near Shrewsbury', *ibid.*, Misc., VI, viii–ix.
'Stone celt from the Longmynd', *ibid.*, Misc., VIII, xi.
'Excavations at White Abbey, Alberbury', *ibid.*, Misc., IX, xii–xiv.
'A day in Bardsey Island', *Observation*, Autumn, 1925, 188–99, figs.

1926

'Bronze implement from Tyddyn Bach, Llanfachreth, Merioneth', *Archaeol. Cambrensis*, LXXXI, Misc., 406–9, figs.

'Bronze dirk found near the Whetstones circle, Montgomeryshire–Shropshire border, with notes on the neighbouring antiquities', *ibid.*, Misc., 409–13, fig.

'Note on perforated stone axe-hammer from Trygarn, Caernarvonshire' (in report of annual meeting of Cambrian Archaeol. Assoc. at Pwllheli, 1926), *ibid.*, 457–9.

'The earliest book of the Drapers' Company, Shrewsbury', *Trans. Shropshire Archaeol. Soc.*, XLIII (part 2), 193–208 (cont. from XLII).

'Notes on prehistoric implements: I. Stone and bronze implements from the Clee Hills, Shropshire; II. Perforated stone axe-hammer from the Severn, Montford Bridge; III. Perforated stone axe-hammer from Aston, near Oswestry', *ibid.*, 233–46, figs.

'The Hoar Stone or Marsh Pool circle', *ibid.*, 247–53, plan.

'Sherry's Meadow, Yockleton', *ibid.*, 254.

'Bronze dirk found near the Whetstones circle, Montgomeryshire–Shropshire border', *ibid.*, Misc., XV, xxvii–xxx.

'The D. G. Goodwin collection of antiquities', *ibid.*, Misc., XVI, xxx–xxxiii, figs.

'Pottery from the Clun district' (appendix to 'Two cinerary urns of the Bronze Age from Little Ryton, Condover', by Clay, R. C. C.), *ibid.*, Misc., XVII, xxxiii–xxxv, figs.

'The Bronze Age trade ways of Shropshire', *Observation*, March and June, 1926, 8–17, 103–9, with map and figs.

1927

'Notes: axe-hammer from Cheshire' (Haslington), *Antiq. J.*, VII, 522–3, fig.

'Perforated stone axe-hammers found in Shropshire', with schedule of 28 specimens, *Bull. Board Celtic Stud.*, IV (part 1), 74–91, figs.

'Dug-out canoes from Shropshire', *Trans. Shropshire Archaeol. Soc.*, XLIV, 113–33 (illustrations issued 1928).

'Bronze spear-head from Petton', *ibid.*, Misc., IV, iv–v, fig.

'Bronze implements found near Castle Bryn Amlwg, Bettws-y-Crwyn', *ibid.*, Misc., V, v–vii.

'Tin scabbard-end found on Watling Street near All Stretton', *ibid.*, Misc., VI, viii–ix, fig.

'The Bronze Age in Shropshire', *Trans. Caradoc Severn Valley Fld. Club*, VII (no. 6, 1926, issued 1927), 203–4.

1928

'The Willow Moor bronze hoard, Little Wenlock, Shropshire', *Antiq. J.*, VIII, 30–47, figs.

'Bronze palstave from the Berwyns', *Archaeol. Cambrensis*, LXXXIII, Misc., 202.

'Bronze halberd said to have been found in Shropshire', *ibid.*, Misc., 209–11.

'Bronze spear-head found near Mellington, Montgomery, 1927', *ibid.*, Misc., 220–2, fig.

'Perforated stone axe-hammers found in Caernarvonshire', *ibid.*, Misc., 223–6, figs.

'Current work in Welsh archaeology: discoveries – prehistoric periods (Irish copper halberd from the Dolgelley region)', *Bull. Board Celtic Stud.*, IV (part 2), 172–3.

'Current work in Welsh archaeology: excavations at Moel Offrwm lower camp, Llanfachreth, Merioneth', *ibid.*, IV (part 3), 279.

1929

'Twin food-vessels preserved at Aqualate Hall, Staffordshire', *Antiq. J.*, IX, 137–40, fig.

'Notes: bronze palstave from Shropshire' (Preeswood), *ibid.*, IX, 253–5, fig.

'Notes on recent acquisitions to the prehistoric section, Shrewsbury Museum', *Trans. Shropshire Archaeol. Soc.*, XLV (part 1), 61–74, figs.

'Stone celt found in Clunton, Shropshire', *ibid.*, Misc., I, i–ii.

'Small perforated stone adze from High Hatton, Stanton-upon-Hine-Heath, Shropshire', *ibid.*, Misc., II, ii–v, fig.

'Bronze palstave from Preeswood', *ibid.*, Misc., III, v.

'Bronze palstave from Knockin', *ibid.*, Misc., IV, v–vi.

1930

'Shrewsbury Museum: prehistoric acquisitions', *Trans. Shropshire Archaeol. Soc.*, XLV, Misc., XIII, xv–xvi.

1931

'Ethnographical specimens reported as Cambrian' (stone celts, Towyn), *Archaeol. Cambrensis*, LXXXVI, Misc., 184–5.

'Notes on air photographs of the district north of Shrewsbury', *Trans. Shropshire Archaeol. Soc.*, XLVI (part 1), Misc., VI, x–xi.

'Archaeology' (report of local discoveries etc. for 1930), *Caradoc Severn Valley Fld. Club Record of Bare Facts*, 40, 3–4.

1932

Distribution maps in *The Personality of Britain: its influence on inhabitant and invader in prehistoric and early historic times*, by Fox, Cyril. Cardiff, National Museum of Wales.

'Archaeology' (report for 1931), *Caradoc Severn Valley Fld. Club Record of Bare Facts*, 41, 3–4.

1933

'A Beaker-like vessel from Bushmills, Co. Antrim', *Antiq. J.*, XIII, 259–65, fig.

'Archaeological notes: I. Bronze looped palstave from Whixall Moss, north Shropshire, fig.; II. Stone implement reported from Buildwas, Shropshire; III. Gold standard weight of James I from Uffington', *Trans. Shropshire Archaeol. Soc.*, XLVII (part 1), 73–7.

'Archaeology' (report for 1932), *Caradoc Severn Valley Fld. Club Record of Bare Facts*, 42, 3–4.

Maps in 'The distribution of Man in East Anglia, *c.* 2,300 BC–50 AD', by Fox, Cyril, *Proc. Prehist. Soc. East Anglia*, VII (part 2), 149–64.

Distribution maps in second edition of *The Personality of Britain*, by Fox, Cyril.

1934

'Amber beads found in Shropshire' (Appendix II to 'Excavations at Titterstone Clee Hill Camp, Shropshire, 1932', by O'Neil, B. H. St J.), *Archaeol. Cambrensis*, LXXXIX, 110–11.

'Archaeology' (report for 1933), *Caradoc Severn Valley Fld. Club Record of Bare Facts*, 43, 3–4.

1935

'The gold torc at Wynnstay' (in report of annual meeting of Cambrian Archaeol. Soc. at Llangollen), *Archaeol. Cambrensis*, XC, 367–8.

'Iberian affinities of a bone object found in Co. Galway', *J. Galway Archaeol. Hist. Soc.*, XVI, 125–33, figs.

'A harvest figure from Yockleton', *Trans. Shropshire Archaeol. Soc.*, XLVIII (part 1), 61–3, fig.

'Report on a bronze spear-head presented to the Hereford Museum', *Trans. Woolhope Natur. Fld. Club*, 1930–32 (issued 1935), lxxxviii–lxxxix.

'Archaeology' (report for 1934), *Caradoc Severn Valley Fld. Club Record of Bare Facts*, 44, 3–4.

Map of South Wales in the Bronze Age in *History of Carmarthenshire*, Vol. I, by Lloyd, J. E., Cardiff, fig. 27.

1936

'Notes: single-faced palstaves in Portugal and in Ireland', *Proc. Prehist. Soc.*, II, 236–8, fig.

'Archaeology' (report for 1935), *Caradoc Severn Valley Fld. Club Record of Bare Facts*, 45, 3.

Distribution map of hill-forts with inturned entrances in 'Excavations at Maiden Castle, Bickerton', by Varley, W. J., *Liverpool Annals Archaeol. Anthropol.*, XXXIII, fig. 3.

1937

'How did the hill-fort builders reach the Breiddin?', with map of hill-forts with inturned entrances in the Welsh Marches, *Archaeol. Cambrensis*, XCII, 129–50.

'The Irish Sea in relation to Bronze Age culture' (synopsis of lecture given to British Association, Section H, at Blackpool), *Trans. Caradoc Severn Valley Fld. Club*, X (no. 2, 1936, issued 1937), 72–4.

'Archaeology' (report for 1936), *Caradoc Severn Valley Fld. Club Record of Bare Facts*, 46, 3–4.

1938

'Notes on the Irish affinities of three Bronze Age Food-vessels of Type Ia found in Wales', *Bull. Board Celtic Stud.*, IX (part 3), 275–83, figs.

'Bronze dagger found on Caradoc, All Stretton', *Trans. Shropshire Archaeol. Soc.*, XLIX (part 2), Misc., i–ii, fig.

'The Berth, Baschurch', *ibid.*, viii–x.

'Archaeology' (report for 1937), *Caradoc Severn Valley Fld. Club Record of Bare Facts*, 47, 3–4.

Distribution maps in third edition of *The Personality of Britain*, by Fox, Cyril.

'Perforated stone axe-hammer from Mathon sandpit' and 'Holed stone implement from Michaelchurch Escley', *Trans. Woolhope Natur. Fld. Club*, 1933–35 (issued 1938), lxxxvi–lxxxviii.

1939

'Flat bronze axe now associated with the Guilsfield hoard', *Archaeol. Cambrensis*, XCIV, 225.

'Archaeology' (report for 1938), *Caradoc Severn Valley Fld. Club Record of Bare Facts*, 48, 3–4.

1940

Schedule and map of ribbed palstaves in 'Late Bronze Age find near Stuntney, Cambridgeshire', by Clark, J. G. D. & Godwin, H., *Antiq. J.*, XX, 63–6.

'Notes: a dug-out canoe from Shropshire: a bogus antiquity', *ibid.*, 288–9.

'Bronze implements from the Oswestry region of Shropshire', *Archaeol. Cambrensis*, XCV, 27–35, figs.

'Bronze implements and other objects from Shropshire in the National Museum of Wales, Cardiff', *Trans. Shropshire Archaeol. Soc.*, L (part 2), 143–54, fig.

'Note on a bone implement from the Ellesmere region', *ibid.*, 155–7, fig.

'Large perforated stone axe-hammer, Stanage Park (Radn.)', *Trans. Woolhope Natur. Fld. Club*, 1936–38 (issued 1940), lv–lvi.

'Perforated stone axe-hammer from Kingston Churchyard (Herefs.)', *ibid.*, xc–xci.

'Archaeology' (report for 1940), *Caradoc Severn Valley Fld. Club Record of Bare Facts*, 49, 3–4.

Distribution maps in *Prehistoric Cheshire*, by Varley, W. J. & Jackson, J. W., Cheshire Rural Community Council.

1943

'Pottery spindle-whorl from Pentrefelin, Caernarvonshire', *Archaeol. Cambrensis*, XCVII, Misc., 232–4, fig.

'Bronze Age cist burial found at Eyton, near Alberbury, Shropshire. Preliminary notes', *Trans. Shropshire Archaeol. Soc.*, LI (part 2), 139–41, figs.

'Two bronze palstaves from Llandrinio, Montgomeryshire', *ibid.*, 146–51, fig.

Distribution maps in fourth edition of *The Personality of Britain*, by Fox, Cyril.

'Herbert Edward Forrest (1858–1942): Obituary Notice', *North Western Naturalist*, XVIII (nos. 1 & 2, March and June), 114–17.

1945

'Archaeology' (report for 1942), *Caradoc Severn Valley Fld. Club Record of Bare Facts*, 52, 3–4.

1946

With Coghlan, H. H., 'The perforated stone hammer – its typology and distribution' (summary), *Man*, XLVI, item 105, 125–7.

1947

'A perforated stone implement from Dudmaston, supplementary note', *Trans. Shropshire Archaeol. Soc.*, LII (part 1), 132–8, fig.

With Fleming, J. T., 'Catalogue of temporary museum' (arranged for annual meeting of Cambrian Archaeol. Assoc. at Rhyl), *Archaeol. Cambrensis*, XCIX, 360–2.

1948

'Harold J. E. Peake: an appreciation', *Trans. Newbury Dist. Fld. Club*, IX (part 1), 2–3.

'Bronze Spearhead from Pennant (Upper Tanat Valley), Montgomeryshire', *Archaeol. Cambrensis*, C (part 1), Misc., 106–8, fig.

'Mound at Little Ness, Shropshire', *Trans. Shropshire Archaeol. Soc.*, LII (part 2), Misc., 248–9.

1949

'Bronze palstave identified as from Clochfaen, Llangurig, Montgomeryshire', *Archaeol. Cambrensis*, C (part 2), Misc., 275–7, fig.

'Flint implements recently found in Shropshire south of the Severn, with a supplementary note on two newly-recorded stone axe-hammers', *Trans. Shropshire Archaeol. Soc.*, LIII (part 1), 24–36, figs.

'Interim notes on subsidiary castle sites west of Shrewsbury, with schedule and map', *ibid.*, 83–90.

'Three unrecognised castle sites in north Shropshire', *ibid.*, 91–3.

'Report on bronze implements stated to have been found at Netherwood, Thornbury, N.E. Herefordshire', *Trans. Woolhope Natur. Fld. Club*, XXXII (1946–48, issued 1949), xlv–xlix.

'La Tène I bronze brooch found in Sutton Walls camp, Herefordshire', *ibid.*, 167.

'Recorder's report on archaeology, 1943–44', *Trans. Caradoc Severn Valley Fld. Club*, XII (parts 1 & 2, issued 1949), 23.

'A perforated stone hammer from Crimpsall, Doncaster', *Yorkshire Archaeol. J.*, XXXVII (part 146), 129–30, fig.

1951

With Shotton, F. W. & Seaby, W. A. 'A new centre of stone axe dispersal on the Welsh Border', *Proc. Prehist. Soc.*, XVII (part 2), 159–67, maps and figs.

'Recorder's report on archaeology, 1944–45', *Trans. Caradoc Severn Valley Fld. Club*, XII (parts 3 & 4, issued 1951), 91.

1952

'Brief Report on the Prehistoric Collections' in *Guide to Rowley's House Museum, Shrewsbury*, revised edition, 3–5.

'Prehistoric and other early finds in the Borough of Shrewsbury' (Appendix by Dunning, G. C.), *Trans. Shropshire Archaeol. Soc.*, LIV (part 1, 1951–52), 105–44, figs.

Bronze palstave found at Pontesbury, Shropshire', *ibid.*, 145–8. fig.

Appendix to 'Preliminary report of archaeological investigations near Radcliffe, Lancashire', by Spencer, A., *Trans. Lancashire Cheshire Antiq. Soc.*, LXII (1950–51, issued 1952), 196–203.

1953

'Bronze axe hoard from Preston-on-the-Weald-Moors, Shropshire', *Trans. Shropshire Archaeol. Soc.*, LIV (part 2), 240–54, figs.

1954

'Prehistory' (Shrewsbury region), *Programme of Annual Meeting at Shrewsbury, 1954* (Cambrian Archaeol. Assoc.), 8–10.

'Caus Castle', *ibid.*, 19–21.

'Offa's Dyke on Baker's Hill', *ibid.*, 33–4.

1955

Appendix to 'Excavations on Stanton Moor', by Heathcote, J.P., *Derbyshire Archaeol. J.*, LXXIV (1954, issued 1955), 128–33.

'Late Bronze Age spear-head from the Great Doward, south Herefordshire', *Trans. Woolhope Natur. Fld. Club*, XXXIV (1952–54, issued 1955), 21–3.

'An expanding flint axe from Lyme Park', *J. Chester Archaeol. Soc.*, 42, Misc., 48.

1956

'Shropshire in relation to the prehistory of Wales' (summary in report of annual meeting of Cambrian Archaeol. Assoc. at Shrewsbury, 1954), *Archaeol. Cambrensis*, CIV (1955, issued 1956), 193–5.

'Caus Castle' (in report of annual meeting of Cambrian Archaeol. Assoc. at Shrewsbury, 1954), *ibid.*, 199–201.

'Annual reports on Archaeology: 1946–50', *Trans. Caradoc Severn Valley Fld. Club*, XIII (1947–50, issued 1956), 34–43.

1957

'An introduction to Shropshire archaeology', report of Royal Archaeol. Inst. summer meeting at Church Stretton, 1956), *Archaeol. J.*, CXIII (1956, issued 1957), 178–85.

1958

'Clun Town Trust Museum', *Programme of Annual Meeting at Presteigne, 1958* (Cambrian Archaeol. Assoc.), 19–20.

'Axehead' (from Hunderton) and 'Axehead' (from Tram Inn) in 'Prehistoric Accessions to Hereford Museum, 1957' by Norwood, J. F. L., *Trans. Woolhope Natur. Fld. Club*, XXXV (part 3), 1957 (issued 1958), 318–20, fig.

1959

Distribution maps in reprint of *The Personality of Britain*, by Fox, Cyril.

1960

'Re-opening of Clun Town Trust Museum, 18 May 1955, *Trans. Caradoc Severn Valley Fld. Club*, XIV (1951–56; issued 1960), 109–13.

'Clun Museum' (in report of annual meeting of Cambrian Archaeol. Assoc. at Presteigne, 1958), *Archaeol. Cambrensis*, CVIII (1959, issued 1960), 155.

'Annual reports on Archaeology: 1950–5', *Trans. Caradoc Severn Valley Fld. Club*, XIV (1951–56, issued 1960), 42–64.

'Polished stone axe', 'Perforated stone pick' and 'Polished flint axe' in 'Prehistoric Accessions to Hereford Museum, 1958–59', by Norwood, J. F. L., *Trans. Woolhope Natur. Fld. Club*, XXXVI (part 2), 1959 (issued 1960), 233–7, (figs 270 by J. N.)

1962

'The Ridgeways', *Programme of Annual Meeting at Newtown, Montgomery, 1962* (Cambrian Archaeol. Assoc.), 17–18.

'Axe' (from Weston Beggard) in 'Prehistoric Accessions to Hereford Museum, 1962–63', by Norwood, J. F. L., *Trans. Woolhope Natur. Fld. Club*, XXXVII (part 3) 1961 (issued 1962), 348–9, fig.

1963

'The Clun–Clee Ridgeway: a prehistoric trackway across south Shropshire', in *Culture and Environment: Essays in Honour of Sir Cyril Fox*, ed. by Foster, I. Ll., & Alcock, Leslie, Routledge & Kegan Paul, 171–92. London.

1964

With Edwards, Elizabeth H., *Index to Archaeologia Cambrensis, 1846–1900*, pp. xiii + 402, Cardiff, Cambrian Archaeological Association.

Distribution maps (1939) in *Cheshire Before the Romans* by Varley, W. J., Cheshire Rural Community Council, 1964.

1965

'Irish bronze axes assigned to the Guilsfield hoard, Montgomeryshire', *Archaeol. Cambrensis*, CXIV, 120–9, figs.

1966

'Notes on a stone pestle found in the River Severn below Ford, west Shropshire' (including report by Shotton, F. W.), *Trans. Shropshire Archaeol. Soc.*, LVII (part 3, 1964, issued 1966), 180–4, fig.

'Tom Hamar of Clun', obituary, 1964, *ibid.*, 273.

'Annual reports on Archaeology: 1955–60', *Trans. Caradoc Severn Valley Fld. Club*, XV (1957–60, issued 1966), 31–84.

1967

'Stone axe (He 46/c) and flint implements from Buckton, N.W. Herefordshire', *Trans. Woolhope Natur. Fld. Club*, XXXVIII (Part 2, 1965, issued 1967), 153–5, fig.

1968

'A bronze looped palstave from New House Farm, Wolverley, near Wem, Shropshire', *Trans. Shropshire Archaeol. Soc.*, LVIII (Part 2, 1966, issued 1968), 101–6.

'Supplementary note on a bronze looped palstave from Bryn Shop, Bettws-y-Crwyn, S.W. Shropshire', *ibid.*, 107–10.

With Coombs, D., 'A Bronze hoard and burial found at Greensborough Farm, Shenstone, Staffordshire, in 1824', *Trans. Lichfield S. Staffs. Archaeol. Hist. Soc.*, IX (1967–68), 1–16, figs.

'Annual reports on Archaeology: 1960–5', *Trans. Caradoc Severn Fld. Club*, XVI (1961–67, issued 1968), 43–84.

1970

Review of *Bronze Age Metalwork in Northern England, c. 1000 to 700 B.C.*, Oriel Press, 1968, by Burgess, C., in *Archaeol. Cambrensis*, CXVIII (1969, issued 1970), 153–4.

INDEX

363

I Stone Basin in Chamber III, Passage Grave tumulus on Baltinglass Hill, Co. Wicklow—Photo: M. J. O'Kelly (see T. G. E. Powell—The Problem of Iberian Affinities in Prehistoric Archaeology around the Irish Sea p. 98)

II a (*left*) Newton Cairn: Cist 1 from the north-north-west, 1969. b (*right*) Newton Cairn: Cist 2 from the north-west, 1969—(see H. N. Savory. Copper Age Cists and Cist-cairns in Wales p. 126)

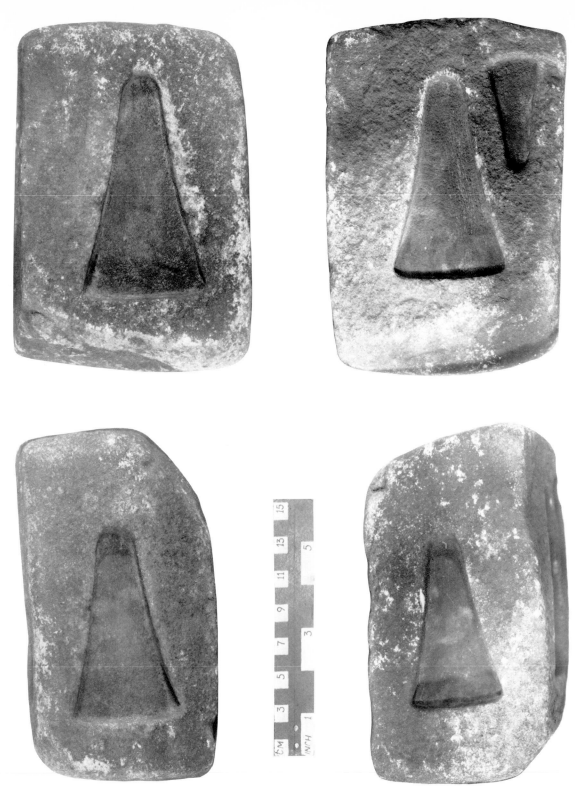

III Axe—mould from the Walleybourne, Longden Common, Shropshire (see Nicholas Thomas An Early Bronze Age Stone Axe-Mould from the Walleybourne, below Longden Common, Shropshire p. 161)

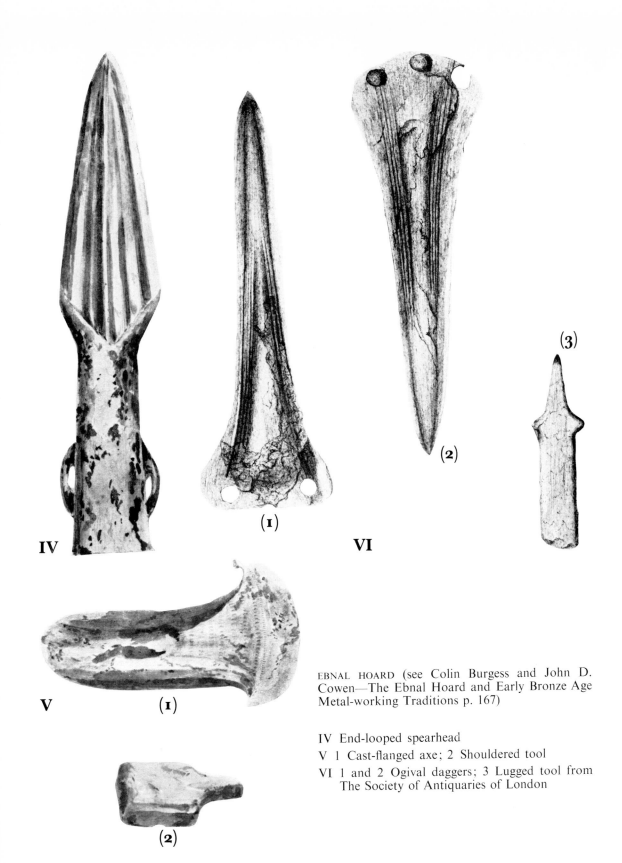

IV

V   (1)

(2)

(1)

(2)

(3)

VI

EBNAL HOARD (see Colin Burgess and John D. Cowen—The Ebnal Hoard and Early Bronze Age Metal-working Traditions p. 167)

IV End-looped spearhead
V 1 Cast-flanged axe; 2 Shouldered tool
VI 1 and 2 Ogival daggers; 3 Lugged tool from The Society of Antiquaries of London

VII

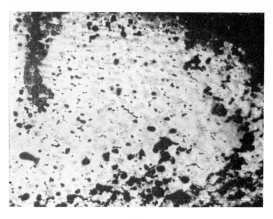

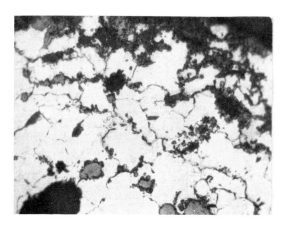

(b)

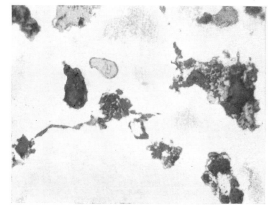

(c)

(d)

(e)

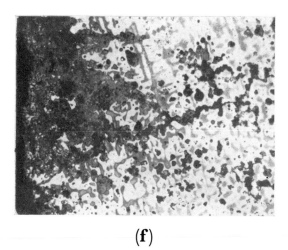

(f)

(a)

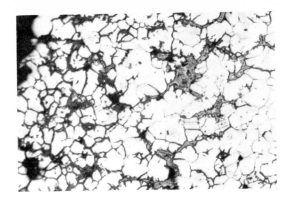

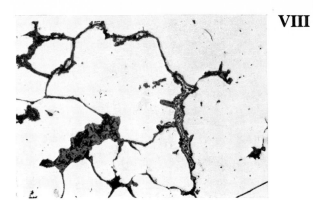

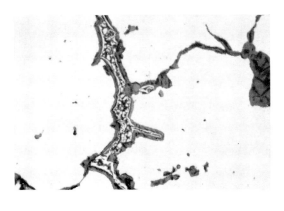

VII *left* Flat Axe OA 229

VIII *above* Palstave S 504 (full size)

IX *right* Socketed axe OA 83 (full size) (see H. H. Coghlan—Three Unusual Implements in the Borough Museum, Newbury p. 183)

X

XI

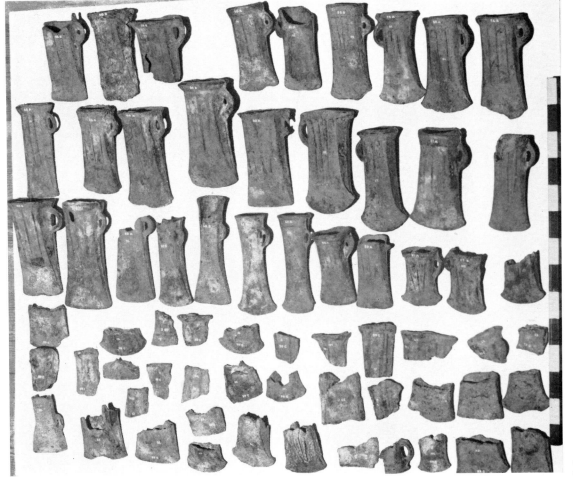

XII

HOARD FROM WICK PARK, STOGURSEY, SOMERSET (see Colin Burgess, David Coombs and D. Gareth Davies—The Broadward Complex and Barbed Spearheads p. 232)

X Spearheads, including fragmentary barbed spearheads (*bottom*), and jets. Ingot metal not shown.

XI Swords (including Ewart Park and Carp's tongue fragments), chape, tools and 'Late' palstaves

XII Socketed axes

XIII *above* Aerial view of the hill-fort on South Barrule, looking eastwards—Photo: Courtesy of the Manx Museum (see Peter S. Gelling—The Hill-fort on South Barrule and its position in the Manx Iron Age p. 285)

XIV Cefn y Castell, Middleton, Mont. (Site No. 25)—Photo: J. K. St Joseph, Cambridge University Collection, copyright reserved (see C. J. Spurgeon—Enclosures of Iron Age Type in the Upper Severn Basin p. 332)

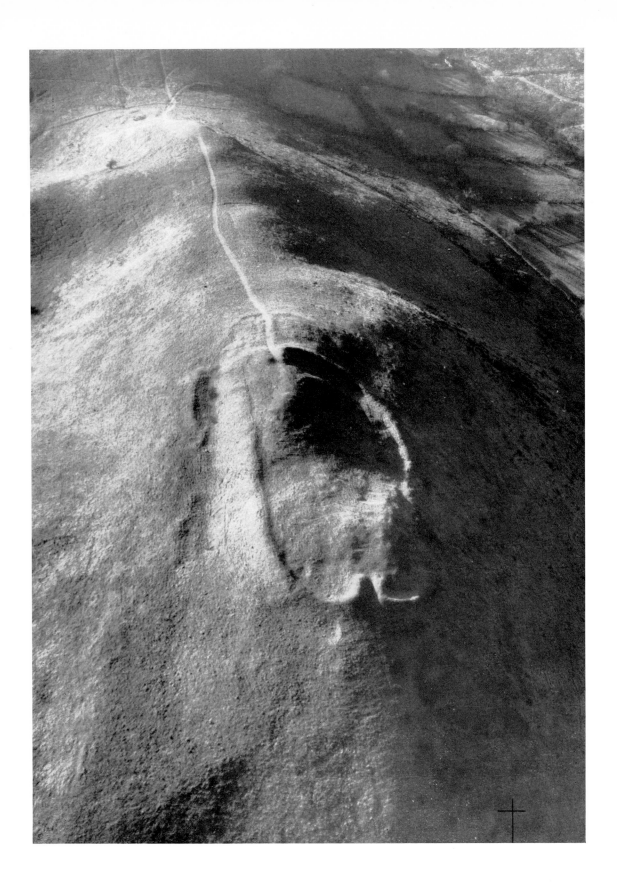

XV *above* Cefn yr Allt, Berriew, Mont. (Site No. 38) (see C. J. Spurgeon—Enclosures of Iron Age type in the Upper Severn Basin p.336)

XVI *opposite* Cefn Carnedd, Llandinam, Mont. (Site No. 44) (see C. J. Spurgeon—Enclosures of Iron Age Type in the Upper Severn Basin p.339)

XVII *right* Pontesford Hill: Lower Camp, aerial view from the south with excavated area visible south-west of centre (see Philip Barker—An Emergency Excavation on Pontesford Hill Camp, 1963 p.345)

DATE DUE

2/28/75			
MY 1 0 '83			
GAYLORD			PRINTED IN U.S.A.